A Community of Writers

A Workshop Course in Writing

A Community of Writers

A Workshop Course in Writing

Third Edition

Peter Elbow
University of Massachusetts at Amherst

Pat Belanoff
State University of New York at Stony Brook

Boston Burr Ridge, IL Dubuque, IA Madison, WI New York San Francisco St. Louis
Bangkok Bogotá Caracas Lisbon London Madrid
Mexico City Milan New Delhi Seoul Singapore Sydney Taipei Toronto

Our cover image depicts a traditional *mola,* a colorful, intricately appliquéd fabric panel created by the Kuna Indians, a tribal society living on a chain of islands off of Panama's Caribbean coast.

McGraw-Hill Higher Education

*A Division of The **McGraw-Hill** Companies*

A COMMUNITY OF WRITERS: A WORKSHOP COURSE IN WRITING

This book is printed on acid-free paper.

1 2 3 4 5 6 7 8 9 0 DOC/DOC 9 0 9 8 7 6 5 4 3 2 1 0 9

ISBN 0–07–303181–X

Editorial director: *Phillip A. Butcher*
Senior sponsoring editor: *Lisa Moore*
Developmental editor II: *Alexis Walker*
Marketing manager: *Thayne Conrad*
Project manager: *Susanne Riedell*
Manager, new book production: *Melonie Salvati*
Senior designer: *Jennifer McQueen Hollingsworth*
Interior designer: *Maureen McCutcheon*
Cover photo: *Copyright 1999 PhotoDisc, Inc. All rights reserved.*
Photo researcher: *Judy Kausal*
Senior supplement coordinator: *Marc Mattson*
Compositor: *ElectraGraphics, Inc.*
Typeface: *10/12 Caslon 224 Book*
Printer: *R. R. Donnelley & Sons Company*

Library of Congress Cataloging-in-Publication Data

Elbow, Peter.
A community of writers : a workshop course in writing / Peter Elbow, Pat Belanoff. — 3rd ed.
p. cm.
ISBN 0-07-303181-X (acid-free paper)
Includes bibliographical references and indexes.
1. English language — Rhetoric. 2. College readers. 3. Report writing. I. Title. II. Belanoff, Pat.
PE1408.E38 2000
808'.0427dc—21 99-43524

http://www.mhhe.com

About the Authors

Peter Elbow

Peter Elbow is Professor of English and Director of the Writing Program at the University of Massachusetts at Amherst. Before writing *A Community of Writers,* he wrote two other books about writing: *Writing Without Teachers* and *Writing with Power: Techniques for Mastering the Writing Process.* He is author of a book of essays about learning and teaching, *Embracing Contraries,* in addition to *What Is English?,* which explores current issues in the profession of English, *Oppositions in Chaucer,* and numerous essays about writing and teaching. His most recent book is *Writing For—Not Against: Essays on Writing and the Teaching of Writing.*

He has taught at the Massachusetts Institute of Technology, Franconia College, Evergreen State College, and the State University of New York at Stony Brook—where for five years he directed the Writing Program. He served for four years on the Executive Council of the Modern Language Association and was a member of the Executive Committee of the Conference on College Composition and Communication. He has given talks and workshops at many colleges and universities.

He attended Williams College and Harvard University and has an M.A. from Exeter College, Oxford University, and a Ph.D. from Brandeis University.

Pat Belanoff

Pat Belanoff is Associate Professor of English at the State University of New York–Stony Brook. She has been both president of the SUNY Council on Writing and a member of the College Steering Committee of NCTE. Pat is a coauthor (with Betsy Rorschach and Mia Oberlink) of *The Right Handbook,* now in its second edition. She has also coedited (with Marcia Dickson) *Portfolios: Process and Product* and (with Peter Elbow and Sheryl Fontaine) *Nothing Begins With an N: New Investigations of Freewriting.* Pat has a doctorate in medieval literature from New York University and continues to teach and publish in this area, too.

Brief Contents

Contents

To the Instructor

We have written *A Community of Writers* for first-year college students in a one-semester writing course.* We've made our book as practical as we can, with lots of hands-on workshop activities. But we don't hide our interest in theory; our book reflects much recent scholarship in composition. And we push students to become thoughtful about their writing process through regular entries in a writing process diary.

We have structured this third edition of our book into 16 *workshops,* each consisting of a set of activities and a writing assignment designed to illustrate an important feature of the writing process (and designed to occupy one or two weeks). The workshops are arranged in a coherent order that provides plenty of direction for teachers who want to follow our lead. (And we've written an extensive instructor's manual for teachers to consult.) But we've also given teachers great latitude by including far too many workshops for one semester and by making each workshop self-contained—so that teachers can completely rearrange the order to suit their own approaches or priorities.

Here's one possible default sequence for a single-semester (12–14 week) course:

1: An Introduction to the Variety of Writing Processes
2: From Private Writing to Public Writing
5: Voice
6: Drafting and Revising
7: Revision through Purpose and Audience: Writing as Doing Things to People
9: The Essay
10: Persuasion
11: Argument
12: Research
16: Autobiography and Portfolio

For a 10-week course, the sequence might be "edited" as follows:

1: An Introduction to the Variety of Writing Processes
2: From Private Writing to Public Writing
5: Voice
6: Drafting and Revising
10: Persuasion
11: Argument
16: Autobiography and Portfolio

* The book is also appropriate for a one- or two-quarter course—and perhaps for a full-year course if supplemented with additional readings. *A Community of Writers* will also be useful for high school seniors or college sophomores or juniors—for we haven't much differentiated our audience in terms of age or skill level. That is, when we work with unskilled or reluctant students, we find they benefit from working on the same interesting, substantive, and sometimes difficult writing tasks we ask of our most skilled students—so long as we explain clearly what we are asking and why we are asking it, and give lots of support. On the other hand, even when we are working with very skilled and experienced students, we give lots of encouragement and take the informal, nontechnical stance you see here. The core of our book is a series of writing activities that we have found appropriate whether we're working with young children or college faculty.

For instructors who prefer more emphasis on process:

- 1: An Introduction to the Variety of Writing Processes
- 2: From Private Writing to Public Writing
- 3: Collaborative Writing: Dialogue, Loop Writing, and the Collage
- 5: Voice
- 6: Drafting and Revising
- 7: Revision through Purpose and Audience: Writing as Doing Things to People
- 10: Persuasion
- 11: Argument
- 13: Interpretation as Response: Reading as the Creation of Meaning
- 16: Autobiography and Portfolio

For more emphasis on genre:

- 1: An Introduction to the Variety of Writing Processes
- 3: Collaborative Writing: Dialogue, Loop Writing, and the Collage
- 6: Drafting and Revising
- 7: Revision through Purpose and Audience: Writing as Doing Things to People
- 8: Writing in the World: An Interview about Writing
- 9: The Essay
- 10: Persuasion
- 11: Argument
- 15: Listening, Reading, and Writing in the Disciplines
- 16: Autobiography and Portfolio

For more emphasis on academic writing:

- 1: An Introduction to the Variety of Writing Processes
- 2: From Private Writing to Public Writing
- 6: Drafting and Revising
- 7: Revision through Purpose and Audience: Writing as Doing Things to People
- 9: The Essay
- 10: Persuasion
- 11: Argument
- 12: Research
- 14: Text Analysis through Examining Figurative Language
- 15: Listening, Reading, and Writing in the Disciplines

For more emphasis on literature:

- 1: An Introduction to the Variety of Writing Processes
- 2: From Private Writing to Public Writing
- 4: Getting Experience into Words: Image and Story
- 5: Voice
- 6: Drafting and Revising
- 7: Revision through Purpose and Audience: Writing as Doing Things to People
- 9: The Essay
- 11: Argument
- 13: Interpretation as Response: Reading as the Creation of Meaning
- 14: Text Analysis through Examining Figurative Language

In addition to the main workshops, there are 12 *mini-workshops*—short pieces each devoted to a smaller feature of writing or usage and suitable to be assigned as outside reading or used for a single class meeting.

We've made some changes from the second edition, but the basic orientation and underlying philosophy have not changed. In this revision, we've emphasized research—especially electronic research—drafting, and public forms of writing more than we did in the second edition. These emphases grow out of our own teaching interests which, in turn, grow out of what we continue to learn from other researchers and scholars in the field of composition and rhetoric.

The final section of our textbook, "Sharing and Responding," is an unusual feature we're particularly proud of: a series of graduated activities designed to help students learn to respond usefully to each other's writing. ("Sharing and Responding" is also available separately.) We've met many teachers who say, "Peer feedback doesn't work." We believe it's really a matter of giving students more guidance; that's what this final section of our book aims to do.

We've tried above all to make a book that is *writerly.* Our overriding principle is that we all learn writing best by writing: writing a great deal, in various modes, to various audiences, and with lots of feedback from diverse readers. This book is not a handbook that lays out rules of grammar or guidelines for good usage—nor even principles of good writing. It is a book of writing activities.

Yet in taking this writerly—even idealistic—approach we have been mindful of the constraints of the classroom setting: grading, time cut up artificially into 50-minute blocks and into semesters or quarters, and the sometimes vexed authority relationships that grow out of teaching a course which, at many schools, is the only one absolutely required of all students.

We spent over a year revising the book for this third edition. We and a number of our colleagues tried out drafts of much of the material in our classrooms, and we have been able to include samples of student writing derived from these trials or sent to us by teachers who used the second edition. We do not intend these samples as models of excellence to imitate or illustrations of pitfalls to avoid, but simply as *examples:* a range of what students have written in response to these tasks. We like these pieces, just as we also like the examples of professional writing that we include with them in the readings. We have purposely mingled the student and professional writing together without differentiation in order to emphasize that we don't think there is anything *different in kind* that distinguishes student writing from professional writing.

The hardest part about this revision was deciding what to throw out from the second edition. We knew we wanted to add some new things, but adding meant leaving out some of what was in the second edition. Otherwise the text would be unmanageable. To keep that from happening, we combined some of the workshops. Some things we simply discarded.

We think this edition is a better book than the second edition. The addition of material on research strikes us as particularly significant: We know that research is becoming more and more important in schools as well as in the business and work world and that the nature of research is changing radically, thanks to new technologies. These new technologies make the pool of resources for research bigger than ever, and the risk of losing one's way correspondingly greater; the mini-workshop on Internet research therefore provides exercises to help students learn to *evaluate* the sources available there in addition to introducing them to the basics of searching and researching.

We've expanded our coverage of drafting, as both teachers and students told us we needed to do more in helping writers with this critical stage of the process. We've added a mini-workshop on writing under pressure, to address a major practical concern student writers have. Finally, in "Sharing and Responding," we're excited with the improvements we've made by changing the two sample student essays and getting new samples of student responses to these essays.

But we didn't follow all the feedback we got. Some teachers wanted us to include more on current cultural and political issues and do less with personal writing. We did add some readings on current social issues, but we did not cut back on personal, exploratory writing because we think that such writing helps us connect to subjects—even social, cultural, and political subjects. Some students told us they wanted us to be more directive, to give more clear-cut assignments, and to devote more space to issues of grammar and form. We did tighten up some of the assignments, but we left most of them pretty open-ended because we think that deciding on an exact topic is part of the whole writing process. We think you need to wrestle with it.

There are many in the fields of writing, teaching writing, and rhetoric who think that all writing should occur in subject-area classes, that no classes should be specifically devoted to writing as a subject. We disagree. In our way of seeing it, students need space and time to work directly on writing: to think about how you go about writing; to try out—with some degree of safety—new approaches, new styles, new forms; and to spend time on sharing and responding to writing.

It is a point of principle with us to treat students as writers: people who deserve to be in charge of what they write, who already know a lot about discourse (even if it sometimes doesn't look like it)—and whose greatest need is *readers*. Feeling ourselves speaking to students as other writers, we have tried to speak honestly about our own writing in a series of "Exploring the Writing Process" boxes scattered throughout the book—excerpts from our own process writing diaries. We've also collected apt pieces of students' and professionals' process writing for these boxes.

Although each workshop is self-contained, we encourage linkage between them, particularly because we want to emphasize revision. After all, most writers can wait a few weeks or even months before revising something they care about. Thus we have designed many workshops in such a way that students can fulfill the assignment by revising or transforming a piece they did for an earlier workshop (see especially Workshops 5, 6, and 7).

About "Sharing and Responding"

When Peter Elbow published *Writing Without Teachers* in 1973, peer response groups were little known and the idea of students working by themselves to give feedback to each other's writing tended to be dismissed as "the blind leading the blind." Since that time, however, peer response has come to be accepted by most writing teachers and theorists as useful and important to the teaching of writing. Yet even now textbooks don't give much specific and detailed help to students for engaging in this complex activity. And students sometimes think of peer feedback as merely an idiosyncratic, experimental activity that their particular teacher happens to like.

Countless teachers have learned that it's no good saying blithely, "OK. Now get into groups and give feedback to each other." Trying it this way—without preparation and sustained help—has led many teachers to announce, "I tried peer response groups and they just don't work!"

We've written the "Sharing and Responding" section to remedy this problem. Students can give each other remarkably useful and productive feedback on their writing. But most of them need substantive help and instruction. And they usually take the process more seriously and do a better job when they see this help laid out carefully in a published book, not just in teacher handouts and oral instructions.

In this section of our text, then, we have gathered together a full and detailed sequence of suggestions for students to use in sharing their writing with each other and giving and receiving useful feedback. We've learned that teachers with the widest range of diverse styles and approaches to the teaching of writing often want their students to learn to use peer response.

We found that our first and second editions tempted some teachers, who had been reluctant to do so or had had unfortunate experiences with it, to try peer responding. For there is often something messy and potentially chaotic about using peer groups. One is always trying to shout one last suggestion while students are moving into pairs or groups, and chairs are scraping, and the hubbub of talk is taking over. *"Oh yes, and don't forget. . ."*—but they don't hear. And one is always running to the photocopy machine at the last minute to copy directions and suggestions. Of course nothing will ever make peer response groups tidy and quiet (we wouldn't want to), but these published suggestions are a good way to give students more specific help: explanations, examples, guidelines, and principles for the complex feedback process. In particular, we like being able to ask students to read about a feedback process *for homework* before we practice it in class.

"Sharing and Responding" contains many more techniques than a student or teacher could use all the time. Our principle in writing the book (and in our teaching) is this: Students need to *try out* a wide spectrum of ways to respond to a text in order to end up finally in the best position to *choose,* on any particular occasion, what kind of feedback to ask for or to give. Different kinds of response are suitable for different writers, different kinds of writing, and for different audience situations.

When we use these techniques for peer responding, we sometimes ask students to work in pairs, sometimes in small groups. We sometimes change groups during the course term; often we stick with stable pairs or groups so that students can build up safety by coming to trust each other. We sometimes try for both goals by keeping permanent pairs throughout the school term, yet sometimes shifting the *pairings* of pairs to make new groups of four.

Before sending students into pairs or groups for peer response, we tend to illustrate and practice each response technique in the whole class on one or two sample texts.

Acknowledgments

We are grateful for help in what (like most writing and revising tasks) has proved to be a bigger job than we expected. We thank our numerous friends and colleagues who tried out early drafts and used the first and second editions, and we thank the students in their classes and in our own. These students and teachers have given us many good comments that have guided us during this revision. As always, we thank the students who have taught us and allowed us to use their work. We thank Lisa Moore, our editor, for all her wise help and encouragement. We thank Susanne Riedell, Michael Warrell, and the rest of the McGraw-Hill production staff for their talent and professionalism. But we feel a special debt of gratitude to Alexis Walker, Development Editor, for her amazingly hard work, deft skill, and discerning taste in seeing the whole process of the third edition through to such swift completion. We feel lucky to have had the chance to work with her. We greatly appreciate the helpful and detailed feedback we received from our original reviewers: Richard L. Larson, Carol Singley, Michael Steinberg, John Trimbur, Maureen Hoag, Susan Kirschner, Jane Terry Lee, Ben W. McClelland, M. Terry Mitze, Betty P. Pytlik, Nancy L. Schultz, and Pia S. Walters, and from those who reviewed the text in preparation for the third edition: Nancy S. Thompson, University of South Carolina; John M. Clark, Bowling Green State University; Veronica M. Keane, St. Peter's College; Mara Holt, Ohio University-Athens; Patricia H. Perry, Virginia Commonwealth University; Yeno Matuka, Ball State University; Richard C. Wing, U. S. Air Force Academy Preparatory School; and Diane Dowdey, Sam Houston State University. Barbara Jones of Sam Houston State University shared with us a journal of her class's experience with the text across an entire semester; many thanks to her and to her students. Joan Mullin of the University of Toledo offered many valuable insights, particularly concerning the approach to visual literacy. Justin Brent of the State University of New York at Stony Brook contributed an excellent review of the text and authored the mini-workshop on "Doing Research on the Web": We extend our sincerest thanks for his fruitful collaboration.

We also thank Doris Alkon, Paul Connolly, Gene Doty, Cami Elbow, Claire Frost, Roni Keane, Laurie Kutchins, Glen Klopfenstein, Irene Papoulis, Marlene Perl, Pat Perry, Debrah Raschke, Valerie Reimers, Barbara Rhodes, John Wright, and Frances Zak.

Peter Elbow
Pat Belanoff

To the Student

Dear Student:

Our goal in this book is to help you write better. This main goal breaks down into several smaller goals: to show you a variety of *ways* to get writing done, to get you to do a variety of *kinds* of writing, and to give you a bit of background theory to help you understand that writing can *produce* ideas and experiences as well as record them. But our main subsidiary goal—in fact, it's almost synonymous with our main goal—is to help you see that writing can be enjoyable as well as useful, fun as well as frustrating.

We enjoyed writing the first edition of this book and revising it for the second and third editions. Our collaboration started when we were both teaching and directing a writing program at the same school (State University of New York at Stony Brook). As we worked together and talked through classroom activities and theories about them, we found ourselves agreeing. In particular, we discovered that both of us wanted some way to make peer feedback and interaction more official and more integral to our classrooms. What was most exciting, though, was our growing recognition that our talk and sharing was leading us to ideas neither of us would have come to alone. When one of us moved to another school (University of Massachusetts at Amherst), our collaboration continued in visits, at conferences, and in hours of e-mail and phone conversations. Both of the revised editions came about that way.

But writing and revising this book was also frustrating and difficult at times. Deadlines to meet. Ideas that just wouldn't come out as good on paper as they seemed in our conversations. Struggling to get our words to sound right to us. Getting fed up with the whole project and how much time it was taking. Proofreading to do. Decisions on readings and on the order of workshops. Little things such as deciding on size of type and where Exploring the Writing Process boxes should go. But it was a pleasure to see the first and second editions finished and printed with all our writing between their covers. We are now looking forward to the same pleasure at soon seeing the third edition.

One thing we have not changed is the title of our textbook: *A Community of Writers: A Workshop Course in Writing.* That title expressed then and continues to express now some of our major thoughts about writing and teaching writing. The key words in it for us are *community, workshop,* and *writer.* Here's why:

Community Language is social and socializing. It's possible for us to write just for ourselves and throw it away—in fact, we're going to try to get you to do that at times in this book. But if you had never had anyone to *talk* to, you would never have developed any language at all, and therefore wouldn't be able to talk or write even to yourself. And the benefits of social language continue throughout our lives. The more we experience the pleasure that comes from communication—listening to others, reading to them, writing to them, talking to them—the better we get at all these skills.

Workshop The only way to learn to write is by writing. Teachers can't teach you directly how to write; they can only create situations in which you learn for yourself from what you're doing. Our book asks for a classroom where students do things under the guidance of a teacher who is a master at writing because he or she has done more of it and thought more about it than students. But your teacher isn't a person who does it in some special, magical way any more than a master carpenter works in a magical way.

Thus the heart of this book is a series of writing situations and assignments. We know that if you can enter into them, you will teach yourself writing. We believe that deep down, most students want to work on their writing, though some of them will resent being made to do so; on many campuses, freshman writing is a required course. If you're resentful, we ask you to put your resentment on the back burner and enter into our assignments. Give us a chance. We think we can help you teach yourself. In truth, the most important piece you'll write in this course may well be the biography of yourself-as-writer which comes at the end of the book. It should contain *what you've learned* and *how you've learned it.* It will be a useful document, particularly if you include advice for yourself for future writing: almost a little individualized textbook.

Writer We assume that all students, including you, will profit from being treated as writers. A writer isn't some peculiar absent-minded genius who goes into a trance and magically produces good writing. A writer is someone who writes a lot and who cares a lot about it. The best writers struggle. You may well already *be* a writer. If not, we can help you become one in this non-magical sense of the word—someone who enjoys writing, cares about writing, and struggles but gets satisfaction from the struggle. Our first step is to start right off *treating* you like a writer.

Here are the things we assume when we treat you like a writer:

- Like all writers, you have lots of words and ideas in you. If it feels as though you don't, that's just a sign that you haven't put down enough words and ideas yet. You may be surprised to discover that the more you put down, the more you'll have left. We'll get you started.
- Like all writers, you own your writing. Only you can know when your words fulfill your intentions. Others—your classmates, friends, teacher, tutors in your school's writing center—can help you see how your words work, but it is you who must decide what suggestions are important and what changes to make (if any).
- Like all writers, you need to share your writing with others. Only by sharing your writing and getting the feeling of what it's like to have an audience by actually reading to one will you begin to know what it means to com-

municate through writing. Part of the problem in schools and colleges is that you often write only for a teacher—writing about topics the teacher knows more about than you do and writing only for a grade. We can't totally eliminate these problems, but we can get you to write for more people than your teacher. After all, writers don't write for just one person. They learn that different people have different reactions to the same piece of writing. That's something you'll discover too from listening to classmates' reactions to your writing. You may even learn that the teacher's comment and grade on the paper is not as valuable in the long run as the reactions of these other readers.

- Like all writers, you're already a sophisticated user of your native language. When you speak, you don't consciously think about words; you think about meaning and the words tend to come out correctly. Unless you are scared, subjects and verbs usually agree, sentence structures work, vocabulary is appropriate. In addition to that, you also react almost intuitively to your social situation—where you are and whom you're talking to. Therefore when you concentrate on your meaning as you write, all these natural language abilities will function in the same way to produce mostly correct language. This natural language ability will also help you make judgments about your writing and the writing of your classmates. You may need to put more trust in these natural abilities.

But it's just as well to acknowledge a difficulty on this score. We say we want you to *own* your writing and to take responsibility for your own choices. But here is a book full of "orders" for you to follow, used in a course where your teacher will also give you "orders." It's easy to feel like you are just doing "our" writing or "your teacher's" writing.

It might seem as though the definition of a good student is someone who's good at following orders. But that's not quite right. The definition of a good student is someone who can *learn the most,* and what makes you learn the most is the ability to *own* even what you are stuck with. Sometimes in order to learn to own, you need to be able to resist. Thus it might happen that we tell you to do *X,* and your teacher compounds it by requiring *Y* in addition, but you realize that you will learn the most if you do *Z.* If you get a lower mark for it, well, you decide that's worth the price—because it's your learning.

About the Structure of this Book

There are three separate sections: the workshops, the mini-workshops, and "Sharing and Responding."

Workshops

The workshops make up the main part of the book. They contain the main activities and writing assignments (one major assignment per workshop). We believe that most of the learning will come from these activities and assignments, not from any ideas or information we give. We assume that most teachers will spend at least a week on each workshop (sometimes longer). There are too many workshops for one semester, so teachers will have to leave some out. Many of the workshops ask you to write something that builds upon what you wrote for an earlier one, but despite these potential sequences, all the workshops can stand on their own. Thus teachers can use the workshops in whatever order suits them. However your teacher arranges the workshops, you'll want to keep all your writing for possible later use.

At the end of most workshops, we have included a section titled "Exploring Theory." In these sections we share some of the thinking we've done that lies behind the workshop. We are wrapped up in these explorations; we think the issues are important. But we have no doubt that the main way you learn is by doing the workshop's activities, not by reading theory. So if you don't feel that these explorations are helping you, skip them (unless your teacher says otherwise).

At the end of every workshop we offer a collection of readings that echo, elaborate, or otherwise comment on that workshop's primary focus. Unless otherwise stated, all readings are student-authored. The large number of such readings and excerpts in our book reflects our belief that they provide the best models for student writers at work. Each of the students whose work is represented in the text actually developed as a writer using the techniques we describe in this book; we hope you'll agree that their results justify our confidence in the techniques.

Mini-Workshops

These short sections can be read or studied on your own or used as the basis of single class sessions. Mini-workshops seldom involve writing assignments.

Sharing and Responding

We've put into one section all the good methods we know for getting feedback from classmates on your writing. You can use these in pairs or in small groups. The ability to give responses to your classmates' writing and to get their responses to your own writing may be the most important thing you learn from this book. You can use it for all writing tasks, in school and out. We talk more about it in a separate introduction to that section. ("Sharing and Responding" is also available as a separate booklet.)

We would like feedback on our book. Sometimes we fear we get too preachy. Sometimes we get carried away with our own ideas. Sometimes we go on about them too long. We want to sound like we're issuing invitations to write rather than orders to write. But we may not always get that tone exactly right. We welcome your feedback about all this as well as about individual workshops and assignments. Maybe someday we'll revise this book again, but our main feeling now is one we're sure you often feel about a writing task: relief at calling it done—at least for now.

Peter Elbow
Pat Belanoff

Introduction

This book has two main messages: Writing is hard. Writing is easy. It's no secret that writing is hard—or at least that writing *well* is hard. But it will help to explore the nature of that difficulty.

Imagine you are having a relaxed, interesting conversation with your best friend. You're in a comfortable room where you both feel right at home. You are both talking away and having a wonderful time. You find you have lots to say because you like talking to this person who likes you and is interested in what you have to say.

Then someone else comes into the room and starts listening to the conversation. A friend. But quickly you feel that something is peculiar because this friend doesn't say anything, doesn't join in, only listens. It makes you feel a little funny, but you keep up the conversation.

Then more people start coming in. Some of them are strangers and they don't say anything either: They just listen.

Then your friend stops talking altogether and asks you to do all the talking yourself.

Then someone pulls out a tape recorder and starts recording what you say.

Finally your friend, even though she won't join in the conversation, starts quizzing you as you are talking and asks:

- "Are you really sure that what you are saying is interesting?"
- "Are you sure that what you are saying is right?"
- "Are you sure you understand what you are saying?"

And she doesn't just ask questions, she gives "helpful suggestions":

- "Make sure that what you say is well organized."
- "Think carefully about who is listening. Are you speaking in a way that suits these listeners?"
- "Watch your language; don't make any mistakes in grammar; don't sound dumb."

This is an allegory of writing. In writing, you must keep on putting out words, but no one answers or responds. You are putting out words for an audience but you don't know how they are reacting. You may know who the intended reader is (probably someone who will *grade* it), but you don't really know who else *might* read it, who any reader might show it to, or who might find it lying around. You are trying to get your thinking right, your organization right, and your language right—all at the same time. And there's spelling and punctuation to worry about too.

No wonder writing is hard.

But we have another message: Writing is easy. Writing is easier than talking because it's safer than talking. For you can "say" something on paper and no one has to see it. If you've ever blurted out something wrong to the wrong person and wanted to bite your tongue off as soon as the words came out of your mouth, you know that you can never undo what you've spoken. But in writing you can blurt out anything and see what it looks like on paper and no one need ever see it. You can even keep yourself from ever seeing it again. In short, writing can be safer than talking.

People expect you to make some sort of sense when you talk; otherwise, they'll stop listening or think you're odd. But you don't have to make any sense when you write. You can go on and on forever when you write; you can't do that in speech because people will stop listening after a while no matter how much they like you.

Writing lets you "talk" about any topic at all, even if you don't know anyone who is interested enough to listen. And there are certain things it's hard to talk to anyone about. Writing lets you "talk" to anyone and tell them anything—and you can decide later whether to show it to them.

Admittedly, in describing how easy writing is, we're talking about writing in itself, not about *good* writing. It gets harder when "good" enters the picture or when you're writing for a tough reader, particularly a tough reader who will judge the writing. But even when your goal is to produce good writing for a harsh judge, you can *start out* this way, just writing for yourself. Afterwards it turns out to be much easier to make it good than you might have thought. For one thing, when you do all that easy writing, surprising amounts of it are already pretty good. Those parts that are potentially good but badly written are often easy to fix up once you've got them down in one form or another. What's really hard about writing is unnecessary: trying to get it right the *first time.*

Behind what we've just said is the fact that writing requires two mental abilities that are so different that they usually conflict with each other: the ability to *create* an abundance of words and ideas; and the ability to *criticize* and discard words and ideas. To write well we need to be both generative and cutthroat. We all know the awful feeling of trying to use both "muscles" at once: trying to come up with words and ideas and at the same time seeing how none of them is good enough. We get stuck. But we can get unstuck by separating the mental processes; we can think of more words and ideas if we hold off all criticism (as in brainstorming); and we can be more critical and tough-minded if we have already piled up more material than we need.

In short, even though writing gets most of us into the pickle of trying to use two muscles that get in each other's way, it is writing that creates the ideal ground for using those muscles one at a time.

A Community of Writers

A Workshop Course in Writing

Workshops

Part I

Ways of Writing

An Introduction to the Variety of Writing Processes

Essential Premises

- Everyone can learn to become comfortable putting words and thoughts down on paper. Writing doesn't have to be a struggle.
- Writing is very different, depending on the situation—especially depending on topic, audience, and kind of writing. It helps to learn different "writing gears."

Main Assignment Preview

We have two related goals for this first workshop. First, we will show you how to get words and thoughts on paper quickly, easily, and productively—helping you realize that there are always plenty more where they came from. In this way we can help you build a foundation of confidence in the face of a blank page—confidence you can draw on later when writing tasks get harder. Our emphasis here is on *generating* words and ideas.

Second, we want to introduce you to a wide variety of kinds of writing—to show you that there is no one thing, "writing," but rather different kinds of writing for different situations.

The heart of this workshop is a series of short writing tasks which involve different writing processes. Some of the pieces will be for others to read and some only for yourself; some pieces will have a specified topic and some will not. Your teacher will probably ask you to do some of this writing in class and some of it at home.

With these short writing assignments, we are introducing a major goal of the whole book: to help you be more conscious of what you are doing and what is happening as you write so that you can take more control of your writing process. By trying out different kinds of writing and reflecting on what is happening each time, you will get over something that causes many people trouble: the tendency to use just one "writing gear" for every writing task.

We won't work much with revising in this workshop, but we'll introduce a minimal kind of cut-and-paste revising to help you end up with a *main assignment:* a "collage" of good passages that will be a miniportrait of yourself as a writer at this point. This will be a piece of finished writing that you can share with others and with your teacher.

A Spectrum of Writing Tasks

1. *Freewriting.* Freewriting means writing privately and writing without stopping. Just write whatever words come to your mind or whatever you want to explore at this moment. Don't worry about whether your writing is any good or even whether it makes sense. Don't worry about spelling or grammar. If you can't think of the word you want, just put in a squiggle. Keep on writing and see what comes. Changing topics is fine. Follow your mind or the words wherever they want to go. If you run out of something to say, just write "I have nothing to say," or write about how you feel at the moment, or keep repeating the last word or the last sentence. Or write swear words. More will come.

Don't worry about trying to write fast and capture *everything* that comes to mind. The main thing in freewriting is trusting yourself and your words: taking a spirit of adventure. The no stopping doesn't mean you have to hurry or be tense. You can write slowly and take your time to breathe and keep your hand or arm from tensing up. Since you don't have to worry about whether there are any mistakes or whether someone else would like or dislike what you write, try to pour your full attention on the feelings and thoughts in your mind.

Invite risks. Remember, you don't have to show freewriting to anyone. There is an example of a student's freewriting in the Readings at the end of the workshop. (We talk about why freewriting is so important to us in the final section of the workshop, "Exploring Theory.")

2. *Focused freewriting.* This is writing where you stay on one topic, but you harness your "freewriting muscle"—the muscle that enables you to pour words down on paper quickly without planning or worrying about quality. You are harnessing that muscle for the sake of exploring one subject. Focused

Exploring the Writing Process

There seems to be a sort of fatality in my mind leading me to put at first my statement and proposition in a wrong or awkward form. Formerly I used to think about my sentences before writing them down; but for several years I have found that it saves time to scribble in a vile hand whole pages as quickly as I possibly can, contracting half the words; and then correct deliberately. Sentences thus scribbled down are often better ones than I could have written deliberately.

Charles Darwin

freewriting is especially useful for the hardest thing about writing: *getting started.* Try 10 minutes of focused freewriting on one of these topics:

- Write about a time when writing went particularly well or badly. What was the topic, and who was the audience? Try to tell in detail how you went about writing and what happened. What can you learn from this example?
- Write about someone who was important to your writing: a teacher or someone else who was helpful or harmful.

3. *Clustering or mapping.* Try a cluster diagram on one of these topics: "What does writing mean to you?" or "What is a writer?" or "Do you think of yourself as a writer?" Put the word "writing" or "writer" in the middle of a sheet of paper and draw a circle around it. Then jot down all around it as many words and concepts as you can think of that you associate with writing. The ones that seem most central you can write closest to your central word; if they seem less central, write them farther away. Try to keep related ones more or less together, but this isn't always possible. Still, you can draw connecting lines between words that seem related. (See Figure 1, an example of someone's cluster diagram of the topic, "reading.")

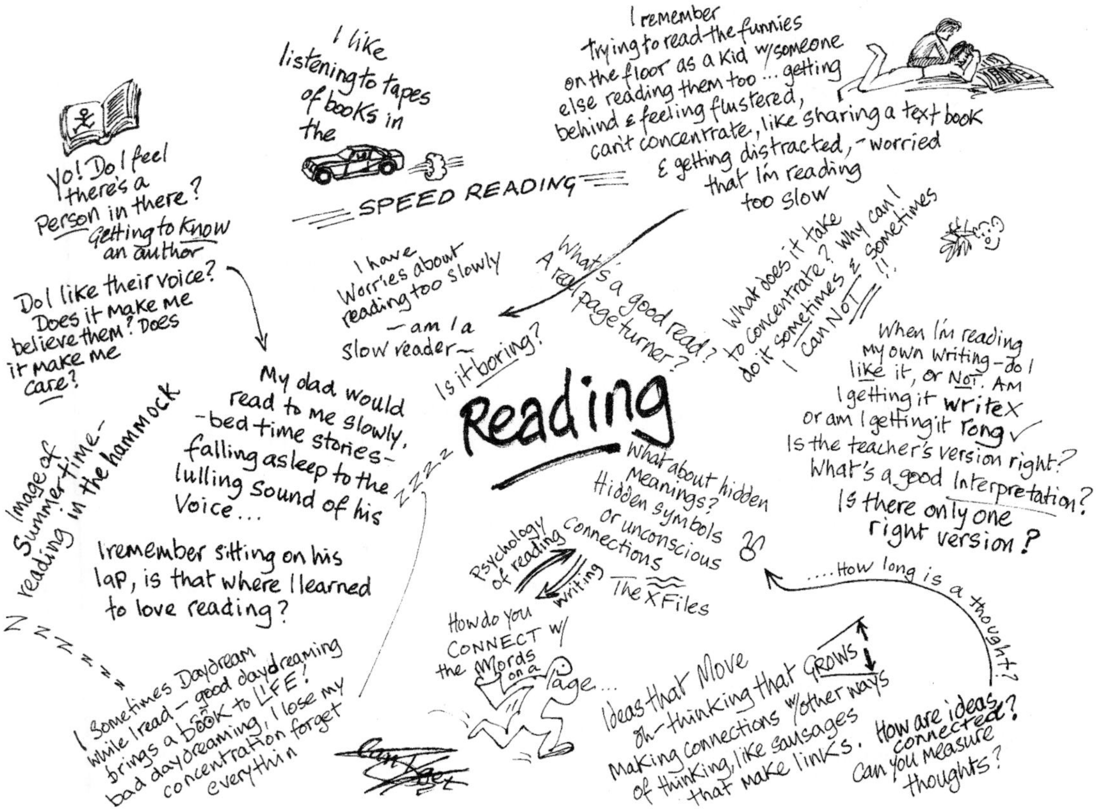

Figure 1 Cluster Diagram

A cluster diagram is thus a "map" of how concepts and ideas and feelings sit in your head. Cluster diagrams are often messy; sometimes you end up with a kind of spider's web of relations. But such diagrams are a good means for quickly getting down lots of possible subtopics and connections and also for giving a quick overview of a large conceptual territory. (You might think of traditional outlines as a more orderly form of clustering or mapping, but they aren't so visual or spatial. For more about using outlines, see pages 313–314.)

4. *Invisible writing.* This may sound odd, but you may actually find it *helpful* to write in such a way that you can't even see the words you are writing. This odd situation is very easy to achieve if you write on a computer: just turn down the screen so it doesn't show your writing at all. Invisible writing is confusing at first, but most people get used to it quickly and then find it surprisingly useful. It makes you write *more* because you can't pause or you'll lose track of what you're saying.

What's more important is how invisible writing increases your *concentration.* It does wonders if you are tired or your mind is wandering too much. It forces you to focus better on what you have in mind—on the emerging meaning in your head. Invisible writing makes most people realize how often they get distracted from their topic in their regular writing: either because something else is on their mind or because they stop too often and look back at what they have already written. Try invisible writing, especially if you write on a word processor. Possible topic for invisible writing:

- Write about the *physical conditions* for your writing. Where and when do you like to write? What implements do you use and why: pen, pencil, typewriter, computer? What kind of pad or paper? Do you need silence and solitude or do you prefer to have music on or other people around?

5. *Public informal writing.* Here is a piece of writing to share with others (in this case with your classmates). It is not for evaluation, but only for the sake of communicating with them. Because it is public writing, you may find yourself pausing and thinking and perhaps changing some things as you go along (as opposed to freewriting, where you never stop but put down whatever comes to mind). Since you probably don't yet know the others in your class, give yourself time at the end to look over what you've written and see whether you want to cross out or change anything. Possible topics:

- Write a short introduction of yourself to others in your class. What would you like them to know? You don't have to tell more than you feel comfortable telling.
- Introduce yourself as a writer. What are your strengths as a writer and learner? What are you proud of? What do you most want to learn? What do you need from others in the class to do your best as a student and writer? What can you contribute to a learning community?

Please read your short piece out loud to a partner, to a small group, or to the whole class. Please read slowly and distinctly. Don't sabotage your work by mumbling or reading too quickly. The sharing will help everyone in the class learn more about the writing process and about each other.

6. *Letter.* Letters are partly public and partly private. That is, they go to a reader, but usually only to one or two readers. Of course there are "open letters" or "letters to the editor," but they feel different from most letters precisely because they are so much more public. Letters to friends and family are often informal and casual. Sometimes we don't even look them over before mailing them. But letters can be just as formal as any writing if they are intended for strangers or for business purposes. Still, even in the most formal letter, we usually write directly *to* the receiver—addressing her* in the second person—which is rare in any other kind of writing.

- Write a letter to your teacher introducing yourself. Say as much or as little as you want at this point. We suggest that you talk about your goals, hopes, and needs for this class: what you want to get out of it, what you can contribute, what you hope will not happen, and what makes you nervous or anxious about the class. This is not writing for a grade; it is writing to communicate. We teachers can teach better if we know more about our students and what they want and need from the course.

7. *Collaborative writing.* Much of the world's writing is done collaboratively. We collaborated to write this book. Probably most writing in business and government and research is done collaboratively. There is often a collaborative element even in individual writing (for example, when your ideas become different as a result of discussing them with others or getting feedback). Collaboration is more companionable, but it can also be more complicated to have to work things out together. What we're asking now is for you to work with one or two others to produce a paragraph or more on one of these topics. Together you can work your way to agreement on what you write (or perhaps you already agree) or write a piece that describes your difference of opinion and experience. (See Workshop 3 for more about collaboration.)

- What are some of the most helpful and least helpful things that teachers have done in assisting you with your writing?
- What makes a good teacher of writing?

8. *Evaluated writing.* Many students have never written except for a teacher, and the teacher has always noted mistakes or given some kind of evaluative comment or even a grade. Have you, like many students, fallen into assuming that writing *means* writing for evaluation by a teacher? We will try to convince you that this is not the most useful way to think about writing. Of course much of your school writing will be evaluated by your teacher, but you've done a great deal of informal writing, some of it not for your teacher. Now see what it feels like to write something that your teacher will evaluate in some way.

---

* Sometimes we refer to persons in general as *she* or *her*, and sometimes as *he* or *him*. We have definite reasons for this policy. First, we want to avoid the sexism of referring to all persons with masculine words; there's no doubt that the gender of pronouns has an effect on readers. But second, we want to avoid the awkwardness of phrases like "he or she" and the vagueness of always going to the plural "they" and "them." The singular pronoun tends to convey a more concrete meaning and thus more force. We'd actually like readers to *see* people when we talk about "she" or "he." Sometimes they'll see female persons and sometimes male persons.

Possible topics:

- Write a short summary of one of our pieces in "Exploring Theory," in this workshop (pages 15–18), or of something else your teacher may suggest. This is a test of careful reading as well as careful writing.
- Briefly describe the differences between speaking and writing.

9. *Revising.* Try revising one of the shorter pieces you have written so far. For now we won't talk about techniques for revising (we will in some later workshops). Pick a short piece that interests you but doesn't satisfy you—perhaps one that you have read aloud. Please don't just change a word here and there; try wading in and making substantive changes—changes even in what it says. Experiment. Notice that "revising" doesn't necessarily mean making something better: It means making it different. You won't learn the difficult skill of making things better unless you are adventuresome about making them different—and perhaps even worse.

10. *Process writing.* Much of what we've asked for in this workshop has already been process writing: an exploration of what happens when you write, which is to say, an exploration of your writing process. But so far we've asked you to explore the writing you've done in the *past.* Now we want you to do some process writing about something you've just written, so that what happened as you wrote is still fresh in your mind. What usually works best for process writing is simply to tell the story of what actually happened with as much honesty and detail as possible. The goal is not to judge yourself or prove anything or reach big conclusions. You are just trying to *notice what happened* in a spirit of calm, benign acceptance. You can trust that if you do process writing regularly (and we will try to twist your arm to make that happen!), you *will* reach plenty of interesting conclusions. You don't have to *try* for them. If you are like most people, you'll have to give some effort to remembering some of the steps you went through and the feelings and thoughts that went on in your head. Notice how this student used the form of a story to remember what was happening in the process:

> First I thought of my brother and the words tumbled onto the paper as fast as I could write. Time went by faster than I expected. I came up with some thoughts that were new to me. Then when I wrote about my mother, I began to feel mixed up and I slowed down and I couldn't figure out what I wanted to say. I knew what I felt about my brother; I wasn't sure of my feelings when I came to my mother. I stopped for a long time and walked around feeling stuck. Then . . .

Sometimes process writing is easier if you do it after two writing sessions and compare what happened in the two. Remember that process writing is not only about the act of writing itself, but also about *everything* that goes into writing: thoughts about your topic way before you start to write, collecting material to use, talks with others, feedback, daydreaming, false starts. Try it now:

- Do a 10-minute process writing about what was happening as you wrote one of the preceding tasks or assignments. Look for the details or specifics of what you did or what happened.

11. *Cover letter.* When writers send their manuscript to a publisher or magazine or editor, they always include a letter introducing it. Many teachers ask for cover letters with all major assignments. We do. We find we can give much more useful feedback if our students tell us a bit about what was going on for them as they wrote (giving us some process writing), and then answer questions like these:

- What was your main point and goal in this paper? What effect were you trying to achieve?
- What do you see as the strengths of the paper, and what would you try to do if you were to revise it some more?
- What didn't you manage to include? Are there other thoughts you'd like to share?
- What feedback or reactions did you get at various times in this paper, and how did you make use of them, if at all? Any other kinds of help—from classmates? teacher? others?

And most important of all:

- What kind of feedback or response would you like from your reader?

It's difficult to hand in a paper you've worked hard on and not say a few words about it. If we give a piece of our writing to someone else—whether it's for feedback or just for information—we invariably say a few things about what we wanted to achieve in the writing. Almost any teacher, scholar, fiction writer, or poet who reads something to an audience *says* something before she starts to read in order to create some link between herself and her audience. We find that cover letters can serve as this kind of link too.

You'll see many pieces of process writing in this book—lots of short "Exploring the Writing Process" boxes scattered throughout the text and in

Exploring the Writing Process

Cover Letter

I had a very good idea of what I wanted to write about the song I picked. This is one of my favorite songs. I like it because of the meaning it has and because of its great rhythm. In starting to write this, the inflow of information just flooded the paper. I kept putting down the things that I felt were trying to be said. After I analyzed almost every detail and every line of the song, I began to question where this song is leading and what he is really trying to say. I began with the idea that this song was about suicide in general and in the end I ended up contradicting that idea and finding a new meaning to the song. I was very surprised at finding this new meaning just from this analysis. I now listen to the song in a different light.

I have to credit a friend of mine who brought out the idea of the threat of nuclear war as the major idea in the song. If he didn't point it out to me, then I really wouldn't have been so interested in trying to find out the deeper meanings of this song.

Please tell me which points are strongest and clearest and which ones don't work for you. Where it doesn't work, is it the point itself or the writing that doesn't work? I feel kind of unsure about the structure. Any suggestions?

Student

the Readings sections. Some are written by students, some by published writers, and some by us. We've put in lots of process writing because we're fascinated by the enormous variation in what happens when people write—differences between people and even between different occasions for the same person. We speak more about process writing at the end of this workshop in the Exploring Theory section. Obviously we take process writing seriously and are trying to give you lots of short but useful examples of people reflecting on how they write.*

Main Assignment: *A Collage about You as Writer and How You Write*

A "collage" in the original sense, as coined by artists, is a picture produced not by painting or drawing but by pasting actual objects on the canvas—objects such as theater tickets, bits of colored paper, cloth, cardboard, or metal. A written collage consists of separate, disconnected bits of writing rather than one continuous piece. Usually there are spaces or asterisks at the "joints" between the pieces of writing.

A collage can serve as a "quick-and-dirty" way to produce a finished piece of writing. That is, you can simply pick out the passages you like best and put them together in whatever order strikes you as most interesting. It is traditional in collages to organize the bits intuitively.

In effect, a collage allows you simply to *skip* what are often the hardest parts of the writing process: revising weak passages (you just throw them away); getting the whole piece unified (all the bits are *related,* but there may not be an exact center); figuring out the best order (you settle for a sequence that seems fun or interesting); and making transitions between sections (there are none). And yet the finished collage is often effective and satisfying. We've provided a number of examples of the collage in the "Readings" for this workshop. The collage by Peter Elbow is *about* collages and will give you help in making yours.

Since the collage we ask you to produce is a portrait of yourself and your experiences in writing, think of your teacher and your classmates as your audience for this assignment: You are introducing that side of yourself to these relative strangers and also helping them learn about how writing is for different people. But think also of *yourself* as your audience: You will manage to tell things about yourself that you didn't know before.

Here are the simple steps you need to follow in making your collage:

- Look through all the pieces you have written so far and choose the ones you like best for giving a picture of how you write. You can choose portions of pieces, especially if the pieces are long.
- Write some more short bits about you and your writing. What you have should suggest other possibilities: incidents, memories, pieces you liked or hated.

---

* In scientific or technical fields, the term "process writing" is often used quite differently; namely, to refer to writing that describes some particular and often technical process—for example, how to analyze blood samples in a lab or how to construct a piece of equipment.

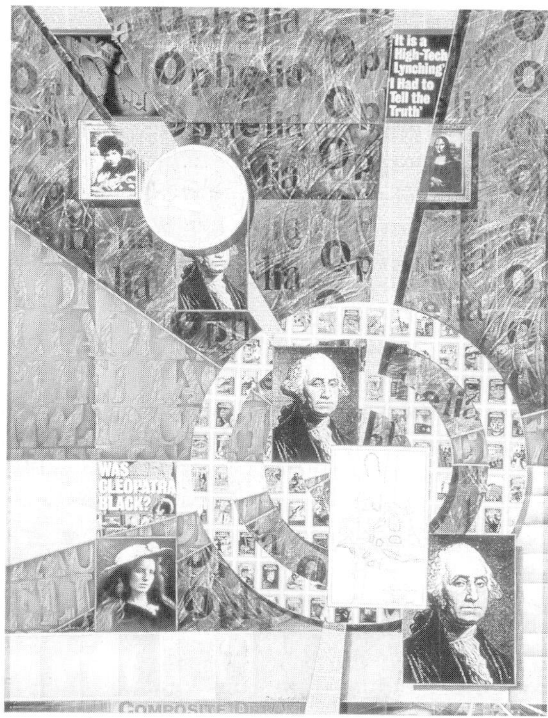

"Composite Dream," © 1992 by John Hertzberg, collage artist, deals with metaphorical abstraction. www.JohnHertzberg.com

The term "collage" usually refers to visual art, as in this interesting modern example.

- Spread them out on a table or on the floor so you can see them all.
- Arrange them in what seems the best order.
- Feel free to do the choosing and arranging by instinct or intuition.
- You might now see the need for one or two more sections. Perhaps other experiences or thoughts come to mind—perhaps an opening or closing piece, but not a traditional "introduction" or "conclusion."
- Next revise it all, but in a minimal and purely "negative" way. That is, don't rewrite (unless there's some particular section you really want to rework). Just *leave out* words, phrases, sentences, or passages that don't work. Instead of trying to make nice connections or transitions between the remaining passages, leave spaces or put in asterisks.
- Copyedit your collage carefully and type it so that it looks its best when your friends and classmates see it. You may need help with copyediting from a classmate, family member, or roommate. You can return the favor by carefully proofreading something of theirs, since most of us have an easier time seeing mistakes or usage problems in someone else's writing than in our own.

Suggestions for Collaboration

The collage form is natural for collaboration. You can take passages from each of several writers and decide collaboratively on which pieces to choose and which order to put them in. You then have a group collage. It is not necessary to look for agreement: Your collaborative collage will probably be even stronger if it shows sharp contrasts between people's experiences and feelings and conclusions. It becomes a kind of dialogue or conversation, not a monologue. More about this in Workshop Three.

Sharing and Responding

We are not suggesting feedback or revising for this first workshop, but sharing is definitely in order: reading your piece to listeners for the sake of communication and enjoyment, not for reactions. You have probably already shared some of the short pieces. It will be a pleasure now to share the whole collage. You will get the most benefit and enjoyment from reading it out loud, perhaps in small groups. It is fun to share a collaborative collage by having the different authors each read their bits. We hear movement back and forth among the different voices. But remember, no feedback at this point, just communication and enjoyment.

If you are not used to reading things out loud to others, you may find it embarrassing or difficult. Timidity and fear get in the way. The trick is to read it as though you *mean* it, as though you *respect* your own words, as though you want to *give* the words to your listeners. Listeners are not supposed to give feedback, but they should stop you and tell you if they can't hear you well. It's all right for them to pester you on this matter. Listen to your voice and enjoy it. If you learn to read your writing out loud so others *get it,* you will see a powerful improvement in your writing. It can also be useful and enjoyable to trade papers and have people read each other's papers out loud.

Process Journal

We ask you to keep a process journal for this course. It might be a whole notebook, a section of a larger notebook, or a folder where you keep separate pieces of process writing. We make regular process writing a requirement in our courses. And we always end our courses with Workshop 16, which asks for a full writing autobiography or case study of your writing and writing process throughout the semester. For this, you can draw heavily on your process journal.

The best time to do process writing is right after you have been writing. The goal is to find out what really happened—the facts of what occurred on that particular occasion. Don't struggle for conclusions; trust that they'll come.

We spoke earlier of doing process writing in the form of a *story* of your writing session. Another good approach is to plunge into an exploration of what was most *difficult* or *frustrating* for you in that session. Explore what happened: What led to this difficulty? How did you deal with it? Tell everything you can. Interesting insights often come. In short, you can use process writing as a way to get some power over what is difficult for you in your writing. As you explore difficulties or frustrations over a number of sessions, you will begin to figure out how to avoid trouble.

In each workshop we'll give you a few questions to help you remember and notice your writing process. If you can remember what is useful and interesting without our questions, feel free to ignore them (unless your teacher asks for answers to specific ones). Here are some possible process writing questions for this workshop:

- What did you notice about trying to write without stopping when you freewrote?
- What did you notice about writing privately and writing for an audience? Were there differences in writing to different audiences?
- Sharing. What was it like reading your words to others? listening to theirs? having your collage distributed?

Exploring Theory: *Freewriting and Process Writing*

1. Why We Think Freewriting Is Important

Why should freewriting be so helpful if it is so easy and invites such carelessness in writing and thinking? And why does it also invite some of our best writing and thinking?

First, let's look at the easiness—in comparison with the difficulty of regular writing:

- Writing is usually judged or even graded, but freewriting is not.
- Writing usually means thinking about spelling and grammar, but in freewriting you can put all that out of mind.
- Writing is supposed to make sense, but freewriting can be incoherent or nonsensical.
- Writing is supposed to stay on one topic and be organized, but freewriting can jump all over the place.
- Writing is usually for an audience, but freewriting is private. Thus, freewriting is even *safer* than speaking, since we almost never speak except when someone's listening.
- Writing is usually supposed to be more important and dignified and "better" than speech. ("Why take the time to write something out unless you are going to try to get it right?") But freewriting is an invitation to let words be less important and less careful than speech—and to see what you can learn from them.

Thus freewriting removes all the difficulties of regular writing. But in one sense, freewriting is *more demanding* than regular writing; it insists on the hardest thing of all: writing without stopping. But it makes that demand in a context of high safety. Thus, freewriting gets you going, gets you rolling. The hardest thing about writing is to make yourself keep putting words down on paper, and that's just what freewriting makes happen.

In addition, even though freewriting allows you to be careless or relaxed, it almost always heightens your thinking. That is, freewriting allows you to stop thinking about the *medium* of writing—about spelling and grammar, forming letters with your hand, choosing words, and being concerned with quality. It makes writing as easy as speaking. And therefore it helps you to devote *all your attention* to what you are trying to say. You need no longer be distracted by the process of writing.

Regular careful writing requires you to take the chaos inside your head and turn it into coherence on paper. But this is too hard for most of us to do in one step. Freewriting provides a helpful middle step: getting the chaos in your head *on paper.* This frightens some people at first, but it is helpful to discover that it's not so hard to get down on paper what's going on in your head. Then it's not so hard to improve once it's down on paper. What's hard about writing comes from trying to *improve* what's in your head while you are in the act of writing it down. With freewriting you get two steps to produce coherence instead of struggling to produce it all in one step.

Thus, freewriting is full of "wrong words." You are writing along and get to a word and have a feeling it's the wrong word but you haven't got time to find a better one so you put it down. Putting down the *wrong* word often leads you to the right word ("I dislike him. No, it's not that I dislike him, it's that I'm always uncomfortable around him.") For some mysterious reason, it usually helps to write down that wrong word rather than to stop writing and search mentally for a better one. Freewriting makes you write it down. You get to notice that it's not quite right, yet still write it down. Then when you come back, you can usually find a much better word.

Despite all this freedom and all these wrong words, we have virtually never seen a passage of freewriting that we couldn't understand easily, while we've seen many passages of careful writing that we couldn't make head or tail of. And most passages of freewriting have a voice and energy and life to them.

Exploring the Writing Process

My free writing is less presentable in handwriting than the public writing. My free writing is a bit more imaginative than the public writing. The public writing seems more formal than the personal writing done in the free writing exercise. I tried to cut down the sentences in my public writing to a shorter type rather than the possible run ons in the long sentences found most presently in the free writing exercise. I seem to be preoccupied with the fact that I have problems with writing. This is reflected in my public writing. I am not at ease with writing publicly and tend to be very formal toward the audience or the reader. New or more complex words tend to pop into my head easier than when I am intent on trying to deal with grammatical problems in my writing. I do understand that shorter and briefer sentences are the best but I like to make my sentences a little more extravagant.

Student

It's not that freewriting is always *good.* Far from it. But interestingly enough, it's easier to tighten and clarify bad freewriting than bad careful writing. Try it. Find a long stretch of bad freewriting and also a piece of careful writing that you struggled over but which is still weak or problematic. Now try to clean up both passages. You'll discover that the careless writing is easier to fix. The careful writing, on the other hand, is sort of delicately glued together and therefore hard to re-glue.

Sometimes a skilled student objects, "But freewriting is for blocked beginners, and I'm a fluent, skilled writer already." It's true that freewriting is good for unskilled students, but we find that *skilled, experienced* writers and teachers get even more out of freewriting. It's an exercise whose payoff increases with the expertise of the writer.

In case you think that only loose, artistic spirits advocate freewriting, notice the following passage from the Official United States Coast Guard writing guide for officers: "Instead of staring at a blank piece of paper, let your mind run freely. Jot down your ideas in sentence form or as an outline without regard to order, grammar, punctuation, or syntax. Keep writing as long as the ideas keep coming."*

You can't predict how freewriting will work for you. Some people start off with coherent freewriting, but as they use it, they gradually drift into freewriting that's more jumpy and surprising. Some people start off jumpy. We've discovered that better writers seem to allow more shifts and jumps into their freewriting—and more talking to themselves. They trust themselves enough to follow their minds where they lead. We sense that people go through stages: perhaps a stage where you write only, "Nothing today, nothing, nothing," over and over—or some other kind of refusal to make meaning. It is important to give yourself permission for this and not measure freewriting by the *quality* of what you turn out. We sense that freewriting "works" in an underground way on what the writer needs to work on, but obviously that's a statement of faith. (We first heard of freewriting from an important pioneer teacher of writing, Ken Macrorie. We've listed a couple of good books by him in Works Cited section at the end of this book. We've also cited a book of essays about freewriting, edited by Belanoff, Elbow, and Fontaine.)

2. Why We Think Process Writing Is Important

Writing usually seems a mystery: Sometimes you slave over something and it comes out awful, and sometimes you dash something off and it comes out good. Yet, dashing everything off won't solve all your writing problems either. Thus, it is common to feel frustrated and even helpless about writing. Frequent process writing can help you understand your mental processes better and give you more power and control over yourself as a writer. You can figure out what specific procedures work for you, under what kinds of condi-

* John V. Noel and James Stavridis, *Division Officer's Guide* (Annapolis, MD: Naval Institute Press, 1989), p. 265. Our thanks to Barbara Barata, a teacher at the Coast Guard Academy, for showing us this passage.

tions, and for what kinds of tasks—and what kinds of procedures undermine your thinking or tend to get you stuck.

If someone asks you out of the blue to explain how you *usually* write, you are very apt to tell lies. For example, you might say, "It always helps me to write an outline first." But what about that assignment when you didn't have time and produced a well-organized piece without an outline? Or that time when you got stuck trying to keep to an outline, which you eventually abandoned anyway? "Words always come slowly and with effort. Writing always discourages me." And what about that time when a whole train of thought bubbled up into your mind as you were writing, and you felt confident as you were writing? How could you make that happen more often?

People's memories play tricks on them, and they succumb to thinking there is one neat pattern to their writing. But if you do regular process writing, you'll discover that the truth is more complicated, and usually much more interesting. And more useful.

Still, it feels odd to some students to write about their writing. It makes them feel self-conscious. "It's hard enough to think about *what* I'm writing without also trying to think about *how* I'm writing." It often confuses people to try to analyze their tennis stroke as they are trying to hit the ball. But process writing doesn't ask you to watch yourself writing while you write, only to think back afterward to what happened.

A sports metaphor is instructive here. In every sport, serious players and coaches make videotapes of the games and later watch the tapes carefully to reflect at leisure on matters of technique they didn't have time to reflect on during the game. Teachers and psychiatrists watch tapes of themselves on the job to see what worked and didn't work. Process writing is a matter of "looking" back at your memory tapes and writing about what you see.

The coauthor of this book, Peter Elbow, became interested in writing because he went through a long period of writer's block. He had to quit graduate school because he couldn't write his papers. The way he got himself going again (five years later) was by doing process writing about almost every writing session—and discovering what was getting in his way. This process writing grew into Elbow's first book, *Writing without Teachers*. But neither of us thought about using this kind of writing as a teaching tool until we learned about it from Sondra Perl in the New York City Writing Project.

Psychologists use the term "metacognition" for thinking about thinking, which is what you do in process writing. Metacognition gives you more power over your future learning and over yourself. By the same token, the most important writing you do in this course may be about your writing. Process writing is what will give you the most control over your future writing and over yourself. It's simple. Just tell what happened. Yet because it consists of self-reflective thinking, it is also the most cognitively sophisticated writing.

Example of a Student's Freewriting

There we go again—am I back in Ms. Wendell's class? freewritg, freewritg, freewritg—freewriting up to my ears—never did learn how to write an essay. I should really learn to write out my ings—I feel like I write like John Madden talks—slow at first, then speeding up the end to a point that one can't even understand what he's says, or with me, what I'm writg. I dont do this as well as I used to. Forget that. I do this better than I used to. I have such a cold—if I dare get any sicker I'll die. I weighed myself today & almost fainted!!! I'll be eatg oranges for months! There is this cute middle-aged woman sittg next to me who looks at us all as if we are in a ecological study—look at this speciment, semi shaved heard—North Edgewick's only punk—but wait—she wears wool sweaters and skirts—ala Princeton Prep! But that must be the influence of livg so near there. Princeton means Bruce—that little park by the Nassau Inn—getting lost in the campus—could always find my way in, could never get out. PRB—Owen's radio show—fallg asleep on this filthy vinyl couch in that creepy dank cellar—listeng to the death of Suzzy Rocke.—Of course Martini. There is no fall in New York City—There were no leaves to kick around like there are in Princeton!! I missed fall. At least I don't sneeze anymore like I used to when the two oak trees would drop leaves in great big piles in my back yard & I'd fall asleep in them & the dust and dirt would make me sneeze until my mother forbade me to romp in the leaves—we used to play that spider game in Elinor's backyard—she had little skinny trees—I had great big oak trees—Sam is sittg next to me as usual—I can't decide whether or not I should put him on my roster. I miss the cats. I know they must be so adorable by now—so fat & stupid—they surely did take my place—when I left. My poor guilty mother over Thanksgiving battling over her love for the cats & her love for me—would she let me die from my allergy from them—or let them all freeze to death out in the cold! didn't the air filter work? Finally the stupid cat had more kittens in the cellar—three more—longhairs too—the father wooed her away for three weeks—what a romance—she finally came back and then had them. I saw him once, he was huge & longhaired, pale yellow—sort of champagne.

Example of a Student's Freewriting

Cristy Cornell

It's a relief to laugh. It takes every part of my body. I like the rush of endorphins or whatever scientists call them. It reduces everyone to a level playing field, a common ground. It's hard to lie I think when you laugh it puts you in touch with something. I don't know what. I think I missed the point of this exercise, what kind of stuff was supposed to be on this list anyway? I saw a thing/show on tv about these british twins who laughed all the time it was really weird. But I started laughing just hearing them laugh. One put a bright colored hat on her head & the other laughed they went around in circles in those revolving doorways they got in banks and they roared like it was the funniest thing they ever heard. It reduced tension for sure. Maybe that's why you laugh when you're nervous. I wonder if anyone's written a poem about laughter. So do I bring a story or poem to this literary round table thing or do I just show up w/some story about my lost passion—how I wanted to be Marie Curie & still wish I had a scientific mind or that I stopped playing the sax because I hated my band director? So, anyway LAUGHTER. Ha Ha Hee Hee. I like how Joey always puts Ha Ha and Hee Hee in his emails. I can hear him laughing that way. Anyway, jokes. I never get them. I think it's in the timing. I have none of that. But laughing. I laughed so hard at a Mark Halliday reading that tears ran down my face. And Brigit Pegan Kelly read with the speed of a freight train. What is this all about anyway? I don't know. I hate questions like these. Laughing. What's it all about? It's about letting go of something. It's a knot unknotting like something unraveling. It's in my lungs I think. It goes with those words a little maybe it's a letting go or a breathing out it's a build up and release. Maybe that's my word? Release? Release in the lungs? Sure. Okay. My feeling is of letting go, or release is that even a feeling? I feel released? No. I'm doing the releasing so that's not right. Is it maybe in the belly? Or maybe inbetween? In the shoulder muscles? Try lungs. I think it's there and so it's a pull in and it's a letting go its putting that breath out there & seeing where it goes or maybe watching what it takes out of the body with it. Yeah, it's in the lungs. Okay that's right. But feeling? I guess release. That's not the right word but it's the best I can think of. Release a letting go, a sending forth into the air it's about making a noise too and you need lungs to do that.

Example of Process Writing

Jennifer Fasulo

As with all writing assignments, I begin with dread. Somewhere Elbow writes that few people will continue to write if they don't find some surprise or pleasure in their writing. Twenty years of trying to be a "good" writer has all but killed my writing pleasure. Now my main goal is to get that pleasure back.

Was there ever a time I took pleasure in writing? I remember my first diary entry. I was 8 years old. It was not the writing per se that I enjoyed, it was merely the act of transmitting my excitement from hand to paper. The audience was important too. Even though it was a private diary, with skull and bones and PRIVATE!! KEEP OUT!! scrawled across the top of the first page, I knew I would share it all with my best friend Kyanne Willis. Noone else. Most of what I'd written was a love poem to her anyway.

Writing was pleasure because it was *communication*—a way to get out the feelings—or actually re-experience them. I remember a long novella of a letter I sent to another best friend, nine years later, after my first romantic kiss. In the letter's conclusion I wrote, "I'm honestly not sure what's better—the kiss itself, or describing it in gory detail to you."

In the second grade, I wrote a short story about a little girl who was the size of a thumb and lived inside a flower in the forest. I'm sure the story was just a poor imitation of several stories my mother read to me and my sister before bed—Thumbelina and Snowwhite and perhaps a few borrowed scenes from the movie *Bambi* which I'd seen about five times. But the story was exhaustive, if not original.

It numbered 12 pages of my blue composition book by the time I was finished—

complete with illustrations. I worked on it faithfully every day for nearly two weeks, in a near frenzy of creative excitement.

My teacher, Mrs. Hinkle, was astounded. I think she believed she had stumbled upon the next Louisa May Alcott. First, my work was held up and praised to the class. Then, I was paraded down to the principal's office and given the ultimate honor of reading my entire story to this towering figure of authority. I don't remember his reaction—the whole experience was too intimidating. But I do remember how Mrs. Hinkle held my hand on the way back to class and squeezed it as she told me how special I was, how I was going to achieve great things in my life. I could barely breathe from the excitement.

This was the beginning of the end in so far as my writing pleasure was concerned. After this incident, I had but one consuming passion; to once again win the praises and adoration of the Adult World. Writing itself was no longer a pleasure, only a means, a tool, a secret passage to the crowning glory of SUCCESS. Each time I sat down to write, it was with this goal in mind. And with it came the fear, like a tiny malignant cell, forming at the base of my spine. Fear of failure. Fear of not being able to write something again that would elicit this spectacular reaction. At first it didn't stop me from writing, but as I grew older, it grew also—as quietly and undetected as a cancer. Eventually, it would keep me from writing altogether.

Collage: Your Cheatin' Art*

Peter Elbow

A TV documentary on cancer. It's really a collage. It opens with shots of a funeral—people standing around a graveside, a close-up of the widow, and then of the coffin being lowered. Cut to a sequence of cells under a high-powered microscope—time-lapse so that we see the cells multiplying and going crazy. A voice-over is telling us how cancer cells behave. Then a man in the doctor's office getting the verdict. Then Ronald Reagan cracking a joke about his colon cancer. Then a young medical student telling how she wants to go into cancer research—why she finds this exciting and all the progress that's being made. We cut from her, bursting with enthusiasm and health, back to a victim, balding and emaciated from the therapy but walking in the woods, obviously drinking in the scene as though he can't get enough. Next a sequence of someone earnestly giving us statistics: how many cases of this and that, how much more than in the past, but also how many more successful treatments and cures. Back now to Reagan going about his work. Then the victim trying to explain things to his child. Finally a sequence of advice about how to avoid cancer.

It's all a hodge-podge—completely "disorganized"—no connectives.

But it works.

• • •

Collage uses the simplest but most effective aesthetic principle: Put things together if they sort of "go." They need to go . . . but not too well. Interest and pleasure increase if there is some friction, resistance, difference. A bouquet is a collage, but a good bouquet needs some clash.

• • •

* A fuller version of this collage is printed in: *Writing On the Edge* 9.1 (1997/1998): 26–40, and also in a collection of Elbow's essays forthcoming from Oxford University Press.

Directions for writing a collage:

1. Do or gather as much of your writing on your topic as you can. Go fast, don't worry. Freewriting is a good idea. Take thoughts in any order that they come.
2. Go through what you have and choose the best and potentially best bits—freely cutting to find long and short sections.
3. Revise what you have, but only by cutting, not rewriting. Cut paragraphs and sentences; cut phrases and words. Of course you can cheat by doing some rewriting, but it's amazing what is possible by just cutting.
4. Figure out a pleasing order for the bits: perhaps logical, more likely intuitive and associative, maybe even random.

Another option: Add fragments of writing by others—as you'll see I have done here.

• • •

Just as Cubism can take a roomful of furniture and iron it onto nine square feet of canvas, so fiction can take 50 years of human life, chop it to bits, and piece those bits together so that, within the limits of the temporal form, we can consider them all at once. This is narrative collage.

(Dillard 20)

. . . two parts of a piece of writing merely by lying side-by-side, can comment on each other without a word spoken.

(McPhee qtd. in Sims 13)

• • •

Collages are cheating because they permit weak writers to produce strong finished pieces.

What's hardest for writers of essays? Figuring out exactly what they are trying to say. And getting everything well unified and well organized.

What is easiest? Getting some good ideas and some good writing. Weak writers can often produce essays with a number of strong points—points that are definitely related and that throw good light on the overall topic. Yet the points don't quite follow each other coherently and the whole piece doesn't really hang together. And then there are those clunky transitions.

• • •

I sit here with seven short pieces of writing scattered around me on the floor. Some are as long as a page and a half, some only a paragraph or a sentence. Some are printed out, some written by hand. A couple of the pieces consist of two smaller pieces taped together. The miracle is that I *like* it all. I want to show all of them to readers.

How could I like all this writing when I didn't feel I was doing anything particularly good this week—just churning stuff out, writing fast, producing assorted blips and pieces?

I didn't *change* a word. Yet now my pile of writing feels strong and right. The secret is cutting, elimination, absence.

• • •

In art, the "collage" seems modern, but consider the typical medieval stained glass window. Or the collection of stained glass windows in a church or cathedral. The walls and ceiling of the Sistine Chapel are a collage.

Symphonies, concertos, and suites don't feel peculiar but they are collages. Why do music critics look for thematic or structural links between movements? Because most movements in most pieces of music are essentially unrelated.

Poetry is the most natural collage form. Poems often don't say what they are really saying, and they jam unlike things together.

Why should the collage be ancient and natural in art, music, and poetry—but not in prose?

• • •

The principle of negativity; absence. Strength from what's left out, not what's put in. Shaker furniture. Spareness—the flavor of old timers and seasoned professionals. The old tennis pro who scarcely moves—he makes his opponent move. The collage makes the reader move. Silence can be most powerful in music; space in art. Picasso's bare line drawings. If everything there is strong, the reader will put in what's not there. The crashing silences in Beethoven's Quartet Opus 18, no. 6.

• • •

I find it helpful to lay out the spectrum that runs from the tightest essay to the loosest collage. This is a story of gradually decreasing explicitness, unity, focus, connectedness, linearity:

- *The school essay.* Slam bam, thank you ma'am. Say what you're going to say, then say it, then say what you said. No surprises allowed.
- *The academic essay.* Academics permit themselves striking liberties that they don't permit to students. Still, their essays are supposed to be smoothly connected and to *say* what they are saying.
- *The essay in the larger tradition of Montaigne.* It's supposed to *get around to* saying what it's saying, but sometimes does not. From Montaigne on, this more expansive genre has served as an invitation to see where the mind goes as it explores something—and to welcome the fact that the resulting path is not tightly logical but instead has a lot of surprises and wandering. Nevertheless, the implicit principle of the essay is to *connect* that wandering, to *lead* the reader's mind from point to point, to create bridges. The principle of the collage, on the other hand, is to blow up the bridges and make the reader jump or swim.
- *The focused collage.* It doesn't say what it's saying, but it implies a definite point.
- *The open collage on a specific issue or topic.* It doesn't even imply a point or point of view. Rather, it presents conflicting and multiple points of view. Many newspaper feature stories and radio and TV documentaries take this form because it's so much easier: no need to choose or decide.
- There are open collages with no topic at all but they hover over a general area. "Sports Roundup." "Medical Breakthroughs in our Lifetime."
- *The collage on no topic at all.* Sheryl Fontaine and Francie Quaas get their students to make collages at the end of a writing course by simply choosing passages they like from everything in their portfolios. This is an invitation to the centrifuge. But what else is a "magazine" but a collage on no topic at all. "Magazine" means a storehouse, classically of gunpowder. Still, there will almost certainly be a lurking theme or issue. As Chaucer says, "The tongue returns to the aching tooth."

The collage process can provide a quicker and easier way to create a draft for a conventional or logically organized essay, and usually the resulting essay is a bit livelier—more raisins in the loaf. Just follow the main steps of quickly writing everything you can think of in any order, then choose the best pieces and clean them up a bit, and, finally, arrange them in a *logical* order (perhaps with the help of an outline) and figure out what is missing.

• • •

Just do it! Things go better with collage. TV ads are often microcollages, functioning as unrelated dingbat interrupters of unrelated programs. As non sequiturs, they are often more vivid and interesting than the programs they interrupt, often better art, and better rhetoric—a more concentrated aesthetic experience.

• • •

I dial the phone. I must choose from a menu of choices. Then I'm on hold. Then I hear a short ad for the company. Then I'm thrust into the middle of a sequence of disconnected pieces of music. Then someone answers and we talk. Then she puts me on hold again. And so on.

Everybody's home page. Indeed the Internet itself is a vast collage.

• • •

In our struggles to teach and to write well-constructed essays, we are constantly reminded of the mind's tendency to disconnect. But if we spent more time seeking randomness—for example, by constructing collages on no topic at all—we'd notice a much stronger tendency in the human mind, namely, to connect. The human mind is *incapable* of not making sense. It is even difficult to program a computer to produce true randomness.

• • •

"That's just the way it is." The phrase always points to bad news:

—The good die young.
—The wicked prosper.
—No dessert till you eat your salad.

Especially in writing:

—You can't communicate unless you use words as others do.
—You won't be taken seriously unless you conform to Standard Written English.
—People won't read it if it's boring or unclear.
—Commas and periods go inside the quotation marks, semicolons and question marks outside—at least on this side of the Atlantic.

So let's celebrate the subversive: "Just the way it is" can also point to good news. Using a collage, we can write a good piece—something people will read—without quite figuring out what we are really trying to say and without figuring out a logical or coherent organization.

And let's celebrate all the other cheating shortcuts we can use in writing and the teaching of writing:

—Freewrite. Don't plan, don't be careful, don't structure. Invite garbage. It often yields good writing—good ideas and language that's alive.
—Stop writing. Take a walk. Forget about it for a while. Stop struggling. *Not doing* is essential for doing.
—Put readers out of mind. The piece may have to work for them eventually, but think about them later in revising. Writing is often stronger when we say "Screw readers."

—Share drafts with others and ask for nothing at all. Get everyone simply to listen and enjoy. We improve our writing immensely just by feeling our words in our mouths, hearing them in our ears, and experiencing the presence of listeners. No criticism, no instruction, no suggestions. Just the pleasure and mutuality of sharing.

—Share our drafts with others and ask them not for feedback or criticism, but for *their* thoughts and ideas on the topic. Our thoughts will usually trigger good thoughts in them that they are happy to give away.

—Write *with* others. Meet at someone's house or in a cafe or restaurant or an empty classroom. One or three hours of writing with short breaks for chatting and tea. The presence of others somehow makes writing more feasible and satisfying. Body heat. Companionship. When we write alone, we are often pulled down by a feeling that says, "I can't do this."

Yes, struggle is necessary and inevitable. No danger of forgetting that. But there's seldom much progress in learning or teaching without sometimes finessing the struggle.

Yes, cheating is unfair. Babies are given everything they need without earning it. Little children get to play all day. Taking the easy way helps us relax and risk. Shortcuts help our minds to jump.

• • •

I read my collage outloud to a friend. He ends up thinking I have the opposite opinion from the opinion I really have. Is it because I wrote so badly? No, it's not badly written. It's because, as a collage, it doesn't try to *say* anything: It only *presents* material. Yes. And I like that about collages. They can settle for throwing live bits at readers and asking them to experience them and make up their own minds.

But my friend's "misreading" leads to a subversive thought. Perhaps he's right. Perhaps, now that I look at my collage again, I don't think what I thought I thought. Perhaps my collage allowed me to find words for what I didn't know. My collage—and my reading it outloud to my friend—are making me wonder if I disagree with my old self.

Works Cited

Dillard, Annie. *Living by Fiction.* New York: Harper, 1982.

Fontaine, Sheryl, and Francie Quaas, "Transforming Connections and Building Bridges: Assigning, Reading, and Evaluating the Collage Essay." *Teaching Writing Creatively.* Ed. David Starkey. Portsmouth, NH: Boynton Cook-Heinemann, 1998.

Sims, Norman, ed. Introduction. *Literary Journalists.* New York: Ballantine, 1984.

Collage about Myself as a Writer

School versus Personal Writing

Tara O'Brien

Ever since I learned to write, I've just written what I think the teachers want to read. When they give the assignment, I write for the grade I want to get. I've always known that I don't want a career in the field, so why should I put any extra effort into my papers? Only my teachers read the work, so I didn't even have to impress my classmates.

• • •

Impressing classmates, however, should be somewhat of a goal. I wonder why teachers don't encourage students to express themselves. Most of the time, kids write thinking that only the teacher will read it. If they were taught at an early age that sharing is the best way to become a better writer, not many grownups would have a problem doing so. I was hardly ever given the opportunity to exchange work with my classmates. I truly believe that if I was, I'd be more open about doing it now. I'm always scared that others will think my writing is dumb or that it doesn't make sense. I might have had a totally different opinion if I had felt comfortable since I was younger.

• • •

I don't mind reading my work aloud in small groups because I know everyone else has to do it, too. In tenth grade my teacher, Mr. Macdonald, assigned us a term paper on the topic of our choice. It was easy to get an 'A' because he basically only cared about mechanics and grammar. In eleventh grade my two least favorite teachers were Mrs. Loiter and Ms. O'Brien. Mrs. Loiter was rude and snobby, and you could easily tell who her favorites were (one of whom I was not!). She thought the world of creative writers and totally disregarded the pathetic rest of us. Ms. O'Brien's class required 15-page term papers on the most boring topics possible. If they were half a page shorter than the required length, the grade would definitely show it. Why do teachers use these methods? Writing should be a comfortable exercise, and it makes me mad to know that some people make it so uncomfortable.

• • •

I can write pretty well when I'm given a topic, but I have the hardest time thinking of one on my own. Sometimes I have trouble with introductions and conclusions in essays or papers. I think writing long reports is extremely boring, plus I can never put thoughts into logical order. I am usually grammar-conscious, though, and I used to be a spelling bee champ! The one thing I'd really like to change about my writing is my tendency to procrastinate. I terribly dislike deadlines, even though I understand the need for them.

• • •

I love journal writing. It's so helpful for anyone with a problem. Writing down my confusing and angry feelings allows me to deal with them much more easily. I can solve and understand my problems better when I see them down on paper. When I know a teacher will be checking up on my journal writing, I keep up with it much more. It seems like every time I try to do it on my own, I get out of the habit after a little while because I start writing pages at a time. It gets tiring!

• • •

Back in junior high, all of the girls used to write each other notes. I have all of them saved in a few shoe boxes in my closet. Ever since then, I've always liked sending and receiving letters. I'm meticulous about sending thank-you and birthday cards (go ahead—call up my relatives!). I don't know how I became like this—my parents are terrible about keeping in touch with people. My mother always asks me, "How do you do it? Really, what's your secret?" No matter how hard I try, she doesn't get it. My boyfriend and I always trade greeting cards. Whenever we fight, writing helps us communicate better. We can understand each other's points of view, even though it's not guaranteed we agree! I think people take writing, as opposed to speaking, more seriously. Sometimes we just blurt out things without thinking previously. But usually when we write, we put a lot of thought into our words. Letters are like conversations that we can keep forever. We may not remember phone calls, but we can always look back on letters and reminisce.

• • •

Maybe as I grow older, I'll mature as a writer. I can see somewhat of a difference in my style over the years, and hopefully this difference will expand. Writing for school, as opposed to writing on my own, brings out another side of me. It's as if my mind goes into auto-pilot! I have been trying to let go of some of my inhibitions when it comes to papers and essays. I do realize that it makes reading much more interesting if the material is personal. For now, though, I'm happy with my cards and letters!

The Feel of Writing—and Teaching Writing

Donald Murray

Donald Murray, a Pulitzer Prize-winning journalist, is the author of A Writer Teaches Writing, *among other works, and an emeritus faculty member of the English Department at the University of New Hampshire.*

Emptiness. There will be no more words. Blackness. No, white without color. Silence.

I have not put down any words all day. It is late, and I am tired in the bone. I sit on the edge of the bed, open the notebook, uncap the pen. Nothing.

Or.

Everything has gone well this morning. I wake from sleep, not dreams, the car does not have a flat tire, I do not spill the coffee grounds, I do not turn the shower to cold instead of hot. The telephone does not ring, and I sit at the typewriter with a clean piece of white paper twirled into the machine. Nothing.

If I can make myself wait, remain calm, ready to write but not forcing writing, then words come out of silence. Out of nothing comes writing.

Now it is hard to keep up with the words which write what I did not intend, do not expect. Often this is the best writing, and I know it, but I never welcome that emptiness, that terrible feeling that there will be no more words.

• • •

The student sits in my conference chair, a Van Gogh miner, his hands clasped and hanging down between his legs near the floor, his head slumped forward. He mumbles. "I didn't write nothing." His head rolls up, his face defiant, and then angry when he sees me smiling at him. "What's the matter?" he snarls.

"You look like me, sound like me this morning. Nothing happened."

"What d'ya do?"

"I wanted to kick the cat, but I don't have a cat, and I couldn't pick a fight with my wife. She was out shopping. So I had to sit there and wait."

"And?"

"The words came. Not what I expected. But words. You want to read them?"

I wait while he reads my uneven, early morning draft. I can see him getting interested and suspect he's saying to himself that he could do as good, or perhaps a bit better.

"You just wait?"
"Yes, it isn't easy though."
"Will it work for me?"
"I don't know. Sometimes it works for me and sometimes it doesn't."

• • •

The writing is going well. Everything is connecting. I need a word, and it is in my ear; I need a fact, and it flows out of my fingers; I need a more effective order, and my eye watches sentences as they rearrange themselves on the page. I think this is what writing should be like, and then I stop. I go for another mug of coffee, visit the bathroom, check the mail.

I wonder about this compulsion to interrupt writing which is going well. I see my students do it in the writing workshop. It's so much of a pattern there must be a reason for it. Sometimes I think it is the workman's need to stand back to get distance; other times I think it is simple Calvinist distrust—when everything's going well something must be wrong.

• • •

My students arrive in class just at the bell, as if they were hurled there by some gleeful giant. They are rushed, harried, driven. They remind me of me. I barely made it myself. How am I going to create a quiet space around us within which we can listen to writing trying to find its voice?

This is the writer's problem: take all the energy you have to fight your way to the writing desk: reject wife, child, friend, colleague, neighbor; refuse to carry out the trash, take the car to the garage, transplant the blueberry bush; leave the mail unopened and the opened mail unanswered; let the telephone ring; do not answer the knock on the door or prepare for class; ignore the message on your desk to call somebody back; do not rehearse the speech that will impress at the afternoon meeting; do not remember, do not plan; use all your energy to get to your desk, and then try to sit there, calmly, serenely, listening for writing.

I hear a teacher asking a student who has just begun to write. "What is your purpose?"

I hope the teacher will not come to my door when I have just begun to write. What, indeed, is my purpose? To make it through the day? To get tenure? (I already have tenure.) To become rich? (I will not eat on this article.) To impress my parents? (That sounds more like it, but they are dead, and would not read what I wrote when they were alive because, true Scots, they knew they would be disappointed.)

I hear more of the teacher's questions. "What is your purpose in this piece? What do you intend to say in the piece you are writing? Who is your audience?" They may be good questions but it's the first week of the semester and the student has passed in his first tentative draft.

He'd better not ask me. If I knew all those things—my purpose, my content, my reader—I wouldn't have to write this. Well, that's not really true. Perhaps I know my audience in a sort of general way, and perhaps I know what I'm going to say. And that worries me, because I want to write to surprise myself. It would be terrible if I knew my purpose, if I knew what I was doing, how it would all come out. That's when I'll know I'm finished. There are few things more dangerous in writing than too much purpose. . .

• • •

My father died with a machine plugged into his chest and a small smile on his face. The police found my mother on the floor of her apartment in a nest of covers tugged from the bed. My daughter, Lee, stands always at the corner of my eye, but at twenty she lay in a hospital bed, a beautiful woman without brainwaves. I made the decision to kill my father, to kill my mother, to kill my daughter, to let them go. I hope they have found more peace than I.

I have never said these words until this moment. I did not know I would say these words. They came out of silence. I heard them and I believe them.

Facing their own silences, my students write of death, of hate, of love, of living, of loss. They put down words which reveal a mother plunging a knife into a father while a girl looks on; a student tells of a failure—to kill herself; another student carries her father in her arms, rocking him, trying to comfort him against the pain of cancer in the night.

I tell them that they do not have to write of these things. I tell them they should write of such matters if it bothers them. They tell me it feels good, and then look guilty. I tell them I know. It helps, somehow, to put words on paper. I tell them it gives me distance, in a way, it makes what cannot be believed, a fact. I tell them I cannot understand why it feels good to write of such terrible things, but I confess it does feel good; that is my way of achieving a kind of sanity.

• • •

A student comes to conference and shows me her new notebook. We marvel over it—a looseleaf notebook has a third arm with a clipboard on it which folds over the notebook. We share our wonder at it, for we share the thrill of writing and know the importance of tools. We are always trying out each other's pens or feeling the texture of a new kind of paper between our fingers. We are writers and we know that there is writing in the paper if we know how to let it out.

• • •

Often I write by not writing. I assign a task to my subconscious, then take a nap or go for a walk, do errands, and let my mind work on the problem. It doesn't do much good for me to think thinking.

I tell my students to write every day, for a short time, going away from it and coming back. The going away is as important as coming back. Read, stare out the window, jog, watch a ballgame, eat, go to bed. Sometimes I feel I have to make a note. It's too bad; for what can be forgotten usually should be forgotten. Writing surfaces from my subconscious, but I push it away, the way I shove an over-friendly puppy from my knee. Go away and work by yourself, writing, and come back when I'm at my desk.

• • •

I can recognize my students' papers without looking at their names. I hope they hear their own voices as clearly as I do, for writing is mostly a matter of listening. I sit at my desk listening to hear what my voice says within my head. Sometimes it speaks so clearly I feel I am taking down dictation while I write.

Voice gives writing the sense of an individual speaking to an individual. The reader wants to hear a voice. Voice carries the piece of writing forward; it glues the piece of writing together. Voice gives writing intensity and rhythm and humor and anger and sincerity and sadness. It is often the voice of a piece of writing that tells the writer what the writing means.

From Private Writing to Public Writing

Essential Premises

- Many people don't feel safe as they write. Lack of safety usually makes it harder to write.
- Private writing is one important way to achieve safety in writing. It is usually easier to express our feeling and thinking and to find words if we write words that are not for the eyes of others. *After* we write privately, we can look back over what we've written and use parts of it for pieces meant for the eyes of others.
- About flexibility of genre: It's not hard to take some writing we've produced in one or two sessions, particularly if it's fairly messy or unformed writing, and use it as the germ for different pieces in different genres. For example, we can easily use the same raw ingredients for making a story or an essay—or for making an analytic essay or a persuasive essay.

Main Assignment Preview

This is a double-barreled workshop. In the first section, we will invite you to do a lot of private writing and show you how privacy can make it easier for you to find more things on your mind and also to write more freely and with less struggle. In the second section of the workshop, we will show you how to *mine* this private writing for various public purposes.

This workshop will give you a feeling for what we think of as the root process in writing something important: starting with the safety of private writing so as to allow maximum freedom, creativity, and exploration, then *working with* what you have produced in private and building it more carefully into the kind of finished product you want—or that some audience wants.

Section I: Private Writing

You may be someone who can write everything you need simply by telling yourself "Write!" Fine. But we suspect that you will learn to produce richer and more interesting material if you try out one or both of the following techniques: Sondra Perl's "Composing Guidelines" and the "Open-Ended Writing Process." Both are somewhat structured methods, but after you have tried them out, you can adjust them to your own needs in the future.

Sondra Perl's Composing Guidelines

Your teacher may ask you to guide yourself through Perl's guidelines by reading them to yourself as you engage in writing at your own speed. In this case, we urge you to follow them with full concentration, making sure to spend enough time to get rolling at the various stages of writing. On the other hand, your teacher may read out loud from the guidelines to lead the whole class through an extended session of writing. Some students feel distracted by having to proceed at the same pace as everyone else, but we have found some of our own best writing sessions occur when someone leads us through the guidelines with a group. It keeps you going. (See the box on page 34 with Pat Belanoff's process writing when she was led through the Perl guidelines.) However you are introduced to the guidelines, remember that the goal is to teach you a process you can use and fiddle with on your own.

Remember that this is private writing. Write with the understanding that this is not to be shown to anyone. You may end up with passages you want to share, but that's a decision to be made by you later.*

1. Find a way to get comfortable. Shake out your hand. Take some slow, deep breaths and settle into your chair. Close your eyes if you'd like to. Relax. Find a way to be quietly and comfortably aware of your inner state. Try to let go of any tension by slow breathing.

2. Ask yourself, "What's going on with me right now? Is there anything in the way of my writing today?" When you hear yourself answering, take a minute to jot down a list of any distractions or impediments that come to mind. If there are noises or other distractions, notice them, and then bring your attention back to yourself.

3. Now ask yourself, "What's on my mind? Of all the things I know about, what might I like to write about now?" When you hear yourself answering, jot down what comes. Maybe you get one thing; maybe a list. If you feel totally blocked, you may write down "Nothing." Even this can be taken further by asking yourself, "What is this 'Nothing' all about?"

4. Ask yourself, "Now that I have a list—long or short—is there anything I've left out, any other piece I'm overlooking, maybe even a word I like, something else I might want to write about sometime that I can add to this list?" Add anything that comes to mind.

---

* We thank Perl for permission to copy these guidelines. We have made tiny modifications—mostly just some cutting. Sondra Perl is a professor of English at Herbert H. Lehman College and founder of the New York City Writing Project.

5. Whether you have one definite idea or a whole list of things, look over what you have and ask, "What here draws my attention right now? What could I begin to write about, even if I'm not certain where it will lead?" Take the idea, word, or item and put it at the top of a new page. (Save the first page for another time.)

6. Now—taking a deep breath and settling comfortably into your chair—ask yourself, "What are all the things I know about this topic and all the associations I have with it? What can I say about it now?" Spend as long as you need writing down these responses. Perhaps it will be a sustained piece of freewriting or stream of consciousness, or perhaps separate bits, or notes to yourself.

7. Now having written for a good while, interrupt yourself, set aside all the writing you've done, and take a fresh look at this topic or issue. Grab hold of the *whole* topic—not the bits and pieces—and ask yourself, "What makes this topic interesting to me? What's *important* about this that I haven't said yet? What's the *heart* of this issue for me?" Wait quietly for a *word, image,* or *phrase* to arise from your "felt sense" of the topic. Write whatever comes. (For more on "felt sense," see "Exploring Theory" at the end of this workshop.)

8. Take this word, image, or phrase, and use it to explore further. Ask yourself, "What's this all about?" As you write, let the "felt sense" deepen. Where do you feel that felt sense? Where in your body does it seem centered? Ask yourself, "Is this right? Am I getting closer? Am I saying it?" If not, ask yourself, "What is wrong or missing?" and keep writing. See if you can feel when you're on the right track. See if you can feel the shift or click inside when you get close: "Oh yes, this says it."

9. If you're at a dead end, you can ask yourself, "What makes this topic hard for me?" Again pause and see if a word, image, or phrase comes to you that captures this difficulty in a fresh way—and if it will lead you to some more writing.

10. When you find yourself stopping, ask, "What's missing? What hasn't yet gotten down on paper?" and again look to your felt sense for a word or an image. Write what comes to mind.

Exploring the Writing Process

I got out this diary, & read as one always does read one's own writing, with a kind of guilty intensity. I confess that the rough & random style of it, often so ungrammatical, & crying for a word altered, afflicted me somewhat. I am trying to tell whichever self it is that reads this hereafter that I can write very much better; & take no time over this; & forbid her to let the eye of man behold it. . . . But what is more to the point is my belief that the habit of writing thus for my own eye only is good practise. It loosens the ligaments. Never mind the misses & the stumbles. Going at such a pace as I do I must make the most direct & instant shots at my object, & thus have to lay hands on words, choose them, & shoot them with no more pause than is needed to put my pen in the ink. I believe that during the past year I can trace some increase of ease in my professional writing which I attribute to my casual half hours after tea.

Virginia Woolf

11. When again you find yourself stopping, ask yourself, "Where is this leading? What's the point I'm trying to make?" Again write down whatever comes to mind.

12. Once you feel you're near or at the end, ask yourself, "Does this feel complete?" Look to your "felt sense," your gut reaction, even to your body, for the answer. Again write down whatever answer comes to you. If the answer is "No," pause and ask yourself, "What's missing?" and continue writing.

How and Why the Guidelines Work

When the guidelines help us write, it's because they help us to focus our attention better and to keep checking back and forth between the *words* we are writing and the felt *meanings* or *feelings* or *intentions* inside—the "felt sense"—that are so often the source for our words.

There's nothing sacred about the exact format or wording of the guidelines. They aren't meant to be a straitjacket. To help you in adapting them to your own style and temperament, here is a short list of the four most productive moments in the process. After you try out the complete set, you could try using them as an abbreviated version of the guidelines:

- Relax, stretch, clear your mind, try to attend quietly to what's inside—and note any distractions or feelings that may be preventing you from writing. Allow yourself to be aware of your body and your physical surroundings.
- Start with a list of things you *could* write about. Often we can't find what we really want to write about until the third or fourth item—or not until that subtle after-question, "Is there something else I might have forgotten?"

Exploring the Writing Process

On Writing When Using Perl Guidelines

Didn't write what I intended to write—intended to be pragmatic—write out what I *needed* to write out. But someway the other topic forced itself on me and became too exciting to ignore. Topic appeared on paper when I searched my head for something I really wanted to write about. Found all the prompts helpful except one.

The nonhelpful one was, "Use image, idea, phrase, and keep trying to get it right"—because it felt right to me already. The spot when I started on metaphor and metonomy. Don't know why I got on that. Doesn't connect in very well—and yet I know there's a connection, and I guess I saw it as relevant. But I did drop it when Peter said, "Where is this going?"

While writing, I found pleasant revealings coming forth and thought, "Gee! These are good ideas!" Thought of typing it up and giving copies to Peter and Don for comment—not sure I was thinking of them as audiences. Didn't really feel I was writing for them as I wrote—they came to mind because I know they have thoughts on these subjects. I'd like them both to think I'm on to something good—but I'm really wanting this idea worked out for myself. Believe they could help me do that.

I did have some feeling of going around in circles, not putting things together into one Bingo result—but I do think there's stuff there to explore. I'm glad I wrote this.

Pat Belanoff

- As you are writing, periodically pause and look to that felt sense somewhere inside you—that feeling, image, or word that somehow represents what you are trying to get at—and ask whether your writing is really getting at it. This comparing or checking back ("Is this it?") will often lead to a productive "shift" in your mind ("Oh, now I see what it is I want to say").
- Finally, toward the end, ask, "What's this all about? Where does this writing seem to be trying to go?" And especially ask, "What's missing? What haven't I written about?"

In the Readings at the end of the workshop, we have printed the writing Peter Elbow did using the Perl guidelines.

The Open-Ended Writing Process

The open-ended process is another way to encourage exploratory, private writing. Where the Perl guidelines help you find words for what is sort of in your mind but not in words, the open-ended process pushes you to figure out entirely new thoughts and ideas that are as yet nowhere near your mind.

The open-ended process consists of a simple movement back and forth between two basic activities: *freewriting* and *summing-up.*

Start by freewriting. (Or, start by listing things you *might* write about and then start freewriting.) Simply explore whatever topics emerge for you while you're doing this unfocused freewriting.

After 10 or 15 minutes of freewriting, stop and look back or think over what you've written. (Pause, take a deep breath, stretch, look around.) Then write down a sentence, phrase, or image to summarize the most interesting or important thing you find in your freewriting. Look for a center of gravity: that piece of your writing that seems to pull on you most strongly. It doesn't have to be an accurate or objective summary of your freewriting. You might focus on some small detail from your freewriting if that seems the most important to you now. You might even write down a thought that didn't occur in your freewriting but occurs to you now as you pause. The point of these summings-up is to provide a springboard for your next piece of freewriting, your next dive into language.

For that's the next step: more freewriting. As you write, learn to keep on writing even if you don't know where you are going. Learn to ride waves of writing for longer and longer periods of time. When words start to run out after only five minutes, force yourself to keep going. Remember, you don't have to stay on the same subject. Write "What else could I write about?" and "What else?" and keep on writing to see what comes. The goal is to lose yourself in language, to lose perspective.

Then stop again to sum up. And so on.

Follow this back-and-forth chain of freewriting and summing-up wherever it leads you. To get the benefit from the process, you need to follow through at least three cycles: three freewrites and three summings-up. More is better.

How and Why the Open-Ended Process Works

The open-ended process gets its power from alternating two contrary kinds of mentality or two opposed ways of producing language. During the freewriting you are *immersed* in your words: your head is down and you are tumbling along in an underbrush of language; you tend to be working more in words than in thoughts. Indeed the *goal* is to get lost in the words and not worry about the thoughts or where they are going.

When you pause and sum up, you use a completely different mentality or way of producing language. You extricate yourself from the underbrush of words and, as it were, climb up a tall tree to see where you have gotten yourself: you seek perspective and detachment. In this process you are trying to work more in thoughts than in words. These summing-up sentences or phrases help keep your freewriting productive. For if you do nothing but freewrite for hours and never stop to climb a tree, you sometimes just go in circles.

As you move back and forth between the two activities, sometimes your writing will change: in subject, in mode, or in style. For example, having written the story of what happened to you, your pausing and summing-up may lead you to see that you now need to write about the *person* who was involved in that event. Let these changes occur. Perhaps you've been writing to yourself, and now you realize you want to write to someone else—a letter, perhaps. You may even want to write a poem or a prayer or a dialogue. Sometimes the open-ended writing will lead you closer and closer to what you were trying to get at from the beginning; but sometimes it takes you far afield to something new that surprises you.

Exploring the Writing Process

Sharing, Privacy, Safety

I want to thank you for emphasizing safety around sharing our writing—for your invitation to keep our writing private when we need to do so. You gave us permission to share or not share, whichever we were most comfortable doing. I have, however, come to realize that there are some powerful sociopolitical factors that complicate the issue of safety for me. I realized that as a member of a minority group, the line between safety and self-respecting survival is frequently blurred. The oppressive powers that foster one's feelings of being unsafe count on fearful silence as a means to continue the oppression. To create a place for myself at the table, I sometimes find that the need to make myself purposely *unsafe* is more important than my instinctive and sensible need to be safe. And thus, I sometimes give myself voice and demand that society acknowledge my existence—I become visible in a world which might otherwise choose to ignore me. As a teacher, I feel the additional care-taking pressures. I begin to feel as though I have an obligation to speak out, not only for myself, but for the children who live in silent fear. This has become a huge issue for me. I know that each individual person has the choice to remain safe in her writing, even an ounce of social consciousness will sometimes drive me to make decisions for the betterment of society—not just for my own safety.

Susan Luppino, in a letter to Peter Elbow after a teachers' workshop

Your teacher may well introduce the open-ended process in class. Sitting and writing privately in a public group might seem odd at first, just as it did with the Perl guidelines. But again, we want you to practice this new procedure *once* with some direction. Otherwise you tend to drift into your usual writing habits. The goal is to learn a *new* writing process so that you can then use it flexibly by yourself.

Process Questions about Private Writing

- What did you notice when you did private writing for this workshop?
- Is private writing familiar to you, or something new? Sometimes, when people haven't done much private writing, they keep thinking about readers even when the writing isn't meant for those readers. Did this happen to you?
- What did you notice using the Perl guidelines?
- Did it make sense to you to pause and look for your "felt sense" of inner meaning or intention—and try to compare that to what you'd written? Did that process lead you anywhere?
- What did you notice using the open-ended process? What kind of path did it lead you on—staying in one area or moving far afield?
- If you did some of this private writing outside of class, did that make a notable difference?
- Did this private writing tell you anything about how you usually write?

Section II: Using Your Private Writing to Create a Piece of Public Writing

In this part of the workshop, we will ask you to use your private exploratory writing as raw material or seeds for a piece of public writing. We'll ask you to do a number of 10- or 15-minute sketches to try out different *genres* or kinds of writing (for example, a description, narrative, dialogue, or essay). We want to show you that there are many diverse possibilities lurking in any piece of rough exploratory writing.

Exploring the Writing Process

In the freewriting we did today, I see some possibilities for subjects to write about. What interested me was that I didn't feel compelled to put the ideas into the final form I intend to use. In the light of this, I was more able to get the flood of thoughts out on paper for observation. I can see what I think and am able to discard things that don't hold my interest longer than a few seconds. There are lots of germs in my open writing. It is a road for me to wander along and maybe pick up bits of dried grass, some flowers, shells and a few rocks.

Jo Ferrell

The main assignment will be to choose one genre or kind of writing and write a full good draft of a public piece of writing to share with others. (Your teacher might specify one genre to use.)

In this workshop, you'll get a feeling for different genres, and how you can make choices about genre to help you take a piece of writing where you want it to go. In the process, you will come away with a better understanding of the tricky relationship between form and content. Sometimes you will feel yourself (putting it crudely) pouring existing content into new containers, and sometimes you will feel that the containers are helping you think of new content. That is, sometimes the exercises will lead you to "revise" or "shape" your private writing to fit different genres. But sometimes the process of thinking in terms of genre will make you think of *new* content or ideas that weren't even in your private writing.

Looking Back over Your Private Writing

Some theorists think that we haven't, in a sense, *finished* expressing any thought until we finally make it public in some form: without communication, a natural cycle isn't complete. We disagree. We think it's perfectly natural to express some thoughts and feelings and keep them to ourselves. We often need privacy in order to explore our thinking and feeling without having to consider what others might think about them. You may well not want to share much of what you got on paper in the previous workshop.

But of course we often *do* want to communicate to others what is private inside our heads. If we've written our thoughts and feelings down on paper, occasionally we can simply hand it over unchanged to readers. But private writing often needs to be revised in order to communicate its sense to others.

The first step is to look back over your private writing just to get it fresh in mind. As you look back, you're likely to have mixed feelings about it. You may feel good about how much you wrote, about how diverse it is, and about how you were able to record your thinking and feeling in a way you'd never

Exploring the Writing Process

I find it is so much easier to say something to a person when, instead of saying it face-to-face, I am able to write the message down. In fact I tried that system just today. I had a problem with my friend, but when I tried to speak to him about it, I just could not find the words, even though I knew exactly what I wanted to say. I complained about the situation to another friend who gave me the suggestion that I write a letter. Even if I didn't give it to him, I would at least have my thoughts expressed on paper. I tried the advice and, believe it or not, it worked. I believe that I got everything down that I wanted to say, completely and honestly. When I didn't have to look at his face and know that he was listening to me at that very moment, I felt so free at the thought of expressing my emotions. I did end up giving the letter to him, but that's another story.

Katie Houston

done before. As you read it over, part of it will probably rematch with the "felt sense" of it still in your head, and the match will feel gratifying to you. Or perhaps you'll be pleased because this "private exploratory" writing is not very much of a mess at all: Some of it may well be clear, shaped, and strong.

But you may also react negatively, at least to part of it: "Yuk. What a mess! What drivel my mind is full of." This reaction often occurs when people first try out private exploratory writing. It's important to remember that you weren't trying to produce good, well-organized writing; you were trying to give yourself the safety to produce, as it were, an accurate brain X ray or mind-dump. Minds are messy. When you produce messy writing, that's not a problem—indeed, in a way it's a *good* sign.

For the mess means not only that you were able to trust yourself enough to record what was actually going on in your mind: It also means that you have begun to learn a powerful way to find things to write (a powerful heuristic). For if you read through that mess in the proper spirit of noncritical inquiry, you will find more possible topics and potential trains of thought for writing than if you had written something careful and well-organized. Messiness means that you didn't keep only to one neat path but let your writing record the many diverse side paths that every mind inevitably considers. You might want to explore some of these paths further now.

We suspect your private writing has some or all of these characteristics:

- *Contradictions.* You might have thought or felt X at one point, but then later on you wandered into thinking or feeling Not-X. If you are going to engage in good thinking, you need contradiction; you need to wrestle with both sides or get both sides to wrestle with each other. In this way you'll come up with new thinking, not just a restatement of your old thoughts.
- *Changes of topic and digressions.* Your writing might have been going in one direction but suddenly veered off or changed direction completely. There's cognitive power in this jumpy diversity: There are seeds for different pieces of writing. But even more interesting than that, *there are important unstated insights contained in every jump or point of change or digression.* Look closely at each jump or shift in your writing. Pause and ask yourself, "How did my mind make that jump? What is the connection?" Even if there is no "real" or "rational" connection (say you jumped from radios to swimming), there was always something in your mind that served as a bridge between radios and swimming. Noticing that bridge will throw some light on both of them. The mind is incapable of pure randomness.
- *Obsessions.* Your writing might have seemed to be in a rut, grinding over and over again in a tiresome or depressing way about the same event or the same feelings. Some people who have not done this kind of private exploratory writing before say, "How depressing!" or "How childish!" or "How irrational!" But remember, if this material came out on paper, it's in your head. You can't get rid of it by not writing it down. Writing it down is usually the best way to get rid of it, perhaps by giving you enough perspective on it to work through it, or perhaps only by giving you a place to "put it down" so you know it's there. You don't have to "carry it" any more in

your head so you can stop thinking about it. Everyone obsesses sometimes. You'll find you can learn things and get perspective on yourself by reading through the obsessions. If they really bother you or get in the way of functioning at your best, you may decide you want to talk to someone you trust about them. And there may well be some useful things in the obsession that you would enjoy communicating—even to people you don't know well.

An Example of Open-Ended Writing

You may ask how it is that we can print this private writing in public? Peter Elbow used the open-ended writing process with a class and went through the whole cycle: from doing private writing to producing a public piece. Everyone did private writing for their own eyes only. But later on Peter (looking for a sample for this book) asked whether any students would be willing to let him see their private writing. He thought Melissa Fogel's was interesting and would serve as a good example, and he asked her permission to use it. You'll see her public writing in the "Readings" at the end of this workshop. We have not corrected any of Melissa's typing mistakes (it was a computer classroom) since we want to highlight that this is informal private writing where there is no concern for mechanics.

Alienation . . . like being alone, like feeling shut out, with no friends, no one to turn to. then there is a light, somewhere down that halll, of someone who feels the same someone who shares in the utter feeling of alone. shes warm and kind and she knows how to feel.

• • •

I called, he was warm and sharing the way he said I love you last noght was with care, like he was beginning to know what it means to say those words, to say them and to mean them. sometimes I feel like I don't have a problem sometimes I feel like my only friend is the city we live in the city of angels lonely as I am together we cry. so becky banged andy. so I have Jeff. I cant wait fgor the dream sequence its so beautiful and lovely, lovely what a cheesy word, its white and red and everything is like the dawn, foggy yet glissening. I cant wait, only a couple of more days. The times I feel alone, are sometimes truthful other times they are brought on by my own anxieties, and that scares me more than being alone. Today is blue and blue, ironic I wear those colors right now. The banquet is tonight. and that horrible horrible neophite ceremony. Why scare others. I don't want others to feel the fear I experience so often. Expose them to sunshine, not thunder storms. The rain was coming down hard, and the crash of thunder was so monstrous, I thought I would hide my head under the pillow. I remember the raccoon, it just jumped right out at me. Initiation is a time to reflect on the meaning of Kappa, it is a time to recognize all the good of sisterhood, I look forward to experiencing the other side of the beauty. Oh joy another hour and a half.

• • •

Who am I? Where do I go from here?

• • •

I am Melissa the great the wonderful, with a face of anger, sometimes happiness, I guess it depends on the mood my life has. The tone of the day almost like writing, whats the tone melissa, why I do not know, the tone today is fun, happy, get it done, eat and merry, be loyal to kappa. Its blue day for gods sake, your favorite color in the world, Jeff's too. Is he far away thinking of me now. I am so shungry right now I wish I had finished that slim fast shake, since we will be here for the entire time. now that I am totally off track. I wonder if I am the only sophomore that is taking this class. Good thing I took, that horrible typing class in the eleventh grade. Well lets try to get deeper . . . If I stay and let myself be subject to the life I create for myself, I accept without hesitation or sigh that life, the one where I stay in Mass. and live on expressing myself through friends and family, that family I call Kappa. If I go I delete that, its just not worth it today anyway, tomorrow ask me again. When I think about jeff he scares me, not because he scares me physically, not even him. Its the idea of having a boyfriend again that scares me. falling in love again means sacrificing my feelings for another, it means taking the risk of somehow being left, being alone again and learning to cope all over again. Danny left me high and dry, now I cant stand him, but I'm over him. gone. Jeff is the sweetest, he's everything a girl could ask for and the physical is slowly slipping into place, which might be better for me, who knows. All I know right now is that I miss him, miss him to death.

• • •

Our hearts meet somewhere along a sea of lonliness, somewhere among the vast mountains of trust. Then my hand grabs his, and we walk the path I call life.

• • •

And so this class drags on. . and on. . Maybe if I try to save her I can. No she is brain washed, lost in the crowd of men who want to take her away from our family. for so long it was tight, together we shared not always with words but with actions and he the masked ass of the century destroyed that closeness in one fell swoop. She is only a child looking for some attention, he could see that in her lost eyes of a sea of blue. See that she was crying out of the term middle, he seized her while she cried, and gave her a shoulder to lean on, why did she fall. Because we all looked away for a split second and she was gone. Now we all pay. . . I just want her to be happy. She wont with him, even though he was there when we were busy, he is a do nothing a go nowhere. and she lives with that, nothing else. Can I stop and help you little girl. Do you need my shoulder to cry on, I won't hurt you in the end, I am sister I will not leave. I am sister, trust me please. My little brat from behind, catch up come play in the yard with us, no I want to swing, swing in the rain. It feels good on my tongue. But it is not safe little girl, don't you see it's not safe. She falls quick, hard under the swing set, we don't see her. Wait I see her. She lies in a pool of mud and blood. Someone help her she is falling. Now she is falling again into another pool of mud and blood. This time the consequences more than a couple of stitches. but wait do you remember sister? The stitces did not hurt the little girl, she asked for a piece of gum, maybe there is hope, maybe she will survive with a smile left on her time beaten face. Maybe she will live and live long with the family, the ones who forgive and forget, nomatter what you do or say, or who you go out with.

• • •

So I am alone and afraid of feeling alone. Should I go and do something about this, or work through it, like so many other times, by myself. I also look forward to the end of this week with all the beauty it possesses. The song the laughter and the fun at the end of it all. I am also fearing the closeness I have with Jeff. It scares me, to think I fall again. Then there is my sister, Will she be o.k. boy you have a lot to think about!!!!

Melissa Fogel

Process Letter

Dear Peter,

I have participated in this exercise before. The amount of freedom is so amazing. The feeling of writing whatever your mind may find deep within its core allows the writer to express herself without any fear of denial. I do believe some of our writing in this fine University of ours is extremely narrow and limited. One has guidelines and rules and finds oneself lacking creativity. This type of writing had me smiling again, with my fingers typing away, yearning for more and more. However, because I am so used to being confined in my writing, my thoughts did not wander as much as they used to. I found myself staying on one topic very diligently. With more practice I could probably find creative aspects of writing lurking behind the closed doorway.

I found that a bunch of my underlying fears of whatever seemed deep in my thoughts, would surface, no matter how hard I tried to retain them. Maybe this sort of writing is a release from the everyday tensions. It did remind me of diary writing: the kind of writing that enables you to let go of your anxieties and fears, to come up with solutions to the problems you write about.

The honesty of my writing today was present. There was a lack of superficial qualities in my writing. I wasn't putting up a front for a professor, or running for a thesaurus to help improve my wording. I was me, a horrible speller and a not-so-great writer. I was creative and I enjoyed the writing experience.

My heart and soul was in this writing today, something I haven't felt in years!!!

Sincerely,
Melissa Fogel

Trying Out Genres

A genre is a widely recognized *form* of writing. Some genres are large, inclusive, and loosely defined—such as poetry and prose. Some genres are smaller and less inclusive—such as essay and fiction. Then there are even smaller, more specific genres—which are the ones we will ask you to try out in this workshop: (1) description or portrait, (2) narrative or story, (3) dialogue, (4) persuasive essay, (5) expository essay, (6) satire or parody, (7) meditation or personal essay, and (8) poetry (we leave this one broad). We could add "letter" to this list, but we assume that most of you probably explored letters in the last section.

You probably won't have time to try out all these genres. Your teacher will give you direction about how many and perhaps which ones to try. As you try them out, notice when you find yourself pouring existing content into various containers and when the containers make you think of new content.

(1) Description or Portrait

Read through or think back over your private writing and try to find a *scene*, an *object*, or a *person* that could be important to you. Perhaps you'll only be able to find the *germ* or *seed* of a scene, object, or person. Do 8 to 10 minutes of descriptive writing. First, close your eyes and try to experience your subject using your eyes, ears, nose, and touch. Then go on to describe it in writing.

Obviously you can't complete a large scene in this short time. But take a minute or two at the end to make a note to yourself about how you'd shape it or organize it if you were to finish it. These are just sketches. The goal is simply to get a start—to test how fruitful it might be to write a longer piece of public writing in this genre of description.

If your private writing is already mostly descriptive or already contains a very full description or portrait, you might skip this exercise. In effect, your private writing already led you to use the genre of description or portrait. Just take a moment more to write about what changes you would consider, if any, to focus on the description and make your piece *public*: Would you shape it any differently? What would be the center? Are there any changes in style or approach you would want to make?

Melissa Fogel discovered that her private, open-ended writing led her finally to an image of her sister swinging on a swing and then falling off—and indeed this image became the germ of her revised public piece of writing. (Just as Eudora Welty's image served as the germ that led her to write "A Worn Path." The story is printed in the "Readings" for Workshop 4, and she describes how it grew from an image in a piece we've printed in the "Readings" for Workshop 7.)

Peter Elbow tried out a fast sketch of an image of himself at the computer:

> His shoulders began to hunch more as he got more frustrated with the computer. He was sitting forward on his chair, his eyes as though drawn toward the screen. Periodically he would stop, lean back, try to take a deep breath and relax, but then as he struggled more, he would hunch again and you could see his muscles

> gradually become tense. On one side of the computer were papers and notes he was trying to write from. On the other side and on the floor around him were the computer manuals—propped open to various pages with random objects: books, pencils, boxes of floppy disks. Behind him a window showed clear, bright blue sky, but he was oblivious to it. At this point, he didn't even live in the same universe with that blue sky.

(2) Narrative or Story

Where are the potential *stories* in what you wrote? Look for crucial events, moments, turning points. These points might not even be in what you wrote, but only implied. For example, perhaps your writing is nothing but your feelings about a certain person or your thoughts about a certain issue. But there are stories that could be *found* or *made* that relate to that person or issue. Start at an important moment in that story—not necessarily the beginning—and just write for 8 to 10 minutes to get the feel for how you might write a story. This may lead you to new material or new insights.

If your private writing is already mostly story or has an extended narrative in it, just take a couple of moments and jot down what shaping and adjusting you'd do to make it a public piece. Would you heighten or play with the plot? the mood? the narrator or that narrator's point of view?

Melissa Fogel tried using her private writing for narrative:

> Once upon a time, in a fast-paced city of lights, action, and turmoil, there lived a family. This family wasn't an average family. For in the big city it is hard to find average families. This family, like every other family in the big city, had problems. These problems had nothing to do with money or violence, like most in the city. This family struggled with emotional stress that revolved around one of the family members, the middle child. This middle child was a beautiful girl, for she had eyes the color of the sky and skin that only a china doll could retain. She had long brown locks of curls, and in the sun you could see the gold highlights glowing. She had unique style and sensitivity, and she would share the world with you if she could. There were other children in the family, an older sister and two younger brothers. They all went about their own lives, sometimes fighting, like normal adolescents. But under the surface fights about clothes and the car, they shared a love and respect that isn't easy to come by in the big city. One day the middle child announced that she had a new love. Everyone was happy for the girl. They knew this boy was a very lucky person. But as time went on, problems with this boy began to appear. Changes in the middle child began to take place, changes that no one could understand, not even the sister and brothers that loved her more than the world itself.

(3) Dialogue

You may not think of yourself as naturally writing "dialogue," but there may well be germs of dialogue in your private writing: places where you said "No" or "But wait a minute" or "I agree" or "Here's one thing for sure." In passages like that, you are really *speaking to* another voice—even if that other voice is just another feeling or opinion in your own head. And there are even more passages that imply a dialogue, such as if you wrote about someone who disagrees with you. And if you wrote, "Then we got into a fight" or "She asked him out for a date," it would be a natural thing to break that out into an actual dialogue or conversation of what they said to each other.

Take 8 to 10 minutes and start a dialogue, perhaps with that person you disagree with, perhaps between two conflicting feelings. Perhaps there are two people in your private writing who had an interchange or who disagree with each other; get them talking. But it's not necessary that people disagree. If they simply have different temperaments, any dialogue they have will be fruitful. Start the conversation and just see where it goes.

Don't forget that you can easily write productive dialogues with *objects* or *ideas:* with a house, a book, a place, a piece of clothing. You can have a fruitful dialogue with anything that is *important* to you in your exploratory writing. The trick is simply to have one member of the dialogue say something to start off. As little as "Hello"—or, "What was it like being the house we've all lived in, and seeing and hearing everything we've all said to each other?" Just see what answer comes; let the conversation proceed. Get your pen moving and the dialogue will unfold and create new material: new ideas that are not part of your original exploratory writing. The dialogue may affect or even change the views or feelings you had when doing your exploratory writing.

When Peter Elbow looked back over his private Perl writing (printed in the "Readings" for this workshop), he realized that he could start a dialogue between himself and the computer.

Peter: Why do you always give me such trouble? Why do you so often mess me up or not do what I want you to do? I paid a lot of money for you. I got instructions. Most of all, why won't you *talk* to me when I need you?

Computer: Actually, I talk to you quite often.

Peter: Yes, you send me messages—"bad command," "insert target disk in Drive B"—worse yet, "FATAL ERROR"—but when I'm really in trouble, you just sit there silent and refuse to do what I want you to do.

Computer: Unfortunately it's you who gives me trouble: you refuse to do what's needed. But I don't hold it against you. I just wait for you to catch on. I do everything you ask me to—no matter how many times you ask me to do it; I never forget anything; I'm never bored or impatient. There's only a problem when you don't know my language or you ask me to do something that is impossible. I'm not programmed to know your language perfectly. It's your job to learn mine. As soon as you speak meaningfully to me, I'll speak meaningfully to you.

Peter: Don't take that superior tone with me! "I never make a mistake. I never make a mistake." Why do you keep saying that to me?

Computer: I didn't say that; I never have. But in fact I never do make a mistake. In our dealings, I'm sorry to say that it's only you who makes mistakes.

Peter:	*SEE*! I won't put up with this arrogance. (Wait a minute; let me get a hold of myself. It's only a machine. Calm myself.) OK, I'll be more reasonable with you. I admit it. Of course I make mistakes. But I'm doing the best I can. I try to do things right; and when something doesn't work, I look at the manual; I go over my steps one at a time and try it again and again. But still it doesn't work. Sometimes I get so mad I want to hurl you across the room. And you just sit there silent, superior, condescending.
Computer:	But that's it, don't you see? You are so irrational. Why do you give me the same order again and again when you see it's not working? And then you get so *angry* because *you're* doing something irrational.
Peter:	But I can't help it.
Computer:	Yes, that's what perplexes me. Why do I bring out irrationality in you? I've been watching you these months. I've never seen you as furious and fuming—as close to violence—with anyone else as with me. Not with your wife or children or students or coworkers. What do I do that brings out your irrationality?
Peter:	That's a good question.

(4) Persuasive Essay

What are some of the important *opinions* or *beliefs* in your exploratory writing? What if you tried to persuade people to agree with you? Are there certain people you particularly want to persuade? You'll find that the persuasive essay as a genre—the process of trying to persuade someone—will often bring up reasons or arguments that you didn't think of earlier when you were just expressing or exploring your opinion for yourself.

Take 8 or 10 minutes now and start the germ of a persuasive essay, beginning perhaps with summing up your point as briefly as possible. Before you stop, jot down quickly as many reasons as you can think of that you might use; and try to sketch out a possible organization for the essay. If what you wrote privately was already more or less in a persuasive mode (or a big chunk of it was), just write for a few moments about what changes you would make to shape it or make it stronger. (Workshop 10 deals more fully with persuasion.)

Melissa Fogel tried using her private writing for a persuasive essay:

> I of all people know what it's like to use a boyfriend for a sense of security and escape. I also know what the consequences are for doing such a thing. Relationships these days are under tremendous stress. The problems one of us decides to take on become a problem for the couple. Sometimes even the smallest problems cause the largest rifts between two people. However to stay involved with someone because it is the easiest thing to do, or because of the fear of being on your own, produces a strain no other problem can compare to. When hiding behind someone, you can lose a sense of identity and pride. You can become so wrapped up in the lie that you can't see the truth, even when people are trying to

tell you so. The lie can fester and create long-term disaster. After a while, you can't see the trouble brewing. This trouble can come in all forms. It can cause fighting between those who are trying to make you see the truth, it can hurt the people that care about you, and most of all it can hurt you. You may give up on yourself—decide that you're not good enough for others. You may stop caring for your health and your appearance. You may even lose the qualities you had when you began the relationship. Sometimes when you're unsure if you are falling into this trap, you should break off the relationship for a while and try to regain your life and self once again. You may find that liking you is more important than whether or not someone else likes you.

(5) Expository Essay

What's the most interesting *question, issue,* or *concept* in your exploratory writing? Most people think of an essay as explaining something that they understand. That approach is common, but if you want the most interesting essay—and want to have the most interesting time writing it—don't look for answers or conclusions or explanations; look for *questions* or *perplexity.* What do you need to understand better? You'll discover that you can produce good writing even though you don't yet really understand the issue you are trying to write about. Remember that many good published essays don't give solutions: They clarify or analyze a question so that others can understand it better and go to work on it.

So sniff out the issue of greatest interest to you and take 8 to 10 minutes to start exploring it. You can think of what you are writing as an example of the general form known as "expository essay": an essay which explains. But if you wish, you can think of different subgenres which represent different *ways* of explaining—each of which could give a slightly different shape to your writing. (Workshops 9 through 16 explore different kinds of essays.)

- *Analysis.* Perhaps your private writing talks about lots of things that are all connected to an incident or related to a topic or feeling, but it's not clear how it all adds up or what the main point is. The basic question is the one that lies behind all thinking and writing: "What sense can you make of this tangled pile of data?" Analysis means untangling a tangle.
- *Definition.* Perhaps your private writing leads to some complex or slippery concept you want to figure out (e.g., selfishness). The clearest and most down-to-earth way to define is "ostensive"—that is, pointing or giving examples. (X and Y are examples of selfishness, but Z is not, and here's why.) This is really the same approach used in zoological definition: *genus* tells how something is like its cousins; *species* tells how it differs from its cousins. Thus the essay of definition is closely related to the next form.
- *Compare-contrast.* It's often hard to define or analyze one thing by itself. It's much easier when you can compare it to others—continually holding them up against each other to find similarities and differences. This gives mental leverage. And your private writing may well suggest two or more people, places, or ideas that invite comparison.

- *"Process essay."* In scientific or technical writing, a process essay explains how to do something (e.g., how to go about making water from hydrogen and oxygen). But process essays are not limited to these disciplines. You can write about the steps you go through, for example, to cook a particular meal or prepare a garden plot in the spring—or to do something less concrete such as convincing a parent or teacher of something. Does your private writing contain the germs of some process that you could explain in a process essay?
- *Research essay.* Does your private writing suggest some areas you'd like to study more? You can now write out some of the questions you would pursue. You could take up the issue again in Workshop 12 about research essays.
- *Five-paragraph essay.* This is a school-invented genre, and unfortunately, it is the only genre that some students are taught. The first paragraph introduces the thesis, the three "body paragraphs" each give a reason and an example, and the last paragraph gives a conclusion that restates the thesis. The five-paragraph essay limits thinking because it is so rigid in form. But it is a handy formula to use in certain conditions where you don't have time to think through or explain any complexities. It can be a handy genre for timed exams: "In 20 minutes, explain the causes of the Civil War."

Select one or more of these essay subgenres and write for at least 10 minutes on each one you pick.

(6) Satire or Parody

There might well be germs of satire or parody in your private writing: moments where you make fun of something or someone. If not, what could your private exploratory writing *lead you* to make fun of? A person you'd like to

Exploring the Writing Process

To write letters to friends & *not to send them*. . . . When you are on fire with theology, you'll not write it to Rogers, who wouldn't be an inspiration, you'll write it to Twitchell, because it would make him writhe and squirm & break the furniture. When you are on fire with a good thing that's indecent, you won't waste it on Twitchell, you'll save it for Howells, who will love it. As he will never see it, you can make it really indecenter than he could stand; & so no harm is done, yet a vast advantage is gained. . . . Often you are burning to pour out a sluice of intimately personal, & particularly private things—& there you are again! You can't make your mouth say them. It won't say them to any but a very close personal friend, like Howells, or Twitchell, or Henry Rogers.

Mark Twain

show as silly? An opinion or view that needs puncturing? Yourself when you realize you did something silly? A situation or "scene" that is on the brink of the ridiculous (e.g., people who show off)?

The essence of satire is to exaggerate or distort. Thus you could satirize someone in your exploratory writing (or yourself) by simply describing, but exaggerating certain traits. Or you could put down the thoughts and feelings that run through the person's head (a monologue) but overdo it—carry the thoughts and feelings beyond the plausible, exaggerate the manner of talking. Or you can make fun of an opinion or view by stating it and even arguing for it, but pushing it a bit too far. Or you could create a tone or voice which is off: be highly dignified about something trivial, or very flippant about something serious.

(7) Meditation or Personal Essay

These are particularly interesting public forms because they often function as a somewhat private genre turned public: an invitation to others to *overhear* our transaction with ourselves. It might well be that a portion of your private exploratory writing could be turned into a meditation or personal essay without having to make many changes at all.

Melissa Fogel's private writing was already meditative and personal. By focusing on one topic, she made a meditative personal essay—included in the "Readings" for this workshop. See Beth Spencer's meditative essay, "The Act of Writing as Prayer" in the "Readings" for Workshop 6.

Peter Elbow began to write a brief meditative piece, building on some of his private Perl writing about using a computer, but also reflecting on ideas he generated in his dialogue. (You may find, as he did, that one genre exploration sometimes prompts or speaks to another.) Here is part of what he wrote:

> He's right. (Or is it she? It?) I do get madder at that machine than at anyone else in my life. Why should that be?
>
> Is it because it's a machine and I *can* get mad at it? I can't let myself get so mad at people? That's a nice thought—me as sensible and rational: that I don't act irrationally toward people since it would hurt them and instead I save it for a machine which can never be hurt by my feelings. That's like the dog who moderates his roughness when playing with a tiny toddler. It's like the toddler who hits his parent as hard as he can in blissful faith that anything he puts out, they can deal with. Can I remember when I first realized I could *hurt* my parents? No; but it must have been an awful realization.
>
> But somehow that's too pretty a story: me as purely sensible and rational. There's undeniably something disturbing about getting so heated up at a machine. Is it that I want to kick it because it's helpless? Little kids often seem to pick on the weak one.
>
> But in a way it's not weak at all. It's so powerful, so much more powerful than I. It can do all these things I can't do. And my frustration mounts because I know what's happening is not its fault. *And* if I harm it, *I* would be the one to suffer and would have to pay to have it fixed.
>
> But that reminds me of other occasions when I feel that way. It's true that I never seem to get as mad at people but I do get almost as mad and frustrated

when I'm trying to *fix* some object or machine and cannot do it. It makes me want to cry with frustration.

Perhaps I was getting at something important in my dialogue earlier: the fact that the damn thing won't *talk* to me. I guess that's the hardest thing for me to bear: it's certainly the best way for someone to torture me—not to talk to me. I need a response from creatures around me. Without that, I find existence intolerable.

(8) Poetry

Young children seem to be naturally drawn to poetry, but most of us become somewhat intimidated by it as we grow older and as teachers talk to us about the complexity of great poetry. We know that some of you have continued to write poetry since childhood, or have perhaps come back to it. We will attempt no formal definition of poetry here; we'll just say that for us, poetry is utterance where the language is special or the voice particularly matters; it is discourse or language one wants to savor. We find that most people can write poetry with a little encouragement if they know they don't have to show it to anyone else. We also believe that the very process of writing poetry brings us to a richer understanding of the potential in all language—including even the language of formal essays.

As you read back over your private writing, you may find language that already seems somehow resonant—words that feel right on your tongue or phrases that recur in your ear. Perhaps you can shape some of this into poetry. Remember that poetry does not have to rhyme or even have a formal design; much modern poetry has neither, at least not in a strictly patterned way. You may find that you can create poetry out of some of your private writing with minimal changes. Or you may want to extract some passages—lines and phrases—and build a poem on them.

Peter Elbow extracted the lines that had resonance for him and played with them and came up with this. He realized in mid process that it was also a dialogue.

Don't make a mess.

    No.

Clean it up.
    I don't want to. I refuse. I love throwing things down.

Throw it away.
    I won't. It's mine. I like it that way.

Make a mess.
    No.
    Wait a minute. What? Don't confuse me.
    What if I don't want to?

Make a mess.
    I'm in a swamp. I'm on the kitchen floor.
    It's slimy with spilled food.
    I'll never get clean.
    Too much chaos.

Change your mind.
  My mind is a mess.
  I'm half in my mind—half out.
  How do I get permission to do it differently?
  Will you make it all right?
  I feel it in my stomach.
  I want a guarantee.
Lots of luck.

See the poem "Autobiography" by the Turkish poet Nazim Hikmet in the "Readings" for an example of how good published poetry can use the plainest everyday language.

Main Assignment: *Developing Your Sketch into a Full Draft*

For your main assignment, take one of the quick sketches you have made and develop it into a full draft. Perhaps your teacher will direct you. (You could also develop two sketches into two drafts so that you can compare more fully the effects of varying the audience or genre. If you do two drafts, they will probably be rougher.)

The simplest way to decide which sketch to work on is to think back and decide which one brought you a "click"—a feeling, even if faint, that tells you that this is an interesting direction (or "container") in which to develop some of your private writing.

After you choose a sketch—that is, choose a genre—look back over all your private writing and take a few quick notes on what you want to include in your first draft. Sometimes you need to do a genuine rewriting: the private writing puts you in a position where you can now start fresh on what you want to say. But don't change more than is necessary. It's amazing, sometimes, how little has to be changed from messy, rough private writing to make it polished and ordered. Inexperienced writers sometimes write lively and interesting rough private writing, but in revision they throw away or ruin the most lively, perky, and individual language and the most adventuresome, powerful thinking and instead go for what is safe and "nice" and conventional. So don't be timid. Look for what has energy and juice and life, and find a way to use it.

Once you have a draft of your major assignment for this workshop, your teacher will either give you an opportunity for more feedback and revision or ask you to set it aside to work on later—perhaps for another workshop in this book.

Suggestions for Collaboration

Full collaboration is probably harder here than in many other workshops, since you are starting from private writing. Still, some of you might find that you have similar themes, issues, or even stories in your private writing and would like to write something together. If so, you are in a good position to write a collaborative collage. See Workshop 3 for how to produce together a collage that explores a theme or issue in a rich and interesting way.

Sharing and Responding

Since you and your classmates are likely to end up with a wide range of diverse kinds of writing in different genres, there are no common feedback questions to suggest. It is probably most appropriate to use one of the first four methods for feedback described in "Sharing and Responding": plain sharing; pointing and center of gravity; summary and sayback; or what is almost said.

It might also be useful to get movies of the readers' minds to find out what is going on moment by moment as they read or listen to your work (see "Movies of the Reader's Mind," in "Sharing and Responding" on page 534). For this kind of feedback, it helps to pause two or three times as you are reading to them (or make them pause as they are reading), and have them tell you what is going on in their minds at that moment.

Process Journal

- How did you feel looking back over your private writing? Encouraged, discouraged, bothered? Why?
- What was it like moving from private to public? Did it make a big difference in how you wrote?
- What was it like doing all those short sketches or trial starts? Could you get yourself to jump in and do one burst of writing and then move on to another? If you found it hard, what would it take to become more comfortable with it?
- How did you decide which genre or audience to use?

Exploring Theory: *Are Genres Form or Content?*

Do you usually start writing by thinking mainly about *what* you want to say or *how* you want to say it? That is, are you thinking about content or form?

Starting with Content

In this textbook we often suggest doing freewriting or exploratory writing without worrying about organization. "Invite chaos," we say; "Worry later about organization or form." In making this suggestion we might seem to be making an interesting (and arguable) theoretical assumption: that first you create content (pure content-without-form, as it were) and then you give it form.

Even though Genesis tells us that God took this approach when He created the heavens and the earth (starting out with "formless" matter), it is only one approach to creation. Yet the approach is remarkably helpful to many people in their writing. Whether skilled or unskilled, many people find it a relief when they allow themselves to produce "raw content-without-form." They find it enabling to turn out pages and pages of writing without worrying about whether it's organized or fits a certain form.

In this workshop we may seem even to have exaggerated this one-sided approach. We asked you to produce, as it were, gallons of formless content, and then we asked you to pour those gallons into various bottles or forms.

Let us now turn around and look at the *other* way of talking about form and content in the process of creation. In the first place, strictly speaking all writing has form: There's no such thing as content-without-form. All that private writing cannot but have *some* form. Perhaps the form is mixed or messy, but that's form too. Besides, what looks messy at first glance is often quite patterned. What you wrote may have a large coherent pattern which is obscured by local clutter, digressions, and interruptions.

For example, if you look carefully at your seemingly chaotic private, exploratory writing, you may see that it is shaped by a single narrative flow—or even by a clever flashback narrative pattern. Or perhaps your exploratory writing has a three-step pattern of moving from *event* to *reactions* to the event to *reflective thoughts* about that event and your reactions. Or maybe you'll find the opposite pattern: a movement from reflective thoughts back to the events behind those thoughts. The point is that if you manage to record what's going on in your mind, you are almost certainly recording patterns. Our minds operate by patterns even when we are confused. The human mind is incapable of pure randomness or chaos. Therefore when you look at your private exploratory writing, don't just respect the chaos as useful and valid (which it is); keep an eye out also for the *order* hiding behind the seeming chaos.

This realization leads to a very practical consequence: there are always organizations and genres already lurking in your seemingly messy exploratory writing—organizations and genres that you can discover and prune into shape (like recovering a shapely tree that has become overgrown). Just because you weren't aware of writing within a particular genre doesn't mean that you wrote genreless material. When you "organize" your chaotic private writing, you probably don't have to create organization from scratch; you can clarify the latent organization that's already there. Or more likely you can choose and develop one of the two or three overlapping organizations that are operating, like overlapping wave patterns caused by two or three pebbles dropped in a pond.

In sum, there's no such thing as "starting with content only"; you can't have a smidgen of content that is not fully formed. But you can *pretend* to start with content only; that is, you can put all your attention on following a train of words or thoughts where they lead and totally ignore consideration of form.

Starting with Form

So too, it's possible to pretend to start with form only. And this too is a very practical approach that can help in writing. That is, it can be helpful to start with an organization or genre and look to content afterward. For a genre isn't just a mold to pour unformed raw writing into or a sewing pattern to lay on top of whole cloth to show us where to cut. A genre can serve as a way to *generate* or invent content. Choosing a genre will make you think of words and ideas that you might not think of otherwise. For example, if you decide to use narrative as a form, you will not just arrange your material in terms of time; you will almost certainly think of certain connecting or even causal events you had forgotten. If you are vacillating between a persuasive and an analytic essay, the persuasive genre will cause you to think of reasons and arguments; the analytic genre will cause you to think of hypotheses and causal relationships.

It's perfectly normal to start by choosing a genre. For example, we may decide to write a letter to someone and not be sure what we'll say. Or we may decide to write an essay with a certain organization (for example, a point-by-point refutation of someone else's view). Or someone may choose a genre for us: "Write a persuasive essay on any topic." In loop writing (next workshop), we start with mini-genres (portrait, narrative, letter, and so forth). In this workshop, however, we ask you to think about these genres or types *after* you have done lots of writing.

Because language is inherently both form and content, we can never really have pure content or pure form. It is only our consciousness which tends, at any given moment, to emphasize one more than the other. If we use process writing to study our tendencies of mind when we write, we will gradually learn when it's helpful to put more attention on form as we write, and when it's helpful to put more attention on content. In this way we can take better control of our writing process.

Process Journal: Using the Open-Ended Process

Manuel Depina

As I was doing the private writing, I struggled tremendously, especially with the open-ended process. I went through the open-ended guidelines. I read them about twenty-five times, and still couldn't come up with anything. I couldn't figure out how to do the mechanics and compose it in a way which I would feel most comfortable with.

I followed everything that was in the guidelines. I shook off my hands, took a deep breath, closed my eyes, and still the paper in front of me was blank. I couldn't get myself to relax and concentrate like I usually do. This was probably due to the different method and procedure that I would normally follow.

Believe it or not, reading the guidelines for the twenty-sixth time, I finally got something down. The word *pressure* came to my mind, and I wrote it down as soon as I could, fearing I might forget it.

After I wrote the first word, it seemed like a bomb waiting to explode. Afterward my pen couldn't keep up with my brain, and the words seemed to fall into their proper places. Meanwhile I felt a pleasant feeling of relief and comfort which propelled me and made me want to write more.

The thing that contributes most to my technique is the listing process. After I had that part done, I simply followed the guidelines. And I must admit it was very helpful.

Example of Writing with the Perl Guidelines

Peter Elbow

Note on this text. *This was Perl writing I did during a workshop—about an hour and a half—demonstrating the Perl process to teachers. I emphasized to everyone that the writing would be private and that they could use it for* whatever *kind of writing they wanted or needed to do. When I started listing things I could write about (I didn't save my list), I was hit hardest by my need to get going on the job currently staring me in the face: writing an overdue essay about writing on a word processor. Most of my previous Perl writing had been personal and exploratory—about some strong feelings or event in my life. Once I even tried writing a story. And usually I don't have much sense of audience during Perl writing. But on that morning I gave myself permission to work on this piece of public, pragmatic, "duty" writing for our textbook.*

Because I was leading the workshop and my mind was somewhat occupied by that role, I didn't have as much concentration for my own work as I would have had if someone else had been in charge. I didn't get so much written. I remember feeling distracted. (Also slightly guilty, for as it were, "doing my homework in class.")

I give here what I wrote that morning—as I wrote it (except for correcting some spelling and filling in some missing punctuation and making a couple of other minor corrections so it's readable). In several places I insert, in capital letters, the Perl questions that my writing is responding to (e.g., WHAT'S THIS ALL ABOUT?)

I'm sitting here writing with my pen. About writing with a word processor. Seems odd. I normally write on my WP, but today I'm in a workshop with other teachers and we have a chance to write together about whatever we need to write.

The two main skills in writing are making a mess and cleaning up the mess.

That is, it's hard to write well unless we are inventive and fecund—open to lots of words and ideas. That means being open and accepting to the words and ideas which come. Not being too quick to reject and say no. When we do that, we make a mess. We write down (or at least consider) too much. ~~We~~ Too many words; we start down too many paths. Branching and complex. We need that mess.

Yet in order to write well we also need to do just the opposite: we need to ~~say no and~~ be skeptical and rejecting—to throw away or change everything that's not the best; to reject what looks or sounds nice but isn't really, in the end, up to snuff.

It turns out that the WP is ideal for both these mental operations. ~~It helps~~

It ~~helps in make~~ makes it easier than with pen and paper to make more of a mess. We can throw down everything to the screen easily in more [I left a few blank lines; I think I assumed I'd come back and say more.]

Yet it also makes it easier than with pen and paper to clean up that mess. It's so easy to throw away what's discarded, fix words and spellings—and come up with neat copy.

Indeed, I would say that the main psychological danger in writing with a WP is that its fixing and cleaning up is so easy—indeed so fun—that it's tempting to stop every time you mistype or misspell a word or change your mind about a word and go back and fix it.

Learn to block that impulse. Learn to sustain your generating. Learn to keep on writing—as though it were pen and ink or typewriter and it were too hard to make a change. Otherwise you will distract yourself from your generating. Learn, in short, to make a mess.

You can let yourself write notes to yourself in your text when you're not sure. Instead of stopping and scratching your head and thinking when you become puzzled, you can keep on writing about your puzzlement. (Because it's so easy to erase them later.) I tend to put these remarks in CAPS—or indent them 5 spaces [in a block that's all indented]. So I can see later that they're not part of the text.

Why that's useful. When you keep writing

But—edit on screen/paper.

~~Start anywhere—cause you can move it around~~

WHAT'S IT ALL ABOUT?

—new power
—new relationship to words
—addiction
—my duty
—new horizons

WHERE DO YOU FEEL IT?

I feel it in my upper stomach.

WHAT'S THE PHRASE?

new power

It's scary: but it leads to addiction. It can change your relationship to writing.

click [I felt a click here; a shift of felt sense. Asking myself what it's about, what's the phrase, and where I feel it—these acts led me closer to what seemed interesting and important. Leading to what follows.]

Screen is something half way between mind and paper.

Mind is a mess: paper is supposed to be neat. When I'm writing on screen, it feels like it's sort of—half—still in my mind. It's a second mind. It's ~~not~~ still partly in me.

Like my mind I can't look at all of it at once, I can only put my attention on one bit at a time. I don't yet have complete detachment from it till I print it out.

It gives me a second mind.

WHAT'S LEFT OUT?

Techniques.

—How to adopt right attitude.

—Not be scared. You can't hurt the machine.

—You can get into trouble by losing text if you aren't careful to back up—but don't be worried.

—Writing as play.

WHAT DO I LOVE ABOUT IT?

—That it lets me get so much down.

—When I have a new idea, I just start writing it (using a carriage return to start a new line). I don't have to worry about putting it in the right order. I can jump back from idea to idea.

—Because you know you can correct, you have permission to write a messier way.

—You can start anywhere, in the middle, add late idea—cause you can move things around.

—It's so easy to revise. I suddenly see a new idea or new arrangement after I'm almost done—and I can wade in and do it—and print out clean copy.

—I can experiment. Leave one version as it is. Copy. Start revising but leave the old one. In case I lose good aspects of the old one in the revising process.

—I can print out 3–4 copies—at middle stage—and give' em to someone else. And they'll be neat and easy to read.

—Spelling and grammar checker. Handwriting and spelling have always been superficials of writing, but they've influenced readers more than anything else. Form of snobbery. If your spelling and handwriting and grammar are bad, I won't take you seriously. Now anyone can turn out professional copy.

WHAT'S HARD/DON'T LIKE

Another mind. Sometimes I make such a mess that I feel in a swamp. Too many options. Once I remember feeling. "Oh, I wish I were writing in ink on expensive velum so that I would just choose a word and be done. Not feel like I have to keep revising and changing. I want something final (I must find that process piece I wrote when I was in that situation).

Sometimes I try to revise too much on screen. Too much chaos in the mind.

It's an enharmonic, changeable medium: it's a mind or it's paper—and it moves back and forth. If on screen, it's fluid—it's my mind; if I print it out, it stops being fluid and changing and I get it still and quiet where I can deal with it. I can take a mind scan.

Need it.

One can move back and forth.

It's like a brain photograph.

Be Brave Sweet Sister: Essay Developed from Open-Ended Writing

Melissa Fogel

My sister Jennifer and I were the closest two sisters could be. We were not abnormal, we had our fights, yet they were fights you'd have with any life-long roommate. All of my childhood memories are filled with her face. Her baby blue eyes, her long curly brown hair and of course her chubby little cheeks. Our days were spent torturing our little brother, playing dress up with mom's clothes, climbing trees, sledding down the back of our yard, riding bikes until we couldn't walk, or just singing along to the radio in our make-believe band. I die a little each time I think that the laughter left our family, or my sweet little sister has vanished from my life.

Jennifer has been dating a man our family has trouble relating to. Although she would love to blame it on the color of his skin, this is far from the truth. My family has trouble relating to his ten-year leap over her age, his twenty-two arrests, and his three times in jail serving longer than six months. Take all the legal problems away and my family will not relinquish their problem with this man. My sister is young, beautiful, and intelligent; however she has very little self-esteem, and seems to let herself get lost in the crowd. The man she dates does not help in this situation; he only lets her hide under his arms. Jennifer needs someone to motivate her in school and life—to show the world that she is an incredible woman with enormous gifts to give. He just hides her, and feeds her fear.

The days without her now are almost empty, almost depressing. She and I fight on the subject whenever one of us can muster up the energy. Some days I want to reach for her thin little neck and start strangling. For the path down this life time she has chosen will only break the rope that ties our hearts together. The anger I feel rises inside of me until I can hardly see straight. My nails bury themselves into my skin and tears cascade down the pale cheeks of my pain-ridden face. I can see the anger in Jennifer as well. Her blue eyes become black and there is no reflection of the sister she once loved staring back at her. I am the enemy, with a black heart and red horns that stick strangely towards the sky. Our clashes have become so ugly, that I began to fear seeing her in the halls of the house—the same halls we used to bang into while playing a fast-paced game of tag. Now these halls are empty, lonely, and ugly.

The pain of losing her is harder to describe than the anger. The pain gnaws on the inside of my heart, making it slowly bleed to death into a sea some call the soul. I have painful reminders of what our relationship used to be like in the back of my mind trying to break free and huddle over the mess we have now. My days at home are so dark. The rooms seem so cloudy, even when the sun peers through the hazy windows. The cloud seems to follow me into every sphere of my life, hanging over my head and gliding along the paths I choose to follow. It shadows my every move and makes others aware through the ugly darkness that covers my face. It seems as if this cloud will never let me free, until I confront the pain that steals my body from a happier existence.

That is where the fear becomes effervescent in the scope of my life. This confrontation that seems inevitable pulls at my sleeve as a nagging child does to her mother. In every scenario I play on the record player of my mind, Jennifer either wins the war, or drives off for good. I can't lose her entirely, I would die without my sister. Yet I can't see her with someone who does not bring out the Jennifer I know and love. I fear the loneliness I will experience without her. I fear the pain she will have to endure in a life under his wing, and I fear the guilt that will creep into my heart if I make her leave him for a life of loneliness.

I remember one rainy afternoon. Despite the warnings we heard from our parents, my sister, brother and I went out to play. We ran over to our neighbor John's house, because he had the coolest swing set. It was wet and I had a really eerie feeling about the day. My sister ran over to the swing set to a bench where four people could sit and began to swing really high. She called me over but I couldn't do it; I didn't feel right about it. So I called her over to come play with me. To no avail: she wouldn't stop swinging. About ten minutes later I heard a scream. I ran over to find my little sister underneath that swing lying in a pool of blood. She was crying. The rest is memory to the adults, because they took over from there. Jennifer was rushed to the hospital, where she was given fifteen stitches in the top of her head. I remember waiting by the window, so scared I would never see her again. She came home with a goofy story about how she was very brave, didn't cry and asked the doctor for gum while he was sewing her up.

The story seems ironic to me now. I'm calling out to my sister, for I have this awful feeling about this boyfriend of hers. Yet she doesn't hear me; she keeps on swinging. I keep calling; she keeps swinging. I want her to come home and every day I wait for her to come back to her big sister. Maybe one day she will come home with a new story of how she let him go, was very brave, didn't even cry and asked for a piece of gum.

A Letter

Published in *Elementary English*

Mark Levensky

Teachers
Perkins School
43 & College
Des Moines, Iowa 50311

Dear Teachers:

This morning, just as I woke up, I remembered something that I have thought about off and on for years. I remembered taking spelling tests when I was in grade school at Perkins. As I remembered this, I experienced some of the feelings that I experienced when I prepared for these tests, took them, and got them back. I experienced fear, anxiety and humiliation.

I remember the spelling books that we used. The color, size and shape of the books. How the words to be learned were grouped on the page. And I can remember how hard I tried to learn these words. Doing just what my teachers said. Printing the words over and over again. Spelling a word to myself with my eyes closed and then opening my eyes to check if I was right. Spelling the words for my parents before bed. Going over them again and again right before the test. I can also remember what it was like to take the spelling tests. A piece of wide margined paper and a pencil. The teacher saying the words aloud. Fear and anxiety. I struggled to remember how to spell each word. Erase. No matter how I spelled a word, it looked wrong. Fear. I crossed out, printed over, went back, tried again. "One minute left." Anxiety. When my spelling papers came back they were covered with red marks, blue marks, check marks, correction marks, and poor grades. It was so humiliating. And it was always the same. No matter how much I prepared or how hard I tried, I couldn't spell most of the words. And no matter how many spelling tests I took and failed, there were always more spelling tests to take and fail. We got a new book of spelling words at the beginning of each term.

At the time my teachers tried to help me. They told me what I had to do in order to improve: "Print the words over and over again. Spell a word to yourself with your eyes closed and then open your eyes to check if you are right. Spell the words for your parents before bed. Go over them again and again right before the test." My teachers also said that unless I learned to spell I would never get into high school, or out of high school, or into college, or out of college. And the last thing that they always told me was that I couldn't spell.

What I want to say to you teachers now is this. I couldn't spell very well then, and I still can't. I got into high school, and out of high school, and into college, and out of college. While my teachers at Perkins didn't teach me to spell, they did manage to have an effect on me. For example, this morning, twenty five years later, I woke up and remembered their spelling tests, and experienced the fear, anxiety and humiliation that I felt when I prepared for these tests, took them, and got them back. If you are still giving children these spelling tests, please stop doing so at once.

Sincerely yours,

Mark Levensky
Associate Professor
Department of Humanities
Massachusetts Institute of Technology
Cambridge, Massachusetts

Autobiography

Nazim Hikmet

Nazim Hikmet (b. Salonica, 1902; d. 1963) is one of Turkey's most important modern poets.

I was born in 1902
I never once went back to my birthplace
I don't like to turn back
at three I served as a pasha's grandson in Aleppo
at nineteen as a student at Moscow Communist University
at forty-nine I was back in Moscow as a guest of the Tcheka Party
and I've been a poet since I was fourteen
some people know all about plants some about fish
                                        I know separation
some people know the names of the stars by heart
                                        I recite absences

I've slept in prisons and in grand hotels
I've known hunger even a hunger strike and there's almost no food
   I haven't tasted
at thirty they wanted to hang me

at forty-eight to give me the Peace Medal
which they did
at thirty-six I covered four square meters of concrete in half a year
at fifty-nine I flew from Prague to Havana in eighteen hours
I never saw Lenin I stood watch at his coffin in '24
in '61 the tomb that I visit is his books
they tried to tear me away from my party
it didn't work
nor was I crushed under falling idols
in '51 I sailed with a young friend into the teeth of death
in '52 I spent four months flat on my back with a broken heart
waiting for death
I was jealous of the women I loved
I didn't envy Charlie Chaplin one bit
I deceived my women
I never talked behind my friends' backs
I drank but not every day
I earned my bread money honestly what happiness
out of embarrassment for another I lied
I lied so as not to hurt someone else
but I also lied for no reason at all
I've ridden in trains planes and cars
most people don't get the chance
I went to the opera
most people can't go they haven't even heard of the opera
and since '21 I haven't been to the places that most people visit
mosques churches temples synagogues sorcerers
but I've had my coffee grounds read
my writings are published in thirty forty languages
in my Turkey in my Turkish they're banned
cancer hasn't caught up with me yet
and nothing says that it has to
I'll never be a prime minister or anything like that
and I'm not interested in such a life
nor did I go to war
or burrow in bomb shelters in the bottom of the night
and I never had to take to the roads under diving planes
but I fell in love at close to sixty
in short comrades
even if today in Berlin I'm *croaking* of grief
I can say that I've lived like a human being
and who knows
how much longer I'll live
what else will happen to me.

About Being a Man: Essay Developed from Private Writing

Charles Miller

In this paper I will discuss, through personal experience, what it is to grow up male and all that is expected of a "man" and why we exhibit these traits.

It all begins as a child. My father treated my older brother and me more like his buddies than his sons. He would be gone for sometimes weeks at a time on a flight and when he would come home, even though we missed him, there were no hugs and kisses. He'd walk through the door and say, very unenthusiastically, "Hello boys" and give us a swift slap on the back or shoulder. Or shake our hands, clenching tightly, making us squeeze back as hard as possible. This was followed by some sort of strength test to see if we had gotten any stronger while he had been away.

We were never allowed to cry in my house: "Men don't cry." Believe me, having an older brother around to beat the hell out of you, it was extremely hard not to cry occasionally. If my father saw us crying he would say "What the hell are you crying for, go outside!" Or if we were already outside it was "Go see your mother!"

Then there was sibling rivalry. My brother and I were constantly getting into fights and I had my share of getting beaten up, and if I ever cried, the taunting from him and his friends was worse than the black and blues. To be called a sissy or a wimp was the worst torture and embarrassment possible. So you learned not to cry, show no pain, "suck it up," be a man about it.

Then there were times on the schoolyard when I found myself walking up to another male classmate and punching him in the gut as hard as I possibly could, only because he may have called me a name or maybe it was because his mom dressed him funny or he had a "girly" lunchbox. All the boys were so hostile towards one another at that age: it seems so horrible now.

And then there was proving oneself. You always had to prove yourself as a young boy. Climb the highest tree, jump the widest stream, ride your bike down the steepest hill, or hold your breath the longest. You always accepted the challenge. Even if you didn't want to, you had to. Otherwise you would be called a wimp and society turned their backs on you. So you go through with it, and if you didn't make it you do it again no matter how bad your knees were scraped from the first try. If you challenged that test of "manhood" and beat it, then you would gain status in this society and become a leader, and it felt pretty good, until someone did something better.

This competition among peers carried on into high school. But for some odd reason it became even more important. When playing sports you were never allowed to show or at least permit yourself to show any pain, no matter how bad you were hurt. "Suck it up. Don't be a candy ass." Sometimes you would be in so much pain you didn't want to move, but you would get up and get back into it. You felt more like a man playing with the pain than sitting out like a wimp. All I got from that manly bull was an unbelievably painful knee reconstruction operation, over a year of therapy, and years of knee problems to look forward to. All for the image I, as a male, am supposed to portray.

I realize now that trying to portray that image is foolish. There is no reason to harm oneself in an effort to be manly. Helpless and in pain is all I felt lying in that hospital bed. With a group of therapists standing around you urging you to move your leg just the slightest bit and struggling to the point of exhaustion without success, you feel anything but manly. If I could go back in time I would stop myself at the first sign of any knee problems and gladly accept being a wimp for awhile, rather than screw up my knee permanently.

If I have a son, just like any other father, I want him to be tough and brave to all challenges. But I will not force these ideals of manliness on him. If he wants to take on a challenge it should be for himself and not to impress me or anyone else. It is far better for him to achieve something for himself rather than do something against his will merely to impress other males and hold true to that portrait of being male.

"Dear Adrienne"

from *The Language of Life*

Adrienne Rich

Adrienne Rich (b. Baltimore, 1929) is an awarding-winning American poet, essayist, feminist, and political activist.

Dear Adrienne:
I'm calling you up tonight
as I might call up a friend   as I might call up a ghost
to ask what you intend to do
with the rest of your life.   Sometimes you act
as if you have all the time there is.
I worry about you when I see this.
The prime of life, old age
aren't what they used to be;
making a good death isn't either,
now you can walk around the corner of a wall
and see a light
that already has blown your past away.
Somewhere in Boston   beautiful literature
is being read around the clock
by writers   to signify
their dislike of this.
I hope you've got something in mind.
I hope you have some idea
about the rest of your life.

In sisterhood.

Adrienne

Loving and Destroying

Marion Milner

Marion Milner (b. London, 1900; d. 1998) was a pioneering British psychoanalyst as well as an accomplished painter. As an author, she is known for her psychoanalytic writings and for her diaries, memoirs, and writing on the process of artistic creation.

This is a short section from Milner's Eternity's Sunrise: A Way of Keeping a Diary. *She describes her book as an attempt "to make public this account of what has been an essentially private enterprise, one growing out of my own need to try and sort out what being alive really means to me" (vii). Much of* Eternity's Sunrise *consists of passages (like this one) from a diary she kept over a number of years. She was "stimulated by reading Montaigne's essays and his insistence that what he calls the soul is totally different from all that one expects it to be, often being the very opposite. It was this that gave me the idea of keeping a diary to see if I could find out at all what this soul of mine was really like" (ix).*

Yesterday, as we drove home in the car with the cat on my lap, he kept driving his claws into my bare knee in what seemed like an uprush of affection, till I took his paws into my hand and just held them gently, a strange delight in just holding them, the little spears safely sheathed. Soon he reared himself up and started butting my chin, rubbing his nose all round it—and then curled up and went to sleep.

There's this feeling of wanting to hug someone so closely that they merge into you. Even the cat. Or especially the cat. I do really want to have for myself his quality of total being, his total relaxation when spread out on my knee and total and complete absorption in washing himself, sticking up his front paw, toes wide spread and luxuriously licking between them, totally at his own pace, such a delight to watch. But demanding that someone should merge into oneself can be destructive of their identity. Like eating them.

The Mass surely recognises the destructiveness hidden in primitive loving. Adonis, Osiris, Orpheus, all torn to pieces. And now I remember the story of the walk to Emmaus, how it is said Jesus was known to them in the breaking of bread. I wonder, did this encounter really happen or was it a poetic invention to express an inner truth, to do with inner nourishment?

Two mornings, stretching out from the bed to turn on the electric kettle, the flow into my fingers, it felt like love, a kind of love affair. That hymn we had to sing every day at the little private school I first went to: 'New every morning is the love/Our waking and uprising prove.' Then, I had no idea what the word proof meant, now of course I know that the very fact of my being able to move at all, be alive, is only because someone gave me love, took care of me.

Now I am told that my cat's pounding when feeling loving is a repetition of how, as a kitten, he pounded at his mother's belly to make the milk come. But of course he hadn't got sharp claws then.

Can I say what is the central thing I have learned from psychoanalysis? Is it about the unlearned morality, that it needs no one to teach us that it's bad to hurt, spoil, harm what one loves? Life does the teaching. And all the ways we find of trying to escape by splitting off the bits that do the hurting, deny them, project them, say it's other people who do it, not me.

That story of the boy who killed a kitten, with people's appropriate horror at such an act of depravity. But then seeing it as perhaps the result of a fierce inner morality which saw the kitten as what he felt to be the bad bit of himself. This was before I had had any patients and found this process going on again and again.

Collaborative Writing:
Dialogue, Loop Writing, and the Collage

Essential Premises

There are three important ways to help you get more involved or "into" a topic you are writing about, and thereby enrich and complicate your thinking.

1. *Collaborative writing.* If two or more people come at the same topic, they don't just *add* to the thinking ("two heads are better than one"), they *multiply* the thinking through the interaction of ideas. Dialogue is one form of collaborative writing.
2. *Loop writing.* If you come at the same topic from different angles and use different writing structures, you will find a much wider variety of ideas and even points of view.
3. *Collage.* If you use a collage structure, you can communicate more richness and complexity in a piece of writing—even contradiction—and still give readers a sense that the piece hangs together.

All three methods are playful. Using a spirit of play in your writing is one of the best ways to make writing more satisfying for you and more effective for readers.

Main Assignment Preview

Students often point to two main problems in dealing with school writing assignments: not being interested in the topic (*"boorrrring"*) and not having enough to say. The activities in this workshop—collaborative writing, dialogue, and loop writing—are powerful ways to overcome these problems. All three techniques are most useful if you want to do a lot of thinking about your topic, if you are having trouble finding things to say, or if you feel bored, unconnected, or alienated from what you have to write about. They are less useful if you already know what you want to say or are in a hurry for a final draft. They tend to make a mess.

Collaborative writing can be difficult, but we can show you some interesting and productive ways to start: ways to learn collaboration and get many of its benefits, yet avoid many of the difficulties. At the same time, you'll learn two other techniques for expanding your thinking about any topic: dialogue and the loop process. You also can use these techniques by yourself even if it is not feasible to collaborate with others.

There are two assignments for this workshop. The first and smaller assignment is to write a dialogue with a partner. The main assignment is to write a collage with one or more partners. (These writing activities are also beneficial for producing a collaborative essay, or a solo collage or solo essay.)

Writing a Dialogue

The dialogue is a venerable form of writing. Plato wrote the most famous dialogues, which recount philosophical conversations between Socrates and some of his fellow Athenians. But Plato got to write both voices in these dialogues (though he is said to have based them on real conversations). We're asking for something more genuinely collaborative from you and your partner: a dialogue in which each of you writes one voice. Your dialogue can be as short or as long and ambitious as you want to make it. Either way, it will serve as a warm-up for the main assignment.

Here's what we suggest. With a partner, decide on a topic or issue that you are both interested in or which you would like to explore through "talking on paper." Perhaps your teacher will suggest a topic. If you have a choice, it's best to choose an issue or topic that you'd like to understand better. One suggestion is to write about your past experiences working with others in some kind of collaborative project or working as a member of a team.

Starting the Dialogue

Writing a dialogue may sound difficult, but you won't have trouble if you realize you are just "having a conversation on paper." Every conversation is really a form of collaboration. We are all practiced at simply *replying* to what someone says and carrying on with an exploration of a topic through talk.

After you have chosen your topic, one of you simply starts. Think about how actual conversations start. Someone just *says* something. One of you might write, "Hi. What do you think about collaborating?" Or "I hate collaborating." Or "I liked social studies group reports. We got together at someone's house and had a lot of fun while we were getting the work done. It was more fun and less lonely." Or "When I was a kid, I always had to do the dishes with my brother and sister. We could never divide up the jobs evenly. We spent more time fighting than doing the dishes. Why did we do this night after night? You'd think we'd have figured out some system." (Also, remember that what you write here is only a rough draft. Before you show it to anyone, you will have a chance to delete and add and change things.)

After one person writes the opening remark, the sheet of paper goes to the other person and she writes her reply: whatever the opening remark leads her to say. (With a computer, you can take turns or pass the keyboard back and forth. If you have networked computers, you can each sit at your own terminal and write the dialogue online.)

It's all right to let the written conversation wander around a bit, much as spoken conversations do. Sometimes one person says, "Yes, I agree." Fine; the other can reply, "What makes you agree? What is your experience?" And in conversations we often say, "No, I disagree" and then say why. This is fine in writing too, and then the two of you can go on to have an argument. Sometimes there's a kind of pause, when a thread of thought has come to an end, and it's up to the next person to start off a new thread; for example, "Well, I can't think of anything more to say about this point. But here's another point I'd like to know your thoughts about."

You can go on this way anywhere from 3 to 23 pages, depending on how much time you have and how long a piece your teacher asks for. Some of the Socratic dialogues are more than 50 pages long; in fact, Plato's *Republic* is a long book in the form of a dialogue. Just make sure you write more in your first draft than you need for your final version. If your teacher asks for a three-page dialogue, try to start off with more pages to choose from.

Here's another way to produce a dialogue on paper. Hold off writing and start by talking. Simply *have* that conversation with your partner, but take notes as you go along to record the most interesting points and issues that came up. Then reconstruct the best parts of your conversation on paper. (This may be what Plato did with the Socratic dialogues.)

Revising the Dialogue

The next step is to look over what you have and decide together how to make a finished product. Remember that dialogues are naturally informal and conversational in tone, as you'll see from the dialogues in "Readings." There's no conflict between an informal tone and careful philosophic thinking. What you want to end up with is a conversation on paper that throws light on an issue and is also interesting to read because it captures on paper the liveliness and voice of conversation. Your conversation might record a disagreement, even a fight, or you might trade your thoughts and ideas and not disagree at all. There is a whole range of possibilities, the full range of ways that people talk to each other in conversation. Conversations and dialogues are particularly satisfying if you can zero in on an issue or a question that you disagree about or want to understand better. The conversation helps you figure things out.

Your teacher might ask you to revise your rough draft carefully and extensively to get it as good as you can make it; she may ask you just to clean it up quickly for sharing and then go on; or she might even ask you to treat it as an exercise and leave it unchanged—as a private conversation between the two of you.

If you revise, whether quickly or carefully, you'll want to consider these questions:

- What are the most interesting parts?
- What is the focus, the emphasis? Have you figured anything out or

reached a conclusion? You may have to write a bit more to give some focus or closure.

- Which parts will you rearrange or discard?

It's interesting to share dialogues, whether for feedback or only for learning. It's particularly interesting to read them aloud: that is, to "stage" or "perform" the dialogue for other pairs or perhaps for the whole class. That helps you notice where you've managed to get your written language to sound natural and where it comes out stilted or awkward.

Finally, take a moment to notice the nature of the collaboration you've engaged in. You produced a genuinely collaborative piece of writing, yet you avoided most of the difficulties of collaboration—that is, you collaborated to agree on a topic and on which parts of the dialogue to cut and keep and what to add or change. But you didn't have to agree on any ideas or write sentences together or find a common voice or style. And you probably produced a lively, useful, and interesting piece of writing. (If not, you can see now what got in the way and how to do it better next time.)

The Loop Writing Process

Loop writing consists of a series of short pieces of writing that help you think more productively and write more interestingly. It is called a "loop" process because as you do many of these short pieces, you allow your mind to slide away somewhat from full concentration on the topic, but afterwards you loop back to focus on your topic as you revise. While doing these loops, you can trust that the pieces will be productive and yield good insight in the end. By turning slightly away from the topic and writing little stories, portraits, and even lies, your mind will find insights that it can't find otherwise. (In the dark we can sometimes see a faint star or the hands of a clock from the corner of our eye that we cannot see head-on.) But these insights are often *implied,* not directly expressed. So you often have to reflect on what you wrote in order to see what it is telling you about your topic.

Your teacher may invite you or your group to choose your own topic, or she may set a topic. Here are a couple of topics we consider useful and appropriate to explore using the loop process:

- Explore the relationship between speaking and writing. What's useful and problematic about each of them? Are there differences between how your mind works when you speak and when you write? Is your language different? Is the "talking on paper" that you are engaged in as you write a dialogue more like writing or talking? What roles do speaking and writing play in your life?
- Consider your gender, race, religion, socioeconomic class, or cultural background (or perhaps more than one) to explore three things:
  —The strengths and virtues they have given you (i.e., what are you proud of in your inheritance?).

—The ways they have tempted people to stereotype you or even be prejudiced against you.

—The ways they might have led you to stereotype or even be prejudiced against other people.

These are not easy topics. They might seem too large or too personal or too academic. We think they are important in themselves, but we also chose them because we want to show you how the techniques of this workshop—dialogue, loop writing, and collaboration—are all helpful when you are faced with a complex topic you didn't choose.

You can use the loop writing whether you are writing collaboratively or alone, and whether you want to produce an essay or a collage. We suggest that you write a collaborative collage for this workshop. The loop writing process will be the same in any case.

We'll show you five general kinds of loop writing. Each one has variations within it.

1. First thoughts, prejudices, preconceptions
2. Moments, stories, portraits
3. Dialogue
4. Variations on audience, writer, and time
5. Lies, errors, sayings

You probably can't use all of the loop processes on one writing task, but it's worth learning them all and becoming comfortable with them. That's why we're asking you to try them out quickly for this workshop. If you are writing collaboratively, make sure that you and your partner use all the varieties (even the variations or subvarieties). See if you can write for at least 10 minutes on each of the subvarieties. The "Readings" contain examples of loop writing and collages made from loop writing. (Hint: when writing your loops, it's best to write only on one side of the paper, so you can cut and paste and rearrange later.)

First Thoughts, Prejudices, Preconceptions

You have already sampled this kind of writing if you did focused freewriting in Workshop 1. It is a matter of putting down whatever first comes to mind about your topic. Focused freewriting might have felt like a "mere exercise," but writing first thoughts is a good way to start out writing a serious essay: You always know more about a topic than you realize. The important thing is to jump in and keep on writing and let yourself get past what you already "have in mind."

A helpful way to write first thoughts is to use what might be called "narrative thinking." Simply write your thoughts in the form of a story about what's happening in your head from moment to moment: "When I think of this topic, what first comes into my mind is a feeling that _______. Then I think of _______. Then it occurs to me that _______. And then I wonder about _______, and so on. This procedure takes the emphasis away from the question of whether your thinking is true or right or sensible. It puts the emphasis instead on a different kind of truth and validity: that these thoughts, feelings, images, hunches, and wishes are going on in your mind, that these are snapshots of what *you* bring to the topic. This approach adds to the sense of adventure in the process and often encourages more exploration.

You might worry that this acceptance of prejudices will lead you to wrong ideas or bad thinking. Remember that you're treating this writing not as "the answer" but as exploration. If you want to do good thinking on a topic, you need to understand your own prejudices and preconceptions. The best way to understand them—and to prevent them from infecting your *careful writing*—is to get these candid snapshots of your initial feeling and thinking out on the table.

For example, let's say you've decided to focus on the relationship between speaking and writing. Let's say further that you're sick of writing and tired of people (like us) glorifying it. You could call this a first thought or preconception. Take it seriously. Explore it: it may lead you somewhere useful. Why are you sick of writing? What about it has been glorified too much? What happens to you when you write? Why do teachers, textbook writers, and journalists glorify writing so much? We think you're more likely to understand writing this way—by acknowledging and exploring your first thoughts—than by pushing those thoughts aside or defending them as gospel.

Give yourself permission to go along with your preconceptions—even to exaggerate your prejudices. You might want to start off by saying something as extreme as "There is no longer any need to teach students to write now that we have telephones." Once you've written this, you may react so strongly against its absoluteness that you'll want to cross it out. But we suggest that you follow through, push it, nurture it a bit, and protect it from your own criticism for a while. As you allow yourself to get carried away by your extreme idea, you may discover some unexpected problems with writing—or why writing has been so important to humankind. You'll begin to understand some

Exploring the Writing Process

I just figured out what it is I'm trying to say—found my point or assertion. I've been wrestling for three days and unable to figure it out—knowing that I've been saying good stuff—knowing that long passages I've been writing are good (some as long as 3–4 pages)—but unable to *say* exactly what it is I'm really trying to say.

I found it when I started to write out a slightly tangential thought. I realized this was a side thought and started a new sentence in parentheses. In midsentence I recognized it was even more tangential than I had realized and almost just stopped and crossed the whole thing out as an unhelpful side road. And then I just said what the heck and kept going, and all of a sudden it led to a sentence that zeroed in on the precise issue that was at the heart of the 15–20 pages I'd so far written but been unable to sum up.

It's simple and clear once it's said. But *I* couldn't see it. Or I couldn't see it till late in the game—and not till I let myself ride on this digression.

Peter Elbow

of the significant differences between talking on the telephone and writing things down. Almost invariably there are interesting insights tangled up with early careless thinking. People seldom come up with good new thinking except through some obsession or exaggeration.

If you are doing a research project and have to do a lot of reading or research before you can write, use first thoughts and prejudices *before* you do that reading and research. By putting on paper all the ideas you already have—even writing out a quick 20-minute fantasy of what you *hope* your research will show—you'll find that your reading and research become far more interesting and productive. You'll already have ideas of your own to compare with what "authorities" say; you won't be reading with a blank mind. You're more likely to remember what you read and have more reactions to it.

Moments, Stories, Portraits

Moments: What times or situations can you think of that somehow seem connected to your topic? Stories: What happenings or series of events come to mind in connection with your topic? Portraits: Quickly describe any people who are somehow central to your topic. It's fine to move quickly and simply sketch in moments, stories, and portraits in short five-minute bursts of writing. But you may discover that one or two of these are so important that you need to write at great length. You can do that now or wait till later. At this point don't spend any time trying to connect separate pieces to one another or to elaborate on the significance of them unless that just happens while you're writing. (You've already sampled this kind of loop writing in Workshop 1 when you wrote moments, stories, and portraits from your past writing experiences.)

The cognitive power here comes from using *experiential* writing (description and storytelling) for the sake of *cognitive* or *expository* writing or thinking. We are often smarter when we tell stories and think about actual people than when we give ideas and reasons. Most of us have had more practice with describing and storytelling than with abstract and inferential writing.

Try testing this idea sometime by asking someone his ideas about the relationship between speaking and writing. After he has said a few things, ask him to tell you some moments, incidents, and people that come to mind when he thinks about speaking and writing. After he's talked some more, ask him to reflect on these moments, stories, and portraits to find insights or implications about speaking and writing in each of them. It's very likely that he'll come up with more and better thinking by means of this roundabout loop path than by starting off directly with "trying to think." He's very likely to surprise himself and discover that what he said about speaking and writing when you first questioned him is different and not as valid as the reflections he has after telling stories and reflecting on people. Loop thinking is concrete and specific thinking that cuts a path around generalities, pieties, and prejudices. Thus writing up remembered moments sometimes works *against* first thoughts in a productive way.

Dialogue

Describing and storytelling seem easier and more natural than abstract or expository kinds of discourse like *explaining, giving reasons,* and *making inferences.* Describing lets us close our eyes and see what to say; storytelling carries us along on a stream of "and then, and then, and then." We've been describing and telling stories from infancy.

But there's an important exception here. Ever since we could talk, we've engaged in *dialogue* too, and dialogue tends to consist of explaining, giving reasons, and making inferences. When someone told us that we couldn't have ice cream before lunch or that we had to go to sleep after our snack or asked us why we thought the flower was "sad," we fell naturally into giving reasons, explaining, and making inferences. We've been doing it ever since. That is, dialogue pops us right into the kind of conceptual and reason-giving uses of language we need for writing essays. (Of course, it doesn't organize that conceptual language and thinking into an essaylike form, but we can do that later.)

There are other powerful advantages to dialogue. A dialogue injects unusually strong energy into language and thinking. A dialogue makes you speak and think from your own point of view and yet forces you to imagine another point of view at the same time. (See the dialogues embedded in collages on pages 89, 91–92 in the "Readings" for this workshop to get a sense of how this works in practice.) A dialogue leads you to the very stuff of essays: assertions, summings-up, reasons, arguments, examples, counterexamples—and probably all in down-to-earth, clear language.

Thus one of the most powerful ways to do exploratory writing for essays is simply to write a dialogue. Probably the easiest way to do this is to find a friend or classmate and write collaborative dialogue between yourselves. But it works fine to write a dialogue with someone all by yourself. In writing this dialogue yourself, you must first choose someone to have your dialogue with. Choose someone who seems important to the topic you want to explore. The person can be real or fictitious, living or dead, someone you know well or someone you've never met. And, as we mentioned earlier, you can have a productive dialogue with entities other than persons.

Exploring the Writing Process

What you finally read in the published text is what's been collaged and montaged (can one use these words like this?) from all my various improvisations. In other words, writing for me is also a way of splicing stuff together. That's real writing for me, and not that initial spontaneous flow of words. That's in the final text too, but buried inside the other levels of improvisation. It's in the various *re*-workings and *re*-writing sessions that the real elements of improvisation (and not inspiration) come, because improvisation is always something that builds on something else.

Raymond Federman

Variations on Audience, Writer, and Time

It is classic advice to write to someone who doesn't understand your topic, even if you are really writing something for experts. Writers have traditionally benefited from writing their technical material as though to children: Dr. Samuel Johnson, one of the most prolific and popular writers of the 18th century, used to read his writing to his unschooled servant and not stop revising till it was clear to her. It's not simply that this process forces you to be clear. The most important effect is that you *see* your topic differently when you direct your thinking to a different audience—and this process gives you new perspectives and new ideas. So, for this topic choose one or two people you would enjoy sharing thoughts with.

You can achieve comparable benefits by varying the *time.* Try writing about speaking and writing as though you were living in the future or during some period in the past. You will notice many things about the topic that you wouldn't otherwise notice.

Varying the *writer*—that is your own identity—will change your perspective even more directly and give you new insights. You might pretend that you've never learned to write, or that you could only write and not speak, or that you are a professional writer. You could imagine you were a court stenographer or a caption writer for TV and spent your work day doing nothing but turning speech into writing.

If you want to end up with something fair and judiciously detached, spend some time writing from the point of view of someone who is extremely biased and involved in the subject. Then write as someone with the opposite bias. Obviously this category can merge into a dialogue.

This mode is good for experimenting: Start out writing to various audiences and at various times and as various people. Find out which are most fruitful to continue with.

Lies, Errors, Sayings

These are just sentences or phrases, not extended pieces of writing. Therefore, lies, errors, and sayings have a kind of coiled cognitive power and energy. After you write them, you can explore the implications of your lies, errors, and sayings. You'll find much more meaning than you expected.

With *lies* it's fine just to write single sentences, but now and then let yourself spin one out a bit more if it intrigues you. Be bold in your lies: "You can trust speech more than writing."

By *errors* we mean ideas that are almost right—assertions that are wrong but tempting. Write down things that many people believe, things you're not sure of, or things you wish were true but might not be: "Speech is more informal than writing," "Writing is more precise than speaking," or "I can always get my thoughts out better in speaking than in writing."

Sayings tend to carry "folk wisdom"; they are worth exploring and questioning. They teach you to squeeze a lot of meaning into a pithy and memorable chunk of language. You can use sayings that already exist: "The pen is mightier than the sword" or "Those are words writ in water." But you get to make up your own sayings and phrases: "Speaking is forever but writing disappears before you know it." You don't always have to know exactly what you mean by sayings you make up. Playing with "proverb syntax" will lead you to formulations that are interesting to explore: "Speak softly but carry a big pen."

If it sounds merely foolish or game playing to write lies, errors, and sayings, try pondering their implications in conjunction with each other. Ask yourself questions like these:

- In what respect is this lie true?
- Why do some people think this idea is true?
- Are there times when this is true and times when it's not?
- What would follow if this were true?
- What is it that makes this untrue?

Discussing lies, errors, and sayings with your partner or group is particularly fruitful. You can also make up good ones collaboratively with them.

Main Assignment: *Using Loop Writing to Create a Collage or Essay*

Our suggestion for this workshop is to produce a collaborative collage. But it's easier for us to describe how to use loop writing if we start with directions for a solo collage (and we also want to emphasize how these techniques are not only for use in collaborative writing).

Read through all the pieces you've written. As you read, decide which passages are the most interesting and successful. Which ones throw the most light on the topic? These passages might be anywhere from a few sentences

Exploring the Writing Process

About our collaborating [with Andrea]. Lots of talk. LOTS of talk. Out loud brainstorming, a woman's conversation, many wandering diversions to create the wide beautiful track, lots of explaining our ideas and that touching off new ideas and coming around in a circle and laughing about not knowing what we were getting to or exactly where we had been. A long time—the clock surprised us by saying it had been over three hours! The logical part of my brain saying at the end of that session: But have we gotten any farther than agreeing mostly on the ideas I came to her with three hours ago? Yes, we had, I believe: We had begun some new entity called Our Project. We had sparked ideas and validated thoughts and begun to shape something—even though it still looked shapeless. Couldn't quantify it, but it was a learning *process* even if it didn't result in a paper right then to judge, or even a definite direction . . . During the second meeting, in the middle of us blabbing on about the paper, I heard myself stop and say, "Do you feel comfortable enough to tell me if you don't like an idea I come up with?" Andrea said yes, which I figured she would say, and I felt that way too. So then we plunged right in again to full speed brainstorming and thinking and discussing.

Jana Zviebelman

THE LOOP WRITING PROCESS

as interpreted by Karen Kurt

THE VOYAGE OUT

This first island stop will help you get your raw thinking out into the open—write all of these down quickly:

FIRST THOUGHTS,
PREJUDICES,
PRECONCEPTIONS.

I hate this, I love that

Of course, we're smarter than they were in the old days.

First I thought this, Then I thought that...

NARRATIVE THINKING
How did you get this idea? Tell it back to yourself.

INSTANT VERSION.

Wow.

Pretend you have got all your data and write a quickie essay.

MOMENTS.
Quickly list memorable scenes connected with your subject.

STORIES.
Record 5-8 stories that somehow relate to your topic.

Just listen to this one

MY TEACHER

PORTRAITS.
Write portrait-sketches of people who remind you of your topic. Was your third grade teacher like a medieval tyrant?

DIALOGUE.

Write a dialogue between the major players in your essay.

I am the Sun King!

LOUIS XVI

Horse feathers.

VOLTAIRE

Reflect on your subject from a different period in time.

VARY THE TIME.

Humans... they'll never last.

VARY THE AUDIENCE.
Say, explain the French Revolution to your boxing coach.

I gotten minutes, kid. Give it to me straight!

VARY THE WRITER.
Pretend YOU are someone different, for example—the person you are writing about.

Now when I wrote the Gettysburg Address I was trying to...

LIES.

All teachers are dumb.

Recording lies about your subject can clear fog and give you new ideas.

ERRORS.

The teacher must know more about it than I do...

Write down dangerous ways of thinking you want to avoid.

SAYINGS.
Playing around with old sayings can give you new insights.

A little danger is a learning thing!

THE VOYAGE HOME

Return, then, to full consciousness of what your goal is.

Figure 1 The Loop Writing Process

to a couple of pages. Keep the good ones and arrange them in whatever order seems most interesting and effective. (If you remembered to write on only one side, you can simply cut out the good ones with scissors, spread them on the floor, and play with various arrangements.)

You can work for three outcomes: an open collage, a focused collage, or an essay. If you want to produce an *open collage,* you can move at this point toward a final version. Just edit your pieces by making minor revisions: cuts, tightenings, changes. Arrange them in the best order—the order that feels most interesting or enlightening or dramatic—not necessarily in the most logical order. Then proofread. Your collage will be a lively piece of writing which will throw good light on the topic. That is, an open collage doesn't have to be completely unified with a clear conclusion. It doesn't have to state explicitly what it is "saying." It can plant seeds in the reader's mind. When such seeds bear fruit, the effect on readers is usually more powerful than if you had told them exactly what you want them to think.

You can produce a *focused collage* by working more with your material. A focused collage is also made up of interesting and diverse short pieces, but it is more clearly unified and has a conclusion: It *says* what it is saying. For this you need to carry your thinking further and force yourself to figure out what all these pieces of loop writing mean. Thus you would have to write one or more additional passages that tell what all the others add up to. These pieces would answer the question "So what?" and would probably come near the beginning or the end. A focused collage is more carefully framed than the open collage: it doesn't leave so much up to the reader.

Either way, however, a successful collage gives its pieces to the reader in intuitive order and lets the reader enter into a kind of interaction or collaboration with the pieces to make sense of them. That is one of the advantages and pleasures of the collage for readers: It's a more participatory form. (Actually, of course, all language has gaps and ambiguity and requires the participation of the reader. The collage highlights this quality of all language.) There are collages in the "Readings" for Workshop 1 and a collaborative collage in the "Readings" for this workshop.

You can also use loop writing to produce an *essay.* Indeed, one of the best ways to understand the nature of the essay as a form is to explore how it differs from a collage. The essay asks for two things that are not necessary in a collage: full explicit unity and full coherence.

- *Unity:* A collage invites you to explore a general territory, and it can be successful if it is "sort of unified"—that is, if all the parts are related, yet don't all connect perfectly to a precise center. But an essay insists that you work out what the center is and keep everything related to it.
- *Coherence:* A collage invites you to jump from point to point with no connective passages, and sometimes to jump quite a distance. But an essay insists that you work out your train of thought so that each part follows smoothly, logically, and with connective tissue.

To produce an essay, then, you have to push your thinking harder: Work out exactly what you want to say and make sure all the parts really fit it; work out your train of thought and make sure all the parts follow. The crucial process will probably be to look back over all the pieces of loop writing you did and figure out more clearly in your mind what each of them is telling you. This is more work, of course, but the benefit is that your thinking is more developed and careful. In other words, the collage is best for *throwing light on an issue* and making people think; the essay is best for *working out your thinking* and reaching a conclusion with as much validity as you can get.

Suggestions for Collaboration

Using Loop Writing for Collaborative Writing

It will probably be obvious by now how to make a collaborative collage from your loop writing, and why a collage is such a helpful way to get used to collaborative writing. First, get together and listen to each other's loop writing or share it on paper. Then decide together which pieces seem most interesting and successful, and which ones you want to choose for your collaborative collage. The pieces don't need to agree with each other or fit in voice or tone. In a collage, contrasts are a benefit: a source of energy that stimulates thinking in readers. In effect, you are putting together a collection of pieces, each written from an "I" point of view, for the sake of a "we" enterprise: a gathering of individuals toward a collaborative purpose. Whether or not you actually use the first person singular in these pieces doesn't matter. If you make it clear to readers on the title page that this work was written by multiple authors and that it is a collage consisting of individual and distinct passages separated by asterisks rather than smoothly connected, readers will get the picture. They will understand what's going on when different "I's" say conflicting things or tell conflicting stories in different voices.

If you want an open collage, you can now move to completion: Agree on an order for your pieces; work collaboratively to edit, tighten, and proofread. If you want a focused collage, you'll have to collaborate a bit further in your thinking. That is, after listening to everyone's loop writing, you need to decide more explicitly on your topic or focus, and decide more clearly how your pieces hang together or relate to each other. You don't have to agree with each other on a single point of view or conclusion; it's fine to disagree completely. But you do need to agree on your disagreement; that is, you'll have to agree on how to describe the *relationship* between your conflicting opinions, and on that basis write a few collaborative passages that represent your larger collaborative or joint view of your disagreements. These collaborative passages would probably occur near the opening and/or the closing. In effect, the focused collage might be a collection of "I" pieces, but they would be framed by some crucial "we" pieces that express joint or collaborative thinking to better focus the whole thing.

If you want to increase the degree of collaboration, you can write a *collaborative essay.* It would consist not of separate blips in separate voices, but an extended piece of writing that readers would feel as more or less connected and single. That is, it needs to consist mostly of "we" thinking and writing, not "I" thinking and writing. Thus when you are writing a collaborative essay, you have to keep discussing your individual loop writing and what it all points to until you can pretty much come to some agreement.

But even in this connected essay, you can use quite a few of the "I" passages from your loop writing, transforming them into examples or "points" for your essay. That is, you might frame some of these passages with wording like this: "One of us had the following experience that illustrates what we are saying here: . . ." Or "One of the authors, however, points out a difficulty with the idea we have just explained: . . ." In short, it would be an essay from the "we" point of view that represents corporate agreement, yet it would have some genuine diversity of thinking and perhaps even plurality of voice. You could even have an essay that clearly explains and explores a *disagreement:* It would be a case of agreement about the terms of disagreement.

Harness the Power of Disagreement for Collaborative Writing—and Also for Solo Writing

Notice how we are introducing you to collaboration by suggesting a progression from less agreement to more. The dialogue and the open collage provide good starting places because, on the one hand, they require *some* agreement—agreement on which pieces to choose and how to arrange and edit them. On the other hand, the dialogue and open collage spare you the two hardest forms of collaboration: reaching full agreement in your thinking and finding a common voice. The focused collage pushes you a bit further into collaboration by asking you to agree in your thinking and find a common voice, but only for a few short passages. Finally comes the essay which asks for *full* agreement.

Or does it? Even for the essay, don't struggle for more agreement than you really need. What we consider the most important point in this workshop lies here. When you are trying to write a single and coherent essay—a "seamless" piece—you don't have to make it too seamless. You can keep some of those conflicting ideas and voices. It's fine in an essay to "break out" at various points with passages that might start like this: "But wait a minute. Let's look at this issue from a contrasting point of view." Or, "Notice what follows, however, when we consider what an opposing voice might say." Or, "There are some serious objections, however, to what we have just been saying." In each case, you can go on for a paragraph or even a long section stating this contrasting idea or arguing this conflicting point of view. And the conflicting point of view can even be in a contrasting voice—with or without quotation marks. Many readers would consider these breaks or this internally "dialogic" quality a strength rather than a weakness in an essay.

Thus we are not introducing these easy forms of collaboration (the dialogue and the collage) simply because they are easy, though that's a big benefit too. These easy forms bring into your writing and thinking a dimension that is often missing in much collaborative writing. A good deal of collaborative writing is weak in its thinking because the writers settle for the few things they could agree on. And much collaborative writing has a weak or fake voice because the writers hid their individual voices. The collage may be easy, but it shows you a way to bring to essay writing what is rare and precious and often lacking: some internal *drama of thinking and voice.*

Indeed, the collage will have the same benefit on your solo writing if you let it because much solo writing—especially by inexperienced writers—suffers in the same way we just described. The thinking is dull and obvious because the writer latched too soon onto one idea or "thesis" and timidly backed away whenever he felt perplexed or came across a conflicting view; he nervously swept the complication under the rug and hoped no one would notice. And the writer tried to use a "proper" or "impressive" voice and came out with something completely fake and stilted. Most *good* solo writing represents a single writer having some internal dialogue with himself—having more than one point of view and using more than one voice. Critics often praise a "dialogic" quality in good writing.

So, if you need to turn your collage into a single and coherent piece of writing, don't make things too "single" or one-dimensional. Look for ways to save as much of the dialogical drama of thinking as you can—even the drama of voices—while still getting it all to hang together. Try for rich thinking and complex voices harnessed to a single and coherent task. Any good passage from your loop writing that fits your topic probably belongs in your essay. It might have to be moved, reshaped, or reframed, but good thinking and lively voices are what most people are looking for in essays.

Some colleagues tell us that this is dangerous advice, so perhaps you should take it with a grain of salt. They would argue that one of the main problems with inexperienced writers is their tendency to save too much—to be too scared to throw things away. But we'd reply that the other main problem with inexperienced writers is their tendency to throw away the lively, perky stuff in their rough writing and replace it with "proper writing"—smooth writing from which all the mistakes have been removed, but writing that is so dull and timid that no one would ever read it by choice.

Down-to-Earth Suggestions for Working with Others

Students have sometimes reacted to what we are saying with frustration: *"But damn it! You two keep putting off the question of how to actually reach agreement and find a common voice. You keep giving us ways to avoid it and telling us it's no problem. But we've suffered in collaborative groups that break down because people couldn't agree. We've been forced to work with people we don't want to work with. We've been taken advantage of by loafers. We've had our time wasted when we could have done a better job alone—and quicker too."*

This is a valid objection. There's no getting away from the real difficulties of working together, whether or not people need to agree. And sometimes you actually need to agree and to find a common voice. For the nitty-gritty difficulty, we offer some nitty-gritty rules of thumb.

- Never try to generate actual prose together. It will drive you crazy. One person suggests a sentence; the person with the pencil writes it down;

someone else objects; the writer erases and writes something different; someone else tries. And so on until everyone is crabby. Don't argue about or even discuss actual wording until you have some rough drafts to work from. Here are some different methods of avoiding this killing situation:

- Use something like the loop process so that everyone produces prose (everyone takes the risk). Then people can proceed positively rather than negatively: Choose the bits they mostly like rather than criticize what doesn't work.
- Brainstorm. Encourage and accept all ideas and have someone take them down. No criticism. Then hear them and discuss and pick the ones that appeal. Have one person take notes on the agreements and then write up a very rough draft. Share it; hear some general kibitzing as to strengths and weaknesses of this general approach. No arguments about wording yet! Have another person take notes on that discussion and write up a slightly better draft. Now that you have this draft, you can start to discuss wording. And so on.
- Meet and discuss the topic and reach general agreement on certain points. But then each person writes up one *section.* Come together to hear the sections; discuss the strengths and weaknesses of the thinking and voice. Then one person does a quick rewrite of the whole thing. Hear it and get feedback. Someone else does the final write-up.
- Here's a risky, difficult method, but it can work well if you have the right mix of people. After only a bit of discussion, one person writes a very rough *discussion draft.* This must be a brave and nondefensive person who can write quickly with very little effort, for much of what she writes will be rejected and virtually all of it changed.

- When hard choices have to be made, of course you will sometimes have to argue against each other's thinking. What helps most is a spirit of supportive cooperation. And one concrete technique is helpful: avoid "God statements" and stress "I statements"; that is, avoid saying, "This is wrong for the following reasons," and instead say, "This doesn't seem right to me because I had the following reactions." In short, remember that you are seeing things from only one point of view and you may be wrong. Be prepared to change your mind. Someone has to change his or her mind or you won't get the job done. But if you are supportive of each other and creative, it won't be fighting where one person "wins" and the other "loses." It will be a process of collaboratively figuring out *new ideas* that are better than those held by any of you individually.
- When you get close to a final draft and are trying to think about a voice, make sure to read things out loud. Get different members to read. Try to hear the different voices in the pieced-together writing. Try reading with exaggeration to bring out different possibilities of voice. Then you can decide which voice (more or less) is the one you want to try for. The person who can "do" that voice is probably the one who should do the final polished version.

- Be concrete and assertive about spelling out everyone's task. Write it down. Collaboration almost never works without an explicit *schedule*. Be tough-minded about insisting that people fulfill their responsibilities, and on schedule. If you are doing more than your fair share, maybe it's because you haven't insisted that others do *their* fair share. Be tough and expect others to be tough about this.

But take hope. Despite the real difficulties, we still think you will do best if you realize that collaboration is not really so hard. It's all a question of getting the right attitude, or spirit, or feeling among you. That's exactly what our introductory dialogue and collage activity—the "easy collaboration"—will do for you: give you practice and experience working together and reaching agreements.

Attitudes or feelings make the biggest difference. If collaborative writing feels weird, stop a moment and reflect on the fact that it is the most common kind of writing in the world. In business, industry, and government, most writing is collaborative. Most research in the hard sciences and social sciences is written collaboratively. And it helps to notice the collaborative dimension even in most "regular" solo writing. Whenever you write something yourself, you tend to use the ideas and voices that you have absorbed from those around you. Collaboration is the natural thing that humans do. It's only in school that people tend to say, "Make sure you don't get any help from others."

It's helpful to realize, by the way, that we all learned collaboration before we learned to do things by ourselves. The collaborative use of language precedes the solo use of language. Babies learn to speak by first having dialogues with parents. Only by means of the language learning they get through these dialogues do they gradually learn to "internalize" language enough to speak or think extended strings of language on their own.

Realize too that moving from difference to agreement is not just a difficulty, it is also an opportunity. If you have to struggle to work out some agreements, that very process will carry your thinking and analysis further. It will help you find weaknesses in your present views and lead you to new ideas that none of you could find alone. Collaboration is the most powerful way to expand your thinking about something because it brings multiple minds to bear on it.

Sharing and Responding

If you are writing collaboratively, you will probably do most of your sharing among yourselves in the process. In particular, as you read over your dialogue in order to edit it and as you share your loop pieces in the first steps toward the collage, remember this: Mostly listen—listen for what is good. Put your effort into picking out the good bits and see if that process will show you what to use so you don't have to spend much time criticizing the ones you don't like. The *spirit* of collaboration is best served if you can make your choices by means of positive enthusiasm rather than by means of negative criticism.

If you want to get responses from others on your dialogue or collage, some of the main questions would be these:

- "Which words or sections or pieces are strongest?"
- "What do you hear the main sections saying?"
- "What do you hear the whole piece saying?"
- "What happens as you listen? What are the steps or stages in your response? That is, tell us how the sequencing of pieces in our collage works for you."

Process Journal

You are trying more processes here than in most workshops—and some of the most unusual and perhaps difficult processes too: dialogue, loop writing, collage, collaboration. You will have your hands full simply talking about the ones that were most important to you: What was helpful and not helpful, difficult and easy, surprising or interesting.

But for future writing decisions it will be helpful to answer these questions:

- Which loop processes did you find the most helpful for getting involved in the topic and expanding your thinking? Are there other loop processes that you sense will be helpful for you if you get more familiar with them?
- Describe the collaboration you engaged in. What were the sticky points, and how could you deal with them better next time?
- How can you get more of the drama of contrasting thoughts and voices into your future solo writing?

Exploring Theory: *Loop Writing versus the "Dangerous Method"*

The Dangerous Method

Many teachers and textbooks say that to produce a "good" piece of writing, you must figure out what you want to say *before you start writing:* "Think before you write," they say. Once you've done that, they suggest that you make an outline of your whole paper. Only then are you to start actually writing.

This advice sounds sensible. But this process of trying to begin by getting your meaning clear in your mind—so that you can write something right the first time—is what we call "the dangerous method." It's dangerous because it leads to various writing difficulties that most of us are familiar with.

- You find yourself procrastinating: "I can't start writing yet. I haven't thought this through well enough. My outline isn't right. I've got to do more reading and studying and thinking."

- You spend hours trying to figure out what you want to say—perhaps even making a very careful outline—but you don't really come up with much that's interesting.
- Even when you *do* figure out much to say beforehand and get it neatly outlined, as you try to write from your outline, you feel constrained. You start to wander away from the outline, which makes you feel guilty. You think of a new idea you love, but it doesn't fit. Or worse yet, your outline starts to unravel as you write: You think of new problems or objections to something in your outline, or you can't quite explain the idea or the transition that seemed so right when it was in outline form.
- You agonize over every sentence in an effort to get it right. You constantly cross out, change, revise, start over.
- *Finally,* when you get a draft written, you can't bring yourself to make major revisions—or throw even a sentence away—because you've poured so much sweat and blood into writing it.

Perhaps you are not troubled by these difficulties. Perhaps you are actually good at the dangerous method of getting everything clear before you start writing. If so, by all means write that way. And of course there are a few writing tasks where you must get your meaning clear before writing, such as for exams that allow no revising time.

But usually when we write, we need to do more thinking about our topic. Even if we believe we understand quite well what we want to say, our thinking can benefit from exploratory writing in order to find new thoughts and new ways of talking about our old thoughts. We seldom see the full implications of our thoughts until we see them concretized in writing.

Of course writing *does* require getting your meaning clear in your mind, often even making an outline. And writing certainly means communicating to others what you've *already* figured out. But these processes usually work best

Exploring the Writing Process

I enjoyed the loop writing. When I first saw the assignment, I thought it would be easy to complete because I had been thinking about how and why I learned to write on and off since this summer. I'd had to write a paper about it last year. I figured I'd be able to use whole chunks of it for this assignment. Once you explained how you wanted us to approach it, though, and after I read the description of it, I decided not to even look at the other paper. The process sounded like fun; I just dove right in.

For the most part it *was* fun. Being compulsive in my fear that I'd forget something important, I began with the instant first draft to get all the "important" details down. Then I felt relaxed enough to do some of the more creative loops and dives. I particularly liked speaking in other voices to myself. I do a lot of talking to myself anyway and this seemed to legitimize the process.

After I finished looping, I went back using the cut-and-rearrange function on the computer and put everything in chronological order. Another compulsion: Somehow things don't seem right to me unless they're in time sequence. And it seemed to work here.

Kathy Reckendorf

after you've already done enough exploratory writing to produce good raw material—and if possible after you've felt the mental click that tells you, "Ah! That's it! *Now* I see exactly what I want to say." This insight is often accompanied by some clues about organization.

"It's Impossible Not to Think of Something"

So wrote the poet William Stafford. Whenever we pay attention to our mind, we find words there; we may not always be satisfied with those words, but they're there nevertheless. If we put these words on paper, other words take their place inside our heads. This process is infinite. But we're quite likely not to believe in it until it is proved to us; we need to record the words we find in our head and realize for ourselves that others take their place. This new set of words may or may not have an obvious connection to the old set of words. And the same may be said for each succeeding set of words. Consequently, the only limit to what we can write comes from our muscles: how long we can sit up, hold a pen, type.

When we write something down and don't stop to look back inside our heads, more words come anyway, and these words begin to appear on the page. If we continue to write, we become conscious of new sets of words only as they appear on paper. This gives us the sense that the words are writing themselves. In truth, almost all writing happens this way, whether it's exploratory or not. We rarely plan any written sentence out entirely in our heads. We start off a sentence with an intention to go somewhere with it and with the faith that we can do that. And we continue the same way when we've finished that sentence.

This is not to say that we don't get stuck. We do. Think of yourself as being in a maze. You come to a junction and are baffled. You could just sit and try to reason through the alternatives, but if you've never been in this maze before, that's hopeless. Your best chance of getting to the end is to try possibilities. Since every piece of writing is unique, you can think of each one as a maze you've never been in—even though you may know something about mazes in general. When you're stuck, it isn't because you don't have words; it's because you're trying to figure out *in advance* whether they're the right words. But the only way to know that is to write them out.

At first they may seem as though they're "wrong" words, but if you keep writing, you may arrive at some good ideas that you would never have gotten to otherwise. Even if you come to a dead end or become irreversibly discouraged, you can always return to the point in the maze where you were stuck in the first place and take a different path. And remember: if your aim is to learn more about mazes themselves, you would deliberately take as many routes as possible.

This, of course, is analogous to loop writing. You start off a certain way that seems to be heading where you want to go, and travel wherever that takes you. If you are blocked in some way or don't like what you're doing, you can return to your original subject and start off from it again in another way. You may well discover that there are quite a few effective approaches to your topic. Once you know that, you have choices. And if your aim is also to learn more about writing, it pays to explore as many paths as possible.

Robert Bingham (1925–1982)

Published in *The New Yorker*

He was a tall man of swift humor whose generally instant responses reached far into memory and wide for analogy. Not much missed the attention of his remarkably luminous and steady eyes. He carried with him an education from the Boston Latin School, Phillips Exeter Academy, Harvard College—and a full year under the sky with no shelter as an infantryman in France in the Second World War. Arriving there, he left his rifle on the boat.

One of his lifelong friends, a popular novelist, once asked him why he had given up work as a reporter in order to become an editor.

"I decided that I would rather be a first-rate editor than a second-rate writer," he answered.

The novelist, drawing himself up indignantly, said, "And what is the matter with being a second-rate writer?"

Nothing, of course. But it is given to few people to be a Robert Bingham.

To our considerable good fortune, for nearly twenty years he was a part of *The New Yorker,* primarily as an editor of factual writing. In that time, he addressed millions of words with individual attention, giving each a whisk on the shoulders before sending it into print. He worked closely with many writers and, by their testimony, he may have been the most resonant sounding board any sounder ever had. Adroit as he was in reacting to sentences before him, most of his practice was a subtle form of catalysis done before he saw a manuscript.

Talking on the telephone with a writer in the slough of despond, he would say, "Come, now, it can't be that bad. Nothing could be that bad. Why don't you try it on me?"

"But you don't have time to listen to it."

"We'll make time. I'll call you back after I finish this proof."

"Will you?"

"Certainly."

• • •

"In the winter and spring of 1970, I read sixty thousand words to him over the telephone."

• • •

"If you were in his presence, he could edit with the corners of his mouth. Just by angling them down a bit, he could erase something upon which you might otherwise try to insist. If you saw that look, you would be in a hurry to delete the cause of his disdain. In some years, he had a mustache. When he had a mustache, he was a little less effective with that method of editing, but effective nonetheless."

• • •

"I turned in a story that contained a fetid pun. He said we should take that out. He said it was a terrible line. I said, 'A person has a right to make a pun once in a while, and even to be a little coarse.' He said, 'The line is not on the level of the rest of the piece and therefore seems out of place.' I said, 'That may be, but I want it in there.' He said, 'Very well. It's your piece.' Next day, he said, 'I think I ought to tell you I haven't changed my mind about that. It's an unfortunate line.' I said, 'Listen, Bobby. We discussed that. It's funny. I want to use it. If I'm embarrassing anybody, I'm embarrassing myself.' He said, 'O.K. I just work here.' The day after that, I came in and said to him, 'That joke. Let's take that out. I think that ought to come out.' 'Very well,' he said, with no hint of triumph in his eye."

• • •

"As an editor, he wanted to keep his tabula rasa. He was mindful of his presence between writer and reader, and he wished to remain invisible while representing each. He deliberately made no move to join the journeys of research. His writers travelled to interesting places. He might have gone, too. But he never did, because he would not have been able to see the written story from a reader's point of view."

• • •

"Frequently, he wrote me the same note. The note said, 'Mr.________, my patience is not inexhaustible.' But his patience *was* inexhaustible. When a piece was going to press, he stayed long into the evening while I fumbled with prose under correction. He had pointed out some unarguable flaw. The fabric of the writing needed invisible mending, and I was trying to do it with him in a way satisfactory to him and to the over-all story. He waited because he respected the fact that the writing had taken as much as five months, or even five years, and now he was giving this or that part of it just another five minutes."

• • •

"Edmund Wilson once said that a writer can sometimes be made effective 'only by the intervention of one who is guileless enough and human enough to treat him, not as a monster, nor yet as a mere magical property which is wanted for accomplishing some end, but simply as another man, whose sufferings elicit his sympathy and whose courage and pride he admires.' When writers are said to be gifted, possibly such intervention has been the foremost of the gifts."

Loop Writing Collage

Darci Jungwirth

Sara was afraid to come home at night. When she got there she would always find the same thing: her father with a beer in his hand and his breath smelling of alcohol. His hair was all messed up and he was sitting in the brown recliner with the ripped seat that he never bothered to get patched after an incident with a cigarette left burning. He always greeted her the same way. "Hi, darling, how was your day?" He would try to be nice first but always ended up getting out of control or going off the handle over nothing. She would end up huddled on her bed, both her body and soul wincing in pain from this man, her father. She lay on her soft old bed with the dusty pink comforter for hours. When she could finally get her strength up she did her homework that had to be completed adequately to avoid another beating.

• • •

Child: Dad, why do you hit me?

Dad: Son, I don't know why. I had a bad day at work and bills are due tomorrow. I had so much tension and anger built up inside me that I was just mad at the world and you happened to be there.

Child: But Dad, you do it all the time; don't you realize that you make me scared to be around you at all. I'm always worried that you are going to haul off and hit me at any moment. You say things that make me feel bad too. I don't think that you love me. I feel like everything that goes wrong in your life is my fault and that I am worth nothing.

Dad: I don't mean to be mad at you son; it is just that I feel so bad myself and then I see you and it makes me feel even worse that you are not happy either. I don't want the responsibility to feed you all the time and to keep you entertained—it all adds pressure to the stress I have already.

Child: What would you do if you didn't have me, Dad? Who would you take your anger out on then? You already went through Mom; that was why she left. You make me feel like the lowest piece of garbage on the whole earth and you made her feel that way too. You need to realize that it is you who needs to deal with your problem first. I am only a child and I should not have to deal with your frustration—it is not my fault. The bruises I get from your beatings will go away on the outside but inside they just keep getting bigger and bigger. They will never heal. The panic and fear I feel when you go off on me cannot be erased from my memory—how can you forget that kind of terror? It is like watching a horror movie. I am watching but there is nothing I can do to help.

• • •

The abuser who comes to mind is about 35 to 40 years of age; he has painful eyes and dark hair. He stands nearly six feet tall, average build. He is your average guy; he does not look like he could ever hurt anyone but after you've seen his anger you can. He is not really a bad person but he has had a hard life. When he was a child the same kind of father did the same kinds of things to him. He always vowed never to turn out like him but for some ironic reason he is the mirror image of that man he hated, the same looks, the same eyes.

He walks a tad bowlegged and seems to have self-confidence. He wears nice business clothes to work and casual clothes at home. On the weekends he takes care of the house and mows the yard. He lives alone with his daughter now. She does all the household chores while he does all the "men's work." He does not lay a hand on the dishes or a pan.

• • •

Your Daddy does not hurt you because he hates you. He loves you very much. He does not want to hit you and say mean things but he is very sad. Since your Mommy left he has been very unhappy and he wishes she would come back. Do you know how you feel when you go to school and the teacher tells you that you have to come inside because recess is over; sometimes you get mad at her because you are having such a good time playing on the playground. You get mad at your teacher but it is not her fault that recess is over. You are not really mad at the teacher but you act like you are mad at her. Well, when your Daddy hurts you, it is the same thing. Your Daddy is not really mad at you; he is just angry about other things that are happening in his life.

You are not being a bad girl or doing anything wrong when your Daddy hits you. When your Daddy does this to you, you need to go tell someone so that your Daddy can get help from the doctor. The doctor will help your Daddy get all better and then he will not hit you anymore. He will be the Daddy you remember who used to take you to the playground and play catch with you in the front yard. You are a very good girl and I am very proud of you.

• • •

The children are victims; they are the ones who have to live with the torture for the rest of their lives and try to deal with an abusive parent along with all the other growing up they are doing that is tough enough already.

The line between spankings as punishment and when they turn into beatings is a very fine line that is difficult to draw. Many people receive spankings in childhood for getting out of line or doing something that is not acceptable to their parents.

• • •

LIES—OPPOSITE VIEWPOINT: The parents are right; there is no such thing as child abuse. It is all a misconception and the people who try so hard to put child abusers behind bars are all people who should mind their own business. They should worry about their own families. The kids were being brats so they deserved to get a good whipping. They are at fault and they can be blamed for everything. Kids are worth nothing and they should be treated like they are nothing. Parents are always right and never do anything wrong. The parents who abuse their children should not be punished; they should be rewarded for doing justice to the whole society. It was the kids' fault that the dog came and wet on the rug and that they did not get A's in every subject at school. It was the kids' fault that their mother ran out and is never coming back; they made her cry and leave. I never hurt her; it was just the damn kids, always screaming and yelling. I was right to hit them. Parents are too lenient on their kids these days. There is nothing like a good whipping to leave purple marks all over their puny little bodies to teach them a good lesson. They will thank me for it when they are older. I hope that they can beat their kids too, or else they will never learn discipline. All the anger I feel right now is because of them. If I did not have the kids in my life everything would be perfect. Kids cause all the problems. Nothing is my fault; it is all theirs. I know I am right.

• • •

They are not just beating their children for the fun of it. The children are scapegoats for their parents' frustration. They need to get help for the sources of the anger that cause abuse in the first place.

• • •

They are still to be held responsible for their acts and it is never acceptable to beat a child.

• • •

Almost more important than counseling for the parents is counseling for the children who actually have to go through this hell. They feel trapped, unable to get out, and helpless. They need a hand to grasp, a person to talk to.

Collage about Human Differences

Amy Vignali

I grew up in a fairly small town in southeastern Massachusetts; middle class is definitely a word you could use to describe it. Most of the kids I went to school with had the same basic middle-class background. But working in a jewelry factory in East Providence this past summer gave me a chance to be exposed to people very different from me in many ways such as education, home life, morals, etc.

At first, I was stared at constantly as every newcomer is, and I'm sure I was viewed as a college snob by many. But as they got to know me, I was accepted by the people I worked closely with. I was known as the little freckle-faced white girl. I didn't mind the name because I knew they didn't mean any harm by it. I became particularly friendly with a black guy named Paul. By talking to him I really began to realize a lot of misconceptions people had about me. He truly believed that my parents gave me money whenever I wanted and that all white people did this. I almost laughed in his face because this is something my parents would never do. My mother once told me she'd choke on the words if she told me not to get a job. Since leaving that job, although we still keep in touch, I haven't had a chance to see Paul again. He believes that this is because he's black and I think that makes him only good enough to talk to at work. He'll never know how mad that makes me when he says that.

• • •

Because I've grown up in the middle class I've always believed in the American dream. I believed that everyone had the chance to be successful and there was a solution to every problem. I remember reading *Native Son* last year and not being able to believe that Bigger could not have straightened himself out. He was given a chance and he blew it, and he would blow every chance he ever had because of the circumstances of his life; he was a born loser.

One day while working at my job in the jewelry factory this summer, I found myself in a conversation with a guy named Bob. I discovered, much to my surprise, that he was well educated and had at one time shared my ambition of law school. But in his last year of school, his father became very ill and Bob was forced to quit school and get a job in order to support his family. I thought it was such a pity that he was wasting his brain doing manual labor. So a few days later I went to Bob to encourage him to finish his education and earn his law degree. But he told me that it was impossible now, he had his own family to support and could never take the time out of work. What a tragedy! Even though Bob wasn't a born loser like Bigger he had also suffered an unfortunate twist of fate and would never be able to realize his dream. I can't imagine what I would do if my life's dreams were dashed apart before my eyes.

• • •

"Hi Bigger!"

"Hi Amy!"

"Bigger, why couldn't you behave when you got that job for the white family?"

"I did behave. It was Mary and Jan who couldn't leave me alone. I just wanted to be left alone."

"Why did you have to go and kill Mary?"

"I didn't want to, I just wanted her to be quiet so her mother wouldn't find me in her room. I did not want to get in no trouble."

"Her mother was a good woman, she would have understood."

"You're stupid if you think that way, especially when it comes to a daughter. I don't trust no white folks."

"I guess I really don't know how you feel. I've always been among mostly whites, and I don't know how it feels to be outnumbered. But I still don't understand."

"There's nothing to understand; that's just the way things are. You can't change them."

• • •

Our similarities as human beings far outweigh our differences.

• • •

Differences. I think they're important. I love to talk to people from different places. I mean, imagine what a boring place the world would be if we all were 5′8″, had blond hair and blue eyes, played racquetball on Tuesdays, ate at 6:00 every night, etc. And if everyone would view these differences as enriching aspects rather than negative ones, I think the world would be a much better place. Furthermore, I feel that everyone has prejudices even if they keep them well hidden. Although I won't deny my own feelings against certain people and things, I must admit that I had never experienced prejudiced feelings toward me until I came to U. Mass. I think it's ironic that a place that's supposed to be teaching open-mindedness is home to some of the worst discrimination.

Process Writing

Peter,
I had a lot of trouble with this assignment at every step. I have no idea what you wanted. Everything I write sounds terrible. I especially had trouble with the dialogue because every time I began a conversation in my head it sounded so predictable. I couldn't think of anyone I could have a conversation with naturally. I revised it as best I could. For some reason I concentrated mostly on the differences between whites and blacks, although I don't consider myself prejudiced.

I really wanted to write the story about Bob no matter what because that really bothered me. I also wanted to include Bigger from *Native Son* because the two circumstances were similar: people being trapped into a pattern they just can't break free from.

I found the stories and prejudices to be easier even though they blended together a lot. I find that I'm even having trouble writing this. I'm putting a lot of time and effort in, but I don't feel that it's showing. I wrote the two articles on the jewelry factory for Tuesday, and although they seemed bad to me, they sounded better when I read them to Karen. I was afraid they would be too boring, but Karen said they really made her think. I guess if I can't make people laugh, I can make them think. I sometimes think of things to write about my boyfriend, but I don't like to mention him too much and have you and the class saying, "Not another Jim story." All my roommate wrote about last semester in her class was her boyfriend, and that's still all she talks about. I'd hate to have my life depending on one thing. Sorry I got off the subject.

I think it sounded better when I read my collage out loud—I guess because I could let my voice help the words. On my second blip I had to explain a lot about what I meant concerning differences. Basically I meant that although I have the chance to go

to college and succeed, not everyone else can, and therefore we are different. There are so many different factors that contribute to it. Also I had a lot of trouble deciding on how to label my town's size. I mean it's small, but not that small. About 12,000 people. It all depends on the size of the town that the person reading it comes from.

Amy Vignali

Who Influences Children More, Their Parents or Their Peers?

Published in *The Guardian*

Bel Mooney and Kitty Dimbleby

Dear Kitty,

Being a parent, as I've often told you, is very difficult, so there has to be something in it for us, apart from love. Why look after you for 18 years, and put your welfare before most other things? Because I made you and I want to go on "making" you. Is it an ego-trip to say my two children are the best things I've ever produced and—yes—I do take some credit (with your Dad) for the kind of people you are.

You can see why it's hard for me to take a new American theory that it isn't us poor old parents, but the peer group which has the most influence on teenagers like you. Judith Rich Harris has just published a book called *The Nurture Assumption,* which says goodbye Freud, goodbye guilt—if your kids turn out bad, you can say it isn't your fault, it's that crowd they hung out with. So we're let off the hook on one level, but does that mean we can shrug off responsibility?

The other side of the coin has to be that if they turn out to be little saints (like you!) we can't take the credit either. What was it all for: that careful parenting, the long talks about life, love and morality? The forgiveness when you behaved so badly (like when you were drunk at 2:30 A.M. and got me out of bed to collect you)? Did I give you all that, so a group of kids can make you in their images? No way.

Love,
Mum

Dear Mum,

Although I understand your views, I feel that you fail to see the importance of friends in a teenager's life. You always tease me about the close relationship I have with my girlfriends, saying it's more like a love affair. Yet we go through everything together—my friends know more about my life than you do and have more influence over me.

They see me outside the home, in nightclubs, in lessons, when drunk . . . I talk to them when I've had a fight with my boyfriend or you. Peer pressure is always seen as a bad thing but this is wrong. When friends criticise or offer advice, it is far easier to listen and take on board than when parents do so.

Many of my friends don't have a stable parental structure and so it's friends they turn to. If I give advice on drugs or sex (areas parents find difficult to face with their own children) my friend will know that what I say is from an equal's view, someone who knows and understands the situation, which a parent can never fully do.

So Mum, although it's you who I call for when I'm ill, my friends are very important to me and have helped shape me into the person I am. I think we both know that you are just the tiniest bit jealous.

Love,
Kitty

Listen Missy,

I admit I am jealous sometimes, because I value our closeness so much. I want you to be *my* friend! I boast that you tell me everything, and then I'm put out when it's proved untrue. Last weekend, Dad and I were walking along Princes Street in Edinburgh and bumped into some girls you were at school with, one of whom had a pierced nose. I said, "Kit would never do that because she knows I hate it." The next night we took your cousins to hear some jazz, and they informed me you'd just had your nose pierced—and were really worried what I would say about it! So, was I wrong about my influence on you? Yes, otherwise you wouldn't have had it done. But you did care what I thought; which is something to celebrate.

The thing is, this nose-piercing (like the panther recently tattooed on your tummy) happened when we were away on holiday and you were with your friends. I'm not saying you bent to peer pressure to decorate your body thus—but sometimes I get fed up with all of you and the "culture" you inhabit. Too much talk about sex and clubbing, too much loafing about watching TV, too little direction, not enough interest in great issues. Sometimes I feel that all of you—lovely, bright girls—drag each other to the lowest common denominator. Or is this unfair?

Love,
Your confused mother

Dear Mum,

That is not only unfair but *wrong*. Far from dragging each other down, we encourage each other. Part of the reason I love and respect my friends is that they are all intelligent, sensitive girls. You say we talk too much about sex. Come on! For the amount of time I spend on the phone I couldn't just be talking about sex—there's not that much to talk about, is there? In fact we discuss everything from the trivial to the bombing in Omagh, when we were all moved to tears. About my tattoo and nose: I am my own person—moulded partly by you but still me, an individual, Kitty. You know I hate it when people think I have only achieved things because of you and Dad—well, I hate it just as much when you attribute what I do to my friends.

I respect you and what you think but I also know (and hope) that you respect and trust me to make wise decisions. You *have* to let me make my own mistakes. I could have been friends with girls who think drugs are cool; instead we all feel they are sad. You've done a good job but I owe the person I am to three "people"; my family, my friends and *me*. There are some parts of my life where you can't be there to guide me, and others where it's only you.

Love as ever,
Kitty

Darling Kit,

So much of what you say is right—and we're both too intelligent not to see there has to be a compromise. Anyway, who always welcomes your lovely friends? But I remember when you were little—bullied at school or miserable because some horrible little cow wouldn't play with you—and I realised there was nothing I could do to protect you from the hurt your peers might do you. Dad and I gave you our genes, and a stable family life, but after that. . .

Yes, you will go on being formed by people you love (both genders), things you experience, books you read, pain you feel. I hope I don't cling to the bright balloon that's tugging in the wind already. But I don't think you should bear children unless you take responsibility and go on mothering forever. Glad I put you first in the past. Is it wrong to feel that in the future, when you've lost contact with friends who are so important now, your old Ma will still be at the centre of your life, and that you will still be influenced by me?

All my love,
Mum

Dear Mum,

Of course it's true and always will be. I hope you'll mother me all your life just as I'll go on loving and respecting you all mine. Yes, I had a hard time when I was younger and just as my grandmother couldn't stop you being called names, you were powerless to help. At my age you realise that far from being the gods of your childhood, parents are flawed. You've made mistakes, and (at times) I've taken care of you. Remember when I forfeited a friend's birthday because you had food poisoning? The mother-daughter role reversed.

You have given me so many of the things I love: literature, theatre, poetry, ideas—sometimes I hear myself speak, and think I am my mother. That doesn't stop me resenting it when you tell me to go and do some work—I'm old enough not to be told. I look up to you so much, and am proud of you as I hope you are of me, not as your child but as another person. Think of me as a jigsaw puzzle—if any part of me were missing (you, Dad, my friends, my boyfriend. . .) I would not be whole.

Your ever loving daughter,
Kitty

Collaborative Collage about Writing a Collage

Laura Corry, Elija Goodwin, Matt Ludvino, Denise Morey, Tassie Walsh

We sat around the table hearing the audible roar of gun blasts and explosions from the video games over at one end of the cafeteria. Several conversations went on at once. We spoke about anything. The work was the last thing on our mind. We were just getting to know each other.

• • •

The first day that we met together as a group alone, I felt kind of awkward. I didn't really know these people. Would I want to spend the semester working with them or would things be strained? I worried that perhaps there might be some kind of "impenetrable barrier" between us. However, as we sat down and began the process of getting to know each other, I began to feel more at ease and comfortable. We talked for quite a while and there was really no awkwardness, no strained moments, no long periods of quiet. As a group we seemed to hit it off. I did not feel shy about saying what I really felt.

• • •

When five people, different in every way, share experiences with each other, there is going to be something there. Different ideas and opinions, mannerisms, and mind-sets, sharing different pieces of themselves with each other. There is something to be learned there. Something intangible will be received whether anyone wants to or not. The ideas were already out there for everyone to see. Something will be absorbed. I have a yearning for knowledge and I have a problem with understanding people: any insight gained is definitely appreciated.

• • •

I think working as a group was hard because no one wanted to. No one wanted to meet for a long time and try to figure out something to write and then sit and write it. We seemed to want to find something we could do on our own and yet put it together as a group. I think part of why this happened is because we did not fully trust each other. Time is very hard for all of us, and it always seems that one person does not show up or cannot stay. How can we put our grade in the hands of a group of peers yet strangers?

• • •

The situation was strange. We all had ideals with no way to express them. Well, maybe it's just me. This group project really brought me down in the beginning. I've never written with anyone else before. I tried to be reasonable but no ideas would come.

• • •

As I sat down at the computer my mind froze up. I had had all these ideas running around in my head and now nothing. I stared at a blank screen. The hum of the computer lulling me asleep at this late hour. I started to write just to get anything down. What came out wasn't what I wanted, but it was a start. I think just the thought of writing with a theme, a topic, for the group was stifling my thoughts and creativity. Suddenly, an inspiration hit me. Yes, that was more like it. But it still needed work and more added. So I saved and shut the computer off to let the ideas ferment a little bit.

• • •

It was a couple of Thursdays ago; we were all determined to figure out what our group project was going to be. We thought about reviewing a book or movie. This was not a unique enough idea. We then as a group talked about writing a play. "Yeah, that's it; write a play." "How will we approach it?" Yes, this would be very creative, but as a group we felt that there was a lack of time to challenge ourselves and make this work. After just telling the group that my brain was dead (mental block), I had an idea.

• • •

I remember when we decided on our collaborative project. Suddenly the mood changed. We all had smiles on our faces and our body movements became more relaxed. It's amazing how decision-making can cause such stress and how the larger the group the harder it is to make a decision.

• • •

It is harder to write in a group. I feel like these writing exercises are helpful, but each time that we are asked to do them I wonder about the content of my writing compared to the others'. I feel like I have a responsibility to the group to write well and please them.

• • •

We shared the writing we did by reading it out loud. This was almost ritualistic when the group met.

• • •

Even in a small group, it is hard to get together at a set time. Everyone is so busy. It got easier when the group got comfortable with each other because we realized that we would do fine even with the absence of one person.

• • •

Everyone must be there and contributing. When one person doesn't show or can't make it, like when I had exams, it really seems to disrupt the group. It is hard to make decisions, and you miss that person's input to bounce off of. Once a group is formed, each piece is sort of essential for it to work. When someone has another obligation, things really seem to fall apart.

• • •

When I work in a group I get very nervous. There have been too many times when I have had to do more work than others and yet we got the same grade. Or, because of something someone else did, I did not get as good a grade as I should have. Because of this, I don't like working in groups. If I have to, I am always the one asking if people have finished their part and making sure that they know exactly what they should do.

• • •

Here I am again, back at the Newman Center, staring mindlessly at the grain of the table top. I can barely hear the others' discussion over the bang of my thoughts. It's not that I don't care; it's just that after a while you get burnt out and need to drain the cluttered pool in your head. I sometimes feel a little suffocated this semester. Not because of this class alone, but because of the combined workload of all my classes. It seems like I'm being held underwater for two minutes at a time. I thrash at the invisible hands until they let me go, but only long enough to catch a gasping breath. Then I'm submerged again in a block of water looking up as the sun's rays hit the surface, distorting the skyline.

• • •

Whenever the group found itself confused about something, I always tried to give my best input and knowledge. In the group, I always made sure that I knew what the assignment was, when it was due, and so on. Knowing myself, I am aware that when I am involved in any group I like to participate in this way. Yet I am shy and I feel timid when I have to speak aloud. This weakness became less noticeable as I became more comfortable with the group.

• • •

When I work in a group I am sort of on the outskirts. I stay fairly quiet, occasionally voice ideas when I feel they are important, support others' ideas when I feel they are good. But when it comes down to making decisions, I usually can be happy and work with any decision that is made, so I let others battle it out while I watch.

• • •

The best part of working in a group is being able to bounce off each other's ideas. When we start talking, even about seemingly unrelated topics, we start identifying with each other or disagreeing, and that makes us think about things in ways we hadn't before. Soon we are coming up with a pretty good description of school and how we have reacted to it. Problems we've had in the past and why. It starts off pretty informally and soon we have a wealth of learning and potential papers.

Two Friends

David Ignatow

An award-winning poet, David Ignatow (b. Brooklyn, 1914; d. 1987) also wrote short stories and a memoir and edited numerous volumes of poetry.

I have something to tell you.
I'm listening.
I'm dying.
I'm sorry to hear.
I'm growing old.
It's terrible.
It is, I thought you should know.
Of course and I'm sorry. Keep in touch.
I will and you too.
And let me know what's new.
Certainly, though it can't be much.
And stay well.
And you too.
And go slow.
And you too.

Getting Experience into Words: Image and Story

Your poetry issues of its own accord when you and the object become one.

Bashō

Essential Premises

- The best way to make your words powerful—to make readers *experience* the meanings in your words—is to make sure that *you* actually experience what your words are about. Finding nice words is all very well, but actually experiencing your meanings—seeing, hearing, and feeling what you are writing about—is another thing. It takes extra energy and concentration.
- A good way to write a story is to let it grow out of a strongly experienced image.

Main Assignment Preview

Our goal in this workshop is to help you make readers *experience* what you are writing about, not just understand it. We're after words that don't just *describe* the tree outside the window, but make your reader *see* it—and hear it and smell it. This means using words that somehow carry some of the life or energy of that tree. This is a magical way of putting things, but in fact it's not so hard to get this valuable quality into your writing if you take the right approach.

The basic principle here—getting experience into words—applies to all kinds of writing, including essays. But it is easier to learn it with descriptive and narrative writing. That is, it's easier to learn how to get visual and sensory experience into words, and know when you have succeeded, than to get cognitive or intellectual experience into words. When you learn the principle we're teaching in this workshop, you'll be able to apply it to essays.

The crux is this: If you want to get your reader to experience something, *you* must experience it. If you want your reader to see something, then put all your effort into *seeing it.* For your reader to hear or smell something, you must hear or smell it. Put all your effort into, as it were, having a vision. Don't worry about words; worry about seeing. When you can finally see, hear, and smell things, just open your mouth or start the pen moving and let the words take care of themselves. They may not yet be elegant or well-organized words, but don't worry about that. You can take care of that problem later. If you are actually seeing and hearing what you are talking or writing about, your words will have some of that special juice that gives your experience to the reader. If you don't see what you are describing, you may find very nice words but they are less apt to make the reader see what you are talking about.

The point of this workshop is *real* description: transporting the thing itself inside readers' minds. Sometimes readers say, "She's so good at describing things; she told me about 15 things in the scene." But those 15 items were often just mentioned or verbally described, not really conveyed into the reader's head.

Your main assignment for this workshop will be to develop an image into a story. Your teacher will let you know whether you should save this piece for revision later in the semester or do an extensive revision immediately.

Workshop Activities for Developing Images

This workshop consists of a sequence of six mini-workshops or focused activities—all designed to help you get more life and experience into your words. Most of the activities involve speaking rather than writing. We suggest even using your hands a bit or gesturing. The goal is not "acting" or "illustrating" things for an audience but rather getting as much as possible of your self invested in the words you use. This is all practice in *giving* words.

You can do these activities in pairs or small groups, but your teacher may well have you do some of them all together with the whole class.

It will be hard to fit all six activities into one session unless you have a long period of time. Thus you may spread them over two sessions. If you do that, be sure to do at least a bit of writing at the end of the first session—writing about whatever image you are currently working on. Don't hold off writing till the end of the second session.

Activity One: Letting Words Grow Out of Seeing

Think of some small object—for now something simple that you know well. For example, you might think of your favorite mug or coffee cup on the

---

Exploring the Writing Process

The most difficult part of your assignment (for me) was the imagined object. My mind just wandered from place to place, trying to think of a simple yet interesting object to describe. Perhaps in the next edition of this text you could include a few examples. [*This was a student comment from the first edition, and we did add examples.*]

kitchen counter. The goal is to describe your mug in spoken words so as to make your listeners *see* it.

What's important here is to take your time and not utter a word until *after* you close your eyes and put all your effort into *seeing* that mug on the counter. Don't try to see the whole kitchen or even the entire crowded counter. Focus all your energy on seeing that mug—hallucinating, if you will. Take your time. Don't worry about words or about classmates listening. The important thing is to wait with your eyes closed until you can really see what you are going to describe. When you are finally having that actual experience inside your head, open your mouth and say what you are seeing, letting the words take care of themselves.

Invite yourself to make some gesture or body movement as you speak. The goal is not so much to act out or illustrate what you are saying (though that's fine too) as to get so involved in your seeing and saying that you just invite some movement to flow naturally. Perhaps you'll find yourself pushing your arm or fist away as a kind of emphasis for certain words; perhaps you'll make a slow gradual movement of your arms as you are speaking. See what your limbs or body "want" to do with your speaking. Standing up will make natural movement easier. Of course you may feel shy or self-conscious about this. If it bothers you too much, you may need to skip this part of the activity. But the truth is that body movement invites language with more presence and involvement.

Perhaps your speech is halting and full of pauses as you struggle to see and hear inside your head—not "literary" or even grammatical. Perhaps you wander around in your description, changing focus as you pause. Perhaps you talk about the mug, then about the flower pattern, then the light on the surface, then the crumbs on the counter, the half-eaten bit of toast right next to the mug. There's nothing wrong with this: It often results from the effort to see. But now pause a moment and look for the center of gravity, the most important point in your scene, and give your description again, trying to get it whole and into one piece of energy. For example, you might end up with:

> I see my favorite mug. It's white with a twining pattern of blue flowers. Kind of oriental pattern. Narrow, small mug, but thick sides. I look inside. Dull gleam on the side of it from the fluorescent light. A few sips of cold black coffee left.

Another example:

> There's a striped towel lying on the cement. It's wet from my lying on it, but only where my bathing suit was. I can smell the chlorine from the pool. I hear splashes and kids' shouts. The towel has some wrinkles on it. The bottom corner is kind of turned over.

Listeners should just listen. No response. This is their chance to enjoy and to get better at listening. Then the next person gets a turn to describe her object. Make sure she too takes plenty of time to *see* it before talking.

This procedure should take just a few minutes for each person; a minute or so for remembering or finding an image, a minute or so for going inside your head and trying to really see it, and less than a minute for saying what you see. Short descriptions are fine, no more than four or five sentences. Here are a few guidelines:

- *No people or big scenes.* People are too big and complicated to describe at this point. (But you might describe the *hand* holding the mug.) For now, keep to more or less one object with no more than those few things that are near the mug or interact with it, such as a spoon standing in the mug, or the page of newspaper underneath the mug.
- *Go easy on feelings.* The goal for this exercise is to present the mug, not your feelings about it. Yes, you can describe the mug "through the lens of your feelings"—how the light was twilight dim and the smell of lilacs drifted in the window—but tell what you see and smell, not your feelings.
- *No stories.* Again, it's tempting to tell the story of who gave you the mug and how you once knocked it off the counter and slopped coffee all over the linoleum. Of course these memories are part of the mug for you, but skip them for now.

Story is tempting because it's the most captivating form of discourse. Everyone feels the basic tug of plot: "and next . . . and next . . . and next." But for this exercise, we are pushing stories away in order to concentrate on the central task of really seeing—not settling for the easy momentum of "and then this happened . . . and then . . . and then." In effect, this exercise asks you to take a snapshot and stick to one instant of time—to tell what could fit in only one still photograph. It's fine to describe the one instant of spilt coffee and mug fragments on the floor, but only that single snapshot/instant. In a little while we'll get to story or moving pictures.

Activity Two: Can Listeners See It?

After everyone has had one turn at presenting a small image, go around again presenting new images, using the same procedures. This time let listeners

Exploring the Writing Process

I didn't even want to do this exercise but felt I had to. Yoon's image was Oriental, although I think I de-Orientalized it as I wrote. I saw the road going down into the woods and I knew at some level that it was only one fork of the road because I seemed to be standing just before the break—but I saw that road more and more, twisting and winding (it was dust-colored) into the trees and forest surrounding it and disappearing into the dark.

But then the leader suggested looking at different parts of the image. I did. And there was the other fork going up a sloping grass-covered hillside toward an open blue sky. Why did I see the "half-empty glass" first? That open blue beckoning sky was there all along.

I was floored by what such a simple game led me to. I certainly won't listen when someone says it's stupid. Is it possible my resistance led me into the forest and obscured the blue sky and when I stopped resisting I saw the blue sky? It was even a different bodily sensation. The tension left my bones and muscles. Wow! And that's an understatement.

Pat Belanoff

give a tiny bit of feedback: Have them tell you which bits or details, if any, they could see (or hear, smell, taste, feel). This is a difficult test. Don't despair if listeners can't really see *anything* of what you described. It happens frequently. Words that carry real experience are rare. Don't give up; don't assume you are incapable. Everyone is capable of seeing what's in mind and describing it so that others will see it too. But it's a slippery skill. And some listeners are harder to get through to than others. Try to notice which details did get through.

The main thing to remember is that if they can't see or hear what you describe, it's probably not a problem of words—wrong words or lack of words; it's a problem of your *not experiencing* your object. You may have interesting ideas or words about your object; you may have strong feelings about it. But if listeners aren't seeing it, you're probably not really seeing it either.

Activity Three: Letting Listeners Give an Impetus

Now give listeners a bigger role. Get them to ask you about details you may not have thought of. For example:

- Tell me about the handle on the mug.
- Tell me about the surface of the counter.

Invite listeners to introduce other senses:

- What do you hear?
- What does the surface of the mug *feel* like?
- What do you smell?

Don't "think up" or "make up" answers to these questions. Look and see what the "real answer" is. That is, if you don't see the handle or feel the surface, pause till you do. Wait for answers to come. Keep the image in mind, look at it inside your head and make *it* give you the new answers.

Activity Four: Letting an Image Move toward Story

Now invite the germ of story or narrative by having a listener ask, "What happens next?" But don't move too fast. Your story will be better if you don't try to *tell a story,* but just try to *enrich an image.* Above all, avoid the temptation to jump into a long story, especially a corny story. "And then a hand drops a poison tablet into the mug!" No. The point is to let the next event be small and real—generated by the image rather than imposed on the image by you. Put the image in charge, not the event. This exercise is practice in standing out of the way, not steering but letting the image steer: letting details and events be generated *by reality,* not imposed by a creator.

So when someone asks you, "What happens next?" your job is easy. Just close your eyes, go back inside your head, and look at the mug and *wait.* Wait to see what does happen next. Don't be in a hurry. Some events may come to your mind that are too "made up." You'll usually be able to tell that they are manipulations of your mind, not products of the mug itself. They'll be too contrived or phony. Let them go. Wait for the event that really happens or really wants to happen. Perhaps it will just be:

> The rock song on the radio ends and a man's voice—fake-cheerful—announces the time, "It's eight forty-seven now, folks."

For your listeners, the question is always, "Do you believe it? Did it really happen, or was it just made up?" Again it is a matter of *experiencing*—applied this time to an event, not just an image: Did you give the experience of the event to the listeners?

Activity Five: Extending the Story through Collaboration

Now your group or pair is ready to try collaborating to develop one image and help it grow into a story.

- One person starts by suggesting a time of day.
- The next person provides an image occurring at that time of day.
- The next person adds a *detail,* but from a different sense (sound, smell, feel).
- The following person tells what happens next.
- Another person gives another detail or tells what happens next.

And so on, as far as you want to carry it. Make your own variations. This sequence of tasks works with a small group or even a pair: Simply go around and around the circle or take turns.

Remember all the things you worked on above: Concentrate on *having* an experience, not on finding words; wait and look; let your image be in charge, don't impose on the image. If you collaborate, you'll all have to hold the same

Exploring the Writing Process

There are two theories of inspiration. One idea is that poetry can actually be dictated to you, like it was to William Blake. You are in a hallucinated state, and you hear a voice or you are in communication with something outside, like James Merrill's new poem, which he says is dictated through the Ouija board by Auden and other people.

The other idea is Paul Valéry's, what he calls *une ligne donnée,* that you are given one line and you try to follow up this clue, pulling the whole poem out of it. My own experience is that a rhythm or something comes into my head which I feel I must do, I must write it, create it.

For example, I recall looking out of a railway window and seeing an industrial landscape, factories, slag heaps, and the line coming into my head: "A language of flesh and roses." The thought at the back of this was that the industrial landscape was a language, what people have made out of nature, the contrast of nature and the industrial, "A language of flesh and roses." The problem of the poem was to work this connection out, trying to go back to remember what you really thought at that instant, and trying to recreate it. If I think of a poem, I may spend six months writing, but what I am really trying to do is remember what I thought of at that instant.

Stephen Spender

image in mind even as it develops. In a sense you are working on a collaborative hallucination.

Activity Six: From Talking to Writing

So far, this has been mostly talking, but it's crucial to *start* a piece of writing right away when all this experiencing is still alive in your head—when you have been exercising your skill at internal seeing. You need at least 15 minutes for this writing, more if possible. (Your teacher may take charge of the timing.)

It might seem most natural to write from your own image. And that is OK. But we suggest choosing someone else's image. Choose an image which somehow feels interesting to you, which somehow intrigues you or resonates or feels perplexing. It's better if you don't even know why the image or description feels right or clicks for you. Writing from someone else's image often liberates your imagination. It gives you practice in relinquishing control and letting the image generate material. It's not *your* image and so you'll have less need to own it or control it, and you'll have fewer preconceptions about it.

Start by putting the image into words. But then keep writing and see where it leads. Carry it further by asking, "And then what happened? And then what?" Let it develop into a story. Don't plan; don't decide where it should go. Just start by re-creating the image and then continually ask, "Then what?" Better yet, ask the question of your developing *story:* ask *it* "What next?" Trust the image to be in charge and trust yourself by standing out of the way. Allow yourself to be surprised. And just as you try not to impose events on the image, try not to impose a meaning on the story. Let the story choose or find its own meaning.

If you have more than one session, it can be helpful to start the later sessions by hearing each other's rough exploratory writing based on images from the previous session. It needn't take much time if you quickly read in pairs or small groups. No need for response. Listen for how the images you heard in the previous session have been enriched and transformed in the writing. (We

Exploring the Writing Process

My task which I am trying to achieve is, by the power of the written word to make you hear, to make you feel—it is, before all, to make you *see*. That—and no more, and it is everything. If I succeed, you shall find there according to your deserts: encouragement, consolation, fear, charm—all you demand—and, perhaps, also that glimpse of truth for which you have forgotten to ask . . .

To arrest, for the space of a breath, the hands busy about the work of the earth, and compel men entranced by the sight of distant goals to glance for a moment at the surrounding vision of form and colour, of sunshine and shadows; to make them pause for a look, for a sigh, for a smile—such is the aim, difficult and evanescent, and reserved only for a few to achieve. But sometimes, by the deserving and the fortunate, even that task is accomplished. And when it is accomplished—behold!—all the truth of life is there: a moment of vision, a sigh, a smile—and the return to an eternal rest.

Joseph Conrad

are grateful for having learned about these seeing activities from John Schultz's work, listed in the "Works Cited" section at the end of this book.)

Main Assignment: *From Image to Story*

You may want to base your draft for this workshop on one of the images you've worked on in class, developing it into a full story. But if you prefer, you can start fresh on some new image since this is your chance to do some of what we tried to stop you from doing during the exercises: to describe a person, a large scene, or your feelings.

But as you do this more ambitious writing, make sure to rely on the techniques we've been emphasizing in this workshop. Above all, don't search out words and make up stories; instead get yourself to have experiences. When you feel stymied, stop, close your eyes, look inside, listen. Go through this root experience again and again, as often as you need to. It is a foundation for good writing, writing that conveys an experience to readers.

Don't worry if this approach leads you to write down words that seem jumbled or awkward—not as nice or polished as the writing you usually do. Trust the words that come. You can take time later, when you get around to revising, to clean them up—to cut, rearrange, and add. This way, you'll be working with language that has more life to it.

When you write your story, you may have the impulse to make it "say" something to the reader; or to "send a message" or a "deep meaning." But we would warn you against this impulse. If you start out with a meaning or moral in mind, the story often comes across heavy-handed or preachy. Almost always you do best to concentrate on what might be called "letting the story tell itself," or "letting the meaning take care of itself." You always have chances later, during revising, to spell out meanings more clearly—or better yet, to help the events *imply* the meaning more clearly. Have faith in the materials you choose, in your vision, and in the power of a story once you set it loose. In fact *you* don't even need to know what a story "means." If you have a strong urge to tell a story, fictional or real, that shows that it means something to you, and often that meaning will be more powerful if you leave it unstated.

Suggestions for Collaboration

A group or pair of you who collaborated on an image and story-germ might want to continue together and write a story collaboratively. In collaborating, you can divide the task by *sections,* where each of you writes a different part of the story. Or you can divide the task by *stages,* where one person starts by doing a rough draft, and each succeeding person takes the draft through the next stage. (We've used both of these techniques in collaborating on this book.) If you collaborate, you may have to give special attention to the problem of making the writing consistent, especially if different members write different sections.

Sharing and Responding

Feedback should focus on the main thing we are working on in this workshop, namely, the ability to make readers and listeners *experience* what you're describing. "Summary and Sayback" will be helpful (in *Sharing and Responding*), but perhaps the following pointed questions, addressed to your audience, will also help:

- "Which parts do you see most? Tell me in your own words what you see."
- "Where do you feel the most energy, voice, and life in my writing?"
- "Which parts are the most believable?"
- "Are there places where you feel me trying to take the image where it doesn't want to go?"
- "What does the story mean to you?"

After you've gotten feedback on your draft, your teacher may ask you to revise it immediately. Or she may ask you to set it aside for revision later.

Process Journal

The mental process we emphasize in this workshop may be new and difficult for you. But it's a vital process for all writing and thus useful to reflect on.

- Was it hard for you to see your object and stay focused on it? Could you get the *seeing* or *experience* to lead to words, instead of your having to look for words? What helped?
- Could you let the image lead to a story instead of your having to make up a story? What helped?
- Were these processes easier in speaking or writing?
- Did you know the meaning the story had for you from the start, or did it sneak up on you—or are you still not sure?

(For more process or cover letter questions, see Workshop 1, page 11.)

Exploring the Writing Process

I began writing about a woman whom I remember from my early childhood and soon realized that I really wanted to write about my grandmother. I was remembering her in the detail it takes to make a reader see a character, and it was a very pleasant experience. She hadn't been that clear to me in years. Even if the piece goes nowhere else, the writing of it was a pleasurable reliving of a long buried time of my life. It was important that I cared for the character I was writing about.

Jo Ferrell

Exploring Theory: *Writing and Getting Carried Away*

Have you sometimes had the experience of getting excited with what you are writing, getting carried away, and later discovering that the writing you produced in that excitement was terrible? Or at least discovering that others thought your writing was terrible? We've certainly had this experience ourselves.

Being carried away can lead to writing that is jumbled or disorganized. The excitement we feel in writing removes all sense of perspective and control and produces a mess—a rich mess, perhaps, but still a mess. "What is your thesis?" "No focus here!" "Sloppy!" are some comments that you might have gotten. Because of this experience, some people try to *avoid* getting carried away. And some teachers warn against it. They conclude that you should write only when you are cool and in control. And yet in this workshop we seem to be advocating getting carried away. When we suggest that you move your hands or body or give a gesture, we are trying to help you get further into your vision and thus, in a sense, to get carried away.

But you don't have to make an either/or choice between being excited and being cool. You can be excited or caught up in your meaning when you are writing *drafts*—and we think you should. Then when you *revise,* you can be coolly controlled and tough. Each of these opposite frames of mind helps enhance the other. That is, if you know you will be tough and controlled as you revise, you'll feel safer about letting yourself get carried away at the earlier stages. And if you know you've let yourself get carried away as you generate, you'll feel tougher about revising, more willing to wield the knife. So the control problem is solvable if you allow a period for being excited and a period for being cool.

But there is another problem with being "carried away." You can get so caught up with your *feelings* that you lose sight of what you are writing about—lose sight of the coffee mug, when the whole point is to see the mug even better.

We're not trying to argue against having feelings as you write; we're not trying to insist on the idea of the artist as coolly detached and paring his fingernails as he looks down on life from a distance. (James Joyce uses this image

Exploring the Writing Process

The actual object section gave me hope—some focus. You were right about the urges to wander! I am a storyteller. Fortunately I can work these descriptions into my stories to make them more vivid. Thank you for *making* us stop to focus as this will help us produce better writing.

The problem with having listeners see it is that some people have no "pictures" in their head. My fiancé, for example, has difficulty imagining anything. It doesn't mean it's a bad description; he just can't engage his imagination at will. Perhaps I need to spend more time forming a "focus," before writing or speaking. Did you know it's harder to imagine one particular small thing than it is to picture an entire beach scene? It seemed *too* focused for me.

Danielle

for the artist in *Portrait of the Artist as a Young Man.* Wordsworth similarly advises recollecting emotion *in tranquillity.*) But you need to use those feelings to "carry you away" to the coffee mug or to the ideas in your essay—to help you see the images and experience the ideas more vividly. If you only get carried away *to your feelings* about the image or idea, readers will get very little. Here's how the Japanese poet Bashō put this idea (in the passage from which we took our opening epigraph):

> Go to the pine if you want to learn about the pine, or to the bamboo if you want to learn about the bamboo. And in doing so, you must leave your subjective preoccupation with yourself. Otherwise you impose yourself on the object and do not learn. Your poetry issues of its own accord when you and the object have become one. . . .
>
> (Bashō, quoted by Balaban 33. See Balaban in "Works Cited.")

Once you get clear about what "being carried away" means—being carried into greater contact with what you are writing about—it makes writing much easier and more enjoyable. We suspect that few writers would continue writing unless they learned to give themselves the excitement of this experience of *contact.* This is the excitement of "inspiration," which means literally "a breathing into." In your process writing, you might notice the occasions when you feel the excitement of making some kind of contact with what you are trying to describe.

Jonathan Swift, the 18th-century author of *Gulliver's Travels,* said that good writing is nothing but finding the right words and putting them in the right places. In a sense, of course, he's right; and this is a fine way to describe good *revising.* But for *producing* or *generating* good writing, you'll find it helpful to think of writing as the other way around (as Bashō does). Don't seek words or worry about where to put them. Put all your energy into "becoming one" with what you are writing about. This principle works for any kind of writing, but it is most obvious and easiest to practice in descriptive writing.

It is a relief to take this approach to writing. It means that you don't need a fancy vocabulary or syntactic complexity to write well. Plenty of good words and good syntax will come of their own accord. Writing turns out to be a richer and more interesting experience this way, less dry or tense because it isn't so much a struggle to find words or correct words, as a struggle to have or relive or enter into experiences. Interestingly enough, some experienced and skilled writers have a harder time taking this approach. They try too hard to find fancy words and elegant phrasing as they write. They forget to put their effort into experiencing what they are writing about. As we read their writing, we are more aware of their nice words than of the meaning or experience of what they are saying.

Image of Ice-Cream Man

Mitchell Shack

My image of an ice-cream man starting as I hear the ice-cream bells ringing the next block away. As he comes closer, he puts on his blinking red lights and his sign, Watch-children, comes out on the driver's side of the truck. I go around the opposite side and find a window about 3 feet square. Around the outside of the window are pictures of bomb-pops, snow-cones, chocolate bar pops, ice-cream cones, shakes, hot fudge sundaes and a bunch of other treats. Next to each of these items is the price, usually about 20 or 30 cents higher than the same item bought in the supermarket. There is a little ledge where the ice-cream man puts down the various items and counts the pennies, dimes, and nickels the children give him. He places the change in a chrome change dispenser he wears on his waist. Inside the truck I see a metal freezer—actually it looks sort of like a refrigerator placed on its back. On shelves over the freezer are boxes of gum, candy, baseball cards and other sweets. The outside of the truck is mostly white, except for the area I mentioned earlier around the window. The shape of the truck reminds me of a modified bread delivery truck. Next to the window is a little cutout where there lies a garbage can on the other side so the kids can dispose of the wrappers. Towards the front of the truck on the passenger's side is a door similar to the kind you find on a school bus. Looking into the truck from the doorway, you can see the driver's seat—it's worn in with a jacket hanging over the chair. There's a big steering wheel and a little metal fan aimed at the seat. There are great big rear view mirrors outside of the window next to the seat and door. Above the front windshield are the big letters spelling ICE CREAM, and next to it is the infamous bell the kids can hear for five blocks away.

Process Writing

I had to think of vivid images of what I see when I think of the ice-cream man. Since there was no ice-cream truck in front of me, I had to rely totally on the images I had from my memory. Since it had been a while since my last encounter with an ice-cream truck, I had trouble remembering some of the details. I found that I could remember more when I closed my eyes and concentrated on what I saw when I looked at the ice-cream man. As I started writing down the major things, more detail popped into my head. I kept on remembering more things as I kept thinking and my picture in my mind became much more vivid. I could remember myself studying the pictures of the various ice-cream cones and figuring out what I could get with the money I had. I remember racing into the house when I heard the bells and running upstairs to get the money.

I tried to remember the most minute details like getting Italian ices with the little wooden spoon and turning over the Italian ice to get to the bottom which was the best part. It almost seemed as if the ice-cream truck was there—too bad, I was getting hungry and would have loved a hot fudge sundae. Anyway, by creating this image in my mind, all the details and little things I forgot over the years came back to me as clear as ever.

Mitchell Shack

An Ice-Cream Man*

Mitchell Shack

It was a scorching hot day in the middle of July, almost 100 degrees outside. I was playing football with a bunch of kids from my neighborhood. We were playing ball for almost an hour and I had worked up a good sweat. My throat was dry and I was in desperate need of an ice-cold glass of iced tea. We went into a huddle and I started daydreaming about jumping into a cold pool. The score was tied at twenty-one apiece and we all agreed that the next team that scores would win the game. We were about fifteen yards out from the end zone (actually the area between my friend's mail box and the pine tree across the street). Our team discussed our options and decided we were going to play on fourth down instead of kicking.

We lined up at the line of scrimmage and I was ready to start the down when I heart a faint sound. It sounded like a mixture between the fire bells in school and the bell I used to ring on my tricycle. I stepped back to throw the ball when I heard the noise again. This time it clicked in my head that what I was hearing was the ice-cream man the next block away. I dropped the ball and announced, "I forfeit! The ice-cream man is coming." I reached into my pockets in search of a few coins, but to my dismay they were empty. "Darn," I thought to myself, "I must have left my money in my pants in my room." I started to run toward my house and looked back to see my friends doing the same. The long game and the excessive heat seemed to have little effect on me, for I was running as fast as I ever had. I turned the corner and started running down my block. I could see my house at the end, and it seemed as if I was never going to reach it. I ran and ran and then sprinted up the driveway. I reached out for the doorknob to open the door and tried to turn it, but it didn't budge an inch. I started banging on my door and ringing the doorbell, hoping my mom would hear.

My mom came to the door and I was halfway up the stairs before she had a chance to yell at me for almost breaking down the door. I ran into my room in search of my pants containing my allowance money. I checked my floor, under my bed, my closet, my hamper, and behind my dresser, but the pants were nowhere to be found. "Mom! Mom! Where are my pants?" I screamed down to her. "I just took the laundry from your room—check the laundry basket," she replied. So downstairs I ran and grabbed the basket from atop the washing machine. I dumped the laundry on the floor and searched for my pants. I threw socks and shirts all over the place before I found what I was looking for. I reached into my pockets, grabbed the change, and flew out the door. Again I ran down the block, huffing and puffing all the way. I turned onto the street where I was playing and saw the truck in the distance. "Oh no, I better hurry—I think he's getting ready to leave," I thought to myself. The truck from far away looked like an old bread truck, but it would not have mattered one bit if it looked like a garbage truck, just as long as it sold ice cream.

---

* Shack developed this story from his description printed above.

I started getting close to it, when the red blinking sign WATCH—CHILDREN went on and the truck began to move. "Stop! Stop!" I yelled as I ran holding up both my hands. I put on my afterburners and ran in hot pursuit of that beat-up white truck. "Stop! Stop!" I continued to scream, but it had no effect and the truck kept on driving. I ran past my friends who were hysterically laughing as they watched me run while they unwrapped the ice cream they had just bought. The ice-cream truck stopped at a stop sign then turned the corner without noticing me at all. I figured I had better take a short cut so I ran through my friend's backyard, hopped a fence and sprinted through a little patch of woods. I noticed that I had ripped the pocket of my pants, probably while climbing over the fence. I was too concerned about intercepting the ice-cream truck to worry about my pants and I came out of the woods and ran in the middle of the street so I could flag down the truck. I held out both hands and screamed, "Stop!" as I saw the truck approaching, but I noticed something looked different. The truck came to an abrupt halt and I ran alongside it. I looked up but instead of a window, I found a sign reading "Bob's Bread Delivery Service." "Oh no, I stopped the wrong truck," I thought to myself as the driver stepped out and asked me what was wrong. "Oh, nothing. Forget it," I said to the driver, "I just thought you were the ice-cream man." He started laughing and pulled away. I felt like an idiot and just sat there on the curb and tried to catch my breath.

I figured I had better get home and clean up the mess I made out of the laundry. I walked about two blocks, when I turned the corner and saw the ice-cream truck on the side of the road. I couldn't believe my eyes. I thought he was gone for good. I ran alongside the truck and knocked on the closed window. I looked at the pictures next to the window and wanted to buy everything he had. The man came to the window and said. "I'm sorry—we're closed. I'm just packing up a few things before I go home." "Oh please," I pleaded with him. "I ran two blocks home, my house was locked. I couldn't find my pants, I wrecked my mom's laundry, I chased after you another three blocks, ran through my friend's woods and ripped my pants, stopped the wrong truck and when I finally catch up with you, you tell me you're closed!" "You did all that just to buy an ice-cream cone—I think we can make an exception," he said as he smiled at me. I said I wanted a hot fudge sundae and he turned around and started to make it.

I watched him as he was making it, and my mouth watered just looking at all the ice cream, lollipops, bubble gum, chocolate bars, Italian ices, and other candy I saw inside the truck. He reached into the freezer to scoop out some ice cream and I started counting my change as I placed the coins on the little ledge outside of the window. He finished making the sundae and handed it to me along with a plastic spoon. I went to hand him my money when he said, "Forget about the money. This treat is on me." "Thanks a lot! Thank you, thank you very much!" I blurted out. He closed the window and drove off. I just sat there eating my ice cream, watching the truck fade away into the distance. I was the happiest kid alive.*

Reverie

Jane Tompkins

Jane Tompkins is a professor in the School of Education at the University of Illinois at Chicago. "Reverie" is from her memoir A Life in School, *in part an appeal for education not just of the intellect, but of the "whole human being."*

---

* See the "Readings" for Workshop 16 for Mitchell Shack's case study of himself as a writer.

In my mind's eye I keep seeing rows. Rows of desks, running horizontal across a room, light yellow wooden tops, pale beige metal legs, a shallow depression for pencils at the far edge, and chairs of the same material, separate from the desks, movable. The windows—tall and running the length of the classroom—are on the left. Light streams through.

The rows are empty.

Now the desks darken and curve. They're made of older grainier wood; they're the kind with a surface that comes out from the back of the seat on your right and wraps around in front. The desk top is attached to the seat where you sit, which is clamped to the seats on either side or to those in front and in back. The desks metamorphose in my mind. Now they are hinged, tops brown and scarred; they open to reveal notebooks, textbooks covered in the shiny green-and-white book covers of Glen Rock Junior High; there's a bottle of mucilage and a pink eraser. On top, there's a hole for an inkwell, black and empty. The seat, when you stand, folds up behind.

Sometimes the desks are movable; more often they're clamped down. Always they're in rows. And empty. The teacher's place is empty, too, another desk, or table-like thing. Sometimes it's a podium on a platform. The blackboard behind.

The scenes are all mixed together—grade school with graduate school—but always the windows along one side of the room, and always the desks in rows.

After babyhood we spend a lot of time learning to sit in rows. Going from unruly to ruled. Learning to write on pages that are lined. Learning to obey. There is no other way, apparently. Even if the desks were arranged in a circle, or were not desks at all but chairs or ottomans, still they would have to form some pattern. We would have to learn to sit still and listen.

The first part of life goes on for a long time. The habit of learning to sit in rows doesn't leave off when the rows themselves are gone. Having learned to learn the rules, you look for them everywhere you go, to avoid humiliation. You learn to find your seat in the invisible rows.

The last part of life, though, is different. It is no longer automatic, your walking in and sitting down. When you see a row, your gorge rises, or you are simply indifferent. When the command comes to be seated, you don't obey. All of a sudden, survival no longer depends on getting to your desk in the ten seconds after the buzzer sounds. It depends on listening only to your inner monitor, which says: You'd better go while the going's good. Time to give up the security of rows.

'Cause you're not *in* the classroom anymore. There is no blackboard with equations on it, no teacher with her pointer to point out what you need to know. No test, no assignment. No three o'clock when the bell for dismissal rings. No after school.

No smell of chalk dust and freshly sharpened pencils, no fragrances of different kinds of paper, gray and white and yellow, blank pages, lined and unlined, inviting you to prove something, yourself . . . I can do this problem, spell that word, name the capital of that country, explain the meaning of that term.

Though there was always fear associated with sitting in rows—am I too different? will I pass the test? does anybody like me?—the desks and chairs and tasks provided an escape from fear by giving me something definite to do. Add the column of figures. Learn the causes of the war.

Now, wandering the world outside of school, having transcended "rows," nothing to do, no place to go, I am terrified. In the huge, dark, unfurnished world without rows, I cower and tremble. Give me back Mrs. Colgan. Let me be in 1B again. Let me learn to add, to subtract, to carry and to borrow numbers. Give me a problem to do.

I see the light-filled classrooms, rows on rows, desks, chairs, waiting to be filled: let the lesson begin. "Our first assignment will be to learn the periodic table." Let me back in. Please. Let me sit down again, open my notebook to the first blank page, start writing. When is the exam?

The Perfect Swing

Joel Southall

For me, the perfect swing happened on the 15th tee at the T.P.C. Scottsdale Desert Course in Scottsdale, Arizona. My father, brother, and I had taken a "guys only" spring break trip to Arizona for a week of golfing and quality male bonding. We had played 18 earlier in the day at the Raven Golf Course, but we hungered for more golf. On the car ride back, we made some calls and got a tee time. Just the three of us. The day was absolutely perfect. We played by ourselves and it seemed that the golden sun of the late afternoon lasted for all four hours of our round. The mountains around us stretched for farther than our eyes would take us. While we played, there was no time, other people did not exist, and we all walked a little bit taller. I had a pretty good round going as I came to the tee of 15, a 420-yard par four dogleg left over a waste area. The thoughts that usually occupy the spaces of my mind were absent. Tension drained out of my body as water trickles off the end of a melting icicle. My body acted on its own, entirely separate from my mind. As I took the club away from the ball, my legs, hips, hands, arms, shoulders, and head all came away as one. The club face rotated at the exact rate that would demand its return to square at impact. The toe of the club nodded to the golden dome above us at the midpoint of my back swing as if acknowledging the perfection of the day. As I began my downswing, there was no delay or stutter. My body began to unwind in synch with itself as the club head traveled towards the ball. The club face began to square itself as my wrists supinated and released the wrist cock I had maintained to perfection throughout my swing. My hands began to release through the ball producing the last bit of energy required for perfection. Though the real power emanated from my hips, on this swing my wrists acted as a spring, perfectly timed. At impact, a burst of power traveled up the shaft of my driver and radiated throughout my arms, literally making the core of my body warmer. After impact, the club rotated my body around its center of gravity, independent of my conscious actions. At that point, it was clear that I didn't fully have control over my swing. Actions and movements I had made earlier in the swing led to the perfect follow through. So it is in life. Hard work and preparation in the early stages of life lead to easier times later in life. As I reflect on the swing, it seems timeless while simultaneously feeling like an eternity of enjoyment. The most striking feature of the swing was the tempo with which it was delivered. It was an automatic action instead of a planned process. As I walked down the fairway, I was in a state of equilibrium which I may never exist in again. I hit my drive about 275 yards, not mammoth by any proportions, but still good enough to leave me an eight iron from 145 to the far left side of the green. It was slightly elevated and well bunkered on the right side with a single bunker short left. A well-struck shot left me a straight 20-foot putt. I two-putted for the best par I have ever had. I went on to shoot 78. Not the best round of my life (pretty close though), but certainly the most perfect. We finished 18 in the dark, went back to the hotel, and talked about the shots we had hit during the day.

At that moment in time, I was perfect. It was the crowning achievement of my golf life that I will never forget. That swing essentially was who I am, when I am at my best. Confident, sure, and in balance. It somehow seems sad, though. Will I never be perfect again? Was that it? No, that is not it. I was perfect for that time in history, but perhaps in the future, I will be perfect again. Even if I do not attain this state of perfection again, I will be satisfied for the duration of my life. To alter a familiar adage, "It is better to have peaked early than never to have peaked at all."

A Worn Path*

Eudora Welty

Eudora Welty (b. 1909, Jackson, Mississippi) is one of America's noted short story writers and novelists.

It was December—a bright frozen day in the early morning. Far out in the country there was an old Negro woman with her head tied in a red rag, coming along a path through the pinewoods. Her name was Phoenix Jackson. She was very old and small and she walked slowly in the dark pine shadows, moving a little from side to side in her steps, with the balanced heaviness and lightness of a pendulum in a grandfather clock. She carried a thin, small cane made from an umbrella, and with this she kept tapping the frozen earth in front of her. This made a grave and persistent noise in the still air, that seemed meditative like the chirping of a solitary little bird.

She wore a dark striped dress reaching down to her shoe tops, and an equally long apron of bleached sugar sacks, with a full pocket: all neat and tidy, but every time she took a step she might have fallen over her shoe-laces, which dragged from her unlaced shoes. She looked straight ahead. Her eyes were blue with age. Her skin had a pattern all its own of numberless branching wrinkles and as though a whole little tree stood in the middle of her forehead, but a golden color ran underneath, and the two knobs of her cheeks were illuminated by a yellow burning under the dark. Under the red rag her hair came down on her neck in the frailest of ringlets, still black, and with an odor like copper.

Now and then there was a quivering in the thicket. Old Phoenix said, "Out of my way, all you foxes, owls, beetles, jack rabbits, coons, and wild animals! . . . Keep out from under these feet, little bob-whites. . . . Keep the big wild hogs out of my path. Don't let none of those come running my direction. I got a long way." Under her small black-freckled hand her cane, limber as a buggy whip, would switch at the brush as if to rouse up any hiding things.

On she went. The woods were deep and still. The sun made the pine needles almost too bright to look at, up where the wind rocked. The cones dropped as light as feathers. Down in the hollow was the mourning dove—it was not too late for him.

The path ran up a hill. "Seem like there is chains about my feet, time I get this far," she said, in the voice of argument old people keep to use with themselves. "Something always take a hold of me on this hill—pleads I should stay."

After she got to the top she turned and gave a full, severe look behind her where she had come. "Up through pines," she said at length. "Now down through oaks."

Her eyes opened their widest, and she started down gently. But before she got to the bottom of the hill a bush caught her dress.

Her fingers were busy and intent, but her skirts were full and long, so that before she could pull them free in one place they were caught in another. It was not possible to allow the dress to tear. "I in the thorny bush," she said. "Thorns, you doing your appointed work. Never want to let folks pass—no sir. Old eyes thought you was a pretty little *green* bush."

Finally, trembling all over, she stood free, and after a moment dared to stoop for her cane.

"Sun so high!" she cried, leaning back and looking, while the thick tears went over her eyes. "The time getting all gone here."

---

* For Welty's comments about her writing process, and especially about the central role of the image in creating this story, see her essay in the "Readings" for Workshop 7.

At the foot of this hill was a place where a log was laid across the creek.

"Now comes the trial," said Phoenix.

Putting her right foot out, she mounted the log and shut her eyes. Lifting her skirt, levelling her cane fiercely before her, like a festival figure in some parade, she began to march across. Then she opened her eyes and she was safe on the other side.

"I wasn't as old as I thought," she said.

But she sat down to rest. She spread her skirts on the banks around her and folded her hands over her knees. Up above her was a tree in a pearly cloud of mistletoe. She did not dare to close her eyes, and when a little boy brought her a little plate with a slice of marble-cake on it she spoke to him. "That would be acceptable," she said. But when she went to take it there was just her own hand in the air.

So she left that tree, and had to go through a barbed-wire fence. There she had to creep and crawl, spreading her knees and stretching her fingers like a baby trying to climb the steps. But she talked loudly to herself: she could not let her dress be torn now, so late in the day, and she could not pay for having her arm or her leg sawed off if she got caught fast where she was.

At last she was safe through the fence and risen up out in the clearing. Big dead trees, like black men with one arm, were standing in the purple stalks of the withered cotton field. There sat a buzzard.

"Who you watching?"

In the furrow she made her way along.

"Glad this not the season for bulls," she said, looking sideways, "and the good Lord made his snakes to curl up and sleep in the winter. A pleasure I don't see no two-headed snake coming around that tree, where it come once. It took a while to get by him, back in the summer."

She passed through the old cotton and went into a field of dead corn. It whispered and shook and was taller than her head. "Through the maze now," she said, for there was no path.

Then there was something tall, black, and skinny there, moving before her.

At first she took it for a man. It could have been a man dancing in the field. But she stood still and listened, and it did not make a sound. It was as silent as a ghost.

"Ghost," she said sharply, "who be you the ghost of? For I have heard of nary death close by."

But there was no answer—only the ragged dancing in the wind.

She shut her eyes, reached out her hand, and touched a sleeve. She found a coat and inside that an emptiness, cold as ice.

"You scarecrow," she said. Her face lighted. "I ought to be shut up for good," she said with laughter. "My senses is gone. I too old. I the oldest people I ever know. Dance, old scarecrow," she said, "while I dancing with you."

She kicked her foot over the furrow, and with mouth drawn down, shook her head once or twice in a little strutting way. Some husks blew down and whirled in streamers about her skirts.

Then she went on, parting her way from side to side with the cane, through the whispering field. At last she came to the end, to a wagon track where the silver grass blew between the red ruts. The quail were walking around like pullets, seeming all dainty and unseen.

"Walk pretty," she said. "This the easy place. This the easy going."

She followed the track, swaying through the quiet bare fields, through the little strings of trees silver in their dead leaves, past cabins silver from weather, with the doors and windows boarded shut, all like old women under a spell sitting there. "I walking in their sleep," she said, nodding her head vigorously.

In a ravine she went where a spring was silently flowing through a hollow log. Old

Phoenix bent and drank. "Sweet-gum makes the water sweet," she said, and drank more. "Nobody know who made this well, for it was here when I was born."

The track crossed a swampy part where the moss hung as white as lace from every limb. "Sleep on, alligators, and blow your bubbles." Then the track went into the road.

Deep, deep the road went down between the high green-colored banks. Overhead the live-oaks met, and it was as dark as a cave.

A black dog with a lolling tongue came up out of the weeds by the ditch. She was meditating, and not ready, and when he came at her she only hit him a little with her cane. Over she went in the ditch, like a little puff of milkweed.

Down there, her senses drifted away. A dream visited her, and she reached her hand up, but nothing reached down and gave her a pull. So she lay there and presently went to talking. "Old woman," she said to herself, "that black dog come up out of the weeds to stall you off, and now there he sitting on his fine tail, smiling at you."

A white man finally came along and found her—a hunter, a young man, with his dog on a chain.

"Well, Granny!" he laughed. "What are you doing there?"

"Lying on my back like a June-bug waiting to be turned over, mister," she said, reaching up her hand.

He lifted her up, gave her a swing in the air, and set her down, "Anything broken, Granny?"

"No sir, them old dead weeds is springy enough," said Phoenix, when she had got her breath. "I thank you for your trouble."

"Where do you live, Granny?" he asked, while the two dogs were growling at each other.

"Away back yonder sir, behind the ridge. You can't even see it from here."

"On your way home?"

"No, sir, I going to town."

"Why, that's too far! That's as far as I walk when I come out myself, and I get something for my trouble." He patted the stuffed bag he carried, and there hung down a little closed claw. It was one of the bob-whites, with its beak hooked bitterly to show it was dead. "Now you go on home, Granny!"

"I bound to go to town, mister," said Phoenix. "The time come around."

He gave another laugh, filling the whole landscape. "I know you old colored people! Wouldn't miss going to town to see Santa Claus!"

But something held Old Phoenix very still. The deep lines in her face went into a fierce and different radiation. Without warning, she had seen with her own eyes a flashing nickel fall out of the man's pocket onto the ground.

"How old are you, Granny?" he was saying.

"There is no telling, mister," she said, "no telling."

Then she gave a little cry and clapped her hands and said, "Git on away from here, dog! Look! Look at that dog!" She laughed as if in admiration. "He ain't scared of nobody. He a big black dog." She whispered, "Sic him!"

"Watch me get rid of that cur," said the man. "Sic him, Pete! Sic him!"

Phoenix heard the dogs fighting, and heard the man running and throwing sticks. She even heard a gunshot. But she was slowly bending forward by that time, further and further forward, the lids stretched down over her eyes, as if she were doing this in her sleep. Her chin was lowered almost to her knees. The yellow palm of her hand came out from the fold of her apron. Her fingers slid down and along the ground under the piece of money with the grace and care they would have in lifting an egg from under a sitting hen. Then she slowly straightened up, she stood erect, and the nickel was in her apron pocket. A bird flew by. Her lips moved. "God watching me the whole time. I come to stealing."

The man came back, and his own dog panted about them. "Well, I scared him off that time," he said, and then he laughed and lifted his gun and pointed it at Phoenix.

She stood straight and faced him.

"Doesn't the gun scare you?" he said, still pointing it.

"No, sir, I seen plenty go off closer by, in my day, and for less than what I done," she said, holding utterly still.

He smiled, and shouldered the gun. "Well, Granny," he said, "you must be a hundred years old, and scared of nothing. I'd give you a dime if I had any money with me. But you take my advice and stay home, and nothing will happen to you."

"I bound to go on my way, mister," said Phoenix. She inclined her head in the red rag. Then they went in different directions, but she could hear the gun shooting again and again over the hill.

She walked on. The shadows hung from the oak trees to the road like curtains. Then she smelled wood-smoke, and smelled the river, and she saw a steeple and the cabins on their steep steps. Dozens of little black children whirled around her. There ahead was Natchez shining. Bells were ringing. She walked on.

In the paved city it was Christmas time. There were red and green electric lights strung and crisscrossed everywhere, and all turned on in the daytime. Old Phoenix would have been lost if she had not distrusted her eyesight and depended on her feet to know where to take her.

She paused quietly on the sidewalk where people were passing by. A lady came along in the crowd, carrying an armful of red-, green-, and silver-wrapped presents: she gave off perfume like the red roses in hot summer, and Phoenix stopped her.

"Please, missy, will you lace up my shoe?" She held up her foot.

"What do you want, Grandma?"

"See my shoe," said Phoenix. "Do all right for out in the country, but wouldn't look right to go in a big building."

"Stand still then, Grandma," said the lady. She put her packages down on the sidewalk beside her and laced and tied both shoes tightly.

"Can't lace 'em with a cane," said Phoenix. "Thank you, missy. I doesn't mind asking a nice lady to tie up my shoe, when I gets out on the street."

Moving slowly and from side to side, she went into the big building and into a tower of steps, where she walked up and around and around until her feet knew to stop.

She entered a door, and there she saw nailed up on the wall the document that had been stamped with the gold seal and framed in the gold frame, which matched the dream that was hung up in her head.

"Here I be," she said. There was a fixed and ceremonial stiffness over her body.

"A charity case, I suppose," said an attendant who sat at the desk before her.

But Phoenix only looked above her head. There was sweat on her face, the wrinkles in her skin shone like a bright net.

"Speak up, Grandma," the woman said. "What's your name? We must have your history, you know. Have you been here before? What seems to be the trouble with you?"

Old Phoenix only gave a twitch to her face as if a fly were bothering her.

"Are you deaf?" cried the attendant.

But then the nurse came in.

"Oh, that's just old Aunt Phoenix," she said. "She doesn't come for herself—she has a little grandson. She makes these trips just as regular as clockwork. She lives away back off the Old Natchez Trace." She bent down. "Well, Aunt Phoenix, why don't you just take a seat? We won't keep you standing after your long trip." She pointed.

The old woman sat down, bolt upright in the chair.

"Now, how is the boy?" asked the nurse.

Old Phoenix did not speak.

"I said, how is the boy?"

But Phoenix only waited and stared straight ahead, her face very solemn and withdrawn into rigidity.

"Is his throat any better?" asked the nurse. "Aunt Phoenix, don't you hear me? Is your grandson's throat any better since the last time you came for the medicine?"

With her hands on her knees, the woman waited, silent, erect and motionless, just as if she were in armour.

"You mustn't take up our time this way, Aunt Phoenix," the nurse said. "Tell us quickly about your grandson, and get it over. He isn't dead, is he?"

At last there came a flicker and then a flame of comprehension across her face, and she spoke.

"My grandson. It was my memory had left me. There I sat and forgot why I made my long trip."

"Forgot?" The nurse frowned. "After you came so far?"

Then Phoenix was like an old woman begging a dignified forgiveness for waking up frightened in the night. "I never did go to school, I was too old at the Surrender," she said in a soft voice. "I'm an old woman without an education. It was my memory fail me. My little grandson, he is just the same, and I forgot it in the coming."

"Throat never heals, does it?" said the nurse, speaking in a loud sure voice to Old Phoenix. By now she had a card with something written on it, a little list. "Yes. Swallowed lye. When was it—January—two-three years ago—"

Phoenix spoke unasked now. "No, missy, he not dead, he just the same. Every little while his throat begin to close up again, and he not able to swallow. He not get his breath. He not able to help himself. So the time come around, and I go on another trip for the soothing medicine."

"All right. The doctor said as long as you came to get it, you could have it," said the nurse. "But it's an obstinate case."

"My little grandson, he sit up there in the house all wrapped up, waiting by himself," Phoenix went on. "We is the only two left in the world. He suffer and it don't seem to put him back at all. He got a sweet look. He going to last. He wear a little patch quilt and peep out holding his mouth open like a little bird. I remembers so plain now. I not going to forget him again, no, the whole enduring time. I could tell him from all the others in creation."

"All right." The nurse was trying to hush her now. She brought her a bottle of medicine. "Charity," she said, making a check mark in a book.

Old Phoenix held the bottle close to her eyes and then carefully put it into her pocket.

"I thank you," she said.

"It's Christmas time, Grandma," said the attendant. "Could I give you a few pennies out of my purse?"

"Five pennies is a nickel," said Phoenix stiffly.

"Here's a nickel," said the attendant.

Phoenix rose carefully and held out her hand. She received the nickel and then fished the other nickel out of her pocket and laid it beside the new one. She stared at her palm closely, with her head on one side.

Then she gave a tap with her cane on the floor.

"This is what come to me to do," she said. "I going to the store and buy my child a little windmill they sells, made out of paper. He going to find it hard to believe there such a thing in the world. I'll march myself back where he waiting, holding it straight up in this hand."

She lifted her free hand, gave a little nod, turned round, and walked out of the doctor's office. Then her slow step began on the stairs, going down.

Voice

Essential Premises

- There's only one way to write a word, but an infinite number of ways to speak it. Speech can call on great subtleties of intonation, rhythm, volume, and so on—all of which carry messages that are absent when words sit silently on the page. And yet written language can make us hear a voice from the silent page, and thereby capture in writing all those subtleties of the actual human voice.
- We can sharpen our "reading ear." In this way we can learn to hear better the "voice" (or lack of voice) that exists in any piece of writing. By noticing the voice or voices in any text, we can usually understand better why it works well or badly on readers.
- We can also sharpen our "writing ear." In this way we can learn to get more of the liveliness and energy of the human voice in our writing, and also gain more control over what *kind* of voice or tone or feeling comes through to readers.

Main Assignment Preview

"Hello." Think of all the messages you can send by speaking just that one word. Say it "normally," and the message is innocuous—perhaps, "Hi, I'm home from school." But almost everyone knows how to say "hello" in such a way as to be saying, "I think you are really attractive." Say it the way Sherlock Holmes or various detectives have said it and you are saying, "That's an interesting fact I never noticed before." Say it with a kind of scornful accent on the second syllable and you are saying, "Wake up and screw your head on straight for a change." Try it out now—in your mind anyway: Try saying it and remembering all the ways you've heard that one word used.

Now try writing the word "hello." In contrast to the huge varieties of ways of saying it, there's only one way to write it. Yes, you can underline it or write in italics or print it in color or use different typefaces. You can try different spellings—"Helloooo." But the possibilities in writing are miniscule compared to the infinite resources of the human voice. Let's think about these resources for a moment. With our voices we have loud and soft, fast and slow, high and low, emphasis and no emphasis, and all the variations in the middle. Or we could use none of them and talk in monotone, and that would carry a message too. We have pauses and rhythms and timbres—breathy, gravelly, whiney and so forth. Written words just sit there silently, mutely.

Spoken words have other advantages over writing too. When we hear someone speaking, it usually seems as though that speaker has done the work of getting the meanings into our heads. But when we read someone's writing, it usually seems as though we have to do the work of getting the meaning into our heads.

In truth, things are not so simple. Writing is not really so impoverished. The point we want to get across in this workshop is that writing *can* have a voice. It is possible to get all those interesting rhythms and melodies of the spoken voice into writing and thereby make it do all the things that speech can do. That is, *some* written words have a live voice: When we read them, we hear the sound of a person in there, we feel the presence of the person, and it seems as though the writer is doing the work of getting the meanings up off the page into our heads. If you get voice into your writing, readers will pay better attention and your meaning will come through stronger. One of the goals of this workshop is to help you breathe a voice into your writing.

There's a sense, however, in which *most* writing can be said to have a voice of some sort. That is, we could say that there's a *potential* voice in all writing if we listen hard enough. And it turns out that one of the most useful ways to talk about the differences between pieces of writing is to talk about the voices in them.

Certain kinds of voice are frowned on in certain kinds of writing. In highly formal kinds of writing such as we find in business reports and scholarly journals, readers and writers seem to want formal voices: quiet, dressed-up, well-behaved, and impersonal voices. "Don't raise your voice; keep it decorous; keep it dignified." With more informal kinds of writing, such as we find in newspaper feature stories and many magazine articles and literary essays, readers and writers invite informal voices: personal, lively, casual, idiosyncratic voices.

And how about writing in school and college? Should it be formal or informal? Can it have a personal, lively, casual voice, or must it be dignified and restrained? As all students know, teachers don't agree. Some teachers are happy to get an informal voice while others want a dressed-up, impersonal voice. And some teachers who are open to both nevertheless don't like a *mixing* of voices: hearing the collision of a casual spoken voice with a formal academic one. Yet some teachers don't mind a mixing of voices if it's done well—as with a well-placed piece of slang to give emphasis in an otherwise formal paper.

Because of this variation among teachers and other readers, too, we have a second goal for this workshop: not just to learn how to breathe voice into your writing, but also how to *vary* or adjust your voice according to the situation or your reader's needs. To do this, you'll also have to learn to listen well to differences in voice in writing.

And there's a third goal we have—one that might have been occurring to you as we've been talking about voice in writing: "I don't want just *any* voice in my writing. I don't want just the *right* voice in my writing. I want *my* voice in there. I want the voice in my writing to fit me! If I adjust my voice to fit different audiences, I don't want to sound artificial or fake. I still want to sound like me." This is a feasible goal. That is, even though people's voices usually change when they talk to different people or are in different situations (we can sometimes tell who someone is talking to on the phone just by the tone of voice he or she is using), some people nevertheless manage to sound "like themselves" even when they use different voices. They always sound genuine, not like they are pretending. Other people sound unlike themselves only when they talk to *some* people; and they sound fake or artificial or unreal when they "adjust" their voice for certain listeners. Most people sound unlike themselves when they are nervous or afraid; but some people sound this way even if they aren't nervous—they have developed certain *roles* they use in certain situations or for certain audiences, and they don't sound natural in those roles.

We have designed the exercises in this workshop to help you learn not only to vary your written voice as needed but also, if possible, to still sound like yourself.

We are suggesting a choice of three different main assignments for this workshop. Your teacher may decide which one or ones you should use.

1. Gather passages from your writing that illustrate different voices you use in it and create a collage of your written voices.
2. Choose a paper you have already written—probably one that bothers you—and revise it with special attention to voice.
3. Write an essay that explores the various voices you find in your writing and in your speaking. Explore how they relate to each other and perhaps how they relate to who you really are.

Exercises to Help You Explore Voices in Writing

We spend a good part of our lives listening to people and noticing *how they talk.* From the earliest age we can "hear" people's moods just from listening to their voices. For example, we can often tell if someone is mad at us even when they say, "No, I'm not mad at you." We can do this even if we are listening to them on the phone and voice is the only cue we have. We have many words that describe how people talk—words for tone of voice: cheerful, chirpy, sarcastic, breathy, haughty, scared, timid, flat.

Written words just sit silently on the page. But writing will speak to us if we "listen" to it well enough—with our ears and our mouths. We need to learn to apply our sophisticated voice-listening skills to writing. The following are three short exercises to help you hear, understand, and describe the voice in a piece of writing. These exercises are done best in pairs or small groups.

1. *What does the voice in the writing actually sound like?* The best way to find out is to speak the words out loud in order to "enact" or "inhabit" or

"render" the voice. That is, don't just "say" the words, but give them a reading that brings out the tone, mood, feeling, or character—the voice—that seems to fit best.

Try to get two or three readings of the same passage. You can do this yourself, but it helps to have someone else work with you. Others can often hear a voice you didn't notice. Of course, you may well disagree about whether a voice is "there" or "fits the text." This is appropriate. Different voicings can be equally "in" the text—but it's always a matter of interpretation. For example, the same passage could be read as sarcastic or straight.

In addition, a single passage can *change* voices or tones as it goes along; for example, gradually building up to more excitement, or suddenly slowing down and becoming quietly meditative—even changing to angry. Since the goal is to hear voices on the page—that is, to explore voice in written language—it's fine to play around, stretch, or even exaggerate a bit. Then you can discuss your reactions to these readings and try to decide when a reading fits the written words well and when it isn't right for the words.

We'll provide a few passages below for you to use, but first we'll illustrate what we are asking you to do with a sample passage:

> Fun. Fun. Did I say this was fun? A curse, that's what the computer is. In process. Nothing's ever done. You can always find a new way to rework things. Example: the ending. That came to me while I was working on another paper. It probably doesn't work, but hell, enough is enough. I've got shopping to do, cards to send, laundry, you name it. I'm calling it quits. OK, so I'll give it one more read tomorrow in school.
>
> Deb DuBock, process writing, December 1991

Since we didn't include a tape recording with this book, we can't give you out-loud renderings of this passage, but we can talk about the renderings we've heard when we've worked with this passage with students. Some students read it with a voice of cheerful, amused exasperation; others heard a voice of serious, hair-tearing frustration; one reader even gave a kind of frenzied Dr. Strangelove voice to the passage—spitting out those first two words ("Fun. Fun.") through tightly clenched teeth like a mad scientist going crazy.

Exploring the Writing Process

I reread the experimental changes (I keep saving each draft under a new file name so if I don't like the changes I've made I can go back to one of the previous drafts) and got disgusted because I was hit over the head with a major issue I hadn't attempted to deal with at all in the previous night's work—the two different voices I was using in the piece. At that point I asked Deb to read it (unfortunately for her, she wandered into the computer lab at just the *wrong* moment . . .). I asked her for just a quick, initial reaction to the tone. She reaffirmed my feeling that it was a schizo piece—a different person took over at the bottom of page two. Then she made a practical suggestion that really helped get me on a steadier track—"Why don't you just delete the first page and three quarters and begin the paper with Voice #2?"

Kathy Reckendorf

Notice the rich possibilities in just those first two words: Some people gave the second "fun" a very different mood or tone from the first one—more angry and sarcastic; others gave the second "fun" a tone of questioning as though the writer had suddenly noticed what she had just said and now is questioning it. ("Fun. *Fun*?"—the second one saying, in effect, "Are you kidding?")

Quite a few people rendered changes in mood in midpassage. A number of students put in a big pause before that last "OK, so I'll give it one more read tomorrow in school." Some of the pausers made that last sentence sound discouraged and dejected, while others gave it a voice of amused self-mocking—the voice of someone who knows that she always gives in to the need for more work and has come to accept that fact about herself. What we see here is what all actors know: that the same words have a number of potential voices in them.

2. *What kind of person talks this way, and how does she see the world and talk about all kinds of things?* To answer this question, try to *get inside* the voice in the passage—try to pretend to *be* that person—in effect, role-playing the speaker in the passage. Now that you have a new voice and are a new person, just talk (or write) in your new voice. Simply talk or write as who you are now. Here's what we wrote when we did the exercise and tried taking on the voice and identity of that same passage by Deb DuBock:

> My mom called me last night. Saturday night! What made her think I'd be here. The nerve! But there I was. I thought it was going to be someone else and I answered all happy. I know she could hear my voice fall when she told me it was her. But what did she expect? She wants me to come visit next weekend. Next weekend! Give me a break. I'm not going, I'm just not going. I'm an adult, OK? I'm earning money. I'm taking care of myself. N. O. No. OK . . . so what are you making for dinner?

3. *How would you describe the voice?* After you have tried inhabiting or enacting the voices in a piece of writing in these exercises, you will find it much easier to find explanatory language to describe the voices you hear in it. What is the tone, character, mood of this voice? Here is one possible description of the voice Deb DuBock used:

> It's a voice of exasperation and frustration. But there's also a note in the voice of self-awareness—that this frustration is not the end of the world—a faint note even of amusement or enjoyment. And that last sentence has a smile of amused self-mocking underneath the discouraged giving in.

With these exercises, we are trying to illustrate a large principle of learning and teaching. You don't actually need to be able to describe voices to be able to hear them, understand them, and use them. People can usually describe and analyze almost anything better *after* they have entered into it or enacted it or "tried it on." Describing the voice requires a somewhat detached and analytic ability. Of course this analytic ability is useful and interesting not only for analytic school assignments (especially in literature classes—see Workshop 13), but also for handling countless situations that come up in life. We've all been in situations where the tone of voice matters a lot—and where people argue about it. ("I apologize. I'm sorry I hurt you." "I don't believe you are really sorry." Or, "Stop being sarcastic with me!" "Oh, come on. Here we go again. I wasn't being sarcastic; I was just making a friendly joke.")

Now try out these three exercises in exploring the voices in a text. Here are a few passages you can use, though you can also use pieces of your own writing or pieces that your teacher suggests. (You could also use passages of our writing. We wonder whether you have sensed some passages as more in Pat Belanoff's voice and others in Peter Elbow's voice.)

a. What's in a name? A reader noticed something funny about Dassant's *New England Pumpkin Spice Bread & Muffin Mix:* It has no pumpkin. Dassant's *Hood River Apple Spice Cake & Muffin Mix?* Yup. No apple. You add those yourself. Moreover, the two mixes list the same ingredients, in the same order. A customer service representative confirmed that the mixes are "basically the same," and gave us permission to put pumpkin in the apple mix, as long as we followed directions on the pumpkin box. "Gosh," notes our reader, "Maybe they should call it New England Pumpkin, Cranberry & Walnut Spice Bread & Muffin Mix. Then they'd suck in the cranberry and walnut lovers . . . without adding a thing to the mix inside!" We didn't have the heart to ask the company what New England and Hood River had to do with anything.

Consumer Reports, Feb. 1999

b. You see, there's a simple reason our elected officials consistently fail to function. They are stupid. (Not all. There are 17 who actually know what they are doing.) Please don't look for anything more complex. They are dumb, that's all. End of story.

As a matter of fact, if you take a close peek at them you will see a herd of peabrains who are today—this very moment—holding the best job they will ever have. And they're lucky to be employed, because who would hire them?

You wouldn't put them behind the counter at the J&J Variety in Waltham because they steal. You couldn't have them wait tables at the Stockyard because they are so slow they could not remember a food order.

Exploring the Writing Process

Toward the end of his life, Mark Twain started dictating his autobiography to a secretary—lying in bed each morning smoking cigars. He wrote about this method to William Dean Howells.

You will never know how much enjoyment you have lost until you get to dictating your autobiography; then you will realize, with a pang, that you might have been doing it all your life if you had only had the luck to think of it. And you will be astonished (& charmed) to see how like *talk* it is, & how real it sounds, & how well & compactly & sequentially it constructs itself, & what a dewy & breezy & woodsy freshness it has, & what a darling & worshipful absence of the signs of starch, and flatiron, & labor & fuss & the other artificialities! Mrs. Clemens is an exacting critic, but I have not talked a sentence yet that she has wanted altered. There are little slips here & there, little inexactnesses, & many desertions of a thought before the end of it has been reached, but these are not blemishes, they are merits, and their removal would take away the naturalness of the flow & banish the very thing—the nameless something—which differentiates real narrative from artificial narrative & makes the one so vastly better than the other—the subtle something which makes good talk so much better than the best imitation of it that can be done with a pen.

Selected Mark Twain

Pick up trash? Why, they take 12 months to do eight hours of work as it is now; your Christmas tree would still be at the curb on Decoration Day.

Park cars? You'd no sooner leave the lot than they would retain one of their idiotic cousins to handle the vehicle because they have this genetic defect that causes them to pack anything—a payroll or the front seat of a Ford Escort—with some relative who couldn't beat Lassie at Scrabble.

Mike Barnicle, *The Boston Globe* 5 Jan. 1993

c. You may not live on the edge, but you can drive right up to it. If you listen closely, you can hear it call your name. It's the night. A bit playful. Somewhat mysterious. Always intoxicating. And with the available V6 power of your new Camry, you're ready to roll into it. By all means. After all, the night is still young.

From an advertisement for the Toyota Camry, *The New Yorker* 8 Feb. 1999 (reprinted on p. 128)

d. *Simplified Method.* The following discussion outlines the rules that apply for using the Simplified Method. *What is the Simplified Method?* The Simplified Method is one of the two methods used to figure the tax-free part of each annuity payment using the annuitant's age (or combined ages if more than one annuitant) at his or her (or their) annuity starting date. The other method is the General Rule (discussed later).

From the Internal Revenue Service's *Tax Guide for 1998: Individuals*

e. INTELLECTUAL WOMAN SEEKS REAL GUY. I'm a 50-year-old babe, slender, divorced, mother of one. You're a smart Mr. Fix-it with muscles. You hate classical music, love Motown, never set foot in a museum, read only when forced to. You like hanging out, eating pizza, and drinking beer. Financially secure. Send note and photo (of you and/or your truck).

Personal advertisement, *New York Review of Books* 18 Feb. 1999

Exercises to Help You Explore Your Own Voices

Our goal here is to give you a better sense of the different voices that already exist in your writing. On the basis of what you learn, you will be able to take more control of the voices you use in order to fit them better to different readers—and to fit them better to yourself.

Start by gathering passages from your own writing. Look among all the pieces and kinds of writing that you can find—writing you've done in this course and writing you've done for other reasons—and find as many passages as you can with *different* voices or tones or moods. Short passages of just a couple of paragraphs will do just fine. You may think that you always write in the same voice, but if you look carefully—listen carefully—you'll find much more variety than you expected.

The pieces you've written in this course on different topics will probably show variations in voice. If you have old papers around, they may show

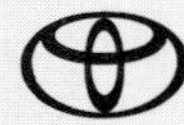

Courtesy Toyota Motor Sales, USA, Inc.

changes in your written voice over time. But don't just look at papers. You've done much more writing. Look at stories, poems, freewriting, early drafts, journal writing, personal notebooks, notebooks you keep for other classes (where you sometimes write notes to yourself or friends), notes to roommates, letters to friends or family, more formal letters you've had to write such as job applications. If you use e-mail and can find copies of things you've written, you'll probably find passages with notable voices. (E-mail is particularly interesting because it is *writing,* but people use it more as though they were speaking. Notice the little smiley faces and "emoticons" people use there to signal tone of voice.)

But don't forget—and this is one of the most important things to investigate—that you can often find different voices in just one paper. Papers often start off in one voice, sometimes a somewhat stiff or neutral or careful voice. Then they may change voice as the writer gets warmed up. Sometimes writers slide into yet other voices when they provide examples, relate anecdotes, and make asides or digressions. (And how about those parentheses? You never know what you're going to sound like once you put in a parenthesis.)

Try to find one or two passages that you feel comfortable with that somehow feel "like you"—sound the way you want to sound. You may be able to find *different* voices that still feel comfortably like you. But try also to get passages that feel *uncomfortable*—to illustrate what happens to your voice when you somehow don't manage to sound as you wish. It can be productive to get a friend to help you look for passages with different voices. Sometimes other people have an easier time noticing differences in voice.

We hope that you'll gather enough passages—at least 10 or more—to make a rich, full collage of your writing voices. But if you are not going to make a collage, you can do the following exercises with only four or five passages in different voices.

The goal now is to work on hearing and understanding your different writing voices better and figuring out how they work. Get into pairs or small groups and try out the three exercises you did above, but this time use them on your own writing.

1. Perform the words to see what the voice sounds like.
2. Inhabit the voice and write in this voice about something completely different.
3. Describe the voice.

The biggest benefit from these exercises will come from the first two exercises because the main way that you learn about voice and develop your voice is not by analyzing but by getting voices into your ear and mouth and body—so that the voices just *come out of you.*

It might feel a little uncomfortable or unsafe to let other people do these role-playing exercises on your writing. Other people are likely to exaggerate or even slip into a bit of parody. So it's fine to do the first two exercises yourself and let others describe the voices they hear in your passages. But if you feel brave and don't mind a little play or stretching of your voices, you will learn a lot from letting others do the first two exercises on your passages.

In any event, the goal is to find the voices in your writing and bring them to life. It helps to experiment and stretch. Remember that your ultimate goal is to get more awareness and control over voice in writing, to use different voices in your writing depending on the situation, and to develop and use a voice that feels right for you—probably one that you feel comes from a deeper part of you. When you get such voices, you and your listeners will often know it right away. They'll feel a click or resonance.

Sometimes a problem crops up. A reader says to you, "Yes, that's it; that's strong; that's you," but you'll feel, "No, that's not how I want to sound; that's not me." This is an interesting dilemma. There are no easy answers. In our experience, voices that are stronger and more resonant with you are not necessarily voices you like. Our strongest voices may not be "nice." In his *Writing With Power,* Peter Elbow observed that sometimes you have to choose between a voice you *like* and a voice that is *strong*—strong enough so that others will actually sit up and listen to you.

Of course, you are not necessarily trying to decide on *one right voice* for you. There probably is no such thing. You need different voices for different situations. Nevertheless, try to get a feel for when a voice feels right for you and when it doesn't. You may begin to get a sense of a kind of voice or range of voices that you recognize as yours, and other voices that seem definitely wrong or unfitting for you.

You may have a final question: "All these exercises are about exploring and listening for voice in writing. What about your first goal: learning to get more voice into my writing?" We haven't forgotten that goal. You'll find that all the trying out, rendering, and inhabiting different voices—*out loud*—will have

Exploring the Writing Process

I feel caught between two cultures. When I have to write a letter to my family and friends back in Korea, I realize that I have lost the eloquence of my native language. In particular, I have forgotten lots of Chinese characters that are used frequently in written Korean. I hardly read or speak Korean these days since I have to write, read, and speak English every day. While I feel sad about losing touch with my native tongue, I also strongly feel that as a foreigner living in this country I must master English in order to survive. Instead of feeling as though I am lost and split between these two cultures, I should feel enriched since I am bilingual and can enjoy both cultures.

I used to write poems when I was in college back in Korea. The colors that emerged from my poems were frequently black and white as I would write about darkness, human suffering, snow, and so on. I remember that I used to be afraid of darkness when I was little, but as I grew up, I became fascinated by the secrecy that darkness implied. While I, as a college student, searched for some meaning in life, black became my favorite color. I thought that black meant negation and nothingness, but it also could be thought of as a point of beginning from which all things can happen. Since I came to America, I have hardly written any poems. I used to feel inspired to write when I was younger. I wonder whether the reason that I stopped doing creative writing is because English is not my native language, or because I am getting older and don't feel inspiration anymore, or because I have to do academic writing all of the time.

I still dream in Korean even though I dream in English most of the time now. Sometimes, I speak in English to my family in my dreams but I don't remember whether they understand me or not.

Eunsook Koo

the effect of helping you breathe more voice into your writing. The crucial thing is to hear more as you write, to get comfortable with your speaking voice, and to be brave about making a noise. If you do these things, your writing will gradually come more alive.

Main Assignment: *Exploring Voice in Your Writing*

There are three possibilities here:

1. Create a collage of your written voices. (See Workshop 3 for guidance in building a collage.)
2. Choose one of your papers that you would like to revise by changing the voice. It could be a finished paper, it could be a draft, or it could be a long fragment from your private writing or freewriting.

Your teacher may direct you in choosing a piece for revision. Try to find a piece where the voice feels bothersome to you or "off." Perhaps it is wooden and stiff—timid writing; perhaps it is writing where you got carried away with a voice you now don't want to use in a final draft—for example, very hostile to the reader; or perhaps the paper seems to be dominated by a strong voice that now feels corny or fake or overdone to you—for example, too jolly or pretending to be 60 years old and wiser than all other people.

The exercises you have done for this workshop will put you in a good position to do this assignment, but there is no right sequence of steps to follow. Perhaps you will start work on this paper with nothing but a sound in your ear and a feel in your mouth for the voice(s) you are trying to create or with some awareness of the voice(s) you don't like. Or perhaps you can start work by describing or explaining to yourself analytically what those voices are. Our only advice is to use *both* kinds of understanding: first, the understanding that comes from inhabiting the voices by speaking them out loud and getting the feel of the words in your mouth and the sound of them in your ear; second, the understanding that comes from analysis and explanation. Use each kind of understanding as a check against the other.

As you do this assignment in revising voice, you might have the impulse to change even the *ideas* or *content* of the paper. Even if this is a faint impulse, listen to it. When you use a different voice, you are being a different person, or at least are taking a different point of view or speaking from a different part of yourself. It's not surprising if this process leads you to think different thoughts. Thus, you might think you are doing only what is called second-level revising, or changing the muscles, but you will probably find yourself drifting into first-level revising, or changing the bones. (More on this in Workshop 6.) When this happens, it's a good sign.

We offer yet another possibility for exploring voice in your writing.

3. Write an essay that explores your voices—the different voices you find in your speaking situations and writing situations—and the question of whether you sense a single voice—"your voice"—in or underneath or behind them all.

The following questions might help you write this paper:

- What are your important voices? Think back to times when your speaking or writing voice was notable or important. Examples: *(a)* Think of a person you feel comfortable and easy talking to. What is your voice with this person? What does it tell about you? What side of you does it bring out? *(b)* Think of a time when you felt particularly awkward in talking—tongue-tied or artificial or "not you." What was your voice like then? Where did that "not you" voice come from? *(c)* Think of a time when you spoke with particular intensity and conviction. Perhaps you were mad or sad or excited. As you spoke, you could feel, "Yes. This is right. I'm saying what I really need to say and damn it, I'm saying it so my listener *has* to hear it." What was your voice like? What part of you was it bringing out? In short, think about how certain people or occasions bring out different voices in you. Try freewriting or role-playing in those various voices. See what those voices want to say.
- What are some of the voices you have heard that have been important in your life: family, friends, teachers, coaches? A bunch of friends who hang around together often start sounding alike. Most of our voices have even been influenced by voices of characters in public life, on TV or radio, in books, in church, and in school—voices we hear often that carry weight or authority. Think of phrases that reverberate in your ear or your memory from some of these people. ("I have a dream." "Winning isn't the main thing, it's the only thing." "Just do it.") Listen to the important phrases in your mind's ear—listen to *how* the person says it—and write about that voice and its meaning for you.
- What voices and parts of yourself do you show in speech but have a hard time using in writing? What parts of yourself come out in writing but don't show in speech?
- Where would you put yourself on this continuum: At one end are people who feel they have a single, "real" voice that represents their real self (despite variations in tone in different situations); at the other end are people who feel that none of the voices they use are more real or "theirs" than any others. In short, what do you see as the relationship between your "real self" and your "real voice"?

Suggestions for Collaboration

Write a collaborative essay comparing the voices of two or three of you. Each of you should start by making a collage of passages of your own writing—passages that illustrate your different voices. This first step can be done individually, but it's helpful to enlist the aid of your partner(s) in choosing among possible passages and deciding what order to put them in. Then write your collaborative essay comparing the constellation of voices each of you has. Possible questions: Does one of you have a wider or narrower range of voices? What are the feelings that each of you has about various voices and their range? How do the voices seem to relate to the person's identity as seen by herself and seen by others? Do certain voices seem less legitimate? Do certain voices have a particular history?

Sharing and Responding

For the Collage Assignment

- Among the various voices in my collage, tell me which are most striking and interesting to you. Describe those voices and tell me why they interest you.

For the Revision Assignment

- Describe the main voice or voices you hear in my revised version. How is it (are they) different from the voice(s) of my piece before it was revised? Try describing the voices in terms of clothing—jeans? baggy sweater? jacket and tie?
- Describe any changes or variations of voice you can hear within the single piece of writing (for example, from confident to timid or serious to humorous). Do these changes or variations work, or are they a problem for you?
- Do you hear any echoes of outside voices—voices that are not mine? Have I made them part of my voice, or do they seem undigested or unassimilated?

For the Essay about My Voice

- What can you learn from my essay that you can apply to your own writing?

Process Journal

- Talk about how you experienced the three exercises for exploring voices in writing: performing a voice, role-playing the person in the voice, and describing the voice.
- Did this workshop make you notice voices of yours that you hadn't noticed before? Or change your feelings about some of the voices you were aware of?
- When you were revising your paper for voice, what changes in content or point of view did you notice?
- Which parts of you are brought out by the voice you used in your revision?
- The questions for the third assignment (see page 132) also make good process questions.

Exploring Theory: *About the Human Voice*

Here are some facts about the human voice. These are not quite "innocent facts" since we intend them to show why *voice* is such a suggestive and resonant term for the understanding of writing. But we think you will agree that they are nevertheless "true facts."

- Voice is produced by the body. To talk about voice in writing is to import connotations of the body into the discussion and, by implication, to be interested in the role of the body in writing.
- People almost always learn to speak before they learn to write. Normally we learn speech at such an early age that we are not aware of the learning process. Speech habits are laid down at a deep level. Also, in the development of cultures, speaking comes before writing.
- We can distinguish two dimensions to someone's "voice": the *sound* of their voice and the *manner* or style with which they speak. The first is the quality of noise they make based as it were on the physical "instrument" they are "playing," and the second is the kind of "tunes, rhythms, and styles" they play on their instrument.
- We identify and recognize people by their voices—even when they have a cold or over a bad phone connection. We often recognize people by their voices even after a number of years. Something constant persists despite the change.
- People have demonstrably unique voices: Voice prints are as certain as fingerprints for identification. This might suggest the analogy of our bodies being genetically unique, but our voice prints are less dependent upon genes than our bodies are.
- Despite the unique and recognizable quality of an individual's voice, we all display enormous variation in how we speak from occasion to occasion. Sometimes we speak in monotone, sometimes with lots of intonation. And we use different "tones" of voice at different times; for example, excited, scared, angry, sad. Furthermore, we sometimes speak self-consciously or artificially, but more often we speak with no attention or even awareness of how we are speaking. The distinction between a "natural" and "artificial" way of talking is theoretically vexed, but listeners and speakers often agree in their judgments of whether someone is speaking naturally or artificially on a given occasion.
- Our speech often gives a naked or candid picture of how we're feeling: Our voice quavers with fear or unhappiness or lilts with elation or goes flat with depression. People sometimes detect our mood after hearing nothing but our "hello" on the phone. Our moods often show through in our writing too—at least to very sensitive readers—but it's easier to hide how we're feeling in our writing. We can ponder and revise the words we put on paper. Speaking is harder to control, usually less self-conscious, closer to "autonomic" behavior. Cicero says the voice is a picture of the mind. People commonly identify someone's voice with *who* he or she is—with their character—just as it is common to identify one's self with one's body. (The

word *person* means both body and self, and thus it suggests a link between the person and the sound of the voice as produced by the body. *Persona* comes from a Greek word for the mask used in dramatic performances, masks which amplified actors' voices.)

- Audience has a big effect on voice. Partly it's a matter of *imitating* those around us; just as we pick up words and phrases from those we spend time with, or pick up a regional accent, so we often unconsciously imitate the ways of talking that we constantly hear. Partly it's a matter of *responding* to those around us; that is, our voice tends to change as we speak to different people, often without awareness. We tend to speak differently to a child, to a buddy, to someone we are afraid of. Peter Elbow's wife says she can hear when he's speaking to a woman on the phone. Some listeners seem to bring out more intonation in our speech.
- There are good actors, on and off the stage, who can convincingly make their voices seem to show whatever feeling or character they want.
- People can become just as comfortable in writing as in speaking. Indeed, we are sometimes deeply awkward, tangled, and even blocked in our speaking.
- Though voice is produced by the body, it is produced out of *breath:* something that is not the body and which is shared or common to us all, but which always issues from inside us and is a sign of life. This may partly explain why so many people have been so tempted to invest voice with "deep" or even "spiritual" connotations.
- Voice involves sound, hearing, and time; writing or text involves sight and space. The differences between these modalities are profound and interesting. (To try to characterize these modalities, however, as Walter Ong has done at length, is speculative; I must resort briefly to parentheses here. Sight seems to tell us more about the outsides of things, sound more about the insides of things. In evolution, sight is the most recent sense modality to become dominant in humans—and is dealt with in the largest and most recent parts of the human brain. Sight seems to be most linked to rationality—in our brain and our metaphors—for example, "Do you see?" But there are crucial dangers in going along with Ong and others in making such firm and neat associations between certain *mentalities* and orality and literacy, especially for the teaching of writing.)
- Spoken language has more semiotic channels than writing. That is, speech contains more channels for carrying meaning, more room for the play of difference. The list of channels is impressive. For example, there is volume (loud and soft), pitch (high and low), speed (fast and slow), accent (yes or no), and intensity (relaxed and tense). Note that these are not just binary items, for in each case there is a huge range of subtle degrees between extremes. In addition, each case has patterned sequences; for example, tune is a pattern of pitches; rhythm is a pattern of slow and fast and accent. Furthermore there is a wide spectrum of timbres (breathy, shrill, nasal); there are glides and jumps; there are pauses of varying lengths. Combinations of *all* of these factors make the possibilities dizzying. And all

these factors carry meaning. Consider the example of the subtle or not so subtle pause as we are speaking, the little intensity or lengthening of a syllable—and all the other ways we complicate the messages we speak. We can't do those things in writing.

It's not that writing is poverty striken as a semiotic system. But writing has to achieve its subtleties with fewer resources. A harpsichord cannot make gradations of volume the way a piano can, but harpsichordists use subtle cues of timing to communicate the *kind* of thing that pianos communicate with volume. Mozart had fewer harmonic resources to play with than Brahms. He had to do a lot with less. To write well is also to do a lot with less. If we are angry, we sometimes press harder with the pen, break the pencil lead, hit the keys harder, or write the words all in a rush. In such a mood our speech would probably sound very angry, but none of these physical behaviors shows in our writing.

A Collage of Passages about Voice

With the people I know very well, I find that all of the emotion which would normally be expressed in the face is there in the voice: the tiredness, the anxiety, the suppressed excitement and so on. My impressions based on voice seem to be just as accurate as those of sighted people.

John M. Hull, *Touching the Rock: An Experience of Blindness*

Ever since I was first read to, then started reading to myself, there has never been a line read that I didn't hear. As my eyes followed the sentence, a voice was saying it silently to me. It isn't my mother's voice, or the voice of any person I can identify, certainly not my own. It is human, but inward, and it is inwardly that I listen to it. It is to me the voice of the story or the poem itself. The cadence, whatever it is that asks you to believe, the feeling that resides in the printed word, reaches me through the reader-voice. I have supposed, but never found out, that this is the case with all readers—to read as listeners—and with all writers, to write as listeners. It may be part of the desire to write. The sound of what falls on the page begins the process of testing it for truth, for me. Whether I am right to trust so far I don't know. By now I don't know whether I could do either one, reading or writing, without the other.

My own words, when I am at work on a story, I hear too as they go, in the same voice that I hear when I read in books. When I write and the sound of it comes back to my ears, then I act to make my changes. I have always trusted this voice.

Eudora Welty, *One Writer's Beginnings*

A dramatic necessity goes deep into the nature of the sentence. Sentences are not different enough to hold the attention unless they are dramatic. No ingenuity of varying structure will do. All that can save them is the speaking tone of voice somehow entangled in the words and fastened to the page for the ear of the imagination. That is all that can save poetry from sing-song, all that can save prose from itself.

Robert Frost, *A Way Out*

That second voice—the distinctive mode of expression, the expected quirks and trademark tone, the characteristic attitude of writer toward reader and subject—has taken over as the meaning of voice in writing today. Hemingway had a voice: spare, selective, easily parodied because readily identifiable.

This is not necessarily the natural voice of the writer; for example, I knock myself out in these language pieces to adopt a scholarly breeziness, respectfully flip and deliciously tedious—a darting-about voice far different from my march-over-the-cliff, calumnious polemics on the op-ed page. Voice is not essence, but is essential to separate the writer from the pack. (That sentence is in a didactic, op-ed voice, and has no place in this light and airy space.)

William Safire, from "The Take on Voice"

“Women’s talk,” in both *style* (hesitant, qualified, question-posing) and *content* (concern for the everyday, the practical, and the interpersonal) is typically devalued by men and women alike. Women talk less in mixed groups and are interrupted more often. By the late 1970s feminist sociologists and historians had begun to describe and contrast the private domestic voice of women with the public voice of men and to tie such differences in voice to sex-role socialization. And Carol Gilligan had begun to write about hearing “a different voice” as women talked about personal moral crises and decisions.

What we had not anticipated [when we began our book] was that “voice” was more than an academic shorthand for a person’s point of view. Well after we were into our interviews with women, we became aware that it is a metaphor that can apply to many aspects of women’s experience and development. In describing their lives, women commonly talked about voice and silence: “speaking up,” “speaking out,” “being silenced,” “not being heard,” “really listening,” “really talking,” “words as weapons,” “feeling deaf and dumb,” “having no words,” “saying what you mean,” “listening to be heard,” and so on in an endless variety of connotations all having to do with sense of mind, self-worth, and feelings of isolation from or connection to others. We found that women repeatedly used the metaphor of voice to depict their intellectual and ethical development; and that the development of a sense of voice, mind, and self were intricately intertwined.

Mary Belenky, Nancy Goldberger, Blythe Clinchy, Jill Tarule, from *Women’s Ways of Knowing*

So poets have been considered unbalanced creatures . . . They are in touch with “voices,” but this is the very essence of their power, the voices are the past, the depths of our very beings. It is the deeper, not “lower” (in the usually silly sense) portions of the personality speaking, the middle brain, the nerves, the glands, the very muscles and bones of the body itself speaking.

William Carlos Williams, from “How to Write”

I am writing a story in my journal . . . I make my way through layers of acquired voices, silly voices, sententious voices, voices that are too cool and too overheated. Then they all quiet down, and I reach what I’m searching for: silence. I hold still to steady myself in it. This is the white bland center, the level ground that was there before Babel was built, that is always there before the Babel of our multiple selves is constructed. From this white plenitude, a voice begins to emerge: it’s an even voice, and it’s capable of saying things straight, without exaggeration or triviality. As the story progresses, the voice grows and diverges into different tonalities and timbres; sometimes, spontaneously, the force of feeling or of thought compresses language into metaphor, or an image, in which words and consciousness are magically fused. But the voice always returns to its point of departure, to ground zero.

Eva Hoffman, from *Lost in Translation: A Life in a New Language*

The Composing Game

A Poem for Two Voices

Sherry Russell

Words	Words
	sharp-edged,
	insolent and
	blind,
delicious,	
round and	
soft,	
insistent, loud and shouting.	insistent, loud and shouting.
	Heartless, rotten
Dazzling, brilliant	
words	words
	sneaking,
streaking,	
	deceptive and spineless,
spicy and strong,	
onto the page.	onto the page.
Words	Words
	like shrapnel,
	tearing and gutting,
like light,	
illuminating,	
powerful,	powerful,
creators.	destroyers.
Oh you	Oh you,
	fickle pretenders!
beautiful dancers	
You,	You,
	ragged tricksters,
elegant allies,	
	hollow charlatans,
magic makers,	
insatiable temptresses,	insatiable temptresses,
I am yours,	I am yours,
	shackled and beaten.
luminous and complete.	
Ripe	Dry
rich	dusty
regal	adrift
smooth	gritty
silky	gangly
sensuous and	awkward and
splendid	angled
	pale
	lifeless
	and thin
startling	
sumptuous	

and alive

lithe

graceful

soaring
pretty pink tutus

noble
dashing
resplendent
strong

passionate and daring

bright, abundant, glorious
words
without borders.
Word warriors

lovers
raging

living
to breathe.

fragmented

opaque

fake

pretty pink tutus
spiky
sharp-edged
rough

homeless
sour, squalid and faceless

drab, weary, neglected

words
without borders.
Word warriors
fighters

raging
struggling

to breathe.

Speak for Yourself

Susan Faludi

Susan Faludi (b. New York City, 1959) is a Pulitzer Prize-winning journalist best known for Backlash: The Undeclared War Against Women *(1991), a book exploring what Faludi sees as the serious remaining obstacles to women's equality.*

> I am at the boiling point! If I do not find some day the use of my tongue . . . I shall die of an intellectual repression, a woman's rights convulsion.
>
> **Elizabeth Cady Stanton, *in a letter to Susan B. Anthony***

"Oh, and then you'll be giving that speech at the Smithsonian Tuesday on the status of American women," my publisher's publicist reminded me as she rattled off the list of "appearances" for the week. "What?" I choked out. "I thought that was *at least* another month away." But the speech was distant only in my wishful consciousness, which pushed all such events into a mythical future when I would no longer lunge for smelling salts at the mention of public speaking.

For the author of what was widely termed an "angry" and "forceful" book, I exhibit a timorous verbal demeanor that belies my barracuda blurbs. My fingers may belt out my views when I'm stationed before the computer, but stick a microphone in front of me and I'm a Victorian lady with the vapors. Like many female writers with strong convictions but weak stomachs for direct confrontation, I write so forcefully precisely because I speak so tentatively. One form of self-expression has overcompensated for the weakness of the other, like a blind person who develops a hypersensitive ear.

"Isn't it wonderful that so many people want to hear what you have to say about women's rights?" the publicist prodded. I grimaced. "About as wonderful as walking down the street with no clothes on." Yes, I wanted people to hear what I had to say. Yes, I wanted to warn women of the backlash to our modest gains. But couldn't they just read what I wrote? Couldn't I just speak softly and carry a big book?

It has taken me a while to realize that my publicist is right. It's not the same—for my audience or for me. Public speech can be a horror for the shy person, but it can also be the ultimate act of liberation. For me, it became the moment where the public and the personal truly met.

For many years, I believed the imbalance between my incensed writing and my atrophied vocal cords suited me just fine. After a few abysmal auditions for school plays—my one role was Nana the dog in "Peter Pan," not, needless to say, a speaking role—I retired my acting aspirations and retreated to the school newspaper, a forum where I could bluster at injustices large and small without public embarrassment. My friend Barbara and I co-edited the high school paper (titled, interestingly, The Voice), fearlessly castigating all scoundrels from our closet-size office. But we kept our eyes glued to the floor during class discussion. Partly this was shyness, a genderless condition. But it was a condition reinforced by daily gendered reminders—we saw what happened to the girls who argued in class. The boys called them "bitches," and they sat home Saturday nights. Popular girls raised their voices only at pep squad.

While both sexes fear public speaking (pollsters tell us it's the public's greatest fear, rivaling even death), women—particularly women challenging the status quo—seem to be more afraid, and with good reason. We do have more at stake. Men risk a loss of face; women a loss of femininity. Men are chagrined if they blunder at the podium; women face humiliation either way. If we come across as commanding, our womanhood is called into question. If we reveal emotion, we are too hormonally driven to be taken seriously.

I had my own taste of this double standard while making the rounds of radio and television talk shows for a book tour. When I disputed a point with a man, male listeners would often phone in to say they found my behavior "offensive," or even "unattractive." And then there were my own internalized "feminine" voices: Don't interrupt, be agreeable, keep the volume down. "We're going to have to record that again," a weary radio producer said, rewinding the tape for the fifth time. "Your words are angry, but it's not coming through in your voice."

In replacing lacerating speech with a literary scalpel, I had adopted a well-worn female strategy, used most famously by Victorian female reformers protesting slavery and women's lowly status. "I want to be doing something with the pen, since no other means of action in politics are in a woman's power," Harriet Martineau, the British journalist, wrote in 1832. But while their literature makes compelling reading, the suffrage movement didn't get under way until women took a public stand from the platform of the Seneca Falls Women's Rights Convention. And while Betty Friedan's 1963 *The Feminine Mystique* raised the consciousness of millions of women, the contemporary women's movement only began to affect social policy when Friedan and other feminists started addressing the public.

Public speech is a more powerful stimulus because it is more dangerous for the speaker. An almost physical act, it demands projecting one's voice, hurling it against the public ear. Writing, on the other hand, occurs at one remove. The writer asserts herself from behind the veil of the printed page.

The dreaded evening of the Smithsonian speech finally arrived. I stood knockkneed and green-gilled before 300 people. Was it too late to plead a severe case of laryngitis? I am Woman, Hear Me Whisper.

I cleared my throat and, to my shock, a hush fell over the room. People were listening—with an intensity that strangely emboldened me. It was as if their attentive silence allowed me to make contact with my own muffled self. I began to speak. A stinging point induced a ripple of agreement. I told a joke and they laughed. My voice got surer, my delivery rising. A charge passed between me and the audience, uniting and igniting us both. That internal "boiling point" that Elizabeth Cady Stanton described was no longer under "intellectual repression." And its heat, I discovered, could set many kettles to whistling.

Afterward, it struck me that in some essential way I hadn't really proved myself a feminist until now. Until you translate personal words on a page into public connections with other people, you aren't really part of a political movement. I hadn't declared my independence until I was willing to declare it out loud. I knew public speaking was important to reform public life—but I hadn't realized the transformative effect it could have on the speaker herself. Women need to be heard not just to change the world, but to change themselves.

I can't say that this epiphany has made me any less anxious when approaching the lectern. But it has made me more determined to speak in spite of the jitters—and more hopeful that other women will do the same. Toward that end, I'd like to make a modest proposal for the next stage of the women's movement. A new method of consciousness-raising: Feminist Toastmasters.

How Can I, a Vietnamese Girl . . .

Minh-Ha Pham

How can I, a Vietnamese girl brought up on food stamps and green stamps, living in a one-bedroom house with an extended family of eleven on El Paseo Street, have a voice?

My mom warned me never to marry a writer. She said that writers are too sensitive and would never make good breadwinners. She said he'd see a wilting flower and be too depressed to go to work—if he had a job. But probably, he'd just sit at home all day and get in my way.

When I decided to be an English major, she was hurt. *"Con hu qua,"* she would say. She would do anything for me, why couldn't I do this for her? Why waste her money reading books and studying writing? Why couldn't I do that on the side, for fun? In the meantime, law school was where I needed to put my mind. This argument continued through my bachelor's degree, through my master's degree, and through the day I moved to Amherst to begin work towards my doctoral degree in English. In some Sunday morning phone calls, law school is still hinted at.

My parents were more invested in our education than any other parents I knew. I would listen to my friends talk to their parents. Their conversations *sounded* like conversations. They would talk about the weather, new boyfriends or girlfriends, new movies, new books, upcoming parties or events. The conversations I had with my parents sounded more like this:

What are you doing right now?

Nothing. I just got up.

Are you eating well?

Yes.

Are you saving money?

Yes.

Have you had any tests lately?/How did you do on the test?

Yes, I did OK.

Just OK?

In these conversations, I never told my parents which books I was reading or what my essays were about. I never told them the discussions that went on in my classes or my thoughts about the canon, literary tradition, or literature. While I reported back grades and results, I never told them what these grades meant. And they never asked.

I was completely alone in my decision to be a student of literature. I don't say this with any bitterness or sadness. It was just a matter of fact. I knew, as I was making this decision sophomore year in college, that my parents could not support this decision in the same way that they supported my sister's decision to be premed or my brother's decision to study chemistry. While I wasn't sad about this, I found that my writing environment wasn't conducive to the liberal and romanticized notion of "the writer" that I was learning at school.

First and foremost, being a writer meant being an author, having an authorial or authoritative voice. This was very nearly an impossible expectation for me. How can I, a Vietnamese girl brought up on food stamps and green stamps, living in a one-bedroom house with an extended family of eleven on El Paseo Street, have a voice, much less an authoritative voice? I think of Gloria Anzaldúa's quandary, "Who am I, a poor Chicanita from the sticks, to think I could write?"* If I were ever to presume the authority to voice my opinion, I would quickly be reminded of the position of my voice by any one of my family members. Clearly, the question of voice would have to be reworked if it was going to work at all.

The second requirement that I learned writers needed was an audience. You're not a writer until you have an audience. Further, your writerliness is measured by your publications—more publications means more audience which means better writer. But what happens when you don't have an audience? Because all of my writing is personally and politically motivated, my main audience is my family and my Vietnamese community. So to rephrase my question more accurately, what happens when your audience believes that writing is a bad use of your time and their time? Who has time to sit around the house and write? And if they had any extra time to listen to me read my writing, don't I think they'd be working overtime like they do every weekend so that they could make ends meet this month? Clearly, the audience question was going to have to be renegotiated as well.

I lay out the terrain from which my writing had to grow in order to map out the conventions of writerliness that I had to displace in order to make writing feasible. The map of writing as it was laid out to me didn't include all the sidestreets and alleys in which my writing had to maneuver. So, what makes me a writer? Why do I write? Probably the best way to answer these questions is to examine the ways in which I'm *not* a writer, to look at the conventions of writerliness and show the ways that my experience breaks with these conventions.

First of all, I don't write because I love it. Writing has caused a lot of pain for me within my family and within my community. Family secrets or abuses are not meant

---

* Gloria Anzaldúa and Cherrie Moraga, *This Bridge Called My Back* (New York: Kitchen Table Women of Color Press, 1984, p. 163.

for the public to know. Talking badly about one's family in public is an unforgivable crime. The subjects that I would consider taboo are topics that many of my peers write about. This is not self-imposed censorship, though, because I don't write to share my experiences or to heal myself either. That has never been a motivation for me. I never wanted to tell anyone about my family's suspicions of writers because it would be misunderstood as a lack of familial support, a suggestion of a domineering family, another nod reaffirming the tired Asian stereotype of a cold, strict family.

I don't write because it is the only thing I know how to do or the only way I know how to express myself. Writing *is* a luxury. It is a devotion of time to selfish reflections, hubris, and fantastical imaginings in a language that is not nearly as rich as my own. I am not too naive to believe that I deserve to write because this would also mean that I deserve to sit and read and think while many of my family members work 14-hour days in factories and assembly lines to barely make ends meet.

Finally, I don't write because I want to be a writer. That term is as suspicious to me as it is to my mother. The delineation of writing as a profession is a difficult category for me to buy into. My mother would never be considered a writer by the conventions I've laid out because she's never been published, her audience is often a private one, and her writing isn't an expression of voice so much as it is a method of communication. Yet, she is a writer. She writes more bill payments every month than she would care to, she writes family members in Viet Nam often to tell them how we're doing, she writes notes to herself to remember to pick up this or that for my dad or one of us. She's constantly writing. In fact, it would be impossible for her not to be a writer because we live in a writing society. We are all writers.

Of course these explanations only cryptically locate my position as a "writer." The

Process

I think I went about this assignment backwards. Rather than feeling inspired to write about my history as a writer, I disdained the thought of having to put this together. Having to piece together my process of "becoming a writer" was more difficult mentally than living through it.

I began with a lot of confusion. I asked myself why I don't get the warm fuzzies talking about writing the way so many people do. I don't feel that sharing my thoughts about writing is useful to me. I often feel that I'm writing for all the wrong reasons.

Being identified as a writer is often embarrassing for me. I call myself a student. That's it. Yes, I write nearly every day but who doesn't? When I speak with my friends or when I go home, we talk about music, who just had to file for welfare, which new immigration laws were going to affect who, who had to re-mortgage a house in order to pay off a hoopty-car that gets them to a minimum wage job, who had another baby, who's pregnant, who died—writing feels like a small corollary to these things. I feel like I took the easy way out. I mainly take care of myself—no one else. While others that I know are responsible for so many others and have no time for themselves, my activities seem selfish.

So as I sat down to think about myself as a writer, I let myself wrestle with all of these thoughts. I thought about the things I generally write about. Almost always home, family, identity. And I thought about the question that my dad always asks me at the beginning of our phone calls, "What have you done to help someone this week?" This essay came out of all of these things.

Four pages took over five hours to write.

Minh-Ha Pham

problems with voice and audience still need attention because my voice is not my own and because audience is not an essential correlative to my writing.

My voice is meaningless if you don't understand where it comes from. It's a traditional Vietnamese voice, it's an immigrant voice, it's a once-middle-class-Vietnamese-turned-lower-class-American-made-back-into-middle-class-now-hyphenated-American politicized voice. It's a female voice. It's the daughter of a first son and second daughter voice. It's an older sister voice and a younger sister voice. My voice never exists on its own. It only exists in relation to the past and my family. I do not own my voice because ownership makes no sense in my family. My voice belongs to my parents who would say that it really belongs to my grandparents who would say it really belongs to my great-grandparents, etc. My voice is a tool, an heirloom, perhaps, that was handed down way before time began. It was important for me to understand this so that I could know how to use this tool, how to cherish this heirloom.

Needing an audience means that the reason I write isn't genuine. I don't write because I want someone to hear me. I write because I have something to say, something to get off my chest. Once it's written, the point of writing has been achieved. The cause of my writing is synonymous with the effects of my writing. There is no need to wait for a response because there's no time for that. And, as I'm reminded, if my intended audience had any extra time to listen to me read my writing, *don't I think they'd be working overtime like they do every weekend so that they could make ends meet this month?*

Voices I Hear

Bryant Shea

Two years ago I read a Charlie Brown comic strip and the last frame read "The worst thing to have is a great potential." Boy, can I relate to that. In four years of high school sports I never lived up to what anyone thought I could do, including myself. Freshman year it was great: "You have great potential," I would hear and even if I screwed up they would let me try again. By senior year, though, it was "He had so much potential." It was ridiculous; I was a two-sport All-Star and had gone to the state finals or semifinal in three different sports. I started for all the teams I played on, but still I did not live up to my "potential." Every time I do poorly at something I hear that voice in my head: "You had so much potential—if only you had worked harder." It rings in my head constantly "you had so much potential . . . you had so much potential." I really wish I could walk into something and have everyone think I sucked. At least this way it would be a surprise that I was good. Instead good is the expected: great is my "potential." Charlie Brown was right: the worst thing to have *is* a great potential.

That is probably the most memorable voice that rings in my head, but there are others as well. Whenever I do anything stupid I hear my mom's voice saying "Oh, Bryant, why?" No matter how old I get, I still remember her saying that all the time when I made a stupid mistake. She did not get upset; she got disappointed, which I think was probably worse. The first time I can remember her saying that, I was about five. I had gone outside and played in the mud wearing my school clothes. When I came in I knew that I had done something stupid and I was getting ready to get yelled at, but my mom just came in the room and said "Oh, Bryant, why? You know better than that." It was worse than getting yelled at; I felt like I had really disappointed her. Now when I hear that voice I do not worry so much that my mom will be disappointed but rather that I have disappointed myself. Another voice that I constantly hear is that of my basketball coach. Whenever I am doing anything physically demanding and I want to quit, I hear his voice in my head saying, "Come on, Bryant, you know you can do this, work it, work it." I think in the six years I knew my coach he said "work it" about a million times. When I first met my coach he was a basketball instructor at my camp. He used to push everyone to the limit and if you gave less than one hundred percent he got mad. By the end of the week we called him the "Work It" man, because he used the phrase so much. Little did I know that I would have to hear it for four more years in high school. I will admit this, though; his voice ringing in my head has pushed me along many times when I thought I was going to give up.

It is funny how you can translate people's voices into your own. The three voices that I talked about above were all from people I know, but when I hear them, it is me talking. I get upset when I do not live up to my potential, I am the one disappointed when I do something stupid, and I am the one pushing myself to do better when I hear "work it." I guess that everyone has the same thing happen to them; it is part of growing up, I would assume.

Along with these voices that I have of other people, my mind has its own voice. It is the voice that I talk to when I have to figure something out; it's the voice that right now is saying, "Okay, think: what else do I have to write about?" This voice is my conscience and it is what I hear when I do something wrong. It says, "Should I really be doing this" or "wow I didn't think you could be so mean." Everyone has a voice like this and without it we would probably be in a lot of trouble. This voice is what interprets the other voices that I hear and then says, "Listen to what they have to say." I think it would be great sometimes to hear what other people are saying to themselves when they're talking to you. The voice inside your head tends to be much more honest than the one that comes out of your mouth, and most of the time we would be better off listening to our inner voice.

A Collage of Passages about Split Infinitives

(A) SPLIT INFINITIVE. The English-speaking world may be divided into (1) those who neither know nor care what a split infinitive is; (2) those who do not know, but care very much; (3) those who know & condemn; (4) those who know & approve; & (5) those who know & distinguish.

1. Those who neither know nor care are the vast majority, & are a happy folk, to be envied by most of the minority classes; 'to really understand' comes readier to their lips & pens than 'really to understand', they see no reason why they should not say it (small blame to them, seeing that reasons are not their critics' strong point), & they do say it, to the discomfort of some among us, but not to their own.
2. To the second class, those who do not know but do care, who would as soon be caught putting their knives in their mouths as splitting an infinitive but have hazy notions of what constitutes that deplorable breach of etiquette, this article is chiefly addressed. These people betray by their practice that their aversion to the split infinitive springs not from instinctive good taste, but from tame acceptance of the misinterpreted opinions of others; for they will subject their sentences to the queerest distortions, all to escape imaginary split infinitives. H. W. Fowler, *A Dictionary of Modern English Usage* (1926)

(B) *Avoid a split infinitive if you can do so without awkwardness.*

DON'T:

SPLIT INF

X It is important to clearly see the problem.

DO:

INF ADV

• It is important to see the problem clearly.

Some readers object to every split infinitive, a modifier placed between *to* and the base verb form: *to clearly see.* To avoid offending such readers, you would do well to eliminate split infinitives from your draft prose.

But when you correct a split infinitive, beware of creating an awkward construction that announces in effect, "Here is the result of my struggle not to split an infinitive." Frederick Crews, *The Random House Handbook,* 6th ed. (1992)

(C) Our attitude toward split infinitives is the same as our attitude toward ending sentences with a preposition: we don't understand why anyone would care, since we can think of no way in which either affects anyone's ability to communicate written meaning. So, all we're going to do here is tell you what a split infinitive is . . .

The truth about split infinitives is that you're not likely to write ones that seem awful to you. But if you need to satisfy a teacher who penalizes you for all split infinitives, you'll have to track them down. Our suggestion is that if you don't like what your sentence sounds like after you unsplit the infinitive, rewrite the entire sentence. Pat Belanoff, Betsy Rorschach, Mia Oberlink, *The Right Handbook: Grammar and Usage in Context,* 2nd ed. (1993)

Drafting and Revising

Essential Premises

- Writing is not just a recording of what you've already thought, but a way of building or creating new ideas on the basis of old ideas; that is: often you cannot start with the ideas you end up with because these ideas only come to you as a result of your writing or revising.
- Most of what we see in print has been revised.
- While all your writing is a product of your own thinking plus what you've taken in over the years through observing, listening, and reading, drafting asks you to pull your thoughts out of what's already in your mind and revising asks you to focus far more pointedly on what others can help you see and add.
- Revising is hard work.

Main Assignment Preview

If you did the preceding workshops, you've already done a lot of drafting and revising. Any writer's first writing on a subject is a draft. Sometimes the final versions are very close to the first drafts; sometimes they're so different as to seem totally unconnected. Most of the time, they're both connected and different. You've probably discovered that for yourself already.

In Workshop 1 you did quick revising (but nevertheless major revising) by simply cutting heavily to make a collage. In Workshop 3 (loop writing), you were faced with a mass of disorganized, rough, exploratory material from which to produce a coherent draft: You had to go through and choose, discard, shape, and rewrite. *All* the activity in Workshop 4 was revising: a series of quick transformations of parts of your private writing to try out audiences and genres, and then a sustained transformation and rewriting as you worked on your main piece of public writing. (Even your story in Workshop 4 probably involved a bit of revision of the image writing you started with.)

Thus, we've already asked for lots of drafting and revising—just treating both activities for what they are: namely, inherent parts of the whole writing process. We don't want to give you the idea that composing is a linear process, proceeding lockstep from early drafts to first revisions to proofreading and final revisions. Sometimes you don't revise at all, sometimes you mostly revise, and sometimes you're doing new thinking and revising all mixed together. But because of their significance, it's worth making drafting and revising the main focus of a workshop's work.

Many people believe that good writers write something and send it off to a publisher, who prints it exactly as it's written. That's not how it works. When we read something published, we have no way of knowing what it first looked like and what changes the author made—first on his own and then on the advice of editors. But many writers testify to how much they revise and what a struggle revision can be. Here are two writers talking about revision:

> I am a witness to the lateness of my own vocation, the hesitations and terrors that still haunt all my beginnings, the painful slowness with which I proceed through a minimum of four drafts in both fiction and nonfiction.
>
> Francine du Plessix Gray

> I had a difficult time revising this piece. I was never sure if my ideas made sense. I wasn't sure of what I really wanted to say. My feedback groups helped a lot by offering opinions on different directions my original paper seemed to be taking. They helped me to see where my thoughts got hidden somewhere in the words I used. After a lot of rethinking and reorganizing (and also with the help of a classmate's "literary analysis" of my paper), I found my way through my thoughts and realized where my paper should go. The revision process was long and difficult, but I feel it did a lot of good.
>
> Stephanie Curcio (student, process writing)

Our goals in this workshop are to help you better understand the ways in which a draft, through revision, becomes a final piece. We also want to help you understand, as a result of actual practice, how important revision is to good writing. Most of all, we want to show you strategies to help you get better at it.

You will have noticed the note of pain and struggle in the preceding quotations, and you may have painful revising memories yourself. There's no way to make revising easy or fun. Inherently it involves going over work again and again, evaluating, criticizing, and throwing away what sometimes seems like part of yourself. Nevertheless, we hope to counteract the tendency to be too grim or tense about revising and show that, like generating, it benefits from a spirit of playfulness. And, when finished, revision can generate immense satisfaction.

Drafting

Drafting is essentially whatever you do first when you begin work on a piece of writing. Some writers make lists; others do some form of clustering; still others (like us) do lots of freewriting. What's important when drafting is to concentrate almost solely on *what* you want to say. Sometimes an early draft is getting ideas clear for yourself even though you may already have an audience in mind. While drafting, you don't need to worry about paragraphing and transitions or spelling. Some writers end up with a plethora of crossings out in a first draft; that's fine. What this should mean is that you're struggling to get at what you want to say. The two of us often hear a little voice in our heads during this early stage which says, "No, that's not quite it; try again." So we'll cross out what we've written (or delete it from the screen) and rewrite. This isn't truly revision at this point, but a search for matching words to intended meaning.

It's important to stay at this stage and not get bogged down in spelling or punctuation or even with writing grammatically complete sentences. Too many beginning writers don't struggle enough at this stage, but move toward conclusions far too quickly. Try holding yourself back by setting your alarm clock for 30 minutes and not allowing yourself to go back to revise until the alarm sounds. And don't forget that at first revision may well make your writing more chaotic rather than less chaotic. Think about what happens when you add eggs to cake batter; at first they make it less uniform and more messy, but if you keep beating, the batter becomes better and better. It's almost as though the eggs disrupt the batter—and revision can sometimes do that, too.

It's particularly important to keep yourself from spending hours on an introductory paragraph, which is often the hardest part of a piece to write. You can always come back to it, and that's often preferable because you may discover, while drafting, that you really want to say something other (and better) than the idea you started with. It's pointless to waste time on introductions which you will have to discard.

Having said that, we recognize that some writers may have trouble getting started if they don't have a fairly solid point from which to start. If you're one of these writers and struggle with opening paragraphs, we suggest that you limit yourself to writing only a thesis statement (which you may or may not use later) and go on from there.

Quick and Dirty Writing

Before we go into greater detail on revision strategies, we want to make you aware that there is something we call "quick and dirty writing." This is writing which merely records something fairly routine whose content you're absolutely sure of. If you want to leave a note for your roommate explaining why you won't meet him as planned, you probably don't need to make a draft and revise it several times. If you want to explain to your parents where you are, you can simply write something like: "I took the dog for a walk—be back soon."

The message in this is that revising is important, but you don't have to revise everything, and revising doesn't have to be a quest for perfection. And sometimes revising may even squeeze the life out of language: "When I arrived home, Fido appeared restless and kept barking at the door, so I took him out for a walk; I didn't want you to worry about where the two of us might be. We certainly will not be gone for long. I'll see you soon."

Quite a bit of the writing that occurs on e-mail networks is "quick and dirty." Those doing the writing sometimes send a correction notice almost immediately if they see they've given the wrong information. In an e-mail message, you may even see a kind of discursive revision: "When I said 19, I really meant 29 in the first sentence" or "but that's not really what I mean—what I really mean is . . ." Some writers apparently prefer not to go back and revise errors; and some systems make such a move impossible. When ideas become complex, what often happens is that the writer is forced to revise what she first wrote because someone will call into question what she has said or may seek clarification. However, such idea-revision does not result in revising the original text, which in any case is already out in cyberspace somewhere. In truth, most writing appearing on discussion lists is "quick and dirty" and stays that way. But we also know of instances where what someone has written in an e-mail message, probably modified and clarified in response to questions, has become a conference paper or a chapter in a book. In other words, the original e-mail serves as an early draft.

Additional Drafts

When you move beyond "quick and dirty writing," drafting begins. We advise, once you have a complete first draft, that you seek feedback. Your teacher may provide time for giving feedback in the class, or she may not. But you can always find readers and ask for feedback. At this early stage, you should ask for feedback directed at the content, rather than the form. Sharing strategies 1 through 9 in "Sharing and Responding" will be most helpful.

When moving through subsequent drafts or moving toward your final draft, you may well find strategies 10 and 11 most helpful. Or you may want to borrow strategies we cover below as part of our discussion of "reworking or reshaping."

Three Levels of Revising

For purposes of the assignment in this workshop, we are going to think of revision as any stage that occurs after you have a complete piece, though—as we've already said—revision usually occurs at all stages of the writing process.

Many students equate revision with "correcting mechanics" or copyediting. Experienced writers never confuse the two. For them, revision means entering into a conversation with their previous thoughts. They match what they have already written against what they *now* wish to say, and create out of the two a new piece which suits their present purpose. For example, now that we're revising this textbook for a second time, we are aware of the need to include instructions for using electronic media. That awareness has generated the need to revise, not just add. What our premises imply is that revision never stops. But of course writers need to finish things for particular deadlines, and so they revise what they have and submit it—usually with the recognition that if they submitted it later, they'd make additional changes.

Since this is how revision actually works, no one can say exactly what revising is. Probably the best definition is that revising is whatever a writer does to change a piece of writing for a particular reader or readers—whoever they may be (e.g., friends, colleagues, an editor at a publishing house, the general reading public of a particular publication, a teacher, or even oneself). But to help us talk about revision, we're going to distinguish three levels:

1. Reseeing or rethinking: changing what a piece says, or its "bones."
2. Reworking or reshaping: changing how a piece says it, or changing its "muscles."
3. Copyediting or proofreading for mechanics and usage: checking for deviations from standard conventions, or changing the writing's "skin."

1. *Reseeing or rethinking: changing the bones.* When you read over something you've written, you often realize that it doesn't say what you now want it to say. You now see you were wrong, or you've changed your mind, or you need more, or you left something out, or you didn't understand the full implications of what you were saying. The process of writing and rereading *changes you.* At its most extreme, this level of revising may mean that you crumple up what you've written and aim it toward the trash basket: The cartoon image of a writer surrounded by wads of discarded paper is not far from the truth. Most writers feel they have to discard lots before they come up with something they can use. When this textbook first came out, Workshop 3, which is now all about collaboration—using the loop process and the collage as methods—had no mention of collaboration. It was only about the loop process. In the intervening years we got more and more interested in collaboration. As we were revising, we saw we could change the whole emphasis of that workshop.

2. *Reworking or reshaping: changing the muscles.* This second level of revising means that you're satisfied with *what* you are saying (or trying to say), but not with *how* you've said it. Working on "how" tends to mean thinking about readers: thinking about how your thoughts will be read or understood by people other than yourself. Thus feedback from readers is particularly useful for this level of revising. One of the most common kinds of reworking is to improve clarity. Perhaps you realize you need to change the order you present things in; or you need an introduction, conclusion, and some transitions; or you've implied ideas or suggested attitudes that you don't want there.* Most common of all, you simply need to leave out parts that may be OK in themselves (or even precious to you) but that don't quite belong

---

* In the reworking level of revising this book, we found ourselves giving a good deal of attention to the subtitles scattered throughout the workshops: adding some and clarifying many. Having finally figured out what we were trying to say—where we were going—we were now trying to improve the road signs others would try to follow.

now that you've finally figured out what the piece of writing is really saying. These passages clog your piece and will distract or tire readers. (You may not believe we left out a lot of the first draft of this book, but we did.)

3. *Copyediting or proofreading: changing the skin.* This third level of revising is usually what you do right before you hand something in or send it to its most important readers. At its simplest, it means finding typographical errors. At a level slightly above that, it means fixing sentence structure and checking spelling, punctuation, subject-verb agreement, and other features of usage. The spellchecker on your computer can help, but be careful about pairs such as *their/there* and noun and verb endings such as *s/ed*. Your spellchecker won't pinpoint these for you.

A writer needs to do all three kinds of revising and ideally in the order we've described them. After all, there's no point in fixing the spelling of a word or the style of a sentence if you're going to cut it, and no point struggling to reword the presentation of an idea until you know you're going to keep it. But of course writing activities don't always stay in a neat order. Sometimes it's not until you rework the presentation of an idea that you realize that it needs to be cut.

Main Assignment: *Revising on All Three Levels*

Choose a piece of writing that you want to revise at all three levels. It probably makes the most sense to pick something that you feel dissatisfied with so that you know you won't mind doing extensive work on it.

There are two principal resources for good revision: time and new eyes. The best source of new eyes is other people; but if you let time go by, you've changed since you did your last draft, so in a sense your eyes are different. You don't see things the same way any longer. This is why it's so important to try to put something aside for a while and do your serious reviewing after a week or more has passed. This is why we've arranged this text so that you revise something a week or more after you first explored and wrote it.

First-Level Revising: Using Others to Resee, Rethink, or Change the Bones

Share your piece with your group and use them to help you discover aspects of your subject which you have neglected or explore possible major revisions: ways in which you might change your mind or disagree with your earlier draft or reach different conclusions. Or perhaps it's a descriptive piece or story,

Exploring the Writing Process

I just figured out that all this stuff about revising is simply "man-talk" for changing your mind—which I have done and been made fun of for my whole life.

Andrea Warren

and you want to change the whole approach. Here are two suggestions to guide your group work:

1. When you've finished reading your piece (and before oral discussion), allow a few minutes for freewriting. You can write down any additional thoughts you have on your topic or story, any doubts you now have about what you've written—anything at all about what the piece says. Those who have been listening to you should simply pretend that they've been assigned your subject and write their thoughts about it. At the end of this freewriting period, each group member can read what he's written. All this can serve as starters for discussion, but since this is your paper, you should guide the discussion and follow up on what is particularly interesting to you. (The others will have this same chance to be in charge when they read their papers.) You may want to ask your group members to give you copies of what they've written so that you can reread them at your leisure.

2. Another way to approach this level of revision is to ask each group member (including yourself) to pick out the most interesting sentences and freewrite about why they are interesting, what they mean, and so forth. For this exercise you'll have to read your paper twice to your group, but reading twice is always a good idea. (It's best not to provide copies for your group since you want them to focus on your ideas, not on specific wording.) While doing this, it isn't necessary or even advisable for any of you to try to stick to your main idea. Remember, you're trying to explore all aspects of a topic no matter how unrelated they might seem at first.

Revision for the sake of revision can be a deadening chore. That's why we ask you to practice first-level revision as a game. Playing the game may lead you to new insights about your subject which you'll want to incorporate into your writing. (Of course, you don't need the game if you discover you actually do see your subject differently.)

Assignment for First-Level Revising

On the basis of your group's discussion, decide what you now want to say, and then rewrite your paper. Don't be surprised if you find yourself doing more revising than you expected. You may even discard the ideas you started to revise with. That's part of what should happen.

If you find this difficult—for example, if you find you don't want to change what you've said or what the story deals with—do some experimenting anyway. Play with your ideas or story. Revision is usually done in a spirit of clenched teeth and duty, but it can be done better in a spirit of play or even fooling around. The most reliable (and enjoyable) technique for changing the bones of your writing is to role-play. Pretend to be someone else who has a different view or outlook on your topic or issue: a real person you know or an imagined person. Then rewrite or rethink your piece from this person's point of view.

Another technique is to pick a paragraph (or even a sentence or image) and build a whole new essay or story around it. In other words, deliberately try to write something different even if you're satisfied with what your original piece says. It helps to start with a fresh sheet of paper or a new computer file to free you from the original way you developed your ideas.

If you give yourself half a chance, you can get caught up in this kind of play. The words you produce will create their own complex of ideas, which in turn will lead to other words, sentences, and paragraphs. Let the process change your mind-set so that you are no longer striving to write something different from the original version; you're working toward fulfilling some new goal or purpose, one that has grown out of the writing itself.

We know that much revision in the working world is probably reworking, not reseeing. If your boss tells you to write a report about a meeting of a special planning group, you can hardly revise it into suggestions for improving company management even it that's what you'd rather write. Still, if you learn that you don't have to stick slavishly to what you've already written, you can free yourself to use the first drafts as seeds rather than constraints. There are always deadlines, of course, so at some point we have to stop new thinking about our subject and focus instead on refining what we've already said. We think that most students, however, get to this second step too soon; they don't recognize the power and pleasure of the prior step. That is why, in this workshop, we require you to do first-level revision even if you are satisfied with what you've already written.

Once you've made your revision, you can decide whether you want to use it or your original for the remainder of the work in this workshop. Remember: Revisions aren't necessarily better—they're different. Once you understand this, you'll be willing to take risks as you revise: changing everything almost totally, exploring something which seems at first odd or silly to you, trying new approaches, developing some ideas that you don't even agree with. You can throw it all away if you want to. Almost invariably, though, you discover

Exploring the Writing Process

I've just written and revised a paper about freewriting I was writing for a conference.

I procrastinated, as I always do, waiting for special inspiration—it didn't come (usually it doesn't). So I forced it, felt like I was stammering on paper. After 10 minutes, though, I was rolling.

After about 30 minutes of this nonstop writing, I had a good amount of stuff on paper, although I still wasn't particularly pleased with what I had come up with. Still, I had to get it done, so I started working with it. As I did that, more and more came out. Soon I had a rough draft of my paper. But I didn't particularly like it, so I fiddled with it some more. Since I had agreed to read it at a get-together of a group of us who meet about once a month to work on our writing, I had to get it in some sort of presentable form.

I told everyone before I started reading it that it sort of did what I wanted it to do; I just didn't think it did it very well. After I finished reading, the members of the group started talking about the ideas in it—not criticizing anything and not giving me many suggestions, just talking about it.

As I drove home that night, it came to me—I knew what I had to do. I had to reorganize, present what I wanted to say as a story of an intellectual quest, what started me on the quest, what I found along the way, and what I concluded when I finished the quest. I don't know why I hadn't seen this before, but I hadn't. Something about sitting in the group and reading it, hearing it discussed a bit, made it (my text) into an object I could look at from a greater distance and shape in a more logical way. The next day I made these revisions with very little effort.

Pat Belanoff

something substantial that you like—something that you'll want to incorporate into your original. Whatever happens, there's no reason to use a revision simply because it's a revision. And you may now decide you've got two pieces you want to finish up.

Second-Level Revising: Using Others to Rework, Reshape, or Change the Muscles

When you've decided which version of your essay to use, you're ready to practice the second level of revision—reworking. For this, prepare a good legible copy of the version you've selected and use very wide left- or right-hand margins—say, about 3 inches. Make copies for your group. Before going to class, write a brief paragraph just for yourself which states briefly your purpose for writing the paper and the reasons why you chose to accomplish your purpose in the way you did. (Our next workshop focuses more on purpose.) Then, on your copy of the essay, write in the margin some notes on each paragraph. These notes should include a *summary* of what the paragraph says and does (its purpose), and how it fits in where it is. Purposes can include introducing, restating, giving examples, setting a scene, building suspense, giving your opinion(s), describing, moving to another aspect of your paper, concluding, and so forth. (See "Skeleton Feedback and Descriptive Outline" in "Sharing and Responding" for more about this powerful activity.) Here's how one student writer summarized the purpose of a paper she planned to revise at the second level:

> I wanted to make readers see the disco scene, so I described it. But I also wanted to show how silly it is—poke fun at the people in it.

And here are the marginal summaries she wrote about the first few paragraphs of her essay. Notice that she had already begun to think of possible changes:

Outside the crowd waits. Guys clad in their outermost layer of skins, their pants, are nervously looking for their "ID's" within their wallets. Of course they make sure every girl sees the big wad of bills. What they don't know is that there is always a girl in the crowd who decides to light a cigarette and upon doing this sees that the big wad of bills is in fact one dollar bills. News travels fast and soon everyone is laughing at the guys. Then there are the young enticing girls. They look about twenty with their make-up caked upon their faces (you'd need a Brillo pad to scrub it all off), skin-tight Spandex and heels. These "women" are in actuality fourteen or fifteen years old; what gives them away is the way they smoke. They simply don't inhale. The drag of smoke enters and exits in the same dense cloud; they need to fan the air with their hands so as not to die of suffocation.	Introducing, setting the scene, describing people. Also trying to set the tone—being sarcastic. I'd like readers to wonder what's going to happen.

The tension is building, and it seems to hang in the air like a low-lying cloud. The people are moving closer and closer to the entrance as if stalking prey. The doors open and everyone pushes in. Suddenly a pink Cadillac screeches to a halt and the driver gets out. The multitude of people stop! It's as if a spell were cast upon them. "It's him!" a young girl cries.

Showing what happens right before the doors open, trying to get suspense going. Paragraph introduces Mr. Big—sarcastic about him too.

He is tall, dark, and rich! He is wearing a white suit (polyester of course) with a black "silk" shirt. His shirt was, of course, opened to his navel in order to display his jewelry. The jewelry consisted of three rope chains, each varying in length and width, and the fourth was an inch-thick rope chain baring the Italian phallic symbol, the horn. The crowd, still mystified, parted like the Red Sea, allowing Mr. Big to enter the disco. The two-ton bouncers who were once mountains of malice became little pups when greeting him. "Can I help you, Mr. Big?" "Your table is waiting for you, Mr. Big." "You look very nice today, Mr. Big," and so on.

Describes and makes fun of Mr. Big. Moves the story ahead a bit. Shows how people react to him and how phony everything is.

Once that awesome happening settled and passed, the crowd went back to pushing and shoving through the doors. It's really ridiculous to see people who are supposed to be grown-ups react like little children when they see a circus for the first time. If they only realized that the circus they're watching (Mr. Big) gets his ears boxed by his mother if he comes home too late.

Gives my opinion about all this, although I'm not sure why I put it here—maybe because I'm now going to move the scene inside.

Once inside, the eardrums shatter like a drinking glass does when it encounters a high-pitched voice. This calamity happens because of the booming music which seems to vibrate the entire building. Ah, there's Mr. Big and his harem. All the women flock around him as if he were a mirror. He'll make his grand entrance on the dance floor later on.

Describing the scene inside, including Mr. Big. I'm making fun of the women who hang around him. I want to describe everything step by step as people would see it when they went in.

Upon entering, the bar is to the left, and a few steps below is the dance floor. By the way, the steps are notorious killers since many, under the influence of alcohol, forget they exist. On the other side there is the seating area consisting of dozens of tables and black velvet, cushiony, recliner-type chairs. They are the type of chairs you lose yourself in.

This is more description of the inside. The thing about the steps is something I always think about when I look down at the dance floor because I fell on them once. Maybe this should all be added to the paragraph before since it's all description.

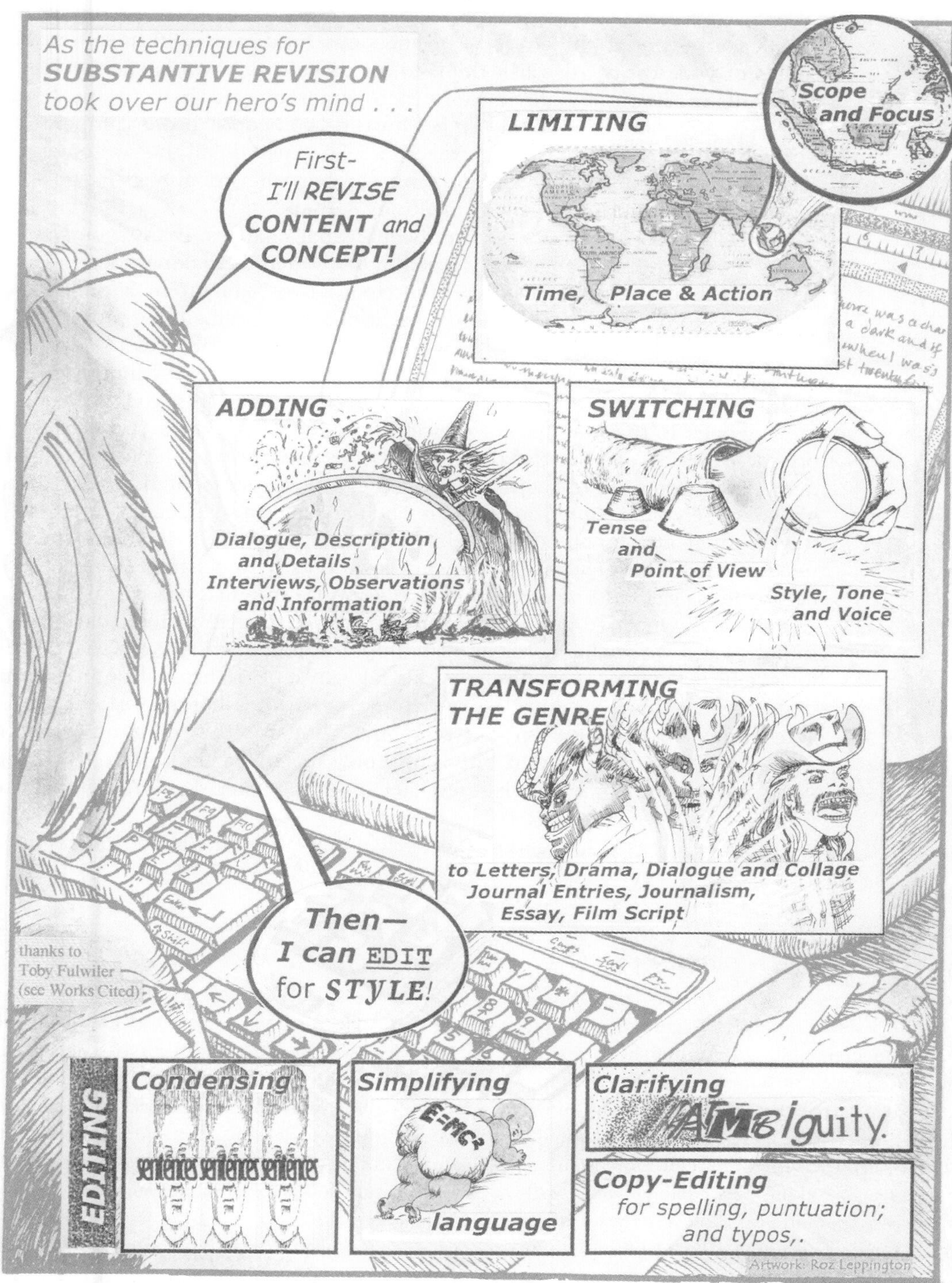

Figure 1 Revision: Start to Finish

Ask your group members to write the same kind of margin notes on their copies of your essay. Also ask them to jot down a few words specifying any emotional reaction they may have to each paragraph: are they curious, bored, annoyed, offended, excited, informed, hostile, etc., and can they pinpoint the words or phrases that cause their reaction? They can do all this at home or in class. If this work is done at home, your teacher will probably give you some time in class to share and get clarification.

Using the feedback you've gotten, decide what changes, if any, you want to make. Most of your changes will probably be aimed at making your meaning clearer. This can include *restructuring* (reordering paragraphs, adding transitions, providing or reworking introductions and conclusions, adding background information), *rewriting* (reworking sentences or phrases to alter their emotional impact or clarify their meaning), and *adding* (everything from new points, to examples, to clarifying phrases). If, while doing this, you find yourself moving back to the first level of revision (altering what you say), don't be surprised. We told you that the three levels of revision cannot be fully compartmentalized. You need to keep in mind, too, that form and content are inextricably linked: changing *how* something is said almost always affects *what* is said.

One final note about this level of revising. Your paper is yours and you need to trust your own instincts about how you say something. We think that before ideas get into words, there is always an impulse toward meaning, a "felt sense." Once we put an idea into words, we test it against that original impulse; and when the words and the impulse match, we know we've got the idea right for ourselves. Sometimes this felt sense of "rightness" comes immediately, sometimes we have to rewrite several times before we feel it, and sometimes we just give up and recognize that, for the moment, we can't achieve it. Our point is that only you know exactly when you've said what you want to say. Someone else may suggest a very nice sentence, but it's no good if it's not what you are trying to say.

In the readings at the end of the workshop we have included drafts and re-

Exploring the Writing Process

Thank you for reading my "rough" (sure took a lot of work to produce something so unfinished—on the computer I lose track of how many drafts I've gone through). When I tried breaking up the exposition, as you suggested, I discovered the need to equally break up the narrative. Then I became more aware of the importance of linking particular episodes with specific discussions (and also discovered a lot of redundancy). I ended up doing a lot of literal cutting and pasting: printed up the whole article, cut it up almost by paragraphs, and then rearranged and taped things together. So I ended up moving from computer back to a physical scroll. (I know the writing process is supposed to be recursive, but doesn't this sound positively retrogressive?) I've never produced anything quite this way before, and I honestly hope that future articles won't be so emotionally demanding. I think I'd now like to tackle some "safe," comparatively dull piece of literary analysis.

Deborah Klein, University of Jos, Nigeria

[*Note: This is the writer's observation after completing a revision of an article that appears in the November 1999 issue of* College English.]

visions of two essays. As you read them, you may want to jot down a list of the changes each author makes. For another example of revising, compare Peter Elbow's Perl writing (Workshop 2, "Readings") and his revision of it into a dialogue in Workshop 3.

Third-Level Revising: Copyediting and Proofreading

When you've finished this second level of revision, type up a final, clean copy of your paper—double- or even triple-spaced. This can be the copy you hand in to your teacher if she uses the proofreading procedure we suggest in Mini-Workshop L ("Copyediting and Proofreading"). Make at least two copies of this final version. You will use them for copyediting and proofreading, the final level of revision. For suggestions on this final, third level of revision, see Mini-Workshop L.

Process Journal

You've probably done some process writing in previous workshops about the revising you did there. But since we haven't until now made revising the focus of a workshop, it's important to try to learn as much as you can about what happens for you in this slippery process. Try to re-create and describe as much as you can of what you did in all the revising activities of this workshop: feelings, thoughts, reactions, things you can learn. If you need help, these prompts may be of use:

- Simply gather as many memories and reactions as you can under the three stages:
  - First-level revising of "bones," or what you said.
  - Second-level revising of "muscles," or how you said it.
  - Third-level, "skin-deep" copyediting or proofreading.
- Freewrite about your own revision processes in the past and about how you feel about revision. Do you revise a great deal? If so, why? What writings of your own are you the most reluctant to revise? Why? When you revise, which level do you most tend to work at?
- At what points in your writing do you tend to stop and fix things? Is it frequent? What triggers you to stop the flow of words and go back to change something?
- Read "Exploring Theory: *Revising and Grammar*" and write in your journal about some of your experiences with grammar.

Exploring Theory: *Revising and Grammar*

Many people think that learning to write means learning grammar. When we ask students at the beginning of a semester what they expect from our course, many say they expect to be taught grammar. They rarely understand that "grammar mistakes" (deviations from standard usage such as subject-verb agreement, spelling, tense forms, and so forth) do not usually lead to a distortion of meaning, though, of course, they can. But deviations from standard usage can be quite *distracting* for many readers. Each of us can probably tolerate a different level of deviation. Some people can read a whole paper in which the final "s" is missing from present-tense verbs and not react. Others will react to even one missing "s."

The real problem with errors in usage is that they force readers into giving attention to the words instead of the meaning. If readers are continually distracted in this way, they begin to believe that the author's meaning is unclear, the organization is poor, or the quality of thinking is mediocre. Or they'll think that the writer is not very committed to the ideas she's presenting, and if that's the case, why should the reader give them much attention?

There is a continuing debate in scholarly and pedagogical journals about whether to teach grammar and usage in writing courses. Here is our position:

- Instruction in grammar cannot serve as a substitute for instruction in writing.
- What students learn from doing grammar exercises rarely transfers to their writing.
- There is a need for discussion about what people mean by "standard usage"—along with its function in society and its relation to nonstandard dialects.
- Elimination of certain usage errors (particularly the dropping of "s"—as in *she see*—and the use of phonetically induced forms—*she could of done it*) is a slow process. We cannot expect students to alter very quickly something so basic to their natural language.
- Instruction in standard usage should focus on the errors students actually make and the contexts in which they make them.
- Students should be forced to articulate for themselves the reasons why they use nonstandard forms. Only in this way can they begin to build different rules into their personal language.
- Students should be required to submit final copies of their revised pieces that are free from errors in typing and usage. We believe in giving students some help in achieving this, but what's most important is making them realize that they have to find whatever help they need. Students who are poor spellers, for instance, may always have to find someone who is willing to check their papers for all misspelled words. Spellcheckers on computers are a godsend for such students. Remember, however, that a spellchecker cannot tell you that "there" should be "their," and it won't tell you that *form* is incorrect when you meant *from*. It may well be that computers will soon be supplied with easy programs for checking some other aspects of usage. In any event, we believe students must find ways to write Standard English whenever they want or need to. This does not mean we consider Standard English superior to other varieties; in fact, we encourage students to

hold on to their native dialects, whatever they may be. Such dialects give language life and often gradually serve to renew Standard English. Nevertheless, students need to be proficient in Standard English if they want to avoid being discriminated against and having certain doors slammed in their faces.

Drafts and Revisions of "The Graham Report"

Kimberly Graham

The Male Bashing Stereotype—Early Draft

Why did we, as a society, need to create a term such as "male bashing"? What is it? Who is guilty of it?

Many women are now feeling dissatisfied with aspects of their lives that they once accepted. They want to be more than housewives. Some want to go back to school in the pursuit of an education and a better job. Many who are in the work force want more power and prestige. Some of these women believe that men are to blame for their dissatisfaction; it was men, after all, who controlled most parts of their lives. They married men and became housewives. Most of their bosses are men. Are women needing a scapegoat? Women are very demanding; they like to intimidate men, and if they do not get what they want, they do not see a future in their relationship with them. To vent their frustrations they resort to male bashing. They blame men for everything. If their car wasn't fixed right, it was because the mechanic was a man. When a crime is committed against a woman, they blame all men. If a female co-worker was sexually harassed by her boss, they assume all male bosses would do the same thing. Male bashing is an overgrown tendency to blame men for every dissatisfaction and to assume all men are alike. It's too bad that we had to come up with this term because it is dangerous and self-destructive.

The media and certain medical circles played a big part in the creation of the term "male bashing." Almost every week on either *The Oprah Winfrey Show* or *Jerry Springer* there is one segment on the state of male-female relationships. Most of the segments include panelists who have just written a "revolutionary" new book, or a group of women (or men) talking about their problems. Inevitably one show turns into a male bashing event because of either a panelist's views or the comments from a participant in the studio audience. One *O.W.S.* was originally about why women marry men who are less financially successful or intelligent than they are. The view at the end of the show turned out to be that women were sick of the games men usually play and they wanted someone they had control over. Men they were used to going out with were egotistical, selfish, cruel, stupid, immature, afraid of commitment, and the list continued. Phil Donahue presented one panel of all men that had formed a "men's club," and the women in the audience felt that they were weak and immature for wanting to be with each other instead of women. There has also been a rapid flow of books written by psychologists and therapists on the state of the sexes. *Men Who Hate Women and the Women Who Love Them* was a bestseller in hardcover and paperback. *Women Men Love, Women Men Leave* is a fairly recent one describing types of women and why men leave them. Books like these give male bashers fuel for their arguments because, as the titles suggest, they put men in a bad light.

One of the most controversial books of late is Shere Hite's new one entitled:

Women and Love: A Cultural Revolution in Progress. It presents the views of 4,500 women and Hite's conclusions from those views. Critics of the book called it inaccurate and false and also think Hite is guilty of male bashing. She based her report on findings from only 4,500 women when the number should have been much larger. She assumed that the views of the participating women were also those of the rest of the female population. For instance, she has concluded that about ninety-three percent of all women are unhappy with their current relationships and about seventy percent are unfaithful but believe in monogamy. It's inaccurate to judge for the many with data from only the few. The book is presented as a testament to the unhappiness of women because of men, and it should be presented more objectively.

The first draft ended here. Following, in boldface type, are questions and comments from the writer's group members and, in regular type, the writer's responses to them.

Do women have a reason to bash and holler? I have to admit—I have met some stupid, immature, egotistical men. But I don't think that all men are alike and I haven't blamed all my frustrations on them. Why do some women resort to mental violence? The media has provided many groupings for men and women. There are the "men afraid of commitment," "the older men only interested in younger women," "the men obsessed with getting ahead in their careers," and "all men in their twenties."

Many women tend to find one fault in a man and turn it into a basis for criticism of all men who have the same fault. Then they find a media grouping and conclude that all men are alike. There are also slots for women: "tired housewives and mothers not wanting sex," "women only interested in having a career," "women living off the men who marry them," and "all women in their forties." If we stopped creating these groupings maybe there would not be bashing against anybody because people would be judged as individuals.

Male bashing is dangerous because it gives men the idea that all women are out to get them. That's not true. Yes, some are, but not all of us are violent militant feminists. It gives society the impression that feminism is to blame and that things were fine before it started. Women guilty of male bashing also put down the concept of feminism. They are fighting for equality, yet they are discriminating against all men for the actions of a few of them. We seem to be going backward in our struggle.

The Graham Report—Middle Draft

What women want—recently there has been a lot of publicity on what women were not getting. And who do we point our lotioned, perfumed hands at? MEN—who else? If we are unhappy, then men, as a race in themselves, are to blame, right? We don't have anyone else to blame. The whole female population is unmistakably guiltless. Why the propensity to turn men into scapegoats?

Him: (While watching the Minnesota Twins win the World Series): Yeah!!! GO, GO, GO!!!
Her: Let's go to a movie or something. Do you want to talk?
Him: Umm.
Her: Was that a yes or a no?
Him: Umm.
Her: Why don't you ever want to talk?

Now, there is a definite problem going on there. The woman (we'll call her June) obviously wanted to talk about something, and she tried to communicate her desire to the man (he's Ward). But her timing was off. Asking her husband, or boyfriend, if he wanted to talk while the World Series was on is like his asking her to meet his mother-in-law while she is applying a deep-cleaning, pore-rejuvenating, look-twenty-years-younger facial mask. Neither the game nor the mask are necessarily important things, but to the person involved, they constitute a sort of livelihood. June could have waited until Ward was done watching the game to ask him to go out. It's common courtesy. Just because it was a man (inarticulately) refusing to talk does not mean that all men would do the same thing. If June had realized how she would feel if Ward did the same to her, then she might have understood his grumbling disinterest. Many frustrated women today are trying to pin the source of their dissatisfaction onto men only, when a more constructive activity would be to look inside themselves and find the core of their pain. It is a difficult thing to do when the easy way out is to blame, accuse, and complain.

A spotlight has been lit on one woman of the last few turbulent decades who has analyzed the state of relationships in the horrendous romantic environment of the eighties: Shere Hite. Her new book, entitled *Women and Love: A Cultural Revolution in Progress,* is fast on its way to becoming a very controversial bestseller. In it she explores the mentality of dissatisfied women and concludes that men play a large, if not total, role in the creation of female frustration.

I say: poop on her. Yes, there are some disgusting examples of the male species—men who proudly and continuously examine just how many decibels their next belch can create (and whether it will crack the tempered glass of their bathroom windows); blind dates who show up displaying their impressionist renditions of nine tattoos scattered extremely artistically upon their mud-splattered arms; college letches who, when confronted with a group of two women and seventeen inebriated fraternity brothers, suggest consuming and emptying all the bottles of Rolling Rock Beer to start a game of strip spin-the-bottle; polyester-clad barflies ambling up to a woman and, in less than two steps, managing to regurgitate the evening's content of alcohol consumed into her lap . . . Need I go on? But it is very important to remember (I know . . . even I am having a hard time after the last sentences) that not all men are responsible for women's anguish. Many people search for scapegoats because they are afraid to admit that they might have made a mistake. A lot of women find it easy to blame men because they know they will receive sympathy from many other women. Ms. Hite has perpetuated the myth of male-created frustration by presenting the views of 4,500 women and applying them to the national population. She has not stated what women want—she has stated what *unhappy* women want.

Why are we bringing up the question of what women want, anyway? Why now? Don't get me wrong; it's not that I think the question is not an important one. On the contrary; I consider it crucial. But why all the clamor now?

I think I have an answer. Now that women have gone out and "done it all"—worked, had babies, entered politics, entered space, developed an argument supporting the metaphysical qualities and the transcendental properties of the color black, drunk a six-pack of Jolt—they are beginning to realize that maybe they overdid it. Stress and burnout are beginning to catch up. In their struggle to prove themselves to society, some women went too far and are now afraid to say, "Hey, I made a mistake. This isn't what I wanted." I can understand why they would be afraid to admit it. Some men would turn around and reply, "You should have stayed in the kitchen where the little woman belongs!!" They have also seen many stressed-out men continue with their struggles, and the women do not want to be the ones to quit. Women have had to prove themselves to society by going beyond what men have done, and for that reason they voice their unhappiness to their boyfriends, husbands, lovers, and so on.

This society would not have to wonder what women (or men) wanted if there were no sexual barriers. Just suppose that there were no physical differences between male and female bodies. Yes, folks, it would be mighty boring, but for the sake of argument, imagine. (Here comes another scenario.)

Ward: Hello Ms. Flintstone. How did the reports on juvenile penguins in the South Antarctic come out on the IBM/PC with color graphics?

Wilma: Just fine, Mr. Cleaver, but I had problems in the area of young penguin street gangs terrorizing the arctic corners.

Ward: Well, why don't you work on it some more and I will get back to you.

Neither Ward nor Wilma has any distinguishing sexual characteristics, so Ward is not wondering what color Wilma's lingerie is while he curses her feminine lack of computer literacy, and Wilma is not wondering if Ward wears boxers or jockeys as she tears apart his masculine egocentricity. Without sexual characteristics people would not be considered men and women separately, but people . . . just people. Then our society would wonder about the wants of everybody as a whole. Definition of this fantasy land: UTOPIA.

The Graham Report—Final Draft

What do women want? Recently there has been a lot of publicity on what women were not getting. WHAT DO WE WANT?? Who has the answers?? Shere Hite? Oprah Winfrey? Ronald Reagan? My plumber? I don't know if I even understand the question.

The original question—what do women want—has turned into the question: What kind of *men* do women want? I cannot speak for the whole female population, but I know what I want in a man—or rather, what I don't want.

I do not desire any man who proudly and continuously examines just how many decibels his next belch can create (and whether it will crack the tempered glass of his bathroom windows). So he drank sixteen cases of Ballantine Ale—big deal! He must be able to control his bodily functions in mixed company. Besides, I do not appreciate his friends' attempting to grade the intensity of the belch by holding up their callused fingers.

Nor do I remain at my door, awaiting blind dates who show up displaying their impressionist renditions of nine tattoos scattered extremely artistically upon their mud-splattered arms. A date is an occasion for which one showers, washes, scrubs, DISINFECTS, FUMIGATES!! And I am not the least bit interested in hearing that the tattoo "artist's" name was Anthony "Michelangelo" Giancanna.

Since I am a female University of Massachusetts student, this next type of man particularly makes me ill. College letches who, when confronted with a group of two women and seventeen inebriated fraternity brothers, suggest consuming and emptying all the bottles of Rolling Rock Beer to start a game of strip spin-the-bottle. What's even more terrifying is when one of them shows up with a Twister mat and a bottle of Mazola. I'm just as fun and exciting as the next person, but, hey, public displays of sweltering lust just aren't my style.

The least desirable of this lengthening list of odd personas is the pseudo-feminist pig who claims to respect Gloria Steinem's every word, while secretly wondering if there exists a small, white, cotton flower embroidered in the center of her brassiere. It is this same sad excuse for a man who, after suggesting an evening at the Four Seasons, thinks convincing a date to pay for a thirteen-course dinner with raspberry crepes and two orders of baked Alaska constitutes a feminist attitude. After all, if she wants to be equal then she should pay for his dinner, theater tickets, Brooks Brothers' suits, an IBM/PC with full-color graphics, a diamond-blue metallic Porsche, a fifty-three-room chateau in the Swiss Alps, etc. The pseudo-feminist pig is also very articulate concerning women's issues and proves it with a phone bill of $3,975.87 to Dial-a-Porn. He is the most dangerous of the undesirables since he has the ability to con unknowing women into thinking that he is compassionate and charming, while secretly wanting to cover them with instant banana Jell-O pudding while handcuffed in the back seat of a mint-green 1974 Chevy Impala.

I do not want to dwell on the above descriptions because, as a feminist, my imagination concerning the various mutant abnormalities of the male species may . . . how can I say it subtly . . . run rampant through the hellish field of sarcastic literary discourse. I have determined what kind of men I don't want. Hopefully these caustic exaggerations will not offend any male egos. As unbelievable as it may seem, I do have a glimmer of hope in the existence of desirable men. But where are they? Do I have to travel to southwest Kansas to find an underpaid tractor salesman who loves to wear the color pink? I suppose there is an Antarctican ice fisherman who is more than willing to relax and enjoy the benefits of my making fifty times more income than he would ever make. Maybe there is a Holiday Inn pool maintenance staff person living in Acapulco, Mexico who knows how to cook homemade turkey soup and double German chocolate cake while diapering an infant. WHERE ARE THEY?

So what does this paper prove? I have come up with an answer to the question of what women want. Or have I? No, the statement is too vague. Society should not generalize—it's an emotional question. I do know what qualities I like in a man: compassion, sense of humor, intelligence, sense of equality toward women, respect for the human race, the ability to read aloud the works of D. H. Lawrence while stirring instant banana Jell-O pudding. . .

Drafts and Revisions of an Editorial for the *Daily Hampshire Gazette*

Kay J. Moran

We see here the role of substantial revising—if not always total rethinking—even in writing that is done fast under a tight deadline. Moran went from her first start to her final version in only a few minutes more than an hour. Normally she works entirely on screen and never prints out copy, but at our request, she pushed the print button periodically and gave us eleven stages to look at. See her cover letter for more about how she works. Here is her first start—which printed out at 9:39 A.M.:

David K. Scott, who grew up on a cold, rocky island off the northern coast of Scotland, was chosen last week as chancellor of the University of Massachusetts Amherst campus.

In July he'll take over at the campus which has made national headlines for its cultural diversity and incidents of racial friction.

Here is what she had a couple of printouts and 15 minutes later (9:54 A.M.):

Many on campus were enthusiastic when David K. Scott was chosen last week as chancellor of the University of Massachusetts at Amherst.

He comes with high qualifications. As a former provost and vice president for academic affairs at Michigan State University in East Lansing, he understands the strengths and problems of a large land grant institution. As a nuclear physicist he can talk to scientists as well as humanists. UMass President Michael Hooker cited as Scott's particular strengths a keen understanding of the role a university can play in economic development, and his knowledge of the emerging world community.

stRon

Story says and humility, honesty and eloquence

to On July 1 he'll take over

who grew up on a cold, rocky island off the northern coast of Scotland, at the campus which has made national headlines for its cultural diversity and incidents of racial friction. Though announcement of his appointment was greeted by many at UMass with enthusiasm, others expressed disappointment and doubt he would be able to improve the racial climate.

He said he believes that, while a public university should reflect the diversity of the whole state, the Amherst campus does not, and he intends to take action after the large

Here is her near-to-final version (10:20 A.M.)—with handwritten changes to show the final version—which was printed at 10:52 A.M.:

A NEW CHANCELLOR

¶indent
Many on campus were enthusiastic when David K. Scott was chosen last week as chancellor of the University of Massachusetts at Amherst, ~~a post he'll assume~~ beginning July 1.

He comes with strong qualifications. As a former provost and vice president for academic affairs at Michigan State University in East Lansing, he understands the mission of a large land grant institution. As a nuclear physicist he can talk to scientists as well as humanists.

¶Scott's particular strengths, said UMass President Michael Hooker, are a keen understanding of the role such a university can play in regional economic development, and his knowledge of the emerging world community. ¶Ronald Story, UMass vice president for academic affairs and chair of the chancellor search committee, cited Scott's humility, honesty and eloquence.

Both are important to the state's — and campus' — future prosperity.

Some on the UMass-Amherst campus, ~~which has made national headlines for its cultural diversity and~~ *where* incidents of racial friction *have made national headlines*, expressed disappointment and doubt last week that Scott, who grew up on a cold, rocky island off the northern coast of Scotland, would be able to improve the campus racial climate.

We urge the doubters to give him a chance. He said last week that racism is an issue which must be discussed; then action should be taken. Furthermore, he said that the Amherst Campus does not now reflect the diversity of the whole state, as a large public university ought to.

For his part, Scott should be careful not to react defensively when he is criticized by those disappointed with his choice, but listen to them carefully. His comment to a reporter last Thursday was a good start: "Those who do not support me remind me of what some of my weaknesses are—and what areas I need to improve."

Cover Letter

My duties at a small daily afternoon newspaper in Massachusetts include the editorial page and writing editorials four days a week. Editorials are unsigned. I write with a police-fire-radio scanner at my elbow, at a desk surrounded by the desks of other editors working on deadline, in a wide-open newsroom. We have to work fast to produce a daily paper. We talk constantly among each other and with reporters. That's part of the job.

You can see on the printout the times various versions of this editorial were printed out. In between, I also edited a page-1 news story for that day's paper, opened mail, took several phone calls and discussed a letter to the editor with a woman who brought it in person. An average morning.

Usually, I think about and research possible editorial topics on weekends and discuss them with the editor-in-chief on Mondays. Research involves reading the news, talking with reporters and others. Hardest are the days I start off with no good ideas, because I still have to produce an editorial.

All writing and editing at the newspaper is done on a computer terminal; I revise and improvise as I go along, as does everybody. The editorial or story develops and is refined as it grows. When it's finished, after a quick final read, I send it (electronically) to the publisher. He reads it, and if he has questions or doubts, we discuss it. Sometimes the discussions get heated, but his is the final decision. In the editorial printed here, he thought describing Scott's island as "cold, rocky" was irrelevant, so he took out those words. I think he was right.

Next, the editorial gets read by two copy editors. Then it is printed out and put on the page.

Kay J. Moran, ***Editorial Page/Business Editor***

Drafts and Revisions of Two Short Book Reviews for *Glamour Magazine*

Laura Mathews, Book Review Editor

What follows is only a small selection from a dozen or more drafts which show a succession of changes—large and small—over a period of a few days.

Drafts of the Review of *A Season in Purgatory*

Figure 1 is a page from Mathews' first, handwritten, exploratory writing. You can see her crossings-out and writings-in. (And what we provide here is neater than her actual page of explorations.)

The first typed draft, which consists of two "draft starts" in the same writing session, follows:

HOW THE RICH GET AWAY WITH MURDER . . . With a daringly identifiable cast of characters, Dominick Dunne's *A Season in Purgatory* (Crown $) informs on a rich and charismatic Catholic family and the murder of a young debutante by one of its wayward sons. Prime witness to the coverup, Harrison Burns is a

~~Famous~~ people

How
The rich and
thin are
different

~~Celebrity spotting...~~

descendants
The ~~children~~ of Joe and Rose Kennedy,
and ~~their~~ numerous cousins, ~~have long~~ been are ~~are~~ favorite models
for popular novelists, ~~including~~ ~~most recently~~ apparently, Dominic
Dunne in his latest outing, A Season
in Purgatory (Crown,). The operative
~~titillating~~ question will be ~~is~~ how literally to take
the novel's ~~unusual~~ ~~murder plot~~ murder plot (though perhaps
not, ~~maybe~~ perhaps, so ~~unusual~~ bizarre from a Kennedy
~~context~~ vantage point). ~~From a~~ ~~In the~~
~~midst of a trial that is 17 years overdue~~,
~~The prosecution's key witness~~
during which a large, rich, insular
Catholic family (here called the Bradleys) marshal their formidable
~~considerable resources~~ a Cardinal? to shut
down ~~the~~ ~~and coverup the~~ an investigation into
brutal slaying of a 15-year-old girl
by ~~their~~ their youngest son ~~the one~~ ~~most likely to~~ ~~to~~
ordained to ~~be~~ of whom great things are expected.

by marriage

Add to the list growing

For ardent Kennedy-watchers,

bizarre

The presumed killer is being tried in a courtroom setting where the
~~As the story progresses~~ the ~~narrative~~ ~~whisks us~~
cash resources, well-maintained ties to the Cardinal, ~~and~~ and local police and, where force is necessary, gangsters

and the loyalty of virtually indentured ~~Irish~~ household retainers

a charismatic ~~but~~ and sexually predatory aggressive 17-year-old prep school student

Figure 1 Mathews' first handwritten, exploratory writing for review of *A Season in Purgatory.*

relatively impoverished prep school classmate of the son's, whom the family plies with hush money in the form of a full scholarship to Yale.

FUN FAKES . . .

Novels inspired by the Kennedys are as commonplace as imitation designer handbags. Titillating in their disclosures, the plots often pass for genuine *romans à clef,* as do *faux* Chanel or Hermès to the undiscriminating eye. A bright red dustjacket evoking Catholic cardinals, blood and flames of damnation announces the arrival of Dominick Dunne's *A Season in Purgatory* (Crown $tk).

The hero is a solemn, fallen saint sort of guy who has carried a burdensome secret since adolescence. Solemn in his disgust, yet transfixed by people whose privilege extends to committing crimes "without consequence."

The typed version that follows is a middle-stage draft. The handwritten additions and changes show how Mathews moved from her middle-stage draft to her final draft. Keep in mind, however, that what you see written by hand is not really one revision; it is the sum of five or six more drafts. Note too that we have not been able to give any indication here of the many scrawled comments and questions from fellow editors that sometimes led Mathews to make some of her changes. That is, the collaborative dimension of writing with fellow editors is invisible here.

• **Rich and Thin** . . .In the "easy reading but not totally ~~sinful~~ junk category," ~~there is~~ A Season in Purgatory (Crown, $tk), is the latest outing by Dominick Dunne (~~An Inconvenient Woman~~). Kennedy-watchers will wonder how literally to ~~take the bizarre~~ interpret the murder plot, in which the Bradley's a rich Catholic clan ~~of sprawling ambition and brawling manners (here called the Bradleys)~~ deal~~s~~ with the mess created by the family's favorite son: ~~Inconveniently~~ Inauspiciously enough,

this future presidential hopeful has smashed the skull of a 15-year-old girl. ~~His weapon:~~ with a baseball bat, ~~identifiable as Bradley property~~ then dragged the body into woods near the family home. /With the help of a visiting prep-school friend ~~who is visiting the Bradley home that same weekend, he has dragged the body into the surrounding woods~~ what follows is a behind the scene primer on the exertion of influence. What does it take, exactly, to silence witnesses and shut down a police inquiry? ~~And how do those in the know live with themselves afterward?~~ The answer comes via ~~in the person of~~ narrator/hero Harrison Burns--the prep school accomplice who, 17 years after is watching his friend confidently deny and get away with murder, ~~has decided~~ decides to break his vow of silence. And talk he does. Writing in his most ~~mea culpa,~~ entertaining, Graham-Greeneish voice, Dunne smoothes any ~~plot~~ raggedness of plot with cunning ~~descriptions of all~~ insights about the little inconveniences of ~~being worth~~ having a lot of money ~~including the privilege of "crime without consequence."~~ and zero integrity.

The following is the final, printed version:

RICH AND THIN . . . In the "easy reading but not totally junk" category, *A Season in Purgatory* (Crown Publishers, $22) is the latest outing by **Dominick Dunne** (*The Two Mrs. Grenvilles*). Kennedy watchers will wonder how literally to interpret the murder plot, in which the Bradleys, a rich Catholic clan, deal with the mess created by the family's favorite son. Inauspiciously enough, this future presidential hopeful has smashed the skull of a 15-year-old girl with a baseball bat, then dragged the body into the woods near the family home with the help of a visiting prep-school friend. What follows is a behind-the-scenes primer on the exertion of influence. What does it take, exactly, to silence witnesses and shut down a police inquiry? The answer comes via narrator-hero Harrison Burns, the prep-school accomplice who, 17 years after watching his friend confidently deny and get away with murder, decides to break his vow of silence. And talk he does. Writing in his most entertaining, Graham Greene-ish voice, Dunne smoothes any raggedness of plot with cunning insights about the little conveniences of having a lot of money and zero integrity.

Drafts of Review of *The Road to Wellville*

Figure 2 is a page or so of Mathews' first, handwritten, exploratory writing. You can see her crossings-out and writings-in. (And what we provide here is neater than her actual page of explorations.)

T.C. Boyle The Road to Wellville

In a story so focussed on gross anatomy (the grosser, the more ~~ex~~ ~~focussed~~ explicit) ~~the woman's organ most conspicuously neglected is the breast~~ ~~emotions are~~ feelings elicited are disgust and a kind of grade school snickering

Lots of emetic, stingy on the tenderness

Too often his ~~contempt~~ ungenial, mocking disdain + cynicism for what his characters are up to, ~~they're~~ their naivete and self-delusions rubs off on them. Then again it's ~~cardboard~~ hard to love cardboard.

~~While~~ Though he redeems them in a final twist spate of ~~selfs~~ ~~discoveries~~ self-discoveries, unmaskings and paybacks

Farcical, lively but not always likable:

A novel destined for the big screen—where casting may add some flesh + warmth to these ~~bare-boned~~ cardboard characters

Emotionally ~~dry as~~ dry as ~~Dry as~~ cornflakes eaten straight from the box

~~His subject~~

American pieties ~~whether~~ ~~have always~~ seem to fascinate~~d~~ + incense T.C. Boyle, ~~and bring out~~ "clean living" being foremost

A familiar complement of Boyle characters: a batty authority figure, a ~~renegade~~ prodigal son, ~~and the~~ a much-put-upon ~~bystander~~ reluctant mediator

Garrison Keillor without geniality, Twain without lovable characters (but maybe Huck grew on us over time)

Caricature without much insight or subtlety regarding motive: People act basically out of greed, lust, vanity or fear

Figure 2 Mathews' first, handwritten, exploratory writing for *The Road to Wellville.*

The typed version that follows is a middle-stage draft. The handwritten additions and changes show how Mathews moved from her middle-stage draft to her final draft. Keep in mind that here too we cannot see all the stages or the comments by others.

Cereal Murder . . . In the early 1900s, fashionable Americans flocked to a famous spa in Battle Creek, Michigan founded by John Harvey Kellogg (inventor of the corn flake and ~~peanut butter~~), to have their colons massaged *by day* and their ears burned *by night* as Dr. Kellogg *delivered his famous vegetarian* ~~exhorted them to renounce beef in his mandatory evening~~ lecture ~~series~~ ("Of Steak and Sin"). Oddly, **T. Coraghessan Boyle** (World's End), seems to be the first ~~novelist~~ to explore the satirical potential of this footnote *to* ~~in~~ America's long obsession with health cures. *His new novel* ~~In the tradition of Ragtime,~~ The Road to Wellville (Viking, $22.50), *is paved with allusions to quack therapies as the story* entwines the quests of three sets of characters: Will and Eleanor Lightbody, a naive young couple ~~from New York~~ who are seeking a cure for Will's indigestion and Eleanor's (unacknowledged) frigidity; the autocratic Dr. Kellogg, *whose adopted* ~~who is tormented by his degenerate~~ son, George *is a meat-eating ingrate in cahoots with Ossining.* ~~the only one of Kellogg's numerous foster children to reject the benefits of five enemas a day; and~~ Charley Ossining, a/n ~~inept~~ confidence man *who hopes to secure* ~~interested in securing~~ the Lightbodys' financial backing *to launch* ~~for a new cereal called~~ "Per-Fo*,*" *a nutritionally perfect cereal; and* Some readers may find Boyle's *humor* ~~comic sensibility~~ too disdainful *and the story's surprise murder too silly.* ~~to hold them in thrall~~. But *at its best, his sending up of* ~~if~~ dietary *fanaticisim* ~~lunacy and medical quackery~~ *cleverly reminds us to the extremes to which Americans will go in pursuit of perfection.* ~~fascinate you, this novel is a health cynic's feast.~~

The following is the final, printed version:

CEREAL MURDER . . . In the early 1900s, fashionable Americans flocked to a spa in Battle Creek, Michigan, founded by John Harvey Kellogg (inventor of the corn flake), to have their colons massaged by day and their ears burned by night as Dr. Kellogg delivered his famous vegetarian lecture, "Of Steak and Sin." Oddly, T. Coraghessan Boyle *(World's End)* seems to be the first to exploit the satirical potential of this footnote to America's long obsession with health cures. His new novel, *The Road to Wellville* (Viking, $22.50), is paved with allusions to quack therapies as the story entwines the quests of three sets of characters: Will and Eleanor Lightbody, a naive young couple who are seeking a cure for Will's indigestion and Eleanor's (unacknowledged) frigidity; Charlie Ossining, a confidence man who hopes to secure the Lightbodys' financial backing to launch Per-Fo, a nutritionally perfect cereal; and the autocratic Kellogg, whose adopted son, George, is a meat-eating ingrate in cahoots with Ossining. Some readers may find Boyle's humor too disdainful and the story's surprise murder too silly. But at its best, his send-up of dietary fanaticism cleverly reminds us of the extremes to which Americans will go in pursuit of perfection.

Cover Letter from Laura Mathews

Dear Peter,

"Glamour Book Editor Tells All"

Here it is—chaos to column, arranged chronologically back to front. If you'd asked to see my drafts from 3 years ago, you'd have received a carton-load. I no longer feel the need to print out every revision I make during the drafting stage. The "hard copy" marked "draft" or "revise" represents the stage of writing where I stop hating my own phrases and feel both focused and productive. I know at that point that the column will get written in a matter of days (or hours) and am willing to let my editor (not the copy editor, but the editor with whom I discuss the month's review choices and my take on them) see a draft. I should point out that, as a writer on staff, I am greatly indulged in terms of deadlines and post put-through revising [revising after going to the printer]. I'm like an addict who'll take advantage of anyone who raises a query: e.g., if the managing editor puts one mark on her galley, I'll answer her question but also use it as an excuse to diddle with other sentences. The point is that there's a great deal more collaboration involved than if I were a free-lancer sending in a monthly dispatch. On the one hand, I have more control over the editing; on the other hand, I'm not as efficient as I'd have to be working on my own (or I suspect that's the case).

One final observation about "voice." When I pick up the issue and turn to the book page to read the final product, what I hear is Glamour's voice, not Laura's.

Love,
Laura

Drafts and Revisions of an Essay, "The Act of Writing as Prayer"

Beth Spencer

Notes and First Drafts

Figures 1–5 consist of Spencer's initial jottings on cards, which she generated when considering what to write about. Figure 6 is her first rough draft, which was handwritten.

Beth Spencer

What are you thinking about now?

- Conversation w/ Bob
- Will's school — a bit irritated
- Ben Mcllellad
- Astrid Daly — high school Biology teach.
- How the edges of trees are starting to turn
- Gerard Manly Hopkins — Pied Beauty
- Day we played PuttPutt in Hadley
- Deceased dog Jaime
- New place, new dynamics, New home
- air conditioning

Figure 1 Figures 1 and 2 show the front and back sides of a card Spencer filled in response to the question, "What are you thinking about now?"

- Rick Bragg's book: All Over but the Shoutin'
- Next two books (1) Dorothy Allison Cavelands
  (2) Kaye Gibbons On the Occasion of my Last Afternoon
- Warm coffee w/ cream
- brown recluse
- minutes, minutes, minutes
- Bob as Will's stepfather — a good match
- ceiling lights here — just like the ones in first grade
- chocolate pudding — lunch

Figure 2

Which one of those do you feel most moved to expand upon? Beth Spencer
G. M. Hopkins Pied Beauty
- Nature, nature of people
- World View
- snakes eye level
- evolution
- vision of the small and intimate
- dream, dream, spring rhythm makes me
- think of Snyder and Edward Abbey
- Desert Solitaire
- Who I am
- Who I am as a teacher

Figure 3 Along with Figure 4 this figure shows Spencer's response to a follow-up question, "Which of those do you feel most moved to expand upon?"

- Spiritual life — expressed as psalm, poem, prayer
- Act of writing as prayer — nontraditional mode
- Bittersweet "and so I did sit and eat"/- Love III
- Being in love colors everything around you.
- Becoming lost in the words and in between the words

william Morris ⟶ PreRap

Figure 4

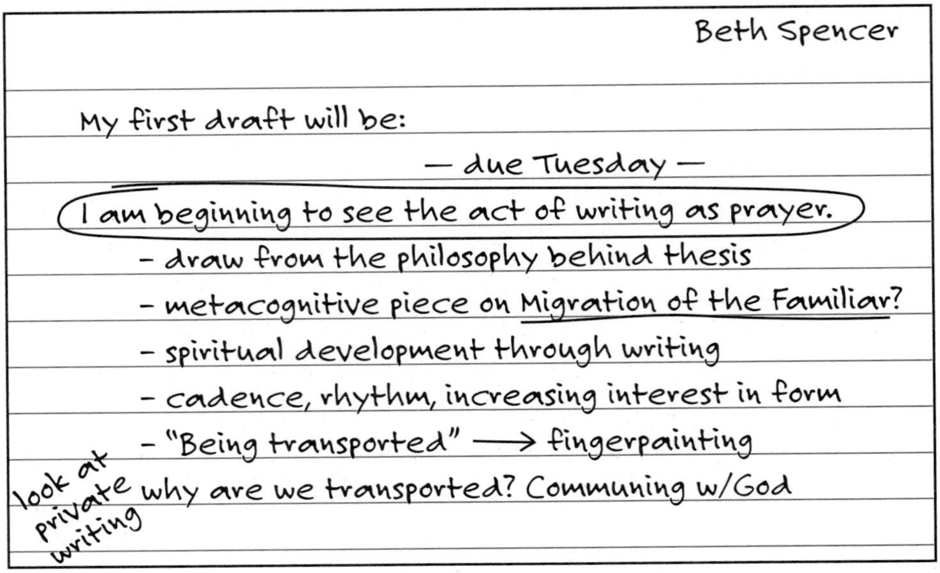

Beth Spencer

My first draft will be:

— due Tuesday —

I am beginning to see the act of writing as prayer.

- draw from the philosophy behind thesis
- metacognitive piece on Migration of the Familiar?
- spiritual development through writing
- cadence, rhythm, increasing interest in form
- "Being transported" ⟶ fingerpainting

why are we transported? Communing w/God

look at private writing

Figure 5 This card shows Spencer's initial thinking on her topic.

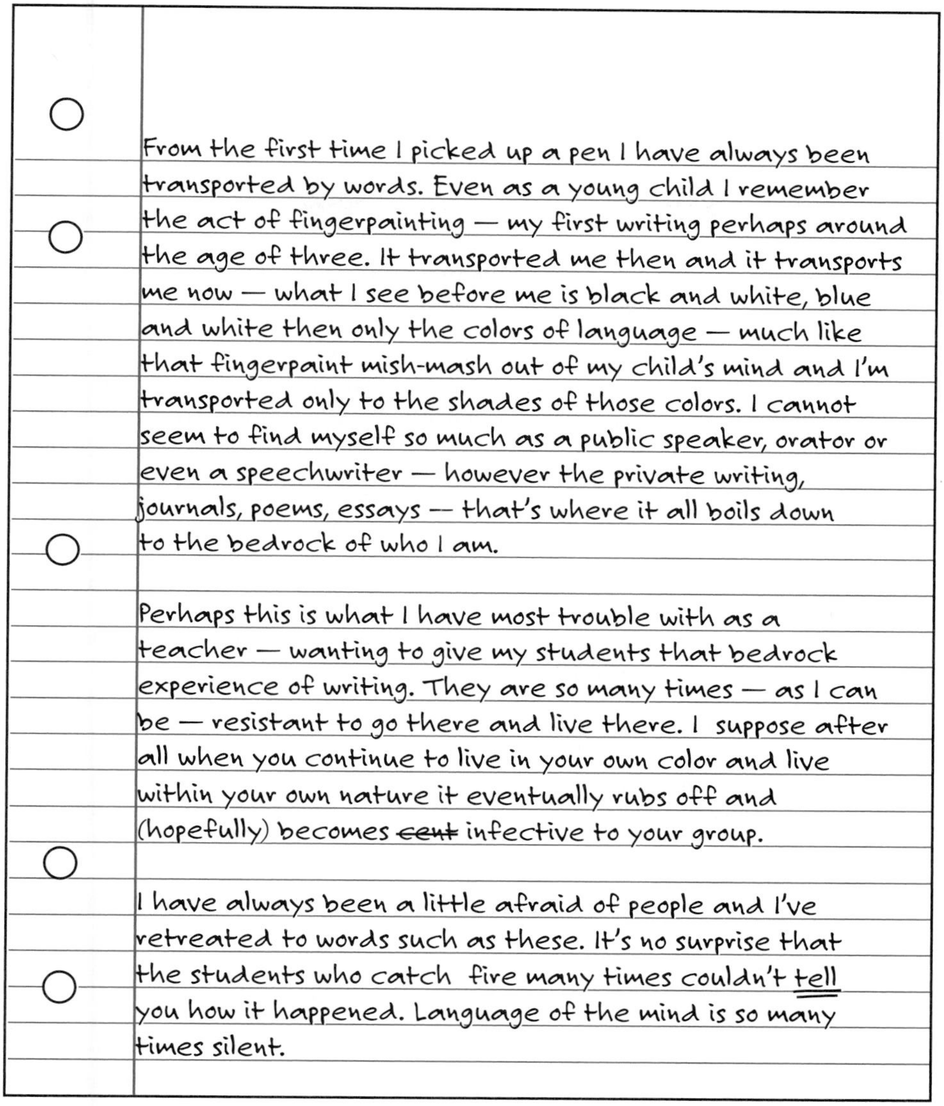

From the first time I picked up a pen I have always been transported by words. Even as a young child I remember the act of fingerpainting — my first writing perhaps around the age of three. It transported me then and it transports me now — what I see before me is black and white, blue and white then only the colors of language — much like that fingerpaint mish-mash out of my child's mind and I'm transported only to the shades of those colors. I cannot seem to find myself so much as a public speaker, orator or even a speechwriter — however the private writing, journals, poems, essays — that's where it all boils down to the bedrock of who I am.

Perhaps this is what I have most trouble with as a teacher — wanting to give my students that bedrock experience of writing. They are so many times — as I can be — resistant to go there and live there. I suppose after all when you continue to live in your own color and live within your own nature it eventually rubs off and (hopefully) becomes ~~cent~~ infective to your group.

I have always been a little afraid of people and I've retreated to words such as these. It's no surprise that the students who catch fire many times couldn't tell you how it happened. Language of the mind is so many times silent.

Figure 6 This is Spencer's first rough draft.

Spencer's first typewritten draft follows:

The Act of Writing as Prayer

Beth Spencer

I am beginning to see the act of writing as prayer. Just a few months ago I sat before three professors, each of whom held a copy of my collected poems in their laps, asking me to explain both the genesis and evolution of my poetry to date. I will never forget the way they looked over their respective bifocals at me: one with a half-grin; one with a mock-scowl and the other with the unabashed delight beaming on his face. There, in that 15 × 25 foot cinderblock office, I recounted how writing had taken hold of me at a young age, the sins of omission and commission admitted through poetic language, and always, always how the act of writing *transported* me beyond my physical body. I tried to explain that it was not so much the words, but the space between the words that compelled me beyond the hard swivel chair and bad lighting to a place which both exhilarated and humbled my spirit. The act of writing for me, then becomes that silent space of fear perfect clarity.

Writing demands that I abandon the notion that I am the source of all creation. I dab words onto the page in fear that I really don't understand what will overtake the process. Journals, lists, couplets, and clusters of words are my markings against a white surface that are like little fists clasped together and pressed to my forehead. They plead with the universe to *show me, show me the way.* Not knowing where I'm going makes the shock of clarity that much more exhilarating. When I am writing, I am pushing against the notion of what I think I know. In the stillness of the morning, I may be moved to describe the beauty of migratory birds: *I have one rose-breasted grosbeak and eight indigo buntings at the feeder. Where will they light next? Will they make the journey back to Central and South America?* At night I fall into sleep scrawling: *a china moon a straw hat and deacons and jackals everywhere. Oh set the coffee maker in the morning. I wish that . . [sleep].* My language always knows where it going; my hand does not.

It is the physical act of going into the unknown that, for me, **is** getting down on my knees and humbling myself at the foot of the bed first thing in the morning. It is sitting in a half-lotus trying to follow my breath. It is letting the trains of thought barrel past me until I am receptive to my breath alone. I am transported away from the clamor of my daily life and into the presence of what churns the universe around. And it seems, without fail, that once I reach that place where the pen takes on a life of its own I cannot imagine wanting to be anywhere else again. I come away from each session thinking *why did I resist? I am intrigued by what is before me. Tomorrow I will unravel it some more.*

Two Examples of Peer Response to "The Act of Writing as Prayer"

First Response

1. Where does the writing really become interesting? Why?

I am captured by your idea!

To me the writing is interesting from the title forward. Comparing writing to prayer is a very interesting idea because, as you state, "Writing demands that I abandon the notion that I am the source of all creation." I don't think a lot of writers would be comfortable looking for practical advice for their writing by beginning with the acknowledgment of their powerlessness. And yet, there it is: We don't control the muse.

Somehow, after reading this piece, I feel that sharing useful or utilitarian insights on how the writing process works for you must "transcend" the idea that all creativity is an impenetrable black box. An interviewer who would ask Miles Davis or any other artist the standard question, "Where does your creativity come from?" is very likely to receive a response that is useless information for the audience in a pragmatic sense, something that will only harden the separation between the viewing and creating art. Prayer, however, is like writing in the sense that we all can and must do it for ourselves first: We can be the ultimate judge of its value. Your comparison of writing to prayer reinforces the private, vital and independent nature of the act of writing.

2. Where does it go flat? Why?

In general, the piece ends too soon for me. I enjoy your creative metaphors, especially the description of "clusters of words" as "little fists clasped together against my forehead."

While one of your strengths lies in your convincing voice speaking through your personal experiences, I keep waiting for you to close the circuit: Can (should) you define prayer more clearly? Could you then compare writing to prayer more directly? Although the creative process is something that traditionally resists interpretation, it seems that you've isolated that act with the act of writing together for the reader to see, but then stop before you really start to draw more specific comparisons of prayer to writing and vice versa. I think that there is room here to be more specific, more literal, about what prayer and writing each involve without becoming pedantic or reductive. It seems like a real wealth of fruit has yet to be harvested . . . what comes next?

3. Do you as a reader make a real connection with the idea of writing as "prayerlike"? Why or why not? What can the author do to illustrate this idea more?

Without turning this into a religious tract, I think that God must be found within this idea. Quite simply, there can be no prayer without a "higher power." I think you hint at this when you remark that "[w]riting demands that I abandon the notion that I am the source of all creation."

That said, how do you talk about that spiritual connection in a way that is honest, and yet doesn't exclude readers who either don't share your religious convictions or, perhaps most importantly, come to your piece seeking a fresh and useful perspective to apply to their writing and not a religious experience? Connecting prayer to writing is an exhilarating and powerful idea that can also misfire if not handled carefully.

What about some good, old-fashioned audience analysis here—whom are you writing to? If it's other writers, my feeling is that they will be captured by the honesty of your experiences—your journals, your morning habits, your feelings of regret for not having written sooner—and yet also demand that you "push" this idea further toward some conclusions. I think I see the evidence of some of the conclusions already: Why do you "fall asleep scrawling" at night? Why do you think the writing habits that you do have tend to work for you?

4. Which areas of this essay need more discussion?

Again, I think that I'd find it helpful to couple more pragmatic suggestions and conclusions with your experiences. Bluntly put: What about writing is like prayer? I think you can return to this conceit time and time again with numerous new avenues each time you compare a specific aspect of prayer to a specific aspect of writing.

This is a powerful idea: You have found an analogy that is revealing some profound truths for you and your readers. Good Luck!

Another Response

Dear Beth,

I like your essay a lot; I'm very intrigued—pulled in. Here are some responses you can think about as you revise. Thanks for the questions. I won't really answer them so directly, but will use them to guide me.

Here is some *pointing:* places that come out strongest for me, hit me, stick in mind.

—The opening image of being with the professors; cinder blocks; glasses. I've been there. Here it's called an "exam" and, though people usually pass, still a little tense.

—"fear"—big word here. And "perfect clarity."
—fists clasped to forehead.
—stillness of the morning.
—those lines about birds.
—my language always knows where it's going.
—churns the universe around.
—why did I resist?

Here are some *movies of my mind* as I'm reading—but also paying attention to your questions:

I get involved in that opening image, having been there. I have feelings about those sessions where I've been a participant. I hate those meetings and discussions about someone's work being framed as an "exam." But perhaps it was dandy and nice for you.

But then somehow I'm moved to a different universe in the second and third paragraphs—not noticing that it's happening—when you start talking about writing as prayer. In your question you asked if I connect to it. Yes, I do, though I wouldn't say that writing is prayer for me. But somehow it feels a *right* and *important* thought. Perhaps I wish it were true for me. And certainly I sometimes feel that writing surprises me and gives me thoughts and even feelings I didn't expect; takes me to the unknown. That's what's most exciting to me about writing; this mystery. So I get excited that you have a different lens for getting at that mystery and excitement.

A simple question flits across my mind. Do you actually get down on your knees to pray? I love the childish simplicity of being on knees with hands to forehead—though I also know that plenty of sophisticated nonchildren do that. I like the combination of frank religious exploration here and the lack of dogmatic language.

Here are some *movies* after I've read again—a day or so later—and more than once—thinking back over it and reflecting.

I'm perplexed by what I experience as a gap between that first paragraph and the rest. I'm in one world and then another. Somehow I can't bridge the gap. Wanting help. Maybe there's something wonderful about that first world being so completely different—so *worldly* compared to the rest of the paper. Writing as satisfying a University requirement vs. writing as prayer! Amazing. But I can't hold them both in mind at the same time.

But I love where the main part of the essay is going. You are giving me language for a vague religious position I feel: that there's something there if we listen and don't resist. And I love the link between that and writing.

And yet at the end I'm not satisfied. I feel there's something missing; I want more or want some change. I feel it could be a lot stronger. But I feel kind of helpless in not having anything concrete or useful to say. But maybe that's a point too: It's not a matter of being clever and figuring something out—it's about being quiet and *waiting* more for what's missing—or at least for what could carry us further.

Maybe I want a bit more concreteness about you and your writing life. It's quite general. What you have is somewhat general. I find the specifics precious: the opening image in that room with those particular people; those particular words or lines that you actually wrote (or said). Maybe I want to see more of your actual writing life. It's "spiritual" but there's not much "incarnation"—embodied particularity. Not sure.

Thanks for writing it and opening a door.

Best,
Peter

Process Writing on "The Act of Writing as Prayer"

Dear Peter:

I think I'm moving into an area with this essay that definitely makes me uneasy—which is always a good indication that the mind is reaching another stage of metamorphosis. As I look over the essay, the thing that strikes me is my capacity to be really honest and not skirt the main issue at hand: spirituality. This is no pat on the back, mind you—it's actually a little unsettling. However, I'd like to be more honest and more to the point of what I'm trying to say. I am very aware that the subject can go awry quite easily and fall off into "dogmatic" language (as you mentioned) if I'm not careful. But I really believe what's driving me in this essay is *attempting to explain* the force of The Spirit and how it guides my life and my writing. Prayer is such an intense and private and potentially volatile subject—I'm sort of wondering how I got here in the first place. But then, if I've really submitted myself to the process then it's not really up to me to worry about the outcome and just remain receptive. Another little shock of clarity, eh? The parallels between the two subjects seem to keep exposing themselves even more as I write. I realize that for the first time in my life I could really write a book on this whole idea.

But then there is fear. It can be such a stranglehold, can't it? But I've discovered if you can really find out what you're afraid of and "get its number" then you are free to write, unfettered and unafraid. That whole section on fear really hit a nerve with me and it felt good to get that down on paper. It was good to enumerate all of the factors that keep me from simply coming forth with my stranger ideas and emotions. I believe that looking at this self-centered fear in my personal life and getting honest with it is the best method to getting honest in writing. It's also definitely something that spills over into the classroom: I can convey a certain confidence to my students when they seem most frustrated and confused with an assignment. I can assure them that they are just where they need to be: in process. I sort of secretly know they are pushing into that mystery I mentioned (I want to say so much more about that!).

I would have to say that if I can narrow down the "sub-themes" of this essay they would be: "fear," "mystery," "the ultimate audience" (thesis committees and the like), "waiting," "The Spirit," and something like "liminality and composition." Writing really does put us between two different worlds if taken seriously and I guess I can only speak to my own experience of negotiating these two worlds. I'm not sure that I've accomplished this exactly in this draft but it is something to bear in mind.

As a parting thought, some feedback that would be helpful from other readers would be the issue of clarity and style. I feel as though my initial draft had more "prose poetry" in it and this subsequent draft is more "essay-ish." Does it water down my first thoughts or help to clarify them? What areas seem to give an "ah-ha" response (felt sense, right?) and what areas make you sort of wince? Any areas where you doze off? Does the spiritual tone become a religious tone at any point? Your ideas are most welcome.

Sincerely,
Beth

Latest Draft of "The Act of Writing as Prayer"

The Act of Writing as Prayer

Beth Spencer

I am beginning to see the act of writing as prayer. Just a few months ago I sat before three professors, each of whom held a copy of my collected poems in their laps, asking me to explain both the genesis and evolution of my poetry to date. I will never forget the way they looked over their respective bifocals at me: one with a half-grin, one with a mock-scowl, and the other with the unabashed delight beaming on his face. There, in that 15 × 25 foot cinderblock office, I recounted how writing had taken hold of me at a young age, the sins of omission and commission admitted through poetic language, and always, always how the act of writing *transported* me beyond my physical body. I tried to explain that it was not so much the words, but the space between the words that compelled me beyond the hard swivel chair and bad lighting to a place which both exhilarated and humbled my spirit. The act of writing, for me, then becomes that silent space of fear and perfect clarity.

I once remember battling a deep resentment towards a person who had probably brought the most pain to my life. I was caught in a thicket of brambles, playing this resentment over and over in my mind. I wanted a way out, wanted to free myself of the barbs that clung to me. The more I resisted, though, the more desperately entangled I became. I forced myself to pray for the person every day for two weeks. I submitted myself to the process, against my better judgment. At first, I remember praying: *please, God, give that sonofabitch what he deserves.* Each day, I prayed a similar sentiment. And each day the words became less and less powerful—revealing that, to my surprise, they were not the truth of my spirit or of my Creator's spirit. By the last few days the prayer changed to *God, bless this person with peace and abundance. I now see, too, that they are as trapped and fearful as I have been.* Again, thinking I knew the truth about a person was changed through prayer. Writing, for me, has the same effect.

Every time I hover above my journal, scrawl a thought on a restaurant napkin or tap out clumps of phrases onto my keyboard, I am submitting myself to an uncomfortable process. Writing demands that I abandon the notion that I am the source of all creation. I dab words onto the page in fear that I really don't understand what will overtake the process. Journals, lists, couplets, and clusters of words are my markings against a white surface that are like little fists clasped together and pressed to my forehead. They plead with the universe to *show me, show me the way.* Not knowing where I'm going makes the shock of clarity that much more exhilarating. When I am writing, I am pushing against the notion of what I think I know. In the stillness of the morning, I may be moved to reach for my pen and describe the beauty of migratory birds: *I have one rose-breasted grosbeak and eight indigo buntings at the feeder. Where will they light next? Will they make the journey back to Central and South America?* At night I fall into sleep scrawling: *a china moon a straw hat and deacons and jackals everywhere. Oh set the coffee maker in the morning. I wish that . . . [sleep]*. My language always knows where it's going; my hand does not.

Prayer, too, requires that I simply submit myself to a process and trust that it will guide me into a deeper sense of understanding. It insists that I pay attention to that stillness of the morning and wait for a nudge. A nudge of clarity at first, and nothing more. *God,* I think. *I do not do not understand your will for me right now. You know me, God, you know me. You know that I need big arrows. Wide maps. Bright colors. I am here. Show me.* Then, when I least expect it, a nudge—no, a push—that moves me from one place to another in my mind; a feeling of powerlessness until I engage in prayer and feel how it transforms me in ways I could never imagine.

Above all, prayer is humble. Prayer keeps me striving for humility just as writing does. Both prayer and writing are a negotiation between humility and ego. I'm not the best at that—I have a tendency to think I have all the answers. And then there are times when I think I know nothing. And, ultimately all I really do know *is nothing* and that is what writing, like prayer, reveals as we go along. It reveals nothing new under the sun and, at the same time, it reveals everything. Revelations about human nature, ourselves, the way our minds work, our prejudices—yes, our prejudices—those wonderful stopgaps that really get us to the door of mystery. I recently found myself thinking a first line of poetry such as "The houses coil together in my mind / the framed yards, bald patches, places marked / with a single acorn" was the most perfect opening to a poem. In fact, I thought, *this is really pretty outstanding. Brilliant, perhaps. How I love it when it comes this easy.* And then I let it sit for a few days—*perhaps* let another pair of eyes take a look at it. And, thank goodness, my focus begins to sharpen. Umm . . . maybe that first line *is* a bit overstated. No, I was wrong. It's *quite* overstated, although I do genuinely feel that the second and third lines give some nice, clean visual images. I'll let them stay for now. Writing through my prejudices, if done long enough, will ultimately paint me into a corner, pull the rug out from under me and *force me to see things differently.* If I can remember that my writing is fed by a dialogue with the God of my understanding, The Spirit, The Muse—whatever you want to call it—I will be able to smile and laugh a little at myself when I move into that shock of clarity: mystery.

Writing and prayer, for me, are connected through mystery. Mystery is what churns the universe around. What's tricky about this connective tissue between writing and prayer is that it is the incentive that gets me *to the keyboard, on my knees, drawing the breath and saying o.k. I really want to enter into this. I'm going to "strap in and close my eyes."* Mystery is the one thing that drives me beyond the fear. Writing, like prayer, only reveals a truth to the writer who is ready, who is putting herself out there with a conviction of faith that constantly pushes through the formidable fear. Fear of being misunderstood. Fear of inarticulateness. Fear of looking and sounding stupid. Trusting and not trusting the muse—moments of weakness where the voice of the potential reader is louder than the voice of The Creator. Fear that someone will take your thoughts and words and twist them into something they were never meant to be, taking the beauty of being vulnerable to the creative process and destroying it with an unmovable, arrogant heart.

It is the physical act of going into the unknown that, for me, is getting down on my knees and humbling myself at the foot of the bed first thing in the morning. It is sitting in a half-lotus trying to follow my breath. It is letting the trains of thought barrel past me until I am receptive to my breath alone. I am transported away from the clamor of my daily life and into the presence of what churns the universe around. And it seems, without fail, that once I reach that place where the pen takes on a life of its own I cannot imagine wanting to be anywhere else again. I come away from each session thinking *why did I resist? I am intrigued by what is before me. Tomorrow I will unravel it some more.*

Revision through Purpose and Audience: Writing as Doing Things to People

Essential Premises

1. Experienced writers know when to think about their audience and when to forget about them. When revising, you need to do both—though not at the same time.
2. All language—spoken or written—has a purpose and all language "does" something, though it may not always be what a writer intended.
3. Revision requires becoming consciously aware of your own purposes, but also aware of the effects your language is having on others.

Main Assignment Preview

The goal of this workshop is to help you learn to shape your writing better by thinking more pointedly about what you want your words to do, and to whom—that is, about purpose and audience. The main assignment is to revise a paper you wrote for some other workshop in this textbook. In Workshop 6, we laid out one way to go about revision. In this workshop, we're going to suggest other ways to work on revision.

We almost always have a *purpose* in mind when we speak. We may be just expressing ourselves ("Ouch!"), making contact ("Hello, how are you?"), conveying information ("It's 10 o'clock"), or persuading ("It's much too hot to work—come to the beach with us"). Even when we talk to ourselves, we probably have some purpose: to buoy our spirits ("C'mon, you can do it"), to keep from being frightened ("It's only the cat"), or to get something off our chest ("I hate him, hate him, hate him!").

In addition, we almost always have an *audience* in mind when we speak: maybe just anyone ("Help! I'm drowning!"), a good friend ("I've missed you"), a parent ("I've studied all week; can I use the car?"), a teacher ("Do you take off for misspelling?"), peers ("Let's do something different this weekend"). And we sometimes just speak to ourselves. Since writing usually takes more time and effort than speaking, we're even more likely to have a purpose in mind when we write compared to when we speak, even if the purpose is mostly to fulfill an assignment for a teacher.

Purpose and audience interact to influence what you say. In all likelihood, if you want to borrow a friend's car, you wouldn't persuade him by saying you had studied all week. You'd be more likely to say, "Are you really my friend?" If you're writing to convey information about the popular music scene to your teacher, you'd probably include more background information than if you were writing an article for your campus newspaper. When we write only for ourselves, though, we can use whatever language and approach we please—and say whatever we want—since there's no fear of hurting or annoying someone or getting a baffled look.

Audience in Writing

Let's work up to purpose by way of audience. Sometimes you know who your audience is, for example, your parents or a particular committee or group of friends. Perhaps your audience is your classroom partner or group.

But sometimes you don't know your readers. You may have to write a letter to an organization or an application to a bureaucracy and not have a clue who will actually read it. You may be writing an essay of application to law school, medical school, or some other special program and have little sense of who the admissions people are and what they are impressed by. Sometimes you know *who* your readers are but not what they're *like*. That is, you may write something for a particular newspaper or magazine that gets all sorts of readers with all sorts of views and feelings. Or perhaps you have nobody and everybody in mind as your audience: You're writing about an issue for people in general or just for yourself.

There's nothing wrong with writing when you are unclear about your audience. Very good writing can be produced in that frame of mind. Besides, you often have no choice: You must write and you don't know the audience. But even when you are very clear about your audience, you may get confused when you think about them; in that case, it pays to forget about them and write your first draft to no one in particular or to a friendly audience. If your audience is not a problem, however, you can usually focus your thoughts and language better if you keep them in mind. (Notice how audience works—or doesn't work—in the Grace Paley story in the "Readings" for this workshop.)

Two Kinds of Audience Analysis

The obvious kind of audience analysis is to think about who your readers are and where they stand on the topic you are writing about. If you are writing something persuasive or argumentative, you will probably think most about where they *disagree* with you: After all, that's why you're writing—to change their minds.

But watch out. Yes, you need to understand the points of disagreement, but your best hope of persuasion is usually to build from a platform of agreement or shared assumptions.* Your audience analysis needs to focus on figuring out some of those points of agreement. Even if your disagreement is very large and even if you feel you are trying to persuade people who are deeply different from yourself, there are probably crucial *assumptions* that you share. (For example, die-hard pacifists and hawks in this country often agree about the desirability of democracy and individual freedom.) To put it another way, if you cannot find any shared agreement or feel some kinship with the "enemy," it's probably a waste of time writing to persuade them.

Often it's difficult to try to decide before you write what your audience is like and where it stands on a particular matter. You'll often discover much more about them if you get a draft written first—and then pretend to be your audience while you read it over: Try to read through their eyes. You'll discover some of their feelings, ideas, and assumptions that you wouldn't otherwise have noticed. Even better, you can enlist other readers to help you read like your audience.

Whether you know your real audience or not, there's a second kind of audience analysis that helps in revising. That is, you can analyze the audience that your writing implies. For if you look closely at any piece of your writing, you can find clues about whom you were unconsciously assuming as reader. For example, does your piece have little touches that imply your readers are smart or dumb? informed or uninformed about the topic? likely to agree or likely to fight you? frivolous or serious?

The "implied reader" is a subtle dimension of a text (and an important, critical concept in literary criticism as well as composition). Most of us need the help of responders to discover the implied reader in what we write. For example, sometimes a responder will show you that your text gives off contradictory audience cues. Perhaps at one point your writing implies that the readers are already interested in your topic, and at another point that they are uninvolved. Perhaps you can carry this off (somehow making it clear that you are writing for all readers), but the contradiction may undermine your writing by alienating *all* readers: Everyone feels, "He's not talking to me."

One of the most common kinds of implied reader is a "reader in the head"—that is, some past reader who continues to be a powerful influence on you. For example, responders may show you that your letter to a newspaper is full of confusing qualifications because you are still unconsciously writing for a teacher who told you never to make a broad generalization when writing about a controversial subject. It's probably not suitable advice for this audience. Or your essay for an economics teacher is full of impressive verbal fanciness that had always won praise from English teachers, but it's inappropriate for this audience. We carry around audiences from the past in our heads, and we need readers to help us notice when we continue to write to them.

---

* Notice how the article by Mona Charen in the "Readings" in Workshop 11 starts from a shared experience of motherhood.

Digression on Teacher as Audience

Teachers read differently from most readers. They read not for pleasure or information, but because it's their job. They read as coach or director. Think about how a director watches a play she's directing—as opposed to how the audience watches it. The director is certainly a *real* audience; she is "really" watching the play, probably more carefully than the "real" audience. Yet, of course, the performance is not for her but for those who buy the tickets. They pay to see the play; she's being paid to watch and kibitz. She's not so much trying to tell the actors how *she* reacts to the play (she may be tired of it by now), but rather how she imagines the audience will react.

School writing situations are often comparable. For example, your writing teacher may specify an audience other than herself for a writing assignment (for example, the readers of the editorial page of the local newspaper). Or she may simply assume that the writing is not only for her but also for general readers or other students in the class. In either case you have some kind of *double-audience* situation, especially if you are graded on the piece.

It is rare that we write something only for the teacher. Notice the difference if you write a letter to her arguing for a change in your grade. Usually you write *for* the teacher who is a stand-in for other readers. Teachers occupy a tricky role as readers. On the one hand, they try to read as coach or editor, telling you not so much how they react but how they think your real audience will react. On the other hand, of course, their own reactions will color their understanding of the reactions of others.

A "coach" or "editor" is a nice image for the writing teacher. For a coach or editor is an ally rather than an adversary. A coach may be tough on you, but she is not trying to be the enemy; she's trying to help you beat the real "enemy" (the other team). There's no point in fighting the coach or being mad at her, or for the coach to fight you. The better you and the coach work together, the better chance you both have of achieving your common goal of "winning" against a common adversary.

But you may have noticed that teachers can easily fall into being *grumpy* coaches. Sometimes it seems as though the only thing we teachers do is criticize your writing. One reason for our attitudes arises from the conditions under which we have to read student papers. As writing teachers we always read student writing in stacks of 25, 50, or 75 papers at a time. Have you ever

Exploring the Writing Process

Though my writing process has certainly changed due to this class, I think that my process of writing is still suffering. My major question: how can we become re-excited by our writing and ideas after the first draft is said and done? I spoke to several classmates during the semester who were having similar trouble reentering and reengaging with their work after setting it aside for a week or two. It seems that a lot of us have gotten used to losing interest in our work, or even deploring it, after it has left us for a bit. And that doesn't seem right.

Leslie Edwards

thought about what a peculiar and unpleasant way of reading this is? Teachers naturally fall into what you might call "schematic" reading. After the 10th or 15th paper (especially if all the papers are on the same topic or in the same genre), we often develop a kind of "ideal paper" in our heads. Instead of reading a paper just to see what is there, we "check it against" that model—looking for certain points that need to be made or certain features that this assignment calls for. We fall into looking at each paper in terms of how well it fits or doesn't fit "what we are looking for." (Notice how we teachers often talk in terms of what we are "looking for," and how you students ask us, "What do you want us to do in this paper?") In "normal" reading conditions, the reader isn't checking what he reads for the presence of something he *already knows;* he's looking to find things he doesn't know.

We're not trying to blame teachers. This kind of reading is an inevitable consequence of the *role* of teacher and the conditions in which we read. A director can't enjoy a play in the way a paying audience can. Frankly, we think most writing teachers are overworked and underpaid. But the role and these reading conditions can lead teachers to be grumpy or to emphasize mistakes. That's why we urge you so much in this book to use your fellow students (in pairs or small groups) as another audience for your writing. Fellow students may not be as skilled in reading as your teacher, but they can read your writing as "real readers"—take it on its own terms and simply look for pleasure or usefulness—and not feel they are reading as a job or duty or to "teach" you.

In short, we want you to get the best of both audiences: Use your teacher for her professional expertise in diagnosis and advice; use your fellow students for their ability to tell you what actually happens when real readers read your words. You get the *worst* of both worlds if you try to get your fellow students to give you professional diagnosis and advice and ask your teachers not to be critical. It is worth having some frank discussions about this tricky double-audience situation in school writing: for students to tell honestly how they experience the teacher as audience, and for teachers to talk honestly about how they experience their situation as readers. It is a painful area, but not one for blaming: There are no right answers here. It's a question of gradually seeing clearly something that, as far as we know, no one yet understands well.

Purpose in Writing

It's hard to imagine a situation in which someone could write and have no purpose at all. Perhaps it's to dump emotion or to get yourself to see some dilemma more clearly. Even so, you can talk about what writing "does" (makes you feel better or understand better). For this workshop, though, we want you to focus on purpose in the sense of what you want your writing to "do" in relation to some audience other than yourself.

We can highlight *purpose* in writing if we consider the interesting situations where writing itself undermines its very purpose. For example, sometimes you can persuade better by *not* writing, by sitting down with your reader and *talking*. If you write to him, that written document may put him off with its formality and distance. Indeed, sometimes the most persuasive thing you can do is not even to talk but to *listen.* Often your only hope of persuading someone is to show him that you respect his thinking and are willing to adjust yours on the basis of what he's saying.

But sometimes writing is a better mode of persuasion than speaking because, in some situations and with some people, speaking just leads to fruitless arguments. A piece of writing can be less disputatious, less intrusive, calmer. Writing can give you a chance to express something quietly to the person without the need for him to answer back to you: a chance to plant a seed and avoid all arguing.

Does this sound like an odd digression—to question *whether* to write at all? Well, the digression highlights the practical and, as it were, nitty-gritty approach you need to take concerning purpose if you want to make an actual difference through your writing. If you really think about who your audience is and what you want to do to them, you may have to rethink a lot of things you took for granted. Most of us tend to stress what words mean, not what they do. Of course, some of the best and most highly paid writers in our society—writers of advertisements—think very much in terms of what words do. There are a number of things that will help you to articulate your purposes more clearly in this concrete and specific way:

- Practice *responding* to writing by telling what the words actually *do* to you—that is, by giving movies of your mind as a reader. (See Section 7 of the "Sharing and Responding" part of this textbook.)
- Hear movies of the minds of readers as they read what you've written. (You'll get more chance for this later in the workshop.)
- Look at advertisements in print and on radio and TV, and analyze them for their purpose: What was the writer trying to make *happen* in us?
- Consider *examples* of specific statements of purpose, such as the following, and force yourself to come up with comparably specific statements for your own writing.
  - To make readers *act* in a certain way (buy something, vote for someone, give a contribution, write a letter to their representative, and so forth).
  - To make them feel a certain way (for instance, to feel sympathy for a particular person), or to give them a vicarious experience—that is, to make them feel as though they've actually been there (to "show" them, not just "tell" them).
  - To make them trust you, or make them laugh.

Exploring the Writing Process

I have a really hard time with writing a diary or journal because I can never figure out who the audience is supposed to be. Is it me? Is it the teacher? I can't write just for myself when I know someone else is going to read it.

Student

- To impress readers (teachers?) that you've really learned a lot of material and thought things through.
- To convince readers that you are right.
- To make readers feel you understand how they see or feel things.
- To bowl readers over.
- Instead of wanting to bowl readers over (with the danger of making them feel threatened or making them want to fight against you), just to plant the seed of a difficult or alien view.
- To give readers information. (But notice that this is falling short of the task. No advertising writer would let herself stop there. Why are you giving readers information? What do you want the information to make them feel or do?)

An Extended Example: Our Purposes in Writing This Textbook

By way of further example, let us list here some of the specific purposes we've had in mind in writing the textbook you hold in your hands. Our audience is students. However, students will never read a course-oriented textbook unless it is chosen and assigned by their teacher. So it turns out we have the same tricky double-audience situation that you often have; teachers aren't our "real" audience, but they "really" are our audience.*

Our purpose is to make things happen in the world, to change behavior. We take our book as a very practical enterprise. Suppose, for example, that some reader should come up to us and say, "I just *love* reading your book. It's so interesting and entertaining. Of course, I never do any of those funny activities you describe; I just continue to write the way I always have." We might feel a glint of pleasure that this reader "loves" our book, but we'd have to admit that we'd *failed* in our main purpose of affecting behavior.

But we can't affect people's behavior unless we can affect their attitudes. We want to make teachers and students trust us. We want to make them think that we know a lot about writing and teaching and that we understand their problems. We want teachers to feel, "This is a smart, sensible book; it will make my teaching easier and more effective."

In the end our major purpose is to *help students become better writers.* Notice, however, that such a broad, pious statement of purpose is not specific enough to be of much use—for revising or helping readers give us feedback, for instance. Here are more down-to-earth statements of what we are trying to do to you to make you better writers:

- To get you over any nervousness or fear of writing you might have.

---

* Double audiences aren't as odd as you might think. A children's book must appeal to grown-ups before children get a chance to read it. You can't get an article or even a letter into the newspaper unless the editor thinks it's suitable. Every book must appeal to an editor before it can be published and be read by an audience. Indeed most books, even after they are published, won't get into many readers' hands unless they succeed at appealing to reviewers.

- To make you trust that you always have lots of words and thoughts available, and thereby make you more confident about writing.
- To get you to *like* writing and thus write a great deal. For we believe that you'll learn more in the end from writing a great deal than from advice or suggestions. And you won't write lots unless you like writing.
- To make you realize that when you have to write something, you have a number of different ways to go about writing it: to feel a sense of choices, options, power.
- To get you to be much more aware of your writing process, to notice the different gears you use and the funny tricks your mind and feelings play—and thereby help you end up with more conscious control over yourself as you write. (Students sometimes think process writing is odd or "merely theoretical" at first, but we want you to feel that it is practical: a method that can help you get unstuck and figure out the best way to tackle the writing task at hand.)
- To help you move comfortably back and forth between being loose and accepting in exploratory writing, and tough-minded and critical as you assess and revise.
- To help you work more independently, without always needing directions from the teacher or the book.
- To help you collaborate better with each other in writing and responding to writing.

Main Assignment: *Analyzing Purpose and Audience in a Piece of Writing*

The assignment for this workshop is to analyze audience and purpose in a piece of writing you have already written, and then to revise that piece on the basis of your analysis. With your teacher's permission, you may even use a paper from another class. You can choose any piece of writing to work on—from a collage to a descriptive piece to an argument (though your teacher may ask you to work on one particular kind of writing). Here are the main questions you need to address in your analysis:

- *Audience.* Whom did you see then as your audience and whom do you see now?
  - If your group members are the wrong audience for this piece, what differences do you think there would be between their reactions and those of the right audience?
- *Purpose.* Were you consciously trying to do something to readers when you were writing your piece? Can you now see any unconscious purpose you had? Would you specify a different purpose now?
- *Actual effects.* What actual effects does your writing seem to have on the readers in your group? What specific words or features seem to cause their reactions?

- *Advice for revising.* Finally, make sure your analysis includes some advice to yourself for revising.

The goal of this analysis is not to *judge* but to *describe.* That is, we're not trying to get you to congratulate or criticize yourself ("I tried to make them laugh but they sat there stone faced!"), but rather to write a paper that describes *purposes* in writers and *effects* on readers—relating those purposes and effects to specific words and features on the page. In making this analysis, you might find it helpful to make references and comparisons to other pieces you've heard and discussed in your group.

Ways to Proceed

There are many ways to complete the assignment for this workshop, but here is a sequence of steps you will probably find helpful.

- Pick out the piece of your writing that you want to analyze. If your teacher gives you free choice, pick whatever piece intrigues you. Perhaps it's interesting because you are pleased with it and want to look more closely at something that worked for you. More likely, it's a piece that still troubles you and needs revision, in your opinion.
- Do some fast exploratory writing about the audience and purpose you had in mind in your original writing. Try to put yourself back into that situation. Do you have any different feelings now about audience and purpose for this piece? Can you now see any unconscious purpose you had? (For example, you might have been trying to persuade politely, but now you can see that unconsciously you were trying to make readers look silly.) Perhaps you were trying to get something off your chest in addition to having some effect on readers.
- Look at any response you got from your teacher on this paper and see what you can learn about the effects your words had on her.
- Share your piece with your partner or group and ask them to tell you in detail about the effects the writing has on them. Ask them to give you careful movies of their minds. It will help a lot if you make them stop periodically and report specifically what is happening to them as readers.
- Then, changing to a more analytic mode, ask them to relate these effects to specific features of the text. If a reader got bored or hostile, can she figure out what words or tone or structural feature in the writing caused it? You can join in on this analysis.
- Then ask your partner or group to talk about whom they see as the audience and what your text implies about audience. Does the text imply that readers are professional or amateur? emotional or cool? Can they see any old "audiences in your head" which led you to shape your writing inappropriately? Again, you can join in.
- If your group is the wrong audience for your piece, ask them to speculate on any differences between their reactions and those of your intended

audience. In this discussion, don't overestimate *differences* between readers. That is, if your intended audience is your teacher or a newspaper editor, your classmates are admittedly different; many of their reactions will be different from those of your teacher or the editor. But you can learn a great deal from seeing what your words did to the wrong readers. For example, your group might say they felt intimidated by your tone. Probably your teacher would not feel exactly intimidated, but there may well be something problematic about your tone. Perhaps it is smug.

- To complete your analysis, ask your classmates for advice about revising. Give yourself advice too: On the basis of what you have learned about audience, purpose, and effects, what changes do you plan for your revision?
- Revise your piece on the basis of your analysis. Show your revision to your group or partner and tell them what you have done and why. Ask them for any further suggestions.

We don't want to leave you with the impression that you need to go through all these steps to revise something you write and make its purposes clearer to your intended audience. But we do believe that good writers have an intuitive sense or "feel" of audience and purpose which guides them as they revise. Our hope is that if you consciously go through the steps we've suggested, you'll discover how attentive you need to be to all of this when you revise. As you develop into a more experienced writer, this sense of audience and purpose may go underground, but it will still be a source of intuition or "feel" for whether your words are matching your intentions. So whenever you're struggling as you revise, look back at the steps we recommend here, and this may get you going again. Take from our suggestions whatever helps you in a specific instance of revision.

Variations on the Assignment

1. Instead of actually revising an earlier paper, make your final piece for this workshop a written *analysis* of that earlier paper. If you select this option, be sure to include an extended proposal for revision.
2. Revise an earlier paper *and* produce a written analysis of it. If you decide to do this, your discussion of specific revisions in the analysis essay need not be as extensive as for variation 1.
3. Instead of concentrating only on analyzing your essay, make your final piece a comparison of your writing with the writing of someone else in your group: the audience, purposes, and effects of *two* pieces of writing. (Sometimes analysis is easier when you have two pieces to compare.)
4. Make your final piece an essay about purposes and audience in *three or four* papers in the group. Obviously you can't write a full analysis of that many papers. Your analysis would have to center on one or two key issues of audience and purpose (for example, trying to get hostile readers on your side or trying to make readers experience a certain emotion), and explore that issue in terms of examples and illustrations from all the papers.

Suggestion for Collaboration

Write a collaborative essay with two or three people in your group whose writing is also being analyzed. This essay can take the approach of either variation 3 or 4 described previously.

Sharing and Responding

To get material for your analysis and revision, you'll need to get feedback from classmates. You already should have some feedback on the paper you're analyzing if it's a paper you wrote for an earlier workshop. Locate that feedback and make sure you get readers to give you emotional as well as logical reactions to the paper you plan to revise. "Movies of the Reader's Mind" (Section 7 of the "Sharing and Responding" part of this text) is probably the best technique for this.

If you are doing this workshop's assignment collaboratively, enlist others outside your group to give you feedback both on the paper(s) you're analyzing and on the essay you produce as a result of the analysis.

For feedback on your analysis, you'll find the following sections of "Sharing and Responding" particularly useful: (3) "Summary and Sayback"; (10) "Skeleton Feedback and Descriptive Outline"; and (11) "Criterion-Based Feedback," especially the criteria traditionally applied to expository writing.

In addition, you might ask your readers and listeners the following questions:

- "Do you agree with me about whom I have identified as the audience of the paper(s)? about what I have identified as purpose(s)?"
- "Do you understand what I would do if I did revise? What other suggestions would you make for revision?"

When sharing your revised paper, ask readers and listeners the following questions:

- "Have I taken my own advice from my analysis of this paper?"
- "Whom do you now see as the audience for my paper, and what do you see as its purpose?"

Process Journal

- Do you usually have a definite audience in mind when you start to write? How do various audiences affect your writing? teachers? your writing group? Which audiences do you find most helpful and most problematic? Do you find it difficult to ignore audience?
- How do you see and experience the teacher as audience?
- Do you usually have some definite purpose in mind when you start to write? Or do you discover purposes after starting? How does purpose function for you as you write?

Exploring Theory: *More on Purpose and Audience*

Purpose, Genre, and an Overview of Rhetorical Terrain

In Workshop 2 we emphasized genre; in this workshop we emphasize purpose. It's worth exploring how genre and purpose are similar and how they differ.

It seems as though certain genres are designed to accomplish certain purposes. If you want to persuade someone, you're likely to assume you should write a persuasive essay, not a poem or a story. (In this case the genre's name even carries the name of the purpose—to persuade.) And yet if you take it for granted that you shouldn't write a poem or story, you should think again. You would be putting too much stock in genre and not thinking concretely enough about purpose.

For really there is no *necessary* connection between genres and purposes. Poetry, for example, may seem to express personal emotion more often than informational essays do, but that's just a matter of how poetry has tended to develop since the romantic period in the nineteenth century. Essays can express personal emotion, and poems can convey information. (Until the romantic period, poetry was treated as an appropriate genre for conveying information, even scientific information. The first version of atomic theory came in a long Greek poem, "On the Nature of Things," by Lucretius. Alexander Pope wrote an important poem called "An Essay on Man"—which is, indeed, an essay.) The important practical point here is that the persuasive essay is not the only way to persuade. Stories, novels, poems, and letters can sometimes persuade better than essays. (Consider the persuasive power of Harriet Beecher Stowe's *Uncle Tom's Cabin* before the Civil War, and see Mark Levensky's use of a published letter to persuade in the "Readings" for Workshop 2.) And the essay can be a form of lyric or autobiography.

It turns out that the grading of writing is often linked to assumptions about genre. If someone says, "This is a poor persuasive essay," he may well mean that the piece violates what he expects of the persuasive essay genre; yet it may in fact persuade many readers. Or a teacher may say, "This is an excellent persuasive essay" (and even give it an A)—and yet not actually be persuaded by it.

Some writers don't care whether their pieces fit the traditional forms and conventions. That is, some story writers don't care if some readers say, "This is a very peculiar story—there's no real ending" (again, see the Paley story in the "Readings" for this workshop), or "I can't figure out whether this is a story or an essay." Some business writers don't care if readers say, "This writer doesn't seem to know the rules for proper memos." Those writers simply want to have a certain effect on readers, and they have decided they can do it better by breaking certain "rules" or "conventions" about genres. Of course, they must recognize the risk in this approach: They will annoy those readers who don't like departures from genre, but it is through this process that genres change. For example, it's no longer clear that the story genre demands a climax or an ending that resolves all the loose ends.

Another way to say this is that there isn't a perfect genre for each purpose. You can do many things with any one genre; for example, you can use a story to amuse, to persuade, or even to convey information. (Think about the purely informational qualities of novels like Arthur Hailey's *Airport* and James Michener's *Hawaii.*) The point is that you need to think concretely and realistically about purpose—and not take things for granted.

Let's stand back and look at the whole terrain referred to as *rhetoric.* We emphasized finding your topic, genre, and audience in Workshop 2 ("From Private Writing to Public Writing"). Now we emphasize purpose and audience in this workshop. It is a good time to stand back and see how purpose, audience, genre, and topic are distinct, yet intertwined.

The figure below shows a traditional diagram called the "rhetorical triangle," or the "communications triangle," that sets out a schematic overview of what we might call the "rhetorical terrain":

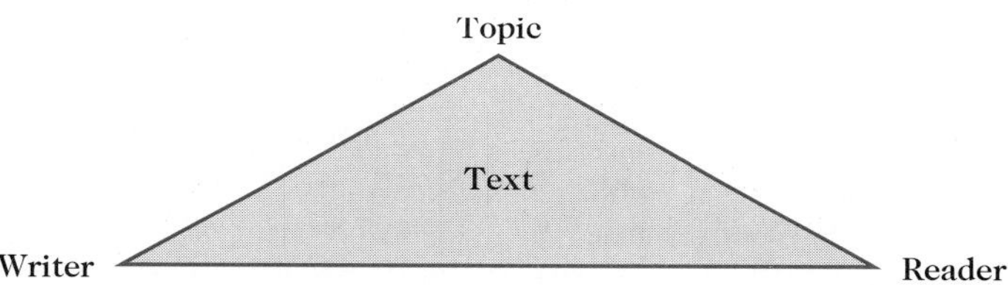

- To focus on purpose is to focus on people—what the *writer* intended and what happens to *readers*—the audience—as they read.
- To focus on the *topic* is to focus on the world or the message.
- To focus on genre is to focus on the *text*—the form and the conventions used. (To think about conventions is also to think about the history of texts; for example, whether stories need to have tidy endings.)

And, of course, you always have to keep in mind the context in which purpose, topic, and genre function: in a classroom, among friends, among enemies, in an office, and so forth. No purpose, genre, or topic exists in a vacuum. When you focus on one dimension, you may leave other dimensions vague or ambiguous for a while. For example:

- We may get quite far in writing a poem about something (thus knowing genre and topic) but not be sure of audience or purpose. There's nothing wrong with proceeding in that manner.
- We may be engaged in writing a letter to someone (knowing genre and audience) but not be sure of the topic or purpose: We know we want to write to them. Fine.
- We may start to write something entertaining about a subject (purpose and topic) but not be sure of the audience or genre.
- Indeed, we may know only that we want to write about a particular *topic* (e.g., an issue or a frightening experience), and remain vague about all three other dimensions: audience, genre, and purpose. We simply need to write in an exploratory way and see where it takes us.

Each rhetorical dimension is related to the other. Any change in one is likely to cause a change in the other. But as we have seen, the lines of connection are a bit rubbery. Thus, before you are finished with any piece of writing, you should be sure of all four dimensions. Indeed, one way to check over a piece of writing and move toward revision is to make sure you are clear and consistent about audience, purpose, genre, and topic (or message).

About Audience

Most teachers and theorists of rhetoric say that you should think about your audience before you write and keep audience in mind while you are writing. Yet we find that it often helps our writing to forget about audience as we write.

When you write, do you prefer to plunge in, exploring your topic on paper without any regard to the readers, and then revise later to fit the readers? Or do you prefer to think about whom you are writing to from the start and as you write?

Your answer may well depend on your temperament. Or it may be that keeping readers in mind is better for certain writing *tasks* (or for certain readers) than for other tasks or readers. The issue of audience is a complex tangle, but an important one. We are going to work toward untangling it here and end up with some practical advice on how to make audience work *for* you and prevent it from working against you.

A Balance among the Four Possible Relations to an Audience

Many students have never written except in school: all their writing has been assigned, read, and evaluated or graded by a teacher. If you never write except for evaluation by teachers, you can drift into unconsciously feeling as though that's what writing *is:* performing for someone in authority in order to be judged. Many students have no sense of writing as a way to *communicate* with real readers. And they may lack any sense of writing as a way to communicate privately with themselves, to explore thoughts and feelings on paper just for the sake of exploring. It is useful to become more conscious of the four main ways of relating to or using an audience in writing:

1. *Keeping your writing to yourself.* This is a case of *not* using an audience—keeping readers out of your way, out of your hair. We hope you have already learned how fruitful it can be not to worry or even think about readers as you write. Many people who were blocked in their writing and then learn the knack of private writing say: "I discovered that the problem wasn't *writing*: it was writing *for an audience.*" If you have kept a diary which you don't intend to share, you have participated in a venerable and traditional form of writing for no audience other than oneself. But of course you can also use private writing to help you produce material which is *eventually* intended for an audience.

2. *Giving your writing to an audience but getting no feedback or response from them: sharing.* Here, too, we hope we have already shown you how much you can learn from this simple, quick, and satisfying way of relating to an audience. When you share but don't get feedback, it emphasizes writing to *communicate* rather than writing to perform or be judged.

Obviously communication is the most common and natural way to use words—the way we are most skilled at.

3. *Giving your writing to an audience for* nonevaluative *feedback or response.* Sometimes in school we fall into assuming that the only thing to do with a piece of writing is to try to talk about how good or bad it is or diagnose its strengths and weaknesses or give suggestions for improvement. It is crucial to realize that we can get helpful responses to our writing without any of that. And we can get it from readers other than a teacher: from peers, friends, parents, and any others who might be interested in us or what we write. Really, one of the least interesting things we can ask about any piece of writing is how good or bad it is. It's usually much more interesting and fruitful to ask questions like these: "What does it seem to be saying? Does it say different things to different readers? Why did the writer write it? Why should we read it, or what can we get out of it or apply to our experience? How is it put together, and how does it function?" We have plenty of suggestions for useful nonevaluative response in the Sharing and Responding section of each workshop and in "Sharing and Responding" at the end of the book.

4. *Giving your writing to an audience for* evaluative *response.* When we use readers in the other three ways just described, then it makes good sense sometimes to get evaluative response from them. Evaluative response is only a problem if that's all you ever get, or if you trust it too much—forgetting that even the best professional critics cannot agree in their evaluations.

Audience as a Focusing Force on Our Minds

Think of audience as exerting a kind of magnetism or focusing force on our minds. The closer we are to our listeners or readers and the more we think about them, the more influence they have on our thoughts and feelings. That is, when we are with people or very aware of them in our minds, we are more likely to feel their concerns or see their point of view. When we go off by ourselves or forget them, we ignore their point of view. Both these situations have harmful and helpful outcomes.

Some audiences are helpful because they make it easier to write. Such an audience usually consists of a person or a group who likes us and respects us and is interested in what we are interested in. People who want to hear what we have to say tend to make us think of more things to say and to write more fluently. Their receptivity opens our minds. And the act of writing to such readers tends to shape and focus what we are thinking about—even if we had been confused before sitting down to write.

But other audiences are unhelpful or problematic because they make it harder to write. Certain audiences intimidate us or make us nervous. Most of us have had the experience of finding it harder and harder to write for a teacher because the teacher did nothing but criticize what we wrote. We may actually find ourselves *unable* to write for this type of person no matter how hard we try. (This happened to Peter Elbow and forced him to drop out of graduate school. It was this experience that got him interested in the writing process.) There are other kinds of problem audiences too. If an audience is completely unknown (for example, an admissions committee or a prospective employer you've never met or someone from another culture) or vague ("the general public"), you may find it hard to write for them.

The trick then is to notice when an audience is being helpful or not helpful so you can decide whether to think about them or forget about them as you write. Occasionally, a frightening or difficult audience is helpful to keep in mind right from the start. They energize us and lead us to be brave. We look them in the eye, and doing so empowers us and clears our minds: we suddenly find exactly the words and thoughts we need to say to them.

Even though audience is a tricky theoretical issue, the practical answer is simple if you think in terms of a little three-step dance with readers: first a step *toward* readers, then *away from* them, and finally *back toward* them.

- *Toward your audience.* Start by bringing your readers to mind. Imagine them; see them. Doing so may help you focus your thinking and your approach to your topic. By bringing readers consciously into your mind, you may well find more to say, just as you would naturally find things to say if you were standing there in front of them and they asked you what was on your mind. If things go well, you simply keep this first relationship to the audience for the whole writing process.
- *Away from your audience.* If you have any difficulty with your writing, it may be because your audience is getting in your way: because they are unknown or intimidating or because thinking about them makes you worry too much about trying to get your writing right. Try putting them out of mind and writing for yourself: Get your thoughts straight in your *own* mind—even if you know that this process is leading you to write things that are not right for your intended audience. If you can once put clearly on paper what you think, then it's not so hard afterward to make changes or adjustments to suit your words to the audience.
- *Finally, back again toward readers.* No matter how clearly you see things for yourself, you must consciously bring your audience to mind again—as a central part of your *revising* process. In doing so you may realize that what is clear for you is not clear for them unless you explain something they may not know about; or you may realize that for them you need a change in approach. You may even decide you need to hide some of your own ideas or feelings when writing to them. This would have been hard earlier, for it's hard to hide something while you are in the act of working it out.

Can We Forget about Purpose and Audience?

We have spoken of the value of thinking about audience and purpose; then we turn around and say it is sometimes useful to forget about audience and purpose if your hands are full just trying to figure out what you think (rather than worrying about how to convey what you think to others).

Does it sound as though we think you can just turn on and turn off all orientation toward audience and purpose—as with a mental faucet? It's important to acknowledge that in a sense one can never avoid orientation toward audience and purpose in any use of language: To open our mouths is to have the impulse to say something to someone for some reason. Our language is often shaped quite well by audience and purpose without our having any conscious awareness of who the audience is and what our purposes are.

But even if we can't get away from audience and purpose (or, putting this in its most general form, even if human intelligence is deeply social and human behavior is deeply purposive), there's still a big difference between *being* conscious of audience and purpose and *not* being conscious of them. There's also a big difference between trying to make your writing *fit* audience and consciously allowing your writing *not* to fit audience and purpose (for example, in exploring a topic). Thus, even if we can't get away from orientation toward audience and purpose, we can get away from trying to think about them and plan for them. In short, there are advantages in trying to plan and know and control what we are doing, but also advantages in leaving quite a lot to intuition or the tacit dimension.

We recognized this same issue when we spoke of organization versus messiness in freewriting. Does doing fast and furious freewriting and not worrying at all about the organization mean you are getting away from organization? No, for it's impossible to get away from organization; everything has organization. But it does mean three important things:

- You are getting away from *thinking* about organization.
- You are inviting messy organization.
- You are inviting your *intuitive* or *tacit* power of organizing—your imagination. For we can often make a more interesting organization by intuition than by careful planning.

Thus, when we forget about audience and purpose, we invite writing that doesn't fit an audience or purpose. But we also invite writing that suits an audience and purpose more cleverly than we could have planned. What it all boils down to is trying to learn to take the best advantages of *both* dimensions of the mind: careful conscious planning and intuition. For even though we are often more intelligent in our unconscious intentions than in our conscious ones, intuition can also lead us down the garden path. Therefore, before we

Exploring the Writing Process

I don't consciously think of audience when I write. In writing for this course, I knew I was going to share my writing with the class but I didn't think of this or imagine them in some way. Right now, I guess I'm directing this writing to you but I'm not really thinking of that. Does this make any sense? I'm not sure where I go in my mind when I write. The feeling I have is of moving upward and to the sky, kind of out of body: a suspended state once I get moving and forgetting time. This is why I tend to write late at night. There are fewer interruptions and the time is more open ended. I do this weird consciousness thing even when I write letters. Then I have a person in mind but I direct the writing to their gut or heart and occasionally their mind. When I first fell in love with my old boyfriend, he was living far away. I wrote to him often and I remember imaging a kind of moving cloud or smoky essence that I directed my writing toward: the part of him I loved and wanted to connect with.

Nancy Blasi

are finished with a piece of writing, we do well to try to invoke the careful and conscious side of our minds: to become clear about audience and purpose and organization. For example, we may have to wrestle with a decision between conflicting aims that our intuition had allowed into our text. "Let's see. Now that I'm finishing this piece, who am I really writing to? What do I really want to do to them? Persuade, yes, but what things do I need to do to them to persuade them? Out of everything I've written so far, what would work best to achieve this purpose? What do I need to discard?"

You'll see an example of analysis on the basis of audience and purpose in the "Readings" for Workshop 10.

Is Phoenix Jackson's Grandson Really Dead?*

Eudora Welty

Eudora Welty (b. 1909, Jackson, Mississippi) is one of America's foremost short story writers and novelists.

A story writer is more than happy to be read by students; the fact that these serious readers think and feel something in response to his work he finds life-giving. At the same time he may not always be able to reply to their specific questions in kind. I wondered if it might clarify something, for both the questioners and myself, if I set down a general reply to the question that comes to me most often in the mail, from both students and their teachers, after some classroom discussion. The unrivaled favorite is this: "Is Phoenix Jackson's grandson really *dead*?"

It refers to a short story I wrote years ago called "A Worn Path," which tells of a day's journey an old woman makes on foot from deep in the country into town and into a doctor's office on behalf of her little grandson; he is at home, periodically ill, and periodically she comes for his medicine; they give it to her as usual, she receives it and starts the journey back.

I had not meant to mystify readers by withholding any fact: it is not a writer's business to tease. The story is told through Phoenix's mind as she undertakes her errand. As the author at one with the character as I tell it, I must assume that the boy is alive. As the reader, you are free to think as you like, of course: The story invites you to believe that no matter what happens, Phoenix for as long as she is able to walk and can hold to her purpose will make her journey. The *possibility* that she would keep on even if he were dead is there in her devotion and its single-minded, single-track errand. Certainly the *artistic* truth, which should be good enough for the fact, lies in Phoenix's own answer to that question. When the nurse asks, "He isn't dead, is he?" she speaks for herself: "He still the same. He going to last."

The grandchild is the incentive. But it is the journey, the going of the errand, that is the story, and the question is not whether the grandchild is in reality alive or dead. It doesn't affect the outcome of the story or its meaning from start to finish. But it is not the question itself that has struck me as much as the idea, almost without exception implied in the asking, that for Phoenix's grandson to be dead would somehow make the story "better."

It's *all right,* I want to say to the students who write to me, for things to be what they appear to be, and for words to mean what they say. It's all right, too, for words and appearances to mean more than one thing—ambiguity is a fact of life. A fiction writer's responsibility covers not only what he presents as the facts of a given story but what he chooses to stir up as their implications; in the end, these implications,

* This is Eudora Welty's analysis of "A Worn Path," included in the "Readings" for Workshop 4.

too, become facts, in the larger fictional sense. But it is not all right, not in good faith, for things *not* to mean what they say.

The grandson's plight was real and it made the truth of the story, which is the story of an errand of love carried out. If the child no longer lived, the truth would persist in the "wornness" of the path. But his being dead can't increase the truth of the story, can't affect it one way or the other. I think I signal this, because the end of the story has been reached before old Phoenix gets home again: she simply starts back. To the question "Is the grandson really dead?" I could reply that it doesn't make any difference. I could also say that I did not make him up in order to let him play a trick on Phoenix. But my best answer would be: "*Phoenix* is alive."

The origin of a story is sometimes a trustworthy clue to the author—or can provide him with the clue—to its key image; maybe in this case it will do the same for the reader. One day I saw a solitary old woman like Phoenix. She was walking; I saw her, at middle distance, in a winter country landscape, and watched her slowly make her way across my line of vision. That sight of her made me write the story. I invented an errand for her, but that only seemed a living part of the figure she was herself. What errand other than for someone else could be making her go? And her going was the first thing, her persisting in her landscape was the real thing, and the first and the real were what I wanted and worked to keep. I brought her up close enough, by imagination, to describe her face, make her present to the eyes, but the full-length figure moving across the winter fields was the indelible one and the image to keep, and the perspective extending into the vanishing distance the true one to hold in mind.

I invented for my character, as I wrote, some passing adventures—some dreams and harassments and a small triumph or two, some jolts to her pride, some flights of fancy to console her, one or two encounters to scare her, a moment that gave her cause to feel ashamed, a moment to dance and preen—for it had to be a *journey,* and all these things belonged to that, parts of life's uncertainty.

A narrative line is in its deeper sense, of course, the tracing out of a meaning, and the real continuity of a story lies in this probing forward. The real dramatic force of a story depends on the strength of the emotion that has set it going. The emotional value is the measure of the reach of the story. What gives any such content to "A Worn Path" is not its circumstances but its *subject:* the deep-grained habit of love.

What I hoped would come clear was that in the whole surround of this story, the world it threads through, the only certain thing at all is the worn path. The habit of love cuts through confusion and stumbles or contrives its way out of difficulty; it remembers the way even when it forgets, for a dumbfounded moment, its reason for being. The path is the thing that matters.

Her victory—old Phoenix's—is when she sees the diploma in the doctor's office, when she finds "nailed up on the wall the document that had been stamped with the gold seal and framed in the gold frame, which matched the dream that was hung up in her head." The return with the medicine is just a matter of retracing her own footsteps. It is the part of the journey, and of the story, that can now go without saying.

In the matter of function, old Phoenix's way might even do as a sort of parallel to your way of work if you are a writer of stories. The way to get there is the all-important, all-absorbing problem, and this problem is your reason for undertaking the story. Your only guide, too, is your sureness about your subject, about what this subject is. Like Phoenix, you work all your life to find your way, through all the obstructions and the false appearances and the upsets you may have brought on yourself, to reach a meaning—using inventions of your imagination, perhaps helped out by your dreams and bits of good luck. And finally too, like Phoenix, you have to assume that what you are working in aid of is life, not death.

But you would make the trip anyway—wouldn't you?—just on hope.

From *A Conversation with My Father*

Grace Paley

Grace Paley (b. 1922, New York City) is a writer of poetry, fiction, essays and journalism. Her work is known both for its attention to the everyday and for its political engagement.

My father is eighty-six years old and in bed. His heart, that bloody motor, is equally old and will not do certain jobs any more. It still floods his head with brainy light. But it won't let his legs carry the weight of his body around the house. Despite my metaphors, this muscle failure is not due to his old heart, he says, but to a potassium shortage. Sitting on one pillow, leaning on three, he offers last-minute advice and makes a request.

"I would like you to write a simple story just once more," he says, "the kind de Maupassant wrote, or Chekhov, the kind you used to write. Just recognizable people and then write down what happened to them next."

I say, "Yes, why not? That's possible." I want to please him, though I don't remember writing that way. I *would* like to try to tell such a story, if he means the kind that begins: "There was a woman . . ." followed by plot, the absolute line between two points which I've always despised. Not for literary reasons, but because it takes all hope away. Everyone, real or invented, deserves the open destiny of life.

Finally I thought of a story that had been happening for a couple of years right across the street. I wrote it down, then read it aloud. "Pa," I said, "how about this? Do you mean something like this?"

> Once in my time there was a woman and she had a son. They lived nicely, in a small apartment in Manhattan. This boy at about fifteen became a junkie, which is not unusual in our neighborhood. In order to maintain her close friendship with him, she became a junkie too. She said it was part of the youth culture, with which she felt very much at home. After a while, for a number of reasons, the boy gave it all up and left the city and his mother in disgust. Hopeless and alone, she grieved. We all visit her.

"O.K., Pa, that's it," I said, "an unadorned and miserable tale."

"But that's not what I mean," my father said. "You misunderstood me on purpose. You know there's a lot more to it. You know that. You left everything out. Turgenev wouldn't do that. Chekhov wouldn't do that. There are in fact Russian writers you never heard of, you don't have an inkling of, as good as anyone, who can write a plain ordinary story, who would not leave out what you have left out. I object not to facts but to people sitting in trees talking senselessly, voices from who knows where . . ."

"Forget that one, Pa, what have I left out now? In this one?"

"Her looks, for instance."

"Oh, quite handsome, I think. Yes."

"Her hair?"

"Dark, with heavy braids, as though she were a girl or a foreigner."

"What were her parents like, her stock? That she became such a person. It's interesting, you know."

"From out of town. Professional people. The first to be divorced in their county. How's that? Enough?" I asked.

"With you, it's all a joke," he said. "What about the boy's father? Why didn't you mention him? Who was he? Or was the boy born out of wedlock?"

"Yes," I said. "He was born out of wedlock."

"For Godsakes, doesn't anyone in your stories get married? Doesn't anyone have the time to run down to City Hall before they jump into bed?"

"No," I said. "In real life, yes. But in my stories, no."

"Why do you answer me like that?"

"Oh, Pa, this is a simple story about a smart woman who came to N.Y.C. full of interest love trust excitement very up to date, and about her son, what a hard time she had in this world. Married or not, it's of small consequence."

"It is of great consequence," he said.

"O.K.," I said.

"O.K. O.K. yourself," he said. "but listen. I believe you that she's good-looking, but I don't think she was so smart."

"That's true," I said. "Actually that's the trouble with stories. People start out fantastic. You think they're extraordinary, but it turns out as the work goes along, they're just average with a good education. Sometimes the other way around, the person's a kind of dumb innocent, but he outwits you and you can't even think of an ending good enough."

"What do you do then?" he asked. He had been a doctor for a couple of decades and then an artist for a couple of decades and he's still interested in details, craft, technique.

"Well, you just have to let the story lie around till some agreement can be reached between you and the stubborn hero."

"Aren't you talking silly, now?" he asked. "Start again," he said. "It so happens I'm not going out this evening. Tell the story again. See what you can do this time."

"O.K.," I said. "But it's not a five-minute job." Second attempt:

Once, across the street from us, there was a fine handsome woman, our neighbor. She had a son whom she loved because she'd known him since birth (in helpless chubby infancy, and in the wrestling, hugging ages, seven to ten, as well as earlier and later). This boy, when he fell into the first of adolescence, became a junkie. He was not a hopeless one. He was in fact hopeful, an ideologue and successful converter. With his busy brilliance, he wrote persuasive articles for his high-school newspaper. Seeking a wider audience, using important connections, he drummed into Lower Manhattan newsstand distribution a periodical called *Oh! Golden Horse!*

In order to keep him from feeling guilty (because guilt is the stony heart of nine-tenths of all clinically diagnosed cancers in America today, she said), and because she had always believed in giving bad habits room at home where one could keep an eye on them, she too became a junkie. Her kitchen was famous for a while—a center for intellectual addicts who knew what they were doing. A few felt artistic like Coleridge and others were scientific and revolutionary like Leary. Although she was often high herself, certain good mothering reflexes remained, and she saw to it that there was lots of orange juice around and honey and milk and vitamin pills. However, she never cooked anything but chili, and that no more than once a week. She explained, when we talked to her, seriously, with neighborly concern, that it was her part in the youth culture and she would rather be with the young, it was an honor, than with her own generation.

One week, while nodding through an Antonioni film, this boy was severely jabbed by the elbow of a stern and proselytizing girl, sitting beside him. She offered immediate apricots and nuts for his sugar level, spoke to him sharply, and took him home.

She had heard of him and his work and she herself published, edited, and wrote a competitive journal called *Man Does Live By Bread Alone.* In the organic heat of her continuous presence he could not help but become interested once more in his muscles, his arteries, and nerve connections. In fact he began to love them, treasure them, praise them with funny little songs in *Man Does Live* . . .

the fingers of my flesh transcend
my transcendental soul
the tightness in my shoulders end
my teeth have made me whole

To the mouth of his head (that glory of will and determination) he brought hard apples, nuts, wheat germ, and soybean oil. He said to his old friends, From now on, I guess I'll keep my wits about me. I'm going on the natch. He said he was about to begin a spiritual deep-breathing journey. How about you too, Mom? he asked kindly.

His conversion was so radiant, splendid, that neighborhood kids his age began to say that he had never been a real addict at all, only a journalist along for the smell of the story. The mother tried several times to give up what had become without her son and his friends a lonely habit. This effort only brought it to supportable levels. The boy and his girl took their electronic mimeograph and moved to the bushy edge of another borough. They were very strict. They said they would not see her again until she had been off drugs for sixty days.

At home alone in the evening, weeping, the mother read and reread the seven issues of *Oh! Golden Horse!* They seemed to her as truthful as ever. We often crossed the street to visit and console. But if we mentioned any of our children who were at college or in the hospital or dropouts at home, she would cry out, My baby! My baby! and burst into terrible, face-scarring, time-consuming tears. The End.

First my father was silent, then he said, "Number One: You have a nice sense of humor. Number Two: I see you can't tell a plain story. So don't waste time." Then he said sadly, "Number Three: I suppose that means she was alone, she was left like that, his mother. Alone. Probably sick?"

I said, "Yes."

"Poor woman. Poor girl, to be born in a time of fools, to live among fools. The end. The end. You were right to put that down. The end."

I didn't want to argue, but I had to say, "Well, it is not necessarily the end, Pa."

"Yes," he said, "what a tragedy. The end of a person."

"No, Pa," I begged him. "It doesn't have to be. She's only about forty. She could be a hundred different things in this world as time goes on. A teacher or a social worker. An ex-junkie! Sometimes it's better than having a master's in education."

"Jokes," he said. "As a writer that's your main trouble. You don't want to recognize it. Tragedy! Plain tragedy! Historical tragedy! No hope. The end."

"Oh, Pa," I said. "She could change."

"In your own life, too, you have to look it in the face." He took a couple of nitroglycerin. "Turn to five," he said, pointing to the dial on the oxygen tank. He inserted the tubes into his nostrils and breathed deep. He closed his eyes and said, "No."

I had promised the family to always let him have the last word when arguing, but in this case I had a different responsibility. That woman lives across the street. She's my knowledge and my intention. I'm sorry for her. I'm not going to leave her there in that house crying. (Actually neither would Life, which unlike me has no pity.)

Therefore: She did change. Of course her son never came home again. But right now, she's the receptionist in a storefront community clinic in the East Village. Most of the customers are young people, some old friends. The head doctor has said to her, "If we only had three people in this clinic with your experiences . . ."

"The doctor said that?" My father took the oxygen tubes out of his nostrils and said, "Jokes, Jokes again."

"No, Pa, it could really happen that way, it's a funny world nowadays."

"No," he said. "Truth first. She will slide back. A person must have character. She does not."

"No, Pa," I said. "That's it. She's got a job. Forget it. She's in that storefront working."

"How long will it be?" he asked. "Tragedy! You too. When will you look it in the face?"

Writing in the World: An Interview about Writing

Essential Premises

- It's interesting and helpful to investigate the remarkable variety of kinds of writing that people do for school, for work, and on their own.
- It's also interesting and helpful to interview people and investigate the different ways they go about writing. It is usually reassuring, whether we discover similarities ("Wow—she has the same experience I do"), or differences ("How interesting—she has a completely different way of going about it").
- Interview essays liven up our writing by getting us to use reported speech in our writing.

Main Assignment Preview

For this workshop we ask you to conduct an interview and find out as much as you can about what and how someone else writes. Our main goal is for you to learn about the great diversity of kinds of writing and ways of writing in the world so that you'll see more options when you approach a writing task. As you hear the interviews written by your classmates, you will gain much more perspective on all the things writing can do.

But we also have other goals for this workshop:

- As you work through this assignment, you'll get practice in how to find or carve out a theme or develop a conclusion from a mass of diverse material.
- You'll also learn to conduct interviews: to ask questions and to listen to what another person is saying, but also to hear what's behind what she is saying.
- School writing and academic essay writing are always in danger of going dead. The interview is good for helping you get lively speech qualities and "voice" into your writing because you will use lots of quoted speech.

- You'll get the chance to begin to think about how writing is often the blending together of your own ideas and the ideas of others into a text you can call your own.

Main Assignment: *Conducting and Writing Up an Interview*

Your main assignment is to conduct an interview and write an interview essay. Here are the three main things that most readers will be looking for in an interview essay:

1. As much information as possible about what and how your interviewee writes and how she thinks and feels about writing—as full a picture as possible.
2. A feel for the person.
3. Your own thinking as you make sense of all your data; a conclusion of your own.

Choosing Someone to Interview

Pick someone who writes a significant amount and cares about writing. Four possibilities suggest themselves:

- An adult professional: either a professional writer or someone who has to write for her job. You could use this assignment to interview a professional in a field you are considering for yourself. (You may be surprised how much people have to write in fields that seem distant from writing. Recent research shows that engineers, for example, spend an average of 25 percent of their week writing.)
- An adult who is devoted to writing though it is not part of her job. This might be someone who writes fiction or poetry or does research in her free time.
- A junior, senior, or graduate student who is majoring in a subject you would like to explore.
- A member of your writing class. (Probably you'll want to pick someone who is particularly interested in writing, though it could also be useful to interview someone who particularly hates writing in order to learn how that can happen to people and what the effects are.)

If you are working in groups, you'll all learn the most if you each choose a different kind of person to interview. Adult subjects make the most sense for students who live at home or off campus, since they can pick an adult from their home environment. But of course there are adults on any campus—and not just faculty—who write seriously, whether or not it is part of their job.

You'll need *two* interviews with your subject (about two or three hours in all). Set up these interviews early and follow through to make them happen. Busy people sometimes have to change appointments, so you may need to push to get your interviews. The important thing is to make sure the person has enough interest in writing to give you the time you need.

A Practice Interview with a Classmate

Some of you may have done some interviewing in the past, perhaps as a reporter for a school newspaper, perhaps as part of an assignment for a particular class. If so, you can help others in the class who haven't had this experience. Interviews can be fun, but they do take some practice and skill, especially if the process makes you nervous. We suggest a short practice interview with a classmate.

This practice session can be as little as 15 or 20 minutes, but it will give you practice at the essential thing in interviewing: asking only a few key questions, holding back and being quiet, listening hard, and taking notes.

The two main questions or requests are utterly simple:

- Please list as many important writing occasions or incidents from your life as you can think of right now.
- Tell me as much as you can about the most interesting or important one.

Your classmate may not be able to think of many occasions in response to the first question, but that's all right. Just get her to pick *one* occasion and tell as much as possible about it. Telling the story of one writing occasion usually makes people think of more. Get the person to choose different kinds of writing.

Your main job is to get your subject talking and to listen. Your best tool for getting the individual to talk is to be genuinely curious and to listen attentively and with involvement. You can show your interest by asking little follow-up questions. ("How did you feel when that happened?" "Was it noisy or quiet?") But don't try to steer too much. Let your classmate determine the direction and the main topics. For your job is to find out how this person sees and understands and feels about the world of her writing.

As you listen take some notes. Don't be shy about it; be proud of it. Most people are flattered that you care enough about what they are saying to take notes. But you don't need to try for full, extensive notes. Simply jot down single words and phrases as each topic or point goes by—words and phrases that are somehow important or striking and that are connected to all the main points. That's enough—as long as you go back over these abbreviated notes

Exploring the Writing Process

Galbraith writes longhand—"That is the speed at which my mind works"—and revises a great deal. It is usually at about the fifth draft, he says, that his trademark note of casual spontaneity enters the prose.

John Cassidy, The New Yorker, ***30 Nov. 1998 [From a profile of John Kenneth Galbraith (b. 1908), one of the most influential 20th-century writers about economy and culture.]***

very soon after the interview in order to flesh them out with fuller notes of what your subject actually said.

If this were a longer interview, you would be going over your notes alone. But for this exercise, do the reconstructing aloud in front of your classmate interviewee. As you go through your notes repeating and reconstructing what she said, she can help you by making corrections. And after you finish, she can mention things that *she* thought important or interesting that you didn't mention—just to give you another perspective on what you recorded.

If this were a longer interview, you would also be jotting down some of *your* thoughts, observations, and trains of thought as you reconstruct the interview. But for this quick in-class exercise, simply *tell* some of these observations after you have reconstructed your subject's words. After this interview-and-reporting-back, switch places and give your classmate a chance to interview you and report back.

You and your partner will also find it valuable to talk about what it was like being interviewed: what approaches made you feel most comfortable and which questions proved to be the most effective prompts for stimulating memory and thoughts.

Option in Threes This same interviewing exercise can be rich and interesting in groups of three. One person interviews another, as before, but with the third person as onlooker, either listening or also taking notes. Then when the interviewer reconstructs his notes, the onlooker can chime in to help capture the words actually spoken or to comment on things he would have tried to record that the interviewer omitted. Or they can both reconstruct notes, compare them, and learn from each other—with, of course, the help of the interviewee.

Your Real Interview—First Session

You may be nervous as you start, but once you get going you'll probably enjoy the session. This interview will be as simple a process as your practice interview for the same two questions or requests are virtually all you'll need. Just go back and forth between getting your subject to remember various writing occasions and getting her to talk about certain ones in more detail.

Exploring the Writing Process

Interviewing made me sort of nervous because I just didn't know whether she wanted to talk to me about this or was just being nice or polite. I took some notes at the beginning but they didn't mean much; when I tried to figure them out I couldn't even remember talking about those things. I was just too nervous. When she started talking about trying to write a novel and how her daughter knocked milk on the pages and then the dog sat on them I just laughed. I remember that and I didn't even take notes. I remember so clearly that she said "My dog's an author!" Then I wasn't so nervous anymore.

Marsha Koons

Again, try to ask broad, open-ended questions and mostly listen. Because this is a longer interview and you are trying to find out more, we suggest three other kinds of questions you can use during the interview.

1. *Supplemental questions* you can toss in as your subject is talking about various writing occasions, especially if he or she seems to run out:
   - What was satisfying or pleasing?
   - What was hard?
   - What was perplexing?
   - What was the occasion (assignment, need, situation)?
   - Was the writing required or voluntary?
   - How high were the stakes for this writing—how much did it matter to you?
   - Tell about the process of getting this written.
   - Did it go through stages or drafts or changes?
   - What surprised you?
   - How did you *feel* about the process of writing it?
   - How did you *feel* about what you had produced?
   - Who was the writing for?
   - What were you trying to achieve with this writing—what effect were you trying to have on your readers (for example to inform them, persuade them, entertain them, impress them, make them realize how you feel, get something off your chest)?
   - Were there other possible readers or past readers in your mind as you were writing?
   - How did readers react?
   - Where did you do this writing and what were the conditions like in that setting?
2. *Conclusions or reflections* from the writer herself. "Do you have any thoughts about all this? What strikes you as interesting about all that you have been telling me?"
3. *A fuller picture of the range of writing* that this person has done. After she has told you about several writing occasions, she'll be in a better position to give an overview of the kinds of writing she does most and the kinds she does least. If you ask for this overview at the beginning, she is more liable to forget about certain kinds of writing that might be

Exploring the Writing Process

This year I had a fight with my best friend, so I'm much more into my studies. For the first half of the summer we had a job, but when we came back to school we weren't talking or anything. I would talk to my mother about what was happening. I guess for the first week she listened, but then she said, "Why are you letting this affect you?" I didn't know what I was upset about, so I went upstairs and I just started writing why that had happened. I felt better about it. I reread it and I saw that it was probably partly my fault. I guess that was a good idea to write it down. I never got a chance to tell her because she was always with her [new] best friend.

***From an interview with "Lisa," in Linda Miller Cleary's* From the Other Side of the Desk: Students Speak Out about Writing**

interesting and important. For example, she might forget that she is a big list maker or a writer of tiny notes to family or friends.

If you feel your interview falling into a lifeless question-and-answer pattern, try to use more open-ended questions, such as "Tell me a story about a time when you were really pleased or disappointed" or "Tell me more about that" or "How did you feel about that?" and so forth. And don't be afraid to wait for a while at the end of an answer. Be willing to leave long silences hanging in the air. People often give their best answers after a long pause for reflection. Remember that one of the best things you can say is simply, "That sounds interesting; talk some more about that."

Tape Recorder You might use a tape recorder for your interview if you prefer, and if you have one available and your subject doesn't object. It will let you quote your subject's words exactly. Most people don't mind being recorded and soon get over being self-conscious. You won't have to take notes during the interview (except perhaps to record your own thoughts and reactions). But a tape recorder doesn't solve your interviewing problems. You'll still have to take notes as you listen to the tape. And taping can deceive you into becoming a lazy listener during the interview. You can capture much more in notes than you might expect, and note taking is an important skill to develop.

Reconstructing Your Notes after Your First Interview

Don't forget: It's crucial to make time right after the interview to go over your sketchy notes.

- Write out explicit notes for the main points. Try to quote some of your subject's most interesting or striking words.
- Don't forget to include a few *physical* details such as the setting (the room and the atmosphere) and the person's appearance (how she was dressed, how she spoke and moved).
- Write out some of your *own* observations, reactions, questions, and trains of thought about what the person has said.
- If you had to decide now on a "moral of the story," what would it be? You don't have to settle it yet, but what's the most interesting conclusion you could draw at this point?
- Work out some new questions for a second interview, questions which follow up on ideas generated as you reconstruct your notes.

If you delay going over your notes for even three or four hours, you will lose many crucial details. It's not too big a job. For right now you are not trying even for a draft of your interview; all you're doing is going over and adding to your notes.

Using Partners or Small Groups to Help You Prepare for the Second Interview It will help you enormously to meet with a partner or small group and share what you have in your notes. Read back the main things your subject told you and all your observations, reflections, and questions. Then you can ask them to give you *their* observations, reflections, and questions. Outside eyes will invariably help you see implications that you didn't see earlier. You need to figure out some conclusions of your own, and others can give you a lot of help.

Your Second Interview

Your second interview will follow comfortably and interestingly from your first one. You can start off by just summarizing for your subject the main things you learned from her, asking her to make corrections and additions. Almost always, your observations will spark other things she will have to say. Afterwards, you can ask her the questions you have worked out on the basis of the first interview: things you want to know more about. Here are a few topics for further questions:

- *Kinds.* Try to cover all the possibilities. For example, if your interviewee is a reporter and if she says she writes nothing but news stories, probe for other writing in her life. And even ask her to explore differences between *kinds* of news stories.
- *Processes.* Try for lots of details here: What happens in your interviewee's mind before she does any writing—during the hours or days before she puts a word on paper? What are her first words on paper? notes? an outline? or just random jottings? Or does she go right to written-out drafts or perhaps even directly to final drafts? What are her feelings throughout the whole process? What about the role of other people? What kinds of feedback help her? And don't settle for a "general story of how I *always* or *usually* write." Probe for differences and exceptions.
- *Audience.* If your first interview didn't touch on this, ask her about her important readers, past and present: former teachers, present friends, supervisors. Get her to talk about what makes an audience helpful or not helpful for her. (Audience is a complicated issue because often, especially on the job, there is more than one audience. The news story may be for people who buy the paper, but the editor sees it first and has to like it; the memo may be for the clients or buyers, but it has to work for the writer's immediate supervisor too.) Does she think a lot or not so much about audience when writing? At which points in the writing process does she think about audience most?
- *Changes.* What important changes have occurred in how she writes and feels about writing? Does she see other changes in the future? Does she have writing goals she hasn't yet met? What are her hopes about these?
- *Functions.* If your interviewee says that the function of her writing is just to inform or just to make money, ask her to think about subsidiary functions within those main functions. Does her writing also serve to persuade, to give orders, to help her understand her life, to give personal satisfaction? Ask her to think about function in connection with audience.

From Interview to Interview Essay

Make sure to find a time soon after your second interview to flesh out your sketchy notes and to write out some of your own observations, reflections, and conclusions. Again, see if you can enlist the help of your partner or small group in responding to your notes.

One way to move toward an essay is to create a collage: Simply choose the most interesting points and quotations from your subject and your own most interesting observations, reflections, and conclusions, and then arrange them as separate fragments into a pleasing or intuitive sequence. Perhaps your teacher will even invite a collage instead of an essay. (See Workshops 1 and 3 for more about the collage form.)

But probably you will need to produce an interview essay—an interesting amalgam. It needs to contain lots of mere *summary* of what your subject told you (using quotations where you can). Yet the overall essay needs to reflect your slant and contain much of your thinking. You have to figure out what observations and conclusions you want to draw from all the material.

There is no single proper way to organize such an essay. In effect, you are writing an "analysis-of-data" essay. Often the easiest way to organize such an essay is to start with the data, summarizing the main things you learned from your interview. Then go on to the analysis: your own observations and conclusions. However, there are plenty of other ways to organize an analysis of data. You can start with *your* main point and then try to explain and demonstrate it with data. Or you can present a bit of data, then some of your thinking, then more data, then more of your thinking, and so on—in effect, telling the story of your thinking.

It will be crucial to get feedback from your partner or small group on a draft of this essay before making your final revision. See "Sharing and Responding" in this workshop.

About Accuracy in Quotation If you used a tape recorder, you can note somewhere that you did so and that your quoted passages use the actual words spoken by your subject. Even so, however, it is customary when transcribing someone's casual speech to do minor cleaning up: leaving out "um's" and "er's" and digressive phrases, and fixing grammar and the like. If you didn't use a tape recorder, do your best to find and reconstruct some actual words, phrases, and sentences and put them in quotation marks. Actual quotations pump lifeblood into an interview essay. But acknowledge that you were working from notes and therefore might not have gotten some of the quotations *exactly* right. (For help with the mechanics of quoting, see Mini-Workshop J.)

Suggestions for Collaboration

This is a particularly good workshop for collaborative writing. You can interview with one or more partners and then write up the interview and your conclusions collaboratively. Another approach is to interview different people and then write a collaborative paper that compares and contrasts your interviewees and draws some conclusions that all of you arrive at collaboratively.

If you have selected or been assigned to write a collaborative comparison essay, do five or ten minutes of focused freewriting about what you see as the conclusions you can draw about your writer on the basis of your interview. Then get together with your partner(s) and trade freewritings as a way to get started on your collaborative analysis. You may want to extend this written conversation through several interchanges as you did in Workshop 3.

It you are studying different writers, here are some questions to consider:

- How alike or different are the kinds of writing our interviewees do?
- In what ways are our interviewees' writing habits alike or different?
- What can we say about each of our interviewees' attitudes toward writing? What effects do these attitudes seem to have?
- How does the writing our interviewees do relate to the writing they did while in school? to the writing we do in school?
- What conclusions can we draw from each of the interviews? Are these conclusions consistent, or do we seem to draw very different conclusions from each of the interviews? If so, what does this suggest?
- What can we learn about our own writing processes from studying these two interviews?

Once you and your partner(s) have discussed or written about these and other issues, you can begin to draft your collaborative essay. (You might want to look back at Workshop 3 for guidelines for collaborative writing.) Keep in mind that you and your partner don't have to agree on every statement you make. Disagreements can be thought-provoking for readers. The more significant the disagreement, the more urgent it is to present it to others.

A Note about Publication It is common for local newspapers and magazines to publish interviews, including interviews with writers. A campus newspaper is a natural place for an interview with a faculty member, administrator, or staff member focusing on the writing they do and how they go about it. Home town newspapers are natural places for interviews with people who live there. You might choose this essay to revise further (perhaps in a revising workshop) and send it off to see if you can get it published.

Sharing and Responding

The most important person to share your essay with is the person you are writing about. It is only fair to let that person read a draft of what you have written. Your interviewee may be so busy that she doesn't care about seeing a draft or the final product, but it's important to make the offer.

Give her a fairly coherent draft so that it is not a chore to read, but be sure it's not a final draft because you need to invite your subject to tell you where she disagrees with you. If she disagrees with you on a matter of fact, you have an obligation to revise according to her feedback; almost invariably she knows more than you do about the facts of her writing, her experience, and her thinking. If she disagrees with you on a matter of interpretation or theory, you don't have an absolute obligation to go along with how she sees things. But you have an obligation to try hard to *see* things the way she does—to play the believing game—and seriously consider changing your mind.

About sharing with members of your class. If you are doing this workshop early in the semester, the main benefit from readers will come from the early forms of feedback: "Sharing: No Response"; "Pointing and Center of Gravity"; "Summary and Sayback"; and "What Is Almost Said." You might also ask readers whether they feel you have fulfilled the three criteria for an interview essay that we mentioned at the start of the workshop:

- Giving as much information as possible about what and how your interviewee writes and how she thinks and feels about writing—as full a picture as possible.
- Giving a feel for the person.
- Giving your own thinking as you make sense of all your data—a conclusion of your own.

You could also ask readers what lessons about their own writing they learned from reading your interview.

Process Journal

You won't need the questions that follow if you can easily write about moments in this week's writing when things went well and badly—and surprisingly. What was going on for you in your thinking and feeling? How did words behave for you? These stories will build a powerful foundation for growth in your writing.

- How did your note taking go? What was it like reconstructing your notes?
- When did your conclusion or main point come to you? Was it a struggle to find one, or did it just seem to appear? Finding the *point* in a great mass of messy data is one of the main cognitive skills involved in learning. On the basis of this workshop's assignment, give yourself advice on ways to develop this skill in the future.
- Compare the goals or functions your interviewee was trying to achieve in her writings and the goals or functions you try to achieve in the various writings you do. How often do you actually think about what your writing *does* (other than fulfill an assignment)?

Interview

Salvatore Bianco

I conducted my interview with my brother, Anthony Bianco. I interviewed him as a person who greatly dislikes writing. Our conversation took place in my bedroom, and it lasted about an hour and fifteen minutes. The atmosphere was a very relaxed, casual one, and, because of this, my brother's opinions were both open and honest.

Anthony is a sophomore in high school and feels that he has had his share of writing assignments. I asked him how he felt about writing, and he said that he disliked it so much to the point where he actually hated it. The main question that I wanted answered was—Why?

My brother told me many reasons for his attitude toward writing. The primary reason, according to him, is that, "I never get the grade I feel I deserve. I've put a lot of effort into some assignments, and they were given bad grades." He told me about the time he was working on a biography about Edgar Allan Poe. Anthony stayed up most of the night, dedicating a great deal of time and effort to it, but all he received for it was a C–. "I did all that work for nothing! I don't even like writing; it's just a waste of my time." When he does do poorly on reports that he knows he has put time and effort into, they come back to him with comments and question marks written all over them. "That gets me annoyed because the way I wrote the sentences seemed right to me; I don't understand what the teachers want from me!"

The actual writing of an essay seems to be a problem for my brother. He finds it difficult to write proper introductions and conclusions. Also, he is unable to recognize when new paragraphs should be started. He is never at a loss for ideas, but he feels that his vocabulary is very limited. Because of this last problem, Anthony usually cannot find the proper words to express his ideas. "I know what I want to say, but I just don't know how to say it."

I then asked my brother what thoughts run through his mind just prior to writing. He often wonders about the length of the essay, what it will be about, when he will finish it, if he will be satisfied with it, and how the teacher will grade it. When he writes, he finds that he really does not concentrate on what he is doing. This is especially true during essay exams. "When I'm being rushed, I can't think straight!"

I thought it was necessary to find out just how he goes about writing something. Anthony told me that if his grades were borderline, he would take "very short" notes on his subject. Then he would write his rough draft before actually writing the final version. If, however, his grades were not borderline, he would just write the essay straight through and only recopy it if the first one was totally illegible.

Although Anthony hates to write, he does prefer some aspects of it to others. He would rather write a composition than, for example, a biography because he feels biographies are boring, yet he finds it easy to make up stories and exaggerates them when possible. He also likes writing at home more than in school because at home there is hardly any pressure for him to deal with. When at home, Anthony prefers to write in either the kitchen during the evening or in the backyard on the picnic table during the late afternoon hours. Noise does not seem to bother my brother's concentration. Yet he does feel that he writes better when there is little noise. But he does not care about writing enough to worry about finding a place to work where it is quiet. Anthony seems to write only for himself, unless grades are involved. He says he does not write for the class because "the teacher doesn't make us get involved with discussing each other's essays." And he does not write for the teacher because "no matter how much I work on my essay, it won't meet my teacher's standards anyway."

In conducting this interview with my brother, I feel that I have learned some things about him and about myself as well. I never realized how dead set my brother was against writing. I can understand how trying one's best but failing to be rewarded for it is enough to discourage most people. I have also learned that no matter how many times he is forced to write, and no matter what grades he receives for his writing, my brother is not going to change his attitude toward writing. What I learned about myself from this interview was that I value writing more than I previously thought I did. Of course, I have had my share of disappointments. But I am glad that I have been able to push myself to do better because writing can be an extremely pleasurable experience.

Analysis of Interview with Ellen Exner

Tyson Peelle

Tyson Peelle illustrates an interesting and useful kind of process writing here: he writes comments by hand in the margin of his essay, telling what he was doing or trying for in this revision.

Ellen said so much at the interview that I ended up w/more than enough information!

Tyson Peelle
Nov. 12, 1996
Writing 113

Decided on this title the night I wrote the rough draft

Ellen Exner: The Devoted Writer!

revised, clearer & smoother

hopefully more accurate

Ellen Exner, a junior at UMass, enjoys writing research papers for her Russian literature class. She particularly likes the huge amount of new information that she learns for every Russian paper she writes. Such pleasure in writing these papers is not only evident by her words. The process and effort that she puts forth shows that she is fully involved in her research papers! Such effort is rewarded by the grades that she receives.

smoother

Before analyzing how Ellen writes her Russian papers, it is important to know what she is assigned to do. Essentially, all of her papers in Russian class are the same format. The teacher requires the students to write 5–10 pages for each research assignment, yet Ellen commented, "He really wants ten pages." There must be evidence of thorough research. The paper must be readable and interesting, "not dry and lame." Also, the student is to include opinions about what s/he has read. Ellen said that the papers must be "very subjective, [with] a lot of [the writer's] own opinions." These opinions must be well-supported with outside sources.

added information that is important, taken from another part of the interview

changed from 1st to 3rd person

Other than these requirements, the research papers for Ellen's Russian class are open-ended. The students are required to pick any topic that is interesting. The topic could be something discussed in class, but it doesn't have to be (assuming it is relevant to the course). Furthermore, the paper need not be in formal research format! For example, it could be poetry, "as long as it's a substantial paper."

added w/o saying "as long as" so that it's not used 2Xs in ¶

Ellen noted that the openness makes the assignment harder. However, this does not cause her to dislike the assignment! She stated, "I [get myself] interested in the topic." As mentioned above, Ellen especially likes the research aspect of the assignments. She said, "This is good because you learn a lot this way."

softens the redundance from ¶1

no revision since perfected in rough draft

The evidence that Ellen enjoys her research papers is by her extensive writing process. Right away, she said, "I'm a big drafter." Ellen does a tremendous amount of writing before going to the computer. To begin an assignment, she writes down some ideas while she is thinking of the topic. Many of these ideas are possible opinions that she might use. She does this throughout the day, no matter how random the idea seems to be.

Ellen begins this process before she does her research. As she reads more articles and literary criticism from the library, she adjusts her opinions or changes them completely! Because of such drastic changes, she does tremendous scratching out, rewriting and refocusing. Throughout this process, Ellen's opinions "expand [as she finds new information], and then narrow again [as she picks out the most important aspects]." This process continues over a period of days.

By the time Ellen has a solid 3–4 pages, she goes to the computer. As she types, she continues to expand her ideas while making a conscious effort to stay on the topic. In the end, however, she always has something different than what she began with. She stated, "It's not necessarily better, hopefully not worse, but it's different." Ellen continues this process on the computer until she is satisfied or until time runs out.

Overall, Ellen sees herself as a perfectionist. She is insistent in having a topic and an opinion in her head right from the beginning. "I never end up using what I have at first," she said. "It's always trash. But, it's a good way to start."

Ellen shared two papers from her Russian literature class as examples. One of her papers was about the writers Tolstoy, Dostoyevsky, and Vladimir Nabokov (which I will call "the VN paper"). The other paper was about Tolstoy and Mozart (or "the TM paper"). With both of these papers, Ellen followed the process described above.

In writing my rough draft, I fell into the perfectionist trap for this whole section. I put forth tremendous effort to make sure this was in chronological order, which is not the order in which I heard things during the interview.

new material

Ellen gave some details on how she wrote these two papers. For the VN paper, Ellen was reading some short stories by Vladimir Nabokov, who wrote literature in both Russian and English. Ellen, being interested in what influenced Nabokov's writing, decided to write a research paper about him.

In her research, she found out that Tolstoy and Dostoyevsky, two other Russian writers, had tremendous influence on Nabokov's writing. Then, she dug deeper, "tracing where Tolstoy and Dostoyevsky's ideas came from" and how they influenced Nabokov. Ellen was able to include a lot of her own opinions of the works of these writers in this paper.

unsure of accuracy

wanted to emphasize where part of deeper analysis was directed

For the TM paper, Ellen noticed that Tolstoy wrote literature in a very similar way to how Mozart wrote music. They were both "precise on how they [did] things." Tolstoy wrote a book titled What Is Art? In this book, he used Mozart as an example of an excellent artist.

wanted to clarify a bit

In order to write the TM paper, Ellen read Tolstoy's book. She also read musicologists' commentaries on Tolstoy's book. This enabled her to form an opinion and back it up with other sources.

clearer, not as if they sat down together and decided

With respect to the two papers mentioned above, both Ellen and her teacher independently agreed that the papers were a great success! "I got A's and I learned," said Ellen. For the TM paper, the teacher complimented Ellen on her "intelligent work" and "thorough research." For the VN paper, the teacher liked her discussion of family affair. For Ellen's personal interest, he suggested that she take a look at Nabokov's lectures on literature.

correct way of doing it (I believe)

Ellen made no mention of this in her analysis, thus I couldn't mention it.

new material, spent some time organizing

Ellen did mention a couple difficulties with writing research papers for Russian literature. Primarily, she noted the difficulty of writing about literature of a foreign culture. "You're just overwhelmed with what you don't know," she said. Ellen also said that literature is difficult to write about because of its subjectiveness. "It's an art form," she noted, "so every one has different reaches on it." For both of these

she said these things in a different order, but this way works best organizationally reasons, she said, "You come into a lot of accuracy problems."

However, she has a positive view of these difficulties. She optimistically stated, "No matter what you do, if you do the research, you learn a ton." She also mentioned, "The more you write [research papers], the better groove you have. There is a better comfort zone."

last quote is not word-for-word

beginning of conclusion

No doubt, Ellen has a very positive view of writing research papers for Russian literature class, and she enjoys it tremendously! This is especially reflected in the effort she puts forth, her extensive writing process. To be honest, I thought that such incredible effort only existed in the professional world of writing. Most students that I meet want to get out of the restrictions of writing assigned papers on topics that they don't care about. This is even true of those who like to write on their own!

at first, I thought all of this would fit into one ¶, I didn't expect 3¶s!

redundant

Before meeting Ellen, I did not believe that anyone goes through such effort for school papers. I am particularly impressed with the fact that she is not a writing major! She is a music major, like I am. The effort and devotion that Ellen puts forth is even unusual for courses related to one's own major! At least, that is according to my observation of other music majors at UMass.

added information

confusing sentence

true

other added information

a little too strong

In general, I thought that my view of school work was unusually positive. Most peers scoff at my view of benefiting and learning from school. But, compared to Ellen, at least with repect to writing, her motivation to benefit and learn from school is far greater than mine! Overall, Ellen Exner seems to enjoy her Russian papers as if she chose to write them for her own satisfaction on the professional level!

better pair of sentences than rough draft

The Social Consequences of Voicelessness

A Profile of Joseph

Linda Miller Cleary

Linda Miller Cleary has written extensively on issues of composition, literacy, and education, in articles and in such books as From the Other Side of the Desk: Students Speak Out about Writing *(1991). This interview is from that book. She is in the English Department at the University of Minnesota–Duluth.*

There's a logical consequence to the heavy "please-the-teacher" mentality that pervaded the successful students' experience. Some students who felt disconnected from the writing they had to do did that work with a touch of anger; a loss occurred for them when the secondary school writing straitjacket was applied. Still other students, however, scared me because they accepted "pleasing the teacher" without perceiving it as a sellout, without seeing it as a loss of personal integrity. They learned to distance themselves from their writing, to please the audience, to be untrue to themselves. Furthermore, they became good at it. Joseph had mastered the art of pleasing his high school teachers.

• • •

In fifth and sixth grade, I got the urge to write a story once in a while. I remember writing about my dog. I guess I don't write for fun anymore. It's just writing for like a teacher or a judge. Most of the writing I do now can go back to learning from sixth-grade composition, like topic sentences of paragraphs and things like that. I guess the past set a good foundation for my writing now, about 50 percent of it, and then I think the rest of the 50 percent came recently, organized it, perfected it, made it easier.

In seventh grade our teacher was tougher, and we did have to do reports every once in a while. Before that we were learning grammar and stuff. We had a textbook with certain stories and interpretation of the stories, and I did really poorly. I didn't know exactly what kind of answers the teachers wanted to particular questions. I didn't really know how you're supposed to go about telling somebody about a story. I started telling the story, and my teacher stopped me and said, "Just tell what mainly happened; go to the end or something." It wasn't that hard to learn once you got the hang of it. You know what the teacher wants, and that would be a good summary. I didn't like literature. I guess I haven't liked it until recently because I didn't do too well. I didn't like spelling until I started doing well in it. I guess I didn't know exactly what was a good answer and what wasn't, and how specific to get. Our teacher was pretty hard.

In eighth grade we did start learning how to write formally, more formally, with the introduction and summary and topic sentences. The first essay that we did for him [was] just a regular article about science. I wrote it, and he brought it up in front of class and said, "This is an example of a good essay." So I guess that was my first. After a while it was actually pretty nice because I liked it better when I wrote better.

We wrote reports, essays, and things like that in ninth grade—more practice and learning new ways of writing. I did have a speech class, and we'd do a lot of writing there: essay, informative, and persuasive. But the first day I can remember in that class, we all stood up and said our names and a hobby that we had, and the next day we had to write an essay on that hobby. I had a friend who had two three-wheelers. That was really fun for me; I liked what I wrote about. That's probably the first time I started speaking in front of a class. It's pretty scary the first time. I always read what I was saying, but we were supposed to ad-lib a little bit. I got *A*'s in the class; maybe she wasn't that strict.

I really have had to worry about what I was gonna write, always worrying if the audience will like it or not. It's been hard because I didn't know what my classmates would accept. The popular ones were really relaxed; I wasn't. I had to worry what I was gonna read in front of class. I'd worry about sounding awkward. I tried to stay away from jokes, I didn't know what kind of joke would work, and I'd get embarrassed if they didn't laugh. I usually tried to stay in the middle of acceptable. I wanted to be creative, but the worst fear was getting too creative. I wasn't writing it for something that I would like. It was more something that they would like. I remember when we had to write an advertisement about a certain product. You had to get creative and that worried me. What if you tried to be funny, and it wasn't funny. I remember in the end I just took a song, and I spoke with the song in an excited way. It was an airline vacation to Europe. They kinda liked it because of the song. It was an acceptable attention getter.

In debate we have to be persuasive and we have to be understandable, make a point that the judges will accept. In an essay it's just writing about something and the teacher grades it, and you are arguing basically. That's what debate is about. We use a lot of analogies, and I've used some of them in writing in English class, for ideas and organization. It's kind of a game. It takes a while to find out how or what exactly the audience is going to believe. In English I usually stay neutral. I used to not like literature, interpreting literature because I didn't know what the teacher would want. But once you debate in speech you know what or which arguments will basically be accepted. When I start writing a speech, I feel strongly for that particular side, and so when I switch over to the opposite thinking, I start believing that side. I wouldn't say that I have any major opinions. A lot of it is presenting arguments that aren't really true. It's just whether or not the other debater can take it apart, or whether the judge will like it or not.

I don't really write for myself. I can't think of any time . . . Oh, okay, I did a voice of democracy thing once. They have a contest at each school where they gave us a topic, and they took the top three people from each school, and the first person got $100, the second got $75, and the third got $50. They'd send the speeches over to judges. And it was called The Challenge of American Citizenship. It was a really tough topic—a lot of ways you could interpret it. There was really no way you could tell what would be a good speech. I was thinking the normal ones would be voting and public service and all that. Voting is so obviously American citizenship that I decided to do something about citizenship and world peace, racism. It was the one time when I didn't do what I thought the judges would like. I did what I thought would be a good speech. I liked it, and I didn't win. People who did win did things like voting. I wish I had won the $100. I thought next time though I wouldn't be so original. I decided to do what would win. School writing is the same basically; I need to get the grade.

I guess with my English teacher it would be better to be original 'cause she'd be looking for that type of thing. When I gave the Voice of Democracy speech, they would be more likely to look at what they would want to hear, while if I was doing it for my teacher, she would take a look at it more objectively, and, "Okay, this is more original." If too many people in the class were going one way, I chose differently. I just wrote this paper on "To Build a Fire." We were supposed to pick a topic sentence from seven that she gave you, and then just write an introduction and conclusion with a couple of paragraphs to support it. The first thing I did was to look at the topics; 90 percent of the class was doing the same topics. I decided to look for other topic sentences and put them together. I've never rebelled about what the teacher wanted us to write about. If the teacher chose something to write about, she usually gives us choices on how to approach it. A lot of kids in the class get mad because the teacher says you have the wrong opinion. I guess I haven't really had any problems with that, I just try to write what the teacher wants. I have my own decision to do it whichever way I want to do it, but still I do it in the general way that she wants.

I don't know, I guess it's nice being a good student. I have friends in debate and in a class like Enriched English, A.P. History. I have other friends, I have to change my line of speaking, and I guess that's a burden. I just have to be easy to understand. I guess respect is pretty important for me. It's important to fit in, to fit into some kind of crowd. I have a best friend, but he doesn't do that well, so I guess I need a group of friends that I can identify with. When I'm in a class that is intellectually oriented, it's really fun to be around that type of environment. In debate for example, I'm getting trophies, winning. The main thing that it does is get respect. When you win, when I bring home a trophy, sometimes I just forget to show it to my parents. I guess it's just respect of fellow debaters.

• • •

When Joseph finished his last interview, I felt a sense of discomfort that went beyond being sick to my stomach; the irony in his words made me sick at heart. At that moment I would gladly have handed over $100 to him if I thought it would have given him back his own voice. He had gone beyond the endeavor of considering what would be compelling to an audience in order to convince them of *his* opinion. Joseph was an earnest young man who was just coming into his own, in his own eyes and in the eyes of his fellow students. I could see him being a future senator in our Congress. Ralph Waldo Emerson said, "Nothing is at last sacred but the integrity of your own mind. Absolve you to yourself, and you shall have the suffrage of the world . . . I am ashamed to think how easily we capitulate to badges and names, to large societies and dead institutions." Joseph had capitulated, and I'm not sure that our democracy can withstand an educational system that rewards capitulation anymore. Has its demise started with the power of grades? Or does it start with the conformity that is permitted to rage rampant in the adolescent years? The forty students in the study did not sense tolerance for their differences, for their diversity and interests. They sought to discover what was "acceptable." If students aren't encouraged to develop their own opinions and to articulate them, I fear for what we call our democracy.

Part II

Kinds of Writing

The Essay

Essential Premises

- The difference between personal and impersonal essays is a matter of focus, whether the focus is mainly on the writer and the way his or her mind works or on the subject matter.
- Most writing you do in school is expository writing, a subcategory of impersonal writing.

Main Assignment Preview

Our aim in this workshop is to introduce you to the essay both as a literary form and as a school form. Along the way, we're going to talk about the differences between personal and impersonal writing and get you to do some thinking about what it means to write "expository" essays in academic language. In workshops 12 and 15, we'll give you other chances to practice slightly different varieties of academic writing.

The main assignment for this workshop will be to draft two essays—one personal, one impersonal—based on the subject matter of another course you're taking and to revise at least one of these into a final version.

We've sequenced this workshop by asking you first to write your own essays and then read and think about the five published essays at the end of the workshop. You or your teacher may want to rearrange this sequence by reading the published essays either at the very beginning of the workshop or at some point in the middle, but keep in mind that the essay is such a flexible form that no one example can be considered an ideal representation.

Main Assignment: *Writing an Essay*

The essay is a slithery form; perhaps (notice we say *perhaps*) we can recognize an essay when we see one, but few of us could actually define the form. That may well be its strength: It permits much; its outlines are pliable. To help you understand the essay better, we present some of our thoughts about it in "Exploring Theory: The Essay" at the conclusion of this workshop and some essays about it in the "Readings" section.

We haven't used the word *essay* much in this textbook; we usually call what you're asked to do "papers" or "writing." "Composition" is a word we also tend to avoid because it's almost always used for writing done only in school—or only in English classes. We're teaching a way of going about writing which is applicable only to school writing. We're hoping we can get you to see that writing is writing: it isn't something you do only for English classes or just for school.

"Expository" has come to be the term used in schools and in academic discourse for essays that *explain*. Expository writing thus tends more toward the impersonal than the personal. Many of your teachers would probably describe the papers they ask you to do by the adjective "expository." We use the word in Workshop 2 to categorize one of the genres you might use to reshape your private writing into public writing. This workshop will ask you to do some variant of that transformation.

First Round of Freewriting: Private Freewriting

Your purpose in this first session of exploratory writing will be to come up with a topic that grows out of something you're studying in another class. This topic or subject should be one you have personal opinions about that you haven't been able to express in that other class. Perhaps you're learning about stages of adolescent growth or about gender roles, and your teacher hasn't asked you how you connect or don't connect to any of this. Perhaps you're taking a geology class and have strong feelings about the environment and business growth which you haven't been able to express. Or maybe your teacher has a particular bias which you find irritating—gives you feminist interpretations of everything you read (or the opposite) and seems to slight women in general.

Everything you learn in school has some relevance to what happens outside school, though we admit that those connections are sometimes hard to uncover. We believe that if you do uncover these connections, you'll learn more in the class. That's part of our goal for the activities of this workshop.

If you have difficulties coming up with a topic, think about the following possibilities:

- If you're taking a sociology or psychology course, how do the theories presented by the teacher and the textbook relate to you, your particular generation, and its interests—for example, music, clothes, sports, media? How do these theories relate to problems such as excessive drug and alcohol use and changing family structures?
- If you're taking a philosophy course, how does what you're learning there connect to your values or beliefs about religion, sexual mores,

and gender roles? Does your approach to these issues differ from that of your parents? your grandparents? Do you know people whom you or others describe as "philosophical"?

- If you're taking an education course, what does that course say about the role of education in *your* life and in the current life of our country? Does it connect to what we so often hear and read about today's young people being less intelligent, poorer writers and thinkers, and less prepared for college work than before? Do you see any evidence that the theories presented in the class have functioned in your education now or in the past?
- If you're taking a botany or geology course, what has it made you think about serious issues like the environment, waste disposal, the diminishing rain forests? Do these scientific fields tend to rely on "facts" and leave little room for intuition and feelings?
- If you're taking a math course, how applicable are the problems you confront there to issues in your everyday life? Math anxiety is said to be prevalent in our society. Do you or others you know suffer from that anxiety? Is there room for creativity and intuition in the solution of math problems? How do you feel about that? Why?
- If you're taking a history or cultural studies course, how does the history or culture apply to you? Do you know the history of your own family? Does your family identify strongly with a particular culture which they call theirs? And does this personal history and culture connect to what you're learning in class? How or how not?

Basically what we're asking you to reflect upon as you freewrite is how some idea you're confronting in one of your classes is important beyond the confines of the class and how it relates to your own life and experience and to the lives of others you know.

Exploring the Writing Process

Curiously, when I am involved in the actual process of writing, I find myself intensely dissatisfied with the act itself—my inability to find the words I want, to visualize a scene, to make it sound smooth enough. For this reason I am almost constantly revising as I go along, sometimes reworking a sentence two or three times before I can go on to the next one. (Though this is almost always at the level of syntax rather than thought. That is, I tend to play with the wording and hardly ever touch the structure or function of the sentence within my argument or development: once something has been written down, even if only partially, I tend to feel committed to the *essence* of that thought and unable to change direction.)

I think this approach is usually a bad one, especially for expository or simple functional writing. Yet it is one I find myself unable to easily discard. The other side of this way of working is that after I've finished even a small section—let's say a paragraph or so—I feel immensely pleased with what I've put down, often more so than I should be. Because of this, it usually takes me at least several days after the fact to recognize that something I've written is not up to snuff.

J. A. Iovine

Second Round: Public Freewriting

Assume that you've been asked to write on your subject by the teacher of the other class: specifically, your assignment is to relate the ideas, concepts, facts, and so forth embodied in your topic to some interest of yours outside the classroom. You will be expected to share most of this second round of freewriting. However, as with all public freewriting, you always have the option of withholding pieces of it.

You will also profit from seeking out others in the class you're writing about. Ask them to respond to what you've written after they read it or listen to you read it. Perhaps they'll lend you their notes. Once you've done this, write out what you've learned as a result and add it to the collection of writing on your ideas.

If you actually have a writing assignment for this class, you have a good reason to go see the professor during her office hours. But even if you don't, she'll probably be interested in what you're doing for the writing class. Maybe you'd like to ask her to help you design a topic which she would consider appropriate for the class. Or if you have established a topic, do some writing and thinking about it first and then ask the professor for some response. Afterward, you can do some more freewriting based on her response.

Analyzing Your Freewriting: Personal and Impersonal Voice

Now we ask you to think about the difference between personal and impersonal writing. We think that you'll discover that this difference is not always the same as the difference between private and public writing. *Some* of what you wrote privately will be impersonal and some of what you wrote publicly will be personal. Keep in mind that it isn't subject matter that determines whether an essay is personal or impersonal: it's the way you approach that subject matter. When you approach a subject personally, you focus more on your own thoughts and reactions to your subject. When you approach a subject impersonally, you focus more on information as a way of "informing" your readers about *it,* not about *you.* In personal writing, who you are comes across more; in impersonal writing, your subject matter comes across more.

Of course there's no absolute difference between personal and impersonal writing. There's almost always some information and some of you in anything you write. Even when you write what seems like "pure" information, your selection was a personal selection. But once you've selected information, you can present it more as *information* or more as *your personal slant* on that information.

Look back over your two pieces of freewriting and mark as well as you can what is personal and impersonal. You might try using a straight line to mark what definitely seems impersonal and a wavy line to mark what definitely seems personal. If you do your drafting on the computer, you can use bold type for the impersonal and italic for the personal—or you can even use different fonts or colors (if your printer has that capacity). Leave unmarked what seems ambiguous. Don't be surprised if this is a harder task than you expected.

You may not find neat separations between whole sections of personal or impersonal writing, or even between sentences. Sometimes you will find a phrase or a single word that is personal within a passage that is largely impersonal—or vice-versa. (You can draw a line under just a word or phrase, or draw a line alongside a longer passage.) You can often get a strong sense of the difference between personal and impersonal tone by reading over sentences or passages aloud and omitting words or phrases or sentences you've marked as personal. It's surprising what a difference a word or two can make. (For example, how would it change the first two essays in the "Readings" section if you removed from both this sentence: "Maybe I should have known from her appearance but I didn't"?)

Bring this material to class and try sharing whatever you are willing to share with your partner or group—to see if they agree with your distinctions between personal and impersonal. (Also, they might have suggestions for enriching both kinds of writing.) But we stress that we're not asking you to share anything you don't want to share.

Keep in mind that your assignment is to discuss the relevance of your topic to the world outside the classroom in which you're studying it. In one version you'll be seeing this connection in personal terms; in the other version you'll be seeing this same connection impersonally.

Revision

Now you're ready to build the personal elements of your freewriting into one essay and the impersonal elements into another. Certain parts of these two essays may be almost identical. Which essay (personal or impersonal) you develop into a final version will depend on your writing teacher's instructions.

It's probably not fair to ask the teacher of the other course to read two versions. But perhaps she will be willing to read and respond to one version if you show her the questions in the box below and assure her they are designed to help her comment quickly and without having to become a "writing teacher." You'll probably want to give her the impersonal version, but don't automatically assume she wouldn't want to respond to the more personal version.

Exploring the Writing Process

Writing comments on students' papers always appears more difficult than it becomes once I start. Just finished doing that—when I finished reading one of the papers, I felt I had absolutely nothing to say and yet I feel it's important to respond—so I have to find something. The wonder is that once I found something—I was off and went on writing and writing as though I too were writing a paper instead of just a response to a student's paper. And, inevitably, having written such a long comment, the student's paper began to look better and better. I feared for a moment that I had said something too negative and went back to try to make it more tactful—but I had written in ink and couldn't. But I rationalized my comments by convincing myself that they had grown out of a long response and the student should see them in that light. Strange, students wonder what our responses will be to their writing—and we worry equally about how they'll react to what we say. Writing responses almost always turns out to be a pleasure once I get going. Much more of a pleasure than grading!

Pat Belanoff

If you can't get comments from the teacher of the subject-matter course, perhaps you can find one or more students in that class who are willing to read your version and give their reactions as readers with some knowledge of the field.

Questions to Help Subject-Matter Teachers Give Feedback More Quickly and Easily

The assignment from my writing course is (1) to explain how a concept or issue in one of my other courses relates to my own life and experience outside that course; (2) to experiment with the difference between making that explanation in personal terms and making it in impersonal terms.

You can give me very helpful feedback if you would please *note* certain passages in my paper:

- Please use a checkmark to indicate phrases or passages where I've got the idea or concept right, and a cross where I seem to be misunderstanding the idea or concept or getting it wrong.
- Please use a straight line below phrases and passages that are clear and effective for you, and a wavy line below phrases and passages that are unclear.
- Please circle words or passages where the language, style, discourse, or approach seems inappropriate for you as a teacher and reader in this field.

If you have time: Are there any other comments you would like to make to me, either orally or in writing?

Alternative Assignment: Analyzing an Essay

Rather than actually producing a personal or impersonal essay for this workshop, your teacher might ask you to write an analysis of the two kinds of writing you've produced for this workshop: personal and impersonal. If you ended up with a fair amount of private writing while you were freewriting, you might want to include an analysis of the differences between private and public writing also—and even some thoughts about how the personal/impersonal dichotomy differs from (or is the same as) the private/public dichotomy.

Optional Assignment: Reading Essays

We selected essays by the four authors at the end of this workshop because they represent a mix of styles and purposes. Another factor in our choice, which will become obvious as you start reading them, is their subject matter.

Earlier we suggested that you read both versions of your essay aloud in order to see how the voice in each creates meaning and tone. You can do the same exercise with these published essays. Choose typical passages from each and do readings. Get more than one person's reading of a passage so that you can talk about the differences in voice you hear. (For example, what can you say about the first two essays in the "Readings" after at least two people have read aloud the first two sentences of each?) But you'll want to talk about the similarities too, so that you can discuss whether or not there are voices "in" the essays themselves. If you decide what voice an essay is written in, does that tell you any other things about the essay?

You can do some writing in response to these essays also. You may want to use the writing-while-reading strategies we set out in Workshops 5, 13, 14, and in the mini-workshops on dialectical notebooks. You can, of course, use some combination of these.

After you've done some reading aloud and some writing on all the essays in "Readings," do some focused freewriting in answer to the following questions:

- Which would you describe as the most personal? the most impersonal? Point to specific features that lead you to these conclusions.
- In which essay does the author seem to speak to you most directly? For which essay do you feel least like an audience? Why?
- From which essay did you learn the most? the least?
- As you were reading, which essay made you feel most like you were inside the author's mind?
- Which essay was the most interesting to you? the least? Why? How do your answers to these questions relate to the questions you've already answered?

Suggestions for Collaboration

The ideal collaboration for this project would be with someone or some others who are in both of the classes you're writing for in this workshop. The impersonal essay could be a traditional expository essay, written collaboratively, with an emphasis on demonstrating an understanding of your subject as it connects to the world outside the classroom. But the personal essay could grow out of a written dialogue or an e-mail interchange, which would allow each (or all) of you the opportunity to describe your experiences and express opinions. The final paper could even *be* this dialogue with collaboratively written concluding remarks.

Of course, another student doesn't have to be in this other class to have personal reactions to its subject matter. You and a partner in your writing class can each write an impersonal essay about a different class each of you is taking (a class you do not share). You can then invite your partner to engage in a dialogue about the implications of the information and concepts in your paper; you, in turn, would engage in a dialogue about the subject of his paper. These dialogues could then be collaboratively smoothed out and transformed into personal essays, or they could remain as dialogues.

Sharing and Responding

When you share your exploratory rough writing (with the exception of those parts you consider private), you'll find the techniques in Sections 2 and 3 of "Sharing and Responding" ("Pointing and Center of Gravity" and "Summary and Sayback") particularly productive. Here are some additional questions you'll find helpful:

- Point to specific spots where the way I think and the kind of person I am is most evident. Where is it least evident?
- What would I need to do to this rough writing to make it more personal? more impersonal?

When you share drafts of your essays, read aloud passages from both the personal and the impersonal versions. Get others to read them too. Talk about the voice in them. Additionally, when sharing and responding to these drafts, you'll find these sections of "Sharing and Responding" most useful: Section 11, "Criterion-Based Feedback"; and Section 7, "Movies of the Reader's Mind." But you may also want to consider the following questions:

- For each essay draft, are there spots where it drifts too far from its basic orientation, either personal or impersonal? Point to specific spots.
- Are the ideas and concepts clear? Point to places where they are the most and the least clear.

Two drafts by everyone in the class create a mountain of writing to respond to; there probably won't be enough time to read and discuss all of them. Early freewriting can be discussed in pairs. For more finished drafts, you may need to bring in copies so that others can take your work home for commenting. Everyone in the group can read all the papers, but write comments on only one set of two drafts. Then when the group meets, each person's writing gets discussed, but the main comments are by the person(s) who wrote comments, and others chime in briefly based on their reading at home.

Process Journal

If you need some help retrieving from memory your experiences and reactions while doing the writing for this workshop, you can use the following questions:

- What did you learn from bringing your writing course to bear on another course? from writing about that subject for this class? from seeing that teacher for help and feedback?
- In what ways did reading aloud help you sense the differences between a personal and impersonal voice?
- Which approach is more comfortable for you: personal or impersonal? Why?

- What did you learn from sharing readings of the published essays with your classmates?

Remember that, for a cover letter, you can almost always use most of the questions we listed in Workshop 1 on page 11.

Exploring Theory: *The Essay*

Historically, the essay as an individual form was born in the 16th century. Its birth occurred during the Renaissance, an age of individualism and new discovery. Thus, the essay is a true child of its times. The Frenchman Michel de Montaigne (1533–1592), who initiated the form, named it *essai,* a French word having its roots in the Latin words *exagium,* meaning a weighing or balancing, and *exigere,* meaning to examine. For Montaigne, the *essai* was "a try," or a kind of "go at" something. In writing about this new form he was developing, Montaigne says that its purposes are deeply personal:

> I desire therein to be delineated in mine own genuine, simple and ordinary fashion, without contention, art or study; for it is myself I portray. . . . Myself am the groundwork of my book.

Francis Bacon (1561–1626) was the first English writer of essays. His essays are quite different from Montaigne's; the first ones are more like notes. It is probably Abraham Cowley (1618–1667) who should be considered the father of the English essay, but it wasn't until the 18th century that the essay became a dominant form in English literature. We won't go on with this history here, but we hope you noticed that in our last sentence we spoke of the essay as "literature."

We invite you to read the essay in the "Readings" section titled "What I Think, What I Am" by Edward Hoagland. In it he notes that "essays . . . hang somewhere on a line between two sturdy poles: this is what I think, and this is what I am." The conclusion of his essay merits repetition:

> A personal essay frequently is not autobiographical at all, but what it does keep in common with autobiography is that, through its tone and tumbling progression, it conveys the quality of the author's mind. Nothing gets in the way. Because essays are directly concerned with the mind and its idiosyncrasy, the very freedom the mind possesses is bestowed on this branch of literature that does honor to it, and the fascination of the mind is the fascination of the essay.

What's so fascinating about the personal essay is that we can find it engaging even when the subject doesn't interest us at all. What engages us is the workings of a human mind. When an essayist gives us that, the subject takes a backseat: It is merely the way of getting into another's mind.

You'll notice that the quotation by Hoagland begins with the words "a personal essay." But there is also something known as the "impersonal essay," an essay which is focused more on *what* is said than on the qualities of the writer's mind. Yet even that is only a relative alteration of the form. Perhaps it's best to think of essays along a continuum from personal to impersonal: Each essay blends these two in its own way.

As you have already realized by reading this far, the personal essay is not usually a school-assigned form. Most teachers are mainly interested in what you know and tend to judge your writing on that basis. There are, of course, classes in which teachers want you to assess the information you present and come to conclusions of your own, but this usually means they're interested in seeing how intelligently you can think about your material.

Changes are appearing, however—particularly at schools and in programs where multicultural and feminist theory is urging teachers not to reject the personal out of hand. It is mainly Western culture that values the detached intellectual stance and prefers that the personal not muddle up the impersonal. Other cultures don't always make such a division. Some feminist theorists take a slightly different tack: They stress the impossibility of separating the personal and the impersonal and the relevance of the context (including the stance of an author) for full understanding of any written text. Teachers guided by these theories might require you to include the personal in papers written for them.

Nonetheless, we still think that the primary interest of most teachers is the substance of your writing, not your mind as it engages the task of thinking about the material. Consequently, you may well write impersonal essays to fulfill school assignments, but you'll not often write a personal essay to do so. The one place where you're likely to write personal essays (other than in a course like this one) is in an advanced composition course. Such courses are often rightly grouped with courses in writing fiction and poetry—because the essay is a literary genre.

Another way we can talk about the essay is in terms we use in Workshop 7, where we present the rhetorical triangle. The personal essay lies close to the writer angle; the impersonal essay lies close to the topic angle.

The impersonal essay moves toward the "article" or "paper." We often speak of newspaper "articles" or "professional articles": articles which usually appear in the periodicals of a particular discipline and manifest the language features of that discipline. But professionals also write articles directed toward a general public; such articles or "essays" are often more personal than purely professional articles.

In an essay in *The New York Times Book Review,* Elizabeth Hardwick writes:

> William Gass, in what must be called an essay, a brilliant one, about Emerson, an essayist destined from the cradle, makes a distinction between the article and the essay. Having been employed by the university and having heard so many of his colleagues "doing an article on," Mr. Gass has come to think of the article as "that awful object" because it is under the command of defensiveness in footnote, reference, coverage, and would also pretend that all must be useful and certain, even if it is "very likely a veritable Michelin of misdirections." If the article has a certain sheen and professional polish, it is the polish of "the scrubbed step"—practical economy and neatness. The essay, in Mr. Gass's view, is a great meadow of style and personal manner, freed from the need for defense except that provided by an individual intelligence and sparkle. We consent to watch a mind at work, without agreement often, but only for pleasure. Knowledge hereby attained, great indeed, is again wanted for the pleasure of itself. (44)

And one more quote. In a review of a collection of essays by Italo Calvino, Christopher Lehmann-Haupt concludes:

> These essays are instructive and often arresting, but it is the responsive play of Mr. Calvino's mind that seduces us. We are invited into a circle that includes the work, its creators and Mr. Calvino as observer.

Untitled Essays

Eleanor Klinko

Untitled 1

I had an inkling of what was going on but when the words were stated to my face it was like an earthquake shattering my world into tiny pieces. My very close friend, the one with whom I have shared so many wonderful times, just told me she was gay.

It was a balmy Wednesday afternoon and my friend and I were driving down my street headed for an exotic boutique. Sitting next to me she seemed jumpy, her hands moving as she talked. I only remember jumbles of what she said about girls and feelings. These words led up to one word that I do remember. I only heard it after I daringly asked, "Are you gay?" I choked on my words.

She replied, "Yes." We were looking at each other face to face. My mind was not controlling my foot on the brake. Realizing this I quickly pressed the pedal to the floor, jerking the car to a stop before hitting the car in front of mine.

I was stunned. The words were a slap across my face. My cheek stung as my mind was bombarded with flashbacks of our days spent together. We would play the guitar, play basketball, go to concerts, listen to music, study history, shuffle through leaves, and shoot coconuts at each other in the snow. These are the activities of two energetic high school girls.

She talked about a young English teacher she liked in school. She had seen her at a gay bar and they danced together. This conversation was awkward, probably because I never had one like it before and never expected to. Weren't two girls supposed to be talking about guys? But I didn't go against her; I actually tried to help her figure a strategy to be with this woman. I don't know why I didn't start yelling and bombard her with questions. I was stunned, a little scared, confused, and really didn't want to accept what she was saying.

There she sat, my friend, in the passenger seat of my car. Her soft pale skin and long thin blond hair did not coincide with her tall muscular body. She really didn't have any feminine features except for her fair complexion and soft hair. She dressed in faded jeans and ripped concert T-shirts. Studded black leather dressed her waist and wrists. Maybe I should have known from her appearance but I didn't. She had masculine features. She used a trucker's wallet which attached to her pants by a chain, sewed a Harley Davidson patch on her leather jacket, wore black leather motorcycle boots, and had four tattoos on her body. She smoked cigarettes and drank beer like a guy. She did not hold and puff on a cigarette the way a woman does.

What do I do now? I loved her and would do almost anything for her, but how could I feel this way now? She might think that I wanted to be more than a friend. But I didn't want to lose her friendship because I didn't want to lose the good times we shared.

I couldn't tell anyone about my situation. I was embarrassed to talk to my father about the subject. He would not tell me to stop my friendship with her because he allows me to choose my own friends. But he would prefer I spent less time with her so my feelings wouldn't be influenced by hers. I didn't tell any other people, partly because it wouldn't be fair to my friend and partly because I feared the rumors that might start about her and me being more than just friends. People in high school love to start rumors, especially if they're not true. People who knew that she and I were close friends might assume that I was like her. And if guys thought I was gay then I would never get asked for a date by a male.

I was in a state of confusion. I wanted to continue with our regular friendship but it felt as if a cloud hung over us. I needed time to think about the situation. Although I liked her for what she was and for being open with me, I didn't like her any more than a friend, and I knew I could never have a relationship with a girl. I told her all this. She accepted. I didn't hold anything against her because I had no right to. She didn't hurt me; she just made me think about a reality of life.

Untitled 2

Three years ago my best friend told me she was gay. We had been friends for over ten years and I had never even suspected it. Perhaps I should have because her soft pale skin and long thin blond hair did not coincide with her tall muscular body. She really didn't have any feminine features except for her fair complexion and soft hair. She dressed in faded jeans and ripped concert T-shirts. Studded black leather dressed her waist and wrists. Maybe I should have known from her appearance but I didn't. She had masculine features. She used a trucker's wallet which attached to her pants by a chain, sewed a Harley Davidson patch on her leather jacket, wore black leather motorcycle boots, and had four tattoos on her body. She smoked cigarettes and drank beer like a guy. She did not hold and puff on a cigarette the way a woman does.

Certainly others have faced this situation, but I didn't know personally anyone who had. I can remember seeing a segment of "Love Boat" where one of the crew member's friends had had a sex change. Part of the story was how the crew member adjusted to that. I also remember that on one of the soap operas there was a family who had to deal with the discovery that the son was gay. I had known about homosexuals for years; in fact, I remember when I thought I could recognize gay men as I walked around the streets of the Village. But later I realized from some reading I did that gays are not identifiable according to some stereotypical image. Gay men can be short or tall, fat or thin, muscular or not. They can be construction workers, truckers, or ballet dancers. They can prefer baseball to cooking. I now know one cannot tell if a man is gay by looking at him. But I didn't know that at the time my friend confided in me.

I knew far less about gay women. My experience suggests that gay women are less likely to "come out of the closet" than gay men. Many of my male friends are sure that they know what a gay woman looks like—and their descriptions are not very flattering. And even though my friend, I now realize, has masculine traits, I suspect that gay women can look as feminine in the traditional sense as straight women. And, also, I know many women who wear just as much leather as my friend does and are *not* gay.

I now realize that when my friend told me about herself, I had three choices. I could accept her and continue our friendship. I could reject her, which I suspect is what my father would have wanted me to do had he known. Or I could simply act as though I didn't know and continue our friendship just as it was. I knew the latter was not really possible since I suspected the lack of honesty between us would kill our relationship. I couldn't reject her because she had been and still was my friend. So I accepted her and was able to tell her how I felt. She, in turn, was able to accept that.

One thing I have learned from this experience is that gay people are more like the rest of us than unlike us. My girlfriend loves her parents, curses her car when it won't start, values honest relationships, wants to do well in school, get a good job, and make a fair amount of money. The biggest difference between us, I guess, is that I want to get married and have a family. Even so, my friend and I still have enough in common to spend hours talking.

The Essay*

Edmund Gosse

ESSAY, ESSAYIST (Fr. *essai,* Late Lat. *exagium,* a weighing or balance; *exigere,* to examine; the term in general meaning any trial or effort). As a form of literature, the essay is a composition of moderate length, usually in prose, which deals in an easy, cursory way with the external conditions of a subject, and, in strictness, with that subject only as it affects the writer. Dr. Johnson, himself an eminent essayist, defines an essay as "an irregular, undigested piece"; the irregularity may perhaps be admitted, but want of thought, that is to say lack of proper mental digestion, is certainly not characteristic of a fine example. It should, on the contrary, always be the brief and light result of experience and profound meditation, while "undigested" is the last epithet to be applied to the essays of Montaigne, Addison or Lamb. Bacon said that the Epistles of Seneca were "essays," but this can hardly be allowed. Bacon himself goes on to admit that "the word is late, though the thing is ancient." The word, in fact, was invented for this species of writing by Montaigne, who merely meant that these were experiments in a new kind of literature. This original meaning, namely that these pieces were attempts or endeavours, feeling their way towards the expression of what would need a far wider space to exhaust, was lost in England in the course of the eighteenth century. This is seen by the various attempts made in the nineteenth century to coin a word which should express a still smaller work, as distinctive in comparison with the essay as the essay is by the side of the monograph: none of these linguistic experiments, such as *essayette, essaykin* (Thackeray) and *essaylet* (Helps) have taken hold of the language. As a matter of fact, the journalistic word *article* covers the lesser form of essay, although not exhaustively, since the essays in the monthly and quarterly reviews, which are fully as extended as an essay should ever be, are frequently termed "articles," while many "articles" in newspapers, dictionaries and encyclopaedias are in no sense essays. It may be said that the idea of a detached work is combined with the word "essay," which should be neither a section of a disquisition nor a chapter in a book which aims at the systematic development of a story. Locke's *Essay on the Human Understanding* is not an essay at all, or cluster of essays, in this technical sense, but refers to the experimental and tentative nature of the inquiry which the philosopher was undertaking. Of the curious use of the word so repeatedly made by Pope, mention will be made below.

The essay, as a species of literature, was invented by Montaigne, who had probably little suspicion of the far-reaching importance of what he had created. In his dejected moments, he turned to rail at what he had written, and to call his essays "inepties" and "sottises." But in his own heart he must have been well satisfied with the new and beautiful form which he had added to literary tradition. He was perfectly aware that he had devised a new thing; that he had invented a way of communicating himself to the world as a type of human nature. He designed it to carry out his peculiar object, which was to produce an accurate portrait of his own soul, not as it was yesterday or

* From an entry in the famous 11th edition of the *Encyclopaedia Britannica,* 1910.

will be to-morrow, but as it is to-day. It is not often that we can date with any approach to accuracy the arrival of a new class of literature into the world, but it was in the month of March 1571 that the essay was invented. It was started in the second story of the old tower of the castle of Montaigne, in a study to which the philosopher withdrew for that purpose, surrounded by his books, close to his chapel, sheltered from the excesses of a fatiguing world. He wrote slowly, not systematically; it took nine years to finish the two first books of the essays. In 1574 the manuscript of the work, so far as it was then completed, was nearly lost, for it was confiscated by the pontifical police in Rome, where Montaigne was residing, and was not returned to the author for four months. The earliest imprint saw the light in 1580, at Bordeaux, and the Paris edition of 1588, which is the fifth, contains the final text of the great author. These dates are not negligible in the briefest history of the essay, for they are those of its revelation to the world of readers. It was in the delightful chapters of his new, strange book that Montaigne introduced the fashion of writing briefly, irregularly, with constant digressions and interruptions, about the world as it appears to the individual who writes. The *Essais* were instantly welcomed, and few writers of the Renaissance had so instant and so vast a popularity as Montaigne. But while the philosophy, and above all the graceful stoicism, of the great master were admired and copied in France, the exact shape in which he had put down his thoughts, in the exquisite negligence of a series of essays, was too delicate to tempt an imitator. It is to be noted that neither Charron, nor Mlle de Gournay, his most immediate disciples, tried to write essays. But Montaigne, who liked to fancy that the Eyquem family was of English extraction, had spoken affably of the English people as his "cousins," and it has always been admitted that his genius has an affinity with the English. He was early read in England, and certainly by Bacon, whose is the second great name connected with this form of literature. It was in 1597, only five years after the death of Montaigne, that Bacon published in a small octavo the first ten of his essays. These he increased to 38 in 1612 and to 68 in 1625. In their first form, the essays of Bacon had nothing of the fulness or grace of Montaigne's; they are meagre notes; scarcely more than the headings for discourses. It is possible that when he wrote them he was not yet familiar with the style of his predecessor, which was first made popular in England, in 1603, when Florio published that translation of the *Essais* which Shakespeare unquestionably read. In the later editions Bacon greatly expanded his theme, but he never reached, or but seldom, the freedom and ease, the seeming formlessness held in by an invisible chain, which are the glory of Montaigne, and distinguish the typical essayist. It would seem that at first, in England, as in France, no lesser writer was willing to adopt a title which belonged to so great a presence as that of Bacon or Montaigne. . . . [Gosse continues by speaking of a variety of English essays, including those of Lamb and Macaulay.] Nothing can be more remarkable than the difference . . . between Lamb and Macaulay, the former forever demanding, even cajoling, the sympathy of the reader, the latter scanning the horizon for an enemy to controvert. In later times the essay in England has been cultivated in each of these ways, by a thousand journalists and authors. The "leaders" of a daily newspaper are examples of the popularization of the essay, and they point to the danger which now attacks it, that of producing a purely ephemeral or even momentary species of effect. The essay, in its best days, was intended to be as lasting as a poem or a historical monograph; it aimed at being one of the most durable and precious departments of literature. . . .

On Essaying

James Moffett

James P. Moffett (b. 1929; d. 1996), one of composition theory's true innovators, wrote many articles, books, and several influential textbooks addressing various aspects of composition pedagogy and such topics as censorship in the schools.

College composition instructors and anthologists of essays have doted for years on George Orwell's "Shooting an Elephant," which they hold up to students as a model of essay or "expository writing." Please look closely at it even if you think you know it well; if a student wrote it, it would be called "personal writing," that is, soft and nonintellectual. Orwell narrated in first person how as a British civil servant in Burma he was intimidated by villagers into shooting an elephant against his will. But so effectively does he say what happens by telling what happened that the force of his theme—the individual's moral choice whether or not to conform to the group—leaves us with the impression that the memoir is "expository,"—that is, chiefly cast in the present tense of generalization and in third person. What we really want to help youngsters learn is how to express ideas of universal value in a personal voice. Fables, parables, poems and songs, fiction and memoir may convey ideas as well as or better than editorials and critiques. Orwell does indeed provide a fine model, but teachers should not let prejudice fool them into misunderstanding the actual kind of discourse in which he wrote "Shooting an Elephant" and other excellent essays, for this leads to a confusing double standard whereby we ask students to emulate a great writer but to do it in another form.

The Essay: An Attempt

Orwell wrote deep in a tradition of English letters, honoring the essay as a candid blend of personal and universal. It was resurrected if not invented during the Renaissance by Montaigne, who coined the term *essai* from *essayer,* to attempt. From his position of philosophical skepticism ("What do I know?") he saw his writing as personal attempts to discover truth, what he thought and what could be thought, in exactly the same sense that Donald Murray or Janet Emig or I myself might speak of writing as discovery. From Burton's *Anatomy of Melancholy* and Browne's *Urn Burial;* Addison's and Steele's *Spectator* articles; through the essays of Swift, Lamb, Hazlitt, and DeQuincey to those of Orwell, Virginia Woolf, Joan Didion, and Norman Mailer, English literature has maintained a marvelous tradition, fusing personal experience, private vision, and downright eccentricity, with intellectual vigor and verbal objectification. In color, depth, and stylistic originality it rivals some of our best poetry. Look back over Hazlitt's "The Fight" and compare it with Mailer's intellectual reportage of the Ali-Frazier fight in *King of the Hill* or "On the Feeling of Immortality in Youth" or "On Familiar Style"; DeQuincey's "Confessions of an Opium Eater" or "On the Knocking at the Gate in *Macbeth,"* which begins: "From my boyish days I had always felt a great perplexity on one point in *Macbeth";* or Lamb's "The Two Races of Men," "Poor Relations," or "On Sanity of True Genius." Consider too a book like Henry Adams's *Education of Henry Adams* for its simultaneous treatment of personal and national or historical.

Some essayists, like Montaigne and Emerson, tend toward generality, as reflected in titles like "Friendship" or "Self-Reliance," but tone and source are personal, and we cannot doubt the clear kinship between essays featuring memoir or eyewitness reportage and those of generality, for the same writers do both, sometimes in a single essay, sometimes in separate pieces; and Lamb and Thoreau stand in the same relation to Montaigne and Emerson as fable to moral or parable to proverb. The difference lies not in the fundamental approach, which is in any case personal, but in the degree of explicitness of the theme. "I bear within me the exemplar of the human condition," said Montaigne. Descending deep enough within, the essayist links up personal with universal, self with self.

Transpersonal, Not Impersonal

Schools mistreat writing because the society suffers at the moment from drastic misunderstandings about the nature of knowledge. Applying "scientific" criteria that would be unacceptable to most real scientists making the breakthroughs out there on the frontier, many people have come to think that subtracting the self makes for objectivity and validity. But depersonalization is not impartiality. It is, quite literally, madness. Einstein said, "The observer is the essence of the situation." It is not by abandoning the self but by developing it that we achieve impartiality and validity. The deeper we go consciously into ourselves, the better chance we have of reaching universality, as Montaigne knew so well. Transpersonal, not impersonal. It is an undeterred faith in this that makes a great writer cultivate his individuality until others feel he speaks for them better than they do themselves. Teachers should be the first to understand this misunderstanding and to start undoing it, so that schooling in general and writing in particular can offset rather than reinforce the problem.

Here are two examples of what we're up against—one from a famous current encyclopedia and one from a leading publisher, typical and telling symptoms. Most English majors probably sampled or at least heard of Sir Thomas Browne, a very individualistic seventeenth-century master of an original prose style, a writer's writer much admired by successors. Of his *Pseudodoxia Epidemica* Funk and Wagnalls *Standard Reference Encyclopedia* says, "Its unscientific approach and odd assemblage of obscure facts typify his haphazard erudition," and then concludes the entry: "Despite Browne's deficiencies as a thinker his style entitles him to high rank among the masters of English prose." What this verdict tells me is that the writer of that entry felt overwhelmed by all the books Browne had read that he had not and that he knew far less than he should have known about the enormously important and complex networks of thought and knowledge, called esoteric, that after several millenia of evolution still had great influence on Newton, Bacon, and Descartes (who displayed at times equally "irrational" intellectual behavior). The encyclopediast's judgment on such a writer as Browne is nothing but smartass chauvinism: permitted to poison basic information sources, it makes "science" as deadly a censor as ever the Church was during its Inquisition.

We can avoid producing Brownes in our school system by having all youngsters read and write the same things—a goal we have closely approximated—and then their approach will not be unscientific, their assemblage odd, their facts obscure, nor their erudition haphazard. And we will have ensured that no one will be able to emulate the great essayists we hold up as models (or even read them with any comprehension). Real essaying cannot thrive without cultivation of the individual. Who would have any reason to read anyone else? (And I want to know how Browne's style could be worth so much if he were merely raving.)

The second example is personal. When I received the edited manuscript of the original edition of *Student-Centered Language Arts and Reading, K-13* back from the publisher, I was aghast. "My" editor had rewritten sentences throughout the whole book to eliminate first-person references and other elements of the author's presence and voice. This included altering diction and sentence structure at times to get a more anonymous or distanced effect. Faced with the appalling labor of restoring all those sentences, I called the editor, furious. She said righteously, "But we always do that—

it's policy." It never occurred to her to exempt, or even to warn, an author who wouldn't be publishing the book in the first place if he weren't regarded as some kind of expert in writing.

Remove the Double Standard

You can't trust your encyclopedia, your publisher, your school administration. And you can't trust yourself until you learn to spot how you too may be spreading the plague, as Camus calls it. The double standard in "Look at the greats, but don't do what they did" naturally goes along with our era of Scientific Inquisition, which is really technocratic plague. Teachers stand in a fine position to spread infection. If you let yourself be convinced that "personal" or "creative" writing is merely narcissistic, self-indulgent, and weak-minded, then you have just removed your own first person.

Essay: What I Think, What I Am

Edward Hoagland

Edward Hoagland (b. 1933) was a serviceman, a firefighter, and a circus hand before becoming a college instructor, most recently at Bennington College. Hoagland is a noted essayist known primarily for his award-winning writings on nature, which display a penetrating knowledge of and an acute concern for the environment.

Our loneliness makes us avid column readers these days. The personalities in The New York Post, Chicago Daily News, San Francisco Chronicle constitute our neighbors now, some of them local characters but also the opinionated national stars. And movie reviewers thrive on our need for somebody emotional who is willing to pay attention to us and return week after week, year after year, through all the to-and-fro of other friends to flatter us by pouring out his (her) heart. They are essayists, as Elizabeth Hardwick is, James Baldwin was. We sometimes hear that essays are an old-fashioned form, that so-and-so is the "last essayist," but the facts of the marketplace argue quite otherwise. Essays of almost any kind are so much easier for a writer to sell now than short stories, so many more see print, it's odd that though two fine anthologies remain which publish the year's best stories, no comparable collection exists for essays.* Such changes in the reading public's taste aren't always to the good, needless to say. The art of telling stories predated even cave-painting, surely; and if we ever find ourselves living in caves again, it (with painting) will be the only art left, after movies, novels, essays, photography, biography and all the rest have gone down the drain—the art to build from.

One has the sense with the short story form that while everything may have been done, nothing has been overdone: it has a permanence. Essays, if a comparison is to be made, although they go back 400 years to Montaigne, seem a newfangled, mercurial, sometimes hokey sort of affair which has lent itself to many of the excesses of the age from spurious autobiography to spurious hallucination, as well as the shabby careerism of traditional journalism. It's a greased pig. Essays are associated with the way young writers fashion a name—on plain crowded newsprint in hybrid vehicles like The Village Voice, Rolling Stone, The Soho Weekly News (also Fiction magazine), instead of the thick paper stock and thin readership of Partisan Review.

---

* This is no longer true. See the yearly publication, *Best American Essays,* published by Houghton Mifflin.

Essays, however, hang somewhere on a line between two sturdy poles: this is what I think, and this is what I am. Autobiographies which aren't novels are generally extended essays, indeed. A personal essay is like the human voice talking, its order the mind's natural flow, instead of a systematized outline of ideas. Though more wayward or informal than an article or treatise, somewhere it contains a point which is its real center, even if the point couldn't be expressed in fewer words than the essayist has employed. Essays don't usually "boil down" to a summary, as articles do, but on the other hand they have fewer "levels" than first-rate fiction—a flatter surface—because we aren't supposed to argue about their meaning. In the old distinction between teaching versus story-telling—however cleverly the author muddles it up—an essay is intended to convey the same point to each of us.

This emphasis upon mind speaking to mind is what makes essays less universal in their appeal than stories. They are addressed to an educated, perhaps a middle-class, reader, with certain presuppositions shared, a frame of reference, even a commitment to civility—not the grand and golden empathy inherent in every man which the storyteller has a chance to tap. At the same time, of course, the artful "I" of an essay can be as chameleon as any narrator in fiction: and essays do tell a story just as often as a short story stakes a claim to a particular viewpoint.

Mark Twain's piece called "Corn-pone Opinions," for example, which is about public opinion, begins with a vignette as vivid as any in "Huckleberry Finn." When he was a boy of 15, Twain says, he used to hang out a back window and listen to the sermons preached by a neighbor's slave standing on top of a woodpile. The fellow "imitated the pulpit style of the several clergymen of the village, and did it well and with fine passion and energy. To me he was a wonder. I believed he was the greatest orator in the United States and would some day be heard from. But it did not happen; in the distribution of rewards he was overlooked. . . . He interrupted his preaching now and then to saw a stick of wood, but the sawing was a pretense—he did it with his mouth, exactly imitating the sound the bucksaw makes in shrieking its way through the wood. But it served its purpose, it kept his master from coming out to see how the work was getting along."

The extraordinary flexibility of essays is what has enabled them to ride out rough weather and hybridize into forms to suit the times. And just as one of the first things a fiction writer learns is that he needn't actually be writing fiction to write a short story—he can tell his own history or anyone else's as exactly as he remembers it and it will still be "fiction" if it remains primarily a story—an essayist soon discovers that he doesn't have to tell the whole truth and nothing but the truth, he can shape or shave his memories as long as the purpose is served of elucidating a truthful point. A personal essay frequently is not autobiographical at all, but what it does keep in common with autobiography is that, through its tone and tumbling progression, it conveys the quality of the author's mind. Nothing gets in the way. Because essays are directly concerned with the mind and its idiosyncrasy, the very freedom the mind possesses is bestowed on this branch of literature that does honor to it, and the fascination of the mind is the fascination of the essay.

Persuasion

Essential Premises

- The first step in persuasion is getting someone to listen; too many words can sometimes keep that from happening.
- Persuasion relies less on formal rational argument than on reaching out to an audience and getting their interest by appealing particularly to experience and feelings.

Main Assignment Preview

The emphasis in this workshop is on writing persuasively: how can *written words* cause people to listen and then change their thinking or behavior? Your assignment is twofold: (1) a persuasive letter to be mailed to an appropriate audience/publication and (2) an explanation of the persuasive qualities of that letter.

We'd like your thinking on persuasion to be grounded in your own experience, not just in theories. Therefore, please stop now and freewrite (this will remain private writing) about an occasion in your own life when someone's words played a big role in affecting how you felt or thought about something—or even changed your action. Or write about an occasion when *your* words affected someone else's thinking, feeling, or behavior. Tell the story of this event in some detail. What really happened? And then speculate about how or why these words managed to be persuasive. If something else besides logic and hard evidence was important, what was this something else?

Your main assignment for this workshop is to write a letter to the editor of your school or local newspaper. You follow up this letter with an explanatory piece for your teachers and classmates about the purpose and audience of your letter. The letter and explanation could be collaboratively produced; many letters to the editor are collaborative. Instead of producing a letter of your own, however, you could expand on your analysis of one of the letters or advertisements from the first part of this workshop. You could write on just one letter or ad, or do a comparison of two or more. This, too, could be a collaborative project. Another idea is to base your main assignment on an analysis of the persuasiveness of Sabra McKenzie-Hamilton's "got violence?" in the "Readings" of this workshop. Or finally, you might decide to tape and analyze a TV ad. Consider why the ad was featured within a particular program and at a particular time. Your task is the same regardless of your subject: How does the writer/advertiser get an audience to look and listen?

Persuasion as Informal Argument

Sometimes people are persuaded by long, formal arguments that somehow "prove" or "settle" an issue by means of incisive reasoning and evidence. But sometimes these good arguments don't work; that is, the reader is somehow not persuaded even though the argument is impressive. (In fact, there is no such thing as pure logic except in closed systems like mathematics or symbolic logic. As soon as you apply logic to real events and natural language, there is always slippage because premises are debatable and situations are never static.) Persuasion always depends on the context: What is persuasive to what audience when. Worse yet, there is always the question of whether a given audience will listen—take seriously or try on what you present. No logic or information can be effective if people have closed their minds to what you are saying or showing them. Thus, at the heart of persuasion is the ability to get someone to *listen* to you.

The focus for this workshop, then, is the process of how people's minds are affected by informal, often short pieces of writing, and by the words and graphics (pictures, spacing, size and color of letters, and so forth) of advertisements. To get someone else to take in or absorb an opinion that differs from his own—to feel it as "interesting," to swallow an advertising claim just a bit even if not actually believing it—is a huge accomplishment. In this workshop we will consider persuasion not as the formal problem of argument and logic but as the human problem of getting someone to listen to your opinion. (In Workshop 11, we focus on more formal, longer pieces of argument.)

At first glance it might seem discouraging that "good" arguments often don't work. It means that if you take your goal to be the complete persuasion of "the enemy," you are almost bound to fail, for people seldom change their minds all at once. Writers of advertisements know this; that's why we see the same ads for the same products over and over again. Advertisers have to attract the eyes before their words can have any effect. But then, of course the words have to keep or provoke a potential buyer's continued attention.

The essence of persuasion in today's world is often embodied in advertisements—in magazines, newspapers, on billboards, radio, and television. Advertisers to the general public usually have only one goal: to get you to buy their products. We admit that some advertisements have a heavy information component, but most advertisements are more persuasion than argument. We've included two here for you to react to, one for the Land Rover Defender 110 and one for DuPont safety products in cars.

TREAD LIGHTLY-DRIVE RESPONSIBLY OFF ROAD. PLEASE BUCKLE UP FOR SECURITY. © 1992 LAND ROVER NORTH AMERICA, INC. *WINCH OPTIONAL. SUBJECT TO AVAILABILITY.

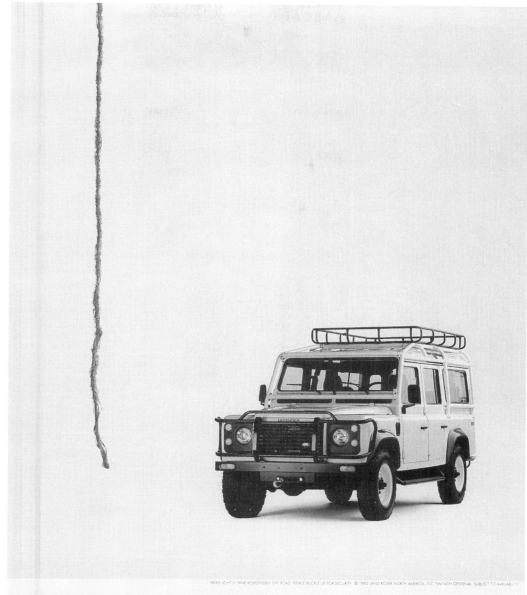

Own one of these legendary forms of jungle transportation.

Many consider it the most exotic vehicle on earth.

It's survived safaris through the jungles of Sulawesi. Madagascar. And the Amazon. Treks across the Wahiba Sands of Oman. The Rub al Khali. Even the Great Rift Valley of Kenya.

It's the Land Rover Defender 110. World renowned for wading through swamps. Crossing savannahs. Venturing deep into kingdoms of the wild.

And even better. Out of them.

There are 500 Land Rover Defender 110s now available in America, more than ready to handle everything the country has to offer.

Including roads.

You can see one of these nearly indestructible vehicles at select Range Rover dealers. For the one nearest you, call 1-800-FINE 4WD.

We realize, of course, that at around $40,000*, it's hardly a frivolous investment. But considering how it's built, it's likely the most solid one you'll ever make.

Because unlike a vine, you won't have to go from one to the next.

Courtesy Land Rover, North America, Inc.

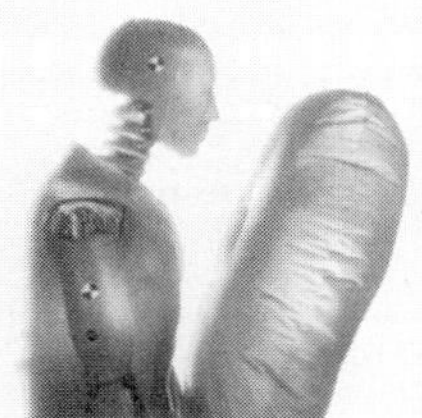

Courtesy DuPont

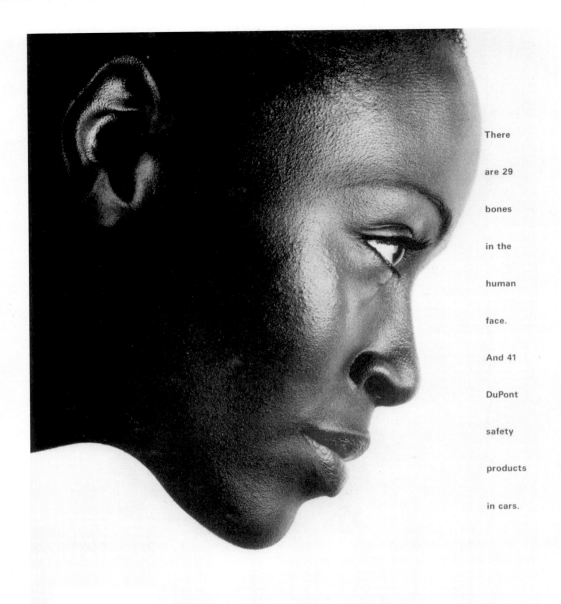

Evaluating Advertisements*

Answer the following questions about the ad you found most visually persuasive.

1. *Most visually engaging.* Which of the two advertisements most drew your eyes, made you look first and return to it the most? Answer the question using quick intuitive judgment. After answering the remaining questions, come back to this one. You may discover you've changed your mind.
2. *Purpose.* What is the ad trying to do? All ads are selling something: some a tangible product, others an intangible service or idea. Determine what your particular ad is selling or advocating.
3. *Focus.* Locate the focal point of the ad. Where do your eyes go first when you look at the ad?
4. *Visual.* Identify the place and objects in the ad and explain the purpose of each. Does the picture illustrate the copy?
5. *Language.* Consider first the headline or "grabber"—the big print that gets your attention first. What does it say, and how does it say it? Next, examine the blurb, or the more detailed written content, and consider *(a)* the language used (paying particular attention to adjectives) and *(b)* the approach used—is it description, comparison, definition, exemplification, testimonial, or something else? Does the written part complement the picture?
6. *Your position.* What was your position, if any, on the topic of the advertisement before reading it? Did you know anything about the Land Rover? Did you know anything about DuPont and its products? How much did the ad change your thinking or feeling?
7. *Assumptions.* What did the advertiser seem to be assuming as true? Do you agree with these assumptions? What does that have to do with your reactions?
8. *Audience.* Do you think you're the audience the advertisers had in mind for their product? If you're the wrong audience, what sort of audience do you think the ad writers had in mind?
9. *Voice.* Go around the circle in your group and read the words of each advertisement at least twice. Does hearing the words change your reactions? Try "entering into" the voice you hear in the words and then write as though you were that person.

Evaluating Letters to the Editor

Consider the fact that more people read letters to the editor in the newspaper than read the news or editorials or even sports. What distinguishes these pub-

* These questions are based on an exercise developed by Alice Robertson of Western Illinois State University, Macomb.

lished letters is that they are short, and they consist of people speaking out to others. If you want the quickest and best way to affect the thinking of the community you are part of, get a good letter published in your student or city newspaper or in a magazine that publishes letters. Here are some examples:

To the Editor:
The women's magazine editors whose Sept. 25 letters criticize Elizabeth Whelan's Sept. 8 Op-Ed article on their health reporting ignore the main point: it is contradictory for magazines presumably concerned about women's health to carry advertising for a product, namely, cigarettes, that brings disease, miscarriages, premature widowhood or death to women.

They declare "we have cautioned women repeatedly about the hazards of smoking," but how can anyone take them seriously when their advertising promotes smoking? If these magazines have women's best interests at heart, they will drop their cigarette ads.

—Louise P. Dudley, *New York Times,* October 12, 1992

To the Editor:
(A previous letter writer) feels women with children should be prohibited from going on spaceflights. If there is to be such a rule, it should also prohibit men with children from going on spaceflights. The loss of a father is just as bad as the loss of a mother.

—*Daily News,* March 20, 1986

To the Editor:
The Oct. 17 killing of a Japanese exchange student in Baton Rouge, La., described in "Another Magnum, Another Victim" (Op-Ed, Oct. 31) could not have been prevented by restricting the Second Amendment rights of Americans to ownership of hunting weapons alone, as the authors recommend. Hunting arms are intended to kill with a single shot, and the .44 Magnum round used in this killing is widely used in low-power hunting rifles. It is unproductive to blame American attitudes about guns for a problem that is rooted in white American attitudes toward members of other races.

I have little doubt that the young victim, Yoshihiro Hattori, would still be alive today had he been as white as his companion the evening of his murder. The white friend of the victim was alongside Mr. Hattori the instant the victim was gunned down, and so gives witness to the murder.

Deterring bias crime by vigorously prosecuting gross incidents such as this one will save more lives than retricting a homeowner's right of self-defense.

—Ludwig R. Vogel, *New York Times,* November 1, 1992
The writer is chairman of the New York State Libertarian Party.

To the Editor:
Mothers Against Drunk Driving Long Island supports New York City's initiative in seizing the cars of drivers arrested on drunk driving charges. There's no question that these offenders are using their vehicles as lethal weapons.

The more than 16,000 deaths every year in the United States from drunk driving accidents attest to the horrific toll of this violent crime. We hope this initiative will lead to more rigorous enforcement of current state law that already allows forfeiture of vehicles owned by repeat offenders.

New York City's initiative will empower the police to seize vehicles from drunk drivers on the first offense. A "first offense" does not necessarily mean the first time an offender is driving drunk. It means that it is the first time that he or she has been caught. The typical offender drives drunk between 200 and 2,000 times before he or she is arrested. Too often the first time they are caught is when someone has been injured or killed. It is better for the offender to lose a car than for an innocent victim to lose a life.

The initiative does involve some legal complications, and even logistic concerns—where do you keep all the impounded cars? But complications or inconvenience should not deter justice; and certainly should not deter any reasonable and positive action that can save lives.

In 1998, law enforcement agencies on Long Island made an estimated 13,000 Driving-While-Intoxicated arrests. MADD Long Island will monitor the progress of this, creative, life-saving initiative by New York City as a possible way to strengthen the dedicated work of law enforcement on Long Island.

Peter Jones, *Huntington Station Newsday,* February 1, 1999
The writer is president of MADD Long Island.

By yourself—or better yet with your group—answer as many of the following questions as possible. (Your teacher may specify how many of the letters you should read for this part of the workshop.)

1. *Most persuasive.* Which letter persuaded you the most? the least? Answer the question using quick intuitive judgment. After answering the following questions, come back to this one. You may discover you've changed your mind.
2. *Claim.* For each letter, state the claim in as short a sentence as possible.
3. *Support.* What is the support for the claim of each letter? Try to summarize it in a sentence. What do you think the writer was relying on: logic, information, example, emotion, language, or something else?
4. *Language.* In each case, did the language add to or detract from the writer's presentation? Try to be specific about exactly which language had what kind of effect on you.
5. *Your position.* What was your position on the topic of the letter *before* reading it? Did the letter change your position? What influence did it have on your thinking and feeling even if you didn't change your mind?
6. *Listening and trust.* Which one made you listen most, even if it didn't change your thoughts or feelings? Why? Was it because you trusted the writer?
7. *Assumptions.* What did each letter writer seem to be assuming as true? Do you agree with these assumptions? What does that have to do with your reactions?

8. *Audience.* For each letter, do you think you're the audience the writer had in mind? How does that affect whether or not you're persuaded? If you're the wrong audience, what sort of audience do you think the writers had in mind?
9. *Voice.* Go around your group and read each of the letters aloud at least twice. Does hearing the words change your reactions? "Put on" or "enter into" the voice you hear, and write as though you were that person.

Conclusion about Informal Persuasion

On the basis of these advertising and letter examples and the answers you came up with to all the questions, can you reach some tentative conclusions about what is most helpful and least helpful in short informal persuasion—in trying to get readers who disagree to listen to you? In trying to get an audience to look and buy? What do you see as the chief difference between how these letters and ads persuade? Keep in mind that complete arguments that "prove" that *our side* is right and *their side* is wrong are usually effective only for our side: for gatherings of our team to help us clarify our thinking, to help us remember why we believe what we believe, and to make us feel better about our position. They are seldom read by the other team (except when they are doing research about why we are wrong).

But this view is not so discouraging if you look closely at how words affect people. After all, it would be odd if people changed their minds all at once. And we see that though progress in persuasion is always slow—and

Exploring the Writing Process

I got the idea for the topic for this piece from something my brother said the last time I saw him. When I first wrote this piece on my brother, I truly loved the way the experience just rolled off my tongue. Yet I knew I needed to work on the grammar. When I read it to the small group in class, I realized that I didn't want to really share this experience with others. But the group had no criticism of my paper at all; they just loved it which really wasn't helpful.

So my next step was I went to the Writing Center and made an appointment with a tutor. She told me that I needed to continue the psychoanalysis of the main character and be more definite in my writing. She also suggested to change the order of the paper. Start with setting the scene of the barbecue and then lower the boom on my brother's dropping out of medical school.

So I revised the paper then making it more descriptive and analyzing the character. At this point I really disliked the whole paper. I believe this is because I enjoyed writing the paper from the point of view of a child rather than an adult. I thought for quite a long time after writing this paper about how to improve it, but I was unable to do so.

Finally after making many appointments at the Writing Center, I truly became disgusted with the paper. The appointments were canceled because of the weather, but at that point I didn't care anymore because I no longer wanted to improve a paper that in the beginning I really loved.

Student

we may not be good at creating airtight arguments—the main act in persuasion is something we *are* all good at: sensing the other person and somehow reaching out and getting the other person to *listen.* Best of all, persuasion doesn't require length. The main task is to get readers to open the door; too many words only make resistant readers close the door tighter.

Main Assignment: *Writing a Letter to the Editor*

Writing the Letter

Spend some time reading and scanning newspapers: neighborhood papers, local papers, school newspapers. Pick several issues out of these newspapers which you feel strongly about and begin freewriting, telling why you feel strongly about them and why you think others ought to as well. In your freewriting, concentrate on *your* reasons for your strong feelings on your topic. Don't think yet about persuading others. It's your own emotional and intellectual commitment that you need to tap now.

One approach is to think back to the time you first became aware of your feelings about the issues you want to write on. Describe the experience that led to your stance. Writing out this experience will help you get a firm grip on why you believe as you do.

Push yourself to write at least 10 or 15 minutes on each topic you select. You might even want to rant and rave about your topics a bit—no harm done; this is not what you're actually going to send off, and the ranting will help you get at the core of your feelings and thoughts. After you've done this exploratory private writing, set it aside for a bit—even an hour helps. Read it over when you come back and decide which issue now appeals to you the most, the one you want to use for your final letter. Isolate the point you want

Exploring the Writing Process

Professors' grades even had the power to change my own opinion about what I'd written. For example, last semester I wrote a nice paper on *The Faerie Queene.* I put a lot of effort into it and really cared about the subject matter . . . However, I received a fairly mediocre grade, the same grade I received on a previous paper that I had spent much less time on. I thought to myself, "Well, all that work went for nothin'." Immediately, I negated the paper just because of the grade I received on it. I started to believe that my paper was worthless. However, looking back on it, I now realize that the paper helped me appreciate *The Faerie Queene.* I don't believe that I would have read it as closely, cared about what the story was telling me, if I hadn't been writing a paper on the poem. In short, I took ownership of the work and I made sure that the paper remained mine as well. I did not let my professor kidnap my paper by putting a grade on it. The paper was important to me, the writer, and that's what matters.

Jerry Boyd

to make about this issue, and state it as directly and concisely as possible so that you can incorporate it into a letter.

Now you're ready to write a first draft for sharing with your classmates. And you must begin to think about your audience. Chances are you may want to address the same audience as the one addressed by the article you're reacting to. Other students in the class can help you characterize this audience on the basis of the original article.

Another good way to approach this first draft is to come up with some possible objections to your views. You may or may not have done this as you were freewriting. But now you can make a list of all the reasons that might keep people from accepting your assertions. To make these clear, try writing a dialogue with yourself where you speak on both sides of your issue. You can, of course, enlist a classmate to write out the opposing side. (For more on the specifics of writing collaborative dialogue, see Workshop 3.)

After you've done your freewriting or dialogue, decide on your focus and whether you want to take objections into consideration. It's not *necessarily* a good idea to answer opposing opinions; sometimes too much responding to objections can make your piece sound defensive and you are better off with a shorter and more direct piece.

Writing Your Explanation

After reading your letter to your group and perhaps discussing it with them, try freewriting answers to the following questions:

- What is my purpose in writing this piece?
- Who is my audience? How do I expect them to react? Why would they react this way?
- What am I assuming to be true? How does that work for my piece?
- What sort of voice have I embedded in my letter? Why did I choose this voice? (We suggest you read your piece aloud and exaggerate the voice you think is there.)
- What claim am I making? How am I supporting it?
- What decisions did I make about the language of my letter? What was the basis for these decisions?

You may also want to reread the exploration of our own purposes in writing this book (see Workshop 7, pages 195–196).

On the basis of your reflections on all these questions, you should be able to produce a solid first draft to share with your classmates.

Publication Your class may want to keep a folder or notebook with copies of all the letters after they've been mailed to the chosen publications. To this folder, everyone can add copies of letters that do get published in addition to any responses to them. This will make interesting reading for everyone.

Suggestions for Collaboration

1. With your classroom group, select (or invent) a product to write an advertisement for, and produce the advertisement collaboratively. In doing so, you'll want to consider visual qualities, too: color, pictures, size of letters, and so forth. You should also decide where your advertisement should be placed (newspaper, popular magazines, specialty magazines, and so forth) to generate the most business. In the "Readings" is a classroom-designed advertisement.
2. Write a letter to a company whose advertisements you find objectionable and explain why. You may even want to suggest changes to the ad.
3. Look at any Web site that includes advertising. You might want to start at Yahoo's home page (www.yahoo.com). Look at the way ads are embedded in the text; consider color, picture, size, dynamism, interactivity, and so forth. Is the effect of this kind of advertising different from the effect of ads on TV, in magazines, or on billboards? Why? How?
4. Do a bit of role-playing: assume that you are an advertising copywriter who wishes to sell the advertisement you and your group designed to the company that produces the product being advertised. Write a persuasive letter to the president of the company explaining why your advertisement is an effective one: who its audience is, what its purpose is, and how it works. Naturally you will include a copy of the advertisement itself. This assignment leads realistically to collaboration since almost all work in advertising agencies *is* collaborative. Two or three of you could thus undertake this assignment jointly. A sample of such a letter is included in the "Readings" for this workshop.

Sharing and Responding

With persuasive texts in particular, we need to see how they work with readers. Thus it is important to get the kind of feedback you need using techniques from "Sharing and Responding" at the end of this book. The main feedback technique might be "Movies of the Reader's Mind" (Section 7), which encourages readers to start by telling you their original opinion on your topic. You can even ask readers to talk about your topic before you show them your piece, and then have them tell you what went on in their minds as they were listening to it. The early forms of feedback (Sections 1 through 5) are useful for an early draft—helping you develop your own thinking. Getting people to describe your voice tells you how trustworthy you sound (Section 6). "Believing" feedback can help you develop your argument further, while "doubting" can help you see what objections readers could raise (Section 9).

You can use the questions we presented earlier in this workshop as strategies for analyzing persuasive letters and ads. Be sure you get your classmates to talk about whom they see as the audience for your letter or ad and what they see you trying to get them to think or do. You can take notes on this to help you with the accompanying explanatory writing.

Process Journal

- How did you choose your topic for the letter assignment? Did you find yourself believing your assertions more and more as you wrote—or less and less?
- About audience: We advised you not to worry about who your audience might be when you started to work on your response to an article or letter. Then we advised you to revise by considering your audience. Reflect a bit on what happened and what you came to notice about your audience awareness. Did we give you bad advice?
- About working in groups: What did you do that helped the group work better? What did others do that helped? Were there things that you or others did that seemed harmful? What would it take to avoid such words or actions next time?
- How would you compare writing an advertisement with most of the school writing you do? Are there ways these two kinds of writing could help one another?

Exploring the Writing Process

Cover Letter

I am, without a doubt, a writer in transition; and this assignment made me painfully aware of this fact. I sat down on Saturday night and wrote 2 pages in the style that I have grown accustomed to; but I was growing more and more uncomfortable with the way it sounded as I went along. At about 1:00 A.M. I threw it all away and went to bed. On Sunday I experienced the worst writer's block that I have ever encountered, writing a paragraph or two and then throwing it away—again and again. This was made all the more frustrating by the fact that I knew exactly what I wanted to say, I just couldn't organize it in a way that "felt" right. I tried freewriting and that went great, but when I tried to take what I'd put down and organize it I found that I couldn't. I spent 12 hrs on the computer (on and off) on Sunday and ended up with *nothing*.

At this point I was panicking. I began to think that maybe I'd jumped out of the leaky boat of my old writing style, and into the water: Wasn't it better to have a leaky boat than no boat at all? With this happy thought in mind I went to bed.

On Monday morning I decided that I would take a deep breath, lighten up on my self-criticism, and plow through it, so that at least I would have something completed that I could work with. By 3:00 when I left for class, to my great surprise, I was more than half done and I liked the way it sounded.

I guess what I was really looking for was a paper that was less uptight than my usual work, and something that had a bit of myself in it. Even though it is really only the introduction of my final paper which is "personal" I feel more like I'm "in there" throughout the paper than I ever have before. The rest of the paper came very easily after I got through the assumptions—it almost wrote itself in response to them.

I'm optimistic and I feel that I have some clear goals to work towards.

Bill Brown

Exploring Theory: *Informal Persuasion and Formal Argument*

We find it useful to lay out two opposite answers to the question of how words can persuade. At one extreme is the *extended, formal argument*—the careful, elaborated "proof"—in which you are as logical as possible and you don't resort at all to feelings or emotional "persuasive language." At the other extreme is *informal persuasion*—more intuitive and experiential. This kind of persuasion doesn't try to mount a full argument; in fact it may not use an "argument" at all, but simply convey an important piece of information or tell a story.

Extended formal argument requires readers to read carefully and at length. They've got to be interested enough in you or in what you are saying to give you lots of time and attention. Extended, careful argument is what you might be expected to write for an audience that is *expert* or *professional*—for example, if you were writing a report for a college task force about the location of a new building or about a particular health care plan. Such an audience isn't interested in emotional arguments or in being persuaded. You don't have to coax them to read and to think carefully about the matter; they're already interested in figuring out what's the best view. It's their job to read with care. They want good analysis and good reasons. If they find you trying to persuade them with an emotional appeal instead of reasons and evidence, they'll likely start to distrust you and say, "What is this pesky writer trying to hide? What are the 'real' reasons he's covering up?" Clever persuasion gets in their way.

Informal persuasion, at the other extreme, is the kind of thing you find in editorials, leaflets, advertisements, short spoken interchanges, and of course letters to the editor in newspapers. It's usually shorter than formal argument, settling for making a couple of the best points, and perhaps giving a reason, some information, and some personal experience all wrapped up together. Often this kind of argument doesn't try to *change* someone's thinking but just to plant a seed. This is the kind of piece you need to write if you are trying to reach readers who have no special reason or commitment to read what you've written.

Brevity is the most common solution to the problem of readers who are liable to wander away at any moment. Whatever you want to say to such an audience, you have to say it fast. You can't take it as your goal to completely change their thinking. Planting a seed or opening a door is probably the best you can hope for.

But informal arguments aren't always short. The crucial thing that marks informal argument is a decision to forgo full argument and instead to *reach* or *interest* readers, perhaps by getting them to experience something or by telling a story. Again, for example, *Uncle Tom's Cabin* is a story that functions as a piece of persuasion, and it had a powerful effect on national sentiment about slavery before the Civil War. Informal persuasion may make "points," but more often it succeeds by conveying *experience* or affecting feelings. Our next workshop concentrates on formal arguments.

Short Letters

Janine Ramaz

People who write short letters to the editors of their local newspapers know that they have to make their points briefly and clearly. Readers of newspaper "Letters to the Editor" sections are mainly interested in knowing what their fellow citizens think on issues the newspaper has printed articles on. If they want to read long, detailed arguments, they will look for them elsewhere in the paper. So letter writers must use few words to get across their opinions. In this paper, I'm going to look at how three short letters do this.

All the letter writers know that they have to say right away what letter or article they're writing about. So they identify that in the very first sentence. This is good because then people who aren't interested in these particular subjects will probably go on and read something else. But then when the letter writer says also briefly what the content is, readers who missed the other letter or the article but are interested will go ahead and read the letter. So every one of the writers of the letters I'm looking at says quickly what the issue is.

This issue is the subject of the letter. The issues of my three letters (pages 260–61) are advertising cigarettes in a woman's magazine, parents on spaceflights, and owning guns. I believe that the most effective of these three letters is the one about spaceflight.

The first of the letters I read, the one about women's smoking, was really too long. The writer of this letter made the same point twice. Furthermore, the second time she says it she uses the words "but how can anyone take them seriously." I hear a whiny voice here which makes the whole letter less strong.

The third of these three letters is criticizing those who are using a particular unfortunate incident to argue against gun ownership. To me, the argument is weak because the writer avoids the whole issue of banning all kinds of guns which might have saved the young man's life. Since I was sure the writer would not approve of banning all guns, his point got weaker for me. And, too, not all accidental gun shootings involve people of different races.

The letter I thought most effective was also the shortest. The writer made his point (I'm not really sure if the writer was male or female because there was no name) in plain simple language: "The loss of a father is just as bad as the loss of a mother." Furthermore I think this letter will have a broader appeal than the other two because the first one would appeal mostly to women and perhaps turn men and non-feminist women off. The third letter appeals mainly to gun lovers, though it would also have some appeal to those with strong beliefs in good racial relations.

The letter about spaceflights really made me think about something I hadn't thought of before and even to come to a new conclusion that parents shouldn't go on spaceflights. It should just be single people or married people with no children. That's the main reason I consider this letter the best: it made me do some thinking after I read it and didn't burden me with unnecessary words.

Letter to a Product Producer

January 8, 1994

Mr. John Jones, President
Wilton Products
5555 Fifth Avenue
American City, American State 55555

Dear Mr. Jones:

We read in *Advertising World* that your company is seeking a vibrant new team to design ads for Wilton's new breakfast cereal, Designer Breakfast. We're enclosing an ad which demonstrates our ability to produce ads for this exciting new product.

Our chief appeal in this ad is to ambitious young men and women who pride themselves on creating unique styles and images for themselves—young people who are already on the road to success. You will notice that we have put the name of the cereal across the top of the page to show how superior it is. The words "You design your outfit every day / why not design your breakfast?" at the top of the page and "You wouldn't wear the same outfit every day / Why eat the same breakfast every day?" come together because they are the same type and echoing structures. The questions challenge readers to participate in the ad itself.

You will note that both figures are stylish in different ways and that both are looking directly at the reader. These are young people secure in their identities. Readers will want to emulate them. The male figure is looking back as though satisfied with the way his day starts. The female figure is moving forward energetically; she has had a nutritious, filling breakfast which gives her the energy she needs to be successful. We also want our ad to appeal to young people who believe both men and women should have careers. We don't really think this is a family cereal.

We've kept the words to a minimum. Readers will want to know what the ingredients are and how the whole idea works. So we've given that information twice. And we added the environment tag at the bottom because again we think that today's young career-oriented people care about the environment. We envision this ad in magazines such as *Newsweek* and *Time,* but also in style publications such as *Vogue* and *GQ.*

We believe that this ad and others like it will sell this exciting new product. If you would like to see more of what we can do, please call.

Sincerely,
Jason Multer
Antoinette Jajee
Martine Oxenham
Ngoyen Nong
Alex Ujibwa

Analysis and Revision of Cover Letter for Advertisement

Using the techniques outlined in Workshop 7, the authors of the previous letter analyzed and revised their letter. Following is their analysis and revision.

Analysis

An analysis of our cover letter for the advertisement we designed as an assignment for Workshop 10 shows us that we do not need to change our audience and purpose: we still need to write to the cereal company for the purpose of getting ourselves hired to produce ads for the new cereal. But we have realized that we need to think more about that audience in terms of our purpose.

When we wrote our original letter, we thought of our audience as people who wanted to make a profit from their new cereal and who were looking for a new advertising firm. After thinking more about this, we have begun to realize that the reader of this letter probably wants as wide an audience as possible for the new cereal. Our problem is that we are not sure whether the cereal company would be more likely to respond to a hard-sell approach—almost like an ad itself—or to a neutral descriptive approach, which is the one we have now except for a few adjectives like "vibrant" and "exciting." As we thought about this audience also, we thought that they are probably more sophisticated about magazines and other places to advertise than we are.

When we read our original letter to our group, they told us that the words "vibrant" and "exciting" stood out and they had a negative reaction to them—as though we were pushing too hard to look good. They also told us that they thought the second paragraph was good and described the ad well. But they reacted somewhat differently to the third paragraph because they thought the male figure could also be seen as someone who looks backward in his life rather than forward. They also wondered about why we assumed so quickly that the cereal could not be a family cereal.

We decided that when we revise the letter, we need to think a lot about the language and whether we should be hard sell or soft sell. We need to think about the sophistication level of our audience and how resistant they might be to advertising language. We also need to worry about how we could make the cereal more of a family cereal.

Revision

Mr. John Jones, President
Wilton Products
5555 Fifth Avenue
American City, American State 55555
Attn: Advertising Department

Dear Mr. Jones:

Your innovative new cereal, "Designer Breakfast," has the potential to appeal to Americans across the board; we are the advertising company that can make that potential realized.

Our young creative advertising team has designed a set of ads to demonstrate our potential to make your product a household word. We suspect that you examined these ads before you started reading our letter and have already realized how strong they are. We certainly don't need to tell you how these ads make

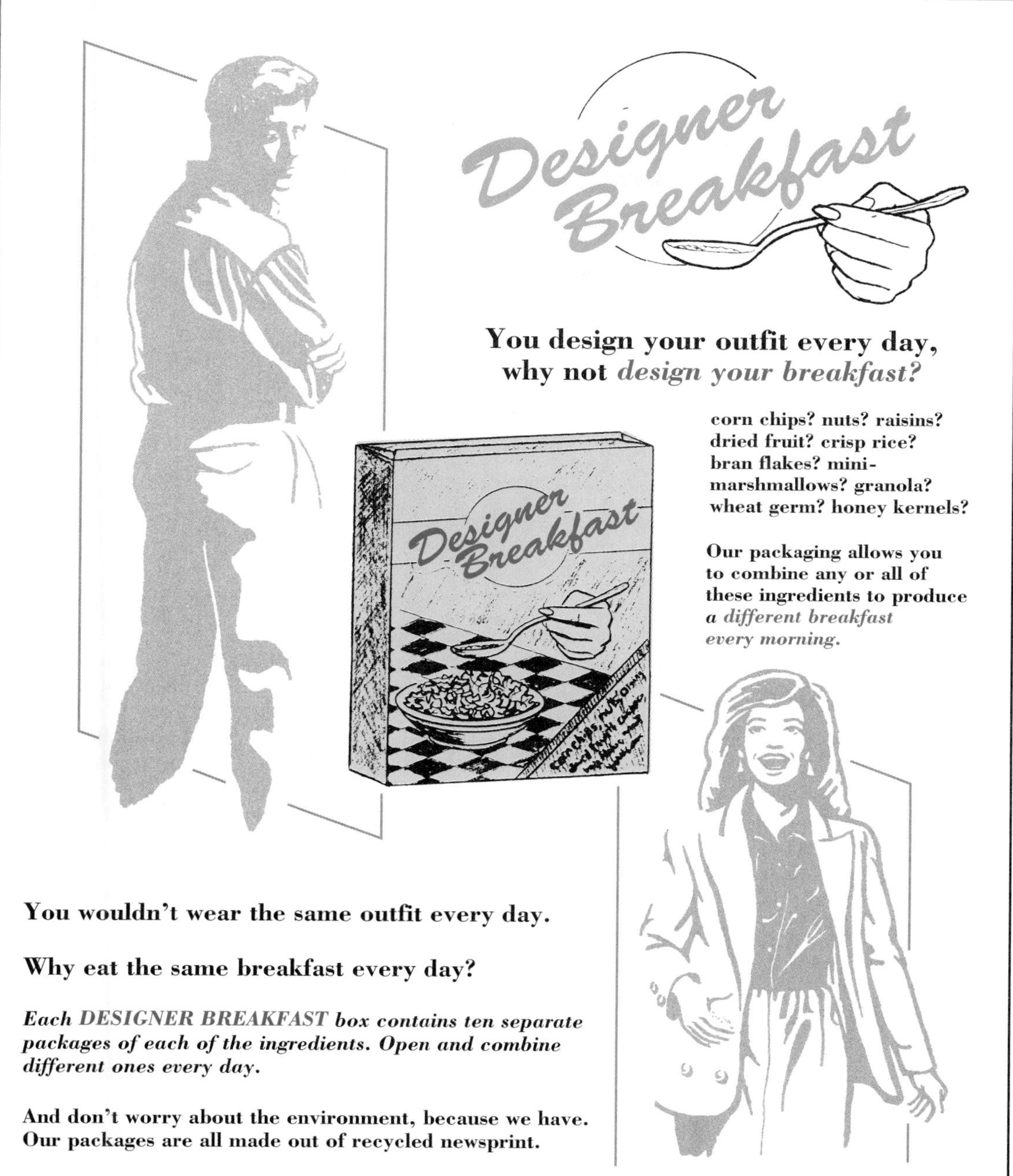

their points: you're quite capable of seeing that yourself. If our ads cannot stand on their own, we don't deserve your account.

Designer Breakfast
You design your outfit every day, why not design your breakfast?
corn chips? nuts? raisins? dried fruit? crisp rice? bran flakes? mini-marshmallows? granola? wheat germ? honey kernels?
Our packaging allows you to combine any or all of these ingredients to produce a different breakfast every morning.
Designer Breakfast
You wouldn't wear the same outfit every day.
Why eat the same breakfast every day?
Each DESIGNER BREAKFAST box contains ten separate packages of each of the ingredients. Open and combine different ones every day.
And don't worry about the environment, because we have. Our packages are all made out of recycled newsprint.

Therefore, in terms of explanation, we're just going to say a few words about how these ads could be manipulated to reach a variety of audiences. For instance, if we keep the same layout, we can change the male and female figures to children bounding out of their houses and heading for a school bus. The figures could also be those of an older man and woman dressed for hiking or golf or tennis. We can substitute figures from the artistic world—carrying musical instruments or canvases. The possibilities are almost endless. An ad campaign designed to alter the appeal within similar frameworks would undoubtedly reach consumers of all varieties. Needless to say, these figures could also be altered to different races and ethnicities.

We are certain we can sell your product. Our past successes attest to that. You probably know that it was our company which designed the highly effective campaign for Labova shoes and the award-winning ads for Lama's new line of soups. This same team can make your product just as successful as these are.

We look forward to talking to you about our ideas.

Sincerely,
Jason Multer
Antoinette Jajee
Martine Oxenham
Ngoyen Nong
Alex Ujibwa

got violence?

Sabra McKenzie-Hamilton

My two-year-old son Adam loves trucks. He is captivated by them. In fact, he currently goes to sleep each night with his miniature orange cement-mixer in hand. It's his teddy bear, and it's adorable.

When we go to the park or walk down the street, his eyes light upon those things with wheels and levers and motors, the toy ones and the real ones. I often end my day wondering when his interests will shift to things that don't just move, but also shoot or explode. There is a time to come, soon ahead, where we, as a family, will face those dreaded gadgets of violence, packaged so artfully that they will be hard to resist.

In light of this, a few weeks ago, while eating cereal for breakfast, I noticed that the milk carton we had purchased bore on its back panel this advertisement for the USS Intrepid Sea Air Space Museum:

"A Day of Adventure & Fun for the Whole Family. $2 Off One General Admission Ticket. Walk the decks of the *Intrepid,* a 900-foot-long aircraft carrier. Enjoy hundreds of sea, air, and space exhibits. Explore dozens of aircraft featuring the A-12 Blackbird, world's fastest spy plane. Tour the top secret command center aboard the guided missile submarine *Growler.*"

It was simple—violence packaged so insidiously, that it was glorified alongside even the most basic elements of daily life. I laughed out loud after reading the milk carton panel, taken aback by the subtle way in which our culture, in my opinion, accepts the outrageous.

I eventually called Tuscan Dairy Farms in New Jersey to hear what they had to say. I spoke to the Senior Vice President of Sales and Marketing, who told me that about 70% of the advertisements on their cartons are public service announcements. These announcements, which are run for a period of two weeks, are selected by a committee, are free of charge and are considered an act of service on the part of the milk company to the larger community. Tuscan barters the remaining advertising space with select amusement parks, Broadway shows and other attractions in exchange for complimentary tickets for its staff. Such was the case for the Intrepid ad.

The man I spoke with was respectful and interested. He saw the ad as a means of honoring war veterans and others who have served our country, a kind of community service if you will, something any milk company would be proud to support. I offered my disagreement, and we ended our conversation, which resembled several I have had with passersby at vigils and demonstrations I have attended at the museum in years past.

Ironically, I agree that the Intrepid is "Not Your Typical Museum," as advertised. I believe, however, it is a monument not so much to history and sacrifice, as it is a glorification of violence, carefully spotlighted in a carnival atmosphere and directed particularly at the imaginations of children. It is a terrible image to behold, that of a child playing on a weapon of death, a sanitized playground of invisible bones. For whether a family sees the Intrepid and what it represents as a support of freedom or the destruction of God's Creation, children ought never be taught to make instruments that kill and maim into objects of fun. At least, this is not the message my husband Joe and I want to teach Adam about how to discern and live in the world around him.

I know this is counter-cultural and perhaps counter-intuitive, if early playground politics is any indication of the challenge we will face in this. It has been a humbling experience thus far to watch our son push other kids and grab their toys, though we ourselves continue to do it in our adult lives in a million, more sophisticated ways. Nonviolence is a practice and a discipline about which we must become most vigilant, lest it fade into mere idealism, or lest we fade into complacency about the violence in our world.

Adam's fascination with trucks will probably dissolve the first time his eyes catch sight of the mammoth, steel aircraft carrier along 46th Street and the West Side Highway. It is an alluring, expensive piece of craftsmanship, only made more glorious by the bloodied, broken bodies that are not shown in its exhibits of smart bombs and video-game warfare, only made more enticing by the festive atmosphere on its flight decks and on milk cartons all over the city.

We don't want our family to be seduced into accepting the concept of war, no questions asked, as we eat our breakfast. In the future, we'll have to be more careful about the products we buy and what they advertise.

The Great Campus Goof-Off Machine

Op-Ed from *The New York Times*

Nate Stulman

Conventional wisdom says that computers are a necessary tool for higher education. Many colleges and universities these days require students to have personal computers, and some factor the cost of one into tuition. A number of colleges have put high-speed Internet connections in every dorm room. But there are good reasons to question the wisdom of this preoccupation with computers and the Internet.

Take a walk throught the residence halls of any college in the country and you'll find students seated at their desks, eyes transfixed on their computer monitors. What are they doing with their top-of-the-line PC's and high-speed T-1 Internet connections?

They are playing Tomb Raider instead of going to chemistry class, tweaking the configurations of their machines instead of writing the paper due tomorrow, collecting mostly useless information from the World Wide Web instead of doing a math problem set—a host of activity that has little or nothing to do with traditional academic work.

I have friends who have spent whole weekends doing nothing but playing Quake or Warcraft or other interactive computer games. One friend sometimes spends entire evenings—six to eight hours—scouring the Web for images and modifying them just to have a new background on his computer desktop.

And many others I know have amassed overwhelming collections of music on their computers. It's the searching and finding that they seem to enjoy: some of them have more music files on their computers than they could play in months.

Several people who live in my hall routinely stay awake all night chatting with dormmates on line. Why walk 10 feet down the hall to have a conversation when you can chat on the computer—even if it takes three times as long?

You might expect that personal computers in dorm rooms would be used for nonacademic purposes, but the problem is not confined to residence halls. The other day I walked into the library's reference department, and five or six students were grouped around a computer—not conducting research, but playing Tetris. Every time I walk past the library's so-called research computers, it seems that at least half are being used to play games, chat or surf the Internet aimlessly.

Colleges and universities should be wary of placing such an emphasis on the use of computers and the Internet. The Web may be useful for finding simple facts, but serious research still means a trip to the library.

For most students, having a computer in the dorm is more of a distraction than a learning tool. Other than computer science or mathematics majors, few students need more than a word processing program and access to e-mail in their rooms.

It is true, of course, that students have always procrastinated and wasted time. But when students spend four, five, even ten hours a day on computers and the Internet, a more troubling picture emerges—a picture all the more disturbing because colleges themselves have helped create the problem.

Nate Stulman is a student at Swathmore College.

Letters to the Editor of *The New York Times*

To the Editor:

Nate Stulman (Op-Ed, March 15) inserts a healthy "byte" of caution into the discussion of classroom technology. New technologies clearly offer great opportunities for learning and research. In my introductory courses, for example, I suggest Web-based resources to help with researching and writing papers.

The problem is that while offering a great time-saving resource for collecting information, the new technologies do not easily teach students how to search in a discriminating manner or how to think critically about the information they download.

Our enthusiasm for cyber-pedagogy should not prevent us from at least recognizing its potential negative impact on students who are far more likely to have surfed the Web than to have visited a library before they enter college.

Mark Cassell Kent, OH, March 15, 1999
The writer is an assistant professor of political science at Kent State University.

To the Editor:

As an undergraduate, I understand Nate Stulman's point that our fellow students spend way too much time on the computer ("The Great Campus Goof-Off Machine,"

Op-Ed, March 15). But Mr. Stulman's notion that universities are doing a disservice by providing Internet access—which will revolutionize the way we live—is downright foolish. High school and college students get in car accidents all the time; does that mean they shouldn't drive?

The bottom line is that college life is a learning experience, a time in which students learn to live independently and to acquire self-discipline. I spend a lot of time on the Internet, and maybe I should be doing my schoolwork instead. But I have also learned to limit my surfing time, spend hours studying, and learn to enjoy life.

Paul Hogarth, Berkeley, CA, March 15, 1999

To the Editor:

I agree with Ernest R. House ("Flunking Students Is No Cure-All," Op-Ed, Jan. 30). Retention programs are no solution to the problems of our educational system. In fact, retention is detrimental to students' mental health; it lowers their self-esteem and their motivation and increases dropout rates.

Early intervention is the only solution. Slow-learning students should be tutored on a regular basis by qualified teachers in small groups from first grade on. It is imperative that students move with their age group, so that they learn social and academic skills from their peers as they move through the grades.

Lore Kramer, Hartsdale, NY, January 31, 1999
The writer is a retired school psychologist.

To the Editor:

Ernest R. House (Op-Ed, Jan. 30) misses the point of forcing underachieving students to repeat grades. The main benefit of such retention programs is not necessarily felt by the few students who are held back but by the many who pass.

Plain common sense shows that students will study harder and longer when the threat of flunking hangs over their heads than they will if their promotion is guaranteed by their birth dates. The broader lesson is perhaps even more valuable than the individual subjects mastered: success is based on active learning rather than on passive presence in the classroom.

Mark Goldblatt, New York, NY, January 30, 1999

Argument

Essential Premises

- There is no single, magic *right* way to argue, with all other ways being wrong. In fact, the nature of argument differs from field to field.
- There are powerful procedures for working on argument that don't depend on the formal study of logic. We'll show you some of these practical procedures in this workshop. If you are interested in the nature of argument, you can turn to the end of the workshop where we talk more about this age-old subject. You may even want, in the process of this workshop, to analyze *that* piece as an argument.
- Good arguments don't have to be aggressive or confrontational.

Main Assignment Preview

In this workshop we focus on argument, on points of view presented through careful reasoning. The main assignment for this workshop will be: (1) an analysis of one of your previous papers, (2) an analysis of a published argument, or (3) an argumentative essay.

In Workshop 10 on persuasion we celebrated short, informal pieces. We emphasized the central skill in persuasion as getting someone to *listen*—to open the door of his mind; we downplayed longer, formal, carefully reasoned arguments. But obviously there are certain situations where it is valuable to use a long, careful argument. We turn to that in this workshop. Our goal is to help you see through any essay to the skeleton of reasoning at its heart in order to better evaluate the arguments of others and to construct better arguments of your own.

We have another goal here too; namely, for you to become more sophisticated about the *nature* of arguments, to become more critical as you read and listen to arguments. That is, even though argument is a subject complex enough for a whole book—indeed for a whole discipline (called "logic" or "rhetoric")—we can give you substantial help with it in this workshop.

An Argument for Argument

Sometimes you are lucky enough to be writing to readers who are ready to listen. A few people are open minded in general, and many people are open minded about issues where they don't have a personal stake. But they won't accept your view unless you can give a good argument, because they are also listening to people who disagree with you.

When you write essays for most teachers, especially essays in subject courses, they won't buy a short, informal burst of persuasion: They're usually asking for a full, careful argument. And teachers are not the only people you'll have to write to whose job is to look carefully at all sides of an argument. Perhaps you need to argue to a person or committee that has nothing against you but nothing for you either. Certainly in the world of work, one often has to write a report, position paper, or memo that carefully marshals the best argument; we might generalize (recognizing there are important exceptions) that for friends and general readers we need to write short, informal pieces of persuasion, but as *professionals* we need to analyze and write more formal and explicit arguments. In the readings at the end of this workshop, there's an excerpt from a dental brochure whose aim is to convince people that dentistry need not be painful. Compare this with the advertisements included in Workshop 10: You'll see directly some of the differences between persuasion and argument.

We suggested in Workshop 10 that experience and feelings often influence us more than careful reasoning, but for that very reason, we need careful argument as an *antidote.* Experience and feelings can fool us: A powerful story, letter, essay, or editorial may win our hearts, capture our feelings, and thus lead us to do exactly the wrong thing. One of the glories of language, especially written language, is that it permits us to consider things more carefully—to help us see whether we should follow our feelings and experience where they lead us. Writing, in particular, permits us to figure out reasons carefully and fully, to stand back from them and consider them one by one. In short, we need to be able to analyze and build arguments in order to make our own minds work well.

Finally, you might not care at all about persuading others, but just need to figure out some issue for yourself. Persuasive "seeds" are not what you need; you need the best reasons and evidence to help you make up your own mind. But it's not an either/or choice between persuasion and argument. Even though you will now be working on longer, more careful argument, that's no reason to forget the skills you focused on in the persuasion workshop to get readers to listen and to try to make your position human.

Analyzing an Argument

Summaries of the rules of reasoning are common, but they (like summaries of the rules of grammar) tend to be wrong unless they are long and complex enough to describe many, many exceptions. Reasoning is too complicated; the effectiveness of reasons in *particular* arguments depends on too many variables. For this workshop, then, instead of trying to give you brief rules, we'll help you harness and extend your *tacit knowledge* (which is enormous and complex): that shrewd common sense you have built up over years of practical reasoning. We'll also help you harness the knowledge of fellow students by working collaboratively.

We present here a simple but powerful method for working on reasoning or arguments. You can learn to use it best if you practice it first on someone else's writing. It is a tool for standing back and seeing writing with detachment, which is harder to do with your own writing because you are so close to it. After learning to use this method with the writing of others, you'll be able to apply it to your own writing.

You might practice this procedure on one of the arguments in the readings at the end of this workshop, on a piece of persuasive writing by a classmate from the persuasion workshop (Workshop 10), on a piece your teacher will give you, or on a speech (either on television or "live").

There are really two different tasks implied by the word "analysis."

- *Breaking down* an argument into its parts. This is a *descriptive* task of learning how to identify and isolate the main elements of an argument: the claim, the reasons, the support for those reasons, the assumptions, and the implications about audience.
- *Assessing* the effectiveness of an argument. This is an *evaluative* task of deciding how effective the reasons, evidence, and assumptions will be with various audiences.

It helps to realize that the first task—seeing what the elements of an argument are—is actually more important and more feasible than the second task of trying to evaluate the effectiveness of those elements. People get bogged down arguing about the effectiveness of an argument—or even of a single reason or piece of evidence—and thereby get distracted from the main job of seeing the argument clearly. Evaluating an argument is usually a matter of unending dispute, whereas seeing it clearly is something you can manage. You can often get agreement among readers about what a reason *is* and what supports that reason, even though they can't agree on how persuasive the reason is.

The Primary Task: Seeing the Elements of the Argument

1. Look at Reasons and Support

Main Claim Read through the argument of the piece you're analyzing, decide what the main claim is, and summarize it in one sentence. Perhaps the main claim is obvious right from the start ("I wish to argue in favor of bicycle paths on campus"; "This law is absurdly overbroad"). If you're analyzing a draft, the main claim may be unclear, perhaps because the author hasn't yet got the claim clear to himself. Even in a finished piece, there may be slippage between an early statement of the claim or thesis and the final summary statement.

Take care to summarize the main claim in the simplest sentence you can manage; wording counts a lot. For example, there's a crucial difference between saying "Terrorism can be countered without violence" and "Terrorism can be reduced if the democratic nations of the world take certain firm actions." Make a note if you find a problem determining the main claim: if, for example, the writer changes claims or if you think the real claim is different from what the writer says it is. You might end up deciding there are actually two slightly different arguments in the piece you're analyzing.

If it's hard to decide on the main claim, go on to the next step and come back later.

Reasons Read through the piece again and decide what you think are the principal reasons that argue for the main claim you have identified—or tentatively identified. It's possible to pick out reasons even when you're unsure of the main claim. Summarize each reason in a *simple short sentence.* A word or phrase won't do because a word or phrase doesn't say anything; it only points. You need a sentence because the sentence forces you to decide what is being said.

Don't be surprised if it's hard to decide just what is a "reason." For a three-page essay, you could choose 3 main reasons or 10. It's a question of how closely you want to examine the thinking. Use your judgment. Try it out different ways.

Don't worry at this point about the order of these reasons. Just summarize them in the order you find them (or out of order if you suddenly notice one you missed on a previous page), even if that makes a jumble. You can reorder them later if you want to examine the reasoning more carefully or if you are analyzing a piece of your own that you intend to revise.

Support For each reason, what support is given? Support might take the form of evidence, illustrative examples, even other "smaller" subreasons that you didn't list as major reasons.

2. Look at Assumptions

What assumptions or unstated reasons does the argument seem to make? You probably noticed some of the assumptions as you looked at reasons and support, but to find important assumptions you need to read through the argument once more with only this subtle question in mind: What did the writer seem to take for granted? Assumptions are slippery and often insidious because the writer gets them into the reader's head without saying them. And if you share the writer's assumptions, you'll have an even harder time uncovering them. For example, the following assumptions might function as unstated

Exploring the Writing Process

Anybody who finds himself in this situation of writing to a prescribed notion or to illustrate or to fill in what he already knows should stop writing. A writer has got to trust the act of writing to scan all his ideas, passions, and convictions; but these must emerge from the work, be *of* it.

E. L. Doctorow

reasons in an argument: "What is modern is better than what is old-fashioned"; "Saving time is always a good thing."

To find assumptions it helps to imagine what kind of person is making the argument—perhaps even make an exaggerated picture of him or her in your mind—and try to think of what that kind of person takes for granted. Finding assumptions in a piece of our own writing is particularly difficult because we usually don't realize we have them. They're just "there."

3. Think about Readers or Audience

What is the implied audience? Does the writer seem to be talking to people who already agree or to people who don't agree? to peers? professionals? teachers? to a large or a small audience?

How adversarial is the writer? Does he take an either/or stand, insisting that others have to be wrong if he's right? Does he use a lot of energy in showing that others are wrong?

And also, how does the writer *treat* the audience? What's his voice or stance? Is he respectful? talking down? distant? hesitant? What does the author seem to want you as a reader or audience to think or do? To get at this, two or more of you can read the argument aloud. For additional help with these questions about audience, you may want to look at Workshop 7, which includes an extended discussion of audience.

The Secondary Task: Evaluating or Assessing

This step involves looking back at what you have figured out in the previous steps: the reasons, the supports, the assumptions, and the audience implications. Try to decide on the effectiveness of each one. As we said, this is the messy and arguable part; there are no rules for what works and what doesn't. Different arguments and supports work for different readers. Some people, for instance, are impressed by tight logic; others are made suspicious by it. But at least you are looking at smaller elements, and so judgments are a bit more manageable. A few techniques might help:

- Look for counterarguments, counterevidence, or attacks that could be made against each reason, support, or assumption. That is, play the "doubting game" with each element.
- Ask what kind of person would agree and what kind of person would disagree with each reason, support, or assumption. What kind of person would "do" or think what the writing seems to be urging? This is a "humanizing" kind of approach that sometimes opens doors.
- See Section 10 in "Sharing and Responding," "Skeleton Feedback and Descriptive Outline," for an example of this procedure used on a sample essay.

If you have done a careful job with the main task of summarizing—and that is feasible—then the task of evaluating becomes more manageable.

Analyzing an Oral Argument

If you elect to analyze a speech, you'll want to tape it so that you can check your response. (You might also want to look ahead to Workshop 15 where we give some suggestions about taking notes while listening.) A speech often gives an impression of careful reasoning which doesn't stand up on second hearing. It's difficult to hold the details of an argument in your mind while continuing to listen to a speech. Speakers can actually rely on that difficulty and fudge their logic. On paper, you can see reasoning better—with more perspective or detachment—especially if it's not your own.

Arguments appear on radio and television in various forms. Sometimes stations air editorials and ask for the public to respond. Sometimes they provide time for elected officials to present pronouncements related to some important governmental issue. During elections, radio and television air political speeches and debates in full. But you need to keep in mind that what appears to be

Exploring the Writing Process

Mid afternoon. I see Hugh as I'm walking back from Ludlow. I'm working on my memo about the goals of the Bard writing program. Rained *hard* all morning and suddenly now it's steamy bright sun with no trace of cloud in the sky.

We're standing in the middle of the path because I decided on the spot to ask him for feedback on the draft of my memo. I stand there with my little canvas briefcase and umbrella between my legs and read my draft out loud to him.

He nods his head at certain points and I nod inwardly: yes, he likes these places; they are strong. But when he speaks I learn they are places he *doesn't* like. He returns to an objection he'd voiced last week when I'd been talking about goals in our meeting. (An objection to my being too pushy and dogmatic in stating goals—trying to claim too much.)

After he's spoken, I know my response immediately. I'm polite, I don't argue, but I know clearly that I want to do it *my* way. I'm not threatened but I'm not in the slightest willing to back down and do it the way he suggests.

Right afterwards I discovered I was missing a crucial page of an earlier draft with a bit I wanted to use. It must be lying in a wastepaper basket on the third floor of Ludlow. I go back, scared I might have lost it. (I am still sometimes hit by feeling that if I lose a piece of writing I've worked on I'll never be able to create it again—it will be a permanent loss of something precious.)

I go back and find it, and while I'm there at my desk, I decide to work on the piece a bit more. With some quick cleaning up I can xerox a few copies and get more feedback—for my session with Hugh made me feel more settled in my mind as to how I wanted it.

I start working—cleaning up and retyping messy bits—and suddenly I realize I need to back down from my position of stubbornness. Chagrined to realize not just that I need to but *want* to. Just what Hugh suggested. For now in reading my memo I can notice a kind of tightness or restrictedness or off-balance in my writing which stemmed from my attempts in the memo to be stubborn and pushy and claim so much. For some reason, I *had* a need to make that claim; for some reason I don't need to make that claim now—and can see it's better not to.

In a nutshell. I got feedback from Hugh; I was forced to see my words through his eyes; I felt secure in rejecting that way of seeing my words; but then in going back to the text with my own eyes, I could no longer see it as I had seen it.

Peter Elbow

purely oral, often isn't. Speakers on television are often reading from a TelePrompter into which a previously written speech has been fed. What radio and television have created is a genre of oral argument based on written scripts.

You can also attend public lectures (or lectures for a large audience at your school) in which speakers are trying to convince an audience of something. Be aware here too, though, that many public lecturers read from typed copy. Government officials and politicians usually distribute copies of their speeches before they actually deliver them. Maybe a courtroom is the one significant place today where oral arguments exist apart from written script. Certainly far fewer great orators exist now than in the past. If you have access to a courtroom, you may want to listen to a lawyer's summation in which she presents a summary of all the evidence supporting her side of the argument.

In Workshop 15 we will focus on the importance of being a critical listener in school, particularly in large lecture classes where discussion is at a minimum. When listening to politicians and others making pronouncements about important public issues either live or on television, you also need a critical ear. This assignment can start you along that path.

While listening to the speaker you select, you may want to take a few notes as you recognize main points, assumptions, evidence, subreasons, and so forth. But even if you don't do that, you should do some writing as soon as possible to record your initial reactions, to record some sense of what your final judgment would be under normal circumstances when you would probably not hear the speech again or read it. Later you can reread your notes and reconsider your initial reactions.

Analysis of an oral argument is a good assignment to do collaboratively. It will give you a chance to see if others "hear" the argument the same way you do. It will also give you more insight into how speakers can mislead because listeners cannot refer back to what was said previously in the same speech. Sometimes two people talking about a speech they've both heard seem not to have even heard the same talk.

Building an Argument

Find an issue to write about that's not completely clear in your own mind: an issue you still have some questions about. Write a dialogue between your own different opinions. For example, you might start off by writing, "Colleges put too much emphasis on competitive sports: Some football and basketball teams might as well be professional." Another voice might answer, "Yeah, but athletics allows some kids to get an education they wouldn't otherwise get."

Remember that arguments don't by definition have only two sides; you can have more than two voices in your dialogue. Another voice can pop in and say, "Sports are good for people: They help them to work cooperatively and keep their bodies in good shape." Once you get started, follow the conversation wherever it leads. We think it will lead you to complex thinking and interesting writing.

But perhaps you want to write an argument concerning an issue about which you feel no confusion. You're convinced you know what is right and you want to convince others. Obviously, there's no internal dialogue here. What you have to do is *imagine* someone who disagrees with you. Perhaps you can think about what kind of life experience would lead someone to feel differently than you do. Be careful not to characterize that person as stupid; you need someone intelligent and fairminded if you're going to get a useful dialogue going. Of course, if you can find someone in your class who disagrees with you, you can write a collaborative dialogue. Make it a dialogue in which you listen to each other, not one where you try to shoot one another down.

If you have trouble coming up with a subject, look back over the freewriting you've done for other workshops. Look particularly for language that is unusually vivid and resonant. Its subject is probably especially thought provoking for you. Look too for issues that reappear; that's evidence that they're on your mind.

Your dialogue should help you come to a clear position on your issue. But a clear position doesn't necessarily have to be a definite pro or con position; you can still write a good argument for a position something like this: "We need to better understand the place of competitive sports in education." A clear position doesn't necessarily mean that your feelings are clear about all the issues.

Once you have your position, you can complete your draft, using material from your dialogue to support it. It's sometimes possible to produce an effective argument by smoothing your dialogue, removing digressions, elaborating on significant points, and providing transitions, an introduction, and a conclusion. In effect, you will be presenting a narrative of the development of your thinking.

If you're aiming for a more traditional essay, you can isolate significant points in your dialogue and build an informal outline before completing your draft. The points we set forth in the previous section for analyzing arguments can help you identify and evaluate various elements in your dialogue: reasons, supports, assumptions, intended audience, and counterarguments.

Revising Your Own Argument

We advised you to practice this analytic procedure on the writing of others, but of course one of the main uses is for revising your own writing: to strengthen the argument in some exploratory writing or in an informal, persuasive piece. If you are revising, you can't just stop with deciding what's strong and weak in your piece; you need to figure out how to improve it.

Here are a few suggestions:

- When you list main reasons, write each one on a 3 × 5 card or a half sheet of paper. That way you will find it easier to play with a different order of points or to restructure the whole piece.
- Define your main claim. If you are not sure, it may take a bit more exploratory writing.

- Finally, figure out the best order for your argument. If you still find this difficult, it helps to realize that even though an argument operates in the realm of "reasoning," this doesn't mean that there's some perfect order you have to find. There are always a host of possible organizations or sequences that could be effective.

It's an important psychological fact that arguments are not necessarily more effective if they present reasons step by step in the most logical sequence, as in a geometry textbook. Obviously it pays to hide the logic in a poor argument, but even a strong argument is sometimes clearer and more persuasive if presented differently from the way a logic or geometry text would present it. So try different orders; you can start with the most powerful reason, or end with it, or give reasons in the order you thought of them (with a kind of narrative thread), or arrange them by resemblance.

In short, don't feel you have to have mastered logic to be good at this process. Use your intuition; follow hunches. Our nose for reasoning is usually more acute than our conscious knowledge of it, just as our ear for grammar is usually more acute than our conscious knowledge of it. Of course intuition alone can be wrong. That's why you need the two powerful tools we suggest here: an X-ray of the skeleton of reasons in the argument and an assessment of the effectiveness of these reasons. And don't forget the value of collaboration in doing all of this.

Main Assignment: *Analyzing or Writing an Argument*

Choose one of the following:

1. Write a paper that analyzes the argument in an essay (yours or someone else's) or the argument in a speech. An alternative would be a paper that compares the arguments in two essays or speeches. (See the "Readings" in this workshop for Janine Ramaz's analysis of her essay in Workshop 10.)
2. Revise a persuasive piece you've already written, with emphasis on strengthening the argument for a particular audience. The most likely one to revise is the persuasive letter you wrote for Workshop 10; you can think of your revision as an editorial rather than a letter. But you could revise an earlier essay if you prefer, since a number of them could be called persuasive. You could even—as a major revision—recast a *non*persuasive piece as an argument.
3. Write a new essay in which you build the best argument you can. Be sure to enlist the help of your classmates in subjecting this new essay to the argument-analysis process we describe in this workshop.
4. Develop some aspect of the activities in this workshop collaboratively.

Suggestions for Collaboration

You can work through analyzing an argument with a partner or with a larger group, discussing each step as you go. Such a process gives you the opportunity to experience directly how productive it is to do joint thinking. But each of you can do this on your own and then compare notes. Or you can divide up the target essay, have each person work on one part or one task, and then put your analyses together. Collaboration can go much further. You and a partner (or even three or four of you) can decide to analyze a given argument separately and then write a collaborative paper which presents the similarities and differences observable in the separate analyses. And, finally, you can always go the route of full collaboration: Do all the work with one or more of your classmates and produce a jointly written analysis.

Sharing and Responding

If you write an analysis, you can ask others to go over it with you point by point, using the items listed on pages 279–81 for analyzing arguments.

If you write an argument of your own, Section 10 of "Sharing and Responding" will give you the best information on your reasoning and structure.

But perhaps—after all this emphasis on reasoning—you should get feedback on factors like voice or stance toward reading. Section 6 of "Sharing and Responding" will be useful for this.

As always, "Movies of the Reader's Mind" (Section 7 of "Sharing and Responding") tends to tell you the most.

When doing sharing and responding on the assignments in this workshop, you should try to give readers written texts of what you write, particularly for later drafts, because it's difficult for them to follow your argument or analysis when they can't read it. It probably makes sense for them to give you feedback in written form, too.

Process Journal

- Do you find yourself more comfortable working with short, informal persuasive pieces or longer, more careful arguments? What was different for you about doing these two different pieces?
- If you analyzed one of your own pieces, what was hardest? How useful was this procedure for revision?
- When persuading or arguing (either orally or in writing), did you find yourself putting more emphasis on why your own view was better or on why the other views were wrong? How did this affect your writing for this workshop?

Exploring Theory: *Nonadversarial Argument, Reasoning, and Grammar*

Nonadversarial Argument

"Construct a thesis; state it forcefully; line up evidence to prove that your thesis is correct; prove that contrary opinions are wrong; conclude by restating your thesis." Are these the kinds of directions you've received for writing an argument? Writing that is structured this way is often seen as the only valid kind of argument—at times, as the only valid kind of writing.

This model of persuasion and argument seems to be grounded in either/or, right/wrong, good/evil stances: "If I am right, you have to be wrong." Consider the result of these approaches: The reader who thinks differently has to define herself as wrong or stupid or bad before she can take your position seriously. This explains why most persuasive pieces and arguments are exercises in wasted energy and tend to become mere displays of the ability to follow prescribed form. We'd like to push for a different conception of argument, a less aggressive, less adversarial conception.

In truth, there may be a way in which writing by definition is monologic and authoritarian—after all, there's one voice speaking. And while you're reading what someone else has written, it has more power than you do because you can't answer it and argue with it and make it change its mind. This power can have two opposing results: Either we can succumb and be submissive to what we're reading, not question it at all, or we can resist it—perhaps even overdo our resistance—because we resent our inability to express our opinion to the author. We can even have both of these reactions to the same piece. The more strongly the author presents opinions, the more likely we are to have these reactions. The question is, "What effect does the author's opinion have on us?" We would answer our own question by saying "very little." If that's the case, the writer has not accomplished much.

One way to encourage dialogue is to contextualize what you're arguing for. Arguments that are absolute—"My point is true for all people in all situations at all times!"—probably provoke the most resistance from readers. If you can set what you're arguing for in a context and acknowledge that what you believe is conditioned by certain circumstances and experiences and present those, you may provoke less resistance from a reader. A reader can enter into the dialogue by bringing up other circumstances and experiences. (In Workshop 12 we stress the importance of contextualizing all research, of recognizing the limits within which all research functions and thus the limits to what one can conclude. This same strategy is important in argument, too.)

Does this mean that you can't argue for something if you believe it's absolutely true: the existence of a supreme being, the necessity for preserving the natural environment, the value of loving others, and so forth? No, of course not. What it does mean is that you're more likely to be genuinely listened to if you say something like, "This is what I believe and this is why I believe it" rather than "I'm right, you're wrong, and this is why."

Another thing we're not saying here is that arguments of the traditional sort are always the wrong way to go. As one kind of argument, they're worth studying and mastering. What we are saying is that argument doesn't always have to be the aggressive sort that hits readers forcefully over the head. An argument for your point of view can be just as effective, perhaps even more effective, if you think of your reader as a partner in discussion and your aim as a desire for conversation that will result in your both being better informed about the issue.

Argument can use its power to create a foundation from which both writer and reader can build knowledge. After all, knowledge is always the result of some sort of collaboration between people, even when those people are long dead and our contact with them is only through written words. The challenge is to write in such a way that a reader is neither passive nor resistant but encouraged to become part of a dialogue. You can show your awareness of opposing opinions, of opposing voices, without belittling them. Once you've set up a tone of dialogue, your reader is far more likely to listen to you. Increasingly, we hear people who are resentful of being forced into either/or arguments, seeing them as a trap which leads to hopelessness. Consequently, they may just tune out.

All of us have a much better chance of being persuasive if we can present a train of thought which says, in effect, "I'm not asking you to give up your beliefs; you can think whatever you like." We might even go so far as to say, "I'll bet your beliefs or opinions make a lot of sense. Continue to think whatever you want. But let me show you some of my thinking that I'll bet you'll find useful and interesting. Don't worry if what I say seems to contradict what you think. We might both be right in some way that we can't yet understand." This approach invites dialogue.

Here's an example. Both of us, the authors of this textbook, think that multiple-choice tests are not only a poor way to test writing but may even be harmful. We could go into meetings with administrators and teachers in charge of testing programs and say, "Multiple-choice tests of student writing are unsatisfactory because they don't ask students to produce language; they present a false picture of what it means to write; they emphasize form above ideas; they are not based on recent research findings," and so forth. But we've had more success getting people to listen to us when we go into these meetings and start the discussion by saying something like, "We've been wrestling with the problem of how to test student writing for a long time" or "Like you, we're interested in finding the best way to test student writing, a way that gives us the information we need, is not too expensive, and satisfies teachers and administrators. Here are some ways other people have come up with that we can talk about."

If it's true that you want your opponent to listen to you, then you have to listen to him. While you're drafting an argument, you can create an opponent as we suggested in this workshop. Writing out his side of the issue will make you a better proponent of your position. Paradoxically, you have a greater chance of arguing successfully with others the more you can enter into *their* position. What you are trying to produce in readers is a glimmer of feeling that says, "Hey, this writer isn't crazy. I can really see why he feels that way." It can be scary for readers to enter into the skin of "the enemy," especially if they think that position is immoral, uninformed, or stupid. The scariness comes from the fear: "Well, if they are right, even a little bit right, then I must be wrong." But this isn't true. It often happens that two opinions or positions which appear to be opposite—and which make people fight tooth and nail—can *both* be right in certain senses. In short, you can argue your position without having to argue that the other position is wrong.

To go back to our example. We often go into meetings of administrators who are talking about testing student writing and simply ask them what they are doing now and what they like and don't like about that. In a similar way, it's possible to start a good argument paper by simply describing the current situation you'd like to see changed. Often faults reveal themselves.

We know there will always be situations where a person has to argue for an absolute acceptance of her point of view and a complete refutation of every opposing opinion—for example, when a lawyer argues against a death sentence for her client. But even here we believe that the principles of nonadversarial argument are worth considering.

Reasoning and Grammar

To figure out what makes good argument is like figuring out what makes good grammar. Indeed, reasoning and grammar are deeply similar: Grammar is a picture of the regularities in the way people use *language;* reasoning is a picture of the regularities in the way people use *thought.*

Take grammar. Though there are certain universals—certain regularities in how people use language whether they speak English or Chinese—for the most part grammar is a story of local peculiarities: Different languages and different dialects are composed of different regularities. Grammar is largely an empirical business; there is nothing but "what native speakers do." That is because at its most basic level, grammar is what makes language possible. "Mistakes" are either momentary lapses or, more likely, not mistakes in grammar but mistakes in *usage.*

If we let grammar include matters of usage (such as whether you may split infinitives or begin sentences with "And" or "Hopefully"), grammar then becomes defined more narrowly: "what *prestige* native speakers *approve of* or call *appropriate for writing.*" At the level of usage, dictionaries may tempt you to think there are right answers, but dictionaries do nothing but record what natives (or prestige natives) do or approve of. Thus dictionaries continually change their minds as the years go by and as people change their habits. At any given moment, dictionaries disagree about the usage and even spelling of certain words.

Although there is no such thing as "correct grammar" built into the universe (or at least very little of it, and it won't help you choose between "who" or "whom"), if you want to get a good grade in most classes, get certain kinds of jobs, or persuade your readers, you have to get rid of what your audience will call "mistakes."

The same situation holds for logic or reasoning. Here too there seem to be few universals. In *The Meno,* Plato stresses the universals, concluding that all humans seem to agree about the rules of geometry or mathematics. But most of our reasoning is not about geometry and mathematics, and it turns out that good reasoning in most realms (like good grammar at the level of usage) depends on what different groups of people *call* good reasoning—that is, upon conventions that are different in different cultures or disciplines. Recently a number of critics have posited differences between feminine and masculine ways of presenting points of view. To reason well is to learn the conventions of a particular community of writers within a particular area of knowledge or practical functioning. And, increasingly, we are becoming aware of the different conventions for successful argument in cultures other than our own.

Are we saying that grammar and reasoning are nothing but a set of random rules to memorize—like batting averages or the capitals of the states? No. There is a rational and orderly science of grammar that you can study and master. It's a lovely science—in a sense the science of the human mind. The same goes for reasoning. But fortunately we don't have to study and master the science of grammar to make our language strong (or to get rid of most of what others call "mistakes"). So, our point in this workshop is that we don't need to study the science of logic to get our reasoning strong (and get rid of our worst mistakes in thinking).

The reason we can do well without studying and memorizing rules is that we've done so much talking, listening, discussing, and writing that we already have an enormous amount of tacit or unconscious knowledge of grammar and reasoning. Can we get good grammar and good reasoning just by putting pen to paper and writing? Don't we all wish! No, we can only benefit from all our tacit knowledge if we go about using it in the right way. In this workshop we suggest tools to harness our tacit knowledge of reasoning effectively and, in doing so, gain more control and conscious awareness of that tacit knowledge.

Here are steps to help you make the best use of your tacit knowledge of *grammar* in the process of writing.

1. Start off writing as naturally and comfortably as possible. *Don't* think about grammar or about any minor matters of phrasing or spelling; think only about what you want to say. *Talk* onto the paper. In this way you are making the most use of your intuitive knowledge of grammar. The most tangled writing almost always results from slow and careful writing: You stop after every three or four words and worry about whether something's wrong—and then think about how to finish the sentence. Or you search a thesaurus for a different word or search the dictionary for a spelling. You lose track of the natural syntax in your head. If instead you can get yourself to talk on paper naturally and comfortably, you will produce mostly clear and correct syntax to start with.

2. Next, using whatever revising process you find best, get your text to say *exactly* what you want it to say—but still without worrying about minor matters of phrasing, grammar, and spelling. Thinking about these things will only distract you from paying attention to what you are trying to say. Why fix up the grammar and spelling in a sentence you may well throw away or rewrite anyway?

3. Now turn your attention to phrasing, spelling, and grammar. Read your draft aloud slowly and carefully to yourself and see what improvements you can make and what mistakes you can eliminate. If you read it *aloud* to yourself—slowly and with expression—you will find even more ways to improve it.

4. Read your piece aloud to one or two listeners: for their help, yes, but also because their presence as audience will help you recognize more problems and think of more improvements.

5. Give your final, typed version to another person to copyedit. In Mini-Workshop L we set out a structured method for getting this sort of help from others.

Thus, in this book we do not summarize the rules of language or grammar or usage for you. You can easily find other books—handbooks—that do so. (Unfortunately, however, such handbooks tend to be wrong unless they are enormously long and complex. Any simple rule will have too many exceptions that depend on the context.) However, you will do a better job of strengthening your language and "fixing your writing" if you work in the more empirical —and more enjoyable—fashion we've just described. The strength of our approach comes from (1) using language unself-consciously to tap your tacit knowledge; (2) examining and revising what you've produced in a self-conscious, systematic, and controlled frame of mind; and (3) collaborating with others.*

These same three steps can make your *reasoning* effective too: (1) write out your argument and its support by talking naturally and unself-consciously on paper; (2) examine and revise what you've written, in the self-conscious, systematic way we've outlined in this workshop; (3) get help from others. By going about writing an argument this way, you use both intuitive and systematic modes of thinking; exploiting them together leads to powerful argumentative writing.

* You will have a harder time at this task if you are not a native speaker or if you don't read a fair amount. But don't underestimate your ear: If you've heard a lot of radio and television, you've heard plenty of Standard English and developed a keen sense of the differences between levels of formality.

Aiming a Cannon at a Mosquito

Mona Charen

Tooling around town with a baby in a stroller gives one a new appreciation for the difficulties of the disabled. Poorly designed buildings, where the elevator takes you to the basement garage only to open upon a flight of stairs—even two or three steps can be impossible for a person in a wheelchair—are the most maddening. It's a small inconvenience for me. I can always take the baby in one arm and carry the stroller in the other. The wheelchair-bound are stuck.

No doubt some well-meaning Capitol Hill staffer had thoughts such as these when she got the idea for a new federal act protecting the "rights" of the disabled. The mental image was probably of a person in a wheelchair, asking only for a chance to work and contribute to society like everyone else.

As with so much liberal legislation, and it is liberal (remember that the next time George Bush touts this as one of the accomplishments of his administration), this law is absurdly overbroad. It attempts to kill a mosquito with a cannon. And the cannon, aimed at American business, will undoubtedly hamper U.S. competitiveness.

The Americans with Disabilities Act is advertised as another in a long line of civil rights bills. But it's more than that. Most state governments already forbid discrimination against the handicapped. The ADA goes further, requiring businesses with 25 or more employees (and in two years, those with 15 or more will be included) to make "reasonable accommodations" for the disabled.

What that will mean—how "reasonable" will be interpreted by the courts—remains unknown. In some easy cases, "accommodation" will mean a simple device on a telephone to permit a handicapped person to use it, or an adjustment to a computer. But in other cases, it may mean having to rearrange work schedules, or hire an extra employee to help the disabled one.

Still, not many Americans would object to paying slightly higher prices for products if it means giving a chance to those who are handicapped. But physical handicaps afflict only 3.3 million Americans. This law is written to cover 43 million. How do they get that figure?

The good folks in Washington have thrown into the "disabled" category those who are morbidly obese ("in rare and limited circumstances" say the regulations), and those with mental and emotional problems.

It's the mental and emotional disorders part of the definition that really opens Pandora's box. For while mental disability is no less real than physical disability, it is far easier to fake.

Most unsettling of all, the law includes among the disabled those who are "in recovery" from drug or alcohol abuse. Not only is an employer forbidden to discriminate against those workers, but they may be forced to permit them to attend support groups or counselling during work hours. Employers may also—though this, too, remains to be seen—be required to cover their medical expenses.

The lesson of Paul Tsongas—that Democrats must learn to be pro-business if they are truly pro-jobs—remains unabsorbed. Mandating ramps and hearing aids is one thing; calling every alcoholic disabled is quite another.

Analysis of My Argument in "Short Letters"

Janine Ramaz

The main claim of my essay "Short Letters" [see "Readings" in Workshop 10] is that the letter about mothers going on space flights is the most effective one. The essay supports my claim with a number of reasons and supporting evidence.

The first reason I give is that a letter directed to the "Letters" column of a newspaper must state its point quickly and briefly. I observe that all three of the letters do this, but I don't really support this by quoting from the letters. Furthermore, since all of the letters are brief and quick about this, this reason does not give particular support to my preference for a particular letter. If I were going to revise my piece I'd have to think about whether this idea should come at the beginning of my essay or more towards the end.

My next reasons are really reasons why the other two letters I looked at are not as effective as the one I preferred. I don't prefer the letter about advertising cigarettes because it is too long. The support for this reason is that ideas are repeated, but I don't really say what the repeated idea is. I also criticize this letter because I hear a whiny voice in it. I'm of course making an assumption that people don't like whiny voices, but I think that's a pretty good assumption.

I criticize the third of these three letters because I don't think the author follows through on his argument. My support for this is that he doesn't talk at all about banning all guns. My second support for the weakness of this letter is that he brings in a side issue: race. This really weakens his argument. But perhaps I was too quick to write off this letter because I'm not a gun supporter. The author may really be quite wise not to bring up larger issues of gun use. And he is also smart in bringing in the issue of race because that may well appeal to a whole different audience than the gun argument.

The other reason I give for stating which letter is best relates to its language. The first support for this is that there are no extra words. The second support is that the language is plain and simple: I quote something as evidence of this. I'm assuming that people like plain simple language, but perhaps I should be careful about that assumption. It's possible that some readers might see plain, simple language as evidence of less education and knowledge.

And my final reason is that the most effective letter is the one with the broadest audience appeal. I support this by talking about the possible audiences or nonaudiences of the other two letters. But if I revised this essay, I think I'd want to reconsider this reason. After all, there's no particular reason why these letters should appeal to a broad audience. Letter writers may just want to appeal to particular audiences.

My essay is not adversarial at all. The main point doesn't even come until over half way through. And I don't really argue strongly against the other two letters. In fact, I start by mentioning a good point about both of them. And I often qualify my statements by words like "I think" and "To me," so I'm not making absolute statements. I'm not an adversarial person, so if I revised this, I don't think I would change my approach very much—though perhaps I ought to think about the effects of phrases like "I think."

The weakest part of my essay is its lack of real audience. This is a paper I wrote for the teacher; I'm not sure why anyone else would think it was interesting. The only possible place where I seem to appeal to a broader audience is in the last paragraph. I do believe that more people care about children losing their parents than about feminist issues or gun support or non-support.

The audience issue would be most important if I revised this. If I rewrote it, I think I'd want to make it an essay which gives advice about how to write an appealing letter to the editor of a newspaper. I'd use these three letters as examples of what to do and what not to do. I think this would give the paper more focus and make it more interesting to readers besides my teacher.

Too Much for Too Little

A Student

When was the last time you sat down and really enjoyed dinner, let alone any other meal in the cafeteria? Can't remember, can you? Neither can I. Don't you think you deserve better service and a higher grade of food? Most students believe they deserve better treatment, so why isn't anything being done? Most students on campus are paying large amounts of money for room and board and also tuition. And a large amount of this money goes towards each student's meal plan during each semester. There's an old saying, "You get what you pay for," but unfortunately we are not.

Did you ever realize how a good meal and quality service affect your attitude and motivation for the day? Sometimes it's the only thing people look forward to. But as of late, most people are left aggravated and hungry after making a trip to the cafeteria. The management on campus is in disarray at the moment. Their poor decision-making and actions cause a great number of hold-ups and mass confusion. If waiting in a long line that moves once every ten minutes isn't bad enough, try finding a seat.

Let's get to the heart of the matter: the food. Lately the quality of the food has gone from mediocre to downright pathetic. Management should put a little variety in their choice of food. They should give students a few alternate choices. Part of the time dinner is cold and sometimes unidentifiable. To cover up they say it's Chinese food. But once you taste it you realize you are eating last week's leftovers. So you say to yourself, "Maybe I'll have a hamburger, they can't mess that up." Wrong again. The burgers are pretty close to hockey pucks, and there are no french fries. The two usually go together hand in hand. And to finish off dinner maybe one would like some dessert—a piece of cake, for example. Well, let's just say when the fork started to bend I kind of figured the cake was not for me.

So when is it all going to change? The school says they improved their food program from the previous year. Well, I guess I should consider myself lucky. If I take into consideration how the food is now, I can merely assume either that last year the food was really terrible or that they just have not made much progress at all. Changes won't come over night, and they may not come at all. It's up to the students to make the choice and to decide what's right. If you like the way the food is now, then by all means enjoy yourself. But I would prefer some better quality food. I'm not asking for shrimp and lobster (though I wouldn't mind). But a little more efficiency in the kitchen may save a lot of aggravation.

Cover Letter

When picking a persuasive topic to write about, it is to the author's advantage to touch on a subject the majority of the readers are familiar with. The aim of the paper was to stir up some feelings and opinions on the student food plan on campus. I went about writing the paper through my own personal experiences in the cafeteria. Because I received no help from anyone, the paper may tend to be one-sided.

Gas Analgesia

From a brochure in the offices of Jack H. Weinstein and Ira H. Abel, 1811 Avenue U, Brooklyn, N.Y.

Fear of dentistry goes back many years to the days when anaesthesia was unknown, and the procedures involved in treating teeth were painful. Today, we have excellent anaesthetics that can successfully eliminate practically all pain involved in dentistry. Novocaine can do this very easily. However, novocaine cannot eliminate the nervousness, the tension and the apprehension of most people. Then too, most people fear the injection of the needle.

Today, people need not stay away from dentists for any reason whatsoever because we have, in addition, *ANALGESIA.*

What is Analgesia?

It is a mild gas with a pleasant sweet odor. We call it *SWEET AIR,* which is inhaled thru the nose. It is pleasant and easy to take for both children and adults.

What Does *Sweet Air* Do for the Dental Patient?

1. It relaxes.
2. It eliminates fear, nervousness and tension.
3. It eliminates most of the pain involved in dentistry, and the rest is so dulled that you do not mind it.
4. It makes you feel WARM and SAFE.
5. It is similar to a light pleasant intoxication.
6. It works three ways, in that you find you are not nervous or fearful BEFORE, DURING, or AFTER your dental visit.
7. If an injection is needed, you will find you don't mind it at all with *analgesia.* It is like a good friend who is with you at all times, close at hand, ready to help you, right at the moment you need him.

There are no after-effects, and you can get right out of the dental chair and go about your business immediately. It is a very safe procedure.

With All Deliberate Speed: What's So Bad about Writing Fast?

William F. Buckley, Jr.

If, during spring term at Yale University in 1949 you wandered diagonally across the campus noticing here and there an undergraduate with impacted sleeplessness under his eyes and coarse yellow touches of fear on his cheeks, you were looking at members of a masochistic set who had enrolled in a course called Daily Themes. No Carthusian novitiate embarked on a bout of mortification of the flesh suffered more than the students of Daily Themes, whose single assignment, in addition to attending two lectures per week, was to write a 500-to-600-word piece of descriptive prose every day, and to submit it before midnight (into a large box outside a classroom). Sundays were the only exception (this was before the Warren Court outlawed Sunday).

For anyone graduated from Daily Themes who went on to write, in journalism or in fiction or wherever, the notion that a burden of 500 words per day is the stuff of nightmares is laughable. But caution: 500 words a day is what Graham Greene writes, and Nabokov wrote 180 words per day, devoting to their composition (he told me) four or five hours. But at that rate, Graham Greene and Nabokov couldn't quality for a job as reporters on *The New York Times.* Theirs is high-quality stuff, to speak lightly of great writing. But Georges Simenon is also considered a great writer, at least by those who elected him to the French Academy, and he writes books in a week or so. Dr. Johnson wrote "Rasselas," his philosophical romance, in nine days. And Trollope . . . we'll save Trollope.

• • •

I am fired up on the subject because, to use a familiar formulation, they have been kicking me around a lot; it has got out that I write fast, which is qualifiedly true. In this august journal, on Jan. 5, Morton Kondracke of *Newsweek* took it all the way: "He [me—W.F.B.] reportedly knocks out his column in 20 minutes flat—three times a week for 260 newspapers. That is too little time for serious contemplation of difficult subjects."

Now that is a declaration of war, and I respond massively.

To begin with: it is axiomatic, in cognitive science, that there is no necessary correlation between profundity of thought and length of time spent on thought. J.F.K. is reported to have spent 15 hours per day for six days before deciding exactly how to respond to the missile crisis, but it can still be argued that this initial impulse on being informed that the Soviet Union had deployed nuclear missiles in Cuba (bomb the hell out of them?) might have been the strategically sounder course. This is not an argument against deliberation, merely against the suggestion that to think longer (endlessly?) about a subject is necessarily to probe it more fruitfully.

Mr. Kondracke, for reasons that would require more than 20 minutes to fathom, refers to composing columns in 20 minutes "flat." Does he mean to suggest that I have a stopwatch which rings on the 20th minute? Or did he perhaps mean to say that I have been known to write a column in 20 minutes? Very different. He then goes on, in quite another connection, to cite "one of the best columns" in my new book—without thinking to ask: How long did it take him to write that particular column?

The chronological criterion, you see, is without validity. Every few years, I bring out a collection of previously published work, and this of course requires me to reread everything I have done in order to make that season's selections. It transpires that it is impossible to distinguish a column written very quickly from a column written very slowly. Perhaps that is because none is written very slowly. A column that requires two hours to write is one which was interrupted by phone calls or the need to check a fact. I write fast—but not, I'd maintain, remarkably fast. If Mr. Kondracke thinks it intellectually risky to write 750 words in 20 minutes, what must he think about people who speak 750 words in five minutes, as he often does on television?

The subject comes up now so regularly in reviews of my work that I did a little methodical research on my upcoming novel. I began my writing (in Switzerland, removed from routine interruption) at about 5 P.M., and wrote usually for two hours. I did that for 45 working days (the stretch was interrupted by a week in the United States, catching up on editorial and television obligations). I then devoted the first 10 days in July to revising the manuscript. On these days I worked on the manuscript an average of six hours per day, including retyping. We have now a grand total: 90 plus 60, or 150 hours. My novels are about 70,000 words, so that averaged out to roughly 500 words per hour.

Anthony Trollope rose at 5 every morning, drank his tea, performed his toilette and looked at the work done the preceding day. He would then begin to write at 6. He set himself the task of writing 250 words every 15 minutes for three and one-half hours. Indeed it is somewhere recorded that if he had not, at the end of 15 minutes, written the required 250 words he would simply "speed up" the next quarter-hour, because he was most emphatic in his insistence on his personally imposed daily quota: 3,500 words.

Now the advantages Trollope enjoys over me are enumerable and nonenumerable. I write only about the former, and oddly enough they are negative advantages. He needed to write by hand, having no alternative. I use a word processor. Before beginning this article, I tested my speed on this instrument and discovered that I type more slowly than I had imagined. Still, it comes out at 80 words per minute. So that if Trollope had had a Kaypro or an I.B.M., he'd have written, in three and one-half hours at my typing speed, not 3,500 words but 16,800 words per day.

Ah, you say, but could anyone think that fast? The answer is, sure people can think that fast. How did you suppose extemporaneous speeches get made? Erle Stanley Gardner dictated his detective novels nonstop to a series of secretaries, having previously pasted about in his studio 3-by-5 cards reminding him at exactly what hour the dog barked, the telephone rang, the murderer coughed. He knew where he was going, the plot was framed in his mind, and it became now only an act of extrusion. Margaret Coit wrote in her biography of John C. Calhoun that his memorable speeches were composed not in his study but while he was outdoors, plowing the fields on his plantation. He would return then to his study and write out what he had framed in his mind. His writing was an act of transcription. I own the holograph of Albert Jay Nock's marvelous book on Jefferson, and there are fewer corrections on an average page than I write into a typical column. Clearly Nock knew exactly what he wished to say and how to say it; prodigious rewriting was, accordingly, unnecessary.

Having said this, I acknowledge that I do not know exactly what I am going to say, or exactly how I am going to say it. And in my novels, I can say flatly, as Mr. Kondracke would have me say it, that I really do not have any idea where they are going—which ought not to surprise anyone familiar with the nonstop exigencies of soap opera writing or of comic strip writing or, for that matter, of regular Sunday sermons. It is not necessary to know how your protagonist will get out of a jam into which you put him. It requires only that you have confidence that you will be able to get him out of that jam. When you begin to write a column on, let us say, the reaction of Western Europe to President Reagan's call for a boycott of Libya it is not necessary that you should know *exactly* how you will say what you will end up saying. You are, while writing, drawing on huge reserves: of opinion, prejudice, priorities, presumptions, data, ironies, drama, histrionics. And these reserves you enhance during practically the entire course of the day, and it doesn't matter all that much if a particular hour is not devoted to considering problems of foreign policy. You can spend an hour playing the piano and develop your capacity to think, even to create; and certainly you can grasp more keenly, while doing so, your feel for priorities.

The matter of music flushes out an interesting point: Why is it that critics who find it arresting that a column can be written in 20 minutes, a book in 150 hours, do not appear to find it remarkable that a typical graduate of Juilliard can memorize a prelude and fugue from "The Well-Tempered Clavier" in an hour or two? It would take me six months to memorize one of those *numeros*. And mind, we're not talking here about the "Guinness Book of World Records" types. Isaac Asimov belongs in "Guinness," and perhaps Erle Stanley Gardner, but surely not an author who averages a mere 500 words per hour, or who occasionally writes a column at one-third his typing speed.

There are phenomenal memories in the world. Claudio Arrau is said to hold in his memory music for 40 recitals, two and a half hours each. *That* is phenomenal. Ralph Kirkpatrick, the late harpsichordist, actually told me that he had not played the "Goldberg" Variations for 20 years before playing it to a full house in New Haven in the spring of 1950. *That* is phenomenal. Winston Churchill is said to have memorized all of *Paradise Lost* in a week, and throughout his life he is reported to have been able to memorize his speeches after a couple of readings. (I have a speech I have delivered 50 times and could not recite one paragraph of it by heart.)

So cut it out, Kondracke. I am, I fully grant, a phenomenon, but not because of any speed in composition. I asked myself the other day, Who else, on so many issues, has been so right so much of the time? I couldn't think of anyone. And I devoted to the exercise 20 minutes. Flat.

Testing in Schools Is Part of Problem, Not Solution

Op-Ed from *The Amherst Bulletin*

Michael Greenebaum

Tests are destructive of education. I don't know how else to say it. Whatever value tests have is offset—indeed, is overwhelmed—by the damage they do to students and teachers, to the structure of schooling, and to the nature of knowledge itself.

Now, when both students and teachers in the Commonwealth [of Massachusetts] are being attacked by testers in the name of reform, is no time to mince words about this subject. Tests are not part of the solution; they are part of the problem. They are emblematic of the problem.

The least of the damage is the language they force us to use. When the state test results were released in December, school officials all over Massachusetts issued statements like those we heard in Amherst, full of words like standards, accountability, basic skills, grade level, succeed. These are heavy and joyless words that have nothing to do with learning; they are words one might expect from Amherst Schools, Inc.

When superintendents and school officials talk about all students succeeding, what can they mean? They must mean doing well on tests, because if they were talking about succeeding in school, they would discover a language that talks about excitement, involvement, questioning, supposing, imagining. The language of knowledge-

and-skills would be joined by the language of expression-and-appreciation. When was the last time you heard a School Committee member talk about expression and appreciation?

You are more likely to hear school officials remind you that tests are good predictors of success in school. Children who do well on tests are likely to do well in school. This is cynicism disguised in its most benevolent robes. Overlooking the tendency of such statements to be tautological, let's just remind ourselves that doing well in school requires doing badly in schools. In order to have an upper half of the class, you must have a lower half.

In a world in which tests predict school success, they also predict school failure. The John Silbers of such a world cry "bad teachers" when scores are bad and "grade inflation" when scores are good. In such a world it is not possible for all students to succeed. Be assured that as test scores rise, the testers are vigilant. Do not suppose that they will rest until substantial numbers fail again. Do not suppose that grade level has any independent existence from test scores.

So the next time you hear a school official talking about every student succeeding, remind him that this is Massachusetts, not Lake Wobegon. If every student succeeds, the testers will be out of business.

This is all terrible, but perhaps it can get worse. Both the President and our governor are talking about testing teachers, not only new candidates but current practitioners. Once again, the language uses words like standards and accountability. It is a little more confusing, because the people who want to hold teachers responsible for their own test scores also want to hold them responsible for their students' test scores. The assumption seems to be that high-scoring teachers will produce high-scoring students.

This is dumb. It is also dangerous. And destructive. High scorers do not necessarily make good teachers. Brilliant teachers are not necessarily good test takers. At the elementary level in particular, the qualities of insight and nurturing, the unique teacherly instinct to intervene or not to intervene, the capacity to inspire, encourage, cajole—these are not only not amenable to testing but are also unconnected to knowledge.

Knowledge is not a bad thing. But it looms large in testing not because it is such a good thing but because we know how to test it. Once again, we are searching for our lost keys under the lamp post where the light is good rather than in the dark street where we lost them.

Humiliation is part of the daily lot of public school teachers. They are not trusted to create their own curriculum. They have little if any control over their own daily schedule, and few have the dignity of a space where they can be alone for a few minutes. They keep reading that the key to a successful school is the principal. And now tests.

The whole testing enterprise is deeply flawed in its assumptions and its logic. It may flow from honorable intentions, but it is not a river, it is a sewer. It corrupts as it compares. Its sole purpose is to rank students. It is rank.

There is much more to be said about it. In this commentary I have discussed its social consequences. Next month I want to indicate its educational costs and then, if I can keep up my head of steam, its philosophical flaws.

Michael Greenebaum, retired, was principal of Mark's Meadow School for 20 years.

Measuring Students' Progress Is Not Antithetical to Learning

Op-Ed from *The Amherst Bulletin*

Gary Stoner and Bill Matthews

In his Feb. 5 Bulletin column, Michael Greenebaum presents a highly critical and misanthropic view of testing in education—both testing of students and testing of teachers. "Standards, accountability, basic skills, grade level, succeed," he writes. "These are heavy, joyless words that have nothing to do with learning."

This stunning statement reflects a deeply flawed understanding of the importance of assessment in the learning process. Greenebaum considers the very notion of measuring student progress somehow antithetical to learning. It follows, then, that assessment of student progress is unimportant in determining the next steps of a student's program of instruction, and that teachers can and should rely instead on intuition. Why bother with assessment?

According to Greenebaum, teaching is linked to learning through insight, nurturing, a teacherly instinct to intervene or not, inspire, cajole, and encourage, and such constructs are neither measurable nor connected to demonstrable knowledge. In other words, we are told what makes a good teacher, and what constitutes learning and knowledge. Then we are informed there is no way to assess the legitimacy of the claims made. Such irrefutable claims are an unnecessary but not uncommon limitation of contemporary perspectives in education.

At this point, one might ask: How can a former principal so misunderstand the essential connection between assessment and outcome in education? Some clues to Greenebaum's perspective are contained in the comments: ". . . doing well in school requires doing badly in schools. In order to have an upper half of the class, you must have a lower half . . . If every student succeeds, the testers will be out of business." These comments reveal two very important flaws in Greenebaum's thinking.

First, his comments suggest the purpose and outcome of educational assessment is solely to rank order students along some dimension, in this case achievement. Certainly, at times the purpose of educational assessment is to rank order students to guide decision making. However, Greenebaum does not recognize other more formative forms of educational assessment that can be used to effectively guide teacher decision making regarding what to teach, and how and when to teach it.

Second, he proposes that "the testers" have control over student achievement. This comment fails to recognize what is essentially a truism in education: The best predictor of a student learning something is the time devoted to and quality of teaching it.

In assessing a child at risk for making poor academic progress, is it Greenebaum's fear that nurturing, cajoling, teacherly instincts and the like may not be enough to improve the child's performance? In essence, Greenebaum suggests that if the academic progress of a child is not assessed, then there can be no failure and perhaps, more significantly, no responsibility for the educator.

Greenebaum implies if one does not ask, then there is nothing to tell. He suggests we can have a child's unmeasurable joy, expression, and appreciation but not a measurement of academic achievement linked to instruction. He implies that we can have only one or the other.

We disagree. Attaining both should be the goal of all educators.

Greenebaum presents a confusing and misinformed perspective on the purpose of education. There is a wealth of empirically valid research on effective curriculum development, instructional design, effective teaching strategies, and assessment techniques related to educational outcomes that can be used to improve the educational performance of students in meaningful ways. This is the purpose of education for which professional educators are paid, and for which we offer no apology.

Greenebaum, alternatively, suggests that improved educational performance ought not to be the goal of education. Whatever his goal, by his own admission, it is not definable or measurable.

Like Greenebaum, we are concerned and annoyed that NES has not released the reliability or validity data, which makes interpreting the teacher test scores impossible. Making decisions about prospective teachers in the absence of the requisite technical data is as bad as making decisions based on Greenebaum's a priori ideological beliefs. We recognize and oppose the politicization of the test scores. However, that entry-level teachers in our society's most important profession should be able to demonstrate basic competency in literacy and in their subject matter seems irrefutable.

That such a test has become necessary reflects a failure in requiring definable academic standards from the first grade on through college. Those of us who are educators must share the responsibility for that failure.

Do high test scorers make better teachers than low test scorers? The question is empirical and requires data to answer, not a priori beliefs.

Greenebaum has summarily dismissed the role of assessment in education. We share some of his concerns, but we believe the available evidence suggests that careful, purposeful assessment has an important role to play in public education.

Gary Stoner, Ph.D. is an associate professor and director of the School Psychology Program in the School of Education at the University of Massachusetts, Amherst.
Bill Matthews, Ph.D. is a full professor in the same program.

Research

Essential Premises

- Research is an integration of what one already knows (through observation and reading and conversation) and what one learns from additional sources.
- The kind of research one undertakes depends entirely on one's purpose and the availability of sources.

Main Assignment Preview

Research results from the desire to know something. What that "something" is determines the kind of research the researcher undertakes and the sources he or she uses. Sometimes research questions lead you to seek information mainly from print sources: books, periodicals, and newspapers. At other times, research questions mainly lead you to observe and interview. And, increasingly, research may lead you to the Internet and the World Wide Web, either to a search mechanism or to an already identified Web site.* Quite often, researchers need data and information from a variety of sources. In this workshop, our goal is to get you to undertake several kinds of research. We hope you'll begin to believe as we do that individual research (observation and interviewing†) and textual research (print, library, Internet) are equally valid; which to use depends on what you want to know.

---

*See Mini-Workshop F for instructions on how to get started with electronic searches.

†When a researcher observes intently (often over a period of time) a particular environment and then writes a fully detailed description of it and what happens there, this is called ethnographic research. It relies on close observation, careful reporting, and rich, "thick" descriptions rather than on a survey of large numbers of examples.

Your main assignment for this workshop will be:

1. To develop a research topic out of a previous piece of writing you've done for this class.*
2. To design a research plan that calls for individual research (interviewing and observing), library or print research, and—if resources are available—Internet research.
3. To write a research paper that combines this information. Your final paper will need to include appropriate documentation.

We're trying to get away from the old "research paper mentality" that makes you say, "Let's see, this is a research paper. Therefore, none of my own thinking belongs here. My job is to find a topic that lets me quote and summarize from the assigned number of books and articles. This is library work: filling out cards, making outlines, pasting it all together, and getting footnotes right." We're asking for a paper that grows out of your own thinking but which joins your thinking, not only to the thinking of others but also to what you can learn from observation and interviewing. In a sense your job is to create and carry forward a conversation: you'll bring the thinking you've already done together with the thinking and observations of others and get all this material talking together.

Main Assignment: *Writing a Research Paper*

Deciding on a Topic

Mainly, in the assignments we've given you so far, we've asked you to write material out of your own head with input from your teacher and classmates in your writing class and in other classes. We think it highly likely that you found—while writing on some of these topics—that you wished you knew more about them. This is your chance to revise an earlier report on the basis of research: interviewing, observing, reading.

Set aside some time for looking back over all the pieces you've done for this writing course. (We hope that, in itself, will prove to be valuable.) As you read, jot down a list of possibilities for research. Perhaps you wrote your narrative about the neighborhood, town, or city where you grew up. Maybe you wrote a description of a frightening dream. We've read quite a few persuasive and argumentative papers on the subjects of college food plans, campus security, and the pros and cons of ungraded courses. And we've read many, many analyses of newspaper editorials, advertisements, and all varieties of literature: poems, plays, novels, and so forth. All of these subjects can be developed into research topics.

To arrive at a topic, try setting up a question for yourself. For example, the student who wrote the argument paper on the college food plan (see readings

---

*We are grateful to Charles Moran, at the University of Massachusetts at Amherst, from whom we first learned of this sensible approach to library research.

for Workshop 11) might ask: "What kinds of food plans are provided by college campuses, and what are the benefits and problems of each?" The student who wrote "Collage about Human Differences" (Workshop 3) might ask "What kinds of differences are there among the students, faculty, and staff on campus?" The students (in the same workshop) who wrote about collaborative writing might ask "How much collaborative writing is there on this campus (or some other site) and who does it?" The student who interviewed his brother for Workshop 8 might ask "What kinds of writing do high school students do and how do they feel about it?"

First Round of Freewriting

Once you've selected a topic and framed a question for your research to answer, reread what you've already said about the topic and do some focused freewriting or clustering about what else you'd like to know. It's quite likely that you'll have more than one topic that seems promising and interesting to you. If so, do some more freewriting or clustering on all of them as a way to discover which presents the greatest complexity and richness for you. If you still can't decide, share this freewriting with others in and outside the class. Their responses will help you decide on your final topic.

When you settle on your final research question, do more freewriting. Push yourself as much as you can to get down on paper what you already know and what your opinions on the subject are. Don't worry about whether what you write is "right" or not. The point is to make clear to yourself exactly where you're starting from. You may be surprised to discover that you actually know more than you think you do and have more opinions about your subject than you're aware of—or, not so positively, you may find out that you have strong opinions and nothing to back them up.

For instance, our meal-plan writer surely knows college regulations: the costs of various plans, the restrictions and privileges of each, his own experience with the food and the experiences of his friends, and his observations of others in the cafeteria. He probably also knows something about changes in the plan, both those which have already occurred and others being discussed by students and administrators. But he may discover that although he thinks the food and the service are awful, when he tries to find specific examples of that, he comes up short.

As you do this freewriting, interject questions as they come up: "Have the prices gone up recently? How much?" "What kinds of plans do other schools have?" "What provisions are made for those on special diets?" "Is there a profit? Who gets it?" "What are the students really complaining about?" Later you can reread and highlight these questions.

Designing a Research Plan

For the purposes of this workshop, we ask you to design a research plan that requires you to do several kinds of research: library, individual, and possibly electronic. This may seem arbitrary to you (it is), but we want you to get some sense of the full range of research strategies and the ways these strategies complement one another. And perhaps it's not as arbitrary as it might seem at first since most subjects can probably be profitably researched in all three ways.

To get started on a plan, make a list of questions you've thought up, starting with your major research question.* If you have a chance to share your freewriting and your list, others will probably come up with additional questions. Decide which can best be answered by library research, which by observation and interviews, and which by electronic resources. Since we're asking you to do all of these activities, make sure you have questions in all categories. Again, your classmates can help here.

Following through on one of our examples, the student who wrote about "Human Differences" might list the following questions:

For interviewing:

1. Do you see yourself as a minority of any kind? because of your race? your ethnic group? your gender? your religion? your physical appearance? your intellectual or social interests? your age? your status as a full-time or part-time student? as a commuting student? as a parent?
2. Do you tend to associate mainly with those who are part of this same minority?
3. In what other ways do you see yourself as different from students here?
4. Do you feel the same difference in your home neighborhood? in your job?
5. Do you think others (students, teachers, staff, colleagues at work, neighbors) treat you differently from the way they treat others? Why?
6. Does your sense of being different in some way affect how you behave? How?

For observation:

1. What sort of differences are visible on your campus? in your neighborhood? at your job?
2. In each of these settings, do people spend most time with those who seem to be most like themselves? In which of these settings is that most true? least true?
3. Do people behave differently depending on whether they're interacting with those most or least like themselves?
4. How do students group themselves in your classes?
5. Do your teachers interact with all students the same way? Do you notice any differences?

*Notice how William Zinsser does this in the excerpt in the "Readings" at the end of this workshop. ("Surely mathematics was a world of numbers. Could it also be penetrated with words?" And "Could a lifelong science boob follow Einstein's train of thought?" And "How does someone write chemistry?")

For the library:

1. Are statistics available about the make-up of the student body on your campus? On campuses across the country?
2. What information can I find about changes in the make-up of college students over the past 100 or so years?
3. Are there books written by people who describe what it's like being a member of a minority group? For example, what's it like to be handicapped in some way? What's it like to go back to college when you're 45? What's it like to be a woman in a mostly male setting? Or vice-versa?
4. Are there articles about the ways colleges (or businesses or neighborhoods) deal with human differences among their members? What seems to work? Not work?

For the Internet:

1. What can I find out about the make-up at particular colleges by seeking out their home pages?
2. Are there special sites for students who see themselves as belonging to minority groups? That is, sites for blind students? For older students?
3. Is there a government site that has information about current college students? a break-down by ethnic group? by age? by gender?
4. Is there some site I can use to disseminate some of my interview questions and thus get input from students on other college campuses?

Once you have this bare-bones list of questions, you'll profit from talking them over with others. Get them to help you devise more questions and refine those you already have. And most important, get them to help you with questions for interviewing and observing. Then you're ready to decide more specifically how to go about your research: what to do first, next, and last.

For example, a student who wanted to find out more about the writing students do in high school might go to the library and look for research studies specifically about this, or for more general articles which describe particular teachers' experiences teaching writing in high school. She could then design interview questions which seek to validate or extend this research. She might want to design a questionnaire for students and teachers to see how similar their reactions or experiences are to the conclusions of the writers of these articles. Or she could reverse these tasks and observe and interview first, perhaps get permission to sit in several high school classes and see what kinds of writing occur there—or even sit in a meeting of teachers as they discuss the place of writing in the high-school curriculum. On the basis of these observations, she could design a questionnaire soliciting information from both students and teachers about their experiences with writing. She could then go to the library and see whether what she has observed and found out is substantiated by other research.

All topics are not alike; some may require that you do a particular kind of research first. The main thing for you in this workshop is to learn to have comfortable traffic back and forth between your own thinking and observing and the thinking and information that others have published. In most workshops we emphasize collaboration with fellow students. Here we want you to understand that you can also collaborate with people you know only through their published works, through interviewing them, or through the words they post on the Internet. What you'll probably realize as you work through this assignment is that you'll need to move back and forth between all these varieties of research.*

Before you actually begin to do the research you've laid out for yourself, we suggest that you write a brief list of some of the things you suspect your research will uncover. This may seem odd to you, but it often makes your research more exciting if you've already got some possible conclusions in mind. This list can be very sketchy—just fantasize that you already know all there is to know about your topic.

A note of caution: Students often think that research papers have to prove something. One of the lessons we stressed in Workshop 10 is that we can seldom prove things: All we can do is get people to listen. Except in rare cases, you're not going to get a final answer to whatever question you pose for yourself. The best you can do is gather data that give you insight into a possible answer, one that will be valid within the limits you set for yourself. You can't come to any conclusions about what American college students think about campus food, but you can reach some conclusions about what undergraduates (or perhaps only freshmen or just male freshmen) on your particular campus think about campus food in particular cafeterias right now. You set up the limits, the context, in which you are doing your research. When you report it, you then let your readers know what that context is.

You can't claim anything beyond what your research shows, but that doesn't mean you can't make suggestions or hypothesize about larger issues. It means you have to acknowledge what your data and information apply to and what they don't. Nor does it mean that your research isn't useful; we suspect that this sort of particularized research would be more interesting to the administrators at your school in charge of food services than more generalized research that might not apply so directly to the decisions they have to make.

Interviewing and Observing

Observing and interviewing are skills; you'll want to make sure you're doing them as well as possible. Before you begin your research through observing, map out where to observe and what sorts of activities to look for. The questions you draw up to further your research will be mainly questions to yourself while you're observing. After a practice run, you may need to alter those

*We've included in the "Readings" for this workshop the "Acknowledgments" Simon Winchester wrote for his book *The Professor and the Madman.* You'll see how he moved back and forth from interviewing to the Internet to libraries of various kinds, all in response to what he discovered he needed to know to continue his research for the book.

questions. Most researchers build a practice run directly into their research plans, knowing that they can't always decide what to look for until they've started looking.

If you're going to design a questionnaire, make sure you try it out on friends or classmates first to uncover whatever glitches it may have. Researchers in the social sciences almost always do this. When you plan your interviewing, it's important to prepare a set list of questions if you're going to draw valid conclusions. You can also do these activities in tandem: first ask your informants to respond to a written questionnaire and follow that up by interviewing a random sample of those who responded. This is also an established research practice, performed, for example, by the U.S. Census Bureau. Also, before you start on your interviews, you may want to look back at some of the advice we gave in Workshop 8.

Your subject may be quite different from those we've been using as examples. We cannot include all possibilities here. Strategies for research are as varied as the questions which can be asked. But you should be able to lay out a plan of action for yourself with the help of your teacher and your classmates. The important thing is to keep your task manageable, to make it into something you can handle within the time you have. Your teacher will let you know how much time that is.

Using the Library

If you're not familiar with your campus library, you'll want to set aside some time to become comfortable finding your way around it. Check whether there's a handout or some other printed introduction available. Many campus libraries set up group tours for students unacquainted with the facility. Sometimes writing teachers or teachers of other introductory courses set aside class time for a visit to the library.

Obviously you cannot "master" a college library on the basis of this one task, but the trick is not to feel intimidated. Few people who use libraries ever master them. Realize that it's legitimate to ask librarians for help—and don't be afraid to ask "dumb" questions. Most are happy to help as long as you treat

Exploring the Writing Process

I decided to write my essay as an informative piece on AIDS, because I feel that the AIDS crisis is a very serious issue that has to be exhausted until everyone begins to care and take precautions. The "Magic" Johnson tragedy really shocked me and instilled a fear in me that made me want to find out more about AIDS, and maybe allow others to learn from my essay. My main goal of this essay is education; to educate myself and others about AIDS.

I took the time to thoroughly read pamphlets and magazines on AIDS. Once I was knowledgeable about the subject I then conducted surveys on some Stony Brook students. I asked them one question; "How is AIDS transmitted?" Only the least knowledgeable (ignorant) students' responses were placed in my essay.

Student

your own questions as occasions for learning, not as requests for them to do the work for you. Also, remember that libraries classify books by subject, so once you've located a book on the shelves, look at the books surrounding it. Libraries are ideal places for wandering and browsing; people who like libraries let themselves pause and glance at books or documents that they are passing. Read a few titles, pick up a book, look at the table of contents, and read a page. Libraries are good for serendipitous finds. Don't give in to the feeling that many people have: "I don't belong here if I don't know where to find what I want."

Here are some of the most promising places to look for information in a library:

- General encyclopedias (e.g., *Encyclopedia Americana* or *Encyclopedia Britannica*).
- Specialized encyclopedias (e.g., *McGraw-Hill Encyclopedia of Science and Technology, International Encyclopedia of Higher Education,* or *The New Grove Dictionary of Music and Musicians*). There are specialized encyclopedias in many areas. Ask the librarian about encyclopedias in your field of interest.
- Almanacs (e.g., *Universal Almanac* or *Facts on File*).
- Biographical dictionaries (e.g., *Dictionary of American Biography* or *International Who's Who).*
- General periodical indexes to short articles (e.g., *Readers' Guide to Periodical Literature* or *Book Review Digest*).
- Specialized periodical indexes (e.g., *Education Index* or *United States Government Publications*). There are many such specialized indexes.
- Abstracts. An abstract is a summary of a scholarly work. Reference rooms in libraries offer online, CD-ROM, or print volumes in various subject areas that include abstracts of articles that appear elsewhere, usually in periodicals. For example, there is a series titled *Psychological Abstracts.* Using this series saves you time because you can usually tell from the abstract whether a particular article is relevant to your research. Abstracts are also sometimes included at the beginnings of articles in certain journals and essay collections. These too can save you time by pinpointing which articles would help your research and which would not.
- Book catalogs. Online Public Access Catalogs (OPAC) are computerized catalogs that have replaced or are replacing card catalogs at most libraries. Almost all are easy to use, and printed instructions are usually available. If not, ask for help from a librarian. Computerized catalogs cut research time immensely. Many libraries' online catalogs also provide access to other libraries' holdings, as well as to such resources as reference works, periodical indexes, and digital text collections.
- CD-ROM and online searches. Most libraries are now equipped with an array of electronic resources ranging from *The Oxford English Dictionary*

or *Newspaper Abstracts* on CD-ROM to dedicated computer terminals providing access to the Internet. (Many of the print resources listed above are now available online or in CD-ROM form, and will in some cases be available *only* in this form in the future.) Access to electronic sources makes it possible for researchers to probe an immense store of material relatively quickly. Generally, this is done by isolating the key terms relevant to your project and plugging these terms into a search engine. Finding the terms that each search engine recognizes and that will yield useful "hits" requires careful study of the user guidelines, but also some trial and error. You will want to give yourself plenty of time to investigate the electronic resources your library offers and to become skilled at using them.

Our list of reference sources is, of course, only illustrative. There are far too many to list here. (A full writing handbook or a textbook devoted to research papers will give more.) To see what more specific resources might be available in your area—and you will often find a reference book that is just what you need—consult a guide like Eugene P. Sheehy's *A Guide to Reference Books* or ask the help of a librarian. The value of reference books is that they give you an overview of your topic and a range of books and articles you can track down.*

The essential skill for doing library research is to learn a *different relationship to the printed (or electronic) word.* We tend to feel we have to *read* articles and books, but in research you need to learn to *glance, browse,* and *leaf* through material. You have learned the main thing if you can tell in a few seconds from a title or an abstract whether something is worth tracking down, then tell in a minute or two whether an article or web site is worth reading, and in two or three minutes whether a book is worth spending an hour trying to "mine" (not necessarily read). To do this makes you feel insecure at first, but give yourself permission to keep on until you feel more comfortable with the process. Instead of feeling intimidated by the weight or mass of what might seem like everything that's ever been written, change gears and think of it as a vast collection of meeting rooms. In each room people are talking about a topic. Imagine that you have an invitation to poke your head into as many rooms as you want for just a moment or two: No one will be disturbed by your coming in for a few minutes or by your leaving in the middle of the discussion. Be sure to jot down a few notes about the conversation you've heard in each room after you leave it.

Of course you have to do some *careful* reading too. Think of it this way: You don't have much time for this research assignment, so you'll want to end up having browsed and dipped into a number of books, articles, and online sources, and having found 50 to 100 pages worth reading carefully for the light they throw on your topic. The main task is to *find* the best 50 to 100 pages to read carefully—and not waste time reading the *wrong* 50 to 100 pages. Inevitably, however, you will do some reading you won't use. This procedure should make you more skilled and comfortable when you have something you want to investigate further. Your goal is to feel that from now on you can wade in and make use of a

---

*You might want to look at Pat Belanoff, Betsy Rorschach, and Mia Oberlink's *The Right Handbook,* which presents a process for working through a research paper that fits well with this workshop.

library whenever you have something that merits the search, whether it's a school assignment or simply something you need to know.

Remember too that you cannot say *everything* about any topic. You always need to limit what you say in some way. Your research is always more convincing and valid to the degree that you realize—and show your reader that you realize—that you are not claiming to have read everything on the subject. This means that you can feel fine about acknowledging what you haven't done. One of the most interesting parts of a research paper can be a section that talks about questions or material you would pursue if you were able to carry on with more research or your suggestions for others who might want to do so. Good researchers almost always do this.

As you read the 50 to 100 pages you've identified as best dealing with your topic in some central way, keep a dialectical notebook as we describe in Mini-Workshop B.

Using the Internet

This section assumes that you have access to a computer with a connection to the Internet and that you have used a World Wide Web browser, such as Netscape Communicator or Internet Explorer. If you have never used a browser, ask your teacher about computer labs at your school that are staffed by a consultant. Once a consultant has helped you open a Web browser and shown you its navigational tools, you probably will have very little trouble getting around the Internet. You will quickly learn to navigate both by clicking on links and by entering an address, or URL (Universal Resource Locator), into the address box. Indeed, the Web's merit lies in its simplicity of navigation and design: Not only can anyone learn to cruise the Web fairly quickly, but practically anyone can learn to make a Web page. Since the Web eliminates virtually all costs of publication and distribution, many people turn to it to publish their work.

Yet the ease of access and distribution also causes problems for the researcher. Because anyone can make a Web page cheaply and with relatively little labor, academically suspect information often masquerades as authoritative research. You can find informed, intelligent discussions of academic subjects, but these pages are in no way distinguished from less reliable pages. Nor is there any conveniently organized card catalog to all academically sound resources on the Internet. In short, when researching on the Web, you have to spend more time discriminating between what is useful and what is useless. For a detailed discussion of finding and evaluating sources on the Internet, please consult Mini-Workshop F, "Doing Research on the Web."

Writing an Exploratory Draft

Once you've done whatever tasks you set for yourself for the first segment of your research (observing/interviewing, library study, and/or surfing the Internet), you're ready to write an exploratory draft. Before beginning, we recommend that you lay out all the notes and writing you've done so far and read through everything. After this perusal, do some freewriting to record what you've learned and how you react to seeing all the material. Think particularly about whether you've discovered any patterns or recurrent themes in your writing and notes.

You may discover at this point that you're not so interested in your original question any more, but in some other question which has arisen as you worked on this project. If this were a rigid assignment, you'd have to continue with your original questions, but we're not being rigid here. If you have come up with a more interesting question or discovered something more thought provoking than what you started out to discover, we hope you'll change your project to follow up on it. (And we suggest that if in other classes you come up with something slightly different from the assignment, you ask your teacher whether you can adjust the assignment to what you've discovered. The worst your teacher can say is no. Many teachers will say yes.)

As you write this draft or after you've finished it, jot down questions for yourself to use as the basis of your next round of research, which may include a return to what you've already done to refine it or a move to another form of research—either in or out of the library.

One of the fallacies about research is that researchers always use everything they find and all research notes they write up. This is simply not true. Remember that research is finding out about something. If you knew what that was going to be at the outset, you wouldn't need to do the research. But since you don't know, you'll read and write a great deal that won't be relevant to your finished research. Researchers almost always throw away more than they use.

Moving Toward a Final Draft

Whenever you decide you have done as much research as necessary, you are ready to write a full draft of your paper. Before beginning, you'll benefit from laying out the writing you've done so far and looking through it again. You may discover—perhaps for a second time—that you're not so interested in your original question any more. Your data may point to something far more intriguing to you. That will probably be fine with your teacher, but you should check with him.

Because the research process gives you lots of notes and rough writing, you may lose direction or perspective. Thus, you may want to make an outline before you start your full draft. Or you may decide instead to make an outline *after* you've written your draft. This can also work well. You could do both. Just don't agonize so long over your outline that you have little time and energy left to write the paper itself. You don't need to spend a lot of time on an outline. It can be as simple as this:

> I'll start by stating why I was interested in my subject and what my original thinking was, move to how I went about doing the research, lay out some of what I found, and end with my conclusions.

Or you may want something as detailed as this:

1. Statement of question.
2. Statement of methods of research.

3. Recounting of observations.
   a. Engineers.
   b. Classrooms.
4. Recounting of interviews.
   a. Engineers.
   b. Undergraduates.
5. Recounting of information gleaned from books and magazines.
6. Reflections on the ways the interviews, observations, and printed sources confirm one another, if at all.
   a. Similarities.
   b. Differences.
7. Conclusions.
8. Possible explanations of conclusions.
9. What I learned and what it means to me.
10. What I'd still like to know.

An important thing to remember about outlines—whether generalized or specific—is that they're only outlines: You need not follow them like a robot. As you begin to write, you may discover some better structure. That may cause you to go back and revise your outline, although you needn't do this if you feel that the structure you're working with is satisfactory.

You can get help from others at this stage. Read or describe your bits of information and data to them and ask them for suggestions about what they see as central and organizing. There are no "right answers" as to how a paper should be organized; it's a question of what works best for readers.* You may want to try out two or three organizations.

A little aside: One way to structure your final paper is to present the story of your search. Tell how you started (including false starts), your original writing and thinking, early hypotheses, what was going on in your head as you worked through the series of steps we've led you through, the order in which you discovered things, what you did, partial conclusions you drew, and what you concluded. In other words, your paper could end up being a mixture of process writing and the results of that process. But to do this, you'll need to do process writing throughout. So we suggest that at the end of each piece of your search, you do some writing in your process journal. Even if you don't decide to use it in your paper, it will be a valuable record for you.

Documentation

You'll need to make sure that you know how to document the information you've used in your paper. If you've used interviews, you must document

*There are some important exceptions here. If you write a research paper for a particular discipline such as chemistry or sociology, there are some conventions guiding how it should be put together, just as there is a standard form for scientific articles in certain fields.

these interviews. Your teacher will tell you what style of documentation she wishes you to use. She may also want to go over some of that technical information in class. If you've used a questionnaire, you should include it plus a tabulation of the answers. If you used the Internet, you'll also need to document that as a source.

Documentation of sources is particularly important in research papers—just as important for personal research as for library research. None of us has the right to claim credit for the ideas and words of others regardless of whether we read them or heard them in an interview. And, from a pragmatic point of view, documentation lends authority to your research paper. If people know that you feel safe in revealing your sources, thus giving readers the

Exploring the Writing Process

The paper I recently sent off to the journal represents the most demanding and most satisfying work of my writing life so far. . .

The project began two years ago, when for the sake of my own sanity I decided to focus on an interdisciplinary project—the interface of ecology and philosophy. I had been drowning in philosophy, condemned to be free. I had no moorings or orientation within philosophy, so I turned to my own experience and concerns to give me a foothold in reality. That allowed me the freedom to explore diverse aspects of philosophy without losing a basic sense of direction and purpose.

Slowly, I began to pull the ideas together. . . Once in a while, I would try to draw my thoughts together into a self-definition, usually a short written statement. What am I doing? How? Why? Invariably my thought would break through that inadequate statement almost before my inadequate word-processor was done printing it. I kept reading and thinking and talking, biding my time.

Last January, I began a period of more focused research, with a paper topic in mind. I don't know when I finally settled on a title, but the topic *was* the title: "How Ecological Is Ecophilosophy?" I read intensively, and scribbled down notes as my thought developed.

At last the time was ripe to begin writing. It was March, almost April. Drawing it all together, making it *fit* was more difficult than I had ever imagined. I was dealing with a lot of material and thought: *patience* became my chief tool. On paper, or on my WP, I worked it through, forcing the thoughts into words, forcing the words into structured forms, on the paper.

Inspiration would strike at odd times. I had to keep pencil and paper handy, just in case I had a flash. . .

During the summer, I ignored it. I told people that I'd buried it in the backyard for the earthworms to edit. When autumn came, the time was ripe once more. Exhumed and reconsidered, with more and more feedback, the paper changed again and again, passing through successive stages of order and disorder. It would arrive at equilibrium, but my thought would break through it, breaking it apart, and it would demand reintegration. . .

A few weeks ago, I was satisfied with my paper: it was good enough to submit for consideration. All I had to do was polish it up. So I read it over and found a dozen things to revise; they were minor points really, but important enough. So I "fixed" them, and read it over again. I found a dozen things to revise. Again and again.

I foresaw no end to it but the slow demise of my paper. If I picked at it ad infinitum it would come apart again, and I doubted I had the energy or the time to rebuild it. My thought was already moving beyond it, to new things. The moment was propitious: I mailed it to the journal.

Bob Kirkman

opportunity to check their validity, they're far more likely to give your words credit.

Quotations

It is possible to do a considerable amount of research and learn from the information and opinions of interviewees and published works—and write a terrific paper of your own without a single quotation or footnote. (Joyce has no footnotes in *Ulysses* for all the details he checked up on.) But for this assignment we are asking for some quotations and footnotes. You should integrate and internalize what you learn into your own thinking, but this is also an assignment in showing to readers that others have said things about your topic. Your reader should not feel he is in a closet with you having a dialogue, but that he is in a large room with a number of people—other voices—involved in the issue. Quotations that allow these voices to come through to your readers will give them a feel for the texture of research on your issue.

For the format and use of quotations in your text, see Mini-Workshop J.

Footnotes Aren't Footnotes Any More

"Footnote" is the word that probably springs to mind when you think of how to document your sources: a *note* at the *foot* of the page. But we are following the recent Modern Language Association (MLA) guidelines for citing sources *without* footnotes. The new MLA citation system makes life easier for both writers and readers and is now standard for academic writing in most of the humanities. (You can still use footnotes for an aside to the reader, but try not to use too many since they can make a reader feel bumped around.)

The citation system that fits the social or natural sciences is the American Psychological Association (APA) system. Some of the essays in the readings in this book, as you've probably noticed, use the APA documentation style. At the end of our listing of examples in the MLA style, we'll list the major differences between MLA and APA.

Documentation procedure has two elements: the *parenthetical citation* in your text as you go along, and the *list of works cited* at the end. When you want to document a source—that is, to tell readers what article, book, or interviewee you are referring to—add a small parenthetical citation. Parentheses show readers where to look for the full information about the article or book in the final list of works cited.

Parenthetical Citations

In parentheses place only the information that readers need for finding the article or book in your list of works cited. Thus:

- Give *only* the page number(s) in your parentheses if you mention the author in your text. For example, your text might read as follows:

  Hammond writes that early jazz recordings contain little if any improvisation,

  contrary to popular conceptions (87).

Note that the parenthesis is *inside* the sentence's punctuation.

- If the author's name is not in your sentence, then add the name to the parenthesis. For example:

  Historians of jazz have pointed out that early recordings contain little if any improvisation (Hammond 87).

Note that there's no comma between the author's name and the page number. The last name alone is sufficient unless you are using two authors with the same name.

- If you cite more than one work by Hammond in your essay, add the title (or shortened title) to your parenthesis; for example, (Hammond, *"An Experience"* 87). But you can skip the title if you mention it in your text. Note the comma after the author's name but not after the title.

Other conventions:

- Titles of articles or chapters are in quotation marks; book titles are underlined with no quotation marks.*
- If the work has more than one volume, specify which one you are citing, followed by a colon and the page number—for example, (1:179).
- If citing a passage from a poem, give line numbers. If citing a passage from a play, give act, scene, and lines—for example, (4.5.11–14).
- If there are two or three authors, list them; for more than three, cite only the first author and add "et al."

In APA style, always give the date of the work, but don't give page numbers unless it's a direct quotation. Thus our first example above, if changed to APA, would be simply: (1970). The second example would be (Hammond, 1970). Note the comma before the date.

Works Cited
This is a list of outside sources you cite in your paper. Place it at the end of your research paper on a separate sheet. Here are examples of the most common kinds of citations:

Print and Other Traditional Sources The items are alphabetized by author and follow this general sequence: author, title, publisher. Here's the order in more detail:

- Author (last name first).
- Full title of the work you're citing. If this is part of a larger work, the title will be in quotation marks.

*Most word-processing programs enable you to italicize titles (which means they would not be underlined). Nonetheless, some teachers probably still prefer you to underline titles; you should check with each of your teachers before submitting a final copy of any piece which contains citations. Probably the most important thing is that you are consistent in your citation style.

- The title of any larger work, magazine, or journal—if the work you're citing is part of a larger work. This title will be underlined or italicized.
- Name of the editor or translator, if any (first name first).
- Edition.
- Number of the volume(s) used. For example, if the work consists of 5 volumes, and you used only volumes 2 and 3, you need to make that clear.
- City of publication.
- Publisher.
- Year of publication.
- Page numbers (if the work you're citing is only a portion of the larger publication).

Note: If the work you cite is unsigned (e.g., an article in an encyclopedia or newspaper), begin with the title. Thus its place in your alphabetized list would be determined by the first letters of the title. If it is an unsigned U.S. Government publication, however, begin with "United States," then the agency that puts it out (e.g., Bureau of the Census), and then the title of the piece—as though the government were the author.

Book

Cameron, Julia. *The Right to Write: An Invitation and Initiation into the Writing Life.* New York: Putnam-Penguin, 1999.

Note that if Cameron had been the editor rather than the author, her name would be followed by a comma and "ed."

Article in a periodical: newspaper

Campbell, Paula Walker. "Controversial Proposal on Public Access to Research Data Draws 10,000 Comments." *Chronicle of Higher Education* 16 Apr. 1999: A42.

Article in a periodical: monthly magazine

Gardner, Howard. "Who Owns Intelligence?" *Atlantic Monthly* Feb. 1999: 67–76.

Article in a periodical: scholarly journal

Gillette, Mary Ann, and Carol Videon. "Seeking Quality on the Internet: A Case Study of Composition Students' Works Cited." *Teaching English in the Two-Year College* 26 (1998): 189–95.

Note that the second author's name is not reversed. Because the pages of this journal are continuously numbered throughout the year, we have "26 (1998): 189–95." If it were a journal where each issue started with page 1, the note would read "26.2 (1998): 189–95." (The "2" here means the second issue of that year.)

Article or other work in an anthology

Gioia, Dana. "My Confessional Sestina." *Rebel Angels: 25 Poets of the New Formalism.* Ed. Mark Jarman and David Mason. Brownsville, OR: Story Line, 1996. 48–9.

Hammond, John. "An Experience in Jazz History." *Black Music in Our Culture: Curricular Ideas on the Subjects, Materials, and Problems.* Ed. Dominique-René de Lerma. Kent: Kent State UP, 1970. 42–53. Rpt. in *Keeping Time: Readings in Jazz History.* Ed. Robert Walser. New York: Oxford UP, 1999. 86–96.

Here we provide citation formats for a poem in an anthology and for a scholarly essay reprinted in a current anthology. The facts of the original publication must be provided for scholarly articles subsequently reprinted: note the abbreviation "rpt." (reprint), which clarifies the relation between the two sources.

Letter or personal interview

Fontaine, Sheryl. Letter to the authors [or "Telephone interview" or "Personal communication"]. 14 Apr. 1999.

Review

O'Neill, Peggy. Rev. of *Reflection in the Writing Classroom,* by Kathleen Blake Yancey. *Teaching English in the Two-Year College* 26 (1998): 202–204.

Electronic Sources The documentation of electronic sources, like these sources themselves, is in a state of constant flux. The general principles mirror those governing the documentation of print sources, but the information itself is necessarily somewhat different. One key difference is the requirement in many cases to include the *date you accessed* a particular site. The general pattern for online sources runs as follows (with each piece of information required only *if applicable* to the particular source and available):

- Name of author(s).
- Title of the work, underlined or italicized. (If the piece you're citing is part of a larger work, then the title would be in quotation marks.)
- Name of editor(s), compiler(s), or translator(s).
- Publication information for any print version of the source.
- Title of the larger work (scholarly project, database, or periodical) in which the cited work appears.
- Name of the editor of the scholarly project or database.
- Version number of the source or, for an electronic journal, the volume number, issue number, or other identifying number.
- Date of electronic publication or of the latest update.
- Name of any sponsoring institution or organization, such as a museum or university.
- Date of access and network address.

For a professional or personal site, the information is less complicated. This is the general pattern:

- Name of author.
- Title of site. If there is no title, use a generic term such as "Home page" (without underlining or quotes). If the page has an official title (for example, *Italo Calvino Page*), it would be underlined or italicized.
- Name of sponsoring organization, if any.
- Date of access and network address.

CD-ROM, Magnetic Tape, and Diskettes These sources are handled somewhat differently; they are closer to traditional print sources in format:

- Name of author(s).
- Title of publication.
- Name of editor, compiler, or translator.
- Publication medium (CD-ROM, diskette, or magnetic tape).
- Edition, release, or version.
- Place of publication.
- Name of publisher.
- Date of publication.

Examples of some of the most common entries follow:

An online database, scholarly project, or personal or professional Web site

Novosel, Tony. *The Great War.* 27 Apr. 1999 <http://www.pitt.edu/~pugachev/greatwar/ww1.html>.*

*The angled marks (< >) used in citations of electronic sources are part of the citation style; when you access the site itself, do not use these marks: type in only whatever is between them.

THOMAS: Legislative Information on the Internet. 9 Apr. 1999. Lib. of Congress, Washington. 25 Apr. 1999 <http://thomas.loc.gov/>.

Voice of the Shuttle: Web Page for Humanities Research. Ed. Alan Liu. 22 Apr. 1999. English Dept., Univ. of CA, Santa Barbara. 28 Apr. 1999 <http://humanitas.ucsb.edu/>.

Material from an online database or scholarly project

Bimber, Bruce. "The Death of an Agency: Office of Technology Assessment & Budget Politics in the 104th Congress." *Voice of the Shuttle: Web Page for Humanities Research.* Ed. Alan Liu. 22 Apr. 1999. English Dept., Univ. of CA, Santa Barbara. 28 Apr. 1999 <http://humanitas.ucsb.edu/liu/bimber.html>.

Article in an online periodical

Herbert, Bob. "The Other America." *New York Times on the Web* 9 Apr. 1999. 25 Apr. 1999 <http://www.nytimes.com/library/opinion/herbert/040899herbert.html>.

Material from a CD-ROM

Whiting, R.M., and Ignace J. Gelb. "Writing." *Microsoft Encarta 98 Encyclopedia Deluxe Edition.* CD-ROM. 1998 ed. Redmond, WA: Microsoft, 1997.

The format of these citations can be hard to remember; we ourselves have to look it up again and again. You could make a photocopy of these pages to keep handy. And we've printed an abbreviated version of this information inside the back cover for ready reference.

Note how citations have "hung margins"; that is, the first line of each citation is "flush left" (all the way to the left margin of type on the page), and succeeding lines of each citation are indented five spaces—as we have shown them. Our examples are double-spaced (as you should type your manuscripts), but citations are usually single-spaced in published or printed matter.

If you are using APA style, you will call the list of sources "References" rather than "Works Cited." The chief differences in style are that initials rather than first names are used, the date of the work appears immediately after the author's name, only the first word of the source is capitalized (although journal titles are capitalized in the conventional manner), and no quotation marks are used for journal articles. Thus, you would have the following:

Cameron, J. 1999. *The right to write: an invitation and initiation into the writing life.* New York: Putnam-Penguin.

Gillett, M.A., and C. Videon. 1998. Seeking quality on the internet: a case study of composition students' works cited. *Teaching English in the Two-Year College,* 26: 189–95.

You'll also notice some minor differences in punctuation.

We have shown here only the most common kinds of citations. You will need to consult a good handbook for more complicated ones, especially for works from unusual sources (such as a television advertisement, record jacket, or map). Truth be told, few readers will care too much about deviations from correct form when it comes to seldom-cited kinds of sources. Still, these must be cited in a consistent manner.

Suggestions for Collaboration

Most researchers know they need to pool their work in order to begin to think about definitive answers. You and another student or even your whole group may decide to focus on one topic, which you can research together. You can then integrate what you've done and turn this workshop into a collaborative writing task. This sort of project will give you a feel for the kinds of collaborative work so prevalent in the scientific and business world today.

If you decide to make this into a major collaborative project, you may want to go back and read over the sections on collaborative writing in Workshop 3.

Sharing and Responding

For your early exploratory freewriting, you might use "Summary and Sayback" (Section 3 in "Sharing and Responding"). This sort of feedback will help you figure out where you are going or want to go. Ask listeners to concentrate particularly on what they see as the implications of what you've written. In addition to "Summary and Sayback," you may find the following questions helpful:

- What do you think I'm primarily interested in finding out?
- Do you think that the task I'm setting for myself is feasible? And if not, how can I alter it?
- How do you think I can go about answering my question or finding out what I want to know?

For later drafts, you'll find "Summary and Sayback" valuable again. But you might also ask your readers to do "Skeleton Feedback and Descriptive Outline" in Section 10 of "Sharing and Responding."

We suggest that you also write out some questions to which you specifically want listeners and readers to give you feedback. Here are some general questions you may find helpful at this stage of your project:

- Have I accomplished what I led you to expect I was going to accomplish?
- Have I given you sufficient evidence to justify whatever conclusions I've drawn?
- Does my organization work? Does my paper seem to be a unified whole?
- What do you hear as my position or point of view or bias in this paper? Do you see me openly showing it or keeping it hidden? Whatever my approach, how does it work for you? How do you react to the relationship between my opinion or feelings here and the information I present?
- Have I made clear the limits of my subject?

Process Journal

What did you notice and what can you learn from:

- How you went about choosing a topic?
- Your first efforts in the library, especially if you had not used a library much before?
- Your first efforts on the Internet, especially if you had not used the Internet in this way before? Using the Internet can be overwhelming because it appears to make so much information accessible—more than one person can hope to master.
- Your success (or difficulties) with integrating your thinking and the thinking or information of others? Did your thinking change much or not at all on the basis of your personal research? your library work?
- What advice can you give yourself for doing future research projects and papers?

Exploring Theory: *The Ongoing Conversation*

> Imagine that you enter a parlor. You come late. When you arrive, others have long preceded you, and they are engaged in a heated discussion, a discussion too heated for them to pause and tell you exactly what it is about. In fact, the discussion had already begun long before any of them got there, so that no one present is qualified to retrace for you all the steps that had gone before. You listen for a while, until you decide that you have caught the tenor of the argument; then you put in your oar. Someone answers; you answer him; another comes to your defense; another aligns himself against you, to either the embarrassment or gratification of your opponent, depending upon the quality of your ally's assistance.

However, the discussion is interminable. The hour grows late, you must depart. And you do depart, with the discussion still vigorously in progress. (Kenneth Burke, *Rhetoric of Motives*)

The usual thing we do when we need to know something is to ask questions. Often what we need to know is very simple: What time is it? How do I get to the zoo? In these cases, we ask someone and that's usually the end of our research. (That we may get the wrong answer is irrelevant since we won't realize that until later.) But once we've gotten an answer, we're in the position of passing it along to others. We can now, for instance, direct someone else to the zoo—and that person can direct another, and on and on. And perhaps the person who gave us directions originally got them from someone else. So we're in the midst of a conversation whose beginning we were not present for and whose ending we're unlikely to be present for either.

But just as often what we need to know may be more complex. How have digital watches affected people's sense of time? Why do people go to the zoo? What do we get out of looking at animals? To get answers to these questions, we need to do more than ask one question of one person. We need to figure out how to ask questions, observe reactions, and draw conclusions. And often what we want to know may require us to seek out information in books and periodicals.

Just as often, though, we can't state precisely what we want or need to know. It may be so fuzzy in our minds that we don't know what questions to ask to start off our research. So, we have to do a fair amount of thinking, talking, writing, and reflecting in order to pinpoint and focus our purpose. In effect, we put ourselves into conversation with ourselves and with others. In a sense, this too is research. More than one philosopher has noted that asking the right questions is often more meaningful than getting the right answers.

However we come to decide what our research will be and how best to do it, when we finally do report it to others, we continue the conversation we had joined when we began our research. In fact, whenever we use language, written or oral, we are joining an ongoing conversation—either with ourselves or with others. Oral conversations tend to move steadily forward since it's difficult for us to have access to what was spoken a year ago, much less centuries ago. But written conversations can span centuries, continents, and even languages.

Almost as far back as we have written records, writers have been addressing issues of human relationships, power struggles, the meaning of life, proper behavior, and so forth. Not one of us can have access to all that has been written on subjects that interest us, but printed materials make possible such access. Still, we can digest only a portion of all that's available. Teachers point us to what our culture and traditions have labeled as the most significant of prior writings on any given subject. Even that changes over time as scholars uncover new documents, reconsider old documents, or understand better the significance of documents once considered unimportant.

When you do print-based research in a library, you are entering into a conversation with those who wrote centuries ago or thousands of miles away. But, to situate yourself within that conversation and to make valid contributions to it, you need to know what has been said in it. This is the basic purpose of most education: to help you find your place in the ongoing flow of history. Unless you show your familiarity with this conversation, most people will not give much weight to your contribution to it. In truth, they probably won't even listen to you. If, for example, you want to write about the role of economics in society, you should probably be familiar with canonical works on the subject: Malthus and Marx and others whom your economics teachers will identify for you. You'll also need to become familiar with what is currently being written on the subject. This knowledge will enable you to make valuable contributions to this particular ongoing conversation. And, if you want to make some permanent impact on that conversation, you'll write your words down so they'll be available for future study. Writing thus allows all of us to talk to the past and the future as well as to the present.

But you can also have an ongoing conversation with yourself. That conversation will obviously draw part of its substance from what you've read and what you've heard from others. A large part of its substance will come from interaction with what you've previously thought and said. This conversation may concern the same subjects as the historical conversations: the meaning of life, human relationships, and so forth. For instance, you probably find yourself saying something like: "I used to think *X* about the difference between Republicans and Democrats, but I now think *Y*." Or: "I used to want to be an engineer, but now I think I'd rather be a teacher."

What we say to ourselves changes as we experience more of the world around us and as that world changes. For most of us, the conversation with ourselves is unrecorded. One of our aims in this book is to push you to record some of this personal conversation in your freewriting and exploratory writing. If you've done this, you've discovered how often such personal conversation can be interesting to others as well as to yourself. So often we've had students who moan that they have nothing to say. They believe this because they haven't yet realized that their personal ruminations can be engrossing for others. (A large part of the appeal of essays is that they foreground the workings of one mind as it treats a particular subject. We talk more about this in Workshop 9.)

Why are we writing about this in Workshop 12? Because we believe that research is a way of integrating our personal conversations with ourselves into our conversations with others across history and geography. Most research becomes both. In articles reporting scientific research, for instance, authors often begin with a review of the literature. Such a review is merely a summing up of the most important writing on a subject. Having done that, the authors move on to report their particular, personal research on that subject. In their conclusions, they often integrate what they've uncovered and what previous researchers have uncovered. These articles in turn will be used by future researchers who desire to join the conversation.

These sweeping conclusions may seem grandiose considering that we got to them from simple questions such as "What time is it?" and "How do I get to the zoo?" But we sincerely believe that most research begins simply and that all research is a combination of personal insights and an awareness of what others have contributed. This is what makes it a conversation. And similar qualities make most writing a conversation with others and with yourself about matters you and they wish to talk about.

When a Child Has Cancer

Kymberly Saganski

When a child is afflicted by cancer, the family members react differently as a result of the initial shock. In the case of my family, my father experienced a typical preoccupation with the trivial things, such as worries about finances. My mother focused on her fear of death. My own reactions included fear, disorganization and even selfishness. These are all common among families dealing with a profoundly ill member.

The ultimate determination that a family member has cancer is never easy to accept, but it seems more difficult when the ill member is a child. At the age of fifteen, my younger brother was diagnosed as having acute lymphoblastic leukemia and lymphoma. In its advanced stages, "leukemic blood cells rapidly glut the bone marrow, pour over into the bloodstream, and invade the lymph nodes, the spleen, and such vital organs of the body as the liver, brain and kidneys" (Levitt and Guralnick 72). It seemed ironic that my father's first thoughts were of his son's high school sports career and the soon-to-be arriving hospital bills. My mother, having watched my grandfather die of the same rare combination of diseases, thought only of my brother's fifty percent chance for survival. In order to avoid the entire situation, I worried about the fact that I was getting behind in work at my Massachusetts school since my mother and I had joined my father and brother in New Jersey where they were living. Peter, my brother, was hospitalized immediately, and the bills started to accumulate from that moment forward.

After this initial hospitalization, the patient often feels lost, helpless and scared. Parents become frantic as they watch their son's or daughter's dreams for the future become unstable and begin to topple. The remaining children fight for their position in the reshuffled family. Although they are not decision makers, their needs are often considered when decisions are being made. Many times, even though there is nothing concrete that they can do to help the situation, the presence of other children is soothing in and of itself.

The patients, themselves, may react in a variety of ways. Sometimes they withdraw from everyone else, repressing their thoughts and emotions. Other times, they become bitter and resentful, blaming everyone and everything for their predicament. Barbara Rabkin, a scientific journalist for *Macleans* magazine, contends that the entire process of "coping with leukemia itself . . . is complicated by the lack of public understanding and acceptance of the disease" (54–5). There are a few patients who seem to accept their condition from the beginning and maintain an open mind and a positive attitude. These cases, however, are few and far between. According to Rabkin, this is the time when the support of other families is the most important. The family members dealing with the cancer need to have contact with unafflicted families in order to maintain their grasp on "real life" (55). I don't happen to agree with this rationalization.

My family dealt with the cancer as individuals. We each reacted in our own separate ways to my little brother's illness. My parents tried to be supportive, as I did, but Pete had decided that his best defense was anger. He was angry at his doctors for misdiagnosing his cancer as an allergy when he had first become sick eleven months earlier. He was angry at himself for not knowing his own body better, and he was angry at all of his friends and relatives for showing him sympathy, which he interpreted as pity. He decided then and there that he was going to hate this cancer until it left him alone.

I had no idea what I should do with myself. My brother seemed to resent the fact that I was up and around while he was hooked up to machines and lying flat on his back in a hospital bed. John Spinetta, writing for *Human Behavior,* contends that this resentment is a natural phase of the cancer acceptance cycle by the patient (49), but I couldn't deal with my brother's rejection of my sympathy. Because I seemed so uncomfortable at the hospital, I was given the choice of missing school for a month and staying in New Jersey or returning to Cape Cod and living alone for an indefinite period of time. That was the least of the decisions that I was asked to assist in making. I delayed my return home in case I could be some help to my parents.

My brother had the option of three different kinds of chemotherapy. He refused to have any input whatsoever, so my parents asked me to put myself in my brother's position and try to imagine living with the various side effects of the different drugs. I had a lot of difficulty with this task, but I tried my best in order to take some of the pressure off my parents. I decided then that even though I seemed to be a comfort to my mother, her worries about my falling behind in school were just added troubles to her already heavy heart, so I returned to school. This return to an almost normal life helped me to deal with the situation, and the fact that I had the added responsibility of living by myself kept my mind from wandering back to Peter constantly.

I was surprised at the amount of time that the social workers on Peter's case spent with my entire family. I had never before realized that an illness such as cancer affects the whole family in such a complete way. Ann Brierly, a social worker at my brother's hospital, believes that the best way to ease the pain of a family illness is to educate all members about the nature of the illness. Once my parents were adequately informed concerning Peter's cancer, they were able to deal with it from a clinical point of view. When people inquire as to Peter's condition, I say that after all we have been through, he is what is so far considered cured. In my heart I feel like I should answer, "We survived," and I hope we will never have to live through such an ordeal again.

Works Cited

Brierly, Ann. Telephone interview. 6 May 1985.

Levitt, Paul M., and Elissa S. Guralnick. *The Cancer Reference Book.* New York: Paddington Press, 1979.

Rabkin, Barbara. "Childhood Leukemia." *Macleans* 23 Apr. 1979: 54–5.

Spinetta, John. "Childhood Cancer: Study of a Family Coping." *Human Behavior* May 1979: 49.

Devoured: Eating Disorders

Concetta Acunzo

"Mirror, mirror on the wall, who's the fairest of them all?" This is the question the Queen, in the classic Brothers Grimm fairy tale *Snow White,* asks as she gazes into her mirror. Invariably telling her what she wants to hear, that she is indeed the most beautiful woman in the land, the mirror's answer one day suddenly changes: the Queen no longer is the "fairest of them all"; instead, her beauty has been surpassed by the younger and lovelier Snow White. The Queen is unwilling to accept the new and unwelcome response; she will go to any lengths to once again attain the original reply. The Queen's scenario is not all that different than the predicament of someone suffering from an eating disorder. She too is not receiving the answer she wishes to hear. She too will utilize all measures to transform herself into the greatest—or thinnest—possible beauty. She too is reaching for an unattainable goal.

Beauty is the defining characteristic of American women. The overwhelming pressure to be beautiful is most intense during early adolescence. Girls worry about their clothes, makeup, and hair, but, most of all, they agonize over their weight. Adolescent girls are taught that obesity equates failure. People are so terrified of becoming fat that a recent study found that 11 percent of Americans would abort a fetus if they were told it had a tendency toward obesity (Pipher, *Reviving Ophelia* 184). Ironically, eating is probably our most ancient form of social activity (Pipher, *Hunger Pains* 17). Food, however, is the cause of much anxiety, particularly among women who have been culturally conditioned to hate their bodies. Eating disorders, resulting from excessive preoccupation with thinness, societal pressures, and various other factors, run rampant in America. The eating disorders anorexia nervosa (*anorexia* is from the Greek for "loss of appetite") and bulimia nervosa (*bulimia* is from the Greek for "ox appetite") are characterized by an implacable and distorted attitude toward weight, eating, and fatness (Hsu 1). Anorexia is self-starvation; bulimia involves a binge-purge cycle. Anorexia and bulimia are not merely consequences of food abuse; they are part of an emotional system that affects every aspect of the sufferer's life (Farrell, Ch. 1).

Each year, over 10 million people are diagnosed with eating disorders in America. Approximately ninety percent of those affected are female, while only 10 percent are male (Felker). The fact that men are more realistic about their appearance and women generally distort their body images is responsible for the disproportion of this statistic. Studies show that 90 percent of all women overestimate their own body size (Pipher, *Hunger Pains* 10); only 25 percent of anorectics and 40 percent of bulimics are actually overweight before the onset of the illness (Hsu 14). In recent years, this size overestimation has been developing in younger girls. Children are growing increasingly preoccupied with weight and appearance. By age five, children select pictures of thin people when asked to identify good-looking others (Pipher, *Reviving Ophelia* 185). Surveys indicate that 50 percent of nine-year-old girls diet. Girls as young as 10 years old are developing eating disorders. Why are children reading nutritional information labels when they should be playing hopscotch or catch?

Society and cultural biases are largely responsible for the escalating obsession with thinness and the stigma attached to obesity. The omnipresent media consistently portrays desirable women as excessively thin—unattainably skinny. (It says something about our society when one of the most popular shows on television is *Baywatch,* where the actors and actresses wear nothing more than skimpy bathing suits.) Watching these women on the television or seeing them in magazines causes real women to loathe their own bodies. Thomas Cash, a professor of psychology at Old Dominion University in Virginia, reports that in 1972, 23 percent of United States women said they were dissatisfied with their overall appearance; today, that figure has more than doubled to 52 percent (Schneider 67). The ever-changing society plays a primary role in this alteration of female thought. In the past 30 years, the voluptuous size 12 image of Marilyn Monroe has been transformed into size 2 models like Kate Moss. Since 1979, Miss America contestants have become so skinny that the majority are at least 15 percent below the recommended body weight, which is also the same percentage to be considered a symptom of anorexia nervosa (Schneider 67). Today, the average model is 5′10″ and 110 pounds; the average American woman is 5′4″ and 145 pounds. As real women grow heavier, models have become slimmer. When unnatural thinness becomes attractive, girls do unnatural things to be slight.

As a traditionally Western civilization problem, anorexia nervosa, to quote Peter Rowen, is a question of "being thirsty in the rain" (Pipher, *Reviving Ophelia* 174). Anorectics are starving while there is food all around them. Anorexia is a disease of control, and suppressing one's appetite or consumption when surrounded by food signifies the ultimate success. Though the word anorexia implies absence of hunger, anorectics, in actuality, are constantly hungry. They are obsessed with food, but, ironically, are starving themselves.

Typical anorectics are the brightest and best young women; it is the good girls, the dutiful daughters, and the overachievers who are at the greatest risk for anorexia (Pipher, *Reviving Ophelia* 174). Anorexia often begins during early adolescence with ordinary teenage dieting; the disease frequently starts with cutting out a certain food or eliminating fat from the diet. From there, anorexia develops into an extreme restriction of caloric intake and often excessive exercising. Instead of concluding the diet when she reaches her target weight, the perfectionist young woman continues on a path to weight obsession and rigidity concerning food.

The anorectic is commonly referred to as looking like "the victim of a concentration camp" (Bruch vii). Anorectics have both the physical and psychological characteristics of starvation. Their abdomens are distended, their hair dull, their nails brittle; amenorrhea—or the absence of menstruation—occurs; they are weak, and prone to infections. Anorexia slows or prevents growth and halts puberty. Emotionally, anorectics are depressed, irritable, pessimistic, apathetic, and entirely preoccupied with food. Anorexia nervosa, or self-starvation, is both physically and psychologically debilitating.

Bulimia is the most common eating disorder in young women. The disease begins as a method of controlling weight, but it evolves into a life-threatening obsession. For bulimics, life revolves around eating, purging, and weight. Like all addictions, bulimia is a compulsive, obsessive, self-destructive, and progressive disorder. Bingeing and purging are the addictive behaviors; food is the drug of choice (Pipher, *Reviving Ophelia* 169).

While anorexia traditionally begins during junior high school, bulimia tends to develop during later adolescence. It is commonly referred to as the "college girl's" disease because the estimates of incidence run as high as one-fourth of all college-age women (Pipher, *Reviving Ophelia* 170). Like anorectics, bulimics are oversocialized to the feminine role (Pipher, *Reviving Ophelia* 170). They are the ultimate people-pleasers; bulimics are generally attractive, with remarkable social skills. Often they are the cheerleaders and homecoming queens, the straight-A students and prides of their families (Pipher, *Reviving Ophelia* 170).

Frequently, the patient enters the bulimic cycle of fasting, bingeing, and purging. The majority, over 80 percent, develop the cycle by first giving in to the increasing desire to eat and thereafter self-inducing vomiting either because the fullness is intolerable or because they want to get rid of the calories (Hsu 15). After a binge, a bulimic is likely to be overtaken by feelings of panic. Though she may have consumed anywhere between 5,000 and 50,000 calories, her preoccupation is with losing weight. She is overwhelmed by guilt and forces herself to purge. About two-thirds of bulimics regularly use vomiting to control their weight, while one-third predominantly abuse laxatives. Many, of course, combine both methods. About 40 percent of bulimics also misuse diet pills. Lastly, many bulimics also take to exercising in an attempt to rid themselves of surplus calories.

Extensive bingeing and purging places young women at risk of serious health problems. Often they have dental problems, esophageal tears, gastrointestinal problems, and sometimes dangerous electrolytic imbalances that can trigger heart attacks. The mortality rates are estimated to be about 3 percent (Buckroyd 24). Psychological alterations are also the result of bulimia. Bulimics experience personality changes as they learn to accept bingeing as the main staple of their existence. Driven by another binge, they become obsessed, extremely secretive, and guilty about their habit. Bulimics have lost their main objective in life: control. As a result, they are typically depressed, irritable, and withdrawn.

Bulimic young women have lost their true selves in a toilet. The "tell-tale" mark, the line that exists on the index finger after repeated episodes of self-induced vomiting, is not the only scar bulimics carry with them. They also possess the knowledge, buried deep within them, that their identities have been devoured by a deadly disease. In their eagerness to please, they have developed an addiction that destroys their central core (Pipher, *Reviving Ophelia* 170); the road to recovery is a long and meandering one.

Margaret Mead defined an ideal culture as one in which there was a place for every human gift (Pipher, *Hunger Pains* 121). This ideal culture would allow its members to grow to their fullest potential. Regrettably, Mead's philosophy has gotten lost in this society where thinness equals success. After all, according to American ideology, "one can never be too rich or too thin." Consequently, women are dominated by a fear of becoming fat which frequently leads to the development of eating disorders. Anorexia, self-starvation, and bulimia, the binge-purge cycle, are rampant. Like *Snow White's* Queen, desperate measures can be taken but, in reality, the end does not justify the means. Just as the mirror will never tell the Queen what she wants to hear, the numbers on the scale will never show the victim of an eating disorder the weight she wants to see.

Works Cited

Bruch, Hilde. *The Golden Cage: The Enigma of Anorexia Nervosa.* Cambridge: Harvard UP, 1978.

Buckroyd, Julia. *Anorexia and Bulimia: Your Questions Answered.* New York: Element Books, 1996.

Farrell, Em. *Lost for Words: The Psychoanalysis of Anorexia and Bulimia.* London: Process Press, 1995. 30 Apr. 1999 <http://human-nature.com/farrell/contents.html>.

Felker, Kenneth R. and Cathie Stivers. "The Relationship of Gender and Family Environment to Eating Disorder Risk in Adolescents." *Adolescence* 29 (1994): 821–35. *Infotrac Academic ASAP.* 30 Apr. 1999 <http://rdas.mmm.edu/bin/rdas.dll/RDAS_SVR=web2.searchbank.com/itw/session/234/538/13014136w5/8!xrn_1_1_A16477233>.

Hsu, L. K. George. *Eating Disorders.* New York: Guilford, 1990.

Pipher, Mary Bray. *Hunger Pains: The Modern Woman's Tragic Quest for Thinness.* Rpt. ed. New York: Ballantine-Random, 1997.

———. *Reviving Ophelia: Saving the Selves of Adolescent Girls.* New York: Putnam-Penguin, 1994.

Schneider, Linda H., Steven J. Cooper and Katherine A. Halmi, eds. *The Psychobiology of Human Eating Disorders: Preclinical and Clinical Perspectives.* Annals of New York Academy of Sciences 575. New York: New York Academy of Sciences, 1989.

Writing Mathematics and Chemistry

William Zinsser

William Zinsser (b. 1922, New York City), journalist, college professor, and editor, is the author of numerous books on writing and American culture. This selection comes from his book Writing to Learn.

One day I got a letter from a woman named Joan Countryman, who is head of the mathematics department at Germantown Friends School in Philadelphia. She had heard about my interest in writing across the curriculum.

"For many years," she said, "I've been asking my students to write about mathematics as they learned it, with predictably wonderful results. Writing seems to free them of the idea that math is a collection of right answers owned by the teacher—a body of knowledge that she will dispense in chunks and that they have to swallow and digest. That's how most nonmathematicians perceive it. But what makes mathematics really interesting is not the right answer but where it came from and where it leads."

The letter grabbed my attention. Surely mathematics was a world of numbers. Could it also be penetrated with words? Could a person actually write sentences that would lead him through a mathematical problem and suggest further questions—different questions from the ones the teacher might raise? It had never occurred to me that the teacher wasn't the sole custodian of mathematical truth. Yet here in the morning mail was a teacher who got her math students to write—a humanist in the world of fractions and cosines. Joan Countryman explained that she was one of a small but growing number of pioneers in her discipline, frequently invited to give workshops to introduce teachers to the idea of writing mathematics. I called her and asked if she would introduce the idea to me. We made a date for me to come to Philadelphia and talk to her and attend one of her classes.

• • •

I put my first question to Joan Countryman as we settled down to talk in her late-Victorian house, a house I had been warmly admiring for its fanciful curves and angles and other eclectic design details.

"What is mathematics?" I asked.

"You've been talking about mathematics ever since you walked into this house," she said. "When you commented on the dormers and the staircase and the circular windows you were making mathematical points."

I said I thought they were aesthetic points. Like Molière's bourgeois gentleman, who was astonished to learn that he had been speaking prose all his life, I was surprised to learn that I had been speaking mathematics.

"Sure they're aesthetic points," she said, "but there are all sorts of interesting mathematics about the way the house is constructed and about the shapes you've been noticing. Unfortunately, most people don't see the world that way because they've been alienated from mathematics and told that it's something apart from what they're able to do."

"So what is mathematics?" I asked, still hoping for a definition.

"What are any of the disciplines but a way in which people try to make sense of the world or the universe?" she said. "Mathematics is one way of doing that, just as literature is, or philosophy, or history. Math does it by looking for patterns and abstracting—that is, by examining a specific case and generalizing from that [. . .].

I asked Joan Countryman when she began to think that there might be another language—writing—which could take students into the subject by a different route.

"When I started teaching math I was thirty," she recalled, "and I had been out working in the field of urban education as a program planner for the Philadelphia school district, so when I got into a classroom I had serious questions about the relationship between what one does in school and what one does in life. I didn't like the isolation of the process of learning math: You study it alone and you take your tests alone and you don't have much to do with other people. I immediately put the kids in groups and made them teach each other and take tests together. I was determined to get them away from the idea that their education is a private experience.

"I also wanted them to be less passive. Math is an active process, and you'll never know that if you sit and wait for the teacher to tell you, 'This is how to do long division—it's a set of specific steps.' The action should begin long before that, with the student initiating a question like 'I've got fifty-three of these things; how am I going to divide them among the people in the room?' Most kids think that the teacher has all the information and they don't have any. I don't like the implications of that—that you aren't capable of finding things out yourself.

"So from the start I got my students to write about what they were doing. My first idea was to ask them to write mathematics autobiographies [. . .]." Another format is for students to keep a journal with a running account of their work. "In a journal," Mrs. Countryman said, "I want them to suspend judgment—to feel free to ask questions, to experiment, to make statements about what they do and don't understand. At first they need help to learn to write without censoring their thoughts—to feel confident that nobody will criticize what they've written."

The following entry, written by a twelfth-grade student named Neil Swenson after a month's exposure to calculus, is typical of how the form lends itself to recording successive stages of thought:

> In my first journal entry I wrote that I believed that calculus is a way of finding solutions to problems that can't be solved with conventional math, by using abstractions. I was partially correct in that many parts of calculus do require abstract thinking. But that's not really what calculus is. Calculus is a way of dealing with motion. It's a way of finding out exactly how something is moving. Without calculus it was impossible for us to know what the instantaneous velocity of something was. We could only know the actual rate of change if it was changing at a constant rate; then its derivative or the slope of its tangent line is equal to the slope of the original line. When we had something that had a variable rate of exchange we tried to find the average velocity, but this was inaccurate [. . .].

Listening to this and other examples, I saw that many of my beliefs about writing and learning also apply to mathematics: that we write to discover what we know and don't know; that we write more comfortably if we go exploring, free of the fear of not being on the "right" road to the right destination, and that we learn more if we feel that the work has a purpose. Motivation is as important in mathematics writing as in every other kind of writing. I asked Joan Countryman how she keeps alive the awareness that math is closely related to life.

"There's no dearth of topics for math papers," she said, "but often students seem to be just meeting an assignment instead of pursuing a genuine interest of theirs. I'm always looking for a connection between mathematics and social questions [. . .]."

• • •

Physiological note: I had been sitting in Joan Countryman's living rooom for two hours talking about mathematics. My pulse was steady, the hand that held my note-taking pencil didn't shake and wasn't even clammy. Where was that old math anxiety? I hadn't been at any loss for questions; they came to me naturally. Like the process of writing, the process of asking questions had been a form of learning, raising further questions and telling me what I wanted to know next. I was genuinely curious. It never occurred to me that this was a subject I wasn't supposed to be any good at. What did occur to me was that mathematics was not some arcane system of numbers; it was a language, a way of putting thoughts together. I might never master the language—my checkbook might still go unbalanced—but at least I had begun to glimpse what the language was trying to say and how it could help people to understand the world around them.

By extension, I thought, this must also be true of engineering, chemistry, biology and all the other special languages that have been invented to express special ideas. They can be at least broadly apprehended. What keeps us from trying is fear; the engineer is as frightened of my language (writing) as I am of his [. . .].

How does someone write chemistry? Here's an explanation I like, taken from *The Journal of Chemical Education,* by Professor Estelle K. Meislich, of Bergen Community College, Paramus, New Jersey. She begins her article by raising the most common bugaboo that science teachers worry about: "Is there some way of requiring good writing from students that will not diminish the science content?" The concern behind the question is twofold: that teaching writing will take time away from teaching chemistry, and that writing in the sciences is "not the same" as writing in the humanities.

Tackling the question, Professor Meislich writes: "Here is a method I have used successfully for the past eight years in courses for both chemistry majors and nonmajors. On every examination I ask at least one and often several questions that require a written response. Students are told that their answers must be written in 'acceptable' English for credit. If I decide that a scientifically correct response is poorly written, the student cannot get credit for the correct answer until it is rewritten in correct English.

"The student has one week to return the rewritten paper for credit. During this time students are encouraged to meet with a writing instructor for help in rewriting. (I send the writing instructor a copy of the examination with correctly written answers to prepare him or her for students' requests for help.) Of course incorrect answers, no matter how well written, cannot be rewritten for credit.

"A paper that requires a rewritten answer will have two grades. The first one is for the originally submitted examination. The second grade, shown in parentheses, is the one that the student will receive if an acceptable rewritten answer is returned on time [. . .]. Once students accept the fact that correct but poorly written answers are unacceptable, most of them write more carefully. Eventually very few of them have to rewrite at all. In this way, writing becomes an integral part of the course without diminishing the chemical content."

Acknowledgments

Simon Winchester

At the conclusion of his book The Professor and the Madman, *the author Simon Winchester details the kinds of research he had to do to complete the book. As you can see, his research included all those kinds of research we advocate in this workshop: personal interviews, observations, the Internet, and print sources. You'll notice too that he asked colleagues and friends to read drafts of the book and give him feedback.*

When I first came upon this story, which was mentioned all too briefly, and just as an aside, in a rather sober book about the dictionary-making craft, it struck me immediately as a tale well worth investigating and perhaps telling in full. But for several months I was alone in thinking so. I had in the works a truly massive project about an altogether different subject, and the advice from virtually all sides was that I should press on with that and leave this amusing little saga well alone.

But four people did find it just as fascinating as I did—and saw also the possibilities that by telling the poignant and human tale of William Minor, I could perhaps create some kind of prism through which to view the greater and even more fascinating story of the history of English lexicography. These four people were Bill Hamilton, my longtime friend and London agent; Anya Waddington, my editor at Viking, also in London; Larry Ashmead, Executive Editor of HarperCollins in New York; and Marisa Milanese, then an editorial assistant in the offices of *Condé Nast Traveler* magazine, also in New York. Their faith in this otherwise unregarded project was total and unremitting, and I thank them for it unreservedly.

Marisa, whom I think a paragon of ceaseless enthusiasm, dogged initiative, and untiring zeal, then went on to help me with the American end of the research: Together with my close friend of a quarter century, Juliet Walker in London, she helped me spin my basic ideas into a complex web of facts and figures, which I have since attempted to settle into some kind of coherent order. The extent to which I have succeeded or failed in this I cannot yet judge, but I should say here that these two women presented me with a bottomless well of information, and if I have misinterpreted, misread, misheard, or miswritten any of it, then those mistakes are my responsibility, and mine alone. My thanks also to Sue Llewellyn, who, as well as copyediting this book so assiduously and with such good humor, also—she reminded me—had worked on my book on Korea ten years before.

Access to Broadmoor Special Hospital, and to the voluminous files that have long been kept on all patients, was clearly going to be the key to cracking this story; and it took some weeks before Juliet Walker and I were allowed in. That we were was a triumph for two Broadmoor employees, Paul Robertson and Alison Webster, who made a persuasive case on our behalf to a perhaps understandably reluctant hospital administration. Without the help of these two remarkable and kind individuals, this book would never have managed to be much more than a collection of conjectures: The Broadmoor files were needed to provide the facts, and Paul and Alison provided the files.

On the other side of the Atlantic, matters proceeded rather differently—despite the best efforts of the splendid Marisa. St. Elizabeth's Hospital in Washington, D.C., is no longer a federal institution but is run by the government of the District of Columbia—a government that has experienced some well-publicized troubles in recent years. And at first, perhaps because of this, the hospital refused point-blank to release any of its files, and went so far as to suggest, quite seriously, that I engage a lawyer and sue in order to obtain them.

However, some while later, a cursory search I made one day of the National Archives pages on the World Wide Web suggested to me that the papers relating to Doctor Minor—who had been a patient at St. Elizabeth's between 1910 and 1919, when the institution was undeniably under federal jurisdiction—might well actually be in federal custody, and not within the Kafkaesque embrace of the District. And indeed, as it turned out, they were. A couple of requests through the Internet, a happy conversation with the extremely helpful archivist Bill Breach, and suddenly more than seven hundred pages of case notes and other fascinating miscellanea arrived in a FedEx package. It was more than gratifying to be able to telephone St. Elizabeth's the next day and tell the unhelpful officials there which file I then had sitting before me on my desk. They were not best pleased.

The Oxford University Press was, by contrast, wonderfully helpful; and while I am naturally happy to thank the officials at the press who so kindly sanctioned my visits to Walton Street, I wish to acknowledge the very considerable debt that I owe first to Elizabeth Knowles, now of Oxford's Reference Books Department, who had made a study of Minor some years before and was happy to share her knowledge and access with me. I am delighted also to be able to thank the irrepressibly enthusiastic Jenny McMorris of the press archives, who knows Minor and his remarkable legacy more intimately than anyone else anywhere. Jenny, together with her former colleague Peter Foden, proved a tower of strength during my visits and long after: I only hope that she manages to find an outlet for her own fascination with the great Dr. Henry Fowler, whom she rightly regards, along with Murray, as one of the true heroes of the English language.

• • •

Several friends, as well as a number of specialists who had a professional interest in parts of the story, were kind enough to read the manuscript's early drafts, and they made many suggestions for improving it. In almost all cases I have accepted their proposals with gratitude, but if on occasion I did, through carelessness or pigheadedness, disregard their warnings or demands, then the same caveat—about the responsibility for all errors of fact, judgment, or taste remaining firmly with me—applies as well: They did their best.

Among those personal friends I wish to thank are Graham Boynton, Pepper Evans, Rob Howard, Jesse Sheidlower, Nancy Stump, Paula Szuchman, and Gully Wells. And to the otherwise anonymous Anthony S———, who grumbled to me that his fiancée had denied him romantic favors one summer morning because she was bent on finishing chapter 9, my apologies, embarrassed thanks for your forbearance, and best wishes for future marital bliss.

James W. Campbell of the New Haven Historical Society gave great assistance in finding the Minor family in their old hometown; the librarians and staff at the Yale Divinity Library told me much about William Minor's early life in Ceylon. Pat Higgins, an Englishwoman living in Washington State, and with whom I corresponded only by e-mail, became fascinated also by the Ceylon and Seattle ends of the Minor family story and gave me several fascinating tips.

Michael Musick of the U.S. National Archives then found most of Minor's military files, and Michael Rhode of the Walter Reed Army Hospital tracked down his handwritten autopsy reports. The National Park Service was helpful in giving me access to military bases in New York and Florida where he had been stationed; the Index Project in Arlington, Va., assisted me in finding additional records relating to his wartime career.

Susan Pakies of Virginia's Orange County Tourist Office, along with the immensely knowledgeable Frank Walker, then took me around all of the important sites where the Battle of the Wilderness had been fought, and later, to cheer us all up, to several of the delightful old inns that are hidden away in this spectacularly lovely corner of the United States. Jonathan O'Neal patiently explained Civil War medical practice at the old Exchange Hotel-cum-hospital that is now a museum in Gordonville, Va.

Nancy Whitmore of the National Museum of Civil War Medicine in Frederick, Maryland, was an enthusiastic supporter of the project and painstakingly dug up a huge amount of highly relevant arcana. Dr. Lawrence Kohl at the University of Alabama was kind enough to take time both to discuss the mechanics of Civil War branding and to speculate (in an impressively informed way) on the effects such punishment might have had on Irishmen who fought in the Union Army—the latter his particular specialty as a historian of the period. Mitchell Redman of New York City filled in some details of Minor's later personal life, about which he had once written a short but so far unproduced play.

Gordon Claridge of Magdalen College, Oxford, had much that was helpful to say about the origins of mental illness; Jonathan Andrews, a historian of Broadmoor, helped also; and Isa Samad, a distinguished psychiatrist of Fort Lauderdale, Fla., told me a great deal about the history of the treatment of paranoid schizophrenia.

Dale Fiore, superintendent of the Evergreen Cemetery in New Haven, then added fascinating footnotes about the end of William Minor's life—the length of the coffin, the depth at which it is buried, and the names of those who surround him in his plot.

Life became a great deal easier once I had tracked down one of the few known living relatives of William Minor, Mr. John Minor, of Riverside, Conn. He was kindness itself, giving me an enormous amount of useful information about the great-great-uncle he never knew, and offering me access to the treasure trove of pictures and papers that had sat for years, undisturbed, in a wooden box in his attic. He and his Danish wife, Birgit, became as fascinated by the story as I was, and I thank them for pleasant waterside dinners and time spent talking about the nature of their most curious relative.

Interpretation as Response: Reading as the Creation of Meaning

Essential Premises

- When we read, we don't so much *find* meaning as build and create meaning—just as we build and create meaning when we write.
- It's helpful to capture our reading process in more detail by observing it closely, which we can easily do by stopping periodically in midprocess and writing what we find in our heads.
- We automatically create an interpretation of a text whenever we *say* it out loud with full meaning or expression. The interpretation we create by entering into a text in this way is often more interesting than the one we come up with if someone asks us directly for "our interpretation."
- One of the most satisfying ways to write a poem—and it is the method that many poets use—is to take a germ or structural element from an existing poem we like and use it as the generative seed for a new poem.

Main Assignment Preview

Reading may *look* passive: we sit quietly and let the image of the words print itself on our retina and then pass inwards to our brain. But the point we want to stress in this workshop is that reading—indeed all meaning making—is a deeply *active* process of exploration. In fact, when we have trouble reading it's often because we've been mistakenly *trying* to be passive—trying to make ourselves like good cameras. We've been trying to become perfect little photographic plates on which the meanings on the page print themselves with photographic accuracy. But since reading doesn't work that way, we don't understand the words very well if we slip into operating on that model. Even the simple act of seeing is exploratory and active. The eye may be like a camera, but the brain cannot "take in" retinal images, only electric impulses.

The important thing to realize, then, is that not only reading but even seeing or "making sense" of what is around us is always a process that occurs in stages. It takes place gradually through the passage of time, not instantaneously like an image passing through a lens. In the first stage, our mind takes in the first pieces of information—the first trickles of electrical impulses—and quickly makes a guess or a hypothesis about what we might be looking at. Then the mind repeatedly checks this guess against further information that comes in. Often we have to change our guess or hypothesis as new information comes in—before we "see what's really there."

Because normal perception occurs so quickly, we seldom realize that this process of first-guessing-and-then-checking is going on, especially since we don't think of vision in these terms. But if you will keep this explanation in mind in the days and weeks ahead and watch yourself in the act of seeing—particularly when you are trying to see something obscure or something you've never seen before—you'll catch yourself in the act of making these visual guesses or hypotheses: "I'm pretty sure that's a yellow car going down the highway," but then in a second, "Oh no, wait. Why is a yellow tractor coming up the highway?" In short, we tend to see what we expect to see until evidence forces us to revise our expectation.

If seeing and hearing are such active exploratory processes, so must reading be: in fact, it's exactly the same process. When we read words or hear them, we *understand what we expect to understand* till evidence forces us to revise our expectation. Even in the process of reading individual words, research shows that as soon as we see a few letters or the shape of the whole word or the phrase that it's part of, we *guess* what the word is and then, as we get more data—or as our guess doesn't seem to fit—we revise our guess. And so the same constructive process goes on in all reading, whether for words, phrases, sentences, paragraphs, chapters, or whole books.

Consider this simple opening sentence: "All the long afternoon, I worked in the windowless office, shivering from the air-conditioning, trying to find the mistake I'd made that morning in the bank's accounts." We get a *bit* of meaning from the phrase "all the long afternoon," but for most readers, that meaning gets slightly modified and reinterpreted when we discover what kind of afternoon it was. "I" gets stashed away with *some* meaning attached to it, but it waits to find out what kind of "I" it is—even what age and gender. "Worked" gives us some meaning, but it too gets a bit of reinterpretation later in the sentence when we discover what kind of work it is.

In this workshop we will show you three different ways of interpreting a poem by means of *responding* and actively creating meaning—three different activities or exercises. There's quite a lot to do here; if your teacher has to skip an activity, we hope you'll experiment with it anyway.

We have two other goals in exploring the reading or interpreting process: helping you do better with hard texts, and helping you use the collaborative dimension of reading.

Your main assignment might be to write an essay explaining what you've figured out about the poem using all three responding activities. Or your teacher might simply ask for the writing you produce as your response to the third activity.

First Activity: Giving Movies of Your Mind as You Read

This activity is a kind of mini-laboratory in the reading process: an exercise to help you become more aware of your conscious and unconscious reactions as you read. In this exercise we interrupt you as you read a poem—we stop you twice in midpoem and ask you what's going on in your mind—so that you can notice your responses and reactions and interpretations as they are in the process of happening. The poem we're using has 15 stanzas. We have printed five stanzas on page 339, five more on page 341, and the last five on page 343. We've done this so that you can notice and write down your reactions to each section before you see the rest of the poem. If this strikes you as highly artificial, you are right. Nevertheless, it is a valuable way to help you capture some of the mental events in your reading and meaning making that you don't usually see.

Capturing Reactions on the Fly

Start, then, and read the first five stanzas of the poem in the box on this page. Read them through once at your normal reading speed. There's no hurry. But when you finish, freewrite for at least five minutes to get down on paper what was happening in your mind as you were reading the stanzas, and after you finished reading them and were trying to make sense of the words. Perhaps you went back and read the words again. What meanings or partial meanings came to mind? What thoughts, feelings, or memories came into your mind? Which words lingered? You could do this whole exercise with a tape recorder, speaking your reactions as you go rather than writing. You might capture more that way.

Of course, sometimes we read something and our only reaction is, "I'm confused." That's fine. Write it down. But try to write a few more words about

"Song" by W. H. Auden

Part I

As I walked out one evening,
Walking down Bristol Street,
The crowds upon the pavement
Were fields of harvest wheat.

And down by the brimming river
I heard a lover sing
Under an arch of the railway:
"Love has no ending.

I'll love you, dear, I'll love you
Till China and Africa meet,
And the river jumps over the mountain
And the salmon sing in the street.

I'll love you till the ocean
Is folded and hung up to dry,
And the seven stars go squawking
Like geese about the sky.

The years shall run like rabbits,
For in my arms I hold
The Flower of the Ages,
And the first love of the world."

what *kind* of confusion this was: frustrated? bored? angry? In any event you'll probably want to read the passage again and see what sense you make this time and what goes on in your mind and feelings. Jot down some notes on this too.

When you finish, go on and do the same thing with the next five stanzas on page 341. Read them and freewrite and record whatever happens in your mind as you are reading, thinking, and trying to make sense—and enjoying the poem, too.

There's an interesting question about the process of reading that is raised here. Should you try to "finish" or "master" or "settle" one section of a poem (or any text) before going on to read the next one? There's no right answer. We all read in different ways—and differently for different pieces of writing. Do what you normally do. However, it's worth pointing out that one of the biggest problems some people have in reading is a tendency to spend too long trying to master one part before moving on. This usually gives you needless frustration since there's often no way to really find out what an early part means until you see a later part. That's how language works.

Notice that there's an interesting correlation here between the reading and the writing processes—that is, a similar problem in both realms: *trying to do it right the first time.* It's an impossible goal. Most people read better and write better when they let go a bit and learn *not* to work so hard to get it right before moving on, but come back again and again. This is really an issue of "revising," and revising is involved in good reading as well as good writing.

Before you have finished, make sure you have read the whole poem at least twice from start to finish rather than in bits. When you read it straight through, you may well have new thoughts about what it means, new feelings, memories, frustrations, associations. Or you may simply become more convinced of how you saw it before. (But even "becoming more convinced" is something going on in your mind.) So make sure you stop after these read-throughs and freewrite for a few minutes to record what is going on in your thoughts and feelings.

What we are asking for is really "process writing"—but it's about your *reading* process. This writing will help you understand better how your mind works when you read: your habits, your preoccupations, your blind spots, your strengths, and the things you'd like to do better. Breaking the poem into parts is like putting the camera on slow motion, so you can see more clearly the details of how your mind gradually makes meaning out of words. Athletes

Exploring the Writing Process

As for inspiration, I've come to believe in it again, after years of devaluing it. But I know that it occurs as much for me in the course of writing a poem, spurred by the words I didn't know I was going to use, as it occurs by events that might precede the poem. . . . After I write a little while, I have some sense of what I'm doing, so I'm going toward something, but I always want that thing I'm going towards to be a surprise for me. Frost says "no surprise in the poet, no surprise in the reader. . . ."

Stephen Dunn

often watch slow-motion pictures of how they function in order to learn to function better. (By the way, it's interesting to notice similarities and differences between how your mind works as you write and as you read.)

You can look at examples of this kind of writing on pages 355–358 of the "Readings" section of this workshop: reactions by students while reading Richard Wilbur's "The Writer" (printed on pages 354–355). What we are asking for is also the same as "movies of the reader's mind"—a method of giving feedback to fellow writers, which we explain and illustrate in a separate section of "Sharing and Responding" at the end of this book.

Share, Compare Notes, Create Meaning with Others

At this point it is useful and interesting to share your reactions with one or two of your classmates. Indeed, it makes sense to do this earlier in the reading process; for example, even after you have read only the first section.

Most people find it interesting just to see how other people's minds react to the same words. It's often a *relief* to see other people's "really rough drafts of reading." Sometimes we feel, "Oh dear, everyone else but me understands it perfectly," and it's fun to see that it's a messy, imprecise process for everyone. And it's common for students to think, "Teachers and critics have a magical ability to see the hidden meaning in poems—whole and complete—but I don't have that ability." As with writing, it's a relief to discover that everyone's mind tends to be a mess at the early stages, no matter how skilled they are. Some people hide the mess more (sometimes even from themselves), but the mess is there. And it's interesting to see that everyone has different reactions and feelings, even when they happen to agree on the main outlines.

In addition, we want to emphasize the collaborative dimension that is inherent in reading and the making of meaning. It's not that we usually read in groups—we

"Song" by W. H. Auden

Part II

But all the clocks in the city
Began to whirr and chime:
"O let not Time deceive you,
You cannot conquer Time

In the burrows of the Nightmare
Where Justice naked is,
Time watches from the shadow
And coughs when you would kiss.

In headaches and in worry
Vaguely life leaks away,
And Time will have his fancy
Tomorrow or today.

Into many a green valley
Drifts the appalling snow;
Time breaks the threaded dances
And the diver's brilliant bow.

O plunge your hands in water,
Plunge them in up to the wrist;
Stare, stare in the basin
And wonder what you've missed.

usually read alone—but we usually discuss what we read with others if we have the chance. Lawyers, scientists, and business people as well as literary critics usually reach conclusions about what something means and implies on the basis of discussion with colleagues. Even when we can't actually discuss our reading with others, we often hold bits of mental discussion with them in our heads anyway.

So find an occasion at some point to share your written reactions with others (though don't feel pressured to share any things that are too private). The goal is to see the poem through their eyes. Then do a few more minutes of writing to record how their reactions and interpretations did or didn't affect how you see the poem. What new meanings, reactions, feelings, or thoughts come to you on the basis of hearing what others wrote? You may experience large changes or only tiny readjustments. Sometimes someone else's memory or association becomes prominent in your mind.

We're not saying you should try to agree with other readers. Just *use* other readers; try out their readings to help you find a meaning or interpretation of the poem that satisfies you. The goal is simply to see and understand the poem better.

Reading "Right" and "Wrong"—Reading with the Grain and Against the Grain

Every piece of writing implicitly asks us to become the *right* kind of reader for it, the reader who will go along and get the meanings and feel the feelings that the writing asks for. When we have difficulty reading something, it's usually a case of "I can't—or I won't—become the kind of reader that this piece asks me to be." Some women, for example, have called attention to how often pieces of writing ask the reader to take on a male point of view, sometimes even asking readers to take pleasure in the criticism or exploitation of women.

We're not asking you necessarily to go along with the poem—to become the kind of reader you feel this poem is asking you to become. It's fine to be a *resisting reader,* to read "wrong," or to read "against the grain." Notice in the "Readings" how Barbara Hales and Julie Nelson are resitant readers of Richard Wilbur's "The Writer." In their dialogue, one of them vehemently refuses to read the poem the way the poem seems to ask to be read. The only thing we ask is that you not stop reading: not stop with "Huh?" or "I hate this piece" or "I hate being the kind of person this poem asks me to be—or having the kinds of feelings it's asking me to have." Please stick with the poem and work out a reading even if it is only a description of what you sense the poem is trying to do to you and why you refuse and insist on having a completely different set of

Exploring the Writing Process

In the actual process of composition or in preliminary thinking, I try to immerse myself in the motive and *feel* toward meanings, rather than plan a structure or plan effects.

Robert Penn Warren

thoughts and feelings. In short, the goal is not to read "right" but to read attentively and capture a record of how your mind makes meaning out of words.

Final Step: Learning about Yourself as a Reader

Read back over everything you have written so far and try to see what you can notice about your habits as a reader. Notice which parts of the poem struck you most and which parts left you unaffected. Try particularly to attend to those parts of the poem you did *not* comment on. How did your reactions differ from those of others? Think about which dimensions of your self or character played a role in your reacting and interpreting. Look in particular for life-themes and life-positions.

- *Life-themes.* Can you see any powerful experiences or interests or preoccupations that shaped your reactions? Here are some examples of life-themes that affect many people's reading: relations between parents and children, love, sex, divorce, eating, the outdoors, fighting, loneliness, adventure, or breaking free of obligations.
- *Life-positions.* How is your reading affected by your age? your gender? the region where you live? your race? your nationality? your class? your sexual orientation? your occupation? We cannot actually step outside of our positions, but reading can be one way to imagine ourselves differently or to enter vicariously into other positions. Nevertheless, our own life-positions exert a strong force on how we read.

"Song" by W. H. Auden

[Note to readers: In the first four stanzas that follow, we are still hearing words spoken by "all the clocks in the city."]

Part III

The glacier knocks in the cupboard,
The desert sighs in the bed,
And the crack in the tea-cup opens
A lane to the land of the dead.

Where the beggars raffle the banknotes
And the Giant is enchanting to Jack,
And the Lily-white Boy is a Roarer,
And Jill goes down on her back.

O look, look in the mirror,
O look in your distress;
Life remains a blessing
Although you cannot bless.

O stand, stand at the window
As the tears scald and start;
You shall love your crooked neighbor
With your crooked heart."

It was late, late in the evening,
The lovers they were gone;
The clocks had ceased their chiming,
And the deep river ran on.

It's interesting to get a better picture of *who we are as readers*—what lenses we read through. There is no such thing as perfectly neutral reading. But insofar as we can get a sense of what lenses we read through, we can get a better sense of what kinds of things we might miss. Do you think, for example, that women read and notice and react differently from how men do? It can be interesting to share this last writing too—about yourself as a reader—but we think it's more important to write these things for yourself. Share only what you want to share.

Second Activity: Interpretation as Rendering or Animation or Performance

Whenever you read something out loud, you interpret it. That is, you can't read something out loud without automatically deciding what the words mean, and that meaning will *show* in your reading (unless you just pronounce the words disconnectedly without any sense of meaning—but that's not what we mean by "reading out loud"). Often we don't have to figure out the meaning before we read out loud because the act of reading out loud in itself *leads us* to figure out the meaning of words that we had been stuck on—puts the meaning there on our tongue, as it were. The mouth can be smarter than the eyes about language. Thus, the minimal task we have in mind here is simply to read the poem out loud in such a way as to make the meaning as clear as possible to readers.

But please don't settle for the minimal task. Critics have often noted that the best interpretation of a text may be a *rendition* or *performance* of that text. To figure out how to "render" a text out loud is usually the quickest and most insightful way to figure out an interpretation. If you read the words with any spirit or animation—if you don't cop out and use a timid monotone—you will convey much more than the meaning of the words. You will convey the spirit or tone of the words—the implications.

Just by trial and error, using your mouth and your ear, you can decide how a line or stanza or whole poem should *sound* (the same for a short story). Once you work that out, you have interpreted it. Then you can work out your interpretation "in other words." You can explain the interpretation you have already enacted in sound. Most important, this interpretation based on voice and sound is usually more insightful and sophisticated than the interpretation you come up with if you go straight to "interpretation talk."

We suggest using groups to put on a rendering or animation or performance of the poem you've worked on in this workshop (or one of the poems printed in the "Readings" at the end of this workshop). It is fine for performances to be playful and even take some liberties with the poem. Here are some techniques that student groups have used for renderings of Richard Wilbur's "The Writer."

- *Using more than one reader and alternating between readers.* You can have the group read the whole thing together—trying to bring out different moods or tones for the different parts of the poem. But it's usually fruitful to vary the voices. For example, one group used all their voices for stanzas one, four, five, and eleven (the stanzas that seem the most "choral"). They used only one reader for the first line of the second stanza and the first two lines of the sixth (where there is an "I" speaking). And they used a pair of readers for most of the second and third stanzas (the extended image of the typewriter and the boat) and for the extended story of the trapped bird.

- *Echoing or repeating lines.* One group had one person repeat certain lines after they were said the first time—quietly and intermittently in the background. This reader repeated "My daughter is writing a story" until the group got to "I wish her a lucky passage"; then he repeated that phrase intermittently until the group got to "I remember" and he kept on with that until he stopped for the last stanza. Another group did an experiment where each reader started one line later than the previous reader. It was like singing a round. They only had three readers and the effect was interesting—almost like waves. As listeners, we understood more than we expected we would. But the goal wasn't to put across a clear understanding: It was to give "musical" or "sound" rendition.
- *Putting parts in different orders.* Some groups experimented by starting with the story of the bird, or the extended image of hearing the typewriter and the boat. When we hear things in a different order, we notice new relationships; we learn more about the text.
- *Using sound effects.* Some groups used the sound of a typewriter either intermittently or throughout the poem. Another got the sound of a bird banging against the window. One group made some "abstract" or nonrepresentational sound effects to go with the rendering.
- *Staging and interpretive movements.* One group had someone "playing" the father—walking meditatively around; another person playing the daughter holed up in a room—struggling with writing; another person acted out the trapped bird in a kind of dance. All this while a couple of others read the poem. A few adventuresome groups always try rendering pieces *entirely* with movement and sound—no words at all. This is interesting and fun. For remember, these performances are for people who already know the poem. For one enactment, a person who knew American Sign Language did a signed version while another person read the words; it was extraordinarily beautiful and moving.
- *Adding words—creating a dialogue with the poem.* One group added words for the daughter to speak. Some groups interjected some of their own interpretive responses, adding thoughts or memories or reactions of their own. In one performance, one person kept interjecting the phrase "Get a life, Dad!" (see Hales and Nelson in the "Readings"). There are limitless possibilities. Any strong reactions or even background material can be added to a performance to make it a *dialogue* between your voice and the voice of the poet.

After the renderings, do some freewriting about what you learned from working out your own rendering and seeing those of others.

This performative approach is helpful in thinking about the question of whether there is such a thing as a "right" interpretation. As you'll see from the performances of your classmates, most sets of words can be performed in more than one plausible way. But some texts lend themselves to a multiplicity of readings or interpretations (these are more "open" sets of words), while other texts seem more "closed" or determined and seem to ask for only a few or possibly only one interpretation. We can usually notice when a reading is implausible and notice the various degrees of pressure when a reading is pulling the text where it doesn't seem to want to go. But sometimes a very talented reader or actor can show us a new reading we never would have dreamed of and might even have called absurd, and succeed in making it seem absolutely plausible. For the purposes of this exercise, however, the goal is not *right* readings but *variations* in reading. It can be helpful to push and pull and even distort the text. Sometimes even a very wrong reading—satiric or parodic—can show us something in the words that we hadn't noticed.

Third Activity: Responding as a Writer: Responding in Kind

In schools and colleges people often assume that writing about literature means writing some kind of *analysis, interpretation,* or *essay* about the work. But it doesn't have to work that way. When *writers* respond and write about a poem, their response often takes the form of another poem: some kind of answering poem that in some way relates to or "bounces off" the poem they read. The way they appreciate a poem is to do a piece of work that somehow shares the same thematic or formal space as the poem. They create a companion poem. Many of the famous poems we read and appreciate (and write essays about) are, directly or indirectly, companion pieces or response poems to previous poems. In effect, the poet is saying, "I found this poem powerful and enabling, and I will write this new poem somewhat in its shadow." Virginia Woolf wrote that the best way to understand a book is "not to read, but to write; to make your own experiment with the dangers and difficulties of words." (See pages 360–361 for Bi Chen's poetry response to Sindy Cheung's poem.)

Perhaps you don't normally write poems and even find it a bit scary to think about doing so. This is true for both of us too; we are in no way poets. What helps us most if we want to write a poem is to find a poem that we like and connect with, and then *use* it or *borrow* from it: Use its theme or some of its words; borrow some of its form or some of its spirit and energy. Try to ride on its coattails to make a poem of your own. What we find most useful is *not* deciding what the poem will be about before hand, but letting the borrowed elements somehow lead us to start writing some lines and writing some more lines and seeing what the poem wants to be about and where it wants to go. It's an exercise in letting the words or the structure *lead* us.*

Here are some suggestions for writing a poem in response to the Auden poem:

- *Borrow some of the texture of Auden's poem to make your own.* Try writing a poem that uses the rhythms of popular songs and poems.

* We've learned about these techniques from Kenneth Koch, Theodore Roethke, and Charles Moran.

Auden seems to mix echoes of ballads and folk songs ("As I walked out one evening"), children's songs and nursery rhymes (Jack and Jill and the Giant—"And the river jumps over the mountain/ And the salmon sing in the street"), and popular songs in general. He also uses the rhymes and the sing-song three beat line that go with those kinds of songs. You could draw on the same sources. But it would be just as good, if not better, to try for echoes, words, and rhythms from more recent popular songs that are loud in your head or that you think might be in the heads of people you would like to write for—even popular love songs or rock songs or rap. We strongly suggest that you *not* try for rhyme unless you enjoy it and are pretty good at it. Poems are often pulled down when rhymes don't come easily. Not only can poems be terrific without rhyme; plenty of songs don't rhyme.

- *Borrow some structural features to lead you to a poem of your own.* Here's one way to see the structure: First, a short section where you speak in the first person and name a time and a place—and overhear someone else saying or singing something. Second, a section written in the voice of that someone. (The poem could be about love, but it could be about something entirely different.) Third, a section that starts with "But" where a thing or some inanimate objects ("all the clocks") speak out in reply or in contradiction to the first speech. These words seem to be addressed directly to us ("O let not Time deceive you" "O stare, stare in the mirror"). Finally, the last section is an impersonal statement rather than spoken words addressed to someone. But it uses a number of words from preceding sections ("lovers, clocks, river")—and one prominent word from the first stanza ("evening").
- *Use some prominent elements.* Here are some elements you could use to spark your mind: Use the name of a street; name two places (continents?) in one sentence; use at least one surprising metaphor where something *is* something unexpected ("the crowds were fields of wheat"); use elements from one or two nursery rhymes; mention a road or path to somewhere and then describe that place ("a lane to the land of the dead. Where . . ."); somehow manage not too obtrusively to repeat words more often than usual (plunge, plunge; stare, stare; look, look, look; blessing, bless; stand, stand; crooked, crooked; late, late").

Exploring the Writing Process

No matter how long I stare out of the window it still won't come to me. Thoughts, ideas—where are you? How should I start? If I look hard enough maybe it'll come or be sent to me.

Brainstorm! Quick, jot down everything you know before it leaves you. Elaborate later—you might forget the good stuff now.

Something, someone, anything please stimulate me. I have writer's BLOCK!

Student

- *Use some actual words.* There are so many striking words here that if you use too many, you'd probably echo Auden too closely. But if you choose a set of six or eight, these could spark you into your own poem. The trick is to pick ones that are interesting but, in a way, random. Here is a possible set that could be generative: pavement, brimming, arch, China, conquer, shadow, coughs, basin, wrist, distress, scald. But it's fine to use your intuition to pick another set. However, try to pick them *before* having any sense of what your poem will be about. Let the words lead you to your poem.
- *Use the theme.* Try writing a poem (it could be a prose poem) where there is some kind of meeting between a belief in love and a doubt that love is real or possible.
- *Reply.* Try writing a poem of reply. What does this poem lead you to want to say? Perhaps something about how this poem makes you feel? Something about your experience with love? A story of a very different dialogue about love?

What's crucial for this process of writing a poem is to put up with being very dissatisfied, perhaps embarrassed. You have to give yourself permission to do something just for the heck of it—to see where the process leads you. When we do this, we have to *force* ourselves to keep writing, almost like freewriting, so that much of what we put down is simply junk or filler. We end up throwing away more than half of what we've written, but we didn't suffer to write it so it doesn't hurt. You have to be playful and not too reverent about the process of "writing a poem."

After you have a draft, you can make big changes so that no one would ever see any relation to the Auden poem. But there's nothing wrong with leaving very direct links to her poem. It's an act of respect to write a poem that has echoes of someone else's poem. (If you have a hard time connecting to this poem, your teacher might allow you to write a poem in response to a different one that suits you better.)

Main Assignment: *An Exercise in Interpretation*

Perhaps your teacher will treat the poem created in the previous activity as the main assignment. Or perhaps she will ask for an essay about your emerging understanding or interpretation of the poem. Such an essay might contain *both* your understanding or interpretation—what sense or meaning you make of all those words—and an account of how you came to understand or interpret it this way through the three response activities. (Don't forget about the role of other people.)

Before we leave this workshop we want to reassure you that we're not trying to persuade you to go through these extensive processes every time you read something. It's fine to read quickly for pleasure. But these processes we are demonstrating here, once learned, will enrich your fast, casual reading. And if you have an assignment to interpret a piece of literature for a class, you might indeed find it helpful to go through all the response steps we've set up. Poetry might even be defined as follows: language that's rich and well built enough that it bears *re*reading and *re*responding. The pleasures and the meanings in poems don't get "used up" in one reading. The more the words are read again, the more interesting the reactions that emerge.

Sharing and Responding

- On a poem:
  —Which of my words and images somehow linger, work, or have an impact on you?
  —What meanings, feelings, and associations do those words produce?
  —What new views, ideas, or insights does my poem give you about the Auden poem?
- On an essay:
  —How do your reactions and understandings of the poem differ from mine?
  —What happened for you as you moved from activities to interpretation? How does that compare to the reactions I described?

Process Journal

- What did you learn about yourself as a reader? About the effect of life-themes and life-positions on how you read?
- What did you learn about yourself from the process of rendering or performing the poem? How did this change your reading?
- Reflect on your process of trying to produce a poem. What would it take to get you to do this more often?
- Reflect on the similarities and differences between your writing process and your reading process.
- How did you respond to the readings and interpretations of others? And they to yours? Do you tend to be a believer or doubter of what others say?

Exploring the Writing Process

How Poetry Comes to Me*

It comes blundering over the
Boulders at night, it stays
Frightened outside the
Range of my campfire
I go to meet it at the
Edge of the light.

Gary Snyder

* Try writing a poem with the same title—or perhaps change the second word of the title.

- How have your prior school experiences with literature influenced how you read and respond to literature?

Exploring Theory: *Reflecting on the Exercise in Interpretation*

About the Artificiality of Our Exercise

These exercises in the reading process might seem odd and artificial to you, so we want to spell out now why we are asking you to use them. Our goal is to illustrate both what you *already do* when you read—and also help you a bit with what you *should do* in the future.

The Exercise as a Picture of What You Already Do

Because we keep interrupting you in the middle of your reading and asking you questions to write about, we are clearly producing an artificial reading process. We may cause you to think of things that you never would have thought of, just reading quietly on your own.

But reflect a moment about these things "we made you think of." We didn't give you anything but the poem, and besides that, we didn't put anything in your mind that wasn't there already. Any "new" thoughts or memories were already in your mind anyway. We merely interrupted your reading and made you pause so that more of what was in your mind came to conscious awareness.

Our point is that these things you would not have noticed would nevertheless have influenced your reading in ways that are below the level of your awareness—*even if you read quickly without any interruptions.* What's new in our exercise are not the thoughts and memories, but your awareness of them.

For example, our "artificial" exercise may have triggered a memory about rabbits us about a time when someone read you the nursery rhyme about Jack and Jill. Those memories might not have come to mind during a fast reading, but they probably *influenced* that fast reading without your noticing it. Research on reading gives more and more evidence of how quick and active our thinking and remembering are when we read—how much goes on below the level of awareness. Since we don't "take in meaning," but rather "make meaning," we do that making on the basis of all the thoughts, feelings, and experiences already inside us, not just on the basis of words on the page.

Think about where meaning comes from. There are no meanings *in* words; only in people. Meaning is what people bring to words—and the meanings people bring are their own meanings—amalgams of their own individual experiences. When readers see the word *chat,* for example, they will bring different memories and associations—all having to do with informal conversation. Some people may have a very warm, cozy feeling about chat. Others, however, might find the word irrevocably colored by an experience when a powerful person said, "I think we'd better go to my office and have a little *chat.*" And yet a French reader will bring to those same four letters, c-h-a-t, meanings having to do with cats.

We might assume that the reading of straightforward prose is "regular reading," while the reading of difficult stories and poems is "irregular" or "exceptional." With difficult literature we have to stop and puzzle things out; we get one idea and then we have to change it when we get to something that contradicts it. But the process of reading difficult pieces simply shows us more nakedly the very same process that goes on quickly and subliminally in all reading. We see the same kind of thing in physics: Cars and billiard balls seem to behave "normally," while subatomic particles seem peculiar—for example, having ambiguous locations and becoming smaller as they move faster. But in fact *everything* behaves according to those peculiar rules of relativity; we just can't see it with cars and billiard balls because they are large and move slowly.

The Exercise as a Picture of What You Should Do in the Future

If you engage now and then in this artificial exercise—going slowly, pausing, looking inside at memories and associations, making hypotheses—you will learn to be more active and imaginative in your fast reading. You will learn to pay more attention to the words on the page and their relationships with each other; and you will pay more attention to the richness—the meanings, reactions, and associations—that you already bring to words. By being more skilled at the active and exploratory process of making meaning, you will simply understand more. You will be better at seeing the meaning even in very difficult pieces of writing.

A Litany for Survival

Audre Lorde

Audre Lorde (b. 1934, New York City; d. 1992), poet, activist, and educator, wrote poetry that dealt among other topics with her identity as a black gay female and with her West Indian heritage.

For those of us who live at the shoreline
standing upon the constant edges of decision
crucial and alone
for those of us who cannot indulge
the passing dreams of choice
who love in doorways coming and going
in the hours between dawns
looking inward and outward
at once before and after
seeking a now that can breed
futures
like bread in our children's mouths
so their dreams will not reflect
the death of ours;
For those of us
who were imprinted with fear
like a faint line in the center of our foreheads
learning to be afraid with our mother's milk
for by this weapon
this illusion of some safety to be found
the heavy-footed hoped to silence us
For all of us
this instant and this triumph
We were never meant to survive.
And when the sun rises we are afraid
it might not remain
when the sun sets we are afraid
it might not rise in the morning
when our stomachs are full we are afraid
of indigestion
when our stomachs are empty we are afraid
we may never eat again
when we are loved we are afraid
love will vanish

when we are alone we are afraid
love will never return
and when we speak we are afraid
our words will not be heard
nor welcomed
but when we are silent
we are still afraid.
So it is better to speak
remembering
we were never meant to survive.

Movies of the Reader's Mind While Reading Audre Lorde's "A Litany for Survival"

Alexander Jackson

When reading the first quarter of this poem I caught the image of a rock shoreline. The words that stuck out the most were "doorways," "futures," and "bread in our children's mouths." That last phrase conjured images of small kids gagged with bread. The overall feeling I got was isolation. I felt this loneliness as a result of the barren and weird images given.

These images made me hear music. I can almost hear Pink Floyd's "The Wall." I felt Lorde's sense of the bleakness of the future. I wanted to disagree. I don't think it's necessarily like this. I think the future is what we make it.

Still, I like the poetry a lot. I like the no-rhyme. It doesn't need rhyme. I like how she gives emphasis to particular words by how she puts them in short lines.

The second stanza felt oppressive to me because it uses imagery of fear and being beaten. The words "mother's milk" and "weapon" stuck out the most in my mind. The ideas of fear and the image of marching boots helped to make me think some authoritative force was repressing me.

She draws me in. I'm not outside, I'm part of it. It's so depressing. I want to say No, it's not true, it's not an illusion of safety, you are safe, you are a baby.

The next stanza keeps holding me to the idea of fear, but elevates the fear to terror. It says we cannot overcome the force of fear. It implies that we are afraid no matter what. In the end it says "we are still afraid," but I'm not sure what we are afraid of. But now I think, "we ARE afraid." Everyone feels it. Fear of what is to come. We don't know.

I'm still hearing Pink Floyd. Almost a marching beat; structured; it marches.

The last stanza is about remembering. The feeling is overcoming your fears. I feel the words strongly: "So it is better to speak remembering that we were never meant to survive."

I feel "remembering" especially—because of how she has it alone on one line.

This is almost the antithesis of everything that's come before. I feel some elation. Let it out. Forget the crap in your life, forget the stupid things, just let it out. I feel catharsis.

As I think back, I notice how much I resisted, but then she brings me along—she brings me through a progression of thinking.

The whole progression of this piece is about being born, learning to fear, and in the end overcoming that fear. It could be a metaphor for life. However, it is all written in the plural form. The idea is that Audre Lorde is trying to teach us to overcome the fears that we have learned as we grew up.

A Litany (With Thanks to Audre Lorde)

Alexander Jackson

For those of us who stare into the morning sun
blinded by silence
The enormous glowing ball slipping slowly over the shoreline
fills our eyes like bread in the children's mouths
For those of us who speak but don't listen
opening the doorways to our minds but shutting the windows to our
hearts
looking outward
For those of us who remember
For all of us who forget
wrinkling our brows in concentration
When will we forget
When will we remember
When will we speak
When will we listen
When will our stomachs be full
When will our eyes be open
But the sun sets
so we sleep again.

The Writer

Richard Wilbur

Richard Wilbur (b. 1921), a Pulitzer Prize-winning poet and former Poet Laureate of the United States, is also a translator, a teacher, a Broadway lyricist, a critic, an editor, and an author of children's books.

In her room at the prow of the house
Where light breaks, and the windows are tossed with linden,
My daughter is writing a story.

I pause in the stairwell, hearing
From her shut door a commotion of typewriter-keys
Like a chain hauled over a gunwale.

Young as she is, the stuff
Of her life is a great cargo, and some of it heavy:
I wish her a lucky passage.

But now it is she who pauses,
As if to reject my thought and its easy figure.
A stillness greatens, in which

The whole house seems to be thinking,
And then she is at it again with a bunched clamor
Of strokes, and again is silent.

I remember the dazed starling
Which was trapped in that very room, two years ago;
How we stole in, lifted a sash

And retreated, not to affright it;
And how for a helpless hour, through the crack of the door,
We watched the sleek, wild, dark

And iridescent creature
Batter against the brilliance, drop like a glove
To the hard floor, or the desk-top,

And wait then, humped and bloody,
For the wits to try it again; and how our spirits
Rose when, suddenly sure,

It lifted off from a chair-back,
Beating a smooth course for the right window
And clearing the sill of the world.

It is always a matter, my darling,
Of life or death, as I had forgotten. I wish
What I wished you before, but harder.

Response to "The Writer": Movies of the Mind While Reading

Elijah Goodwin

[Written after reading only the first quarter of the poem.] The sea imagery gives the act of writing power. I feel as though his daughter is writing something passionate. I almost picture a ship in a storm or a ship crashing through large waves. She is adventuring and exploring through her writing. What she is writing is something that she believes in, is excited about, rather than an assignment or the like. The chain hauled over the gunwale represents the lifting of her mental anchor as she is free to write. It represents freedom of ideas and creativity. She has let go of the anchor that holds back the creativity.

[Written after reading only the second quarter of the poem.] Each moment in life is important and can be very incredible. Even though she is young, she has had a lot of experiences, good and bad, and she carries them with her. It is possible for a young person to have a more incredible meaningful life than an old person. Sometimes I feel that way myself. That if I died tomorrow, I would die contented, knowing I have lived a full life.

[After reading almost to the end of the poem.] It keeps reminding me of the subject that I have been thinking of, the struggle to live freely. We will continue to batter ourselves against the walls as the bird continues to struggle to make the wrong choices and to recover and try again. And perhaps we may make it to the freedom of flight before we hit that wall or window one too many times. To find that entry into the wide open.

[After finishing the poem.] The romance of the ocean has always held a place in my heart. When I was young and even now, I travel to the ocean often, so I reacted right away because of the powerful effect the ocean imagery had on me. Lately I have been almost obsessed with the idea of being free and exploring. Being open to experiences, opening my mind, taking my body to its physical limits. I have been looking for the ultimate sensory and mental overload. To experience things so purely that you threaten to just burn out. And this is the angle I approached this poem with. I pictured the girl freeing her mind from pre-conceived ideas and pressures and the blocks of society. It was easier for me to react to the poem in pieces than as a whole. It is because of the way I think. Quick, fleeting, powerful images, glimpses through a window at high speed. It is not a matter of attention span; it's just that simple is more powerful.

Response to "The Writer": Movies of the Mind While Reading

Tassie Walsh

The first thing I do is picture the scene. At first I imagine a young girl, but as I am told she types, I picture her to be a teenager in high school. She has a sunny room with her window open and the lace curtains blowing. It is late afternoon in the late spring or early summer. Her room has old teddy bears, mirrors, and pictures.

Her father is middle aged. He wears slacks and a shirt and a sweater without sleeves. The stairwell goes up then turns left. The stairs are carpeted beige and there are old family pictures on the wall going up.

I don't want to be here [at school]. I want to be in my sunny room. I want my home. I want warmth. I want my room. I want my bears and my mirrors and pictures. I want my dad to be interested in what I am doing.

It is about a wish for life. He wants his daughter to fly. He wants her to keep trying. It will be hard, she will fall, but he wishes her a lucky passage.

Collage Dialogue on "The Writer"

Barbara Hales and Julie Nelson

The father is proud of his daughter who has chosen the solitude of her room to write a story. He's curious and thinks she's too young to be interested in writing. She's excited, can't sleep and started writing even before the dawn arrived. She doesn't want to be disturbed and has sent the message out to her world by shutting the door. The keys continue at a steady pace. She's driven to get her thoughts and feelings onto the paper. The father stops by her door to listen. He continues to wonder what could possibly entice her from sleep at that early hour.

ALL THIS NOISE OF CHAINS!
WHY CAN'T HE GET ON WITH HIS OWN THING AND STOP FUSSING ABOUT HIS DAUGHTER.
I SENSE HIM THERE—OUTSIDE THE DOOR—
I WANT TO BASH HIS FACE IN.

Her struggle for freedom reminds him of the day they together witnessed the hurt and fear of a starling caught in that very room. They assisted only by raising the sash and staying present to send their healing energy to the bloody bird. They were delighted to watch it regain its strength and fly to freedom.

YUCK
"HUMPED AND BLOODY"—COME ON, IT WOULD DIE OF SHOCK IF IT WAS THAT BADLY OFF.
HOW ABOUT FATHER OWNING HIS OWN FEELINGS. HE IS ASSUMING THIS STRUGGLE IN HIS DAUGHTER—IT MAY OR MAY NOT BE TRUE.
THIS ASSUMPTION ANNOYS ME.
I IDENTIFY WITH THE DAUGHTER WHO WOULD BE FURIOUS IF SHE SENSED HER FATHER HOVERING OUTSIDE THE DOOR AND WOULDN'T BE ABLE TO WRITE.

Life will present traumas—even small things will sometimes feel like a matter of life or death. The father would like to protect her from the harshness and pain of life's experiences. But from the wisdom of his years, he knows wishing her a lucky passage is all we can ever do for another person.

. . . *the concerned, supportive parent.* . . .
. . . *the child fighting, albeit prematurely, for her independence.* . . .
. . . *the eternal "generation gap".* . . .
. . . *the eternal parent/child dynamic.* . . .

Some Thoughts about "The Writer" on the Occasion of the Death of Isaac Bashevis Singer

Laura Wenk

I read the poem "The Writer" by Richard Wilbur just after hearing of the death of the great Yiddish writer, Isaac Bashevis Singer. My interpretation of the poem is wound around the feelings I had at that moment.

For me the poem is about the ways that, while the young and old cannot always truly communicate—cannot be fully in each other's worlds—there can be a knowing. There can be a true, felt sense about each other's lives that can be gratifying, that can fill our hearts and give us hope. So, it is a poem about connections, although imperfect ones. As such, it is also a poem about being able to let go and feel oneself as separate.

The father in the poem had given as much as he could to his daughter. He had helped her build a solid sense of self and let her follow her own heart. To my mind this means that, among other things, he must have given her a sense of the past—of who she is as understood by what has happened to those who came before her. For growth and understanding of self is connected to understanding one's parents, and them their own parents—so a chain is built.

In reading this poem, I became the daughter. Isaac Bashevis Singer became the father. He stood watching through the door along with other people who have been important in creating an atmosphere in which I could grow to be a strong, independent person. I sat inside typing, secure enough in my past to feel the turbulence of the present and dream of the future.

Even though I must do my own writing, I want to know that I am not entirely alone. I want to know that there are people near me—people who have come before and will come after—who are thinking clearly and acting out of a place of conscience.

I want to feel a thread running from the past to the knot where I hold it and onward into the future. I want this thread to sometimes become a live wire. There have been people who can turn on the current for me. They tell me that, while I, like the starling in Wilbur's poem, must find my way through that window alone, they have opened the window wider for me and will watch my flight through it.

There have been writers, like I. B. Singer, who have helped make the world of my grandmothers real to me—that have let me look back through that window to understand just how I got into this room to begin with. There have also been family members, friends, and political activists whose presence, stories, and work have strengthened my understandings, and made solid the ground on which I walk. I mourn the death of each living link to this rich past, and worry that in their absence the looking back will become impossible—the thread will be severed.

My grandmothers formed another link to a much more personal history—a family history. Each in her own way helped me to see patterns woven by the threads of their sisters and brothers, parents and grandparents. They wove a nest from which it was safe for me to venture outward—no matter how tentative my starts.

I don't think I will ever understand how my grandmothers found the strength to test their own wings in an air so filled with blood—so many losses. What lampposts lit their way through pogroms and gas chambers? How did they manage to trust that I could have a "lucky passage"?

Elsie, you were brave to open a window for me that you were too frightened to look out yourself.

Gerti, I still plant columbine and violets for you, and the smell of linden brings me to your side.

Quiet Until the Thaw*

From the Cree Indians

Her name tells of how
it was with her.
The truth is she did not speak
in winter.
Everyone learned not to
ask her questions in winter
once this was known about her.
The first winter this happened
we looked in her mouth to see

* This and the following are Cree Indian "naming poems." You can write a naming poem for yourself or someone else. It might help you get going to borrow the first line, "His/her name tells of how it was with him/her." (You can drop it later.)

if something was frozen. Her tongue
maybe, or something else in there.
But after the thaw she spoke again
and told us it was fine for her that way.
So each spring we looked forward to that.

Rain Straight Down

From the Cree Indians

For a long time we thought this boy
loved only things that fell
straight down. He didn't seem to care
about anything else.
We were afraid he could only HEAR
things that fell straight down!
We watched him stand outside
in rain. Later it was said
he put a tiny pond of rainwater
in his wife's ear
while she slept, and leaned over
to listen to it.
I remember he was happiest talking
about all the kinds of rain.
The kind that comes off herons' wings
when they fly up from a lake. I know
he wanted some of the heron rain
for his wife's ear too!
He walked out in spring to watch
the young girls rub wild onion under their eyes
until tears came out.
He knew a name for that rain too.
Sad onion rain.
That rain fell straight down
too, off their faces
and he saw it.

I Am Sorrow

Sindy Cheung*

Who will listen to my feeling?
Who will listen to a useless land?
After the war, my skin has been damaged,
There are craters in my body.
Although I was sad, sorry, and suffering
  Who will listen to my feeling?
I am sad, sorrow, and suffering
  Who will know my feeling?
I am not sad about my harmed body.
I am sorrow because of the people, who can't use me rightly.
Who will know my feeling?

Wishing in the Dark

Bi Chen†

Looking out of the window,
A maze of eyes I see,
They are little
Yet,
So bright. Each reveals
Thoughts that sneak through the mind
Leaving behind
An unknown face.

"I am sorrow,"
That voice of yours I heard.
Looking up to search,
I found nothing
But endless shiny stars.
Are they not gorgeous?
Are they not amazing?
Are they not
The brothers of life?

Sitting here miles away from you,
Holding the heart of yours
In the hands of mine,
Begging the stars
To take your sorrow away.

---

* When she wrote this poem, Sindy Cheung was a high-school-age "boat person" from Vietnam living in a refugee camp in Hong Kong.

†Bi Chen was an eleventh grader in San Jose, California, when he wrote "Wishing in the Dark" in response to Sindy Cheung's "I Am Sorrow."

May you have to face
No more sorrow,
I pray.
Search for the brightest star
In the dark.
There, you will find
My warmest blessing.

Text Analysis through Examining Figurative Language

Essential Premises

- Metaphors and other kinds of figurative language represent language at its most creative or generative.
- If we locate the metaphors and imagery in any poem or story, we almost always find places where the most central meanings are being born.
- If we simply write about the metaphors and imagery that we connect with most in a poem or story, we can usually find a good way to zero in on what's important in the work and what's important in our response to it.

Main Assignment Preview

Since there are a number of sections on analyzing texts in this book, you've probably tried at least one approach already. Our aim in presenting these various approaches is to expand your options when you're asked to analyze a text.

In this workshop we specifically want to help you see the value of focusing on figurative language: metaphor, simile, image, and symbol. Figurative language usually reveals what is *implied* in a text rather than what is *said.* In addition, figurative language is usually a center of intensified energy and meaning in a text. You've undoubtedly focused on figures of speech in your English classes as a way of getting closer to the meaning of fiction or poetry. But looking at figurative language can also help you analyze expository writing such as essays and editorials. All this close examination of texts should make you more consciously aware of how words and phrases carry secondary as well as primary meaning.

Your assignment for this workshop is to write an analysis of a text based on its figurative language. Before we describe more specifically how to do that, we're going to talk a bit about figurative language itself to give you some background for your analysis.

Figurative Language

Metaphor

Metaphor is the most basic or universal kind of figurative language. A metaphor is a word or phrase used (to put it bluntly) "wrong" but on purpose—used in something other than its normal or usual fashion, and used not literally but figuratively. If we say, "The farmer *plowed* the field," "plowed" is literal. But if we say, "The student *plowed* through his homework," "plowed" is figurative. To use a word metaphorically awakens us to new possibilities of meaning. By saying that the student "plowed" through homework, the speaker forces us to realize that "plowing" cannot mean what farmers do in the fields. Therefore, we are forced to create or remember a sense of plow that *fits* the sentence. ("Oh, I guess he went through his homework slowly, methodically, and persistently.") We have probably heard the word "plow" in this metaphorical sense before so that we can't feel much "wrongness." We don't have to ask ourselves directly, "Let's see; what can you do to homework that is like what a farmer does to a field?" This is a tired metaphor and it doesn't waken us to many new possibilities of meaning.

When we hear a metaphor we've never heard before, however, we are forced to forge new meaning. "In her room at the prow of the house . . ." writes Richard Wilbur in his poem "The Writer," printed in the "Readings" section of Workshop 13. Most of us probably haven't heard this metaphor before. This use of "prow" asks us to see a house in a new way—as a ship—and to sense one room as somehow forging forward. But the usage is not *so* odd and the meaning not so new because we have probably heard "prow" used metaphorically for various things besides ships, if not for houses.

We have to work harder to make new meaning in these lines by Dylan Thomas in "Poem in October" about his 30th birthday:

> I rose
> In rainy autumn
> And walked abroad in a shower of all my days

The "shower of all my days" metaphor is so "wrong" that it's hard to interpret. Our hunch (given the context) is that the poet is inviting us to feel something about walking in a light rain in October as also causing us to feel and remember our past days.

If we keep talking about people "plowing through" things, we will someday cease to experience that use of "plow" as a metaphor. We will call it literal, just as we probably experience "She *upset* me by being late for dinner" as equally literal with "He *upset* the glass of wine at dinner." When the time comes that the metaphorical meaning becomes literal, we will say that "plow" means "to push methodically and persistently through something"—a meaning just as literal as what farmers do to fields.

Though we can usually tell the difference between what is literal and metaphorical, there is no hard-and-fast way to decide in a fuzzy case—in the case of a metaphor that is so common that we can't decide whether to call it literal. Many of our literal meanings started out as metaphorical.

Whether a word is metaphorical depends on whether people experience that usage as metaphorical—was there any "wrongness" or blockage of meaning? Consider "leg of a table." Is "leg" a metaphor or not? Probably not for most of us, but if you feel "leg" as a word that applies only to living beings, not tables, then you will feel a wrongness that gives the word a metaphorical force. (In the Victorian period, people sometimes put skirts on tables to cover their legs, showing that they experienced the animal or human connotations of legs.) So we call it a metaphor whether the meaning is obvious as with "plow through homework" or more obscure as with "shower of my days." In both cases a word is being used wrongly in order to bring in new meaning.

Simile

We move from metaphor to simile when we use "like," "as," "seems"—or some similar word—to signal a comparison. Thus we can change Wilbur's metaphor to a simile by saying, "Her room, *like* the prow of a ship . . ." In one sense the difference between metaphors and similes is trivial, just a matter of sticking in a "like" or an "as." But it's interesting to note that deep down, metaphors and similes represent different orientations to reality. Metaphors insist on bending reality or telling lies, and thus in a sense represent magical thinking: Houses have no prow. Similes refuse to bend reality; they insist on being literal. They say only that the room *resembles* a prow or makes us think of a prow. Metaphors can thus be said to represent a different and more metaphysical view of reality.

Exploring the Writing Process

Why I Am Not a Painter

I am not a painter, I am a poet.
Why? I think I would rather be
a painter, but I am not. Well,
for instance, Mike Goldberg
is starting a painting. I drop in.
"Sit down and have a drink" he
says. I drink; we drink. I look
up. "You have SARDINES in it."
"Yes, it needed something there."
"Oh." I go and the days go by
and I drop in again. The painting
is going on, and I go, and the days
go by. I drop in. The painting is
finished. "Where's SARDINES?"
All that's left is just
letters, "It was too much," Mike says.

But me? One day I am thinking of
a color: orange. I write a line
about orange. Pretty soon it is a
whole page of words, not lines.
Then another page. There should be
so much more, not of orange, of
words, of how terrible orange is
and life. Days go by. It is even in
prose, I am a real poet. My poem
is finished and I haven't mentioned
orange yet. It's twelve poems, I call
it ORANGES. And one day in a gallery
I see Mike's painting, called SARDINES.

Frank O'Hara

When we meet them in the flesh, however, metaphors and similes often don't function so very differently; similes can be just as startling or resonant, even magical, as metaphors: "I was like a tree in which there are three blackbirds," Wallace Stevens wrote in "Thirteen Ways of Looking at a Blackbird."

Image

Images need not be metaphors or similes at all; they need not involve any comparison or anything figurative. Images are simply picture-words—words that set something before our eyes. However, so frequently do metaphors and similes carry picture-words or images that critics often use the word "imagery" when they mean "metaphors, similes, and images." Critics say, "Let's look at the imagery of this poem," and they mean all the figures.

Here is some rich imagery that contains no metaphor or simile—nothing is compared to anything:

> We stacked the bales up clean
> To splintery redwood rafters
> High in the dark, flecks of alfalfa
> Whirling through the shingle-cracks of light
> Itch of haydust in the sweaty shirt and shoes
>
> —from "Hay for the Horses" by Gary Snyder

Snyder gives us not only pictures for the eye, but even tries to make us feel itchy and sweaty feelings on our skin. Images can also appeal to the ear—"grasshoppers crackling in the weeds"—indeed to any sense. This rich imagistic poem, which has virtually no metaphor or simile, is printed in its entirety in the "Readings" for this chapter.

The distinguishing mark of an image is that it appeals to our senses, not just our minds. It's a showing, not just a telling—a re-creating of something palpable, not just a naming or explaining. Here too, of course, there is no firm dividing line between something shown and something told. Thus the following three phrases would probably not count as images for most people because they are scarcely more than naming:

> the notes of bells, the sounds of musical instruments, the noises of wind, sea, and rain. . . .

Exploring the Writing Process

The idea started as the oyster starts or the snail to secrete a house for itself. And this it did without any conscious direction. The little note book in which an attempt was made to forecast a plan was soon abandoned, and the book grew day by day, week by week, without any plan at all, except that which was dictated each morning in the act of writing.

Virginia Woolf

But you could argue that they are small images. Dylan Thomas continues his list, however, with three more items which, though short, are so artfully phrased as to bring a sound to almost any reader and thus make us count them as strong images:

> the rattle of milkcarts, the clopping of hooves on cobbles, the fingering of branches on a window pane. . .

Let's look at Thomas's whole sentence—a long singing one—and notice how it combines the three figures we've talked about: image, simile, and metaphor. The whole thing is an extended simile or comparison. Many of the compared items are images, and one of those images contains a metaphor, "fingering of branches." (He is speaking of his childhood experiences while reading.)

> And these words were, to me, as the notes of bells, the sounds of musical instruments, the noises of wind, sea, and rain, the rattle of milkcarts, the clopping of hooves on cobbles, the fingering of branches on a window pane, might be to someone, deaf from birth, who has miraculously found his hearing.

Symbol

The symbol is a word or phrase that *stands for* ("symbolizes") something. It conveys a comparison but doesn't state it; it only *implies* a comparison. Thus a symbol gives us a comparison between *x* and *y* but only gives us *x*. The symbol symbolizes by virtue of *resembling or partaking of* what it stands for. Thus the circle has often been a symbol of infinity or perfection, the rose a symbol of beauty or of the Virgin Mary, the sun a symbol of reason. The symbol is inherently more mystical than the metaphor or simile: It resonates with the life and significance of what it symbolizes. It contains the juice of something other than itself.

If we have a piece of writing where circles turn up frequently—not in metaphors but in literal description (for example, a dream poem where birds fly in perfect circles), and if we feel that the way the writer uses these circling birds is somehow *loaded* or *resonant*—so that the writing seems to point beyond mere birds flying in circles—then we could say that these descriptions are functioning as symbols. Then we can ask ourselves what their symbolic meaning might be. Perhaps we would conclude that they symbolize perfection. Remember, however, that symbols do not carry automatic symbolic meanings that you can look up in a dictionary. Admittedly there are dictionaries of symbols or of dream symbols, but you shouldn't trust them. They tell only what some alleged authority pronounces the symbol to mean; for example, whenever you dream of bread or houses you are dreaming of your mother. Sometimes yes, sometimes no. It depends on how symbols are used. Symbols give us a good glimpse of the values that a culture takes for granted. When Malcolm X looked up "black" in the dictionary, he noticed how it was taken to symbolize what is evil or inferior. And things that are soft, yielding, and passive have tended to symbolize women.

The Wallace Stevens poem that we quoted in the section on similes opens with what some readers might call a symbol:

Among twenty snowy mountains
The only moving thing
Was the eye of the blackbird.

Or later in the poem:

The river is moving.
The blackbird must be flying.

Others might say there are no symbols here, merely evocative literal statements. Such arguments cannot be settled conclusively. The key is whether we sense a word or phrase *standing for* or *symbolizing* something—and doing so not arbitrarily but by virtue of its own nature and the way it relates to its linguistic context. Once we sense the words being used in this way, we try to get at what they stand for or symbolize.

It's usually a mistake to try to translate a symbol. It makes more sense to talk about symbols causing additional meanings to *hover over* a text. For example, the moving river linked to the flying blackbird might imply or symbolize change being everywhere and all changes somehow linked to each other. But this is arguable. Not all readers are going to agree about whether any passage is resonant with implied meaning. And even if they agree that the language is being used symbolically, they will often disagree about what the symbol means. For this reason—and because we are sometimes asked by teachers to agree about symbolism that seems far fetched to us—people sometimes conclude that "symbolism is just English teacher baloney." Yet it's undeniable that we are all users of symbols. We all dream every night and when we can remember a dream, we almost always feel that some elements of it carry extra unstated meanings.

Main Assignment: *Analyzing a Text by Focusing on Figurative Language*

What follows is a somewhat schematized procedure for writing an analysis of a text. We suggest these steps because writing analysis is difficult, and there is a particular danger of jumping too soon to conclusions without examining enough evidence from the text. The power of the following steps for exploratory writing is that they force you to do the bulk of your writing *before* figuring out what your main points are or how you will organize your final essay. When you do this noticing and exploring before you stop to work out what it all means, that working out is almost invariably more interesting and intelligent. It builds on richer thinking. (Be sure to do your exploratory writing on only one side of the paper so that you can cut and paste later.)*

This process is intended to help you with two goals that often seem to be at odds: to pay close attention to the language of the text you are analyzing, but

*We are indebted to the Bard Institute for Writing and Thinking for help in working out this approach to analyzing a text.

also to relate what you see to your own experience and values—to build bridges between the text and yourself.

Reading the Text

Read the text you want to analyze at least twice. Try to read it with pleasure but also with care. Don't worry about analyzing it now, just *immerse* yourself in it as much as you can. At this stage the goal is not "figuring out" but *noticing.* Best of all is to read it out loud; try out a few variations and hear others try a few different readings.

Writing a Draft

1. Put the text aside and list the figurative words, phrases, or passages that come to you as memorable, important, or intriguing. Don't worry about whether these are really figurative or about what kind of figurative language they might be. Simply list words or passages that seem especially *alive.* More often than not they will have figurative language.
2. Circle three or four phrases or passages that somehow seem the *most* important or intriguing.
3. Choose one that is most interesting to you. Briefly describe it and go on writing about it—as much as you can. Relate it to other parts of the piece but also be sure to relate it to your own experience, memories, or values. What does it make you remember or think of? How do you find yourself reacting to this passage? (You might want to look at the text again.)
4. To end this piece of writing, simply decide on the main thing you want to say about this passage.
5. Now go through steps 3 and 4 for the other phrases or passages you circled.

Exploring the Writing Process

Stories tend to appear to me, not as formal ideas, but as metaphors, and these metaphors seem to demand structures of their own: they seem to have an internal need for a certain form. [*Questioner: Can you say something more about these metaphors that your fiction grows out of?*] They're the germ, the thought, the image, the idea, out of which all the rest grows. They're always a bit elusive, involving thoughts, feelings, abstractions, visual material, all at once. I suppose they're a little like dream fragments, in that such fragments always contain, if you analyze them, so much more than at first you suspect. But they're not literally that—I never write from dreams. All these ideas come to me in the full light of day. Some, when you pry them open, have too little inside to work with. Others are unexpectedly fat and rich. Novels typically begin for me as very tiny stories or little one-act play ideas which I think at the time aren't going to fill three pages. Then slowly the hidden complexities reveal themselves.

Robert Coover

6. Reread the whole text and then write about what these three or four phrases or passages have in common. What do they tell you about the text? How could you relate them to your own experience?
7. Write also about what these passages do *not* have in common. Are there other passages in the piece that seem interesting to you now or to call for attention? How does your experience seem different or contradictory to the piece? In effect, this step asks you to write about what is puzzling or doesn't seem to fit what you wrote before. (It always helps our thinking to pay attention to what is not neat and tidy.)
8. Now read or think back over what you have written and do some "So what?" writing. Figure out the main thing you want to say about how this text works: how it works in itself and how it works on you.

It helps to go through these activities in a class or workshop with others, not only for the encouragement and company but so that at various points you can share some of what you've written and hear what others have written.

Revising

Now you have already produced the makings or ingredients of a draft of an analytic essay. To revise, we suggest these steps:

- Look back over the text. Read it aloud again to see if you hear it any differently now.
- Look back over what you have written.
- Make up your mind now about what you really want to have for your main point. (Perhaps you've already done this in step 8.) In truth, there are good published works of literary analysis that consist of nothing but a succession of good but unconnected observations or insights. But most critics and teachers feel that you don't have a critical essay unless you reach some conclusion that ties together most of those smaller points.
- In the light of your main point, cut and paste the better parts of what you've already written into the order that makes the most sense.
- Now read over your cut-and-paste draft and wrestle with it to get it the way you want. Perhaps you'll only need to change words and phrases to make it clearer and to move a few parts around. But you may find you have to make major structural changes—and perhaps even change your mind about what you are saying.

Sharing and Responding

If you share a piece of first-stage writing—such as the writing you produced during the eight steps—look for feedback that carries your thinking forward: "Pointing and Center of Gravity" and "Summary and Sayback" in "Sharing and Responding" may help you see more clearly what you said and almost said in your early draft. The following questions will help too.

- Does my draft reach a conclusion, or is it just a collection of insights? If I have no conclusion, get me to talk until I find one, or tell me some points you hear implied.
- Do I manage to make you see the text as I do? Is my analysis convincing to you? What parts or aspects of the text do you feel I don't pay enough attention to?

Process Journal

- Was your reading of a text changed because you knew you'd have to analyze it or write about it? If so, what was gained? what was lost?
- Did our sequence of steps help or get in your way?
- Did the words and phrases that came to your attention seem to be figurative language? If not, what kinds of things made the language memorable or interesting?
- Were you able to pay close attention to the language of the text and still relate the text to your own experience or values?

Exploring Theory: *Figurative Language as a Window on the Mind*

People often believe that "regular language" says what it means while literature (especially poetry) has "hidden meanings" that only teachers and critics can find by some mysterious process. This is an unhelpful view of language because "regular texts" aren't so regular, and literary texts aren't so odd or unregular.

If you think that figurative language occurs only in literature, you've been misled by the fact that people may *talk* about it most in the study of literature. Figurative language is universal. Listen closely to any extended conversation. Better yet, record it so you can really examine the language. You'll find many metaphors, similes, and images in the words people speak as they go about their lives. You'll probably find even more in sports writing and political speeches. Slang is peppered (note the metaphor) with figurative language.

Figurative language appeals to the mind at a deep level, perhaps for many reasons. When figurative language tells us what something is *like* rather than what it is, it's taking a path that is natural for the mind. It's in the nature of the mind to see things as *like* other things or standing for other things. Indeed that's how we *do* see. It's virtually impossible to see any chair exactly in its uniqueness; we tend to see it as an instance of *chair.* To think is to use concepts or categories, but that means clumping things together as "the same" when they are not really the same. (Read Lakoff and Johnson in the "Readings" for this workshop on how metaphor permeates our language and thinking.)

So the distinction between metaphorical and literal language becomes problematic. Literal language is a lens, and it distorts—like any lens. But we are so used to literal language that we think it is clear glass. Literal language is nothing but a lens that we don't notice anymore. Although we are used to literal language, most of us realize deep down that distortion is going on. We know there are things we aren't seeing—or saying—with the common lens, and that if we tried out other lenses, we'd see some new things. Most of us feel that we can't say things just as they are with our literal or regular language. Words don't ever seem to get at what we are trying to say with complete accuracy; there is always some slippage. So we all have the impulse to find other words (or other media) to capture things we cannot say quite right; we find ourselves calling things by the "wrong name" because we can sometimes feel that wrong name getting at what is important. "Your knees are a southern breeze—or a gust of snow," wrote William Carlos Williams ("Portrait of a Lady"), trying to get closer to what he saw and felt than he could manage with "regular" literal language.

We cannot make up *new* words; no one will understand them. But we can use the old words in new ways, and that does bring out aspects of our experience that we cannot capture otherwise. A new lens brings new distortions, but it helps us notice what we didn't notice with the old lens. Thus we all use metaphors to make sense of things that are hard to make sense of.

And why images? If we see something that is powerful or important (or hear it or touch it), we have the impulse to put our experience into words for ourselves and to tell others. We see this phenomenon most clearly when someone has been in a terrible accident or has experienced something frightening: He has an impulse to tell about it again and again. The same is true if something wonderful happens:

> "Did I tell you about what happened at third base? The ball bounced out of Schmitt's mitt and into the catcher's. You should have seen the look. . ."
>
> "Yes, you've already told me three times."

The truth is we all need to talk about what is important—and tell it again and again. The telling helps us digest and make sense of our experience.

Thus if we hear the metaphors and images in the conversation of a friend, we'll usually find the most interesting places, the places where his mind *reveals itself* the most. If these are new metaphors—metaphors he created (and people do it all the time)—they will represent the making of new meaning: places where he wasn't satisfied with the regular use of words, usually places where his mind is the most in touch with what he wants to say.

If they are *used* metaphors—metaphors he found handy—they will represent places where you usually get the quickest and surest picture of the attitudes that he lives inside of—the meanings that shape his mind. For example, if someone says he "scored a touchdown on the physics exam" (or that he "scored" last night on a date), he is showing that at some level he thinks of school and dating as competitive games, where the object is to win. To notice the metaphors in someone's language is to notice the keys to how he understands the world.

If you find the places where someone lingers for a moment over a detail and gives a bit of an image for it—where he doesn't say he went to a restaurant but tells how the candles looked or how the waiter spoke—you can find some of the experience that the person probably felt the most and considered the most important.

Passages of figurative language often have the strongest effect on listeners. If someone tells you, "For me, playing music is like flying over snow-capped mountains," this probably affects you more than if he said something literal like, "I am utterly involved in the excitement of playing music."

We are taking here a *cognitive* and *functional* approach to figurative language, not a *decorative* approach. That is, some critics talk as though figurative language is important because it "beautifies" thought. Some venerable theorists of poetry say that the poet first finds her idea and then "clothes it" in "rich fabric" or in the "colors of rhetoric"—meaning figurative language. Though some writers work that way—and all of us sometimes stop and search for a colorful word when we want to dress up something we are saying—figurative language is much better understood as reflecting the way the mind works.

This is why we suggest that the quickest way to get to the heart of what's interesting and important in a conversation—or in a political speech, an advertisement, a story, novel, or poem—is to look at the figurative language.

My Mother, That Feast of Light

Kate Barnes

Kate Barnes (b. 1932) is the poet laureate of Maine. Barnes lives on a farm in Appleton, Maine. Her collected poems, Where the Deer Were, *was published in 1994; her latest volume is* Crossing the Field *(1996).*

My mother, that feast of light, has always sat down,
Composed herself, and written poetry, hardly
Reworking any, just the way she used to
Tell us that Chinese painters painted; first they
Sat for days on the hillside watching the rabbits,
Then they went home, they set out ink and paper,
Meditated; and only then picked up their brushes
To catch the lift of a rabbit in mid-hop.

"If it didn't come out I would throw it away."
Oh, she
Is still a bird that fills a bush with singing.
The way that she lifts her tea cup, the look she gives you
As you sit across from her, it is all a kind
Of essential music.
I also remember my father
Alone at the dining-room table, the ink bottle safe
In a bowl, his orange-red fountain pen in his big
Hand. The hand moved slowly back and forth
And the floor below was white with sheets of paper
Each carrying a rejected phrase or two
As he struggled all morning to finish just one sentence—
Like a smith hammering thick and glowing iron,
Like Jacob wrestling with the wonderful angel.

My Mother, That Beast of Blight

Amber Moltenbrey

The three pieces that I have picked out from the poem "My Mother, That Feast of Light" all relate together in the image of a story. The story begins to unravel with the line "If it didn't come out I would throw it away." This sentence brings the introduction of the mother, that beast of blight. I imagine the mother in the poem as a bottomless well of words, which she forms together to produce a feast of interesting phrases—only, at the completion of a piece, to cast it aside as a reject of her own senses, a work that she has no desire to keep.

The sentence "I also remember my father/Alone at the dining room table . . ." brings to me a feeling of sorrow or pity, and leads me to side with the father in this tale of literary unrest. The father in the story is what starts my mind rolling. I do not see the father as a poet, or anything close to one, for that matter. I see him as a struggling businessman, trying to manage the farm efficiently, as he writes a letter to the local bank explaining a late payment.

In the line "As he struggled all morning to finish just one sentence. . ." the father seems to be performing a chore rather than a pleasant ritual. It is here that I see the father resenting the mother for her writing ability; and her, a blight to all of his efforts. This becomes the plot-thickening ingredient in the poem.

In the story I see the mother as very well respected by her children, writing poetry when the mood strikes her, only to abandon it as something she had never written. I see the father as a one-man-band in the family. The piece of the poem that states "the look she gives you/As you sit across from her [. . .]" makes me wonder why no one sits across from the father as he writes. Maybe a boost of confidence is all that is needed for the father to complete a piece of writing successfully. It seems it is a wondrous occasion when the mother writes (and only then to throw it away), but when the father writes it is a thankless task "to finish just one sentence [. . .]." It is as though the father has no one to stand by him, no one to share his problem with, no one there to offer help. I feel that the father has been left out of a family secret, or something special that the whole family should share.

The story in my mind leads me to think about the literary unrest that occurs in the poem. The mother, having seemingly no problems producing a piece of writing, and the father struggling to construct a respectable sentence, create a symbolic contrast that gives the poem an added feature. This twist makes the story more intriguing and leads the reader to dig deeper into the meaning of the poem.

The aspects that have been neglected by my story are the ones that might prove that the mother has any sensitivity. The story of the Chinese painters gives a hint of sentimentality that I don't care to relate in my story, although it may very well be an important part of someone else's interpretation. Jacob wrestling the "wonderful" angel is not incorporated in my story either because of the "wonderfulness" of it. I don't see the children of the family ever relating their father to something "wonderful."

The effect of this piece of poetry has hit me like few others. I find it difficult to read and comprehend an average poem. This poem worked because of the many images that focused in my mind. Not only the ones I have written about, but other images that I didn't have time to develop. The figurative language in the poem adds color to the story. I also believe that the author leaves room for many interpretations in the poem by using the different methods of figurative language.

Writing Styles in "My Mother, That Feast of Light"

Karen Daley

The poem "My Mother, That Feast of Light" by Kate Barnes is a comparison between two very different writing styles. Barnes poetically describes her parents while illustrating their unique methods for writing. Her mother is presented as a natural writer who has the ability to transform her thoughts and images onto paper. She spends a great deal of time just thinking through what she wants to write before she actually picks up her pen, allowing her words to flow freely onto her paper, not revising a single word. Her father has a much more tedious writing style. He knows what he wants to write, but the words that come out of his pen are much different, often awkward and unclear. He struggles with every word until his thoughts and images are presented in a creative manner.

As the poem begins you can see how Barnes illustrates her mother possessing such a creative and natural writing ability. "My mother, that feast of light" is a phrase that stands out, creating a positive view of her mother. A light is something that shows you the way in the dark; it is warm, bright, and alive. When it is used to describe her mother, the reader tends to develop a favorable opinion of her because the word "light" is associated with many positive images. Another phrase that eloquently presents her mother as a talented writer is "To catch the lift of a rabbit in mid-hop." The mother possesses the special ability to refer back to her own memory and create a vivid picture of a rabbit hopping, through the use of her carefully chosen words. The mother has this special ability due to the fact that she spends a great deal of time reflecting upon her vivid memories before she actually begins to write.

"I also remember my father alone at the dining-room table." The word *alone* stands out from the rest of the sentence. It conjures up negative feelings, forcing the reader to sympathize with the father. The phrase is written in common, everyday language lacking the imagination and creativity that was present in the first sentence describing the mother. Barnes seems to change her own style of writing when describing each parent. She describes her parents the way they might describe themselves: the mother who is very confident and expressive as opposed to the father who is unsure and always struggling with his words. Barnes writes with great detail and imagination, reinforcing the image of her mother as a talented poet. Her style changes when she describes her father. Her images become plain and uncreative, presenting her father as a struggling writer.

The idea that her father is a hard-working writer is reinforced once again. "The ink bottle safe in a bowl, his orange-red fountain pen in his big hand." Why is her father so persistent? It must be because he has ideas in his head that he wants to express on paper. Unfortunately he has a great deal of difficulty doing so. "The ink bottle is safe in a bowl" symbolizes the thoughts and images that are trapped in his head; he must struggle with them to get his ideas onto paper. Often the way he writes is awkward, which seems due to his large hand. We assume that the word *big* represents the difficulty he has with writing his thoughts down clearly. Fortunately, he does not allow his big hand to keep him from writing, although writing is much more of a struggle for him than for his wife.

Both of these writers are equally gifted, but go about writing in two totally different ways. Their thoughts are dreamlike (vivid but unreal) and until they reach paper their readers cannot see and feel the thoughts that they are trying so hard to share. The mother's method appears very carefree and simple, making her come across as a confident writer whom many readers may envy. The father struggles through his writing. His frustrations dealing with poetry are very common and familiar emotions that cause the reader to empathize with him. As you can see, Barnes uses her words not only to illustrate the two different writing styles but to force the reader to feel the same emotions that she, as a writer, is trying so hard to get across.

One Art*

Elizabeth Bishop

Elizabeth Bishop (b. Worcester, Massachusetts, 1911; d. 1979) was best known as a poet, educator, and translator. Bishop won virtually every major prize awarded to poets in the United States.

The art of losing isn't hard to master;
so many things seem filled with the intent
to be lost that their loss is no disaster.

Lose something every day. Accept the fluster
of lost door keys, the hour badly spent.
The art of losing isn't hard to master.

Then practice losing farther, losing faster:
places, and names, and where it was you meant
to travel. None of these will bring disaster.

I lost my mother's watch. And look! my last, or
next-to-last, of three loved houses went.
The art of losing isn't hard to master.

I lost two cities, lovely ones. And, vaster,
some realms I owned, two rivers, a continent.
I miss them, but it wasn't a disaster.

—Even losing you (the joking voice, a gesture
I love) I shan't have lied. It's evident
the art of losing's not too hard to master
though it may look like (*Write* it!) like disaster.

*Notice how this poem is answered by Adrienne Rich in the following one.

[It's true, these last few years I've lived]

Adrienne Rich

Adrienne Rich (b. Baltimore, 1929) is an award-winning American poet, essayist, feminist, and political activist.

It's true, these last few years I've lived
watching myself in the act of loss—the art of losing,
Elizabeth Bishop called it, but for me no art
only badly-done exercises
acts of the heart forced to question
its presumptions in this world   its mere excitements
acts of the body forced to measure
all instincts against pain
acts of parting   trying to let go
without giving up   yes   Elizabeth   a city here
a village there   a sister, comrade, cat
and more   no art to this but anger

Hay for the Horses

Gary Snyder

Gary Snyder (b. San Francisco, 1930) teaches literature at the University of California at Davis. Snyder was associated with the Beat poets in the 1950s, traveled widely, and lived in Japan for a 12-year period, studying Zen Buddhism and translating Buddhist texts. Snyder is an avid outdoorsman well known for his nature poetry. He has published 12 volumes of poetry and prose.

He had driven half the night
From far down San Joaquin
Through Mariposa, up the
Dangerous mountain roads,
And pulled in at eight a.m.
With his big truckload of hay
  behind the barn.
With winch and ropes and hooks
We stacked the bales up clean
To splintery redwood rafters
High in the dark, flecks of alfalfa
Whirling through shingle-cracks of light,
Itch of haydust in the
  sweaty shirt and shoes.
At lunchtime under Black oak
Out in the hot corral,
—The old mare nosing lunchpails,
Grasshoppers crackling in the weeds—
"I'm sixty-eight," he said,

“I first bucked hay when I was seventeen.
I thought, that day I started,
I sure would hate to do this all my life.
And dammit, that’s just what
I’ve gone and done.”

The Book of the Grotesque

Sherwood Anderson

Sherwood Anderson (b. Camden, Ohio, 1876; d. 1941) decided to make his living as a writer somewhat abruptly in 1912, leaving a manufacturing business, his wife, and two young children behind in Ohio and moving to Chicago. There he met Theodore Dreiser and Carl Sandburg and began writing the short stories and novels for which he became famous. Winesburg, Ohio *(1919) is generally considered to be his masterpiece.*

The writer, an old man with a white mustache, had some difficulty in getting into bed. The windows of the house in which he lived were high and he wanted to look at the trees when he awoke in the morning. A carpenter came to fix the bed so that it would be on a level with the window.

Quite a fuss was made about the matter. The carpenter, who had been a soldier in the Civil War, came into the writer’s room and sat down to talk of building a platform for the purpose of raising the bed. The writer had cigars lying about and the carpenter smoked.

For a time the two men talked of the raising of the bed and then they talked of other things. The soldier got on the subject of the war. The writer, in fact, led him to that subject. The carpenter had once been a prisoner in Andersonville prison and had lost a brother. The brother had died of starvation, and whenever the carpenter got upon that subject he cried. He, like the old writer, had a white mustache, and when he cried he puckered up his lips and the mustache bobbed up and down. The weeping old man with the cigar in his mouth was ludicrous. The plan the writer had for the raising of his bed was forgotten and later the carpenter did it in his own way and the writer, who was past sixty, had to help himself with a chair when he went to bed at night.

In his bed the writer rolled over on his side and lay quite still. For years he had been beset with notions concerning his heart. He was a hard smoker and his heart fluttered. The idea had got into his mind that he would some time die unexpectedly and always when he got into bed he thought of that. It did not alarm him. The effect in fact was quite a special thing and not easily explained. It made him more alive, there in bed, than at any other time. Perfectly still he lay and his body was old and not of much use any more, but something inside him was altogether young. He was like a pregnant woman, only that the thing inside him was not a baby but a youth. No, it wasn’t a youth, it was a woman, young, and wearing a coat of mail like a knight. It is absurd, you see, to try to tell what was inside the old writer as he lay on his high bed and listened to the fluttering of his heart. The thing to get at is what the writer, or the young thing within the writer, was thinking about.

The old writer, like all of the people in the world, had got, during his long life, a great many notions in his head. He had once been quite handsome and a number of women had been in love with him. And then, of course, he had known people, many people, known them in a peculiarly intimate way that was different from the way in which you and I know people. At least that is what the writer thought and the thought pleased him. Why quarrel with an old man concerning his thoughts?

In the bed the writer had a dream that was not a dream. As he grew somewhat sleepy but was still conscious, figures began to appear before his eyes. He imagined the young indescribable thing within himself was driving a long procession of figures before his eyes.

You see the interest in all this lies in the figures that went before the eyes of the writer. They were all grotesques. All of the men and women the writer had ever known had become grotesques.

The grotesques were not all horrible. Some were amusing, some almost beautiful, and one, a woman all drawn out of shape, hurt the old man by her grotesqueness. When she passed he made a noise like a small dog whimpering. Had you come into the room you might have supposed the old man had unpleasant dreams or perhaps indigestion.

For an hour the procession of grotesques passed before the eyes of the old man, and then, although it was a painful thing to do, he crept out of bed and began to write. Some one of the grotesques had made a deep impression on his mind and he wanted to describe it.

At his desk the writer worked for an hour. In the end he wrote a book which he called "The Book of the Grotesque." It was never published, but I saw it once and it made an indelible impression on my mind. The book had one central thought that is very strange and has always remained with me. By remembering it I have been able to understand many people and things that I was never able to understand before. The thought was involved but a simple statement of it would be something like this:

That in the beginning when the world was young there were a great many thoughts but no such thing as a truth. Man made the truths himself and each truth was a composite of a great many vague thoughts. All about in the world were the truths and they were all beautiful.

The old man had listed hundreds of the truths in his book. I will not try to tell you all of them. There was the truth of virginity and the truth of passion, the truth of wealth and of poverty, of thrift and of profligacy, of carelessness and abandon. Hundreds and hundreds were the truths and they were all beautiful.

And then the people came along. Each as he appeared snatched up one of the truths and some who were quite strong snatched up a dozen of them.

It was the truths that made the people grotesques. The old man had quite an elaborate theory concerning the matter. It was his notion that the moment one of the people took one of the truths to himself, called it his truth, and tried to live his life by it, he became a grotesque and the truth he embraced became a falsehood.

You can see for yourself how the old man, who had spent all of his life writing and was filled with words, would write hundreds of pages concerning this matter. The subject would become so big in his mind that he himself would be in danger of becoming a grotesque. He didn't, I suppose, for the same reason that he never published the book. It was the young thing inside him that saved the old man.

Concerning the old carpenter who fixed the bed for the writer, I only mentioned him because he, like many of what are called very common people, became the nearest thing to what is understandable and lovable of all the grotesques in the writer's book.

From Metaphors We Live By

George Lakoff and Mark Johnson

George Lakoff, professor of linguistics at the University of California-Berkeley, and Mark Johnson, professor of philosophy at the University of Oregon, have co-authored Metaphors We Live By *(1980) and, most recently,* Philosophy in the Flesh: The Embodied Mind and Its Challenge to Western Thought *(1999).*

Metaphor is for most people a device of the poetic imagination and the rhetorical flourish—a matter of extraordinary rather than ordinary language. Moreover, metaphor is typically viewed as characteristic of language alone, a matter of words rather than thought or action. For this reason, most people think they can get along perfectly well without metaphor. We have found, on the contrary, that metaphor is pervasive in everyday life, not just in language but in thought and action. Our ordinary conceptual system, in terms of which we both think and act, is fundamentally metaphorical in nature [. . .].

Primarily on the basis of linguistic evidence, we have found that most of our ordinary conceptual system is metaphorical in nature. And we have found a way to begin to identify in detail just what the metaphors are that structure how we perceive, how we think, and what we do.

To give some idea of what it could mean for a concept to be metaphorical and for such a concept to structure an everyday activity, let us start with the concept ARGUMENT and the conceptual metaphor ARGUMENT IS WAR. This metaphor is reflected in our everyday language by a wide variety of expressions:

Argument Is War

Your claims are *indefensible.*
He *attacked every weak point* in my argument.
His criticisms were *right on target.*
I *demolished* his argument.
I've never *won* an argument with him.
You disagree? Okay, *shoot!*
If you use that *strategy,* he'll *wipe you out.*
He *shot down* all of my arguments.

It is important to see that we don't just *talk* about arguments in terms of war. We can actually win or lose arguments. We see the person we are arguing with as an opponent. We attack his positions and we defend our own. We gain and lose ground. We plan and use strategies. If we find a position indefensible, we can abandon it and take a new line of attack. Many of the things we *do* in arguing are partially structured by the concept of war. Though there is no physical battle, there is a verbal battle, and the structure of an argument—attack, defense, counterattack, etc.—reflects this. It is in this sense that the ARGUMENT IS WAR metaphor is one that we live by in this culture; it structures the actions we perform in arguing.

Try to imagine a culture where arguments are not viewed in terms of war, where no one wins or loses, where there is no sense of attacking or defending, gaining or losing ground. Imagine a culture where an argument is viewed as a dance, the participants are seen as performers, and the goal is to perform in a balanced and aesthetically pleasing way. In such a culture, people would view arguments differently, experience them differently, carry them out differently, and talk about them differently. But *we* would probably not view them as arguing at all: they would simply be doing something different. It would seem strange even to call what they were doing "arguing." Perhaps the most neutral way of describing this difference between their culture and ours would be to say that we have a discourse form structured in terms of battle and they have one structured in terms of dance.

This is an example of what it means for a metaphorical concept, namely, ARGUMENT IS WAR, to structure (at least in part) what we do and how we understand what we are doing when we argue. *The essence of metaphor is understanding and experiencing one kind of thing in terms of another.* It is not that arguments are a subspecies of war. Arguments and wars are different kinds of things—verbal discourse and armed conflict—and the actions performed are different kinds of actions. But ARGUMENT is partially structured, understood, performed, and talked about in terms of WAR. The concept is metaphorically structured, the activity is metaphorically structured, and consequently, the language is metaphorically structured.

Moreover, this is the *ordinary* way of having an argument and talking about one. The normal way for us to talk about attacking a position is to use the words "attack a position." Our conventional ways of talking about arguments presuppose a metaphor we are hardly ever conscious of. The metaphor is not merely in the words we use—it is in our very concept of an argument. The language of argument is not poetic, fanciful, or rhetorical; it is literal. We talk about arguments that way because we conceive of them that way—and we act according to the way we conceive of things.

The most important claim we have made so far is that metaphor is not just a matter of language, that is, of mere words. We shall argue that, on the contrary, human *thought processes* are largely metaphorical. This is what we mean when we say that the human conceptual system is metaphorically structured and defined. Metaphors as linguistic expressions are possible precisely because there are metaphors in a person's conceptual system. Therefore, whenever in this book we speak of metaphors, such as ARGUMENT IS WAR, it should be understood that *metaphor* means *metaphorical concept.*

Some Further Examples

We have been claiming that metaphors partially structure our everyday concepts and that this structure is reflected in our literal language. Before we can get an overall picture of the philosophical implications of these claims, we need a few more examples. In each of the ones that follow we give a metaphor and a list of ordinary expressions that are special cases of the metaphor. The English expressions are of two sorts: simple literal expressions and idioms that fit the metaphor and are part of the normal everyday way of talking about the subject.

Theories (and Arguments) Are Buildings

Is that the *foundation* for your theory? The theory needs more *support.* The argument is *shaky.* We need some more facts or the argument will *fall apart.* We need to *construct a strong* argument for that. I haven't figured out yet what the *form* of the argument will be. Here are some more facts to *shore up* the theory. We need to *buttress* the theory with *solid* arguments. The theory will *stand* or *fall* on the *strength* of that argument. The argument *collapsed.* They *exploded* his latest theory. We will show that theory to be without *foundation.* So far we have put together only the *framework* of the theory.

Ideas Are Food

What he said *left a bad taste in my mouth.* All this paper has in it are *raw facts, half-baked ideas,* and *warmed-over theories.* There are too many facts here for me to *digest* them all. I just can't *swallow* that claim. That argument *smells fishy.* Let me *stew* over that for a while. Now there's a theory you can really *sink your teeth into.* We need to let that idea *percolate* for a while. That's *food for thought.* He's a *voracious* reader. We don't need to *spoon-feed* our students. He *devoured* the book. Let's let that idea *simmer on the back burner* for a while. This is the *meaty* part of the paper. Let that idea *jell* for a while. That idea has been *fermenting* for years.

Understanding Is Seeing; Ideas Are Light-Sources; Discourse Is a Light-Medium

I *see* what you're saying. It *looks* different from my *point of view.* What is your *outlook* on that? I *view* it differently. Now I've got the *whole picture.* Let me *point something out* to you. That's an *insightful* idea. That was a *brilliant* remark. The argument is *clear.* It was a *murky* discussion. Could you *elucidate* your remarks? It's a *transparent* argument. The discussion was *opaque.*

Love Is Magic

She *cast her spell* over me. The *magic* is gone. I was *spellbound.* She had me *hypnotized.* He has me *in a trance.* I was *entranced* by him. I'm *charmed* by her. She is *bewitching.*

Love Is War

He is known for his many rapid *conquests.* She *fought for* him, but his mistress *won out.* He *fled* from her *advances.* She *pursued* him *relentlessly.* He is slowly *gaining ground* with her. He *won* her hand in marriage. He *overpowered* her. She is *besieged* by suitors. He has to *fend* them *off.* He *enlisted the aid* of her friends. He *made an ally* of her mother. Theirs is a *misalliance* if I've ever seen one.

Listening, Reading, and Writing in the Disciplines

Essential Premises

- Although there are traits essential to all good writing, each discipline has its own additional standards.
- Writing can serve as a way to learn something as well as a way of explaining what you already know.

Main Assignment Preview

Our aim in this workshop is to get you to do some thinking about the differences between writing for a general audience and writing within a specific discipline. We also hope you'll begin to understand the importance of learning to write within your chosen discipline and the ways writing differs from one discipline to another.

But this workshop is a bit different from most of the others in our book because we have an important goal apart from completion of the main assignment itself: we want to get you to practice some writing techniques which will help you become a better learner. That is, we want to show you how you can use informal writing to *learn* subject matter, not just to demonstrate that you know it. (In the "Readings" for Workshop 12, there's an excerpt from William Zinsser's *Writing to Learn* that presents the results of some of his research on using writing to learn mathematics and chemistry.)

Your main assignment will be to draft two pieces with the same topic—a topic you are studying in another class. One piece will be written for members of your writing class; the other for members of the other class (including the teacher). For each finished piece, you will be expected to prepare a cover letter explaining why you consider the piece appropriate for the class for which it was written.

In Workshop 9 we asked you to write about connections between your school work and nonschool life for two different audiences. Our aim there was for you to begin to understand that it's possible to take both a personal and an impersonal stance toward connections between school and your experience outside of school. We also encouraged you to do some audience analysis, especially as a guide to revision.

This workshop is similar to Workshop 9 in that we're asking you again to draft papers for two different audiences: one that is studying the subject you are writing about and one that isn't. But here we emphasize the subject itself. Your main purpose is not to connect the subject with your experiences out of school but to pick out a difficult or interesting concept and explain it to a general and a professional audience.

In the "Readings" at the end of this workshop, there are several pieces on the same subject written within varying disciplines. On pages 390–391 there are suggestions to help you analyze these readings and revise your assignment for this workshop. Your teacher may ask you to do this reading and analysis before you begin any work on the assignment itself.

Main Assignment: *Writing in Different Disciplines*

Getting Started

Probably the chief task in most of your college classes is to sift through a great deal of material and single out what's most important from what's less important. There's no way any of us can remember *everything* we hear and read; we're always involved in selecting. This assignment foregrounds that whole process.

Listening and Taking Notes

From the outset of this course, we've been asking you to listen to your classmates and others who hear or read your papers. The more carefully you listen, the more resources you'll have for revision. And the more carefully you listen to others read their pieces, the more likely you'll give them good advice for revision—if that's what they're seeking.

But we've also stressed reading aloud to others from whom you ask *no* response because we think that having an audience physically present and listening somehow enables you to view your paper differently. Having a listener can be powerful: We're sure you've said or heard others say something like, "I like to talk to her because she's a good listener."

You've done a lot of listening to teachers in the past twelve years of your life. Taking notes in class seems to come naturally to some students, while others struggle. Your writing teacher may decide to give you practice in taking notes by giving a short lecture on some subject relevant to the class and then asking you to write out your notes as fully as you can and discuss the whole process. This will give you a chance to see how others take notes and how all of you can give one another tips. Here's some of what you might discover:

- It isn't wise to try to write down "word for word" what your teacher says. You usually end up losing track of the main thrust of the lecture.

- It's usually better to put things down in your own words if you can, since your teacher's words may not mean much to you when you reread your notes.
- If you've been given a reading assignment in preparation for a teacher's lecture, it's useful to read the assignment both before and after the lecture. You'll be surprised to discover that the "after" reading often produces different understandings than the "before" reading. But doing the "before" reading almost always makes the lecture more comprehensible and the note taking easier.
- It helps as you're taking notes to put question marks next to facts and concepts you don't "get." This will allow you to keep going and yet know where you had troubles. This will also help you focus your second reading and pinpoint what to ask questions about. And if the teacher doesn't allow for questions, you can write up some questions based on these pinpointed spots and ask them during the professor's office hours.
- Perhaps the most important thing a good note taker does is sit down and flesh out or rewrite notes as soon as possible after class. You'll recall that we gave you this same advice for the interview workshop. The general ideas are still in your head to help you put together what might lose meaning in the following hours. Being forced to write out ideas has a way of making them stick.

You may want to add to this list what you've learned about yourself as a note taker and talk about that with your classmates too.

Listening and Taking Notes in the Other Class

Choose a class for this assignment; we suggest you choose the class you're having the most difficulties with because what we're asking for will help you learn the material better. But perhaps you'd rather choose a class you really enjoy and want to get even more out of. It needs to be a class in which the teacher lectures quite a lot or our assignment won't work out.

Take notes in the class as you usually do. Rewrite those notes as soon as you can after class. Read your notes aloud to your partner or group members and ask them to tell you what they "hear" as the main ideas of the class.

We know students (especially students whose first language is not English) who tape classroom lectures and then study from the tapes. If you do this, here are a couple of suggestions:

Exploring the Writing Process

The first time I write a draft of a paper for a course, I totally let go and rant and rave and say unprofessional things, including swear words. Later I go back and change it to something more acceptable for my academic audience. My theory is that the new, more "professional" words will still carry underneath them the original energy (even anger) of the first draft, and so even my final, "academized" version will have more oomph than if I tried too hard to control my initial reactions the first time around.

Kathy Cassity

- Keep your notebook and pencil handy while listening to the original lecture. Not having to catch everything frees you to pick out and jot down what comes through as particularly important.
- Take your notes from the lecture tape. You can listen to it as many times as necessary. But writing up the notes will help you learn and remember the material as well as prepare you to write short-answer exam responses and papers. Remember what we said earlier: You can't remember everything; the effort to take notes will force you to separate what is most important from what is least important.
- Next, take notes on the chapter or unit in the textbook (or other reading material) that the teacher assigned as preparatory or follow-up reading for the lecture you took notes on. (See Mini-Workshop B for a good technique for note taking, the "double-entry" process.)

Moving to Drafts

During the course of this workshop, you've collected a wealth of data to use in completing your assignment. You should have the following:

- Rough and written-up notes taken during a lecture and during your reading.
- Responses to these notes from classmates.

Before you actually start writing your drafts, you may need to do some exploratory freewriting to settle on your topic. In contrast to your task for Workshop 9, your main purpose here is not to connect what you're learning to your own life; your purpose is to pick out a difficult or interesting concept from your freewriting and dialectical notebook and explain it to two different audiences. Once you've picked it out, it may help to discuss it directly with these two audiences, and perhaps later to write directly *to* them. The goal is to heighten your sense of contact or relationship with these two audiences so that your thinking and language will relate well to each of them.

The audience for one of your drafts will be the teacher and classmates of your

Exploring the Writing Process

I was surprised that Professor _________ said he'd read my paper on the problems of Marxism because there are so many students in that class. Guess it's good they aren't all doing a 101 paper on economics! He seemed to think he had to point out grammar errors even though I'd told him he didn't have to. But I'm not sure some of those were really grammar mistakes. Oh well. I fixed them up anyway. He seemed to be kind of a rough grader so I'm glad in a way that I wasn't writing it for him.

Now I have to revise and I don't know which paper I want to revise. Somehow it did feel different writing the two papers because I worried more about *what* I was saying in the paper for Professor _________. But I think when all is said and done I care more about the paper for this class—so guess I'll revise that one—maybe get more of the "facts" in there.

Jonah Swartz

writing class. You can think of them as equivalent to a general or lay audience. The audience for the other draft will be the teacher of the other class. This is a more specialized audience. We suggest that you talk to this other teacher during her office hours, tell her what you're doing, and ask her if she would be willing to read a draft of the paper which you consider appropriate for her class. If she agrees (and even if she seems reluctant), show her the form we included in Workshop 9 (page 239) as a possible guide to her response.

Your teacher may ask you to polish both drafts or only one. Another option is for you to polish neither of these drafts but instead write an essay which analyzes the differences between the two drafts. The questions you use to analyze the readings at the end of this workshop will be helpful here. These appear in this workshop on pages 390 and 391. If this alternative is pursued collaboratively, you and your partner(s) could analyze more than one set of drafts.

Preparing Your Cover Letter

Your teacher may have asked you to add cover letters to every assignment you hand in to her. If not, you may want to look back at our discussion about these in Workshop 1. We're putting a bit more emphasis on cover letters in this workshop, but we think they're important for all assignments. Your particular purpose for this cover letter will be to reflect on how the two different audiences influenced:

1. Your stance toward your subject and the organization, method of reasoning, vocabulary, and style of the paper.
2. The thinking, drafting, writing, and revision of the final paper(s).

Obviously you can't cover all this in the 200 words or so that fit on one cover page. If you find you have too much to say, select what seems the most interesting to you and save the rest for your process journal.

Examining Differences

A good way to begin to understand differences between the discourses of various disciplines (as well as differences between language directed at specialists and nonspecialists within a discipline) is to look at several pieces of writing on the same subject. Included in "Readings" at the end of this workshop are four pieces about women and gender differences. As you read through the four professional articles, record your reactions in your process journal. Don't edit these reactions; put down whatever comes into your head as you read, just as you do when you give a "Movies of the Reader's Mind" response to a classmate's paper (see "Sharing and Responding," Section 7). Another way to analyze each piece is to put down in semi-outline form what each section says and does, a strategy we describe in Section 10 of "Sharing and Responding." Some of you may prefer to use the double-entry notebook approach described in Mini-Workshop B.

Using the thinking and writing generated by these ways of responding, do some freewriting about all four pieces. Your teacher may suggest that you do this work collaboratively in groups of four; all of you would read all the pieces, but each of you would freewrite about only one. Then you can pool your observations and discuss the differences you've observed. Focus your freewriting on the following topics:

- *Comprehension.* What is particularly puzzling for you: the language and vocabulary, your lack of background knowledge, an inability to understand the underlying assumptions or the purpose?
- *Reasoning or thinking.* What kinds of reasons or arguments does the author use? What sort of information does the author give to back up what she or he is saying? Do specific examples or personal experience count as evidence? What assumptions is this author making?
- *Structure.* How does the writer organize material? Perhaps deductively (starting with a stated position and then giving reasons, evidence, and examples)? Perhaps inductively (starting with reasons, evidence, and examples, and then stating a conclusion)? Perhaps musing on a theme in a more meditative, wondering way? Perhaps there is a narrative structure. Does the writer tend to use partial summaries at the end of segments of the writing? How does the author use formatting to structure material (subheads, bullets, indenting, and so forth)?
- *Purpose.* Why is the author writing this piece? To explain? To persuade? To express himself?
- *Audience.* Do you feel like an audience for the piece? If so, is the author addressing you as a colleague? a friend? an educated layperson? If not, whom do you think the piece is written for?
- *Personal and impersonal.* How personal is the writer in the presentation of material? Is the writing completely impersonal, or can you identify spots where the writer becomes more personal—and figure out why? How does the personal or impersonal quality of the writing affect your response?
- *Writer.* What kind of person do you think the writer is? This question doesn't mean that you should go out and try to find out about the author. What we're asking is that you try to characterize the writer on the basis of the piece of writing itself. Starting with an imagined physical description helps.
- *Language.* Are sentences complex in structure? Do they tend to be long or short? Does the author use straightforward language? Does the author use specialized vocabulary? How would you characterize the language in general?
- *Feelings.* What kinds of emotional reactions do you feel as you read the piece? Do you think these feelings are what the writer wanted you to have? How do these reactions influence your reading?

Exploring the Writing Process

The "problems" of my country [South Africa] did not set me writing; on the contrary, it was learning to write that set me falling, falling through the surface of "the South African way of life."

Nadine Gordimer

- *Evaluation* How would you describe the strengths and weaknesses of this piece of writing? Would people in all fields call these strengths and weaknesses?

What we're asking you to do is difficult; it will require time and considerable thought on your part. We suggest that you not try to do it all at once, but use several sessions to give yourself some breathing space.

In addition to thinking about how these four pieces differ, we also want you to think about how they're alike. Much of what makes for good sociological writing also makes for good natural science writing. Nor can we say that a particular discipline has only one form of writing associated with it. Within each discipline there is a formal and an informal style (at the very least) and a style used for those in the field and for those out of the field. After all, it is important for specialists in any field to be able to talk to nonspecialists too. Yet common to those different styles (or "registers," to use the jargon of linguistics) within each discipline is a *way of thinking* that is characteristic of that discipline: a way of arguing or an agreement about what counts as reasons and evidence. If you're interested in the theory behind our aims, you can turn to the "Exploring Theory" section at the end of this workshop.

We need to put in a disclaimer. We've picked the four essays to be analyzed and have specified the fields in which they're written. You must realize, however, that there is plenty of variation within discourses in any one field.

Suggestions for Collaboration

This is a good assignment for working collaboratively. The ideal collaboration, of course, would be to find one or two students from this writing class who are also in the other class. Then both or all of you can take notes and compare them. You can each read your notes to the same audience and ask that audience to tell you what they "hear" as the same in your notes and what they "hear" as different. One nice side effect of this collaborative work is that you'll discover the benefits of working in small study groups with others in your classes. Research has demonstrated that students who participate in informal study groups usually do better in school.

There are a number of ways you could take the assignment from this point, including writing collaborative drafts and final papers. Or you might want to produce either collaboratively or individually a comparison of how two (or possibly even three) of you take notes and read textbooks.

Sharing and Responding

Because there's so much to share in this workshop, your teacher will probably not be able to give time for all of it during class. Perhaps she'll suggest that all group members exchange drafts, but that each person in the group be given chief responsibility for responding to one other person's two drafts. This way, each writer will get some written response. If everyone reads everyone else's drafts, though, all can participate in the discussion of each paper. Focused freewriting in response to questions about the published pieces can be exchanged in class and read outside class. Or your teacher may decide to devote extra time to this workshop so that much of the work can be done in class.

You'll find "Pointing and Center of Gravity," "Skeleton Feedback and Descriptive Outline," and "Criterion-Based Feedback" (Sections 2, 10, and 11 in "Sharing and Responding") most valuable for this workshop. Following are two more questions which you can address to your group members:

- What do you see as the main point of my paper(s)? Does it get lost? Does it have enough support?
- Are you clear about the subject matter of the lecture and reading I used for this workshop? Do you agree with me about what seems the most significant? What parts need more explanation?

Process Journal

- How did you experience the writing out of your lecture notes? Were you able to make everything clear for yourself?
- How has this assignment affected (if at all) your work in other classes? How might it affect that work in the future?
- What makes an audience easy or hard to write for?

Exploring Theory: *Writing (and the Teaching of Writing) in the Disciplines*

Knowledge and Writing within Discipline Communities

One of the most important things you learn while you're in college is to speak and write in new ways. You've undoubtedly noticed already that the language of your readings and the language of your professors' lectures are different from the language you're accustomed to. You may have noticed too that the way people write about poems and stories is usually different from the way they write about atomic particles. It isn't just that the subject matter of the writing is different or even that the style is different. It's that the *kind* of writing is different because of differences in thinking itself: how the writer presents material differs from one subject to the next.

You need to learn to write in ways acceptable within various fields, particularly within the field of your chosen major. Learning to do this requires, of course, that you learn the subject matter. If you're majoring in physics, you have to learn a lot of physics. But in the process of doing that learning, you'll absorb almost unconsciously the language and ways of thinking of physicists. You'll begin to use that language and thinking when you're talking about subjects within the field. You'll also begin to use them when you write about such subjects. A large part of being a good physicist is being comfortable with the *way* physicists talk and write about their subject. If this seems like a strange idea to you, we hope this workshop will help you begin to understand what we're saying.

All this doesn't mean that you'll write exactly like other physicists; some of your personal ways of putting words and ideas together will stay with you. Even within physics—often considered one of the least subjective of sciences—writers often have an individual style, and others within the field can often identify a writer by that style.

Most of your learning about how to use the methods of different academic disciplines may not occur until after your freshman year. But all of you take courses in some of these disciplines during your first year in college; perhaps now you're taking a math course or an introductory psychology or sociology course. If so, you're already absorbing the language and thinking of these disciplines along with the knowledge. The real and essential "knowledge" *is* the language and thinking, not just some list of facts. If you write papers for the course, your professor will expect you to demonstrate not only what you know but also how skilled you are in the ways of writing in that discipline.

You needn't actually worry about acquiring the language of a particular field; that happens gradually and usually imperceptibly. But you do need practice at it. That's why it's important for writing and speaking to be a part of all disciplines from engineering to philosophy. If, when you reach your senior year, you were to compare papers written in an advanced course in your major with papers you wrote in an introductory course in the same discipline, you'd probably be startled at the differences—differences that have been produced by small changes throughout your college years. You'll realize that you now sound more "academic" than you used to.

But even in your senior year in your major—as a "member" of the field—you will still find yourself making adjustments in your writing (after you've clarified ideas for yourself on paper): one set of adjustments for people in your field and another set of adjustments for nonacademics or for academics not in your field. Given the increasing isolation of specialties in our society, we believe strongly that academics need to develop language that is accessible and comfortable for those not in their fields. Some of the very best scholars in a discipline often write in the most accessible way.

Within our field (the teaching of composition), we have a special language too—our own jargon. We've tried not to use too much of it in this book because it requires explanation. Also, if you're like us, you find it annoying when people in a particular field—one you're not in—use the language of that field in their conversations with you. But in this workshop, we do need to rely on one word which is often heard within our field: "discourse." One of the ways this word is used is to designate the language and thinking of a particular discipline; you'll hear us and our cohorts talking about "the discourse features of sociological writing" or, more succinctly, "the discourse of sociology." "Discourse" means both written and spoken language *and* ways of thinking.

It may sound as though we're saying that first you get facts or ideas about some subject, say, economics, and then you make them conform to some artificial form deemed acceptable by economists. But this is far too simple a conclusion. In a very important sense, the way economists talk and write *creates* economic knowledge. Just as we saw in Workshop 2 that a genre can lead you to see new facts and ideas, not just shape ideas you already have, so too a particular discourse can lead you to see new facts and ideas, not just shape ones you already have. Think of it this way: economists, psychologists, and mathematicians can all look at the same phenomena—for example, the transition to the new millennium—and come up with different knowledge. That knowledge is a product of their particular angle of vision, their kind of language and thinking, and their kind of questions. Consequently you can never truly write appropriately within a discipline until you have become immersed in its ways of perceiving, thinking, and constructing knowledge.

One further caveat: The modern university or college with its various departments is a fairly recent creation, at least viewed against hundreds of previous years of formal education. Dividing knowledge up into segments—calling some physics, some philosophy, and so forth—is a human act. Since that's so, we need to leave room for the possibility of segmenting knowledge into different categories from the ones we now use. If all of us get locked into the language of our own fields, we're not so likely to see possibilities in the interaction of disciplines or for the creation of new disciplines, new ways of thinking, new ways of seeing.

Another problem with this strict departmentalization is one you may be experiencing: It's often difficult for you to integrate the separate pieces of your education. What you learn in one class often seems to have little relevance to what you learn in another. This outcome has led many universities and colleges to set up interdisciplinary courses where the interaction of science, art, religion, and history, for example, becomes evident.

An Argument for Freshman Composition

Because of the close marriage between language and knowledge in any discourse field, many experts in the teaching of writing advocate abolishing freshman composition and having all writing occur within disciplinary or subject-matter classes. We don't agree. We think there are certain things common to all writing. Chief among these is the process of writing things out for oneself—for *one's own purposes* before adjusting that writing to others. How you go about doing this constitutes your personal writing process. But no matter what you're writing and for whom, you'll benefit from going through both of these steps. It's too difficult to work things out for yourself and for others at the same time.

In the previous paragraph we spoke of writing for one's own purposes. The truth about school writing is that you are often writing to get a good grade; the subject matter can be secondary. And the truth is that it's hard to write well when your subject is not important to you. In subject-area classes, you may have to write papers on topics that have little interest for you. This can be true in your writing class too. One thing a writing class can do (for which there isn't time in most other classes) is to help you find ways to make a subject your own in some way, find some angle on an assigned subject that grabs you. Freewriting, Perl writing, and open-ended writing can all help here. But you'll never believe that unless it actually happens for you. A writing class can provide that opportunity.

Thus, attention to your writing process as *process* is essential. Perhaps you work things out best for yourself by freewriting (we do); but perhaps you find list making more productive or drawing cluster diagrams or outlining or meditating. Perhaps you use several of these on the same task. Perhaps you alter your ways of working out ideas according to what you're writing. Maybe you always do it the same way regardless of your subject. No matter. There's always a process of some kind. And when you actually sit down to make something clear for yourself, it doesn't matter much if the stuff in your head comes from your personal experience, from reading in a textbook or professional magazine, or from lectures by your professor. What you've learned must still *pass through you* somehow and come out on the page in words chosen and ordered by you.

Once you've worked out something for yourself by whatever process you prefer, you need to have processes to check for audience. Maybe you cut and paste, maybe you put aside what you've done for hours or days, maybe you read it or give it to someone for feedback, maybe you make one draft, maybe you make three or more. Again, whatever you do may be invariable—not dependent at all on your subject or audience. Or maybe you vary this part of your process according to what you're writing and for whom. As you become a better observer of your own writing and revising processes, you'll probably be fairly certain about some things you need to do: Make sentences and paragraphs longer or shorter, keep an eagle eye out for repetitions and slips in logic, check whether you have too many or not enough examples, and so forth. How much of each of these you do may depend on whether your way of writing for yourself is closer to an academic style or closer to a casual style. Thus, depending on your audience, you may need to "academize" your writing or "unacademize" it. Our point is that attention to process is important. (If you've gotten this far in our textbook, we really didn't have to tell you that!)

This is what we believe to be common to all writing. Whether all writing shares certain features such as clarity, logic, voice, and so forth, is a debate we're not entering at this point (though we think there are features all good writing has). The existence of language universals—truths that underlie all languages—has been debated for centuries. Do all languages have ways of expressing subjects or agents of action? Do all languages have ways of expressing action apart from the agents of action? Do all languages have expressive, communicative, persuasive, and poetic capabilities? That's another debate we hardly have room for. Here we're arguing something much less broad: that underlying any writing one does is a process for getting that writing done. Our aim in this book is to help you find *your* best processes.

What a writing class can do for you is help you discover your own best writing processes, modify them if necessary, and become adept at using them. Subject-matter classes and teachers don't, and some teachers say they can't, devote time to this often messy task. You'll need to make changes in your writing processes as you move through your college years and into a career, but your writing class can help establish a firm foundation for doing that.

We have another reason for advocating separate writing classes: They give you the opportunity to do a kind of writing you won't be doing in subject classes. In subject classes, you do writing connected with those subjects. But much of the writing in the world cannot be specifically categorized according to the way universities have divided up knowledge. Lots of writing in the world doesn't have anything to do with school at all. Writing classes can give you the chance to do this sort of writing; in the long run, it may be the kind of writing that matters to you the most and that you do the most of for the rest of your life.

From Eve's Rib: The Biological Roots of Sex Differences

Robert Pool

Robert Pool is a science writer based in Arlington, Virginia. His most recent book is Beyond Engineering: A New Way of Thinking About Technology, *published in June 1997 by Oxford University Press.*

One weakness of much of the research on sex differences is that, like Lytton and Romney's work, it focuses only on Western societies. There are few studies of sex differences in Eastern countries, such as Japan, China, or Korea, and fewer still that are performed in Third World countries, where the cultures are much different. Do women have better spatial ability than men in Bangladesh? Do men outscore women on mental rotations in Botswana? We don't know.

Yet it is particularly helpful to compare men and women in different cultures. We know, for instance, that there are very violent peoples, such as the Yanomamo of Venezuela, and very peaceful peoples, such as the Semai of Malaysia. Do sex differences in aggression exist in either of these tribes? If not, we should ask what it is about our culture that brings out such a difference. And if anthropologists were ever to discover a group of people in whom the women are clearly more aggressive than the men, we would suspect that sex differences in aggression are created by how males and females are raised, not because of biology.

This is the basic idea behind cross-cultural studies. If a certain human behavior is culturally determined, it should differ from one society to the next. To take a rather silly example, suppose somebody told you that there is a biological reason why women wear dresses and men wear pants. It's a natural, hormone-driven sex difference, this person says. To test this claim, all you need to do is gather data on a number of human societies from around the world. When you find that men wear skirtlike clothing in a number of cultures, you can discount the hormone-clothing connection.

Conversely, if you find that a particular behavior is universal, or nearly so, across cultures, you can be pretty sure there is some biological predisposition for it. All human cultures have spoken languages, for instance, which means that speaking is something humans do quite naturally. On the other hand, not all cultures have written languages, implying that writing isn't nearly so natural.

How natural are sex differences? We can get a good idea by looking for patterns across cultures.

The most consistent cross-cultural evidence concerns aggressiveness. In all cultures known to anthropologists, the male is more violent than the female. In the United States and other Western societies, men are responsible for the lion's share of the homicides: about 86–88 percent of those arrested and charged with homicide in the United States are men. And when a woman does kill somebody, it's almost always a husband or a boyfriend, not a stranger. Nor is the male's near monopoly on murder just a Western phenomenon. Consider the peaceful !Kung San of the Kalahari Desert, a tribe of hunter-gatherers who live much as anthropologists believe all humans lived ten or twenty thousand years ago. (The "!" is a phonological symbol denoting a clicking sound that has no equivalent in English.) Among the !Kung San, a tribe known for its sexual equality, every one of the twenty-two homicides documented by one researcher was done by men—and all but three of the victims were men. Some societies are more violent and aggressive than others, but within each society the pattern remains the same: men are the more savage sex.

Unanimity of this sort can only mean that a biological mechanism is at work. It's possible to debate whether a given society exaggerates or dampens the natural difference in aggression between the sexes, but a difference there is.

Other social sex differences are not as pronounced across cultures, but a few are consistent. Perhaps the best cross-cultural study of sex differences is the 1973 report by Beatrice Whiting and Carolyn Pope Edwards on behavior in children aged three to eleven in six countries around the world: Kenya, Okinawa, India, the Philippines, Mexico and the United States. Besides finding that boys were physically and verbally more aggressive around the world, Whiting and Pope saw several other reliable patterns.

Girls were more "dependent" than boys. The younger girls, three to six, were more likely to ask for help than boys, although the sex difference disappeared as they got older. And all of the girls were more eager for physical contact, touching, holding and clinging to others more often than the boys. The boys, however, had their own form of "dependency," Whiting and Edwards noted. They sought attention and approval more, especially as they got older, trying to get either a positive or negative reaction from people nearby. In short, males and females have different ways of interacting with other people, differences that are apparent at an early age and are consistent across very different cultures.

The other major difference was that girls were more nurturing to other people than boys. They consistently scored higher both on offering help, such as food, tools, or toys, and on offering emotional support and comfort. The difference increased as the children got older, and Whiting and Edwards attributed the trend to the societies training girls to be more nurturing toward infants in preparation for motherhood. As evidence the researchers pointed to two exceptions to the rule, societies where boys and girls were equal in offering help and support. Both exceptions were cultures that didn't expect girls to participate more than boys in caring for infants—Kenya, where young boys shared in helping care for infants, and a small town in New England, where families were small and the girls did little baby-sitting.

Whiting and Edwards conclude that sex differences in aggression and touching behavior are most likely to arise from biology. The sex difference in nurturance, they say, is at the very least exaggerated by cultural expectations and may be due mostly to young girls being expected to help with children.

Concerning sex differences in mental abilities, there have been few cross-cultural studies that targeted people outside North America and Western Europe because such research is expensive and time-consuming, but one recent test did compare sex differences in the United States and in Japan, a decidedly non-Western culture. Working with three collaborators from Japan, Virginia Mann at the University of California at Irvine created a battery of tests in English and Japanese and gave them to high school students in the two countries. In both countries males outscored females on mental rotations, while females outperformed males on word fluency (coming up with words that start with a given letter or, in Japanese, kana character) as well as story recall and digit-symbol, a common test of memory.

This research clearly demonstrates that nurture can play a large role in how people perform on tests: the Japanese students—who are pushed to excel by parents and teachers—consistently outperformed the Americans, and the difference was so large on the mental rotations test that Japanese girls outscored American boys. On the other hand, nature was just as clearly playing a role in creating differences within each culture: despite the fact that children are raised quite differently in the United States and Japan, the students from these two cultures had very similar patterns of sex differences in their cognitive abilities. It would be nice to have more cross-cultural studies like this, with students from Paraguay or Pakistan or Pago Pago, but even without them we can clearly see that similar sex differences appear in quite disparate environments: an indication of nature at work.

• • •

What differences would remain between boys and girls, men and women if our society were sex-blind, so to speak—if people were treated as individuals, not as members of one sex or the other? Boys would still be boys, with their rough-and-tumble play and their fascination with manipulating objects, from playing with blocks and trucks to building model airplanes and competing on video games. Girls would still be more people-oriented than object-oriented and would still like playing with dolls. The psychological differences that Carol Gilligan and Deborah Tannen have identified—females paying more attention to people's needs and to the web of relationships and males being more attuned to rules of right and wrong and to dominance hierarchies—might still hold, assuming that they are somehow connected with the person/object difference in interests between females and males.

Females would retain much or all of their verbal superiority, and males would still have an edge on spatial skills. Some of the male advantage in higher-level mathematics would likely fade away, since it seems to have been decreasing slowly over the past couple of decades anyway, but boys would probably retain much of their lead among the very top scorers on math tests. Males would continue to be more variable in intelligence than females.

Men would still be more aggressive and commit more violent crimes than women. Women would still be more nurturing to infants, although it's possible that in most other ways males and females would be similar in nurturance. The evidence implies that much of helping behavior among both males and females is taught, and often girls are taught more of it than boys.

All this may make it seem as if the world would not be much changed if the sexes were treated equally, but I don't mean to imply that at all. Although these statistical sex differences would remain, many if not all would probably be smaller. And the consequences might be quite large for some individuals. There may be many girls, for instance, with a knack for spatial ability and mathematics who never pursue these interests and never develop their talents because they're intimidated by venturing into a "male" field.

And I have said nothing about how much of the differences between the sexes might be erased by active intervention. We know that spatial ability can be improved by training, so the sex difference in spatial skills might be decreased if both boys and girls were given this training. The same is likely true for other areas. In a society that taught nonviolence to all its children, males might still be more aggressive than females, but the difference might well be smaller.

In general, I've written little about the massive amount of research that has been done on how environment and socialization affects boys and girls. That is not because it's unimportant, but simply because it is another book. The question here was what type of role nature plays in creating differences between males and females. The answer is: a major one.

A Plethora of Theories: Biological Storytelling

Anne Fausto-Sterling

Anne Fausto-Sterling is a developmental geneticist on the faculty at Brown University. She is perhaps best known for Myths of Gender: Biological Theories about Women and Men *(1985), from which this selection is an excerpt. Her latest book is titled* Sexing the Body *(1999).*

Despite the small size of sex-related differences in verbal and spatial skills, their existence has elicited numerous studies aimed at explaining them on the basis of biological differences between the sexes. Scouring the ins and outs, curves and shapes, capacities and angles of the human brain, hoping to find traits that differ in the male and female is a pastime in which scientists have engaged for more than a century. Early studies, which discovered that male brains were larger than female brains, concluded that the female's smaller size resulted in her inferior intelligence. This logic, however, ran afoul of the "elephant problem": if size were the determinant of intelligence, then elephants and whales ought to be in command. Attempts to remedy this by claiming special importance for the number obtained by dividing brain size by body weight were abandoned when it was discovered that females came out "ahead" in such measurements. The great French naturalist Georges Cuvier finally decided that intellectual ability could best be estimated by the relative proportions of the cranial to the facial bones. This idea, however, ran aground on the "bird problem," since with such a measure birds, anteaters, and bear-rats turn out to be more intelligent than humans. Some brain scientists believed that the frontal lobe of the cerebrum (the part that sits in front of the head just above the eyebrows—see Figure 1) was an important site of perceptive powers and was less well developed in females than in males. Others argued that even individual brain cells differed in males and females, the cerebral fibers being softer, more slender, and longer in female brains.

As neuroanatomists became more and more convinced that the frontal lobe was the repository of intelligence, an increasing number of reports appeared claiming that this lobe was visibly larger and more developed in males. One report, in 1854, concluded that Woman was *Homo parietalis* (after the parietal lobe, which lies toward the back and to the side of the head—Figure 1) and Man *Homo frontalis*. In time, however, the parietal rather than the frontal lobe gained precedence as the seat of the intellect, a change accompanied by an about-face on sex differences in the brain: "The frontal region is not, as has been supposed, smaller in woman, but rather larger relatively. But the parietal lobe is somewhat smaller."

Other female brain "deficiencies" found in this same period include the supposedly smaller surface area of the corpus callosum (a mass of nerve fibers that connect the left and right halves of the brain), the complexity of the convolutions of the brain, and the rate of development of the fetal cerebral cortex. These beliefs were held until 1909, when anatomist Franklin Mall used new statistical techniques developed in the budding fields of psychology and genetics to refute the existence of such differences.

From the period following the end of World War I through the first half of the 1960s, psychologists and biologists developed few additional theories. A new outbreak began in the late 1960s, and since then hypotheses have come and gone rapidly. The popular press fanfares each entry with brilliant brass, bright ribbons, and lots of column space, but fails to note when each one in its turn falls into disrepute. The number and variety of theories that have come our way in the past fifteen years are truly remarkable, and an account of their advent, an analysis of their scientific basis, and a view of their demise instructive. I've listed seven of these biological hypotheses in

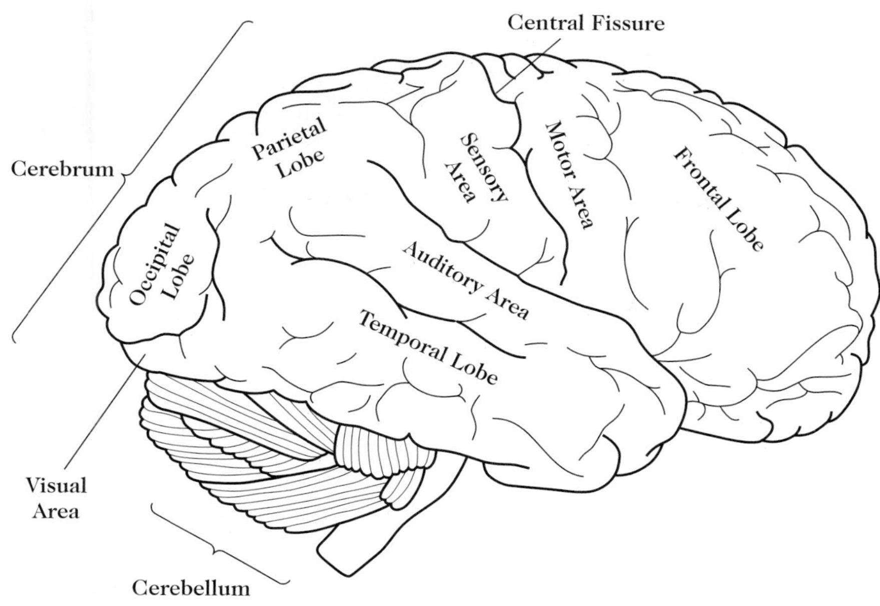

Figure 1 Cerebrum and Cerebellum
Localization of function in the human cerebral cortex. Only the major convolutions of the cortex are drawn. They are remarkably constant from individual to individual, and provide landmarks in the task of mapping the distribution of special functions in different parts of the cortex. Note especially the sensory area which lies posterior to the central fissure (or convolution), and the motor area which lies anterior to the central fissure.

Table 1 along with their current status and references for studying them in more detail. The pages that follow focus attention on two of the most popular and currently active ideas—the claim that spatial ability involves a pair of X-linked genes and that male and female brains have different patterns of lateralization.

Space Genes

In 1961 Dr. R. Stafford suggested that humans carry two different X-linked genetic sites, one influencing mathematical problem-solving ability and the other affecting spatial ability. Similar to Lehrke's X-linked variability hypothesis, Stafford's theory proposed that males need inherit only one X chromosome in order to excel in math or spatial tasks, while females need a math and a space gene on each X chromosome, a less frequent possibility.

If his hypothesis were true, one would expect a smaller percentage of females than of males to be good at math and spatial activities. A number of studies have tested predictions about parent-child correlations in mathematical problem solving—predictions that geneticists made from Stafford's theory. Before 1975 some small-sized studies seemed to support Stafford's contention, although the experimental results rarely obtained statistical significance (unless, in a highly unusual procedure, groups from different studies done by different research groups were pooled to increase sample size). Large studies performed since the mid-1970s have failed to find evidence to support the X-linked hypothesis. The most recent study I found concluded that "[s]ince the previous evidence from small studies cannot be replicated, it appears that the X-linkage hypothesis is no longer tenable." Even more recently, Dr. Hogben Thomas, a researcher at Pennsylvania State University, pointed out that the approach used to

Table 1 Biological Theories to Explain Sex-Related Cognitive Differences

Year of Initial Publication	Name of Theorist	Basic Tenet	Current Status of Theory
1961	Stafford[g]	Spatial ability is X-linked and thus males show it more frequently than do females.	Clearly disproven,[h] although still widely quoted. Current authors still feel the necessity to argue against this genetic hypothesis.
1966	Money and Lewis[c]	High levels of prenatal androgen may increase intelligence.	Disproven by Baker and Ehrhardt in 1974.[d]
1968	Broverman et al.[a]	Males are better at "restructuring" tasks, due to lower estrogen levels, greater activity of "inhibitory" parasympathetic nervous system.	Actively critiqued in early 1970s. Not cited in current literature.[b]
1972	Buffery and Gray[j]	Female brains are more lateralized than male brains; greater lateralization interferes with spatial functions.	No evidence; not currently an important view.
1972	Levy[k]	Female brains are less lateralized than male brains, less lateralization interferes with spatial functions.	Currently in vogue; dominates the field despite a number of cogent critiques; no strong supporting evidence.
1973	Bock and Kolakowski[i]	Supplements Stafford's theory. Sex-linked spatial gene is expressed only in the presence of testosterone.	Clearly disproven,[h] although still widely quoted. Current authors still feel the necessity to argue against this genetic hypothesis.

Table 1 ***(continued)***

1976	Hyde and Rosenberg[e]	High blood uric-acid levels increase intelligence and ambition. Males have more uric acid than females.	Not widely cited, no supporting evidence.[f]

[a] Donald M. Broverman, Edward L. Klaiber, Yutaka Kobayashi, and William Vogel, "Roles of Activation and Inhibition in Sex Differences in Cognitive Abilities," *Psychological Review* 75(1968):23–50.

[b] Julia A. Sherman, *Sex-Related Cognitive Differences: An Essay on Theory and Evidence* (Springfield, Ill.: Charles C Thomas, 1978); Mary Parlee, "Comments on 'Roles of Activation and Inhibition in Sex Differences in Cognitive Abilities' by Broverman et al.," *Psychological Review* 79(1972):180–84; G. Singer and R. Montgomery, "Comment on Roles of Activation and Inhibition in Sex Differences in Cognitive Abilities," *Psychological Review* 76(1969):325–27; Donald M. Broverman, Edward L. Klaiber, Yutaka Kobayashi, and William Vogel, "A reply to the 'Comment' by Singer and Montgomery on 'Roles of Activation and Inhibition in Sex Differences in Cognitive Abilities'," *Psychological Review* 76(1969):328–31.

[c] John Money and V. Lewis, "Genetics and Accelerated Growth: Adrenogenital Syndrome," *Bulletin of Johns Hopkins Hospital* 118(1966):365–73.

[d] Susan W. Baker and Anke Ehrhardt, "Prenatal Androgen, Intelligence, and Cognitive Sex Differences," in *Sex Differences in Behavior,* ed. R. C. Friedman, R. M. Richart, and R. L. Van de Wiele (New York: Wiley, 1974).

[e] J. S. Hyde and B. G. Rosenberg, *Half the Human Experience: The Psychology of Women* (Lexington, Mass.: D.C. Heath, 1976).

[f] Julia A. Sherman, *Sex-Related Cognitive Differences: An Essay on Theory and Evidence* (Springfield, Ill.: Charles C Thomas, 1978).

[g] R. E. Stafford, "Sex Differences in Spatial Visualization as Evidence of Sex-Linked Inheritance," *Perceptual and Motor Skills* 13(1961):428.

[h] Robin P. Corley, J. C. DeFries, A. R. Kuse, and Steven G. Vandenberg, "Familial Resemblance for the Identical Blocks Test of Spatial Ability: No Evidence of X Linkage," *Behavior Genetics* 10(1980):211–15.

[i] D. R. Bock and D. Kolakowski, "Further Evidence of Sex-Linked Major-Gene Influence on Human Spatial Visualizing Ability," *American Journal of Human Genetics* 25(1973):1–14.

[j] A. W. H. Buffery and J. Gray, "Sex Differences in the Development of Spacial and Linguistic Skills," in *Gender Differences: Their Ontogeny and Significance,* ed. C. Ounsted and D. C. Taylor (London: Chirhill Livingston, 1972).

[k] Jerre Levy, "Lateral Specialization of the Human Brain: Behavioral Manifestation and Possible Evolutionary Basis," in *The Biology of Behavior,* ed. J. A. Kiger Corvalis (Eugene: University of Oregon Press, 1972).

test Stafford's hypothesis may be fundamentally flawed and that the X-linkage theory of spatial ability may simply be untestable.

Furthermore, there is a very different source of data that appears to contradict the X-linked hypothesis, one recognized some years ago by two other scientists, Drs. D. R. Bock and D. Kolakowski. Rather than discard Stafford's hypothesis, however, they modified it, turning counter-evidence into support. On occasion, individuals are born with no Y chromosome. Doctors call them XOs. Since they are born with female genitalia, XO individuals are usually raised as girls, and in many respects are quite normal, although they can sometimes be recognized by their short height, webbed neck, and failure to develop fully at puberty. XO individuals, said to have Turner's Syndrome (named after the physician who first described it), have spatial abilities well below the normal range, a fact that contradicts Stafford's hypothesis. If the X-linked hypothesis were correct, Turner's Syndrome patients would not differ from XY males, expressing their spatial ability more frequently than XX females, because their single X chromosome is not "covered" by a second X. In order to get around this uncomfortable fact, Bock and Kolakowski proposed that the space gene is not only X-linked but is also sex-limited, depending for its expression on high androgen levels which circulate throughout the body in higher concentrations in men than in women. (A familiar example of a sex-limited gene is baldness, expressed only in men because it depends for its expression on higher androgen levels than are present in most females.)

The sex-limited hypothesis represents a clever stab at saving the game, but it too runs counter to the data. Psychologist Julia Sherman has offered the most succinct demolition of the theory, and Table 2 represents some of her work. Turner's Syndrome patients have lower than normal estrogen (a hormone found in higher concentrations in females) and androgen levels. Bock and Kolakowski argue that the gene coding for spa-

Table 2 Verbal and Performance IQ's of Individuals with Sex Chromosome and/or Hormone Abnormalities

Number of Individuals Tested	Sex of Rearing	Sex Chromosome; Constitution	Adult Hormone Levels	Average Verbal IQ Scores	Average Performance IQ Scores
45	F	XO	low estrogen low androgen	106	86
15	F	XY	intermediate estrogen, androgen-insensitivity	112	102
3	M	XY	intermediate estrogen, androgen-insensitivity	117	119
23	M	XXY	intermediate estrogen, intermediate androgens	105	88
12	M	XXY	intermediate estrogen, intermediate androgens	66	76
20	M	XYY	unknown	79	88

Note: Julia Sherman, *Sex-Related Cognitive Differences: An Essay on Theory and Evidence* (Springfield, Ill.: Charles C Thomas, 1978), 84. Courtesy of Charles C Thomas, Publisher.

Figure 2

tial ability requires a certain cellular concentration of androgen in order to function. In XO individuals, they suggest, too little androgen is present, and thus Turner's Syndrome girls have poor spatial abilities. To shore up their position, they cite another study of individuals with androgen insensitivity syndrome (AIS)—people who possess both X and Y chromosomes but who are unable to respond to androgens. AIS patients are often born with femalelike genitalia. Fifteen such persons, all raised as females, were tested and obtained an average Verbal IQ of 112 and Performance IQ of 102.* Although both scores fit in the normal range, Bock and Kolakowski inferred from this test that inability to respond to androgen lowered spatial IQ. But who can say whether the Verbal IQ might not have been abnormally high rather than the spatial IQ being unusually low? Furthermore, Bock and Kolakowski ignore additional data from the same study. Three AIS patients reared as *males* scored well above the normal range on both verbal and spatial IQ tests. If androgen really improves the expression of spatial genes, how is it that three androgen-insensitive individuals performed above average on a spatial test?

Chromosomal abnormalities affect mental functioning. All people born with either one too many or one too few chromosomes show some degree of mental impairment. The information in Table 2 makes this clear. Only AIS patients, who have a normal chromosome complement, score consistently in the normal range on both Verbal and Performance IQ. The data in Table 2 thus suggest that good performance correlate with normal chromosome complements, *not*—as Bock and Kolakowski suggest—with hormone levels. By any scientifically acceptable standards, this attempt to save the X-linked space gene theory fails.

As a study in the sociology of science, however, the Stafford hypothesis remains interesting. From the point of view of a geneticist, the idea that two specific genes govern a complex, continuously varying trait is dubious to begin with. As we have just seen, the available data is either categorically inappropriate or lends no support to the idea. Yet since its initial publication in 1961, the X-linkage hypothesis has shown considerable tenacity, appearing as fact in some textbooks and showing up in highly political articles as part of larger arguments about the genetic incapacity of females for certain sorts of work. The real fact is that many people, both scientists and nonscientists, just plain *like* the idea and go to considerable lengths to salvage it because it fits so

* Performance IQ is used by some scientists as a measure of spatial ability, although it is not a test designed for this use.

neatly into the entrenched stereotype of feminine inferiority. It constitutes a not uncommon example of how social views influence the progress of science.

From American Experience

Vern L. Bullough

Vern L. Bullough was founding director of the Center for Sex Research at California State University–Northridge, and he is an emeritus professor of history at the same university. He is a prolific writer and researcher who has authored more than 50 books, the latest of which is How I Got Into Sex *(1998).*

When the wife of Governor Hopkins of Connecticut [. . .] became mentally ill, her insanity was blamed upon the fact that she had spent so much time in reading and writing. "If she had attended her household affairs, and such things as belong to women, and not gone out of her way and calling to meddle in such things as are proper for men, whose minds are stronger, etc., she had kept her wits, and might have improved them usefully and honorably in the place God had set her."[1] Those women who attempted to exceed their assigned role usually found themselves in hot water. A good illustration of this is Anne Hutchinson (1591 to 1643), who was banned from Massachusetts because she had exceeded "woman's place" by holding informal weekly meetings of women to discuss the sermons of the previous Sunday and to interpret them for her listeners. Such activity was held to be "a thing not tolerable nor comely in the sight of God nor fitting" for a woman to do. When Mrs. Hutchinson retorted that the Bible gave permission for women to teach the young, she was warned that such teachings were to be restricted to teaching young women "about their business to love their husbands," not religious views that differed from the majority.[2]

The Puritans in New England found biblical justification for their subjugation of women in the fifth commandment and its reference to honoring a father and mother. Though both sexes were clearly mentioned in the commandment it was held that "father and mother" were to be interpreted as meaning not only parents but all superiors and since the husband was the superior of the wife by the law of conjugal subjection, as well as by nature, she had no choice but to respect his wishes.[3] When one New England woman wrote a book her brother publicly rebuked her by stating that your "printing of a Book beyond the custom of your sex, doth rankly smell."[4] Anne Bradstreet (1612 to 1672), America's first woman poet, conscious of the male hostility to the educated female, prefaced her book:

> I am obnoxious to each carping tongue
> Who says my hand a needle better fits.
> A poets pen all scorn I should thus wrong,

[1] John Winthrop, *The History of New England 1630–1649* (2 vols., Boston: Thomas B. Wait, 1826), vol. 2, p. 216.

[2] David Hall, ed., *The Antinomian Controversy, 1636–1638* (Middleton, Conn.: Wesleyan University Press, 1968), pp. 312, 315–316.

[3] For a discussion of this see Thomas Cobbet, *A Fruitful and Useful Discourse Touching the Honour Due from Children to Parents* (London, 1656), p. 18.

[4] Thomas Parker, *The Copy of a Letter Written to His Sister* (London, 1650), p. 13.

For such despite they caste on Female wits:
If what I do prove well, it won't advance,
They'l say it's stoln, or else it was by chance.[5]

Even when women went to school they often read special textbooks prepared for them in order to limit the strain on their faculties. Such titles as *Newton's Ladies Philosophy, The Lady's Geography, The Female Academy, The Ladies Complete Letter Writer,* and the *Female Miscellany* were often advertised.[6] Women were not always happy with such restrictions and Anne Bradstreet was one of those who protested against the generalizations about female inferiority. She pointed to Queen Elizabeth as an example of a woman who had made considerable contributions to civilization and concluded:

Now say, have women worth or have they none?
Or have they some, but with our Queen is't gone?
Nay Masculines, you have thus taxt us long,
But she, though dead, will vindicate our wrong.
Let such as say our Sex is void of Reason,
Know tis a Slander now, but once was Treason.[7]

Women of course were invaluable as economic adjuncts to their husbands and they did other jobs which either required no formal education or little technical knowledge. Others served in more skilled capacities as private tutors, as school mistresses, or as midwives and herb doctors. Many served as nurses but usually as a sideline rather than a real occupation. Women were also shopkeepers, although their shops were usually run from their own homes. Maria Provost, wife of James Alexander, kept one of the largest shops in New York City. One evening in 1721 she gave birth to a daughter after having spent the day behind the counter and the next day with the help of her sixteen-year-old apprentice she opened the shop and sold thirty pounds worth of merchandise from her bed. Her husband bragged that he was very lucky to have such a good wife who "alone would make a man easy and happy had he nothing else to depend on."[8] Women, of course, served as seamstresses, milliners, laundresses, dyers, and stay-makers, but they also had other occupations; Jane Inch of Maryland was a silversmith, while Mary Willet took over her husband's pewter business after his death. In South Carolina Anna Maria Hoyland advertised that she would do any kind of "braziery and tinwork" as her mother had done. Maria Warwell mended china and Cassandra Ducker of Maryland owned and ran a fulling mill.[9] It was only when cities grew larger and occupations more specialized and professionalized that women were cut out of most jobs. This was because as cities became larger the business districts centralized and it became much more difficult for women to run a store from their home or to compete with the specialized stores. As specialization increased in impor-

---

[5] Anne Bradstreet, *The Works of Anne Bradstreet,* ed. by John Harvard Ellis (New York: Peter Smith, 1932), p. 101.

[6] Julia Cherry Spruill, *Women's Life and Work in the Southern Colonies* (Chapel Hill: University of North Carolina Press, 1938), p. 202.

[7] Bradstreet, *Works,* p. 361.

[8] Alice Morse Earle, *Colonial Days in Old New York* (Port Washington, N.Y.: Friedman, 1962), p. 163.

[9] Spruill, *Women's Life,* p. 288.

tance, more training was required and women were denied the opportunity to be apprentices or in the cases of the professions to attend the necessary colleges or universities. Continental ideas about what constituted the fashionable woman also exercised more influence as Americans reached higher levels of prosperity. Increasingly those women who pretended to any culture or status imitated their English cousins in their ideas about women's role.

Still the vastness of America often allowed different norms to be followed. On Nantucket Island, for example, the whaling fleets kept the men away from home on voyages from two to five years in length, with the result that much of the island's business was handled by the women. Status for such a woman came from her ability to best make or protect her husband's money during his absence. Under such conditions it was very difficult for a woman to be a "clinging vine," if only because as one islander remarked, there were "no sturdy oaks" for her to cling to. Though mainlanders characterized Nantucket women as "homely and ungenteel," and their Quakerism kept their dress plain, they performed many of the tasks reserved for men in other parts of America. One preserved anecdote, perhaps apocryphal, tells the tale of a good wife who while at a store decided to buy a whole barrel of flour rather than make several trips to the store, and then to save delivery time, picked up the barrel and carried it home.[10] It was perhaps no accident that women from Nantucket contributed out of proportion to the leaders of the women's rights movement in the nineteenth century. Lucretia Mott, one of the early feminists, and Maria Mitchell, professor of astronomy at Vassar and militant champion of a new place for women, were both natives of the island.

A New World beyond Snow White

Sandra M. Gilbert and Susan Gubar

Sandra Gilbert, professor of English at the University of California-Davis, and Susan Gubar, professor of English at Indiana University, together authored the groundbreaking The Madwoman in the Attic: The Woman Writer and the Nineteenth-Century Literary Imagination *(1979), as well as the three-volume* No Man's Land: The Place of the Woman Writer in the Twentieth Century *(1988–94). They contributed this comment to* The New York Times.

In 1979 we dramatized the dilemma of 19th-century women, especially women writers, through a discussion of "Snow White." There was a good queen who pricked her finger with a needle, watched blood fall on snow, gave birth to a girl, died and was replaced by a wicked queen, who became stepmother to Snow White.

When a mother figure becomes self-assertive in a society that discourages independence, we suggested in our analysis of the story, it is as if the good mother dies and is replaced by a wicked stepmother. Thus, the tale illuminates the conflict between socially prescribed femininity and the rebellious woman artist's desire for power.

But now too much has happened for the story of sexuality and its discontents to be summarized along the classic lines of "Snow White." Increasing numbers of women

[10] William Oliver Steven, *Nantucket, the Far Away Island* (New York: Dodd, Mead, 1966), p. 103.

have entered the workplace. They have been through the sex wars associated with the modern liberation movement. And many American families have been transformed by a second wave of feminism.

If a '90s storyteller, a contemporary Scheherazade, were to meditate on the story of "Snow White," then, what new plots might she weave?

She might continue the story like this:

"Who is the most powerful of them all?" the queen asked her husband, resenting his smug sense of superiority. The king quickly answered that he was 10 times more powerful than she and her stepdaughter Snow White put together. So she and the lovely girl plotted to kill him.

They lured the king into a dark forest, planning to tear out his heart. But a passing huntsman rescued the majestic man and brought him to a male sanctuary where seven dwarfs and a prince disguised him as a statue of God in a glass coffin.

Meanwhile

What the reader imagines as an outcome of this revision clearly depends on which side he or she is on in the battle between the sexes.

Can the king and the queen make love, not war? Another rewriting might focus on current controversies about the erotic, and in particular on recent re-imaginings of women's desire.

"Who is the fairest of them all?" the queen asked, and her mirror said Snow White was the sexiest girl in the realm. So the queen set out to perfect the child's charms. She hired a huntsman to take the girl to a finishing school run by dwarfs where she would be taught costuming, hairdressing and how to stay on a diet. The queen hoped her stepdaughter might become Miss Dark Forest of 1992.

But en route to the school the handsome huntsman seduced Snow White. By the time she finally arrived at the mansion of the dwarfs, she was quite adept in the arts of love. Indeed, she was ready to teach the dwarfs a thing or two.

As this version suggests, changes in sexual standards have a double meaning for women: On the one hand, our heroine's erotic urges have been liberated; on the other, she risks becoming no more than a marketable commodity.

Because heterosexuality is so problematic here, our Scheherazade might want to use the old tale to explore alternative sexualities. "Who is the fairest of them all?" the queen asked, and when the mirror said Snow White was the most beautiful, the queen realized that she loved the girl with a love surpassing the love of man.

But as the two grew closer, the king became suspicious and plotted to kill Snow White. He hired a huntsman to take the girl into a forest and tear out her heart. The queen, though, got wind of his plans and arranged for Snow White to hide in a commune run by kindly dwarfs, where she could study her maternal heritage and receive nocturnal visits from the queen (disguised as a huntsman).

But the king, determined to stop these unnatural activities, arranged for a mercenary prince to capture the girl. This clever fellow disguised himself as a medical man and offered her three gifts to heal her of what he asserted was a neurosis: a feminine costume, a new hairdo and the fruit of his knowledge.

Depending on our storyteller's views about alternative sexualities, this third revision might result in a blissful union between the queen and Snow White (or maybe a happy-ever-after pairing of the king and the prince).

But given the increasing indeterminacy of our plot, the final retelling of the story could well represent many recent speculations about the artificiality of such traditional categories as gender, race and identity.

"Who is the fairest of them all?" the queen asked her mirror, for she realized that she was a mere mask. So were Snow White and the king. Who and what were they all, anyway? Merely signifiers, signifying nothing—or so she thought in her bleakest moments.

Or were those her wisest moments? Because everything seemed so indeterminate to the royal couple, they decided to send their brilliant daughter to a seminar run by bookish dwarfs who pondered the riddle of gender identity. Accompanied only by a philosophical huntsman, the girl made her way through circuitous paths into a bewildering forest of no names. "Am I no more than a glass coffin?" she wondered aloud.

Despite the tales our modern Scheherazade might produce, there is one constant: Snow White is of woman born and, even in an age of in vitro fertilization and surrogate motherhood, she would still be of woman born. What sort of woman could be her mother now, though? Mightn't Snow White as easily be born to the ambitious second queen as to the more dutiful first?

Because contemporary women are no longer inevitably silenced and domesticated, perhaps there need be no murderous conflict between Snow White and the second queen. And because women can negotiate between procreativity and creativity more easily today than they could 50 years ago, perhaps there need be no split between Snow White's biological mother and her rebellious stepmother.

In fact, many of the women poets and novelists who came to prominence after World War II were mothers—as were a great many other postwar women professionals—and these writers frequently focused on maternity. How might one of these mother-writers tell the old story of "Snow White"? Would she tell it all, or would the major cultural changes she represents so transform the basic outlines of the tale that its plot would no longer be recognizable?

There was a good queen who pricked her finger with a needle, watched blood fall on snow, gave birth to a girl named Snow White and lived to rear her. Sometimes when this queen looked into the mirror of her mind, she passed in her thoughts through the looking glass into a forest of stories so new that only she and her daughter could tell them.

What Keeps an Airplane Up?

Version for General Readers or Students in the Writing Class

Gary Kolnicki

At least once in the course of your life while sitting in an airplane, you must have asked yourself, "What keeps this thing from falling out of the sky?" You may think you understand. You've probably studied it or had it explained to you. But ask yourself, as you sit there looking out at nothing but clouds, if you can explain it to yourself and the answer will probably be No.

Two dynamic effects supply the lift for an airplane in flight. The simplest and most obvious source is what is called "the kite effect." Because the wing of the plane is slightly tipped upwards like a kite (see Figure 1), and because the plane is moving forward through the air, molecules slam with high speed into the *bottom* surface of the wing, pushing it upwards. Clearly there would be no kite effect if the plane were not moving forward. (It's true that the kite may not seem to be moving forward, but in fact it is moving forward with respect to the air around it—for the kite only flies if there is a good breeze.)

But the kite effect supplies only about one-third of the lift in an airplane. Two-thirds of the lift comes from what is called the "dynamic lift effect." This effect also

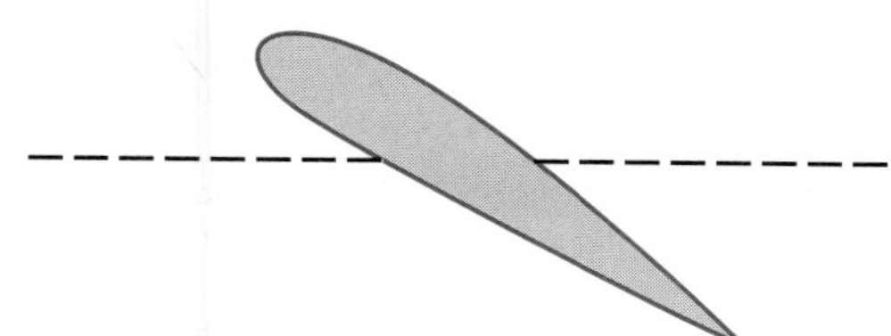

Figure 1 Cross Section of a Wing

depends upon the plane moving forward very fast. (Thus planes don't try to take off till they have a good velocity.) But to understand the dynamic lift effect, the major source of support for an airplane, you need to understand how gas particles exert pressure at a microscopic level.

Air is a gas that consists of a very large number of particles or molecules in high-speed motion. These molecules travel in straight lines in all directions. Because air is so dense, these molecules continuously collide with one another, bouncing off in all directions in zigzag paths. But because there are so *many* molecules moving randomly in this way, it turns out that at any given moment about the same number of particles are moving in all directions—with a result that there is no net movement of air. There's lots of motion, but as a whole it's getting nowhere.

But these molecules do exert pressure on any surface that they run into (and the more molecules, the more pressure). For when the randomly moving molecules hit the wall, they transfer their momentum to the wall—causing pressure. In an air-filled box, for example, an empty cigarette box on the table, the air exerts an *equal* pressure on all the walls since there are an equal number of particles bouncing off each wall. Thus the box stays where it is on the table: all those molecules are hitting on all walls equally.

An airplane wing is shaped in such a way as to make an "airfoil." It is rounded in the front, and arches to a point in the back. Because of this airfoil shape (and because it is somewhat tipped upward) there is an *imbalance* of pressure as the wing passes through the air.

As the wing passes through the air, the air takes two distinct paths across the wing: above and below (see Figure 2). Since the upper stream travels a longer path than the lower stream, the lower stream reaches the back of the wing first.

Because the upper stream hasn't yet reached the back, the air above the rear of the wing has lower pressure, causing the lower stream to curl up and back rather than to continue in the same direction. The upper stream meets this curling stream and forces it in a circular flow, called a vortex (see Figure 3). The upper stream is accelerated due to the lower pressure under the vortex.

The Bernoulli principle predicts dynamic lift under these conditions. According to this principle, a higher speed results in lower pressure. The stream above the wing has

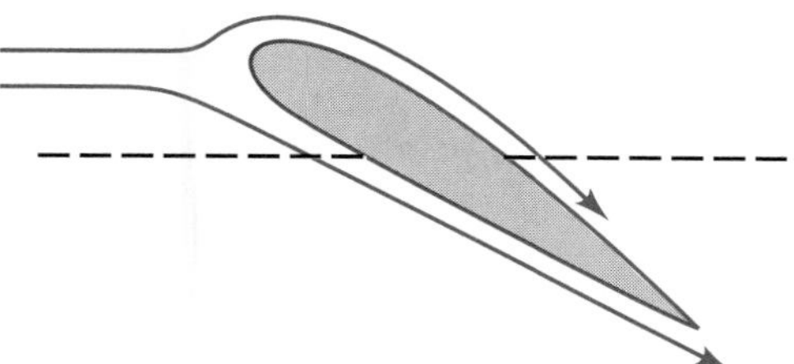

Figure 2 Path Difference

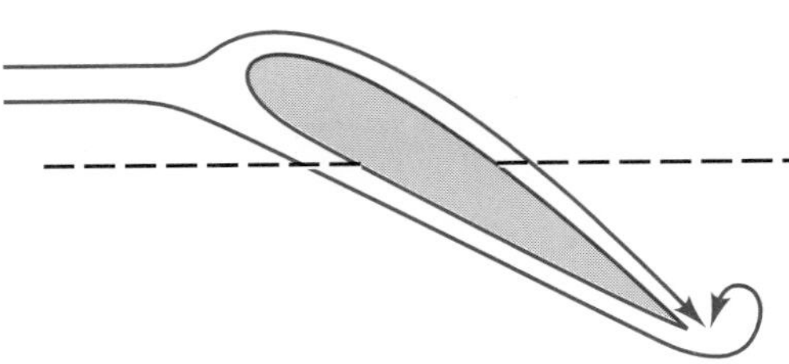

Figure 3 Vortex

a higher velocity and produces a lower pressure—thus a net upward force or lift. Remember that this effect is all being produced by molecular collisions at the microscopic level.

To illustrate this principle more schematically, consider a piece of paper in horizontal position with three volumes of air: one below, one above, and one in front, as shown in Figure 4.

This picture describes a case in which no motion results. Look now at Figure 5 with the top box moving to the right. The force which moves the upper box must result from an imbalance in pressure between it and the larger box in front. Since the large box's pressure hasn't changed, the upper box must have a lower pressure in order to be moved to the right. It follows that the faster the motion, the lower the pressure. The lower pressure above results in a net force upwards, or lift.

Flaps, moveable deflectors at the trailing edge of the wing, control the amount of lift. If a flap is in a downward position, it increases the curvature of the wing and thus makes the path difference between upper and lower flows even greater. This results in a process similar to the one just described and lift increases. The opposite occurs if the flap is in an upward position.

Of course, more can be explained about the complicated subject of flight. Basically, however, the physical processes described above prevent an airplane's falling out of the sky. Though not magical, the effects which describe the way air alone can hold up a jumbo jet are quite fascinating, complicated, and unexpected. Even a person with basic physics knowledge may not be aware of the sources of an airplane's lift on a fundamental level.

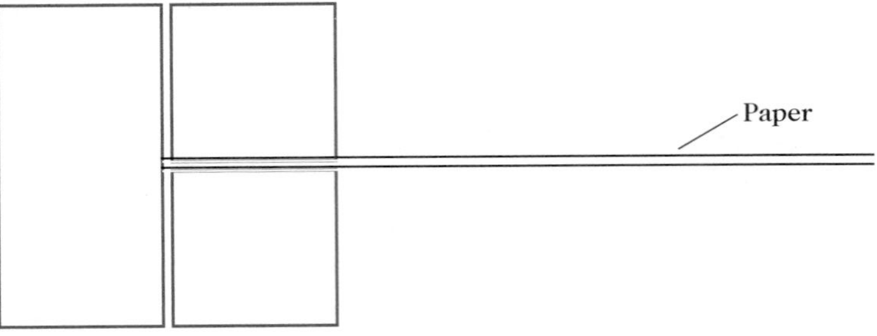

Figure 4 Small Volumes of Air

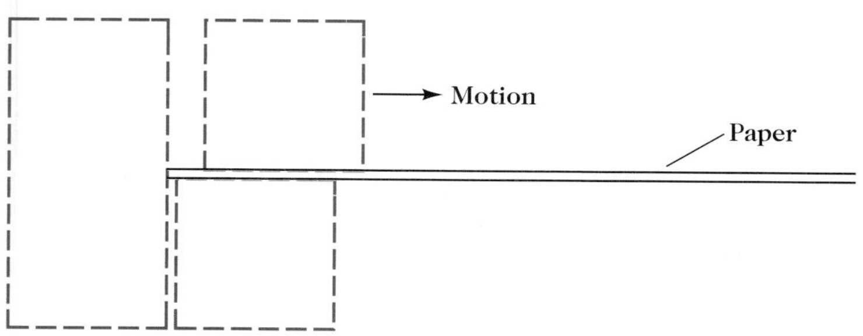

Figure 5 Motion from Pressure Imbalance

What Keeps an Airplane Up?

Version for Teachers or for People Who Know a Bit about Physics

Gary Kolnicki

Even though many people believe they understand the way an airplane flies, very few truly know the physical processes which occur.

Two dynamic effects join to supply nearly all the support, or lift, for an airplane in flight. For an airfoil or wing, dynamic lift and the kite effect provide nearly all the lift.

Instrumental in understanding dynamic lift and the kite effect is a fundamental understanding of the gas particle theory along with a concept of pressure at a microscopic level. The Bernoulli equation predicts that these two effects will bring lift but does not aid in explaining them.

Air, a gas, consists of a very large number of particles in high-speed motion which travel in straight lines in all directions. Because air is so dense, particles continually collide with one another, bouncing off into other directions, in zig-zag paths. Since there are a large number of particles in this random motion at any one time, about the same number of particles move in all directions causing no net movement of air.

Pressure of a gas on a surface is a force due to collisions of molecules of the gas with that surface. As the molecules in random motion move in a way so that they hit the wall and transfer their momentum, pressure results. Therefore, the more particles in the gas, the more particles that will be moving in that certain direction, colliding with the wall, and putting more pressure on it. In an air-filled box, the air exerts an equal pressure on each wall, since there are an equal number of particles bouncing off each wall.

An airfoil is shaped and oriented so that an imbalance in pressure results as the wing passes through the air. The following effect accounts for the majority of this pressure imbalance. It is called dynamic lift.

A wing's cross section appears in Figure 1. It is rounded in the front and arches to a point in the back. Figure 1 also illustrates the upward direction in which the wing points.

As the wing passes through the air, air takes two distinct paths across the wing: above and below. Since the upper stream travels a longer path than the lower stream, the lower stream reaches the back of the wing first. This is illustrated in Figure 2. Because the upper stream hasn't yet reached the back, the air above the rear of the

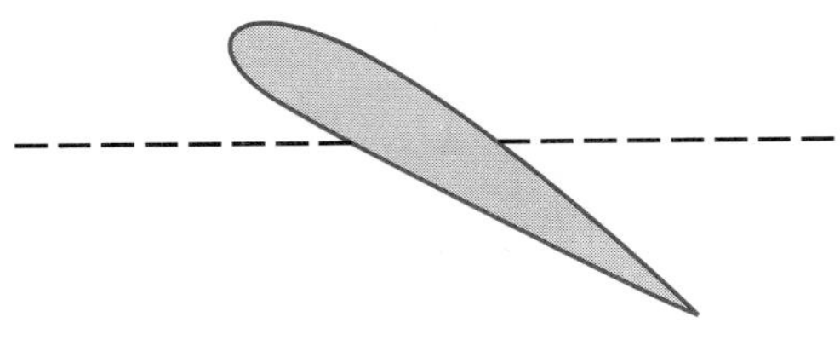

Figure 1 Cross Section of a Wing

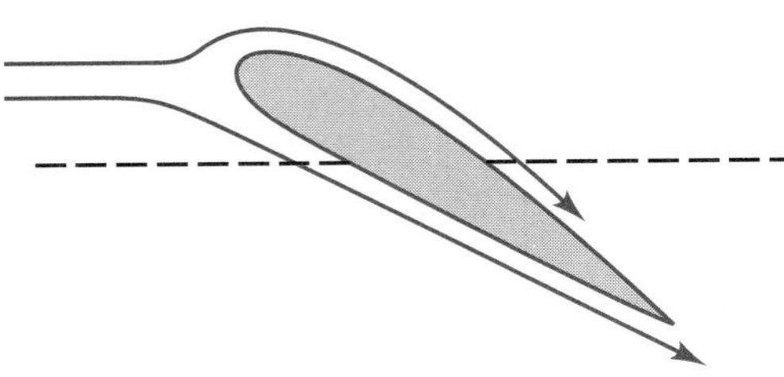

Figure 2 Path Difference

wing has lower pressure, causing the lower stream to curl up and back rather than to continue in the same direction. The upper stream meets this curling stream and forces it into a circular flow, called a vortex. Figure 3 shows this flow. The upper stream is accelerated due to the lower pressure under the vortex. Once the upper stream has reached a velocity so that the upper and lower streams simultaneously reach the trail end of the wing, a pressure difference will no longer exist to curl up and back the lower stream. The vortex then moves away and dissipates, leaving this continuous flow of air above the wing.

The Bernoulli principle predicts dynamic lift under these conditions. A higher velocity results in lower pressure, according to this principle. Above, a stream with higher velocity than the lower produces lower pressure. Therefore, a net upward force, lift, results.

Microscopically, this effect is caused by molecular collisions.

Consider a piece of paper in a horizontal position with three volumes of air: one below, one above, and one in front (see Figure 4). This picture describes a case in which no motion results. Focus now on Figure 5 with the top box now moving to the right. The force which moves the upper box must result from an imbalance in pressure between it and the larger box in front. Since the large box's pressure hasn't changed, the upper box must have a lower pressure in order to be moved to the right. It follows that the faster the motion, the lower the pressure.

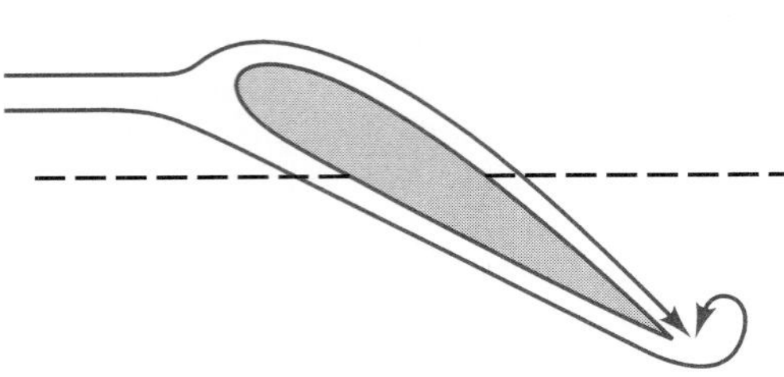

Figure 3 Vortex before Constant Flow

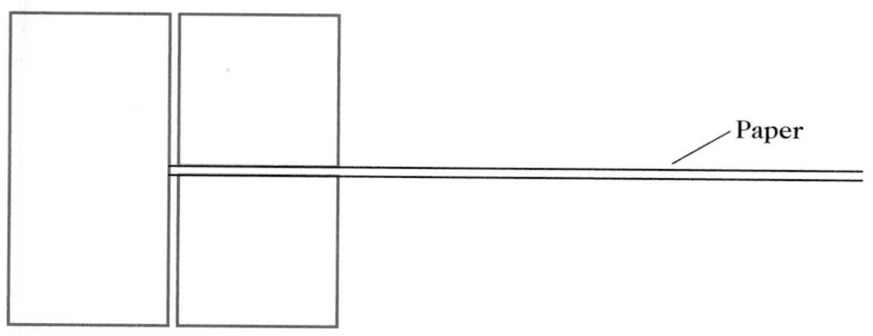

Figure 4 *Small* Volumes of Air

Now, think of air passing across a wing in steady flight. As shown earlier, the upper stream has a higher velocity than the lower stream. Since the air in front of the wing exerts the same pressure on both these streams, similar to Figure 5, the upper stream must have a lower pressure than the lower stream. The greater velocity is the result of a larger force, or greater pressure imbalance. The lower pressure above results in a net force upward, or lift.

The kite effect is also described in a microscopic way. This effect occurs due to the upward orientation of the aircraft's wing. As the wing proceeds through the air, molecules slam with high speed into the slightly upturned bottom giving more lift to the plane.

The kite effect accounts for about one-third of total lift. Dynamic lift claims the majority of lift—almost two-thirds. Aircraft velocity is necessary for both these effects, and, therefore, thrust must be supplied. For this reason, aircrafts are designed to minimize friction. In some ways, an airplane is designed to slip through the air like a paper airplane.

Flaps, moveable deflectors at the trailing edge of the wing, control the amount of lift. If a flap is in a downward position, it increases the curvature of the wing and thus makes the path difference between upper and lower flows even greater. This results in a process similar to the one just described and lift increases. The opposite occurs if the flap is in an upward position.

Of course, more can be explained about the complicated subject of flight. Basically, however, the physical processes described above prevent an airplane's falling out of the sky. Though not magical, the effects which describe the way air alone can hold up

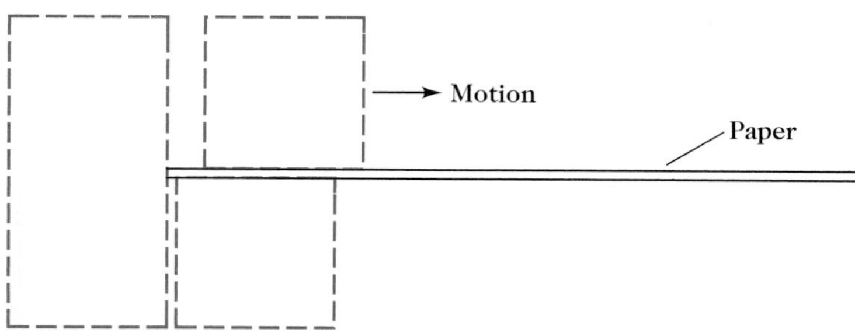

Figure 5 Motion from Pressure Imbalance

a jumbo jet are quite fascinating, complicated, and unexpected. Even a person with basic physics knowledge may not be aware of the sources of an airplane's lift on a fundamental level.

Bibliography

"Aerodynamics." *Britannica Online.* Vers. 99.2. April 1999. Encyclopedia Britannica. 25 May 1999 <http://search.eb.com/bol/topic?eu=3920&sctn=1>.

"Airplane." *McGraw-Hill Encyclopedia of Science and Technology.* 8th ed. 1997.

Halliday, David, Robert Resnick, and Jearl Walker. *Fundamentals of Physics.* 5th ed. New York: Wiley, 1996.

Autobiography and Portfolio

Essential Premises

- Examining one's writings and the processes that went into composing them is a valuable learning process that can lead to improved writing and thinking.
- Writing is not just a school activity; it has a role to play in one's private and public life outside the classroom.

Main Assignment Preview

Our experience has taught us that writers learn the most by becoming students of their own writing processes. Thus, our major aim in this workshop is to get you to learn something about yourself and your writing process that will be useful when you are doing future writing tasks in school. But we also hope the activities of this workshop will help you see some role for writing in your life outside of school assignments. Along the way you should discover for yourself that writing leads to learning.

Main Assignment: *Creating a Portfolio and Your Autobiography as a Writer*

Your main assignment will be to create a portfolio of the work you've done during this school term and add to it an autobiography of yourself as a writer. And since you will be using the writing you've done throughout the semester as a basis for your autobiography, this workshop will encourage you to look back on the term and assess honestly what happened to you and your writing.

For many of you, this will be your final assignment of the term. It will help you solidify and benefit from what you have been learning all this term. Some of what you've learned you've been explicitly aware you were learning; but you have learned many other things in an intuitive, unconscious way. This autobiography will help you see and consolidate *all* you have learned. It needn't be too much work, yet you can discover much about your own learning and how it has affected the way you write.

The theme of your autobiography is the theme of the course: *the writing process*. The autobiography will help you see the writing process in detail and empirically, not just settle for generalizations. The *facts* about what you actually do when you write are probably somewhat different from what you *think* you do. Discovering these facts almost always makes your writing easier and better.

Creating Your Portfolio

Your teacher may have asked you at the beginning of the term to start a portfolio and keep everything you write in it. Or she may have asked you to put only certain things in it. Perhaps she has looked at it—even evaluated it—once or twice already. In our classes we like our students to put a wide variety of kinds of writing in their portfolios: some journal pieces, freewritings, exploratory writings, responses to readings, drafts, peer responses, and process writing, as well as finished pieces. We like also for students to put into their portfolios other pieces of writing we haven't asked for that they may be particularly proud of: pieces written for other classes and even pieces written for pleasure.

Your teacher will tell you what she would like you to include in your portfolio. Chances are that if she is going to use the portfolio to help decide your grade for the term, she won't want everything in there and will ask you to make some selections either with or without help from her and your classmates. These pieces will serve as a basis for your autobiography, which in turn will serve as a kind of cover sheet for your portfolio.

Your first task for this workshop is to assemble the portfolio your teacher asks for. Once it's all together, read back over it and do some freewriting about what you see there.

Possible Ingredients, Issues, or Themes for Your Autobiography

The following are methods and topics to help you bring together material for your autobiography. Some of these issues you've already written about in your process journal throughout the term. Perhaps you've already reread your journal as you were assembling your final portfolio. If not, you should now look back through your journal and identify these passages. The freewriting you did after preparing your portfolio will also probably touch on a number of these issues. You will not have written on other topics we suggest in the following list. You should begin writing on any or all of the topics and see what happens. Looking at the contents of your portfolio may help you come up with specific ideas and examples. For now, the important thing to remember is that you're not trying to draw conclusions; you're still in the data-collection stage.

Moments What important incidents do you remember from past writing experiences?

Stages Intuitively divide your life as a writer into a few stages or periods; then ask yourself what characterizes each of those stages.

Kinds What kinds of writing have you done in the past and what kinds do you do now? Remember that there are many more kinds of writing than those you've done in school. Making lists is writing; so is graffiti. What is different about your experience with different kinds of writing?

In-School versus Out-of-School Writing Do you go about both of these the same way? differently? Do you feel the same way about both? Why or why not?

Audience Who are the important people you have written for? (Not just teachers.) What effects have these different audiences had? on your feelings? on your writing? Which audiences helped you the most or held you back? How often do you feel yourself to be the only audience of what you are writing? (Don't forget "ghost audiences" or audiences we carry around in our heads and unconsciously try to please—usually left over from experiences with past audiences.) Many people remember bad audiences more than good ones. Is that true of you? Why?

Physical Where do you write? When? How fast or slow? What are the effects of using pen, pencil, typewriter, or word processor? How do you hold and move your body? Do you feel tense or relaxed after a session of writing? Tell everything that could be figured out from a complete video recording of your writing from start to finish.

Exploring the Writing Process

Since graduation, I have been working administratively. When I began the job, I feared that I would unwillingly convert to a bureaucrat, and begin to write as one. I may be wrong, but I think the office work has actually improved my writing skills, particularly in correspondence. My writing is now more direct, clear, and assertive. I regularly write to people asking for things, and I ask in a specific, shameless, and brief manner. Sometimes I feel bossy while I do it, but nobody seems to mind, so I keep doing it.

In my office, it is common for an important letter written by either me or a co-worker to be proofread by at least six sets of eyes. This has made criticism and evaluation less painful for me. I have come to learn that it's the page, not the writer that is important, that people have more important things to think about than what a piece of writing has to say about me. Before this job, I was much more apprehensive about showing my writing to other people. As an undergraduate, for instance, I would wince and apologize excessively when handing papers in. Now I am less embarrassed by mistakes and I do not try to explain them.

Donna Whicher

Process Try to isolate specific steps in your writing process—for example, generating words and responses, copyediting, publishing. Nonwriting counts too: sitting and thinking, talking to people. Which of these give you the most trouble? the least? the most satisfaction? the least? Why?

Intervention In what ways have others intervened in your writing? ("Here, let me show you!" "Do it this way." "You must start by making an outline." "You must start by freewriting.") How has intervention affected your writing?

Response and Feedback What kinds of response and feedback have you gotten—and not just from teachers? What effects did this feedback have on you? (Don't forget no response and nonverbal response—silence and laughter.)

Writing for Other Classes versus Writing for This Class If you've written papers for other classes this term, what's different about how you went about it? Did you do any freewriting, produce a draft which your teacher responded to either verbally or in writing, revise one or more times, copyedit? Compare the total effort involved in that project and the total effort involved in writing a piece for this class. Pay attention to any differences in feelings or attitudes toward the two pieces of writing. If you did not use the techniques we've been stressing in this book, do you think you could have or should have? Why or why not?

Problems Stuck points and breakthroughs. What's hardest for you or what gets in the way most? How have you made or not made progress? Where have you made the greatest progress?

Myths What are some of the feelings or ideas that you've had about your writing (or that most people seem to have) that you now see are *false?* Where did these myths come from? What purposes did they serve and what effect have they had on you? What follows from abandoning them?

The Word "Writer" Who do you think of as a writer? What are the characteristics of a writer? Can you think of yourself as a writer? If not, why not?

Temperament or Character Do you see any relation between your writing process and your temperament, character, or feelings? Does your writing process show you to be "loose" or "tight," vulnerable or confident? In general, do you think that someone's writing process reflects his or her character?

Making a Draft

You should now have much raw material—some developed, some just bits. Read through all of this and all your process writing from the term. (You probably have more than you realize; some of your assignments have been process writing or include bits of it. You'll find other bits here and there. Some will be in notebooks for other subjects.) Mark the bits that are interesting and useful. You can probably use some of this process writing as part of your paper if you choose and cut well.

Next, consider what all this process writing is telling you. Do some freewriting, outlining, or note jotting to figure out what your autobiography might focus on.

Two additional things we consider particularly important in any writer's autobiography. One is a mini-study or close look at a single specific piece of writing. The second is an analysis of how your present writing process differs from the way you used to write. We could have included both of these in our earlier list, but we wanted to give them special emphasis.

1. For your mini-study, choose something that you wrote this term. Choose that piece which—as the psychologists say—you "cathect" most, that piece you have the strongest feelings about or feel the strongest connection with. You can learn most from looking honestly and in detail at such a piece. You might also, however, simply pick the piece for which you have the most process writing—the most evidence about what actually was going on as you wrote. Evidence maximizes learning. Spend some time reconstructing how you wrote this piece from beginning to end in as much detail as possible; look at the writing itself, the various drafts, and see what they tell you. Select specific passages that you can quote and comment on. Do some freewriting, outlining, and jotting about what you figure out as you study this piece.

2. Think back on the writing you did before this course. (Some of your process writing will be about that too. You might have included it in the collage you did early in the term about your writing history.) What does that early writing tell you? Many of you have probably saved papers written in high school. You might want to look at these and see how much you can remember about writing them. This should lead you to some conclusions about the similarities and differences between how you used to write and how you write now. This, in turn, should make clearer the effects of this term's work on your writing.

Now you have the ingredients for producing a draft. You can do some cutting and pasting and arranging, but make sure to let this draft making be a process of *new discovery,* not merely an assembling of what you already

Exploring the Writing Process

Each man has his own way. After all, most writing is done away from the typewriter, away from the desk. I'd say it occurs in the quiet, silent moments, while you're walking or shaving or playing a game or whatever, or even talking to someone you're not vitally interested in. You're working, your mind is working, on this problem in the back of your head. So, when you get to the machine it's a mere matter of transfer.

Henry Miller

have. Look at all this material that you now suspect belongs in your draft. What does it mean? What does it add up to? What emphasis, claim, focus, shape, approach, spirit do you want your case study to have? If you keep these questions in mind, you will find new answers as you write and paste.

In making your draft, you are finally ready to ask the practical question: What useful advice or suggestions can you give yourself for future writing? What are the dangers for you as a writer? What do you wish someone would whisper in your ear as you undertake writing tasks in the future?

A good writer's autobiography can be structured like a story or like an essay. That is, you can build it around either of the two major structural impulses for writing:

- *Narrative, temporal.* ("And then, and then, and then . . ."—with scattered "so what's" that tell the point of the story.)
- *Expository, conceptual.* ("Here's my first point and what it means and why it's important; here's my second point . . . , and here's my third point . . ." and so on.)

If you choose the story mode, make sure there is enough "so what." Don't let it be just a story. If you are clever, you can make some of the "so what"—the significance—be implied or unstated. But some of it has to be explicit. Of course, there's nothing wrong with "just a story"—*as* a story—but this assignment asks you to spell out some of the meaning or significance. If you choose the essay or expository mode, don't let it get too dry, abstract, or generalized. Keep the life in it by using specific examples, telling mini-stories, and incorporating descriptions, including particulars and quotations from writing you did, feedback you got, and so forth.

Try to emphasize for yourself that this task can be fun, not just work. Remember:

- You are the authority on you.
- You've done lots of writing and thinking this term about yourself as a writer. What has been the most interesting and useful to *you?*
- Your audience is not only your teacher but also yourself. What you can figure out for yourself is really more important than what you can fig-

Exploring the Writing Process

In general, my writing has always been considered horrible by others. I have never received praise from anyone. Yet I remember my preteen years being filled with poetry. I would write about everything that I could. There was a poem hiding behind everything. It was like heaven. Just being able to pick up a pen and have those wonderful words flow, as if by magic, onto my paper. I never read them (my poems) out loud, for fear that I would not be able to truly express the feeling of each. Each word, phrase, and sentence had a special aura about it. I could never be able to give them their due. Those words from my hands were like heaven.

Ngozi Allick

ure out for your teacher. Your classmates are an additional audience. Your teacher will probably give you a chance to share your autobiography, but if not, find a way. Autobiographies are almost always a treat to read and hear.

Minimal Guidelines

Make certain your autobiography includes at *least* the following. Undoubtedly you'll want to do more; this is just a foundation for you to check your draft against.

1. Examination of your writing both *before* taking this course and *during* this course. That is, the autobiography should function somewhat as a way of talking about how this course affected or did not affect how you write.
2. Examination of one piece or episode of writing in some detail. Indeed, you could center the whole autobiography around your examination of one piece of writing, bringing in the other parts of your autobiography in relation to this piece.
3. Quotations from your writing. Show how these examples of words on the page illustrate (or do not illustrate) what you are saying about your writing process. That is, explain the relationship between your process and your product—between *what*'s on the page and *how* it got there.
4. Examination of comments or feedback by others. Comments can be from teachers, friends, or classmates, from this course or other courses.
5. A bit of advice for yourself: On the basis of all this exploration, what suggestions can you give yourself to make your writing go better in the future? Give your autobiography a *practical* dimension. Make it something that you will find useful to read over in the future when you are engaged in writing.

Sharing and Responding

The most useful feedback is probably what's produced by using the techniques in Section 2, "Pointing and Center of Gravity," and Section 3, "Summary and Sayback," in the "Sharing and Responding" part of this book. But you may also want to get some comments on how your structure is coming across, especially when you've gotten to the final draft. To get some feedback on this, you can use the "Sharing and Responding" sections grouped under structural responses.

Here are some more specific questions to use, but the important thing is for you to ask for the kind of feedback *you* feel most useful.

- What changes do you see in me as a writer? What do you think I've learned during this term? What do you think I need to work on most? What do I seem most confident about? least confident about?
- Do you think some of what I've recorded contradicts any conclusions I've drawn? Do you feel gaps, something missing that would make the picture of me as a writer more complete?

- What do you find the most surprising or unique about my autobiography?
- What did you find helpful for yourself as a writer from my autobiography? What did you learn from me that you find the most valuable?

Process Journal

As always, these are merely suggestions. You may want the last segment of your autobiography to consist of comment on and analysis of what it was like writing it.

Exploring the Writing Process

From *A Case Study of Myself*

The funny thing about the feedback that I received in this course is that I don't think I ever immediately understood what it was saying. The typed feedback letters were immensely helpful. But, I've realized after reading back through them all that what I read and what you wrote in the first place are two different things entirely!

For example, there are sentences which I swear I never read before, suddenly appearing on the page when I go back two weeks later to read it. Also, it seems that what I took your point to be—what you were trying to emphasize—when I first read the feedback and what I understand your points to be now are not the same, either.

I think that I have come up with an explanation for this phenomenon. It seems to me that a piece is very important to me when I write it, when I hand it in, when I get feedback on it, and for about one week afterward, because a piece of writing in this class is sort of representative of just where I am in the class right then—how I'm feeling.

The feedback is sort of like an affirmation that what I wrote was valid or "good." I guess that I've been trained this way. And even though I know that your feedback doesn't aim to say "yes" or "no," "good" or "bad," I still can't help reading it that way. So the feedback sheet comes to me and I say, "Did he like it?" instead of just taking in what you've said.

Because of this, when I get a sheet back and interpret what you've written, I almost end up changing your intention. The words on the page get translated through my own agenda (read: did he like it?) and I lose (or even fail to see!) what you're actually saying. Going back and reading through the sheets, it seems that many things that I took to be negative weren't. They just weren't worded in that "yes, this is an A or this is very good" way that I was expecting.

This, to me is shocking. I've always thought of myself as a person who takes constructive feedback of any sort exceptionally well. But now I realize that I don't take *any* type of feedback well, except for the sort of polar feedback that grades or extreme "yes" or "no's" produce. I used to think that I was an open-minded student, evidenced by the fact that I enjoy getting specific, negative feedback almost more than I enjoy positive feedback. I was proud of this.

But now I realize that I *like* that feedback because when I get it, it's spelled out for me—"what I did wrong." I don't have to evaluate myself or question my writing at all. I just have to take the expert's word for it. And this is easy.

I used to think, being a prospective teacher (sort of), that giving meaningful feedback would be simple: just be specific. But now, having evaluated my own responses to feedback, I wonder: Will being specific with feedback and asking for revisions make for a better writer, or just make for a better paper? And which is more important?

Victoria Malzone

- How did you feel about this assignment before you started it? Did you think you would enjoy doing it? find it a bore? feel unable to come up with enough material? What were your feelings when you were finished?
- Were you able to come up with genuine advice for yourself—advice that you think will be truly useful?
- If you had a chance to hear or read the autobiographies of others, what were your reactions? Did you sense mainly similarities or differences between theirs and yours?
- Do you think *how* you write makes a difference? Why or why not?
- Do you think writing is or will be important to you? What evidence do you have for your answer?

Exploring Theory: *Autobiography and Metacognition*

Writing autobiography is a form of metacognition. Perhaps you've seen the word *metacognition* before you started this course—maybe in a psychology or education class. *Meta* is a prefix that comes from Greek; one of its meanings is "going beyond" or "higher." Thus metacognition literally means going beyond cognition or knowing; metacognitive theories, then, are those that consider our ability to know what we know.

Kenneth Burke, a modern rhetorician (we used some of his words to start the "Exploring Theory" section in Workshop 12, "Research"), writes in *Permanence and Change* of the trout who, having escaped once from a hook embedded in bait, is afterwards warier. The trout may miss out on some genuine food because something about it looks like what almost caught him. And the trout may also fall for bait offered in some other way. No matter: the trout's behavior has changed.

Human beings, Burke goes on to say, can go one step farther than a trout, for we "can greatly extend the scope of the critical process"; we are the only species "possessing an equipment for going beyond the criticism of experience to a criticism of criticism. . . we may also interpret our interpretations." The "equipment" which allows us to criticize our criticism and interpret our interpretations is language. And writing, we add, allows us to physically see that criticism and those interpretations. It allows us to observe our observations.

Research suggests that our unconscious mind is both cognitive and emotional. Events we have not perceived can affect how we behave. In extreme cases, they may lead to psychosis that can be eradicated only if the patient becomes aware of the unconscious roots of the psychosis. We don't want to suggest that writing is psychosis, but we do believe that our unconscious affects how we write. No one teaches any of us how to put the words "round," "big," "box," and "green" in the right order, but as native speakers we are going to come up with "big round green box" unless we're deliberately seeking a particular effect. (And even that proves our point, because we wouldn't get that particular effect if readers didn't automatically "know" the usual order.) Our unconscious mind stores much complex "knowledge" we don't quite understand but can learn to tap. But our unconscious mind can also lay traps for us which we may not understand. Analyzing our own writing behavior and actual pieces of our own writing can help us understand the ways that our unconscious helps and hinders. This, too, is a way of knowing what we know.

Metacognition is not only valuable for mental activities. Athletes and their coaches are well aware of the power of metacognition, of studying and analyzing physical behavior. Football teams watch videos of prior games as a way to improve performance. Often when teams have had a particularly disastrous day, a coach will sit them down immediately after the game—even before they take showers—and insist that they "replay" crucial moments while they're still fresh in their minds. The coach does this to show them not just what they did wrong but how they can do better the next time. Video technology has developed to the point where gymnasts' movements can be digitalized on a screen so that athletes and their coaches can analyze them minutely. Ballet dancers practice before mirrors so that they can see themselves. Exercise therapists even tell us that exercise is more effective when the person exercising thinks about what she is doing—thinks about the movements of the muscles and limbs. When you write, you're exercising a kind of muscle. We believe that a muscle becomes stronger if you look at its actual movements on a regular basis.

Students sometimes become bored with process writing: they've told us so; their teachers have told us so. But we are not dissuaded. We continue to believe that if you can learn what process writing really is—not just mechanically going through the questions in every workshop, but actually probing the steps of your own writing—your writing will improve. The Russian psychologist and learning theorist Lev Vygotsky concluded after years of observing children's learning behavior that human beings are far more likely to move to higher learning if they understand what they've already learned; that is, if they know what they know.

Thus we think that you can best come to conclusions about ways to improve your writing process by studying your writing process—by collecting as much information as you can about it and drawing conclusions about it *only* as a result of discovering patterns in it. This is the philosophy that lies behind the assignment for this workshop. We use our students' autobiographies as guides to helping us design our courses and assignments. Obviously we cannot design a course for one individual, so we seek common elements in the autobiographies we read. In other words, we generalize in an effort to come to conclusions that are valid for many student writers. Despite this, however, we recognize that each student's writing process is slightly different. We recognize the importance of specific data even as we make attempts at generalizations. But your task (at least right now) is different from ours. Your concern is to improve your writing. Thus your autobiography needs to focus solely on you and to draw conclusions solely from your personal experiences and specific interactions with others in a variety of writing environments.

We'll conclude this section and the main body of our textbook with a quotation from the *Notebooks* of Samuel Taylor Coleridge, who has much to say about imagination and creativity:

> Consciousness . . . mind, life, will, body, organ (as compared with machine), nature, spirit, sin, habit, sense, understanding, reason: here are fourteen words. Have you ever reflectively and quietly asked yourself the meaning of any one of these, and asked yourself to return the answer in *distinct* terms, not applicable to any of the other words? Or have you contented yourself with the vague floating meaning that will just save you from absurdity in the use of the word, just as the clown's botany would do, who knew that potatoes were roots, and cabbages greens? Or, if you have the gift of wit, shelter yourself under Augustine's equivocation, "I know it perfectly well till I am asked." Know? Ay, as an oyster knows its life. *But do you know your knowledge?*

A Case Study of Myself as a Writer

Leah K. Clarkson

The first thing I realized about writing was that it had to be done quickly and well. I understood, as a child, that writing and reading were indispensable, and that the sooner one mastered both, the easier life would be. I also understood that one needed to be good at these things to be considered "smart." With this knowledge firmly instilled in my subconscious, I set out to become the fastest, cleanest writer I could be. I knew that spelling was important, and topic sentences, and I knew that tone stood for a lot. I knew that writing for school was not like speaking, and that scribbling a letter or yet another diary entry was not the same as constructing an essay for class. I took incorrect spelling personally. My writing had all of the trappings of goodness. It was clean and clear, and generally precise, although in college I did go through a period of convoluted verbosity as I struggled to meet the minimum page requirements for papers.

I have to say, then, that my early experiences with writing were not traumatizing in the least. I was fortunate enough to have very good teachers who encouraged me to write. I can recall no nightmarish writing episodes in which an evil professor destroyed the spirit of joy in my writing by humiliatingly pointing out my shoddy grammar or sloppy presentation. The only mildly interesting event I can recall occurred when I was in the third grade. I got a C in penmanship because I had transferred from a French school to an American school, and I couldn't write in the Palmer method of handwriting, although my alternate, eurocursive was actually quite nice. I knew that this was unfair and my parents agreed, so, again, I incurred no lasting trauma. I do remember always feeling a little as though I was getting away with something because I could get praise simply by stringing together a coherent sentence. All of this changed when I got to college.

In college I began to get scared when I saw the labor that was going on all around me. Friends of mine would suffer and get extensions and then stay up all night and suffer some more just to turn out eight to ten pages about something they would probably never study again. I began to worry because my system, where I sat down with a pad for a few hours, wrote out my paper, then retyped and revised in an hour or two, seemed too easy. And it was. It was too easy. It was as though my brain would abandon me, and my common sense, during the few hours that I spent cobbling together my papers. I would spend far more time making pretty sentences and paragraphs, putting punctuation in all the right places, figuring out good words to use, than I would actually trying to communicate my point. I've realized, now, that this system emerged not simply out of laziness, but out of fear. The fear that if I paid attention to my writing I would find it to be substandard. The fear that if I began to work on my prose I would be so overwhelmed that I wouldn't finish the paper on time. The fear that if it came down to the last minute before the deadline and I absolutely had to complete my paper I might miss the opportunity to do something more fun. I wrote my papers chronically early and woefully speedily. And I pretty much continued to get away with it, although now I had many more misgivings to repress.

I should state here that for most of my life I considered myself an actor. I lived to ape and pretend and mimic and mock and entertain. I loved it because I knew that a good actor can safely cloak himself and still have power. The shell of the actor performs while his essence sits back and delivers ironic commentary on the action. My last year of college I decided to give up being an actor for many reasons too banal to go into. I decided to write a creative BA thesis, and then the focus of my writing shifted entirely. I became a "fiction writer" with a whole host of issues separate from those that dictate grammar, punctuation, main point. All of a sudden, it didn't matter so much that I knew how to say something—what mattered was that I thought that I had something to say. But the acting wasn't easy to let go of—and it's difficult now for me to write fiction without considering all of the ways in which being an actor has affected the way that I write.

When I think about my writing now, I realize how much of my development of a writing "style" involved the simultaneous emergence of a nonstyle. Even though I knew how to say things well, I though that I had very little to say. I was afraid of taking up space, which is one of the reasons that I quit acting in my third year of college. I quit acting because I was tired of being on display, and I thought that writing fiction would be a more subtle way of making my presence known to the world. Unfortunately my distaste for expansiveness led to a major problem in my fiction writing—essentially, that I take up too little space. My writing is tight and constrained. Everything correctly spelled and commas in all of the right places, but not enough on the page. Too few flights of fancy.

Since beginning the MFA program a month ago, I've also been thinking a lot about voice. I've kept a journal for most of my life, since the fourth grade, and I can look back through them and know exactly what I was reading at the time. There's the *Anne of Green Gables* period where everything is written flowery and sugary-sweet with lots of italics, there's the *Diary of Anne Frank* period which is very earnest with a lot of sweeping generalizations about the state of the world and what it means to be a young girl in it (I think I even embarrassingly called my diary Kitty for a while, but later went back and crossed it out because I realized what a cheesy rip-off that was by the time I was in Junior High.) Anyway, the list goes on. Unfortunately, the same thing happens to me now. I read a short story and if the voice clicks with me, I'm in it, and I can't get out for a few weeks. I can't read Salinger at all—it's a death-knell for my writing, and Amis and Waugh throw me into paroxysms of imitation that also take months to work out. This seems to be a leftover from my acting days, and the realization that I do this leads me to another observation: writing fiction means writing yourself onto the page.

This is incredibly frightening.

I took my first fiction writing class during my second year of college. The professor was Richard Stern, a notoriously crusty professor and writer at the University of Chicago. We had to turn in a writing sample before the first meeting and, during the first class, Stern read aloud the names of people who had NOT made the cut. They had to get up, one at a time, and leave the room. The silence was excruciating. Finally, it came down to thirteen people, all of us sitting holding our breath as though we were in some sort of academic beauty pageant. We waited for the final three names to be called. Stern called out two more names, and two more flushed students shoved their filofaxes into their backpacks and slunk out the door. One more name to be called. "Clarkson." he said. I prepared to leave. "Can I see you out in the hallway?"

Once in the hallway Stern told me that he thought I could take the class, but that I was very young, and so might want to consider waiting another year. Somehow, in the face of his very frightening professorial demeanor, to this man who reeked of Bellow, to this staple of Chicago fiction, I found the guts to say "I think I can do it. I want to do it." And he let me in. And the first piece I got back from him was almost illegible because he had put so many red marks on it. Some of my favorite comments were

"Learn how to write." and "Enough with this semi-poetic drivel." But I appreciated it. I liked it because I felt as though I'd been caught out, finally, as though it was a relief that someone finally knew that I was only pretending to know how to write well. I think that class was what made me decide definitely to quit acting, although I wouldn't do so for another year. Because acting was easy. And writing fiction was hard. I was really grateful to Stern for being a tyrant. And believe me, nothing anyone says about my writing now hurts my feelings. They can't be harder on it than Stern was, and Stern taught me to be hard on myself.

Being hard on myself has been a problem, though. Because I'll know that something isn't working but my only solution is to scrap the whole thing or remain stalled because it seems that what's frequently wrong isn't just a sentence or a paragraph or a segue but the whole voice of a piece. Even writing this right now I'm annoyed by the tone I feel I've assumed, a tone appropriate to a piece titled "A Case Study of Myself as a Writer."

Often in my fiction I feel like I sound cutesy and preachy and like I'm writing a kiddy novel, which maybe I am, because I read quite a bit as a child and I worry that the years of reading all of those books over and over and over have basically ruined me as a writer. And I'm scared to death that I'll wake up one morning and find myself writing children's fiction the same way I woke up and found myself teaching drama to Junior High kids in a Catholic school in downtown Chicago with people shouting "Miss Clarkson, Miss Clarkson" all the livelong day. I DON'T WANT TO BE JUDY BLUME. I DON'T WANT TO WRITE FOR KIDS.

If I don't want to do this, though, I have to let the real me out onto the page. I have to stop self-editing, I have to stop stopping myself before I've even started. I have to learn again how to take up space, and yell for attention. I have to kill that little voice in my head that insists on broadcasting an ironic play-by-play whenever I sit in front of the computer writing fiction.

It's hard to know how to conclude this paper, because I'm more aware than ever now that my writing, and myself, are experiencing mysterious permutations with every passing day. I have to resist the urge to boringly sum up the points that I have stated in the last few pages (often repetitively). Perhaps I'll end on a less formal note, and include this e-mail that I wrote recently to a friend of mine. I think it expresses my current frustrations pretty well, and it expresses them in something a little closer to my true "voice." Please excuse the expletives:

> Dear Melissa,
>
> I've plopped down into a crisis of sorts, my first big writing debacle here at UMASS. It all started—well, it all started a long time ago, which is what I'm discovering. But basically here I was, writing along like gangbusters, busted out three stories and then turned around to find out that what I had in my hands was a pile of utter crap. And that's no lie.
>
> Now. Don't get me wrong. I'm not whining about how I can't trick out a pretty phrase or cobble together a pleasing stream of witty prose. This I can do. But to what end? To

no end. I write stories about nuns and hookers and lepers and have no idea what I'm talking about. I feel like my stuff stinks and I sound like a goddamn Judy Blume novel and I can't bear the thought of becoming just another Elizabeth Wortzel writing about depression and eating disorders and the guy who hurt me and etc. The world just don't need another one of those. So I'm discussing this with a friend and he says, "Why don't you just give me something to read?"

So I hi my ass home and spend four hours finishing the nun story. I go back and change all of this stuff and feel like "Hmm. This story still reeks but at least I realized I was going the wrong way and now I'm going the right way & etc." I even feel kind of proud because, you know, even if it's crap it's 15 pages Times 11 font 1.5 spaced crap. And the commas are all in the right places.

Well, he pointed out that my writing was incredibly anal (my words, not his, I think he said "tight") and he said he couldn't believe it was a first draft because there should be a lot to excise in such a thing but there wasn't anything. I realized that for the last few years I've been praying just like good old Dottie Parker "Please, GOD let me write like a man" and it ain't happening. I'm all bound up about what people will think of me because unless you're a grade-A primo genius writing is you. It's you, baby, splayed out on the table and that-scares-the-shit out of me. Acting my God, acting was so easy. And I was better at it. I was a maestro at that. So what am I doing? I think it all has to do with being a girl. With being a stupid girl, you know? It's so unfair that that's the case, that somewhere along the line I got it into my little blondish head that if I wasn't a stud rock star at something that I'd better just run in the other direction or if I decided to give it a go anyway I'd better be as ironic about it as possible.

So I had a bit of a breakthrough this morning. I was lying in bed, still thinking all of this over (thank God I was on the sauce last night or I wouldn't have slept a wink) and I was thinking: What should I write? What can I write that's honest? And everything I thought of, I realized, I simultaneously brought the hammer down on, smashing its soft little skull into oblivion. Feeling ugly NO being crushed-out NO what to wear on a date NO how it feels to be rejected NO the time I went to XYZ NO. And I've got to stop that. I just have to. I have to make that leap.

Jesus, I'm sorry, Melee. What a rant.

Love,

Leah

Process Notes

Sunday, 1:30 PM: I just free-wrote six pages to start this paper. I had a hard time letting go and just writing. I was too worried about what the point of my paper should be. But I was determined to try this new style of composing, determined to try and get at the meat of what I really wanted to say. So now I have six baby pages.
Tuesday, 11:45 PM: I looked at my six pages for the first time since Sunday and I underlined the stuff I liked. I cut out about four paragraphs and made a list of different points that I think I'm trying to make. Figured out where I think this is going and wrote a few more paragraphs on that subject. But now I have a pile of stuff just slapped onto the screen and I'm trying to resist feeling panicked. This is why I never wrote this way—just to avoid the stress of not being done, or done in time. Hey, maybe I'll write about that in my paper. I'm resisting the old urge to just write whatever, check the structure, and be done with it. I'll let it sit some more.
Wednesday, 1:45 PM: I talk to Leslie about our papers. We talk about what we want to say. It helps. A little.
Wednesday, 6:00 PM: In two hours I have a date. I go through a second printout of the paper and start hacking away. I leave at eight for dinner frustrated at the ever more confusing pile of writing before me. I'm wondering if I should just start from scratch.
Thursday, 12:45 AM: I've been mangling this piece even further for about an hour. I'm frustrated by this new method. I keep thinking that if I'd just written the damn thing well on Sunday I'd be done now. I don't really know how to proceed. I think I'm best at flow—and this has disrupted my flow. Plus, I'm starting to make myself sick with all of this talk about me. I'm going to bed.
Thursday, 12:45 PM: It's done. I added an e-mail that I wrote for a friend and I wonder if that was the best idea. I don't have a real conclusion so I don't feel much closure. I keep reminding myself that I'll still get to revise it one more time after today. I had to go through and start at the beginning and write a lot more to try and get back the safe linear feeling of progress toward a final point. I still feel the issues are a little disconnected, but I've said some things I needed to say. Jury's still out on this one.

Leah K. Clarkson

Case Study

Mitchell Shack

I hate to start out on a negative comment, but I feel I must say that I don't like to think of this as a case study. It makes me feel as if I am preparing a report for a doctor or psychiatrist. Actually I would like to think of it as simply an expression of my feelings about my accomplishments and struggles of being a writer.

In order to write such a paper, I must remember not only works I have written this semester, but also ones that I have written in the past years. Remembering the latter bunch is not such an easy task; not just because of the time difference between now and when they were written, but because I would rather not remember some of the papers. The papers were not actually bad, but I have bad memories of my writings in those days. What I mean is that those papers were written because I was forced to write them; not because I wanted to write them. The papers accomplished the task that they were supposed to do, but they did little more. They were quite boring and uninspired works. Actually the word "works" is an accurate description of those writings because that's exactly what I thought of them—as doing work.

Most of my writings—correction—all of my writings, were assignments in high school, usually English essays. These papers were usually about a book we read in class, or an essay on a test. My style of writing was simple. I just stated the facts, one right after another, and somehow linked all these facts together to form an essay. There was little creativity at all and it was amazing that the teacher didn't doze off before reaching my closing paragraph.

Well, that's how I stood coming into this class, and I anticipated little change in my attitude upon completion of this class. As a matter of fact, I thought that I was going to hate writing even more than I already did, if that was even possible. Much to my surprise my attitude took a complete reversal during the span of this course. "What brought about that change?" you may ask. I think it is because I began to write about things that I wanted to write, not things that other people wanted me to write. I began to even enjoy my writing; something that was previously all too painful just to think about. My writings have drastically improved because of this change in attitude. My papers have become more creative and not just a list of facts anymore. My style of writing has become more natural. It has become smoother and I have "opened up" more so that I can get what I'm thinking in my head down on the paper. That may not seem like a big task to some people, but it would have seemed almost impossible to me just a few months ago. My papers have changed from simply stating what happened to explaining how I felt when it happened. I have also learned new techniques and methods of writing which I will pick up on later.

So far I have been telling you about changes that have come as a result of taking this course, so I think I should give some examples of these changes to prove my point. The paper that I like the best was a descriptive narrative about my favorite person of my childhood, the ice-cream man, so I think it's only fair to talk about that piece. I enjoyed this piece because I was able to open up and explain how I felt and what I was thinking at that time and not just give a plot summary. For example one line from the story says, "The truck from far away looked like an old bread truck, but it would not have mattered one bit if it looked like a garbage truck, just as long as it sold ice cream." The same line written before this class would have probably looked more like "The truck was white and looked like a bread truck." I changed from just putting down facts to putting down feelings along with those facts. This brightens up my papers greatly, gives a more personal feel to it, and makes it much more interesting and entertaining to read. I accomplished this task in an "Image of an Ice-Cream Man," and that is why I feel this paper is a representative of not only one of my better papers, but also of my improvements in writing over previous years.

There are many techniques that I learned which I can attribute to my change in writing. One such thing is the use of freewriting. I have never before used freewriting, and early in the semester I just thought it was a waste of time. In looking back over my papers and some of the freewriting I did that led to those papers I realized I was mistaken. Many of my ideas came as a result of freewriting; some of which I may not have thought of if I just sat down and wrote the paper. I used freewriting in the "Image of an Ice-Cream Man," and the paper benefited from its use. For example, I wrote, "I watched him as he was making it, and my mouth watered just looking at all the ice cream, lollipops, bubble gum, chocolate bars, Italian ices, and other candy I saw inside the truck." This line and many of the others were taken right out of my freewriting. The freewriting allowed me to open up and "look back" in my mind and remember things that I have forgotten over the years. In the line above, using freewriting allowed me to remember in my mind exactly what the truck looked like and what I saw when I looked in it. Another thing that I like about freewriting is that I am not restricted to a topic or an idea. I can let my mind wander and go where it wants to go. I don't even have to worry about punctuation, grammar, or anything else that can inhibit my thinking. The result is usually writing that "flows" and seems natural, and this type of writing can enhance any paper.

Another useful technique which I learned is the loop writing process. I only used this process for one paper, and I must admit that what resulted was one of my weakest papers. This was not because of the loop writing process, but it's because of what I did in actually writing the paper after using the loop writing process. To tell you the truth, the loop writing process worked too well. The process consisted of using all different ways of thinking about a topic to get ideas on that topic. This included my first thoughts, prejudices, dialogues, lies, stories, and portraits about the topic. I used this process in writing "How Death Motivates Us in Life," and my problem was that I came up with too many ideas about the topic. The loop writing process allowed me to think of so many different aspects of the topic and for each aspect come up with several ideas pertaining to it. The problem came when I tried to write an essay which incorporated all these ideas in them. I mentioned all these ideas, but because of the great number of them, I didn't go into any single one in great detail. This resulted in a lot of superficial ideas, but no depth to my paper. What I should have done was pick out the ideas that proved my point the best and go into depth with those items. What I am trying to get across is that the loop writing process is very helpful, especially with topics that you seem short on ideas to pursue. But I have to be careful and not get carried away with myself and try to fit every single idea that I come up with into my paper.

So far I have been talking about methods I learned which aided me in my writings, but I haven't really talked about how I go about using these methods in actually creating a piece. Believe it or not, my favorite way of writing is to compose my paper directly on my computer. This may seem odd or difficult to some people, but to me it works fine. Actually I usually start by freewriting on the topic, or using the loop writing technique if I'm short on ideas. Next I usually make a rough outline of what I am going to say. I try to think about how I want my paper organized and in what order each point should go, and then I create the basic form of an outline. I then go back and jot down a few examples under each argument to prove it. I don't write in sentence form; I just scribble down a few key words and later on when I actually write my paper I look over these key words and then write about them.

This is the part when my computer comes into play. I load up my word processor, set my margins, and start writing. I like using the computer rather than a typewriter or pen and paper because I can edit directly as I go along. I can switch sentences around, delete words, add phrases, and do many other operations immediately. The words look on screen as they will on paper so I can see the structure forming and know how the finished product will look. I can go back and change my paper three weeks or three months later without having to retype it since it is saved on disk. Also my word processing program contains a spelling checker which I find very useful since I am far from being the world champion in spelling bees, and it contains a thesaurus so I can have some place to turn to if I get stuck [. . .].

One thing that I haven't already mentioned and I feel is a major reason why I enjoyed taking this course is that I was actually able to tell a story. I was able to relate an experience that over the years didn't seem important enough to tell anybody. This year I got the chance and just being able to do that has made this course worthwhile for me.

From Hunger of Memory

Richard Rodriguez

Richard Rodriguez (b. 1944, San Francisco) is an editor and the author of several books and numerous articles for print, television, and radio. His best known book is probably Hunger of Memory *(1981), an autobiographical work that explores his Mexican-American heritage and his development as a writer.*

At school, in sixth grade, my teacher suggested that I start keeping a diary. ("You should write down your personal experiences and reflections.") But I shied away from the idea. It was the one suggestion that the scholarship boy couldn't follow. I would not have wanted to write about the *minor* daily events of my life; I would never have been able to write about what most deeply, daily, concerned me during those years: I was growing away from my parents. Even if I could have been certain that no one would find my diary, even if I could have destroyed each page after I had written it, I would have felt uncomfortable writing about my home life. There seemed to me something intrinsically public about written words.

Writing, at any rate, was a skill I didn't regard highly. It was a grammar school skill I acquired with comparative ease. I do not remember struggling to write the way I struggled to learn how to read. The nuns would praise student papers for being neat—the handwritten letters easy for others to read; they promised that my writing style would improve as I read more and more. But that wasn't the reason I became a reader. Reading was for me the key to "knowledge"; I swallowed facts and dates and names and themes. Writing, by contrast, was an activity I thought of as a kind of report, evidence of learning. I wrote down what I heard teachers say. I wrote down things from my books. I wrote down all I knew when I was examined at the end of the school year. Writing was performed after the fact; it was not the exciting experience of learning itself. In eighth grade I read several hundred books, the titles of which I still can recall. But I cannot remember a single essay I wrote. I only remember that the most frequent kind of essay I wrote was the book report.

In high school there were more "creative" writing assignments. English teachers assigned the composition of short stories and poems. One sophomore story I wrote was a romance set in the Civil War South. I remember that it earned me a good enough grade, but my teacher suggested with quiet tact that next time I try writing about "something you know more about—something closer to home." Home? I wrote a short story about an old man who lived all by himself in a house down the block. That was as close as my writing ever got to my house. Still, I won prizes. When teachers suggested I contribute articles to the school literary magazine, I did so. And when I was asked to join the school newspaper, I said yes. I did not feel any great pride in my writings, however. (My mother was the one who collected my prize-winning essays in a box she kept in her closet.) Though I remember seeing my byline in print for the first time, and dwelling on the printing press letters with fascination: RICHARD RODRIGUEZ. The letters furnished evidence of a vast public identity writing made possible.

When I was a freshman in college, I began typing all my assignments. My writing speed decreased. Writing became a struggle. In high school I had been able to handwrite ten- and twenty-page papers in little more than an hour—and I never revised what I wrote. A college essay took me several nights to prepare. Suddenly everything I wrote seemed in need of revision. I became a self-conscious writer. A stylist. The change, I suspect, was the result of seeing my words ordered by the even, impersonal, anonymous typewriter print. As arranged by a machine, the words that I typed no longer seemed mine. I was able to see them with a new appreciation for how my reader would see them.

From grammar school to graduate school I could always name my reader. I wrote for my teacher. I could consult him or her before writing, and after. I suppose that I knew other readers could make sense of what I wrote—that, therefore, I addressed a general reader. But I didn't think very much about it. Only toward the end of my schooling and only because political issues pressed upon me did I write, and have published in magazines, essays intended for readers I never expected to meet. Now I am struck by the opportunity. I write today for a reader who exists in my mind only phantasmagorically. Someone with a face erased; someone of no particular race or sex or age or weather. A gray presence. Unknown, unfamiliar. All that I know about him is that he has had a long education and that his society, like mine, is often public *(un gringo)*.

• • •

"What is psychiatry?" my mother asks. She is standing in her kitchen at the ironing board. We have been talking about nothing very important. ("Visiting.") As a result of nothing we have been saying, her question has come. But I am not surprised by it. My mother and father ask me such things. Now that they are retired they seem to think about subjects they never considered before. My father sits for hours in an armchair, wide-eyed. After my mother and I have finished discussing obligatory family news, he will approach me and wonder: When was Christianity introduced to the Asian continent? How does the brain learn things? Where is the Garden of Eden?

Perhaps because they consider me the family academic, my mother and father expect me to know. They do not, in any case, ask my brother and sisters the questions wild curiosity shapes. (That curiosity beats, unbeaten by age.)

Psychiatry? I shrug my shoulders to start with, to tell my mother that it is very hard to explain. I go on to say something about Freud. And analysis. Something about the function of a clinically trained listener. (I study my mother's face as I speak, to see if she follows.) I compare a psychiatrist to a Catholic priest hearing Confession. But the analogy is inexact. My mother can easily speak to a priest in a darkened confessional; can easily make an act of self-revelation using the impersonal formula of ritual contrition: "Bless me, father, for I have sinned. . . ." It would be altogether different for her to address a psychiatrist in unstructured conversation, revealing those events and feelings that burn close to the heart.

"You mean that people tell a psychiatrist about their personal lives?"

Even as I begin to respond, I realize that she cannot imagine ever doing such a thing. She shakes her head sadly, bending over the ironing board to inspect a shirt with the tip of the iron she holds in her hand. Then she changes the subject. She is talking to me about one of her sisters, my aunt, who is seriously ill. Whatever it is that prompted her question about psychiatry has passed [. . .].

What did my father—who had dreamed of Australia—think of his children once they forced him to change plans and remain in America? What contrary feelings did he have about our early success? How does he regard the adults his sons and daughters have become? And my mother. At what moments has she hated me? On what occasions has she been embarrassed by me? What does she recall feeling during those difficult, sullen years of my childhood? What would be her version of this book? What are my parents unable to tell me today? What things are too personal? What feelings so unruly they dare not reveal to other intimates? Or even to each other? Or to themselves?

Some people have told me how wonderful it is that I am the first in my family to write a book. I stand on the edge of a long silence. But I do not give voice to my parents by writing about their lives. I distinguish myself from them by writing about the life we once shared. Even when I quote them accurately, I profoundly distort my parents' words. (They were never intended to be read by the public.) So my parents do not truly speak on my pages. I may force their words to stand between quotation marks. With every word, however, I change what was said only to me.

"What is new with you?" My mother looks up from her ironing to ask me. (In recent years she has taken to calling me Mr. Secrets, because I tell her so little about my work in San Francisco—this book she must suspect I am writing.)

Nothing much, I respond.

• • •

I write very slowly because I write under the obligation to make myself clear to someone who knows nothing about me. It is a lonely adventure. Each morning I make my way along a narrowing precipice of written words. I hear an echoing voice—my own resembling another's. Silent! The reader's voice silently trails every word I put down. I reread my words, and again it is the reader's voice I hear in my mind, sounding my prose.

When I wrote my first autobiographical essay, it was no coincidence that, from the first page, I expected to publish what I wrote. I didn't consciously determine the issue. Somehow I knew, however, that my words were meant for a public reader. Only because of that reader did the words come to the page. The reader became my excuse, my reason for writing.

It had taken me a long time to come to this address. There are remarkable children who very early are able to write publicly about their personal lives. Some children confide to a diary those things—like the first shuddering of sexual desire—too private to tell a parent or brother. The youthful writer addresses a stranger, the Other, with "Dear Diary" and tries to give public expression to what is intensely, privately felt. In so doing, he attempts to evade the guilt of repression. And the embarrassment of solitary feeling. For by rendering feelings in words that a stranger can understand—words that belong to the public, this Other—the young diarist no longer need feel all alone or eccentric. His feelings are capable of public intelligibility. In turn, the act of revelation helps the writer better understand his own feelings. Such is the benefit of language: By finding public words to describe one's feelings, one can describe oneself to oneself. One names what was previously only darkly felt.

I have come to think of myself as engaged in writing graffiti. Encouraged by physical isolation to reveal what is most personal; determined at the same time to have my words seen by strangers. I have come to understand better why works of literature—while never intimate, never individually addressed to the reader—are so often among the most personal statements we hear in our lives. Writing, I have come to value written words as never before. One can use *spoken* words to reveal one's personal self to strangers. But *written* words heighten the feeling of privacy. They permit the most thorough and careful exploration. (In the silent room, I prey upon that which is most private. Behind the closed door, I am least reticent about giving those memories expression.) The writer is freed from the obligation of finding an auditor in public. (As I use words that someone far from home can understand, I create my listener. I imagine her listening.)

My teachers gave me a great deal more than I knew when they taught me to write public English. I was unable then to use the skill for deeply personal purposes. I insisted upon writing impersonal essays. And I wrote always with a specific reader in mind. Nevertheless, the skill of public writing was gradually developed by the many classroom papers I had to compose. Today I *can* address an anonymous reader. And this seems to me important to say. Somehow the inclination to write about my private life in public is related to the ability to do so. It is not enough to say that my mother and father do not want to write their autobiographies. It needs also to be said that they are unable to write to a public reader. They lack the skill. Though both of them can write in Spanish and English, they write in a hesitant manner. Their syntax is uncertain. Their vocabulary limited. They write well enough to communicate "news" to relatives in letters. And they can handle written transactions in institutional America. But the man who sits in his chair so many hours, and the woman at the ironing board—"keeping busy because I don't want to get old"—will never be able to believe that any description of their personal lives could be understood by a stranger far from home.

From A Case Study of Myself as a Writer

Jean Shepherd

When I begin writing, I compose the first sentence in my head. As I put pen to paper, words begin to rush into my mind. For a few seconds, I can hardly write fast enough to get them all down, but after a brief period, maybe after several sentences, I pause and read what I have written. Possible revisions of words and phrases occur to me, and I write them anywhere I can—to the side, above, or below appropriate sections of the text, often with arrows pointing to their future positions. I reread once more to get the sound of my writing in my head, and then I'm off again in a frantic race with my mind to get the words on paper before they are gone. I use this write, stop, read, revise, read, start again process until I am through writing or until I come to a good stopping place.

At this point, my paper looks like a plate with words and arrows spilled over it in different directions. No one else could ever read this draft, and if I wait a day, I won't be able to read it either. Therefore, I must begin immediately to copy over, selecting words and phrases out of the choices I have given myself on the previous writing. Sometimes new word options and ideas occur to me as I rewrite; during this stage I seem to be more aware of sentence rhythms, and I try to write more slowly this time so I will put the endings on my words. The result of this stage is what I call my rough draft. If I get too caught up in rewriting and again write too fast, I may have to copy it over a second time.

The rough draft often contains ideas that never occurred to me before I wrote. It is obvious that during the first stages of writing I move pen on paper, think of words, spell words, punctuate, see relationships between ideas, invent new ideas, hear the sound of my words, read, and revise all at the same time. The pen becomes an extension of my mind, and unfortunately, my fingers can never move as quickly as my thoughts come, so I am always in a race to the end of a sentence. While producing this rough draft, I am unaware of anything around me. My body is tense with concentration as I rush to record my ideas. During this stage, my thinking is almost unconscious.

The next step of writing, the first revision, is a more conscious stage, and I am more relaxed as I progress. At this point, I correct sentences and sometimes continue to add ideas. I may mark out phrases or entire sentences to avoid wordiness. I change forms of subordination, usually making dependent clauses into phrases, and check coordination to see if it should remain as it is or if it should become subordination. At this point, I am very aware of sentence rhythms and variety, and I try to avoid awkward repetitions of words. I have the poor speller's habit of avoiding words I can't spell, so at this stage, I make a conscious effort to use whatever word I really want. Sometimes, when I get toward the end of the paper, I will think of words to add at the beginning, so I go back and put them in the margin. When I have gone over my paper once this way, I read again, making a few more minor adjustments, and then my first revision is complete.

For the next revision, I am calm and quite relaxed. This is the mechanical stage. I go through the paper and check all punctuation. Then I go back for my most hated task, checking spelling. I underline every word that may not be spelled correctly. Then I look up each one in a word book or dictionary. Oddly enough, I still may change some words or add a phrase even at this stage; I always seem to be aware of the sound of my writing. When this stage is complete, I am ready for the last step, typing.

My evaluation of what I've written is constantly changing as I go through all of these stages. During the first two steps of my rough draft, I feel excited. I'm sure that everything I am saying is clever and imaginative. I am convinced that I've written something that everyone will enjoy and admire. If I am writing for a class, I am sure that I will make an A and that my paper will be the best in the class. When I begin the first revision, my heart sinks. I am embarrassed by my own words and feel confident that anyone else who reads it will laugh and think me a fool. If I am writing for a class, I am sure that I will fail. I have to force myself to go on and not throw the paper out, telling myself that I have to turn in something and that I don't have time to begin again.

After I type a paper, it seems very separate from me. When I read it over, I find words and ideas that surprise me. I can't remember having written such words or having conceived of such thoughts. At this point, I become pleased with parts of my writing, but I have no idea how it will seem to someone else. I have never turned in an assignment with any notion of what grade it may earn.

A Look Inside: Case Study of Myself as a Writer

Greg Teets

Mind—Before

In the beginning thoughts
were formless and void,
often misguided.

For semester's term paper
I have a list of possible
topics. They range from
a comparison of
Shakespeare's tragedies
to an evaluation of Greek
poetry.

Purpose was unclear.
Structure was unthought of.

Follow the guidelines
given on page 427 of the
Warriner's textbook.

Ideas moved randomly colliding
with each other, destroying
each other.

A discussion on the
economic problems in
Hamlet.

Among the good thoughts garbage drifted adding to the confusion. In the last minute rush for perfection, junk was pulled out and used instead of the good.

The paper is due tomorrow. I haven't started. This sounds good.

From the start, order was plain, passive, and predictable. Methodically, ideas and lessons were communicated.

For this essay we will be using the five paragraph format.

Emotion did not exist. All subjects were treated with cold, formal objectivity.

Remember, this is a formal essay. Be objective and don't use slang or contractions.

Feelings that were suddenly displayed were quickly covered-up.

Your feelings on the subject are not relevant to the meaning of the story.

When he finished he looked
and saw that it was not
pleasing to his eyes.

New System

Freewriting: A technique used to remove the garbage from one's head and get real ideas flowing.

Artists. Paintings, sculpture, poetry. They work magic. Their fantasies become reality because they do it.

Exploratory Draft: A piece of writing in which one discovers how they feel and what they know about a topic.

Artists are interesting people. They have learned to place their intangible into tangible objects.

Rough Draft: An organized and structured revision of an exploratory.

Artists are magical people. They can put their ideas into things like sculpture, poetry, or paintings.

Final Copy: The end result of the three processes above. Usually, it is radically different from all previous versions.

Artists are magical people. They have learned to direct their intangible thoughts into tangible objects like poetry, sculpture, or painting.

Mind—After

In the beginning thoughts are always vague, unexplored. What do I write the essay on?

Freewrite. Go. Unconnected thoughts. Don't worry about grammar, structure, punctuation. Take a snapshot of your thoughts.

Gradually, things move together. Look over freewriting. See the natural connections. Don't box yourself in.

Exploratory. Begin to pull thoughts together. Get a feel for the topic. Add a little structure.

The purpose is to tell a story. Who is my audience? What do they need to know? Communicate with them.

Rough Draft. Organize. Make ideas cohesive. Show them your insight.

Reread essay. Is this really what I want to say? Do I make my point? Will the reader understand what I am saying? Check mechanics of the paper.

Add emotion. Add depth. Final Draft. No contractions. Does this feel right? Am I happy with the end product? Yes.

Process Journal

"The piece moved and grew like it was alive.

"I'm beginning to think that nothing is ever finished . . . unless it's written down.

"The 'felt sense' clicked and it became easy to express my emotions on paper and I wasn't ashamed or afraid.

"The 'invisible' writing makes me focus on what is popping up in my head, not what's happening around me.

"Now, I find writing fun and relaxing.

"[I]t seems like there is a lot of garbage in my head. I can write it down and it goes away.

"I've discovered that I am a very spontaneous thinker. The momentary ideas are usually the best.

"For days I've been
trying to think of a
narrative, but nothing satisfied me.
Finally, boom, big revelation,
bingo!

"Now, I am able
to release my thoughts.
Instead of trying to
structure them and
then write them down
I do the reverse.
The 'Doty'* system
works much better
than my old system."

Genesis

In the beginning, God created
the heavens and the earth.

And the earth was formless
and void,

Blank paper, pen, ink,
blank screen, keyboard,
mouse, blank mind.

God said, "Let there be light."

Alphabet.
c,m,p,g,n,x,n,q,y.

And God separated the darkness
from the light.

Syllable, word, phrase.
Sentence, paragraph,
essay.

God created man in his own
image.

Final paper, hidden
meaning, my mirror,
myself.

And God saw that it was good.
It was very good.

---

* Eugene Doty was this student's teacher.

Mini-Workshops

Part I

More on Writing and Research

Writing Skills Questionnaire

To help you get more out of our text and take more control over your own learning, we've made a list of specific skills we are attempting to teach. Filling out the questionnaire will help you notice better what you are learning and not learning—and help us teach you better.

You will benefit most from this questionnaire if you fill it out three times—at the beginning, middle, and end of the course. This way you'll be able to see more about what changes are taking place. (The second and third times you use this form, you may want to cover your previous answers.)

Use the numbers 1 through 4 to stand for your responses: 1—"Yes"; 2—"Fairly well"; 3—"Not very well"; and 4—"No." If you don't know the answer—which may often happen at the start of the course—use a question mark.

When you complete the questionnaire at the beginning of the course, fill in the *left-hand* column of blanks. In the middle of the course, use the *middle* column. At the end use the *right-hand* column.

Attitudes toward Writing

___ ___ ___ Do you enjoy writing?
___ ___ ___ In general do you trust yourself as a person who can find good words and ideas and perceptions?
___ ___ ___ Do you think of yourself as a writer?

Generating

___ ___ ___ On a *topic of interest to you,* can you generate lots of ideas and words fairly quickly and freely—not be stuck?
___ ___ ___ On a topic that *doesn't* much interest you (perhaps an assigned topic), can you generate lots of ideas and words fairly quickly and freely—not be stuck?
___ ___ ___ Can you come up with ideas or insights you'd not thought of before?

Revising

___ ___ ___ Can you revise in the literal sense of "resee"—
and change your mind about major things you hav
___ ___ ___ Can you find a main point in a mess of your disorgan
writing?
___ ___ ___ Can you find a *new* shape in a piece of your writing which you had previously organized?
___ ___ ___ Can you find problems in your reasoning or logic and straighten them out?
___ ___ ___ Can you write your sentences so they are clear to readers on first reading?
___ ___ ___ Can you make your sentences lively? Can you give them a human voice?
___ ___ ___ Can you adjust something you've written to fit the needs of particular readers?

Copyediting

___ ___ ___ Can you get rid of *most* mistakes in grammar, spelling, punctuation, and so on, so readers would not be put off?
___ ___ ___ Can you get rid of virtually *all* such mistakes?

Feedback

___ ___ ___ Can you enjoy sharing with friends a draft of what you've written?
___ ___ ___ Can you read out loud to listeners a draft of your writing so that it is really clear and "given"—that is, not mumbled and "held back"?
___ ___ ___ Can you openly listen to the reactions of a reader to your writing and try to see it as she sees it, even if you think her reactions are all wrong?
___ ___ ___ Can you give noncritical feedback—telling the writer what you like and summarizing or reflecting what you hear the words saying?
___ ___ ___ Can you give "movies of your mind" as a reader—a clear story of what was happening in your mind as you were reading someone's writing?
___ ___ ___ Can you give "criterion-based feedback"—telling the writer how the draft matches up against the most common criteria of good writing?

Collaboration

___ ___ ___ Can you work on a task collaboratively with a partner or a small group: pitch in, share the work, help the group cooperate, keep the group on the task?

Awareness and Control of Writing Process

___ ___ ___ Can you give a *detailed* account of what is going on when you are writing: the thoughts and feelings that go through your mind and the things that happen in the text?

___ ___ ___ Can you notice problems or "stuck points" in your writing and figure out what the causes are?

___ ___ ___ Can you vary the way you go about writing depending on your analysis of your writing process, or depending on the topic, audience, type of writing, and so on?

Double-Entry or Dialectical Notebooks

All there is to thinking . . . is seeing something noticeable which makes you see something you weren't noticing which makes you see something that isn't even visible.

Norman Maclean, *A River Runs Through It*

One of the goals of this book is to help you pay more attention to the *way* you write—what actually goes on as you put words down—how you make meaning and change meaning. Thus all the process writing.

It turns out to be just as useful to pay attention to the way you *read*—and interestingly enough the central activities are the same: making meaning and changing meaning. In this mini-workshop we will show you a simple and practical way to take notes on what you are reading. In the short term, a double-entry notebook helps you understand better the particular piece you are reading; in the long term, it improves your skill in reading. There will be more about the theory in the "Exploring Theory" section.

Keeping a Dialectical or Double-Entry Notebook

Let us quote Ann Berthoff, who devised this procedure:

> I ask my students (all of them: freshmen, upperclassmen, teachers in graduate seminars) to furnish themselves with a notebook, spiral bound at the side, small enough to be easily carried around but not so small that writing is cramped. . . What makes this notebook different from most, perhaps, is the notion of the double-entry: on the right side reading notes, direct quotations, observational notes, fragments, lists, images—verbal and visual—are recorded; on the other (facing) side, *notes about those notes,* summaries, formulations, aphorisms, editorial suggestions, revisions, comments on comments are written. The reason for the double-entry format is that it provides a way for the student to conduct that "continuing audit of meaning" that is at the heart of learning to read and write critically. The facing pages are in dialogue with each other.

That's all there is to it. But if you do this regularly, you will notice how that dialogue—that continuing audit of meaning—gradually helps you read more accurately and more creatively and thus helps you get more out of your reading.

Try it (1) on a piece of reading, then (2) on a piece of your experience.

1. Choose a piece of reading that you can learn from and reflect on—not just something you read to pass the time. Start reading it and, as you do, pause to write down (on the right-hand side of your notebook) words, details, images, or thoughts that strike you. You're not "taking notes." Don't clench

and try to capture or summarize everything; just encourage yourself to write about what you notice in the reading and in your own reactions to the reading. If you find yourself reading more than a few pages without any writing, stop and ask yourself what you noticed in those pages you just read, or how you were reacting. At the end make a few more notations to capture quickly what's in your head as you finish reading.

If possible, let an hour or a day go by and then read over these entries slowly. As you do, jot down on the left-hand side of your notebook whatever comes into your mind as you read the right-hand side. There is no "right" way to do this, but here are some suggestions of entries you could make:

- Second thoughts. What further ideas do your recorded notes suggest?
- How do your notes relate to other parts of your life—to your deepest concerns or interests?
- Reactions to your reactions. What do your notes tell you about how your mind works or what you are interested in?
- Dialogue with the author. What do *you* have to say? How would he or she reply?
- Who do you want to talk to about these things? What would you tell or ask them?
- Summary. What's the most important thing you notice about your notes as you read them over? What kinds of connections can you find in your notes? What conclusions about your reading do your notes make possible? What parts now seem particularly important or unimportant? (It's wise to consider carefully what *seems* unimportant: something about it attracted your attention.)

Don't worry about the exact difference between what to write on the right and on the left. There's no rigid distinction. Mainly it boils down to time: As you are reading something for the first time, whatever you write goes on the right-hand side. As you read this over, whatever additional thoughts you have go on the left. Thus the important thing about this process is to get your *thoughts to be in dialogue with each other.* The dialectical notebook makes it possible for you to exploit the advantages of being two people at once—having two different viewpoints or having discussions with yourself. (Thus it is like our exercises in writing dialogues.)

2. Try the same thing with a recent experience: an important conversation, argument, or interchange with someone; a walk that was important to you (perhaps in a beautiful place or at a time when you needed to think something over); an activity that was important to you (such as participation in a deciding game, taking a crucial exam, surviving a harrowing ordeal, or being invited to a party with new friends). On the right-hand side, put down first-stage notes: what you can remember, what you notice. Then go on to write second-stage reflexive *notes on those notes* on the left-hand side of your notebook.

If possible, share both sides of your notebook with others and listen as they read theirs. This will give you some hints about the ways others read, ways you may want to try out. Others will learn from you in the same way.

Exploring Theory: *Dialectical Notebooks and the Parallel between Reading and Writing*

The dialectical or double-entry notebook reinforces the parallel between reading and writing. The central activity in both is the making of meaning. We tend to think that "meaning" is "out there," that our task in reading and writing is to discover it, not to make it. But even though it looks as though writers have meanings which they put into the words, and then readers take the meaning out at the other end, this is an illusion. We don't fully have a meaning until we have words for it. But even this does not encompass the complexity: words cannot have or contain meanings—only people can; words are only meaningful insofar as people *attribute* meanings to them. In short, words cannot transport a writer's meanings into our heads; they can only give us a set of directions for creating our own meanings in our own heads—meanings which, if all goes well, will resemble what the writer had in mind.

It's as though the writer has movies in her mind and she wants to *give* us her movies. But in truth she cannot. She has to hope that she has been clever enough to create a set of directions that leads us to create movies in our minds that are like the ones in hers. Needless to say, that's hard. This little allegory explains something we all know about language: that it's hard to make people truly understand what we have in mind.

This view of language and communications as complex shows us something important about reading (or listening): Reading is not finding meaning but *making* meaning—not hunting for messages that are already there, but building messages. If you have the wrong idea of reading, you tend to feel (if things go well), "Oh goody, I found it"—as in an Easter egg hunt. And if things don't go well you feel, "Oh dear, where did they hide it?" When you are having difficulty in reading, it's counterproductive to think of it as a problem in finding a pesky little hidden secret; it's better to think of it as a problem in building or creating.

We're not going so far as to say (as Humpty Dumpty did to Alice) that words can mean anything—that we can build any meaning we want out of a set of someone else's words. There are rules for doing this building which people have to obey, or they build all wrong. We all know the difference between being involved in successful communication and unsuccessful communication, though most of us would be hard put to articulate *how* we know this. The trouble is that the rules for building meanings out of words are unstated, and they are continually in the process of negotiation. For that's a picture of a natural language (such as English): a game played by a large number of people where they follow unspoken rules which (because they are unspoken) are continually in the process of slight change. Can you remember games like Pass the Scissors where you join in and play before you know the rules—and the process of playing is the process of trying to learn the rules? That's how it is with language. And that's why critics and ordinary readers are able to find new meanings even in much-studied classics such as *Hamlet.*

Therefore to help us read better—particularly when we are reading something difficult or our reading is not going well—we need to pay more attention to the *process* by which we build meanings out of other people's words. A dialectical notebook helps us do that. It can help you assess what happens when you engage in making meaning from a text. Do you have strong feelings about the subject matter? about the writer? Are you bored by it? What associations jump to mind as you read? How does this writing relate to other things you know and other things in your life? Do you tend to create mental images as you read or relate what you're reading to other things you have read? Do you attend mainly to ideas or to the way something is written? What things impress you? What things do you tend to overlook? We cannot know the rules for building meaning—no one does—but we can watch more closely as we go about building meaning. We can learn to be more sensitive and insightful as we read, and perhaps learn to detect what doesn't fit the meaning we're gradually building up. (What doesn't fit often provides clues to the need for us to shift our sights a bit.) We can learn something about *how* and *why* we construct the meanings we do construct. All this we can do instead of just saying, "Where is the meaning? Where did the writer hide it?"

• • •

This mini-workshop draws heavily on Ann Berthoff's "A Curious Triangle and the Double-Entry Notebook; or How Theory Can Help Us Teach Reading and Writing." The notebook is her idea. But see also Peter Elbow's "Methodological Doubting and Believing" in *Embracing Contraries*. (Full listings for both works can be found in "Works Cited.")

The Difference between Grammatical Correctness and a Formal, Impersonal Voice

Many students confuse *correctness* and *formality,* so when something has to be correct, they try to write in a formal voice and their writing becomes stiff, awkward, and artificial—and their thinking often gets cramped and uninteresting too. In this mini-workshop we will try to show you two simple principles that can have a big effect on your final drafts: (1) Writing can be correct without having to be formal and impersonal; (2) writing can be formal and impersonal without being stiff or artificial.*

For this workshop you need a short passage of casual, informal, comfortable writing with plenty of mistakes in spelling, grammar, and usage. A half page or a couple of paragraphs will do. It's fine to use a piece of journal writing, exploratory draft writing, or freewriting you already have on hand. Or you could now do 10 minutes of freewriting about something that's interesting to you. (Of course some fast freewriting doesn't have a comfortable casual voice: Sometimes freewriting gets tangled and garbled. But don't use a passage like that; find one that really is informal and comfortable.)

Try the exercises below to learn more about correctness and voice in your own writing:

Exercise One: Writing Correctly

This is an exercise in how to make your writing correct without having it be formal or impersonal—how to get rid of all the mistakes and still keep your writing personal or informal.

Go through your passage and make whatever changes are necessary to get it clear; get rid of all the mistakes in grammar and usage, *but make as few changes as you can!* Therefore, when you find a mistake or a place that doesn't

*We lump "formal" and "impersonal" together as categories, but we acknowledge that, strictly speaking, there is a difference. That is, you could use informal language yet have no personal references at all; or use formal language, but use that language to refer to yourself and to personal experiences. Most of the time, however, formality and impersonality go together. Indeed, the very use of casual, informal language tends to give a personal flavor.

make sense or doesn't say what you want, don't rewrite the whole passage. Simply make the smallest change you can and use as much of the original, comfortable language and voice as possible. (You might get a fellow student to look for mistakes you've missed.) What you should end up with is a passage that is not only *absolutely correct* but completely *informal, casual, personal,* and *comfortable* in voice. It will have no mistakes in what we call "Standard Written English."

Peter Elbow did this exercise with a piece of his informal, private freewriting. Here is a passage from his original, fast, casual writing (the full piece is in the "Readings" for Workshop 2):

> Screen is something halfway between mind and paper.
>
> Mind is a mess: paper supposed to be neat. When I'm writing on screen, it feels like it's sort of—half—still in my mind. It's a second mind—It's not stll partly *in* me. Like my mind I can't look at all of it at once, I can only put my attention on one bit at a time. I don't yet have complete detachment from it til I print it out. It gives me a second mind.
>
> Another mind. Sometimes I make such a mess that I feel in a swamp—too many options—once I remember feeling Oh I wish I were writing in ink on expensive velum so I would just choose a word and be done. Not feel like I have to keep revising and changng. I want something *final* (must find that process piece I wrote when I was in that situation.
>
> Sometimes I try to revise too much on screen. Too much chaos in the mind.

When he did minimal revising to get rid of mistakes and get the passage clear—but to make as few changes as possible—he came up with this:

> What's on the screen is halfway between thoughts and feelings in my mind and writing on paper. Mind is a mess; writing is supposed to be neat. But when I'm writing on screen, the words seem half in my mind. The computer is a kind of second mind. The words are still partly *in* me. The computer text is also like my mind because I can't look at it all at once. I can only put my attention on one screen at a time. I don't have complete detachment from it until I print it out.
>
> Another mind. Who says two minds are better than one? Sometimes I make such a mess with my two minds that I feel in a swamp—too many options. Once when this happened I remember feeling, "Oh, I wish I were writing in ink on expensive vellum so I would just have to choose each word and be done, and not feel as though I have to keep revising and changing. I want something *final*." I still have some process writing I did when I was in that situation.
>
> Sometimes I try to revise too much on screen. This makes for too much chaos in the mind.

Correct writing doesn't have to be formal or impersonal or stiff in any way. When a teacher says, "I want your paper to be absolutely correct," you may think that she hates an informal, personal voice, whereas all she hates is *mistakes.* In such a situation (and this is also the situation for most magazine and newspaper writing and many committee reports), your best route is the one you take in this exercise: Write in your most comfortable voice and then correct and clarify it afterwards. Of course you can't use slang or ungrammatical constructions if the audience wants correctness, but you can keep an informal personal style nevertheless: There is no conflict between writing in an informal voice and writing correctly.

Here is Peter's process writing—reflecting on the choices he made in trying to get rid of mistakes but keeping the informal voice he started with:

> Plenty of the decisions were easy. I felt easy about keeping contractions. I consider them definitely correct: no conflict with what we think of as "Standard Written English"—though I know that some teachers or stylists disagree. I also felt clear that I had to change "feel *like* I have to keep revising" to "feel *as though* I have to keep revising." "Feel like" sounds like a definite mistake to me and to most English teachers, though plenty of literate people let it go by these days as correct informal writing.
>
> I felt pretty clear about keeping my two-word, verb-less sentence ("Another mind."). It's not awkward and it doesn't sound like a mistake. But plenty of teachers would disagree with me about it. Language is a matter of social negotiation, and "rules" about what is correct are slowly but constantly shifting like the coastline.

Exercise Two: Writing Formally (But Still in Your Voice)

We can carry the same principle farther now and show you that writing can even be formal and impersonal without being stiff, awkward, or artificial. It can still sound like you.

Sometimes teachers or other readers don't just ask for correctness, they ask for writing that is impersonal and formal. (When some teachers ask for correctness, they really mean "make it formal.") And when you set out to produce formal or impersonal writing, you often write language that feels awkward and artificial. But that's not necessary. You can have formal, impersonal writing that still seems comfortable and sounds like you if you go about producing it in the right way.

The crucial process here is to start out informally in a voice that feels comfortable for you. Don't worry about correctness or the need for formality. After you've written it, go through and remove *only* the personal and informal features (just like you removed only the mistakes in the earlier exercise). You will end up with something quite formal that is not dead; it will still have your voice in it. But if you start off trying to *write* it in a formal voice, your language will often feel very stiff and uncomfortable.

Here is what Peter Elbow came up with when he removed the personal, informal elements.

> What's on the screen is halfway between the thoughts and feelings in our minds and writing on paper. Mind is a mess; writing is supposed to be neat. But when we write on screen, the words still seem half in mind. The computer is a kind of second mind.
>
> The computer text is also like our minds because we cannot look at it all at once. We can put our attention on only one screenful at a time. We don't have complete detachment from what we've written until we print it out.
>
> Are two minds really better than one? Sometimes we make such a mess with

> our two minds that we feel caught in a swamp. We can feel as though we have too many options. We can wish we were writing in ink on expensive vellum so we simply have to choose each word and be done with it. When we feel we have to keep revising and changing, we wish for something *final.*
>
> Revising too much on screen can make for too much chaos in the mind.

Here is Peter's process writing, reflecting on the choices he made:

> When I looked for informal or personal elements to remove I came up with these: contractions; dashes as punctuation; sentences without a verb; conversational words like "till" and "bit"; conversational expressions like "just have to choose" (changed to "simply have to choose").
>
> It was also informal to write in the first person ("I") and refer to my own individual experience. I decided I could make it fairly formal and impersonal by changing to first-person *plural* ("we"). Perhaps others would disagree.
>
> I could have made my language more definitely formal and impersonal by talking about "people" instead of "we," but that seemed needlessly stiff and stuffy.
>
> I got interested in my question, "Who says two minds are better than one?" It gives a personal flavor because it is addressed directly to the reader. First I changed it from a question to a statement ("Conventional wisdom tells us that two minds are better than one"), but that also felt needlessly stuffy. I decided I could keep it as a question if the question isn't pointed so directly at the reader ("Are two minds really better than one?"). That seems a way to have a kind of formality and impersonality while still keeping things livelier and closer to my voice.

Our point in this mini-workshop is that your writing (and your sanity) will benefit enormously if you remember these distinctions. You can have writing that is perfectly correct, but is still personal and informal. And you can have writing that is impersonal and formal but is still lively and sounds more or less like you, not stiff, awkward, and dead.

Therefore, here is our advice: Always start off writing in a way that feels comfortable for you—in a voice that feels like the right voice for you (unless you are actually trying to mimic someone else's voice). Don't worry about correctness or level of voice. Afterwards you can go through and do the minimal revising needed for correctness—or perhaps even for formality. If you try to start off writing in a formal voice, you will often get tangled and artificial language.

On the other hand if you really want to sound like someone different from yourself, someone with a completely different character (perhaps someone older or more formal or more authoritative), *then* it may pay to start out trying to *use* that voice from the beginning. Try to imagine and see that person in your mind's eye and hear them talk in your mind's ear. Try a bit of speaking as that person would speak. Role-play that character a bit: How would the person sit or stand or walk or hold his or her head? Try to enter the role and *be* the person—and then write from within that role. But you don't need to pretend to be someone else just to write something correct or formal.

One additional piece of advice: When it comes to correctness, formality, and voice, a great deal depends on the first few paragraphs or the opening page of a piece of writing. If you can start by establishing the voice and the level of formality that you want, many readers will not notice differences in the rest of the piece. And readers are a bit more forgiving about mistakes if the first page or two are clean. In short, if you get the beginning right, you have more leeway in what follows. Look around, for example, at formal pieces of writing (perhaps scholarly essays or business memos), and you'll see that they often establish their formality in the first page or so and then actually lapse gradually into some real informality. When the informality is in the beginning, readers say, "This writer can't write formal prose." When the informality comes later on, many readers say, "This writer has a real facility with formal writing."

Midterm and End-Term Responses to a Writing Course

As teachers we don't benefit much from students' telling us we are terrific or awful teachers. But when students can give us a specific picture of what they've learned and noticed and of what our various teaching activities have made them think and feel, that's pure gold. You may not realize how much we teachers are in the dark about the effects of our teaching. The essential principle in responding to teaching is the same as that in responding to writing: Instead of trying to *judge* or to give objective evaluations or God-like verdicts, it's much more helpful to give *honest and accurate information about what happened,* that is, to tell about the effects of the teaching on you.

Another essential principle from writing also fits teaching: the person *giving* feedback learns as much as the person *getting* it. Think of the responses you write for this mini-workshop, therefore, as being for your benefit as much as for the benefit of your teacher. People don't usually learn unless they are reflective and thoughtful about their experiences. Thus the best way to increase learning in schoolwork is to reflect back on *what* you've learned, *how* you've learned it, and what it *means.*

As teachers we always try to build into our courses some quiet retrospective moments to help students pause and reflect on their learning. We find that these moments help students get in the habit of being more reflective about their learning in all areas. And it turns out that our students' reflections on their learning are usually the most useful kind of feedback for us as teachers.

Not Just at the End of a Course but in the Middle Too

Traditionally teachers ask for these kinds of responses at the end of a course. But we've found that they are also helpful—in some ways more so—at the middle point in a course. Of course, you cannot judge the whole course when it's only half over, but at the midpoint there's still time to talk to students about something in our teaching that may be confusing and time to make adjustments in our teaching. Many issues come out in midcourse responses, and they need talking about. Sometimes they can lead to a change of procedure; sometimes they show us that we need to discuss and clarify something we had been taking for granted. Almost always they help.

Turning from the teacher's benefit to your benefit, if you pause at midcourse for some retrospective reflections on the weeks that have gone by, you may notice a habit of yours that is getting in your way. Perhaps you realize that you tend to be preoccupied while writing with whether you will please the teacher. As you reflect on those feelings, you will probably see more clearly how much they get in the way of doing your best writing. Or perhaps this midcourse writing will help you reflect on your dissatisfaction with the course. You may realize that your dissatisfaction is indeed justified. But your reflections may also help you realize that you only have two choices: learning something despite the dissatisfaction or not learning anything. It all depends on how you deal with your dissatisfaction. Your midcourse explorations may show you how to get the best out of a bad situation instead of letting yourself pay the penalty because someone else isn't meeting your needs or expectations.

Here then are questions to help you write responses that will be useful both for yourself and for your teacher. We've given far more questions than you can use for a short document. Perhaps your teacher will specify certain ones you should answer—or leave the choice up to you. Probably your teacher would like to see some of these responses, but it is helpful to write them with utter honesty for yourself first, leaving until later the question of which ones you will show to others.

Questions for Response

1a. Which moments come to mind when you think back over the class? good moments? bad moments? perplexing moments? Quickly sketch in a small number of such moments. Two or three sentences can easily sketch a moment; often one sentence will do (indeed you can sometimes point with just a phrase to a moment that your reader will obviously remember—e.g., "That morning you lost your temper about people coming in late"). Just take the moments that come to mind.

1b. What do these moments tell about you as a student, about the teacher, and about the course?

2. What are you most proud of about your own effort or accomplishment in the course? What are you not satisfied with, or what do you want to work on improving?

3. What are the most important strengths or skills you brought to this course?

4. What has been your greatest challenge?

5. Tell about the effects of the course on your writing. Talk about:

    - Changes or lack of change in the quality of *what* you write
    - Changes or lack of change in *how* you write
    - Changes or lack of change in your attitudes and feelings about writing

6. What have you learned other than about writing—perhaps about yourself or about people or about learning?
7. What has been the most important thing you've learned? If you wish, you can just circle something you've already written.
8. What do you most need to learn next?
9. What was the most and the least helpful about:
   - In-class activities
   - Homework assignments
   - Group work
   - Comments on papers
   - Readings
   - Conferences
   - Grading procedures
   - How the course is structured
   - How the teacher operates
10. What aspects of you has the course brought out? What aspects did it leave untapped or unnoticed?
11. Imagine this course as a journey: Where is it taking you?
12. Imagine this course as a detour or setback in some larger journey. Explain.
13. Describe the climate and weather of the course. Has it remained the same or gone through cycles?
14. Describe the course as a machine, as a living organism, as a slow-acting poison, as an *X-Files* script.
15. If you could start over again, what would you do differently? What have you learned about how to learn better?
16. Do you have any suggestions about how the course could be made more helpful?

Another Format for Writing Responses

A Letter to Your Teacher The questions are helpful because they pinpoint many important issues and permit relatively short answers. But you may find it more helpful to read through the questions slowly and then write a letter to your teacher. There's something powerful about starting off on a blank piece of paper with "Dear———." To write a letter is to be faced with the best question of all: "What do I need to say to this person?" Because it's a letter and because you are writing very much to her, you cannot help treating your teacher as a person (not just a role or an authority figure). This awareness may lead you to certain insights you wouldn't get from "answering a questionnaire."

Still Another Format for Writing Responses*

It's useful to build evaluation directly into classroom activities so it's ongoing. Teachers who think this way may develop several strategies. A simple one concentrates not on judging what either you or the teacher is doing but on making suggestions for changes. For instance, the teacher can distribute a form like the following and ask you to draw a directional arrow on each line:

Students should be less involved in class.	—|—|—|—|—|—	**Students should be more involved in class.**
We should do more group work.	—|—|—|—|—|—	**We should do less group work.**
I'd like to do more reading.	—|—|—|—|—|—	**We're asked to do too much reading.**
We should be able to choose more of our own topics.	—|—|—|—|—|—	**I'd rather be given more assigned topics.**
The teacher should write fewer comments on our papers.	—|—|—|—|—|—	**The teacher should write more comments on our papers.**
Teacher's comments should be less directive.	—|—|—|—|—|—	**Teacher's comments should be more directive.**
We should do less in-class freewriting.	—|—|—|—|—|—	**We should do more in-class freewriting.**
There should be more attention to grammar.	—|—|—|—|—|—	**There should be less attention to grammar.**

Your teacher may ask you to respond to a form such as this several times during the semester, and may even ask each of you at some time to work with several others in compiling the results of the form and leading a discussion based on these results at the next class.

---

*This form and the procedures connected to it are based on one developed by Bob Boice and Lyle R. Creamer, psychologists who specialize in learning theory and writing.

Writing under Pressure: Midterms, Finals, and Other In-Class Writing

There are two kinds of pressure that often make writing difficult. Most of us have experienced both kinds: (1) writing when you have sharply limited time, such as when you are taking an exam, and (2) writing when you are anxious or confused and therefore can't think straight.

Writing When You Have Limited Time

In this textbook we stress writing as a complex process of thinking something through: Start by exploring and only gradually work your way through to the point where you finally understand what you want to say. Invite chaos and then work gradually toward coherence. Clarity of mind is not what you start out with but what you end up with. This is indeed the best way to get to new thinking and to your best thinking, and to produce writing that is the most intellectually alive.

But this long and messy process is a luxury you can't afford when you have only 30 or 60 minutes for writing an essay on an exam. If you have a longer essay exam of two or three hours, you can invite a little of this process, but not much. There's a technological issue here too; if you can write your exam on a computer, you can do more revising than if you have to write by hand.

When time is short, and especially if you are writing by hand, you need to start off establishing clarity of mind. We suggest the following steps:

Read the Question Carefully Slowly. Repeatedly. The most common cause of low grades on exams and other assignments is neglecting or misunderstanding the question. Unless the exam question is extremely simple and straightforward, you need to take yourself in hand and force yourself to think hard about what is being asked. It's best to jot things down for a couple of minutes. Ask yourself questions like these:

- What is the instructor really asking? What's the essential question?
- Is there more than one question or a question behind this question?
- What does the question *assume* or *imply*?

It's fine to question the question and go behind it to talk of something not explicitly mentioned in it—as long as you show that you have really understood the question and that your approach is a way of getting to the heart of the matter.

Make an Outline If you know pretty much what you want to say on the basis of your pondering of the quesion, you can go right to a one-step outline. If you find the question difficult and you can't yet see what you want to say, then you need a two-step outline. We'll explain both approaches in a minute.

In either case, make sure it's an "explicit outline"; that is, make sure that each item in your outline is an *assertion,* not simply a point; a *sentence,* not just a word or phrase. Just listing points, words, or phrases may be quicker and easier—like this:

- Speech/writing
  - Audience
    - Speech audience
    - Writing audience
  - Effects

But this kind of *non*explicit outline doesn't spell out your thinking clearly enough and can often get you lost or confused. It's worth forcing yourself to write actual sentences. It's fine for them to be simple—that's even better—and it's okay to skip some words. But make each one feel like it's saying something or doing work, not just pointing in a direction. Your goal is not an abstract, static structure, but a *moving story of thinking—thinking that leads your reader on a path from the question to your conclusions.* Here's an example:

- I'll compare speech and writing.
- Audience is a big factor.
- In speaking, audience is live in front of us (usually).
- In writing, audience is usually absent.
- Therefore, in speaking we usually feel the audience more; we fit words to them better.
- In writing we often don't feel the audience and don't fit words to them or we forget about their point of view.

Some people don't think you can have an outline unless there is *indenting.* But the point is to make your list of sentences tell a story of thinking that works without the aid of indenting. Sentences help you *feel* the logic and movement of your train of thought.

When you write any outline, leave some space between items so that later you can put in points you realize you need at various spots.

One-Step Outline If you have a pretty good sense of your direction, jump right in and start making the sentence outline we describe above. But make sure you are using the outline to focus on one main, overarching point.

A main point doesn't have to be a simple point. For example, your main point could be that there are three important causes/influences/results, or that two opposite arguments are equally valid. In addition, the *path* to your single main point doesn't have to be simple; you can treat a number of subissues and side controversies to build up to your single main point. But as you are taking that path toward your main point, give your readers some hints about the main point. Don't let them feel lost. In short, most teachers are looking for what most good thinkers are looking for—both simplicity and complexity. They'll mark you down if it's merely simple, and they'll mark you down if it's complex but confusing.

Two-Step Outline If you aren't sure yet what you are going to say, you need two steps.

The first step is a preoutline or proto-outline—a kind of "grab bag" nonoutline: Write down every point you can think of that somehow seems to pertain to this question. Write your points down in whatever order they pop into your mind. Again, try for sentences or assertions, not just single words or phrases that don't say anything.

Once you have your list of ideas or assertions—once you have quickly jotted down every point or idea you can think of that pertains to the question—then you have arrived at the moment of decision. Check the exam question again and then your list of points. Perhaps the process of reading over all the points you put down will help you see a main point you haven't yet written down. That's an exciting development. But even if that doesn't happen, you should now be able to see which points are primary and which are secondary.

Now you can go to the second step and make your real outline. Put your points in an order that tells a story, an order that leads your reader on a clear path from the question to your answer.

If you find this process difficult, don't frustrate yourself by assuming that you have to find the single, perfect train of thought or path. There are always various interesting and valid paths. Feel yourself not so much trying to solve a problem in geometry as trying to find a good story to tell.

Writing out Your Essay If you are writing by hand, write on every other line so that you can come back and make additions or corrections. Don't worry about using up a lot of paper. Writing on alternate lines is also easier for teachers to read—which is an important factor.

This may be more or less one-draft writing where you can't simply freewrite garbage. But don't agonize over small details of wording. The best method is to get yourself *talking onto the page,* rather than trying to construct grammatical sentences. This talking will lead to some informality in your wording, but that's perfectly acceptable in most exams. And don't spend much time thinking about spelling either. Just make sure you save some time at the end to go back over what you've written and make a few corrections in mechanics.

Follow your outline and make sure to give your readers lots of "signposts" to identify your structure. (Here are some examples of the kinds of sentences or phrases that help save readers from getting lost: "In this essay I will be making one main argument, but to back it up, I need to consider two side issues." "My first point is this." "My last point might seem surprising but it is as follows." "I see a disagreement between two ideas that many people think are in agreement.") Don't run away from blunt, even clumsy phrasings that spell out what you are doing. Try to help readers feel the logic of your train of thinking with signpost words like "in addition," "moreover," "however," "on the other hand," and "you might think so-and-so, but really, it's thus-and-such."

Writing When You Can't Think Straight

We often have to write a paper even though something in our life has derailed us: Someone we care about is ill or has jilted us, and we are seething with hurt or anger. There are many situations that can short-circuit our brain.

The most obvious solution is to put the writing task aside for a while and let the circuits reestablish themselves—to allow the mind to heal. Take a hike and let a day or two pass. But if there's not much time, the most curative activity is to get a trusted friend to listen while we talk about everything that has upset us. Make it clear that his or her job is to listen and be supportive, not trying to think of answers or cures for our problem. If we speak and our friend listens supportively, we can usually find the perspective we need to put our upset aside for a while. Indeed, the process often shows us how to deal with the situation.

If such a friend is not available, *create* a friend out of blank paper. Simply freewrite about what has upset you. Spill your feelings on paper. This too will usually help you to clear your mind and feelings and to feel fresh again.

But what if you are still having trouble thinking clearly? Perhaps the paper is due tomorrow morning. It's 1:30 A.M. now, no friends are awake to listen to you spout off, you've tried freewriting for two 15-minute sessions—and you still can't think straight. The problem is that your upset is causing your mind to have trouble holding on to more than one thought at a time. When you try to think two thoughts or think about a connection between two or three ideas—especially if you try to create a train of thought—your mind shuts down. This happens to all of us.

The best help for writing under these conditions comes from the two-step outline. Start with the "grab bag" nonoutline process and write down every point that you can think of that pertains to your topic. Don't write them on a piece of paper. Instead get a pile of cards or cut up pieces of $8\frac{1}{2}$-by-11-inch paper into eighths and write each point on a separate card or slip of paper. Write them as they come to you—in any order. That way, you only have to think one thought at a time. But try to make each one a sentence, not just a word or phrase.

After you've written out this pile of thoughts, lay out the slips around you and begin to group them together according to your feeling of which ones "sort of go together." In effect, you are now moving gradually into the second step of creating an outline.

Next, choose one clump of cards or slips of paper—perhaps the one that appeals to you most—and gradually coax your mind into figuring out why this clump goes together. In effect, you are trying to feel the idea in each clump. Write it out (if you have not already done so) on one of the cards. Do this for all your clumps.

Next, try for sequence. Try to feel which clumps or main ideas go before or after the others. Again, remember you aren't doing geometry or algebra, you are trying to tell a story—a story of thinking.

As you are working out a sequence and a story, figure out your main, overall point. Make sure to write that out too on a slip or card. Once you've written out a one-sentence main point, look back at your sequence or story and make sure it fits your main point. You may make changes in the sequence of your cards or slips of paper, but you're not aiming for perfection. Given your fragile state of mind, you are trying to get by with something acceptable or decent.

Notice the process you have been using. You are upset and your mind cannot hold onto more than one idea at a time or think about relationships among ideas. Therefore, you give your mind a break by using a simple calculating machine that consists of movable slips of paper. Throughout the process, your mind never has to deal with more than one thought.

Now you know pretty much what you are going to say and pretty much the order for saying it. You are in a position to start writing your draft. See if you can take some time away from your paper at this point to clear your head before you try to write out a draft. Even a half hour can help.

Writing out a Draft Even though you are probably feeling much better now, you may well find it difficult to write clear, well-constructed sentences. Give yourself permission to write ugly, ungainly, absurd, broken *non*sentences. The goal is to get your thoughts into "sort-of prose." It's fine to use sentences like these: "I'm not sure, but it seems like . . ." "Here's something that I want to say: . . ." Try to talk your thinking onto paper; the more you can talk it, the easier time you'll have.

As you are writing, don't get stopped or tangled trying to fix sentences or stymied by fussing over a grammar or usage problem. Keep slogging forward. Keep following your outline and writing out your thinking. It will probably get better.

Again, clear your head with a short break that will distance you a bit from your language and help you examine it more objectively. After you have a draft of the whole thing, you'll be surprised how easy it is to go back through it to clarify and clean up the language. Your best tool is your voice, using your actual mouth and throat. Force yourself to speak every phrase and sentence aloud. As you do so, you'll find it easy and natural to change words and phrases so that they fit more comfortably in your mouth. Keep in mind that there is usually no need for complete rephrasing or rewriting: The sentence often becomes strong and comfortable if you just omit many of the words you used earlier as you were fighting to produce "sort-of prose."

You might find it helpful to take another tiny break so you can come back to check the spelling, punctuation, and grammar with fresher eyes.

Exercise: Practicing the Technique

So far in this mini-workshop, we have just been explaining general processes. Now we urge you to practice these activities. You'll find it easier to use them under exam conditions or when you are upset and anxious if you try them out under safer conditions first. You need to get the feel of them. Try following the steps we have proposed, but if it helps you to make some adjustments, that's fine. Your goal should be to mold *our* processes to *your* needs.

Set yourself a deadline of a half hour or one hour to write a practice essay exam. Choose a topic where you'll have to struggle a bit to figure out what you want to say. That is, choose a topic that forces you to use the two-step outine process. See if you can find one that is both meaty and difficult for you—choose a topic where you don't yet know your thinking so that you will have to fight your way to a new train of thought. Perhaps your textbook lists questions at the ends of units. Here are a few topics we can suggest:

- Think of two or three different courses, subjects, or disciplines that interest you. Perhaps they are possible majors for you. Compare and contrast the ways of thinking, the assumptions, and the values in these fields.
- Discuss the advantages and disadvantages of traditional gender-role upbringing for men and women doing careers in science.
- Describe an opinion, attitude, or point of view that seems highly valued in our culture—and one about which you have divided feelings. You see the value in it, yet you have misgivings too. Write an essay in which you try to clarify your thinking on this matter.
- In comparing humans to (other) animals, what is more important—the ways they differ or the ways they are the same or similar?

Doing Research on the Web

The purpose of this mini-workshop is to discuss some strategies for finding useful Web-based sources.

Finding Sources

Many of the best online sources cost money, but before you break out your credit card—or decide that your project isn't worth the expense—find out what online publications your school's library has purchased. Go to your library's home page and look for a list of online sources available to students. You may be able to conduct online searches through a database of online articles. If so, then you can probably print out any articles that you find in the database. Online scholarship that is purchased by your school is generally, though by no means always, more reliable than other sources you find on the Internet. Your librarians have already researched the publications to ensure that they meet certain academic standards. If you ignore your library's resources and go straight to the Internet, you will have to perform the same evaluative activities that librarians are trained to do!

It often happens that your library's online resources will be inadequate, and you'll have to turn to the public domain of the Internet. Although the task of finding Web-based sources is more difficult, the art of refining your search and discriminating between useful and useless resources can be rewarding. But be prepared to invest some time in learning how to refine your online searches, ferret out relevant sources, and determine their relative usefulness. Just because a Web page looks professional in its presentation doesn't mean that its content is worthy of citation. There are a few tricks to help you ascertain the authority of a page, but in most cases you'll have to depend on your own close reading skills.

If you've ever used an Internet search engine before, you probably have experienced the frustration of retrieving a huge number of URLs (Uniform Resource Locators) with little or no relevance to your own topic. If you haven't had this experience, use your browser to find a search engine (see Table 1) and type in your search topic. In many cases, the search engine will return a great number of links related to your topic. Instead of paging through thousands of links, you need to learn how to supply the search engine with more information about your search. Some search engines supply a form

Table 1 Search Engines

Search Tool	Description
AltaVista http://www.altavista.com	Comprehensive **full-text search engine.** Searches Web and Usenet. Can limit returns by date, location(s), language; retrieves large number of results (not always relevant). Use when doing a specific search for obscure information.
Excite http://www.excite.com	**Search engine.** Offers in-depth subject arrangement and concept searching (automatically searches related terms) and indexes Internet sites and Usenet.
Infoseek http://www.infoseek.com	**Full-text search engine.** Searches Web, Usenet, gopher sites, e-mail addresses, current news, company listings. Results displayed with good organization by relevance. Use for searching the entire Web or when a large number of results are desired. Also allows specific questions.
Lycos http://www.lycos.com	**Search engine.** Can limit returns by title, pictures, sounds, URL, language. Results returned with good organization by relevance.
MetaCrawler http://www.metacrawler.com	**Metasearch engine.** Searches multiple engines at one time (currently, AltaVista, Excite, Infoseek, LookSmart, Lycos, The Mining Co., WebCrawler, and Yahoo!). Consolidates results, ranked by a score derived from the rankings of each of the search engines listing each site.
WebCrawler http://www.webcrawler.com	**Search engine.** Offers an easy-to-use search form and compact results. Searches Web, Usenet, gopher, ftp sites, but only for title, keywords, URLs. Results returned with good organization by relevance. Use when searching for popular sites and documents or information likely to appear in title and keywords of a site, or when wanting a manageable number of results.
Yahoo! http://www.yahoo.com	**Subject directory** to selected resources, rather than a full-text search engine. Searches for Web, Usenet sites, using keywords only. Numerous directories available; passes on searches to full-text search engine. Use when browsing, for subject categories, overviews of topic. Returns not organized by relevance.

page, with drop-down menus and check boxes that allow you to delimit the properties of your search. Others provide a list of symbols that help you limit your search. Here is a description of some of the most commonly used symbols:

- Quotation marks (“”) designate *phrases* that must appear in the search results. If you type in *deviant behavior,* the search results will include all documents related to “deviant” and all documents related to “behavior.” If, however, you type in *“deviant behavior”* you will receive only those documents containing both words, in the prescribed order.
- A plus sign (+) before a word (e.g., +gun +laws) indicates words that must appear in the search results, though not necessarily in any order.
- A minus sign (–) before a word (e.g., –stock “car racing”) indicates that you wish to exclude results containing that word. The example in parentheses would return results for car racing, but would exclude sites concerning stock car racing.
- An asterisk (*) or wildcard allows you to search for words with various endings. For instance, the search term *bibl** will return any pages with *bible, bibles, biblia, biblical,* but also *bibliography, bibliophile,* and so on.

In addition, all search engines support Boolean operators, such as the following:

- AND returns all documents containing the words separated by AND (i.e., Chinese AND checkers AND rules).
- OR returns all documents containing either the word proceeding or the word following OR (e.g., “Louis XIV” OR “Sun King”).
- NOT returns all documents containing the first word and excluding the second word (butter NOT margarine). For some search engines, you will have to type “AND NOT” rather than “NOT” to perform this function.
- Parentheses allow you to group together search terms, in order to perform more complicated searches (e.g., “Pope John Paul” AND (abortion OR contraception).

Boolean syntax often returns more results than a simple idiomatic phrase will return, and most of these results won’t be related to your topic. If possible, use a phrase instead of words connected by Booleans (e.g., “deviant behavior” instead of deviant AND behavior). Booleans, however, remain useful when combining phrases in your search (“deviant behavior” AND “clinical studies”). Before using any logical tags, you should find out which ones are recognized by your search engine. On the page of the search engine, look for links that say “advanced searches,” “refining your search,” or “help.” These links lead you to descriptions of how to get the most out of your searches.

Once you have learned how to refine your search, you will begin to return a more reasonable number of results. As you skim through the results, bookmark those that may be potentially useful. If you’re using a computer on campus, you may not be allowed to use the bookmarking tool. In this case, drag down the File menu option to “Save as” and save the page to your own disk. If you still are unable to find anything relevant to your source after refining your search in several ways, try another search engine. No two search engines will return the same results. Some will offer you subject headings that help you to restrict your search. Others will offer key words that you can add to your search in order to refine it. Still others will break your search into a list of conceptual components, so that you can include or exclude any of the components. If one search engine proves to be unhelpful, chances are that another one will point you in the right direction.

Evaluating Online Sources

Once you have a list of useful bookmarks (or pages), it's time to do some close examination of each source you've uncovered. To determine the potential usefulness, read through it and ask yourself the following questions:

1. *Is the source authoritative?* In most circumstances, your teacher will expect you to quote and paraphrase sources that follow academic guidelines. This means that the page should indicate who the author is. If you don't see an author on the page of the article, try to find out information about the Web site that "publishes" it: Pursue links toward the home page of a site until you find information about where the article comes from. Articles that don't identify the author often turn out to be perfectly acceptable, but you must determine the reliability of the organization responsible for publishing the article and consider how carefully it screens its submissions. If you feel an article is more authoritative than the publication information suggests, don't be afraid to e-mail a question to the person who maintains the site. They may point you in the direction of more useful sources. Obviously, the more information a site provides about authorship of its articles, the more authoritative it is.

Once you have gathered information about authorship and publication, you can move on to other questions: Does the article cite other relevant articles for the information it provides? Has it been published in a printed journal or magazine? Has it been read and approved by other scholars in the field (a process called peer review)? Is the author a recognized authority in the field? You may not find answers to all of these questions, but you can be much more confident of sources for which the answer is yes. If you are finding lots of untrustworthy sources, try to limit your search again or use a different search engine. Pages lacking academic authority should not be ruled out, but they need to be treated differently in your research project (see point 4 below).

2. *How impartial is the source?* You should not rule out a source just because it takes a strong stand on a controversial issue, but opinionated pieces often have not taken the time to research all sides of an issue. If you come across a page of this nature, you want to present it in your own research as one of several possible arguments, not as the final word on the subject. Once again, finding out information about who "publishes" the page is essential. If you are writing a research paper on the issues of human cloning, you don't want to limit yourself to articles listed on the Human Cloning

Foundation's home page, which calls itself "the official site in support of human cloning." In general, web addresses with an ".edu" (educational) or ".gov" (government) suffix tend to be more neutral and therefore more reliable. Commercial (.com) and not-for-profit organizations (.org) are more likely to have a vested interest in your topic. If a web site is trying to get you to join an organization or to sell you a product, then the articles it publishes are less likely to be impartial.

3. *Is the source presented in a professional manner?* Although a professional presentation is no guarantee of a reliable source, it often indicates a site's level of commitment to the articles it publishes. First and foremost, look for an indication of the time a page was last updated (usually at the bottom of a site's home page). If it has not been modified in the last six months, then you should question its reliability. Consider these issues as well:

- Are there links in the site that don't work?
- If there are images on the page, do any of them fail to load up in your window?
- Is the text hard to read because of the background color, or because it is cut off by images?
- Does the visual presentation of the page distract you from the text of the article?

The more that you answer "yes" to these questions, the less likely it is that this source—or the web site that publishes it—will be around tomorrow.

4. *Is it useful?* Up to now, we have been asking questions to find out how reliable a source is. Ultimately, these questions are not nearly as important as the question of usefulness: What aspect of your topic interested you in the first place and what does this online source contribute to your own position? The sources that are the most persuasive and informative often cause us the most trouble since we are inclined to repeat their ideas rather than articulate our own. When you find such a source, it is a good idea to ask yourself how relevant this information is to your main point. As for the sources you don't understand—even after several readings—you are probably better off not using them at all.

By the same token, if one of your searches turns up an insightful discussion in a page with no academic credentials or institutional affiliation, the lack of formal authority for this discussion should not preclude you from using it. Many search engines, for instance, will return results which were originally posted in newsgroups.* If you read such a newsgroup posting and learn something extremely interesting about your topic, don't automatically dismiss it for lack of credentials or professional presentation. You may want to e-mail the person who posted this message to find out how he or she learned so much about the topic and where you might find these sources. This person may be willing to be interviewed. If you are worried about whether an informal

*Newsgroups work very much like a bulletin board: Anyone can "visit" a newsgroup and post a message to it. But since each newsgroup usually focuses on a narrow topic, there are often very informative messages posted to them.

interview or newsgroup posting is sufficiently reliable, then ask your teacher. Most teachers will permit you to use this kind of source, so long as you follow correct citation standards and indicate the person's credentials. They recognize that a source which stirs your interest and reminds you of why you chose to write about a topic is far more *useful* than one which confuses, bores, or leads you astray.

Citation of Online Sources

The proper method for citing online sources remains a topic of debate; this does not, however, excuse you from the obligation of citing online sources. Find out from your teacher the citation style that you are expected to use. If you are using the MLA style, we recommend the following practice. Parenthetical citations within the body of your essay should include the author's last name—"(Paglia)"—and exclude the page number, since web pages typically do not have page numbers. As explained in Workshop 12, "Research," parenthetical citations refer the reader to a specific entry within the list of works cited at the end of the paper. Since the works cited alphabetizes by the last name of the author, your parenthetical citation usually needs no further information.

We list here examples of two basic entries:

An Online Database or Web Site

Author. *Title of database or site.* Editor. Version number. Date posted or last updated. Sponsoring institution. Date of access <network address (URL)>.

Ishikawa, Akihito. *American Literature on the Web.* 1 Jan. 1999. English Dept., Nagasaki College of Foreign Languages. 21 Apr. 1999 <http://www.nagasaki-gaigo.ac.jp/ishikawa/amlit/index.htm>.

An Article in an Online Periodical

Author. "Title." *Title of periodical.* Volume or issue number and date of publication. Number range or total number of paragraphs, pages, or sections (if numbered). Date of access <network address (URL)>.

Paglia, Camille. "Butler vs. Nussbaum." *Salon Magazine Ivory Tower* 24 Feb. 1999. 8 Mar. 1999. <http://www.salonmagazine.com/it/col/pagl/1999/02/24pagl.html>.

Many web sites will not provide all of this information. In citing such sources, you will have to leave some information out of your works cited entry. But make sure that you have searched the site thoroughly for all the information there.

We cannot devote space in this mini-workshop to the proper citation of other Internet sources, but Workshop 12, "Research," provides several more models, and there are numerous web sites dedicated to this topic. The following list of online citation guides will get you started:

- "MLA Style" (http://www.mla.org/main_stl.htm) is maintained by the Modern Language Association and provides examples for several kinds of web pages, as well as answers to some of the more common questions about citation format.
- "The McGraw-Hill Guide to Electronic Research and Documentation" (http://www.mhhe.com/socscience/english/compde/guide/) by Diana Roberts Wienbroer provides the full text of a McGraw-Hill guide to citing online sources, which also offers strategies for evaluating web sites and conducting online research.
- "Basic CGOS Style" (http://www.columbia.edu/cu/cup/cgos/idx_basic.html), by Todd Taylor and Janice Walker, provides excerpts from their book, *Columbia Guide to Online Style* (New York: Columbia University Press, 1998) on how to site online sources.
- "Documenting Electronic Sources" (http://owl.english.purdue.edu/writers/documenting.html), which is part of Purdue's Online Writing Lab, offers citation information for MLA and APA styles, as well as links to several other sites with information about citation.

Two Short Exercises on Evaluating Online Sources

Learning to assess the value of online sources is a difficult process that most of us have trouble doing on our own. Nevertheless, if you fail to evaluate your online sources carefully before using them in your paper, the results can be disastrous. The following two exercises are intended to develop your critical skills. Both of them break down the process of evaluation into manageable steps. As long as you have a computer with a connection to the Internet, you can do the first exercise by yourself. The second one requires you to work with other students in a computer lab. Both exercises will require you to switch back and forth between a web browser and a word processing program. If you don't understand what this means, ask a computer lab consultant for help. Once someone opens up the programs and shows you how to manipulate them, you should be able to complete the first exercise on your own.

Exercise One: Evaluating a Web Source

- Open up your Internet browser and a word processing program. You will use the word processing window to compose the evaluation of your potential source.
- Now open your Internet browser. Using your browser, locate a search engine (see Table 1) and find an online source that is relevant to your topic. Once you have found one, use the information on the page to create a proper bibliographic entry at the top of your word processing window. When you are done, save your document.
- Read through the source with an eye to the evaluative questions listed above in the section, "Evaluating Online Sources." While you are reading, note down in your word processing window any features that suggest the relative authority of this page. Who is the author? When was it last updated? What organization is responsible for publishing it? What does the text of the article tell you about the author's competence in this field? Remember that you will have to visit other neighboring pages to find out more about your source.
- Spend some time with each of the other three concerns: How impartial is this source? How professional is its presentation? And most important, how potentially useful is it to your own project? As you record your notes in the word processing window, remember to save before returning to your browser.
- Once you have considered all of the evaluative criteria, return to your word processing window, review your notes, and come to some conclusion about the usefulness of this source. With this conclusion as your thesis, organize your notes into points of support. Don't be afraid to conclude that this source won't be very useful for you: We don't expect you to find the perfect source *today!* A sober description of this source and its relation to your own research project are much more important.
- When you finish, save your work and find out what your teacher wants you to do with the document. If your class will be continuing with the collaborative workshop, then you can skip the first three steps below.

Exercise Two: Collaborative Feedback

Each group should contain three to four students.

- In a word processing window, type your name and describe your research project in a sentence or two.
- After you have saved this description, leave the word processing window open. Launch a web browser of your choice and use a search engine to find a source relevant to your topic.
- Now switch back to your word processing window. Below your description, type in a bibliographic entry for this source (see Workshop 12, "Research," for help with this format). Save this document and leave it and the browsing window open.

- Now swap seats with someone else in your group. Read through the description of his or her project. Check over to the web browser and read through the other student's source.
- While you are reading, note down in the word processing window any features that suggest the value of this page as a source—that is, is it authoritative, impartial, professional, useful? Note these down beneath the other student's bibliographic entry and leave at least two blank spaces between your comments and the bibliographic entry. Since you will have to do this for every group member, try not to spend more than 10 minutes on this.
- When you have finished, proceed to another student's computer and follow the same steps. When you have responded to every student in your group, return to your own station and print out a description of your project, along with everyone else's comments.
- Assemble with other group members and discuss which student had the most useful source. If there is time, present your group's conclusion to the rest of the class. What made this student's source superior to those of your other group members? What were the weaknesses of this source?

Part II

Editing

The Sentence and End-Stop Punctuation

Exercise: Identifying Sentences

Look at the following groups of words and decide whether or not each one is a sentence. Don't agonize over the decision; just read each one quickly *out loud* and let your instincts tell you yes or no.

Sitting on the doorstep.
Go.
With careful analysis and painstaking research.
Stupid!
To the door.
The people at the end of the block who have been living there for years.
Jane and John were the kind of people who remained good friends even if you hadn't seen them for ten years.
Jennifer and her mother.
Come and visit with us whenever you can find the time.
John lost.
Let's go.
All the way around the block, into the building, up the stairs, and into the apartment.
Because it's dark.
But only if you have finished your work.
While all of us were sitting on the beach, watching the sun sprinkle sparkling lights on the calm waters of the inlet and feeling far away from everyday cares.
And then there were none.

After you've decided which of these are sentences, check to see if others agree.

We began this workshop asking you to do this exercise because linguists tell us that native speakers of a language recognize complete sentences in their language. In fact, many linguists believe that children as young as two have intuitive knowledge of what a sentence is. Our beginning exercise is a way of testing this premise. We suspect that you and your classmates agreed on almost all your responses. In other words, we believe that linguists are right: native speakers of a language do "know" what a sentence is. They know in the sense that they can intuitively produce and recognize sentences.

If what we're saying is true, why do so many native speakers have problems with incomplete and run-on sentences? We can think of two important reasons.

First, knowing what a sentence is doesn't mean we know how to demonstrate that information when we write. This is one way in which spoken and written language differ greatly. Our voice punctuates our speech so that others can understand it; on paper we have to use punctuation marks. That is, we often need to turn intuitive knowledge into conscious knowledge. That may sound easy; it usually isn't. Second, no sentence exists in a vacuum; sentences always have a context. In speech that context includes the words we have already spoken, but it also includes our physical surroundings and our own gestures. If you're sitting on a beach, watching a beautiful sunset, you can gesture toward the setting sun and say "Beautiful!" Anyone listening will consider that a complete sentence because of the context which allows them to fill in the missing words: "The sunset is beautiful." Or in conversation, if someone says, "Why are you leaving?" and you answer "Because I'm hungry," anyone listening will consider your words a complete sentence because they can fill in the missing words: "I'm leaving because I'm hungry."

These are called fragments—understood words are missing—and in writing they are often called *wrong,* even though they are fine in speech. That's what causes trouble. Most teachers and editors would consider the following wrong:

> The senators refused to withdraw their proposal to ship wheat to the drought-stricken countries. A proposal unpopular with the chairperson.

Even though most of us would agree on mentally inserting the words "this was" before "a proposal," this agreement isn't enough in a piece of writing; most teachers probably want the words to be there on the page.

Maybe you think this is being picky, but it really isn't. We think everyone who reads our piece will automatically insert the intended words, but sometimes we're wrong. In speaking we can see our audience and tell whether they "get" our omitted words, but in writing we don't know how our reader is doing. If we're wrong, our reader may either find our writing incoherent or—what may be worse—misconstrue our meaning.

Nonetheless, good writers use fragments, and you can too, provided you don't confuse your readers. If you want to make sure that none of your fragments are confusing or awkward to readers, always ask a couple of people to read what you write before you hand it in. Ask them to let you know if they're confused. If it's a fragment that's causing the confusion, you'll probably want to fix it. Keep in mind, however, that your friends may not notice fragments that are *not* confusing—fragments that function as complete sentences even though they're missing an explicit subject or a verb. It's a good idea to find out how your teacher feels about fragments such as these.

Let's reconsider the "test" we started with. When linguists say that all native speakers know what a sentence is, they mean that native speakers can recognize sentences when spoken and in context. You may have had some disagreement on the "test"—and perhaps even some downright "mistakes"—because (1) it's harder to tell what's a sentence if it's not spoken, and (2) it's difficult to deal with any set of words which have no context since such a condition doesn't match our own experience. (In extended pieces of writing, the issue is even more complicated. The sentences are in a context, but for the sake of punctuation we have to act as if they are not—act as if the sentences stand alone even though they don't. This runs counter to our intuition.) Still, it needn't take much for you to learn to *adapt* the sentence-knowing skills you have to these harder conditions.

Fragments earn their name because they lack words that complete them. Run-ons display the opposite fault: They contain too many words, enough words, in fact, for two sentences. Run-ons are never a feature of the spoken language of native-born speakers. We all indicate sentence division in speech by pitches and pauses. This being true, we can correct written run-ons by reading aloud. The only problem is to decide what mark of punctuation to use at the point of sentence division: an end mark, a semicolon, a colon, or a conjunction with a comma. Thus you can use your intuition to avoid run-ons only up to a certain point. Beyond that, you're going to have to know some of the rules.

Some Practice Exercises and Some Rules

Grammar books usually define a sentence as a group of words that contains a subject, a verb, and a complete idea. The problem with "complete idea" is that it's often difficult in practice to decide what a complete idea is, where it starts, and where it ends. "A sentence is a group of words that can stand alone" probably works better as a definition because it allows you to rely on your implicit knowledge of what a sentence is. Thus once you decide that a group of words can stand alone, you need look only at whether it has an explicit subject and verb.* The only kind of English sentence that doesn't need a subject is an order ("Come here, please") since the understood subject of all orders is "you," and our grammar doesn't require us to make this "you" explicit.

Exercises: Using End Marks

Here are a few exercises you can do to make you think explicitly about the use of end marks in written prose.

1. Read through the following paragraph and decide where end marks should go; that is, decide which groups of words make complete sentences.

> The essayist does not usually appear early in the literary history of a country he comes naturally after the poet and the chronicler his habit of mind is leisurely he does not write from any special stress of passionate impulse he does not create material so much as he comments upon material already existing it is essential for him that books should have been written, and that they should, at least to some extent, have been read and digested he is usually full of allusions and references, and these his reader must be able to follow and understand and in this literary walk, as in most others, the giants came first: Montaigne and Lord Bacon were our earliest essayists, and, as yet, they are our best.

---

*If you have difficulty identifying subjects and verbs, you'll need to spend some time with a grammar book. Try to find one which identifies parts of speech by position (for example, a noun is a word that can replace the x in the following: The x is here) and by form (for example, a verb is a word that can take the following as endings: *s* or *es, d* or *ed,* and *ing*).

After you've completed this exercise, compare the way you did it with the way others in your group did it and arrive at a consensus about each punctuation mark. If there's class time for more comparisons, all the groups in the class can compare results and work toward a class consensus.

2. Pick out a paragraph from a piece you're currently working on and give an unpunctuated copy of it to someone else. Ask him or her to follow along as you read the passage aloud, and insert appropriate punctuation marks. When you've finished reading, you and your listener can compare the two copies and work out whatever discrepancies exist. But don't argue if you disagree.

When you and your partner have made your decisions about what to agree and disagree about, bring your paper to your entire group for possible resolution of differences. What your group cannot resolve to the satisfaction of everyone, you can save for a full-class discussion. At this point you may also want to consult a grammar book or handbook for help.

In disputed cases remember that you are the author and should make the choice that seems best to you. Not everything is hard and fast, even in the world of grammar. There are exceptions to many usage rules, and choices can depend on context.

One of the most important things you'll discover from doing this exercise is that your voice can help you make decisions about punctuation. As you listened to others read, you undoubtedly heard their voices drop in pitch at the ends of sentences and then pause briefly before continuing.

3. Decide whether you think the following groups of words, all punctuated as sentences, are in fact sentences. One way to do this is to read the passage aloud and force your voice to take its cues from the punctuation. That is, let your voice drop off in pitch whenever you see a period and then pause before continuing with the next sentence.

> I knew I couldn't think. All I knew then was what I couldn't do. All I knew then was what I wasn't, and it took me some years to discover what I was.
>
> Which was a writer.
>
> By which I mean not a "good" writer or a "bad" writer but simply a writer, a person whose most absorbed and passionate hours are spent arranging words on pieces of paper. Had my credentials been in order I would never have become a writer. Had I been blessed with even limited access to my own mind there would have been no reason to write. I write entirely to find out what I'm thinking, what I'm looking at, what I see and what it means. What I want and what I fear. Why did the oil refineries around Carquinez Straits seem sinister to me in the summer of 1956? Why have the night lights in the bevatron burned in my mind for twenty years? *What is going on in these pictures in my mind?*

After you've made decisions about the end marks in the excerpt, talk with your group members about their decisions. There are fragments in this passage. Did you have problems with them? Did others?

Exercises: For Those Who Need Extra Practice

If you have trouble marking sentence endings in writing, you're going to have to do a fair amount of extra work. We suggest the following approach:

1. Read your piece of writing backward (that is, read what you take to be the last sentence, then the preceding one, and so on). That sounds strange, we know. But sentences in a piece of writing often sound complete to us because we are in possession of whatever information prior sentences have given us. Thus we read individual sentences in the context of what precedes them. This is, of course, exactly what we should be doing, but it can blind us to the grammatical incompleteness of a particular sentence. Reading backward makes it impossible for us to apply previously given information to a sentence.

Start by reading the last sentence of your piece. When you've made a decision about that, go to the second-to-final sentence and read that, and so on. If certain sentences are problematic for you, write them out on a separate piece of paper and give them to someone else to read. This way they'll have to deal with the sentence in isolation—and for this purpose, that's exactly what you want them to do.

2. Check a good handbook for the rules on punctuation. We think the following rules are crucial:

- Complete sentences can end with a period, a semicolon, a colon, a question mark, or an exclamation point.
- If you use a semicolon after a complete sentence, make sure that a complete sentence follows the semicolon also.
- Do not use a comma to separate complete sentences. Most teachers will not approve. This error is usually called a "comma splice" or a "run-on." (Such creatures regularly appear in published prose, but they are often considered unacceptable in academic writing.)

Commas

Comma rules are the hardest of all. We'll give you some rules, but almost all commas rules have exceptions. Effective use of commas requires you not only to know the requisite rules but also—at least some of the time—to make decisions.

Rules for the Use of Commas

Rule 1. Use a comma before the conjunction in a compound sentence:

This is the first clause in a compound sentence, and this is the second clause.

There are two exceptions:

- If the clauses in a compound sentence are short, you can omit the comma:

  That is short and this is too.

- If both clauses in a compound sentence have the same subject—and there is no chance for misreading—you can omit the comma.

  This clause is independent and it's short too.

Rule 2. Use a comma after introductory words, phrases, and clauses:

After these introductory words, you should use a comma.

Second, you need a comma here also.

When a sentence begins with a dependent clause, put a comma after the clause.

There is an exception:

- If the introductory segment is short, and there is no chance of misreading, you can omit the comma:

  After this you don't always need a comma.

  But beware of skipping the comma and ending up with a sentence that leads the reader to say it wrong:

  After this writing will never be the same.

Rule 3. Use a comma to separate items in a series:

> A series can be made up of any items that are parallel: sentences, clauses, phrases, or words.

Note that the final comma—the one after *phrases*—is optional, but you should be consistent.

Rule 4. Use a comma to separate nonrestrictive or nonessential parts of a sentence from the main part of the sentence.

> An embedded clause, which is what this is, can be either restrictive or nonrestrictive.

> An embedded clause which is restrictive should not be set off by commas.

Commas and Pausing

These rules don't quite cover all comma use because sometimes we sense the need for a comma in a certain spot just because we "feel" a pause in the structure or rhythm of a sentence. This usually means that if we read our piece aloud, we'd pause at this spot. The pause we make as we speak helps our listeners understand our words. The comma performs the same function in written language. Even when we're reading silently and not physically hearing words, we often "feel" pauses, and it's reassuring to see commas in these spots. Conversely, when we see a comma at a spot where neither structure nor meaning requires a pause and where a pause would disrupt meaning, we're confused. Our comprehension of what we're reading then suffers.

So the best advice we can give you about commas is to read what you've written aloud and notice where there are pauses. You can then examine each

Exploring the Writing Process

Workshop

oh god she tells me
to unpunctuate
unstructure
and my stomach
jellies
for years
i've been comfortable
with commas tight
as rosary beads
circling my throat
with semi-colons stuffing
my nostrils like cloudy incense
with periods clinging like black robes
blocking my eyes
how the hell
can i get this old
boulder off my back
without some skin
coming with it
it's been grooved to the wings
of my shoulders
if i throw it off
i will be weightless
lighter than air
a red balloon
floating over paris

Barbara Hoffman

spot to see if a comma is advisable. Another way to do this is to give someone else a copy of your writing and let them mark the text wherever you pause. In this way you won't break the flow of your words by stopping to mark pauses. Still another way to do this is to read your piece into a tape recorder and mark the pauses yourself as you listen to the playback. These are particularly good exercises to use if you tend not to use enough commas.

Another tactic is to read aloud your writing and pause slightly at each comma (or ask someone else to read it aloud this way). This is probably the best tactic if you tend to overdo comma use. If commas (and periods and semicolons, for that matter) match the speaking voice and sentence structure, your readers (even a diligent teacher!) will probably find no fault. In fact, research studies have shown that teachers are unlikely to notice mechanical errors of any kind if what they read truly engages their interest. So that's the main advice we can give you: Make your writing interesting to your readers.

A Historical Note

Historically commas (and other punctuation marks) developed to mirror certain qualities of oral language which convey meaning but are not represented by recording the sounds of words. These qualities include pauses and variations of pitch and stress. At the end of a sentence, for instance, we usually pause and slightly lower the pitch of our voices. Periods in written language are the equivalent of these speech features. At the spots where commas appear, we often pause (although this pause is usually shorter than that at the end of a sentence), but pitch usually stays the same. Read the following excerpt aloud, and you'll get some sense of how this works:

> Of course we're here an hour before the game starts. I don't mind, though. Now I can see all the other crazy Syracuse Orangemen basketball fans beside me! My brother and I sit down, taking the whole scene in. The Carrier Dome is a massive building with a white, balloon-like roof. It can hold a 100-yard football field, but today there is a blue curtain cutting the area into two parts. One half has vendors selling refreshments and Syracuse University paraphernalia. There is also a stage with two men singing, tables with important patrons clad in orange, and a giant-sized screen which will show the game for the unfortunate fans sitting behind the blue curtain.

When written language began to be considered as important as spoken language (or more important), punctuation began to have quite a different function: *to show the grammatical structure of sentences.* Quite a few rules came into existence to do this, but through the years this list has usually been reduced to the four we listed at the beginning of this mini-workshop.

These two systems of punctuation now exist side by side: to guide us in pausing and to show the grammatical structure of sentences. But usually they do not conflict. It's easy to see why, since the structure of sentences has a great deal to do with where a speaker pauses. In fact, the two systems often work harmoniously together. We often decide whether to use a comma after introductory words on the basis of whether we "hear" a pause:

> In August, I'll go.
> In August I'll go.

There really is no right or wrong here, but the two sentences shouldn't sound alike when read aloud.

Exercise: Using Commas

Here is a part of the first paragraph of the essay "What's Wrong with Black English?" in "Sharing and Responding." We've printed it here with no commas. See if you can put in commas and give a reason for each one. You can then check what you've done against the writer's punctuation.

> Not only the fashion, they also love rap music reggae soul music and Carribean music. When a famous rap musician came to Budokan the biggest concert hall in Tokyo twenty thousand fans rushed to fill it. Every Sunday Yoyogi Park the central park of Tokyo is filled with groups of young people dancing to rap music. They perform so wonderfully that many people stop and watch them. Huge crowds along the street enjoy these performances. Because of the revival of the 60s films of Martin Luther King Jr. and Malcolm X were big hits. Black of America and their culture has the power of attracting people especially young generations.

Once you've practiced on this paragraph, you can select one of your own and do the same thing. Perhaps your teacher will give you a chance to do this in class so that you can work with others. If all the members of your group punctuate at least one paragraph written by each group member, you'll have the basis for a lively and profitable discussion about commas.

Note There are a number of fine points about commas—tiny rules and exceptions which we have chosen not to include in this short treatment. You need to check a comprehensive handbook for difficult cases. But if you really master the main things we treat here, you will seldom get into trouble.

Apostrophes

The apostrophe is a peculiar punctuation mark. No language uses the apostrophe the way English does. Basically it performs two functions in written language: it takes the place of deleted letters, and it shows possession. The first of these functions usually causes no problems for most writers:

she[i]s = she's
I[ha]ve = I've
can[no]t = can't

But the use of the apostrophe to show possession causes problems for most inexperienced and even for some experienced writers. Speech is no help at all: we can't hear the difference between *boys, boy's,* and *boys'.* We use *context* to tell us what the sounds mean.

The boys left early.
The boys left hand is stronger than his right.
The boys left hands were tied behind their backs.

Speech thus trains us to use context to determine the meaning of the *s* sound at the end of words. Having learned this, we tend to transfer this strategy to written language and allow the context to guide us here also.

But, standard written English requires that we use apostrophes even though they may be unnecessary for meaning. That's probably why apostrophes are so hard. You *do* need to get them right though, because whether we like it or not, teachers and most other people regard someone who makes mistakes with apostrophes as an illiterate.

Apostrophes to Show Possession

The basic rules seem simple. An apostrophe indicates that the preceding word possesses something: *boy's* indicates that *a boy* possesses something: *boys'* indicates that *boys* possess something. One way to help yourself is to use an *of* phrase to test whether the apostrophe is appropriate:

The boy's left hand is stronger than his right.

The "left hand of the boy" is what "boy's left hand" means, so the apostrophe is appropriately placed.

The boys' left hands are tied behind their backs.

The left hands of the boys is what *the boys' left hands* means, so again the apostrophe is correctly placed.

Exercises: Using Apostrophes

Look at the following paragraphs and see if you can get apostrophes where they belong:

1. I wholeheartedly believe in the value of education, but sometimes it seems to be more trouble than its worth. I transferred to this school from a small college upstate in order to get a better education and to extricate myself from a situation I felt I had to reassess. (That, however, is a different story!) Since my parents home is an hour and fifteen minute drive from Stony Brook, the logical thing for me to have done was to get some form of housing nearer to school. This I proceeded to do, by moving into an apartment that was way beyond my means, and glibly signing a years lease in the bargain. My roommate was a good friend from high school who was dying to get out of her mothers house. We received countless warnings on the dangers of friends living together, but we brushed off those of little faith, knowing it would be different for us.

• • •

2. As it turned out, there had been a mistake, and I would get the loan, but only after reapplying for it, as the computer had erased me. "It will only take eight to ten weeks to process," the polite voice informed me sweetly.

"Oh, no, thats not possible," I laughed airily. "You see, my rents due next week, and theres nothing in the house to eat, and. . ."

Im sorry," she interrupted firmly, "That is the length of time it takes to process a loan."

"But I havent even bought my books yet!" I said desperately.

"Im sorry," she replied crisply, and hung up.

• • •

3. Our friendship definitely benefited from the situation. Since weve been home, theres no tension over who *always* has to clean the bathroom, and over who used up the last of the mayonnaise and didn't get more. Were almost on the same footing as when we moved in together, which makes us both very happy. The commuting isnt too bad either, as I enjoy driving. Who knows? Maybe next year Ill live at home and use my loan for updating my wardrobe.

You can check what you did against what the writer did by turning to the end of the section on apostrophes.

Apostrophes for Other Uses

It's only fair to warn you that apostrophes also appear in other sorts of places. Some handbooks advise using them for plurals of letters and numbers:

I cannot read her 7's.
The 1960's are both praised and maligned.
I particularly like the A's on that sign.

Other handbooks, however, prefer no apostrophes in these sentences:

I cannot read her 7s.
The 1960s are both praised and maligned.
I particularly like the As on that sign.

We also want to warn you that the apostrophe is not always an indicator of true possession. *An hour's stay* doesn't really mean the hour possesses the stay, but the test we suggested above still works: *an hour's stay* equals *a stay of an hour.*

If you have real problems with apostrophes, you're going to have to do some hard, rather tedious proofreading which will require you to check every *s* that comes at the end of a word. We do think, though, that if you do this conscientiously for a while, you'll find yourself beginning to put the apostrophe in with greater regularity as you're writing.

Note We haven't done a survey, but we bet most apostrophe errors occur with *its* and *it's.* Just remember that *it's* equals *it (i)s* and *its* is a possessive. That last one seems contradictory, since we associate the apostrophe with possessives, but *hers* and *theirs* and *his* don't have apostrophes either. The it's/its conundrum is similar to two others:

who's (who plus *is)* and *whose*
they're (they + are) and *their*

Answers to Exercises: Apostrophes as the Writer Used Them

1. I wholeheartedly believe in the value of education, but sometimes it seems to be more trouble than it's worth. I transferred to this school from a small college upstate in order to get a better education and to extricate myself from a situation I felt I had to reassess. (That, however, is a different story!) Since my parents' home is an hour and fifteen minute drive from Stony Brook, the logical thing for me to have done was to get some form of housing nearer to school. This I proceeded to do, by moving into an apartment that was way beyond my means, and glibly signing a year's lease in the bargain. My roommate was a good friend from high school who was dying to get out of her mother's house. We received countless warnings on the dangers of friends living together, but we brushed off those of little faith, knowing it would be different for us.

• • •

2. As it turned out, there *had* been a mistake, and I would get the loan, but only after reapplying for it, as the computer had erased me. "It will only take eight to ten weeks to process," the polite voice informed me sweetly.

"Oh, no, that's not possible," I laughed airily. "You see, my rent's due next week, and there's nothing in the house to eat, and. . ."

"I'm sorry," she interrupted firmly, "That is the length of time it takes to process a loan."

"But I haven't even bought my books yet!" I said desperately.

"I'm sorry," she replied crisply, and hung up.

3. Our friendship definitely benefited from the situation. Since we've been home, there's no tension over who *always* has to clean the bathroom, and over who used up the last of the mayonnaise and didn't get more. We're almost on the same footing as when we moved in together, which makes us both very happy. The commuting isn't too bad either, as I enjoy driving. Who knows? Maybe next year I'll live at home and use my loan for updating my wardrobe.

Quotation and the Punctuation of Reported Speech

Quotation marks are the primary way to show in writing *exactly* which words were said or written by someone other than you. Notice how this works:

> Elizabeth Kinney, a student who read an earlier draft of our book, said about it, "I think the idea of considering all of us as writers is absurd, and I don't think any student really takes that notion seriously."

The quotation marks tell you exactly which words are Elizabeth Kinney's and which are ours.

The Conventions for Using Quotation Marks

The conventions for using quotation marks can be tricky, but if you master them and end-stopping (getting periods where they are needed and keeping your reader from shouting "sentence fragment!" or "run-on sentence!"), you have mastered 95 percent of what you need to know about punctuation. (Colons and semicolons are infrequent and easy; commas are hopelessly arguable.)

1. *Periods and commas go* INSIDE *quotation marks.* If the quoted sentence doesn't end where you end your quotation, you should include four dots with spaces between them to show that you stopped quoting before the person finished her sentence:

> Elizabeth Kinney, a student who read an earlier draft of our book, said, "I think the idea of considering all of us as writers is absurd. . . ."

(Notice that the first dot has no space before it. British editors use an alternative style: They put periods and commas outside quotation marks. Perhaps you've observed this practice in some books. We think it best to follow the style used by American editors, since that is probably what your teacher will prefer.

If you omit words in the middle of a sentence you're quoting, use only three dots, with a space before the first dot and after the last one:

> "I think . . . considering all of us as writers is absurd. . . ."

2. *Semicolons and colons belong OUTSIDE quotation marks.* To show what this looks like, we've rewritten our original excerpt slightly.

> Elizabeth Kinney, a student who read an earlier draft of our book, said, "I think the idea of considering all of us as writers is absurd"; then she went on to disagree with us further.

3. *Question marks, exclamation points, and dashes sometimes go inside and sometimes outside.* They go *inside* the quotation marks if they're part of the quotation and *outside* if they're not.

> Do you think she was right when she said, "Considering all of us as writers is absurd"?

The question is ours, not Kinney's, so the question mark belongs outside the quotation marks.

> We had to think about our position again when Kinney asked, "Do you really want all students to think of themselves as writers?"

This time the question was hers, and so the question mark belongs inside.

4. *Quoted material that blends directly into your words needs no extra punctuation mark.*

> Elizabeth Kinney said our idea of treating students as writers "is absurd."

5. *When you use a phrase of attribution (for example, "she said" or "John insisted on announcing"), place a colon or comma after the phrase of attribution.* Generally colons appear before formal statements and commas before informal ones. Levels of formality, however, are difficult to assess. What you should keep in mind is that using a comma before a quotation suggests less formality to your readers. If that's what you want, the comma is probably correct. In other words, the choice is mostly a stylistic one. Thus both of these are correct; the comma in the first passage keeps the tone slightly informal:

> A student reader of our text said, "I think the idea of considering all of us as writers is absurd, and I don't think any student really takes that notion seriously."

> She went on to say: "Even if you define a writer as anyone who writes, the public thinks of a writer as a professional who is capable of writing and doing a good job of it."

6. *If the phrase of attribution follows the quotation, a comma is needed—unless the quotation ends with an exclamation point or a question mark.*

> "When you propose that all students can think of themselves as writers, it sounds patronizing," said Elizabeth Kinney.

> "When you propose that all students can think of themselves as writers, it sounds patronizing!" said Elizabeth Kinney.

7. *With a quotation within a quotation, use regular quotation marks for the main quotation and single quotation marks for the inner quotation.*

She went on to say: "Even if you say 'a writer is anyone who writes,' the public thinks of a writer as a professional who is capable of writing and doing a good job of it."

8. *If you quote a long passage—three lines or more—it's usually clearer if you indent 10 spaces from your left margin and OMIT the quotation marks.* Precede the quotation with a colon. Thus:

Here is a comment from a student who used an earlier draft of our book:

> Even if you say a "writer is anyone who writes," the public thinks of a writer as a professional who is capable of writing and doing a good job of it. When you propose that all students can think of themselves as writers, it sounds patronizing.

Exercises: Using Quotations

1. Now that you've read over these conventions, we suggest that you look closely at the student and professional interviews in Workshop 8 and analyze these writers' use of punctuation relative to quotations. Have they followed the conventions?

2. Bring in a paragraph you're working on (even if it isn't from a final draft) which contains a fair quantity of quoted words. Put in punctuation and then read through the paragraph with a classmate or two, explaining to them why you used each mark. Since class time may be limited and your teacher will want to use most of it for substantive matters (like discussing content, organization, tone, and so forth), you may not have time for in-class work on these conventions. But you can still get feedback—from a friend, classmate, family member, or tutor in your school's writing center. If something's particularly problematic, you may want to check it with your teacher.

Spelling

Spelling, like punctuation, is solely a feature of the written language. And for many it's a very important feature. Many people, not just teachers, will think you are not only illiterate but stupid if your spelling is poor. Research studies have demonstrated that spelling has little to do with intelligence, but spelling is highly tied to reading; we get our sense of correct spelling from *seeing* words, not from hearing them. Thus if you do a lot of reading, you're more likely to spell more words correctly. Consequently, readers tend to think that anyone whose spelling is poor has not read much; that is, the person is illiterate.

Nor do we want you to think we're minimizing the importance of spelling. If each of us spelled our own way, writing would become totally chaotic. Misspelled words can block communication. And most readers, including us, get annoyed by misspellings. Our annoyance causes us to get mad at the writer, and this hostility blocks our intent to focus on meaning. We react this way because we feel that if someone really wanted to communicate with us, he or she would take the trouble to spell correctly.

English is basically a phonetic language. What this means is that written English words represent sounds, not things. For example, *house* represents the spoken word "house," which in turn represents a building or structure people live in. The symbol ☗, on the other hand, would represent the building or structure directly. (Despite this phonetic base, most of us probably do not need to hear the word *house* when we read it to know what it means: We probably go directly from the marks on the page to the idea of "house.") In some languages, like Chinese, written words are not a record of the spoken language. Chinese characters represent things without reference to the way a speaker would represent them.

Even though English is phonetically based, it is not *purely* phonetic. The letter *A* in English represents various sounds. And conversely the sound that in the International Phonetic Alphabet is represented as /e/ and pronounced like the vowel sound in *say* is represented in a number of different ways in written English.

Why has English slipped from being fully phonetic? Evidence suggests that our writing was once totally phonetic. Old English scribes probably recorded, or tried to record, the sounds of the language directly. We know this because scribes from different regions spelled words differently, depending on the accent or dialect of that region. When printing was introduced in England during the 14th century, printers began to feel the need for standardization of spelling. The *sounds* of the spoken language continued to change, but the *spelling* of words did not. And so, today, for example, the word *says* is pronounced more like sez, but you don't see it written like that except in special circumstances.

All this explains why our spelling can cause difficulty, but it is of no help at all as you seek to deal with that difficulty. Some people seem to be chronically poor spellers (even if they do read a lot), and others seem to be good spellers without much effort. Most of us fall somewhere in between. Certain words give us trouble and other words—usually those we use all the time—give us no trouble at all. Consequently, all we need to do is to look up new words when we want to use them.

But for those of you who are poor spellers, dictionaries are often not much help because you just don't know which words to look up. And, needless to say, looking up all the words you use would be enormously onerous. Some handbooks and secretarial manuals give lists of frequently misspelled words, and there are some special spelling dictionaries which help you find words even if you look them up under the wrong spelling. But these do not solve all one's problems. So what do you do? Our best suggestion is to learn to use a word processing program on a computer and equip your computer with a spelling checker.

Nevertheless you'll still need to check for "correctly spelled mistakes" such as using *effect* for *affect* or *except* for *accept*. You'll want to gradually compile a list of these homophones (sound-alikes) that trip you up, and make your spelling checker flag them for you, along with those special words that you have difficulty with that may not be built into the spelling checker itself. On the market now are credit-card-sized spelling checkers which look like small calculators and can contain up to 80,000 words. Buying one of these may be a good investment for anyone who is a chronically poor speller.

Our second best suggestion is to enlist the aid of a friend, roommate, or family member who is a good speller and ask him to read through whatever you plan to submit for grading. All he needs to do is mark the misspelled words. It is your job to look them up. This may be a lot to ask of someone, particularly if you are a really bad speller. But perhaps there's something you can do for this person to return the favor. Even if you only read through whatever he writes and give him your reactions to it, you'll be doing something important for him.

There's something sociable and communal about getting help from a friend, but there's also something attractive about *not* getting help from a friend. That means spending money. Some typists are skilled spellers and will simply fix all your spelling. You may have to pay a bit extra. But look long and hard enough—perhaps insist on references—until you find one who really is expert.

Frankly, other than that, we can't give you much help. We do believe that the more you write and the more you look up words, the better speller you'll become. But you may never become good enough to give up relying on help.*

---

*Note: For testimony to this, see the Levinsky letter in the "Readings" for Workshop 2.

Finally we may be able to help you somewhat with the following account of the major spelling problems. We suggest that you keep a special place in your notebook and see if you can group your spelling errors according to the following list. Undoubtedly you'll also need to set up some personal categories—along with a list that gathers together the uncategorizable words. This may help you gain some control over the problem even if you can't eliminate it. Furthermore, such lists may also prove to you that you're not making a lot of errors, just some of the same errors over and over.

Here are special areas of difficulty for most poor spellers:

1. Doubling Letters

This causes the most difficulty when you're adding endings to words. The basic rule is to double the final letter of a word before adding a suffix if it meets the following three conditions:

a. The ending to be added to the main word must begin with a vowel: *-ing, -es, -ed, -y.*
b. The word must either be a one-syllable word (such as *sit, tap, slip*) or end with an accented syllable (such as *admit, begin,* and *prefer*).
c. The word must end with a single consonant that is preceded by a single vowel. (For example, occur ends in a single consonant that is preceded by a single vowel, so we get *occurred* and *occurring.* The word *creep,* on the other hand, ends in a single consonant, but that consonant is not preceded by a single vowel, so we get *creeping.*)

Exceptions:

- *qu* is considered one consonant sound, so *equip + ing = equipping.*
- *x* is a double consonant sound since *x* is really the two sounds *k* and *s*, so *fox + es = foxes.*
- Think of both *y* and *w* as vowels, so *toy + ing = toying.*

Exercise Test yourself: add *-ing* to *forget* and *compel;* add *-ed* to *shop* and *drape;* add *-y* to *cat;* add *-er* to *plan;* add *-ance* to *remit;* add *-ent* to *repel.* (Answers are at the end of this mini-workshop.)

2. Dropping the Silent *E* before Adding Endings

The basic rule is to drop a silent e when adding a suffix that begins with a vowel: *bite + ing = biting.*

Exception: Keep the silent *e* which occurs after c or *g* if the added ending begins with an *a* or *o: change + able = changeable.* (This exception grows out of the pronunciation rules of English. Most of the time we pronounce the *g* or c before *a, o,* and *u* differently from the way we pronounce it before *i* or *e: gin* and *gone;* necessary and *case.*)

Other exceptions are *dyeing* (meaning to change color), *acreage, mileage, truly, judgment, acknowledgment, ninth, wholly.*

Exercise Try some: *outrage + ous; manage + able; love + able; race + ed.* (Answers are at the end of this mini-workshop.)

3. Adding *ify/efy*
Verbs are formed by adding *ify: classify, justify, amplify.* There are only four exceptions: *liquefy, stupefy, rarefy, putrefy.*

4. Words Ending in *sede/ceed/cede*

a. Only one word ends in *sede: supersede.*
b. Only three words end in *ceed: exceed, succeed, proceed.*
c. All other words ending with the "seed" sound, end in *cede:* for example, *concede, precede, recede.*

5. Distinguishing *ie/ei*
The old jingle is probably the most helpful:

> *I* before *e* except after *c* or when sounded like *ay* as in *neighbor* or *weigh.*

Thus *priest* and *niece,* but *ceiling* and *perceive.*

Exceptions: *neither, either, leisure, seize, weird, sheik, financier, foreign,* and *conscience.*

Exercise Try these: *theif* or *thief, deceit* or *deciet, piece* or *peice, consceince* or *conscience, frieght* or *freight.* (Answers are at the end of this mini-workshop.)

6. Adding *able* or *ible*
The rules here are so complex that they're more confusing than helpful. Your best tactic is simply to keep a list. In general, common words add *able: eatable, readable, comfortable.* Less common words usually use *ible: admissible, ineligible, accessible.* There are many exceptions though, such as *possible.*

7. Adding *ance* or *ence*
Again, just keep two separate lists.

> ANCE: abundance, acquaintance, appearance, brilliance, endurance, guidance, ignorance, importance, maintenance, reassurance, remembrance, repentance, significance, tolerance
>
> ENCE: absence, audience, coincidence, conference, confidence, consequence, competence, convenience, correspondence, dependence, difference, essence, excellence, existence, experience, inference, influence, intelligence, magnificence, occurrence, patience, permanence, preference, presence, reference, severence, residence, sentence, violence

8. Words Ending in *ary* or *ery*
Only two commonly used words end in *ery: cemetery* and *stationery* (meaning the stuff you write letters on).

9. Changing *y* to *i* before Adding Endings

a. Change *y* to *i* before adding to any ending not beginning with *i.* Thus *happy + ly = happily; jolly + er = jollier; pity + ful = pitiful;* but *pity + ing = pitying.*

b. Keep the final *y* if it is preceded by a vowel: *play + er = player.*

c. Exceptions occur when adding *ness, ship, like,* or *ly: shyness, citylike, ladyship, slyly.*

Exercise Try some: *beauty + ful; marry + ing; fly + er; history + cal; ninety + eth; lonely + ness; copy + ing; victory + ous; delay + ed; dry + ness.* (Answers are at the end of this mini-workshop.)

10. Learn to Look for Homonyms—Words That Sound Alike but Have Different Meanings or Use, Such as *berth* or *birth*

Any good grammar book or handbook will have lists of these words, usually under some heading like "Words Commonly Confused."

Final Word Spelling can psychologically discombobulate some people more than any other dimension of writing. The thing to keep in mind if you are troubled by spelling is that it is not necessary to know spelling. It is only necessary that for certain important pieces of writing *you must*—by hook or by crook or by spell-checker—*get the spelling right.*

Think of it like this. When you submit writing to someone, often it must be in some printed form, not handwritten. That doesn't mean *you* have to type it or word-process it on a computer. There's nothing morally wrong with hiring someone to do either of these tasks. However it's nicer and cheaper if you can do the work yourself; you don't feel dependent on others. This is exactly how it is with spelling.

Answers to Exercises

1. forgetting, compelling, shopped, draped, catty, planner, remittance, repellent
2. outrageous, manageable, lovable, raced
5. thief, deceit, piece, conscience, freight
9. beautiful, marrying, flier (or flyer when it means *leaflet*), historical, ninetieth, loneliness, copying, victorious, delayed, dryness

Copyediting and Proofreading

Your teacher probably won't be able to provide time in class for you to proofread and copyedit every paper you hand in. But you should find the time for it. You may be able to make arrangements with classmates to do this outside class. Otherwise, ask your roommate, a friend, or a family member. You can even hire a tutor to help. Very few of us are able to edit ourselves; most of us can do a better job on someone else's paper than on our own. (Every published writer gets help copyediting from editors—as we did on this book.) Typographical and usage errors can destroy the best piece of writing; once you've spent a lot of time getting your thoughts straight and in good order, it's foolish not to take a little extra time to make them readable. Surface flubs can make readers decide not to read at all or to read in a hostile mood.

Exercise: Copyediting and Proofreading

Bring to class a typed copy, or copies, of the final draft of a paper you plan to hand in. Another student will copyedit and proofread your paper, and you will do the same for her. If there's time, you will want to exchange papers with at least two people. Your teacher may allow time for this in class, or she may ask you to do this work at home.

Read your classmate's paper very carefully, and pencil in any corrections you think appropriate. You are looking for *all* errors in mechanics or typing (capitalization, underlining, abbreviations, and so forth) and *all* violations of the rules of standard written English. You'll particularly want to check spelling, punctuation, sentence structure, subject-verb agreement, and pronoun reference. If you aren't sure about a change you've made, put a question mark by it. If a sentence doesn't sound right to you—and you can't pinpoint exactly what's bothering you—draw wiggly lines under it. Be sure to sign your name to the paper as editor. Your teacher may want to collect all edited copies of each paper in order to pinpoint particular students' problems.

When you're finished, select two of the corrections you've made and write a rule for each. Don't look up the rule in a handbook; just state the rule in a way that explains why you made the correction. Here's some of the essay we quoted from in Workshop 6, with copyediting changes added, as well as two rules written by the student-editor:

Once that awesome happening settled and passed, the crowd went back to pushing and shoving through doors. It's really ridiculous to see people, who are supposed to be grown-ups, react like children when they see a circus for the first time. If they only realized that the circus they're watching (Mr. Big) gets his ears boxed by his mother if he comes home too late.

Upon entering, the bar is to the person's immediate left and a few steps below is the dance floor. By the way, the steps are notorious killers since many, under the influence of alcohol, forget they exist. On the other side, there is the seating area consisting of dozens of tables and black velvety, cushiony, recliner-type chairs. They are the type of chairs ~~you~~ one lose ~~your~~ oneself in.

Rule: Don't use slang in a school essay.
Rule: Don't use "you" in an essay.

Once you get the copies of your paper back, you'll need to make a decision about each correction or comment made by your editor(s). If you're sure they're right (perhaps your mistake was carelessness or poor typing), make the correction neatly in ink on your good copy. If you're sure they're wrong, don't erase the change; leave it, so that your teacher will know what you've made a decision about. If you're not sure one way or the other, you'll have to check in a handbook. If your teacher hasn't recommended one for you to buy, you should ask her for a recommendation.* If you can't find what you need in your book, you'll need to find some other authority: a classmate, your roommate, a family member, your teacher, or a tutor in the Writing Center.

Sometimes the best strategy for dealing with problems you can't clearly define is to rewrite the problem sentence in a different way. Try to think yourself back into the idea you had when you wrote the sentence, and see if you can write it in a way that matches your idea more clearly. Say what you mean aloud to yourself, talk it through, and then try writing it again. You may want to rewrite the sentence several ways. You'll probably recognize which one is the best. If you do rewrite an entire sentence, you should reread the paragraph it's in to make sure you haven't disrupted the flow of the ideas and language. If, when you've made decisions about all suggested changes, you discover you've made so many that it's hard to read your paper, ask your teacher if she'd like you to retype it or make the changes on your computer and

*For help with understanding how grammatical and usage rules work, see *The Right Handbook*.

reprint the paper. If you have to retype it, remember it needs proofreading again. (This is one advantage of writing on a computer.)

If your teacher gives you additional class time, you can share your findings and problems with others in the class. All of us store rules about language in our heads, even though we may not be consciously aware of them. If we didn't have such rules, we couldn't talk or write at all. If you can become consciously aware of the rules you use, you can discard or alter those that are unacceptable (as defined by your teacher or the grammar book you are using) and sharpen those that are valid. Class discussion will make you aware of which you should keep and which you should discard.

If you make a relatively high number of usage errors, you'll need to do some extra work. Set aside several pages in your journal or notebook to list the errors you make. In this way, you can discover which errors recur and concentrate on avoiding them. What you'll probably discover is that you're not making many different errors, but the same errors over and over. Your teacher may expect you to do some extra work to begin clearing up your particular set of errors.

Sharing and Responding

Cover Letter

Dear Students and Teachers,

In this "Sharing and Responding" guide we present a variety of methods for sharing your writing and getting helpful responses. First we'll give a brief overview of the methods; then we'll explain them in more detail and illustrate their use on two sample essays.

Our goal is to help you become comfortable and skilled at asking for feedback and giving it. We think this may well be the most valuable part of the *Community of Writers* workshop course, the part you are most likely to use after the course is over.

Suggestions for Using "Sharing and Responding"

There are more techniques here than you can use on any one occasion. But we want you to try them all out in order to learn the wide range of options you have for feedback. Then you will be in a position to ask for the kind of feedback that is right for you, depending on your preferences or temperament, the kind of piece you're working on, and the stage it's at. Many people don't like getting feedback on their writing because they feel they are "on the chopping block." They don't realize how many options they could ask for, and so they end up helplessly putting themselves in the hands of readers. "Sharing and Responding" will help you take charge of the process of getting responses.

We also urge you to try out these techniques in order. They go from quicker to more time-consuming, from easier to harder, and from safer to riskier. This progression builds a feedback situation of support and trust. Don't assume, though, that the later kinds of responding are better: Some of the earliest ones remain the most useful despite being quick and easy.

Our Underlying Premises and Convictions

We find that most students are reluctant to judge or evaluate each other's writing and give advice about how to improve it. We think they are right. Evaluation and advice are not what writers need most. What writers need (and fortunately it's what all readers are best at) is an *audience:* a thoughtful, interested audience rather than evaluators or editors or advice-givers. In the long run, you will learn the most about writing from feeling the *presence of interested readers*—like feeling the weight of a fish at the end of the line. You can't trust evaluations or advice. Even experts on writing usually disagree with each other. And even when they agree about what is weak, they often disagree about how to fix it.

Therefore we urge you to follow a crucial principle for feedback: Don't let anyone give you evaluation or advice unless they also give you the perceptions and reactions it is based on, that is, unless they describe *what they see* and *how they are reacting*. For example, if a reader says, "The organization is confusing in your piece," make sure she goes back and describes the sequence of parts in your piece as she sees them, and/or the sequence of her reactions as she was reading: When did she first start feeling confused, and what kind of confusion was it? What was going on in her mind and feelings at different points?

Many students have never written except in school, never given their writing to anyone but a teacher, and always gotten some kind of evaluative response. But it's hard for writers to prosper unless they give their work to a variety of readers, not just teachers, and get a variety of responses: no response, nonevaluative responses, evaluative responses. The suggestions here will give you the variety of audience relationships you need to develop a more productive sense of audience.

You will improve your writing much faster if you let us and your teacher help you build a community in your classroom: a place where people hear clearly even what is mumbled, understand what is badly written, and look for the validity even in what they disagree with. Eventually you will learn to write to the enemy—to write surrounded by sharks. But you will learn that necessary skill better if, for a while, you practice writing to allies and listening to friends.

Two Paradoxes of Responding

First paradox: the reader is always right; yet the writer is always right. That is, readers get to decide what's true about their reactions—about what they see or think or feel. It's senseless to quarrel with readers about their experience of what's happening to them (though you can ask them to explain their experience more fully).

Nevertheless, you as the writer get to decide what to do about any of this feedback from readers, what changes to make, if any. You don't have to follow their advice. Just listen openly and swallow it all. You can do that better if you realize that you get to take your time and make up your own mind.

Second paradox: the writer must be in charge; yet the writer must sit quietly and do nothing. As writer, you must be in control. It's your writing. Don't be passive or helpless. You get to decide what kind of feedback, if any, you need. Are you trying to improve this particular piece? Or perhaps you don't care so much about working on this piece any more but just want feedback on it to learn about your writing in general. Or perhaps you don't want to work on anything but just enjoy sharing this piece and hearing what others have to say. Don't let readers make these decisions for you. Ask for what you want and don't be afraid to stop them if they give you the wrong thing. For example, sometimes it's important to insist, "I'm still very tender about this piece. I just want to hear what it sounds like for now and not get any feedback."

Nevertheless you mostly have to sit back and just listen. If you are talking a lot, you are probably blocking good feedback. For example, don't argue if they misunderstand what you wrote. Their misunderstanding is valuable, and you need to understand it in order to see how your words function. If they want to give you feedback you didn't ask for—or not give you what you ask for—they may have good reasons. If you aren't getting honest, serious, or caring feedback, don't blame your readers. You may not have convinced them that you really want it.

How We Wrote "Sharing and Responding"

In our first drafts of the *Community of Writers* book, we put all our sharing and responding suggestions in the workshops themselves. But then we ran into a dilemma. We realized that we wanted to give students and teachers lots of choice of which workshops to use and what order to use them in. Yet we didn't want to give that much choice about which feedback techniques to use and which order to use them in. For it's crucial to us that you go through a progression that gives the best learning and builds the most trust. Because of this dilemma, we hit on the plan of having a separate "Sharing and Responding" guide (though we have also kept a few suggestions in each workshop).

Also, this part in the first edition of our textbook was too complicated: too many kinds of response were arranged in groupings which were too complex. We realize now that as we worked out this book for the first time, we built too much of our background thinking into the structure itself. Writers often speak of the principle of "scaffolding": structures put up in order to help construct the building in the first place—but which can be taken down after the building is done. We had too much scaffolding in the first edition. You'll find the same thing sometimes happens to you. You'll write something and it comes out complicated; but once you've got it written, you finally understand it better and you can then revise to make it simpler.

And, now for this third edition, we have changed the sample essays. Some of our students and reviewers told us it would be helpful to have essays on topics more relevant to today's world and the kinds of problems they might meet up with in their own lives. We think the two essays we selected confront such problems. We hope you agree. But whether you do or don't, we'd like to have responses from you since, like you, we can profit from readers' responses. Please feel free to comment on any part of this textbook. (You can write to us at the publisher's address.)

Peter Elbow
Pat Belanoff

Summary of Kinds of Responses

Here is an overview of 11 different and valuable ways of responding to writing and a few thoughts about when each kind is valuable. We will explain them more fully later and illustrate their use on sample essays. After you have tried them out, you can glance back over this list when you want to decide which kind of feedback to request.

1. Sharing: No Response

Read your piece aloud to listeners and ask: "Would you please just listen and enjoy?" You can also give them your text to read silently, though you don't usually learn as much this way. Simple sharing is also a way to listen better to your own responses to your own piece, without having to think about how others respond. You learn an enormous amount from hearing yourself read your own words or from reading them over when you know that someone else is also reading them.

No response is valuable in many situations—when you don't have much time, at very early stages when you want to try something out or feel very tentative, or when you are completely finished and don't plan to make any changes at all—as a form of simple communication or celebration. Sharing gives you an unpressured setting for getting comfortable reading your words out loud and listening to the writing of others.

2. Pointing and Center of Gravity

Pointing: "Which words or phrases or passages somehow strike you? stick in mind? get through?" Center of gravity: "Which sections somehow seem important or resonant or generative?" You are not asking necessarily for the main points but for sections or passages that seem to resonate or linger in mind. Sometimes a seemingly minor detail or example—even an aside or a digression—can be a center of gravity.

These quick, easy, interesting forms of response are good for timid or inexperienced responders, or for early drafts. They help you establish a sense of contact with readers. Center of gravity response is particularly interesting for showing you rich and interesting parts of your piece that you might have neglected, but which might be worth exploring and developing. Center of gravity can help you see your piece in a different light and suggest ways to make major revisions.

3. Summary and Sayback

Summary: "Please summarize what you have heard. Tell me what you hear as the main thing and the almost-main things." (Variations: "Give me a phrase as title and a one-word title—first using my words and then using your words.") Sayback: "Please say back to me in your own words what you hear me getting at in my piece, but say it in a somewhat questioning or tentative way—as an invitation for me to reply with my own restatement of what you've said."

These are both useful at any stage in the writing process to see whether readers "got" the points you are trying to "give." But sayback is particularly useful at early stages when you are still groping and haven't yet been able to find what you really want to say. You can read a collection of exploratory passages for sayback response. When readers say back to you what they hear—and invite you to reply—it often leads you to find exactly the words or thoughts or emphasis you were looking for.

4. What Is Almost Said? What Do You Want to Hear More About?

Just ask readers those very questions.

This kind of response is particularly useful when you need to *develop* or enrich your piece—when you sense there is more here but you haven't been able to get your finger on it yet. This kind of question gives you concrete substantive help because it leads your readers to give you some of *their ideas* to add to yours. Remember this too: What you imply but don't say in your writing is often very loud to readers but unheard by you and has an enormous effect on how they respond.

Extreme variation: "Make a guess about what was on my mind that I didn't write about."

5. Reply

Simply ask, "What are *your* thoughts about my topic? Now that you've heard what I've had to say, what do *you* have to say?"

This kind of response is useful at any point, but it is particularly useful at early stages when you haven't worked out your thinking. Indeed, you can ask for this kind of response even before you've written a draft; perhaps you jotted down some notes. You can say, "I'm thinking about saying *X, Y,* and *Z.* How would you reply? What are your thoughts about this topic?" This is actually the most natural and common response to any human discourse. You are inviting a small discussion of the topic.

6. Voice

(a) "How much voice do you hear in my writing? Is my language alive and human? Or is it dead, bureaucratic, unsayable?" (b) "What kind of voice(s) do you hear in my writing? Timid? Confident? Sarcastic? Pleading?" Or "What kind of person does my writing sound like? What side(s) of me come through in my writing?" Most of all, "Do you trust the voice or person you hear in my writing?"

This kind of feedback can be useful at any stage. When people describe the voice they hear in writing, they often get right to the heart of subtle but important matters of language and approach. They don't have to be able to talk in technical terms ("You seem to use lots of passive verbs and nominalized phrases"); they can say, "You sound kind of bureaucratic and pompous and I wonder if you actually believe what you are saying."

7. Movies of the Reader's Mind

Ask readers to tell you honestly and in detail what is going on in their minds as they read your words. There are three powerful ways to help readers give you this kind of response: (a) Interrupt their reading a few times and find out what's happening at that moment. (b) Get them to tell you their reactions in the form of a *story* that takes place in time. (c) If they make "it-statements" ("It was confusing"), make them translate these into "I-statements" ("I felt confused starting here about . . . ").

Movies of the reader's mind make the most sense when you have a fairly developed draft and you want to know how it works on readers, rather than when you're still trying to develop your ideas. Movies are the richest and most valuable form of response, but they require that you feel some confidence in yourself and support from your reader, because when readers tell you honestly what is happening while they are reading your piece, they may tell you they don't like it or even get mad at it.

8. Metaphorical Descriptions

Ask readers to describe your writing in terms of clothing (e.g., jeans, tuxedo, lycra running suit), weather (e.g., foggy, stormy, sunny, humid), animals, colors, shapes.

This kind of response is helpful at any point. It gives you a new view, a new lens; it's particularly helpful when you feel stale on a piece, perhaps because you have worked so long on it. Sometimes young or inexperienced readers are good at giving you this kind of response when they are unskilled at other kinds.

9. Believing and Doubting

Believing: "Try to believe everything I have written, even if you disagree or find it crazy. At least *pretend* to believe it. Be my friend and ally and give me more evidence, arguments, and ideas to help me make my case better." Doubting: "Try to doubt everything I have written, even if you love it. Take on the role of enemy and find all the arguments that can be made against me. Pretend to be someone who hates my writing. What would he or she notice?"

These forms of feedback obviously lend themselves to persuasive essays or arguments, though the believing game can help you flesh out and enrich the world of a story or poem. Believing is good when you are struggling and want help. It's a way to get readers to give you new ideas and arguments and to improve your piece in all sorts of ways. Doubting is good after you've gotten a piece as strong as you can get it and you want to send it out or hand it in—but first find out how hostile readers will fight you.

10. Skeleton Feedback and Descriptive Outline

Skeleton feedback: "Please lay out the reasoning you see in my paper: my main point, my subpoints, my supporting evidence, and my assumptions about my topic and about my audience." Descriptive outline: "Please write *says* and *does* sentences for my whole paper and then for each paragraph or section." A *says* sentence summarizes the meaning or message, and a *does* sentence describes the function.

These are the most useful for essays. They are feasible only if the reader has the text in hand and can take a good deal of time and care—and perhaps write out responses. Because they give you the most distance and perspective on what you have written, they are uniquely useful for giving feedback to yourself. Both kinds of feedback help you on late drafts when you want to test out your reasoning and organization. But skeleton feedback is also useful on early drafts when you are still trying to figure out what to say or emphasize and how to organize your thoughts.

11. Criterion-Based Feedback

Ask readers to give you their thoughts about specific criteria that you are wondering about or struggling with: "Does this sound too technical?" "Is this section too long?" "Do my jokes work for you?" "Do you feel I've addressed the objections of people who disagree?" And of course, "Please find mistakes in spelling and grammar and typing." You can also ask readers to address what they think are the important criteria for your piece. You can ask too about traditional criteria for essays: focus on the assignment or task, content (ideas, reasoning, support, originality), organization, clarity of language, and voice.

You ask for criterion-based feedback when you have questions about specific aspects of your piece. You can also ask for it when you need a quick overview of strengths and weaknesses. This kind of feedback depends on skilled and experienced readers. (But even with them you should still take it with a grain of salt, for if someone says your piece is boring, other readers might well disagree. Movies of the reader's mind are more trustworthy because they give you a better picture of the personal reactions *behind* these judgments.)

Summary of Kinds of Responses

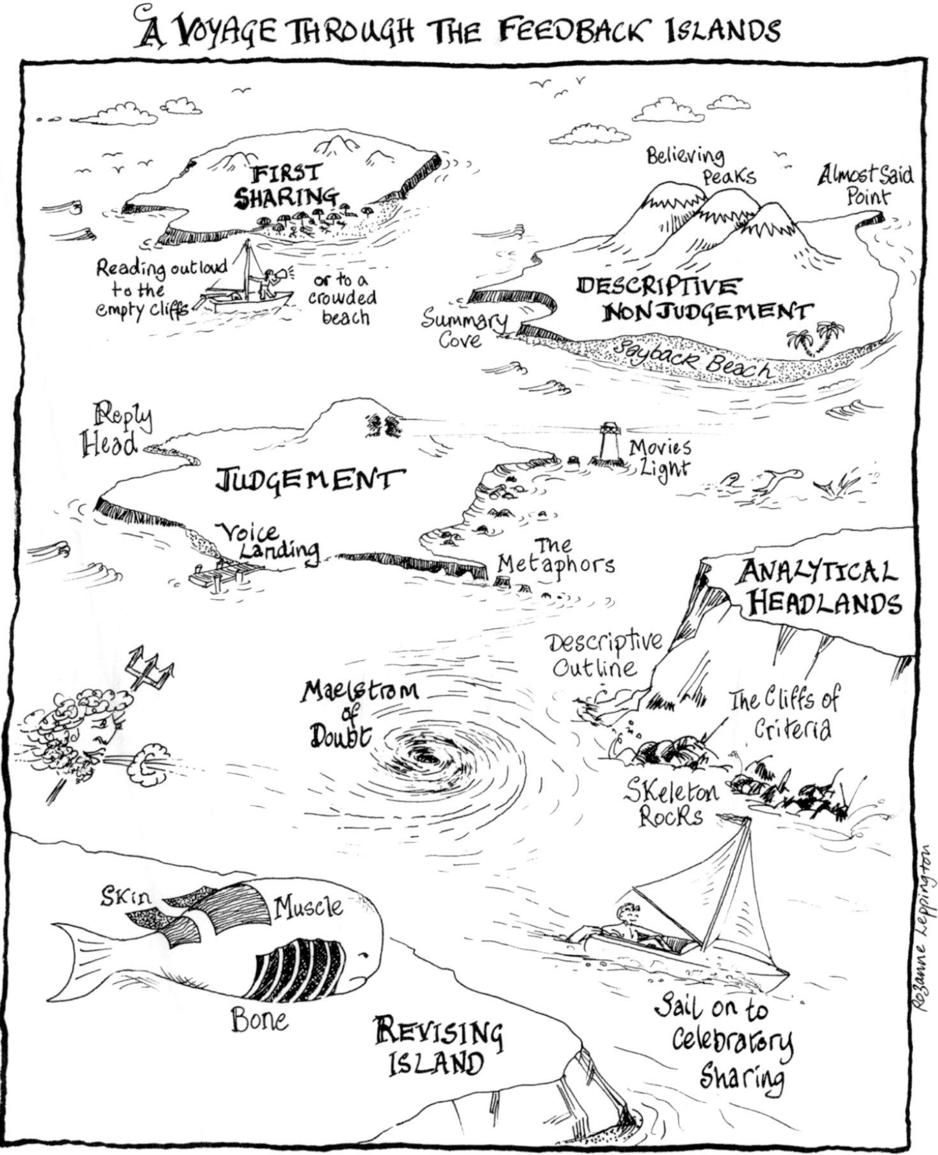

Procedures for Giving and Receiving Responses

We've briefly summarized your choices among *kinds of response*. Now we want to emphasize that you also have important choices among *procedures for getting responses*. It's important to test these out, too—to see which ones are the most helpful for you in different situations.

Early or Late Drafts?

Responses are helpful on both early and late drafts; indeed, it's a big help to discuss your thinking even before you have written at all. (For very early drafts, these response modes are particularly helpful: pointing, center of gravity, summary, sayback, almost said, and reply.) At the other extreme, it can be helpful and interesting to get feedback even on *final drafts* that you don't plan to revise any more: You will learn about your writing and about how readers read. When poets and fiction writers give readings, the goal is pleasure and celebration, not feedback. (Keep your eye out for notices of readings by poets and writers in local schools, libraries, and bookstores. They can be fun to attend.)

Pairs or Groups?

On the one hand, the more readers the better. Readers are different, and reading is a subjective act so you don't know much if you only know how one reader reacts. On the other hand, more readers take more time and you can learn a lot from one reader if she is a good one—if she can really tell you in detail about what she sees and what goes on in her head as she reads your words. Also, it's easier to build an honest relationship of trust and support between just two people. (If you know you are working on something important and will want to get feedback at various stages, you can use your trusted readers one or two at a time.)

You can have it both ways too—getting the multiple perspectives of groups and the trust and support of pairs—by first getting brief feedback from a group and then dividing into pairs for fuller responses (or vice versa).

New Faces or the Same Old Faces?

If you change readers, you get variety and new perspectives. But good sharing and responding depend on a climate of safety and trust. Certain things can't occur until reader and writer have built up trust, and that takes longer than you might think. Most writers find one or two trusted readers or editors, and rely on them over and over.

Share Out Loud or Give Readers Copies on Paper?

The process of reading out loud brings important learning: You can feel strengths and weaknesses physically—in your mouth as you pronounce your words and in your ear as you hear them. And you can tell about the effects of your words by watching your listeners. Reading out loud is more alive. But if your piece is very long or time is short, you will need to give paper copies. Paper texts give readers more time to read closely and reflect on your writing, especially if the material is technical. Remember, however, that if listeners can't follow your piece as you read it out loud, it is probably not clear enough.

Perhaps the most efficient way to get the most feedback in the shortest time is to circulate paper copies around a group; at every moment, everyone is reading someone's paper and writing feedback. (You have the choice of whether to let readers see how previous readers responded.) But efficiency is not everything; this method is not very sociable. You can also combine the two modalities by reading your paper out loud but giving listeners a copy to follow. (Computers and photocopy machines make it easier to create multiple copies.)

Writers have always used the mail to share writing with readers and get responses, but electronic mail and fax machines have encouraged many more people to "meet" across hundreds and thousands of miles. Some people use these media not just for transmitting pieces of writing and responses but even for "real time" conversation about the writing.

About Reading Out Loud

You need to read your piece twice. Otherwise listeners can't hear it well enough to give helpful responses. But if you don't want to read it twice in a row (which can feel embarrassing), there is a good solution. Have each person read once for no response; then have each person read again for response. Listeners need a bit of silence after each reading to collect their thoughts and jot down a few notes; this way no one will be too influenced later by hearing the responses of others.

Also, it can be interesting and useful to have the second reading given by someone other than the writer. This way listeners get to hear two different "versions" of the words. When someone reads a piece of writing out loud, that in itself constitutes feedback: it reveals a great deal about what the reader sees as the meaning, emphasis, implications, and voice or tone of the piece. Some critics and writers say that a set of words is not "realized" or "complete" until read out loud—that words on the page are like a play script or musical notes on a page, mere ingredients for the creation of the real thing, which is a performance.

Some writers get others to give both readings, but we think that's sad because you learn so much from reading your own words. If you feel very shy or even afraid to read your writing, that means it's even more important to do so.

Responding Out Loud or on Paper?

Both modes are valuable. Spoken responses are easier to give, more casual and social. And it's interesting for responders to hear the responses of the others. Written responses can be more careful and considered, and the writer gets to take them home and ponder them while revising.

There's an easy way to combine written and spoken responding. First, all group members give copies of their paper to everyone else. Then members go home and read all the papers and take a few notes about their responses to each one. But each member has responsibility for giving a careful written response to only one paper. When the group meets for sharing responses, the person who wrote out feedback starts by reading what he wrote (and hands his written feedback to the writer), but then the others chime in and add responses on the basis of their reading and notes. This method is particularly useful if there isn't much time for group work or if the pieces of writing are somewhat long.

How Much Response to Get?

At one extreme, you'll benefit from no response at all—that is, from private writing where you get to ignore readers for a while, and from mere sharing where you get to connect with readers and feel their presence but not have to listen to their responses.

At the other extreme, it's crucial sometimes to take the time for extended and careful response—perhaps in writing—from at least one or two readers. We urge you to create some occasions where you ask a reader or two to take your paper home and write out at least two or three pages that provide (a) a description of what they see (skeleton or descriptive outline, description of voice, and so forth); (b) a description of how they reacted (movies of their minds—what the words *do* to them); (c) what they see as strengths and weaknesses of your paper and suggestions for improving it. If your teacher asks for this extensive approach to feedback, she will probably ask you to write out your reactions to those responses, in particular whether you think their evaluation and advice make sense or not and why.

A middle course is to get two to four minutes of response from each reader. This won't give you the complete story of the readers' perceptions or reactions, but it will give you the most powerful thing of all: the leverage you need to imagine what your piece of writing looks like through someone else's eyes. Sometimes just one tiny remark is all you need to help you suddenly stop seeing your words *only* from your own point of view and start experiencing how differently they sound to someone else.

Ways to Help Response Pairs or Groups Work Better

When it comes to people working together on difficult activities (and nothing is more "difficult" than showing your own writing), there are no magic right methods. But there are some helpful rules of thumb.

First, remember that even though you may feel naked or vulnerable in sharing your writing, especially if it is an early draft, readers will be just as naked and vulnerable if they give you good feedback. To give accurate movies of the mind is a generous gift: honest readers are willing to be guinea pigs and let you see inside their heads. And this kind of honesty goes against many habits and customs of student life. Classmates won't give you this gift unless you treat them with great respect *and* are very assertive about insisting that you really want good feedback. (As teachers, we used to shake our fingers at students who weren't giving much feedback and try to cajole them into being "more responsible responders." But that never seemed to help. We discovered we could get better results by turning back to the *writer* and saying: "Are *you* willing to put up with not getting feedback? *We* can't make them do it. Only you can.")

Try to avoid arguments between responders or between writer and responder. Arguments waste time, and they make responders less willing to be honest. But most of all, you usually benefit from having different and unreconciled points of view about your text. Don't look for a "right answer" but for how your writing looks through different sets of eyes. And when readers disagree, that brings home the central principle here: *You* get to make up your own mind about how to interpret the feedback, how seriously to take it, and what changes to make, if any.

When working in groups, always make sure someone agrees to watch the time so that people at the end don't get cheated.

Spend some time talking about how the feedback process is working. Try taking a few moments now and then to write out informal answers to these questions.

- What works best in your group?
- What is not working well?
- Do you wish members were more critical of your work? less critical?
- Which has been the most helpful to you, oral or written responses?
- Does your group work best with detailed instructions? with little guidance?
- Is there someone who always seems to take charge? or who doesn't participate much? How do you feel about this?

You can share these responses yourselves and identify problems and discuss ways to make things work better. You can make these comments anonymous if you wish by giving them to another group to read to you. Your teacher may ask for these responses and use them as a basis for full-class discussion.

Final Note

Does this seem too complicated? All these kinds of responses and ways of giving them? There is, in fact, a lot to learn if you want to get useful responses and give them. But *after* you and your friends have tried out all these techniques and built up a relationship of trust, you can make the whole feedback process become simple. You don't have to decide on any particular kind of feedback to ask for; you can just say, "Tell me about your responses" or "Just write me a letter." You can trust them to give you what is most valuable. But if you leave it wide open this way *before* readers have practiced all these responding techniques, you often get nothing—or even get something hurtful or harmful. It won't take you too long to try out the 11 kinds of feedback, especially since you can sometimes use more than one in one session.

Full Explanations of Kinds of Responses—With Samples*

1. Sharing: No Response or Responses from the Self

If you've never done freewriting before—writing without stopping and not showing your words to anyone at all—it can feel peculiar. But most people quickly find it comfortable and helpful. Similarly, if you've never done sharing before—reading your words to someone without getting any response at all—that too can feel peculiar. When you read your words aloud (or give people a copy of your writing), you probably have an urge to ask them how they *liked* it—whether they thought it was any good. Because all school writing is evaluated, we sometimes assume that the *point* of writing is to be evaluated. But when we speak to someone, do we immediately ask them how good our words were? No. We want a reply, not an evaluation. We speak because we are trying to communicate and connect.

With sharing we're emphasizing writing as communicating and connecting, rather than performing for a judgment. You'll find that it's a relief to give your writing to others (aloud or on paper) just to communicate, just for the fun of it—so they can hear what you have to say and learn from you. It's a relief to say (on some occasions, anyway), "The hell with whether they like it or agree with it. I just want them to *hear* it." If you practice sharing in the right spirit, you will soon find it as natural and helpful as freewriting.

And what is the right spirit? In sharing, the goal is for writers to *give* and for listeners to *receive.* Writing is gift giving. When you give someone a gift, you don't want her to criticize; you want her to use it and enjoy it. If you happen to give someone a gift he doesn't like, do you want him to complain? No, you want him to thank you all the same.

We stress reading your words aloud here, especially at first, because you learn so much by using your mouth and ears. And there is a special psychological benefit from learning to say your words aloud: You get over the fear of making a noise with your written words. But it is also useful to share silently, by giving readers a copy of what you've written. Many teachers periodically create a class magazine. Sometimes they set this up officially with a lab fee to cover costs; sometimes they just ask everyone to bring in multiple copies of a piece. If you single-space your piece, you can often fit it on one sheet,

*For sample peer responses, we are indebted to Alexander Jackson, Arun Jacob Rao, Christine Schnaitter, and others.

back-to-back. Also, you'll find it a pleasure to make a little magazine at the end of the course of your favorite three or four pieces of your own writing (with a nice cover), and give copies to a handful of friends and family.

We suggested earlier that as you try out different kinds of feedback, you might try out more than one kind in one session. But don't combine sharing with feedback (not at first, anyway). The whole point of sharing is to get *no* response. Even if it feels odd at first, try to notice the benefits of it.

Guidelines for the Writer Who Is Sharing Aloud

- Take a moment to look at your listeners, relax, and take a deep breath. Say a few introductory words if that helps.
- Read slowly, clearly. *Own* your writing; read it with authority even if you are not satisfied with it. Concentrate on the meaning of what you're reading. Don't worry about whether listeners like it.
- Take a pause between paragraphs. Let people interrupt to ask you to repeat or go slower, but don't let them give you any feedback. After you're finished, just go on to the next person.

Guidelines for Listeners

- Your job is to receive without comment. Give no feedback of any kind.
- If the writer is racing or mumbling so you can't understand, interrupt him appreciatively but firmly, and ask him to read more slowly and clearly.
- When the writer has finished reading, thank her and go on to the next person. If there is time after everyone has read, you might want to hear the pieces again—especially the more complex ones. Or you might agree to discuss the *topics,* but don't let the discussion turn into feedback on each other's writing.

Exploring the Writing Process

I felt good about reading my piece of writing to the response group yesterday. It was good for me to be in control, by being able to specify what kind of response I wanted to receive. One thing that frightens me as a writer reading my stuff, is that once it's out there, I'm terribly vulnerable. It is often like sharing a secret part of myself. Or like giving birth. As long as the idea stays within me, it is protected, but once it is "born," it is vulnerable. I think of getting my Shakespeare paper back from M. with the *B+* and the marks all over it. I had a very hard time starting the next paper. I didn't trust my ability. I felt the unseen censor's heavy presence. I know that his intentions were to help me to improve my writing, but my problem was to get past the roadblock of my damaged ego [. . .]. I can't change how the world deals with my writing, so maybe the key is in working on my own attitude toward the criticism I get.

Jo Ferrell

2. Pointing and Center of Gravity

These two kinds of feedback fit well with two readings of your piece. After the first reading, listeners can point to the words and phrases that struck them or seemed most memorable. This is a way of letting a writer know which bits of his writing got through or made the strongest impression.

Then after each person's second reading, listeners can tell where they sense any *centers of gravity:* spots they sense as generative centers or sources of energy in the text. They might not be main points. Sometimes an image, phrase, detail, or digression seems a point of special life or weight in the piece.

When you read, don't rush, even though you might feel nervous. Allow a bit of silence after each reading. Give listeners time to collect their impressions.

Why Would Anyone Want Wholly Descriptive Feedback without Criticism or Advice?

This and the next two kinds of response ("Summary and Sayback" and "What Is Almost Said?") ask for description without evaluation or suggestions. If this feels odd, consider the following reasons:

- We benefit most from feedback on *early* drafts, but it doesn't make sense to evaluate an early draft. When we put off feedback until after we've slaved over something, it's hard to revise because we've invested too much sweat and blood. Nonjudgmental feedback gives us early feedback and new ideas and simply ignores the fact that, of course, there are obvious problems in our early draft. It makes readers into allies rather than adversaries while they help us see our still evolving text better and give us new insights.
- Perhaps we're trying out a new kind of writing or an approach that we're weak at: We're trying to break out of the rut of what we can already do well. Or we're working on something so difficult but important that we don't want criticism yet. We just need some *perspective* on our piece. We need a reader to trust us, to trust that we can see faults ourselves and work through them. And frankly we also need some encouragement and support in seeing what's right or strong in the piece.
- We may want feedback from someone who is a good reader but who can only criticize. It's her only gear. We need her perceptions but not her knife. Asking for descriptive responses is a way to nudge her out of her judgmental rut.
- We often need to give feedback to a weak or inexperienced writer or to a writer in a rut. Often we sense that criticism and "helpful advice" are not what he needs. Sure, his writing has serious problems, but what he needs is encouragement and confidence. We often sense that the very thing that's been undermining his writing is too much criticism: He's been clenching too hard; he's been criticizing and rewriting every phrase as he writes it until all the energy and clarity are gone from his writing. He'll

write better when he trusts himself better. Nonjudgmental feedback will help.

SAMPLES OF FEEDBACK: POINTING AND CENTER OF GRAVITY

The sample essays will be found on pages 553–557.

Pointing for "What's Wrong with Black English?":
One Reader:

- Big saggy pants and knit caps.
- America is cool.
- Blacks of America and their culture have the power of attracting people.
- Banning Black English and forcing them to learn Standard English only hurts the children's identity because it means to the children that their language and culture are rejected in the public place.
- "Children have the right to their own language." This is a quote used in the paper, but it is strong and direct and stands out.
- Feelings of public separateness do not come from the language only.
- The advocates of nonbilingual education may believe that the only culture in this country should be the one of the dominant white middle class.

Another Reader:

- Black children should be taught both in Black English (Ebonics) and the Standard English.
- Forcing them to learn Standard English only hurts the children's identity.
- Their language and culture are rejected.
- Children have the right to their own language.
- Language is a culture.
- If you lose your language, you lose the way of expressing yourself.
- Standard English . . . white middle class rules and codes are necessary tools for success.
- Like it or not, they [the white middle class] mark the place where "power" currently exists.
- The reason people love America is its diversity.
- Melting pot of many ethnic groups.
- Coming from the racially homogeneous country like Japan, I see the standardization of America as a great loss to today's diversified world.

Pointing for "The Power of Sprinkles":
One Reader:

- I don't want to do this.
- Our GPA will suffer.
- E-mail isn't the same.
- If you can write for that then why can't you write for this?

Another Reader:

- I don't want to do this I don't want to do this I don't want to do this!
- We have to do this.
- I hate writing!
- You argue all the time.

- Stupid messages aren't just stupid—they're fun!
- And what about the diary?
- It doesn't count.
- Well, if you can write for that, why can't you write for this?
- Because this is assigned!
- Minimum length is good. It tells us how much detail we're supposed to go into and how much we should say about something.
- Adding more would make it worse. It's hard putting in bull_ _ _ _.
- We never do things my way.
- We don't always have to do things the way we're supposed to. Sometimes it works much better if we do our own thing, and just make it look like what it's supposed to be.
- As soon as it's over, we can get a Smurf sundae.
- With sprinkles?
- Of course.
- It's a deal. Let's get started.

Centers of Gravity for "What's Wrong with Black English?": One Reader:

- The image of Japanese kids with baggy sagging pants and girls braiding their hair with beads and huge crowds dancing to rap music.
- Vicious circle of uneducated, poor, single mothers and lives depending on the welfare.
- Destroying a language is destroying people.
- In the 19th century, many people came to the New World because they saw this country as a melting pot of many ethnic groups, and they thought there would be room for them to live their lives.

Another Reader:

- When the bilingually educated blacks are the majority of the black population of America, it will again change white people's ways of thinking and the history of the country.
- Advocates of nonbilingual education may believe that the only culture in this country should be the one of the dominant white middle class.
- The reason people love America is its diversity.

Centers of Gravity for "The Power of Sprinkles": One Reader:

- Examples the writer gives to demonstrate the necessity for communication in life.
- Reasons why students get marked down on papers.
- Reasons why writing for an assignment is not fun.

Another Reader:

- The fact that essays don't have to be long and boring. You can use your imagination to have fun while writing essays.
- Sprinkles.

3. Summary and Sayback

These two kinds of response are similar. Try them both and see which one feels more useful to you (or perhaps work out some combination of the two). If your piece is not too long or complex, you can get summary feedback after the first reading and sayback after the second. (If your piece is long or complex, you need two readings even for summary feedback.)

Summary is a way to find out how readers understand your words—whether your message got through. Many needless misunderstandings come about because readers are arguing about the strengths or weaknesses of someone's ideas without realizing they have different interpretations of what the piece is saying. The procedure is simple: Ask readers for a one-sentence summary, a one-phrase summary, and a one-word summary. (You can even ask for two versions of these summaries: one version that uses words from your writing and one where listeners must use their own language.) Another way to ask: "Give me a couple of titles for this piece."

Sayback (or active listening) is a simple but subtle variation. The author reads and the listener "says back" what she hears the writer "getting at." But she says it back in a slightly open, questioning fashion in order to invite the writer to restate what she means. In effect the listener is saying, "Do you mean. . . ?" so that the writer can say, "No, not quite. What I mean is . . ." Or "Yes, but let me put it this way . . ." Or even—and this is pay dirt—"Yes, I *was* saying that, but *now* I want to say . . ." Sayback helped her move past her original thinking.

In short, sayback is an invitation to the writer to find new words and thoughts—to move in her thinking. Sayback helps the writing continue to cook, bubble, percolate. It helps the writer think about what she hasn't yet said or even thought of.

Thus, though sayback is useful any time, it is particularly useful at an early stage in your writing when you have only written in an exploratory way and things haven't jelled yet.

Here's an important variation: *Sayback to help you figure out what you are doing*. Get your listener to tell what he senses as your *goals* (the effects you want your writing to have) and your *strategies* (how you want to achieve those effects with language). Use his guesses as a springboard to help you talk out your goals and strategies for this piece. The best thing for revising is to get clearer in your mind what you're trying to accomplish and what language strategies you want to use. Take plenty of time to talk and take notes.*

To the Listener Giving Sayback

- Don't worry about whether you like or don't like something: That's irrelevant here. Listen and get engaged with what you hear.

---

*We are grateful to have learned about the use of sayback responding from Sondra Perl and Elaine Avidon of the New York City Writing Project.

- After listening, try to sum up in a sentence or two what you feel the writer is getting at. For sayback, say your response in a mildly questioning tone that invites the writer to respond. Think of yourself as inviting the writer to restate and thereby to get closer to what she really wants to say.

To the Writer Asking for Sayback

- Listen openly to the listener's sayback. If the listener seems to misunderstand what you have written, don't fight it. Use this misunderstanding as a spur to find new words for what you are really trying to say. The process of listening to a misunderstanding and then saying what you really mean often helps you find new key words and phrases that get right to the heart of the matter and prevent future misunderstanding.
- Don't feel stuck with what you've already written; don't defend it. Keep your mind open and receptive: think of this as help in shifting, adjusting, and refining your thinking.

SAMPLES OF FEEDBACK: SUMMARY AND SAYBACK

Summary for "What's Wrong with Black English?":
One Reader:

- Black English is very important and it should also be taught to black children together with standard English.

Another Reader:

- You admonish whites and society for saying that Black English is bad. It is useful and is part of the cultural identity of a portion of the people; thus it should be taught in schools. This is a part of the cultural diversity that makes America great.

Summary for "The Power of Sprinkles":
One Reader:

- The statement behind this essay is that sometimes it is hard to write, especially when you are told to. You may feel like you want to put it off or not bother. But it serves a purpose. A good way to write is to say what you know and feel, and then mold that into what is required. You may have to bribe yourself, but if that is what it takes to get you started, then do it.

Exploring the Writing Process

Group work is really interesting now. I never liked sharing before I took this class but now I even look forward to it. English was always not one of my better subjects, especially writing anything other than letters to my friends or opinion papers. I never wanted to share my writing because I felt stupid and like I wasn't a good writer. It's really easy to share my work now and I met great people in the class. Sharing and working together is a way to get to know people better and gives you a group of people that you can feel comfortable with and even become close friends with.

A Student

Another Reader:

- The writer talks the problem out in detail with herself, comes to a solution, and then moves on.

Sayback for "What's Wrong with Black English?":
One Reader:

- I hear you saying that Black English is very popular because some people in Japan like it? You are saying that it is going to be easy for black children to learn both kinds of English?

Another Reader:

- I understood the writer to be arguing in support of Ebonics in the classroom. The writer assumes Ebonics to be a language of Black Americans, and she asserts that although Ebonics is considered a lower class language, children should be taught it in schools so the children may gain confidence of their culture. The writer was stating that when the language of Blacks is rejected by society, it is a rejection of their culture in the American society. In the middle of the paper, the writer essentially argues that Blacks cannot communicate or express themselves through the English language, so they should be taught in Ebonics in order to gain cultural confidence. She concludes that bilingual education should be implemented in schools so Black culture can remain alive and strong and continue to add diversity to America.

Sayback for "The Power of Sprinkles":
One Reader:

- Writing can be a struggle. I hear you giving a picture of the opposing forces in all of us that promote procrastination, especially when we don't exactly want to do the work. Sometimes it is necessary to reason with ourselves to do something. A bribe may be necessary, but it is a small price to pay for the reward we get from a job well done. I wonder if you are implying that it may not work this way for everyone.

Another Reader:

- You are having an ongoing conversation with yourself, an internal dialogue complaining to yourself about why you hate to write. Your inner voice reminds you of the positive aspects of writing, how you write on an everyday basis, how writing skills are essential for communication in life. You agree with your inner voice but say that such daily writing is fun because you are free to say what you want; you wonder why teachers ask for extended "bull_ _ _ _." You talk about not being able to express your true opinions for fear of getting your grade docked by a disagreeing teacher. Toward the end, the two voices agree that you can be unique and dare to add creativity; sometimes when you do that, the finished product is much better because you invested yourself; you can add humor and silliness and the quality only improves.

4. What Is Almost Said? What Do You Want to Hear More About?

This response technique moves slightly away from what's in the text. No text can ever tell readers everything they need for understanding it; all texts assume that readers already know some of what the writer knows. Literary theorists speak of what's not there as "gaps." When readers respond to a piece of writing by telling you what's almost said or implied, they are telling you how they are filling in your gaps: what they feel hovering around the edges, what they feel you have assumed.

A surprisingly helpful and playful variation is to ask readers to guess what was on your mind that you *didn't* write about. This kind of feedback often gets at an undercurrent or mood or atmosphere that is only faintly present in your writing but which has an important subliminal effect on your readers.

SAMPLES OF FEEDBACK: WHAT IS ALMOST SAID? WHAT DO YOU WANT TO HEAR MORE ABOUT?

What Is Almost Said? for "What's Wrong with Black English?":
One Reader:

- Opponents of bilingual education are cultural suppressors who are striving to keep underclass blacks underclass.
- Teaching Black English in schools is the only way to help Blacks feel important in society.
- Standard English is white.
- Language keeps culture alive.

Another Reader:

- Communication and unity in the U.S. won't be harmed if Black English is taught.
- Japan and other countries don't have much diversity.
- You like to hear Black English.

What Is Almost Said? for "The Power of Sprinkles":
One Reader:

- Teachers like to make writing tedious, uncreative, boring.
- Restriction of creativity is oppression.
- Bribery works—even on yourself.
- A lot of students do an awful lot of writing other than what is assigned in school.
- To do anything well, you have to break the rules.
- To do anything well, you have to bribe and compromise.
- To do anything well, you have to get the different parts of yourself to work together cooperatively.

Another Reader:

- Writing essays can be like doing other common everyday things we do without thinking.
- Everyone consists of at least two people—a "we." You never need to be lonely.
- The voice that says you need to write is the real you.
- The voice that doesn't want to write is the real you.
- e.e.cummings has made a great literary impact and his poetry is limited by nothing.
- In life you don't just have to learn to get along with other people, you have to learn to get along with yourself.

What Do You Want to Hear More About for "What's Wrong with Black English?":
One Reader:

- How many schools are presently doing that? teaching bilingually?
- What is the dropout rate for Black students compared to white students?

- I assume Black English is a slang or loose form of regular English. You imply it's a whole language. Is this true? I'd like to hear more about this.
- I'd like to know the story of some particular students. What was it like when they couldn't use their own language? What was it like when they were invited to use their own language?

Another Reader:

- I'm interested in what you say in the 2nd paragraph: "When the bilingually educated Blacks consist of the majority of the Black population of America, it will again change the white people's ways of thinking and the history of this country." I want to hear how you think it will change people's thinking. How will the emergence of a middle class Black population influence others?
- What do you mean in the fifth paragraph when you say, ". . . an understanding of white middle class rules and codes are necessary tools for social success"? What rules and codes are you referring to specifically?

<u>What Do You Want to Hear More About</u> for "The Power of Sprinkles":
One Reader:

- What sort of essays do you write with "silly stuff"? How about using pictures for writing essays?
- What are some tricks for getting teachers to accept creative and silly and fun writing?
- It sounds like you basically enjoy writing—if the conditions are OK. Is that true? How did you manage that?

Another Reader:

- Do you often write dialogues in your head?
- Do you really have these dialogues silently in your head—or was this just a way to write something? Do you ever talk out loud to yourself?
- Which voice is most you? Or are they both equal?
- Can you use this technique about other difficulties, like whether to go out with someone?
- Which voice wins the most battles?

5. Reply

When you ask readers to reply to what you have written, you are asking for the most human and natural kind of response. And you are also asking readers to treat your writing in the most serious way: to engage with it at the level of substance. In effect, you are saying, "Please take my writing and my thinking seriously enough to reply to what I have said instead of ignoring or sidestepping my ideas and just talking about how clearly or well I have presented them. Reply to my text as a human, not as a helper, teacher, evaluator, or coach." When you ask for a reply, you are really inviting your listeners to enter into a discussion with you about the topic. You are thus also inviting them to leave your writing behind as they get involved in the issues themselves. Nevertheless, such a discussion can be one of the most helpful things of all for your writing. Since you are inviting a discussion, you should feel free to jump in and take full part. For this kind of feedback, you don't need to hold back and mostly listen.

Reply for "What's Wrong with Black English?": One Reader:

Dear Yoko,

Although I liked reading your essay, I want to argue against it. I have always considered Ebonics a type of slang, but now I'm not sure. Is it a real language? Does it follow a specific set of rules? Also, how is society hurting children's identity by not teaching Ebonics in schools? I agree with you that "children have the right to their own language," but it can be spoken at home, with friends, and in the neighborhood. The language will not die if it isn't taught in class. The arguments against bilingual education you use in the essay seem rather extreme to me. I feel like you have limited your options by so forcefully arguing for bilingual education. Perhaps your argument would be even stronger if you could mention more opposing arguments to bilingual education. This way, I would know you have at least considered them and then rejected them.

Another Reader:

- All through my schooling, teachers corrected my mistakes in language. Especially in writing, but sometimes even in speaking. I'm white so they weren't "black" mistakes. They were just "mistakes." I've never thought that maybe I have a "right" to my mistakes. It sounds crazy, but

Exploring the Writing Process

I spent a long time writing a good draft of a memo to teachers in the writing program. I was making suggestions for an evaluation process I wanted them to use. (I wanted them to write reflectively about their teaching and visit each other's classes.) I worked out a plan very carefully and at the end I really *wanted* them to do this—realizing of course that some would not want to. The more I thought about it, the more I felt I was right. I ended up putting it very strongly: They *have* to do it.

I read my draft out loud in a staff meeting to Pat, Bruce, Jeff, Aaron, and Cindy. Wanted feedback. People were slow to bring up that final bit (that they *have* to do it), but finally Cindy brought it up bluntly as a problem. Some disagreed and said, in effect, "Yes, we've got to insist." But Bruce and Jeff thought the way I wrote it went too far—would get readers' backs up unnecessarily. ("I don't want to be inflammatory," I said, and Aaron replied, "But you seem to want to make a flame.")

I wanted to defend what I wrote, but I held back; but the impulse to defend kept recurring. Finally I saw that I *could* make my point more mildly—and it would get my point across *more* effectively. I could see it was better the milder way. Finally, I ended up feeling, "That's what I *wanted* to say."

I tell the story—it came to me this morning as I woke up early—as a paradigm of how feedback can and should work, of writing as a potentially collaborative social process. That is, it now strikes me that I *needed* to write those things; I needed to punch it to them. But by having the chance to read it out loud to this surrogate audience rather than the real one—an audience of peers with whom I felt safe—I could "get it said." And then listen; and finally hear.

By the end, I felt comfortable and grateful at the outcome—even though of course some little part of me still experienced it as having to "back down" and "accept criticism." Yet by the end, it didn't feel like backing down and "doing it their way." By the end it was what *I* wanted to say.

In short, the process of reading a draft to a safe audience and getting feedback wasn't just a way to "fix" my draft. The main thing was that *it allowed my mind to change.* My intention ended up being different from what it had been.

Peter Elbow

it's fun to think about. I never thought about all these corrections as hurting my cultural confidence, but they sure hurt my writing confidence. I grew up feeling dumb and feeling I could never have a job that required writing. I think I could have done better if teachers had respected my language more and not considered me dumb because I made so many mistakes.

Reply for "The Power of Sprinkles": One Reader:

Dear Gabrielle,

I love your essay. I often talk out problems to myself also. I could relate to your confused feelings about writing. I can remember writing essays in high-school English classes and wondering if I should express my full opinions or be safe and write what I knew would receive an *A*. I have noticed since I've been at college, however, that professors encourage freedom in writing and creativity. This makes me think further about what high-school teachers want students to learn. By restricting students to follow a format, teachers are oppressing students' abilities. I really enjoyed the outcome of the dialogue when both of your voices agreed to challenge the teacher's expectations and write a creative essay.

Another Reader:

- It looked as though you were having fun with this. I enjoy reading it, but I'm jealous and actually it makes me mad. People like you could always get better grades with your creative tricks. I can't find ways to worm out of the actual assignment as it is spelled out. I do what I'm supposed to do, I work harder than you, and I always get a worse grade.

6. Voice

Voice is a large, rich concept that you can explore more fully in the workshop we devoted to it in Workshop 5. But to get feedback about voice you can ask two questions that get at two dimensions of voice in writing: (a) "How much voice do you hear in my writing? Is my language alive, human, resonant? Or is it dead, bureaucratic, silent, unsayable?" (b) "What kind of voice or voices do you hear in my writing? Timid? Confident? Sarcastic? Whispering? Shouting? Pleading?" There are some interesting variations on the second question: "What kind of person does my writing sound like?" Or "What kind of person do I become in my writing?" Or "What side of me does my writing bring out?" Keep in mind that there are often *several voices* intertwined in a piece of writing. If you listen closely, you may hear someone move back and forth between confidence and uncertainty, between sincerity and sarcasm. The writing may draw out the various sides of the writer. Multiple voices need not be a problem; we all have multiple voices. The issue is whether they work well together or get in each other's way. In the case of essays, it's important to ask, "Do you trust the voice or person you hear in my writing?"

Responses about the voice or voices in a piece of writing are remarkably interesting and useful. They go to the heart of what makes writing work for readers, since our response to writing is often shaped by our sense of what kind of voice we are hearing. And voice gets to the heart of how we as writers come up with words, because we often write best when we feel we are "giving voice" to our thoughts; and we often revise best when we sense that the voice doesn't sound right and change it to get closer to the voice we want. In short, our *ear* may be the most powerful organ we have for both reading and writing. But some readers need a bit of practice in learning to hear and describe the voices in writing.

Make sure, as always, that everyone's piece gets two readings—perhaps by having one straight read-through and then a second reading for response.

Feedback about voice lends itself particularly to what is one of the most useful forms of feedback: rendering or enacting your words. You might get a listener to do your second reading, or even two listeners to do both readings. Or get listeners to read short bits where they hear a voice. It's interesting and fun to ask readers to bring out the voice or voices as they read. They'll have an easier time if you are willing to invite them to exaggerate or play around a bit: to read it as if they were whining or arrogant or depressed, or whatever the voice suggests to them. This can lead to some parody and silliness, so you mustn't take offense. The goal is to help you hear the various voices and potential voices in your words. If you are willing to invite this kind of performance, it will become the most lively and enjoyable of all forms of feedback.

SAMPLES OF FEEDBACK: VOICE

Voice for "What's Wrong with Black English?":
One Reader:

- Your voice starts out relaxed, friendly, and casual and then gets more authoritative as you start arguing by giving citations and examples to support your claims. This makes it sound like a research essay written for a tough class. Then at the end your voice gets back to the more relaxed tone it had in the beginning.

Another Reader:

- The tone of the voice in your paper is strong, assured, and confident. It seems it would be impossible to sway you in any other direction—you seem absolutely convinced about your argument. It almost comes across as stubborn. Your voice is sincere and even passionate about the topic—almost devoted to proving to your audience that you are right. I don't hear any trace of wondering or doubt in your voice.

Voice for "The Power of Sprinkles":
One Reader:

- The whole essay is in quotes and uses a lot of *"I."* It's all in an out loud voice—like speaking more than like writing. The writer is frustrated and annoyed toward writing essays and is arguing with herself. The voice is very strong and challenging as the author is arguing.

Another Reader:

- The voice that doesn't want to write the essay is always changing: whining, arguing, thinking of clever points, being angry, making jokes. The voice that says you have to write the essay always has an answer; in the end it's a little smarter or a little better at handling the troublemaker voice. It's like the mommy who knows how to handle the quick-thinking rebellious child. It's just like a mommy to avoid an all-out fight and to use ice-cream as a bribe.

7. Movies of the Reader's Mind

What we need most as writers is not evaluation of the quality of our writing or advice about how to fix it, but an accurate account of what goes on inside readers' heads as they read our words. We need to learn to *feel* those readers on the other end of our line. When are they with us? When are they resisting? What kind of resistance is it—disagreement or annoyance? When are their minds wandering?

Movies of the reader's mind is the form of response that really underlies all other forms—the foundation of all feedback. After all, everything anyone might say about a text grows out of some reaction. Suppose, for example, that someone reads your essay and says she doesn't agree with your main point or doesn't like your voice in this piece. You need to ask her to back up and give you the movies of her mind that led to this conclusion: What did she understand your main point or your voice to be? Her movies may reveal to you that she doesn't disagree with you or dislike the voice; she *misunderstood* them. Therefore the cure (if you decide you want to adjust the piece for this reader) would not be to change your point or your voice but to make them stronger so that they are not misunderstood.

It's not so easy to give good movies of the mind. For example, a reader might tell you he feels your tone is too aggressive and wants you to soften it. But what were his *reactions*—the movies of his mind—that led to this reaction? Perhaps at first he can't tell you. ("I don't know. I was just bothered; that's all.") But if you ask him to ferret out those too-quick-to-notice reactions behind that conclusion, he might tell you that he felt irritated by what he thought were some sly digs you were making about people you disagree with. Once you learn what was actually happening in this reader, you can draw your own conclusions instead of having to buy or resist his. After getting back to his reactions, you may decide that the problem was not the "digs" themselves but the slyness. You might well decide that the solution you need is not to remove or soften what he felt as sly digs but to make your disagreement with others much more frank and blunt.

Movies of a reader's mind can be confusing until you are used to them. They consist of nothing but facts or raw data, not conclusions; and the same piece of writing causes different things to happen in different minds. What you get is messy. But movies gradually help you develop your sensitivity to what your words are likely to do inside readers' minds.

Movies do not require experts. Indeed, sometimes you get wonderfully clear and helpful movies from children or very naive readers. Sometimes sophisticated readers have a hard time getting behind their judgments and conclusions to the feelings and reactions that led to them. You need honesty and trust.

Here are some ways to help readers learn to notice and describe their reactions while reading:

- *Serialize or interrupt your text.* Read your writing to listeners one section at a time (or hand them your text one section at a time). At each interruption, get them to tell you what's going on in their heads right at that moment. These "stop-frame movies" are particularly important near the beginning of your piece so that you can find out how your opening affects readers. In particular, you need to know whether your opening has made them resist you or go along with you. That is, readers' reactions to the rest of your piece often depend on whether they became friendly or unfriendly during the first few paragraphs. For the rest of your piece, either they are pedaling with you and helping you along or they are dragging their heels and seeing every possible problem. If you give them a written version of your piece to read at home, persuade them to interrupt their reading at least two or three times and take a few notes of what's actually happening in their minds at the time of each interruption. This technique helps them capture their reactions "on the fly."

- *Get their responses in story form.* Get readers to tell you their responses in the form of a story; that is, "First I felt this, then I thought that," and so on. The story form prevents them from falling into useless global generalities like "I enjoyed it" or "It was exciting" or "I was bored."
- *Get "I-statements."* If a reader says, "You should change this word or move that paragraph," you don't know what was happening to him: Was he bored, confused, or in disagreement? Get readers to tell their reactions in sentences starting with "I."

We have held off movies of the reader's mind until now—until you've tried other kinds of feedback and, we hope, developed trust in yourself and a relationship of trust and support with your readers—because movies are not always easy to listen to. If readers tell you honestly what went on as they were reading your words, you may well hear something like, "I was getting madder and madder because I felt lost—starting in the first paragraph. And I felt your voice was arrogant too, and so I wanted to quarrel with everything, even when I agreed with your actual points." It's hard to benefit from responses like that unless you feel them coming from a friend or ally.

When a reader gives you movies of reactions that are very critical, remember that she is not trying to be fair or impartial (as in "evaluating by criteria," which comes later in our sequence). She is just trying to tell you accurately what was occurring in her. She is not pretending to be God making an objective judgment. These are simply her subjective reactions, and they might be different from those of most other readers.

Here are some other suggestions for getting movies of readers' minds:

- Don't make apologies or explanations of your writing before they hear or read it and respond, because these will heavily influence how they react.
- Don't quarrel with what a reader says, even if he's utterly misunderstanding what you wrote. You're not trying to educate readers about your text; you're trying to get *them* to educate *you* about your text.
- Invite exaggeration or parody. This can be scary, but also a big help if your readers are having trouble telling you what's happening as they read or if they seem to be beating around the bush. For example, readers might feel vaguely bothered by something in your writing but be unable to explain what they feel. "It's OK," they'll say. "I pretty much liked what you

wrote." But you can feel some hesitation or reservation. If you feel brave enough to invite them to exaggerate their reaction, they will often find words for what's going on and say something like this: "If I were to exaggerate, I'd say you are beating me over the head here." You need to feel fairly secure before you ask for exaggeration because it may lead to a strong statement. But an element of play or humor can keep things from getting too sticky. For example, another helpful question is this: "What would a *parody* of my paper look like?" They might then reply: "Well, I guess it would be a three-page soapbox rant that's all one breathless sentence." You can reassure them that you know this is not an accurate or fair picture of your piece, but this distorted picture captures a *tendency* in your piece.

- Movies of the mind requires honesty from readers and reveals as much about them as about your writing. If you aren't getting honesty, perhaps you haven't convinced your readers that you really want it.

SAMPLES OF FEEDBACK: MOVIES OF THE READER'S MIND

Movies of the Reader's Mind for "What's Wrong with Black English?": One Reader:

- When she said that some Japanese liked the fashion of blacks, it reminded me of my friend in Singapore who liked rap music so much that he was willing to pay high prices for it.
- Isn't "African-American" more acceptable than "Black"?
- I could not see the link between music and English when she was talking about blacks attracting people and then suddenly moved to the debate about language among educators.
- I felt that the tone was authoritative when she said that black children "should" be taught in both Black English and Standard English. But I didn't quite agree with the point, as it is not easy to master two kinds of English simultaneously.
- I could see images of minds of confused and disappointed black children when they are told that their culture is not accepted in the public.
- I felt the quotation made a very good point—that the schools have to change, not the children.
- I felt that the statement, "You cannot abandon language just because it is spoken by poor people," has a lot of meaning. It brought the title of the essay back into my mind.
- I completely agree that language is culture. It reminded me of another class I'm taking (about the interpretation of meaning) where that was exactly what I have argued.
- I definitely agree that in today's society, power exists in Standard English, and I can see the importance for black children of learning Standard English as well.
- At the end I get reminded of the introduction as she addresses the Japanese liking of American culture because of its diversity. But in my mind I actually doubted that.

Another Reader:

- The first paragraph grabbed my attention immediately. The writer talks about African-American cultural influence in Japan. The writer, being Japanese herself, gives an insider's view, and she goes on talking about personal observations which intrigued me even more. I wanted to hear more about American black culture and how other cultures imitate it. I wondered how else "blacks of America and their culture have the power of attracting people." I am eager to hear more.

Note: Our normal method of collaborating on the first edition was for one of us to start a unit—do a very rough draft—and give it to the other to work on. The second person would just take it over—make it his or hers, make extensive changes—especially because the first version was often still quite unformed. Then what the second person produced would go back to the first person for more revision. All this usually on disks rather than on paper.

In this way we often lost track of who started something and who "owned" a section or an idea. We pretty much drifted or fell into this method: we were in a hurry, we knew we had a lot to write, and we didn't have time or energy to "protect" everything we wrote. Most of all we trusted each other. It worked remarkably well.

But for this particular unit we proceeded differently. Peter had worked out a fairly full outline and I took on the job of writing a draft from that outline. Then, instead of Peter taking it over from there—as we normally did—he wrote marginal feedback and gave it back to me to revise. Thus we drifted into a problematic arrangement for this unit: I was writing a unit which felt like Peter's—and getting feedback from him about how to revise what I'd written.

I'm revising according to feedback and angry. Why doesn't he write the damn thing himself if he knows so surely what he wants? It's insulting—giving it back to me to do *his* way. I can't do it. I feel as though I'm not into it, not into the ideas—just into superficial stuff, trying to make it what someone else wants it to be. I'd like to just give it back to him and say that: "Here, you have such a sure idea about what this should be, why give it to me to do? I'm not a typist." Does he think I'm inept? stupid? Maybe he's right. Maybe I'm no good at this and he's saying these things so he won't have to say that. He doesn't think "Life is unfair" is good. But I like it and I'll keep it. He wants this to be mainly a paper handed in to a professor in some other class, not an explanation for the self of something difficult. But I prefer the latter. So I kept trying to make the unit into what he wanted, while still thinking my idea was good.

But somehow (because he's a nice guy I guess) I kept on working with the suggestions. And as I wrote, I got caught up in thinking about getting students to see something two different ways: for themselves and for others. An interesting problem presented itself to me for solution. Could I make it work out that way? I began to explore, and suddenly it was *my* idea; although it wasn't suddenly—just my realization of what had happened seemed sudden. Apparently I was writing according to the feedback, and the idea became mine. I saw an interesting way to develop it, potential for the unit I hadn't seen before, ideas I had never written before. I got excited about it because it was good. Then I could write again without anger or resistance.

The feedback was gone; I really didn't look at any more of the marginal comments because they no longer mattered. I had my own way to go. I just forgot the way it had been done. When I finished up and polished it a bit, I looked back and who'd believe it! I had, on my own, come to saying almost exactly the same thing he said later on in the part of the feedback I hadn't even read. That's eerie! This must be an instance of authentically situated voice—somehow using the words and ideas of others and forging them in the furnace of my own word hoard. The ideas I got caught up with seemed to begin to write themselves out. But they also produced an interesting intellectual challenge to me. And there was something very satisfying about discovering that the two of us had been on the same wavelength—or close anyhow. His good ideas had fertilized my good ideas, and we ended up with something that was undoubtedly better than anything either of us could have done alone. It has been worth working through the anger.

Pat Belanoff

- In the second paragraph, I am beginning to disagree with the writer when she says that banning Black English only hurts children's identity and is a public rejection of their culture and language. Because this is my first disagreement, I notice myself doubting the writer more.
- As I read the third paragraph, I become confused. I don't understand the author's reasoning. How can public separation be brought about by a culture feeling shame because of their poverty? The writer argues that instilling pride in the next generation of blacks (teaching them Ebonics in school) will help them climb the socioeconomic ladder. Now I am lost again when the writer says America will view blacks differently when the majority of them become middle class—and the way they become middle class is through learning Ebonics. Why will it change the view of blacks in America? How will it change the view?
- As I read the fourth paragraph, I feel offended when I get to the point that "Standard English and an understanding of white middle class rules and codes are necessary tools for social success." This upset me. I never realized that middle-class rules and codes set by the middle class ensure success. However, I suppose I felt offended because I am white and middle class. I think I would have felt better if she broadened her view by at least bringing in arguments criticizing bilingual education. She can still reject them, but I would have felt more place for my views and feelings.
- As a read back over it all, I feel unsettled. I still resist but I see I have to think more and find out more. It wasn't till I read back over it more carefully that I realized that she said clearly that she was arguing for also teaching Standard English to black students.

Yet Another Reader:

- The first time I read "What's Wrong with Black English?" was by accident. I was flipping through the 1997–1998 Writing Program anthology and just happened upon it. The title caught my eye instantly. Then I read it. It felt racy and I liked how it expressed racial issues bluntly; I'd never heard anything like this before. Most of this piece was admonishing whites and teachers for believing "Black English" was incorrect. I was raised to believe that was true. I liked that Ms. Koga used opposing view points in her argument; it shows the other side of this issue.

<u>Movies of a Reader's Mind</u> for "The Power of Sprinkles":

One Reader:

- What is going on? was my first reaction, and then it all became very clear.
- I felt that the repetition of "I don't want to do this" conveyed a strong force of feelings.
- I could picture the two sides of a person's mind debating over what should be done.
- I could relate to almost everything the author talks about, as these are all common, everyday things that all college students do.
- I felt that there is little chance of disagreement with the essay since both sides of everything mentioned is presented almost immediately.
- I found the essay fun to read as I was getting involved by taking one side of the author's mind and trying to see if my arguments are being countered. I felt as though I were arguing with my own mind.
- When the author said "because this is assigned!" I was saying to myself, Exactly! and thus I agree that something we are told to do by a specific deadline is different than deciding to do something by ourself.
- I got a little bored at the part about "making an essay longer or shorter"—since I don't feel problems about that.
- The "green eggs and ham" things reminded me of the fiction essay I wrote, and I agree that it was fun.
- The ending made me smile and reflect back to the title. Till then I didn't think about the title. I suddenly felt that the author thought of the title only after completing the essay.

Another Reader:

- As I read the first part of the paper, I automatically associate myself with the writer since she is addressing an issue I deal with as well (as a student). Therefore I automatically have trust in the writer and am interested in reading the rest of the essay. As I read and the two voices continue to fight about writing the assigment, I begin to hear the argument in my head and I notice myself emphasizing the words. When there is an exclamation point, I read the sentence with energy and emphasis.

  As I read further into the paper, I only become more involved and more supportive of voice one. The voices converse with each other about teachers who attach so many limitations on writing that it isn't fun. While reading, bad memories came to my mind of high-school days when I had to conform to the writing teacher's requirements. I, too, would get back essays that I labored over saying it didn't meet the length requirement, and the score would drop one letter grade. I can relate to the frustrations of voice one. I was proud of the voices at the end of the essay when they decided to write how and what they wanted. The voices valued freedom in writing more than following rules. I felt really positive when I finished reading the essay. I thought to myself, She's right, you can beat the system if you're clever!

8. Metaphorical Descriptions

It turns out that you can usually see a faint star better out of the corner of your eye than when you look at it directly. The same thing happens in the middle of the night when you try to see the faint luminous dial of the bedside clock: a squint from the corner of your eye usually shows you more. So too, we can often capture more of what we know about something if we talk *indirectly*—through metaphor—than if we try to say directly what we see. For metaphorical feedback, get readers to describe what you have written in some of the following terms:

Weather(s). **What is the weather of the writing? sunny? drizzling? foggy? Try noticing different weathers in different parts of the writing.**

Clothing. **How has the writer "dressed" what he has to say? In faded denims? In formal dinner wear? In a carefully chosen torn T-shirt?**

Shape. **Picture the shape of the piece—perhaps even in a drawing.**

Color(s). **If the writing were a color, what would it be? Different colors at different spots?**

Animal(s). **Ditto.**

Writer-to-reader relationship. **Draw a picture or tell a story with the writer and the reader in it. See what kind of relationship seems to get implied between writer and reader.**

To give metaphorical feedback, you must enter into the game. Don't strain or struggle for answers: just relax and say the answers that come to mind, even if you don't understand them or know why they come to mind. Some of the answers may be "off the wall," and some of the good ones will seem so. Just give answers and trust the connections your mind comes up with.

The writer, too, must listen in the same spirit of play: listen and accept and not struggle to figure out what these answers mean. The writer, like the responder, needs to trust that there is useful material in there, even if it's mixed with things that aren't so useful. An owl swallows a mouse whole and trusts her innards to sort out what is useful and what's not. You too can eat like an owl: Listen in an attitude of trust that your mind will use what makes sense and ignore what does not.

There's a side benefit to this kind of feedback. It highlights an important truth for almost all feedback: that we are not looking for "right answers." We're looking for individual perceptions—ways of seeing. And it all works best if there is a spirit of play and trust.

SAMPLES OF FEEDBACK: METAPHORICAL DESCRIPTIONS

Metaphorical Descriptions for "What's Wrong with Black English?":
One Reader:

- This essay reminds me of a fast moving thunderstorm. It starts off as dark clouds on the horizon. Then the patter of rain begins. Suddenly the wind picks up and lightning splits the sky. The soft sound of rain is transformed into hard pellets as it punishes the earth, slamming into the ground. But just as quickly as it came, the storm passes. The roiling clouds move on to reveal the sun glinting off the newly wetted earth.
- Shape. Polygon.
- Animal. Squirrel.

Another Reader:

- If the essay were an item of clothing, it would be a brand new pair of jeans that don't quite fit right and that have a few holes that weren't apparent at the department store when the jeans were bought.
- If the essay were a type of weather, it would begin as a sunny day which then turns into fog with scattered rain showers.
- If the essay were an animal, it would be a mischievous cat.
- If the essay were a shape, it would be a hexagon.

Metaphorical Descriptions for "The Power of Sprinkles":
One Reader:

- If the essay were an item of clothing, it would be a reversible, warm, colorful down coat with lots of hidden pockets for gum and Chapstick.
- If the essay were weather, it would be a refreshing cool sprinkle on a hot, sticky, humid day.
- If the essay were an animal, it would be a monkey.
- If the essay were a color, it would be chartreuse.
- If the essay were a shape, it would be a diamond.

Another Reader:

- Weather. It's like thunder and lightning at the beginning during the argument and it calms down to the smooth waves of the sea at the end.
- Clothing. Plain T-shirt and shorts.
- Shape. Triangle.
- Color. Light green.
- Animal. Mongoose.
- Picture of the writer-to-reader relationship. It's as if the author is constantly talking to me, but actually ignoring me because she is arguing with herself.

9. Believing and Doubting

This kind of response zeros in on the content or ideas in your writing. It invariably gives you more ideas, more material. The obvious place to use it is on essays, but if you ask readers to play the believing and doubting game with your stories, you'll get interesting feedback too.

Believing

Simply ask readers to believe everything you have written, and then tell you what they notice as a result of believing. Even if they disagree strongly with what you have written, their job is to *pretend* to agree. In this way, they will act as your ally: They can give you more reasons or evidence for what you have written; they can give you different and better ways of thinking about your topic.

Doubting

Now ask readers to pretend that everything you've written is false—to find as many reasons as they can why you are wrong in what you say (or why your story doesn't make sense).

Here are some techniques that help with doubting and believing:

- *Role-play.* Instead of being yourself, pretend to be someone else who *does* believe or doubt the piece, and think of the things this person would see and say. It's a game; just pretend.

Exploring the Writing Process

Why can't I deal with this? The feedback from both of them is enormously useful, but it makes me uncomfortable and mad. I'm all stirred up. It leaves me upset and unable to sleep or relax. I think the crucial factor is that it doesn't feel like it's coming from an ally. I feel I have to fight. That's the main response: Wanting to fight them. Energized for fight. Aggression. Unable to relax. Unable to put it aside. Caught.

I guess you could call that useful. It certainly triggers a piece of my character that is strong. I'm a fighter. My intellectual life is, in a way, a fight. (Perhaps I should talk about this in the Believing essay. I'm in combat.) But it's so exhausting always to be in combat. Yes, it is energizing; it keeps one going. But is it really the best way to go? I wonder if it brings out the *best* thinking. Thinking with my dukes up too much?

Compare the effect of this feedback with the effect of the feedback I got from Paul on the same draft. It was so energizing and comforting. But not sleepy comforting. It made me go back to my thoughts and ideas. It got me *unstuck* from the adversarial defensive mode where I'm trying to beat these guys. It sent me back into my thoughts and simply had me explore what I had to say.

The comparison casts an interesting light on the public and private dimensions of writing. Feedback from ________ and ________ keeps me fixated on *them*—on audience. I want to beat them. Paul's feedback sends me back into myself and helps me forget about audience.

Peter Elbow

- Imagine a different world where everything that the piece says is true (or false): Enter into that make-believe world and tell what you see. Or tell the story of what a world would be like where everything that the piece says is true (or false).

Usually it makes the most sense to start with the believing game. So first, ask your readers to find all the possibilities and richness in what you have written: build it up before tearing it down. But if readers have trouble believing, they might need to start with the doubting game. This can get the doubting out of their system or satisfy that skeptical itch, and afterward they might find themselves freer to enter into a way of thinking that is foreign to them.

You don't necessarily need to get both kinds of feedback. If you are working on an early draft—or you feel very fragile about something you have written—it can be very useful to get *only* believing responses. This is a way to ask people frankly to support and help you in making your case or imagining the world you are trying to describe. Conversely, if you have a late draft that you feel confident about and are trying to prepare for a tough audience, you might ask only for doubting.

Readers will benefit from a spirit of play in giving this kind of response, and you will, too, as a writer, especially when you are listening to the doubting response. People can get carried away with the skeptical wet-blanket game. (School trains us to doubt, not to believe.) You might hear lots of reasons why what you wrote is wrong. Taken as a game, doubting needn't bother you. What's more, this play dimension helps you take all feedback in the right spirit. For feedback is nothing but help in trying to see what you have written through various lenses—to see what you can't see with your lens.

SAMPLES OF FEEDBACK: BELIEVING AND DOUBTING

Believing for "What's Wrong with Black English?":
One Reader:

- Children should be proud of their own language. They can't be expected to speak a different language in the school and a different language at home while thinking that the latter is inferior. Schools should see that Black English is popular not only in the U.S. but also in other countries and should teach it. Students can't use language well if they are ashamed of their real language. Teachers would be more successful in helping all students have confidence and enjoy reading and writing if they learned to honor Black English.

Another Reader:

- A predominantly white middle class is oppressing the cultures of the poor, or anyone different. The white middle class is afraid of the coming of values from a different culture, they persecute it; they don't want a shift in power.
- Language is culture. All should be taught in our public schools. The country will be stronger when we can benefit from all citizens and all cultures.
- The English language is actually already a mixture of all kinds of different languages, slangs, and dialects. That's what makes it a rich language. Honoring Black English will eventually make Standard English more vibrant.
- Some of the best contributions to U.S. music have come from black culture, especially jazz and much popular music. The same thing can happen with language. Black language is turning up in literature.
- We'll see that the concept of "standard language" is a problem, and just talk instead about "good and effective language."

- Black students will be able to help white students understand language better because they'll have two languages and be good at switching, especially when this switching happens as part of school, not as a hidden process.

Believing for "The Power of Sprinkles":

One Reader:

- There is a sense of nobleness in challenging people's expectations of you.
- Writing is fun. We can make jokes even with what is unpleasant.
- If you avoid the straightforward path, things will be easier and more fun.

Another Reader:

- We all argue with ourselves like this.
- There is no "I"—only a "we." We are nothing but a collection of shifting voices.
- Writing is usually a struggle, but there are always ways around the struggle. If we really talk to ourselves honestly, we can find a way to handle things.
- Life is essentially a playful game.

Doubting for "What's Wrong with Black English?":

One Reader:

- Black students will benefit more from having to use Standard English in schools. Teachers can help black students use Standard English and still not put them down or make them feel that there is something wrong with them or their language. And black students can still use their own language at home and with friends.
- Another language in our crappy school system would overtax our resources.
- Standard English will be enriched better by Black English if black students have to use it.

Another Reader:

- Well, when you speak of Japan, how many people in Japan enjoy Black English? And that has nothing to do with the schools in the U.S. not teaching Black English. How is it possible to teach both forms of English in one school when there are white students also in the classes? And even if they did teach both forms of English, how would it be fair for black children to have to learn both the languages and still cope with their other school work while the white students have less burden?
- A single unifying language is necessary for any country to be whole. America was based on the idea of a ruling middle class. It just happens that a significant portion of the middle class is white. I know many African-American middle-class people, and most of them do not use Black English. Your assumption that Standard English is white is incorrect. Standard English is just middle class in accordance with the values that our society holds.

Doubting for "The Power of Sprinkles":

One Reader:

- You can't just write anything silly and claim that you have written an essay. An essay should spell out your thoughts, and they must be carefully crafted and properly refined in order to make a good essay.
- Why do you have to wait till the last minute to do your homework—until when your friends are watching a movie? How can you concentrate on the essay this way?

Another Reader:

- Not everyone has problems writing.
- Are you schizophrenic?
- Planning time to do your homework might help; it makes things easier.

10. Skeleton Feedback and Descriptive Outline

In literature classes we tend to describe what is going on in a story, poem, or novel, rather than judge it or find mistakes. Inherent in such an approach is *respect for the text,* and the response is a way to see the text better, allowing the text to speak on its own. You will benefit from asking for the same kind of respect for your writing, and from showing that kind of respect to the writing of others. We suggest here two ways for describing a text.

Skeleton Feedback

A good way to analyze the reasoning and the structure in almost any essay is to get readers to answer the following questions:

- What do you see as the main point/claim/assertion of the whole paper?
- What are the main reasons or subsidiary points? It's fine to list them as they come—in any order.
- Taking each reason in turn, what support or evidence or examples are given—or could be given—for it?
- What assumptions does the paper seem to make about the topic or issue? That is, what does the essay take for granted?
- What assumptions does the paper seem to make about the audience? Who or what kinds of readers does the writer seem to be talking to (and how are they most likely to react to the ideas in the paper)? How does the writer seem to treat the readers? as enemies? friends? children? In short, what is the writer's stance toward the audience?
- Finally, what suggestions do you have? About the order or organization? About things to add or drop or change?

It probably makes the most sense for readers to answer these questions in writing and at leisure—with the text in hand. However, you could get this kind of feedback orally if you have a group that will cooperate in working out shared answers to the questions.

Descriptive Outline

This procedure (developed by Kenneth Bruffee) involves a sustained process of analyzing the *meaning* and *function* of discourse. You can't really do a descriptive outline unless you have the text in hand and take time: This is a kind of feedback that needs to be written.

The procedure is to write a *says* sentence and a *does* sentence for each paragraph or section, and then for the whole essay. A *says* sentence summarizes the meaning or message. A *does* sentence describes the function—what the paragraph or piece is trying to do or accomplish with readers (for example, "This paragraph introduces the topic of the essay by means of a humorous anecdote" or "This paragraph brings up an objection that some readers might feel, and then tries to answer that objection").

The key to writing *does* sentences is to keep them different from the *says* sentences. Keep them from even mentioning the content of the paragraph. Thus, you shouldn't be able to tell from a *does* sentence whether the paragraph is talking about cars or ice cream. Here is a *does* sentence that slides into being a *says* sentence: "This paragraph gives an example of how women's liberation has affected men more than it has women." To make it a real *does* sentence, remove any mention of the ideas or content and talk only about function: "This paragraph gives an example" would do. Or perhaps better, "This paragraph gives an example designed to surprise the reader."

The power in both skeleton feedback and descriptive outlines comes from the distance and detachment they provide. Thus, they are useful for *giving yourself* feedback—particularly when you feel all tangled or caught up in your piece from having worked long and closely on it.

SAMPLES OF FEEDBACK: SKELETON FEEDBACK AND DESCRIPTIVE OUTLINE

Skeleton Feedback for "What's Wrong with Black English?": One Reader:

Main point:

- Allowing black children to be taught in Black English will give them cultural confidence which will in turn help them rise in society.

Other points and support:

- Blacks of America are influential worldwide.
  —Writer's experience in Japan.
- Forcing black children to learn in English is hurting their identity.
  —They see their culture is rejected in public.
  —Also, the quotation from Delpit.
- Speaking a language felt as lower class makes people feel ashamed of themselves and causes public separation of groups.
  —Supported by a quotation from Rodriguez.
  —But the writer doesn't agree with this point.
- Language keeps culture alive.
  —Appeal to common sense. I don't see others supporting this point.
- White middle-class rules and codes are necessary for success.
  —Appeal to common sense. I don't see others supporting this point.
- The United States is admired for its diversity.
  —Appeal to history and national pride.

Assumptions:

- Ebonics is a language.
- Public separation is due to cultural groups feeling inadequate.
- When the majority of blacks become middle class, America's whole way of thinking will change.
- Opponents of bilingual teaching trying to put blacks down.
- The audience is knowledgeable about Ebonics.

Assumptions about audience:

- The writer seems to treat us in a friendly open way. She is strongly sincere in her argument, but she seems to assume that we will agree with her when she gives her reasons. She's using reason and quiet emotion. Even though she's making an argument, I feel she would be surprised that I am still resisting her.

Suggestions:

- Spend more time understanding and dealing with resisting arguments. I'm confused at her wording in her use of the first quotation. Give me some examples or stories of how this is actually needed or would actually work.

Skeleton Feedback for "The Power of Sprinkles": One Reader:

Main point:

- Writing doesn't need guidelines and it doesn't have to be formal to be a good, solid, effective piece of work.

Other points:

- Teachers discourage writers from expressing sincere opinions by forcing them to write about topics which they hold no interest in.
- Teachers discourage freedom in writing by setting length limits and maximums.
- The writer only enjoys writing when on a daily basis for fun and writing for a class should not be different.
- Personal satisfaction is much greater when one is allowed to write creatively, the way she wants.

Assumptions about audience:

- The writer assumes we can get along without any explanations of what's happening. She assumes we'll go along with the playfulness and not worry that we don't know till the end what the title means.

Suggestions:

- I can't think of any suggestions. It works so well.

Another Reader:

Main point:

- We can get this paper written if we learn to talk to each other, listen to each other, and work together.

Other points:

- I don't want to write.
- There are positive aspects of writing. You write every day. Writing skills are essential for communication in life (e-mail, memos, lists, directions, notes, letters, journals, etc.).
- Yes, but such daily writing rituals are fun because I am free to say what I want and at whatever length I want. Why do teachers ask us to add more to papers, when they are only asking for extended "bull_ _ _ _." I'm not free to express my true opinions due to fear of getting my grade docked by a disagreeing teacher.
- Sometimes I can be unique and creative even on school assignments. Sometimes when I do what I want instead of what I am told, the finished product is better. I can add humor and silliness to papers and the quality improves.
- Let's work together and do it just this once—and give ourselves a treat for a reward.

<u>Descriptive Outline</u> for "What's Wrong with Black English?": One Reader:

- Says, essay as a whole: Black English is necessary in the classroom in order for poor blacks to improve their position in society.
- Does, essay as a whole: Does present an argument.
- Says, first paragraph: Blacks are admired worldwide; their culture will die or suffer if their "language" is not used in school.
- Does, first paragraph: Gives an observation or example from a great distance—and doesn't even bring up the issue of the essay.
- Says, second paragraph: Schools need to foster black pride in African-American children.
- Does, second paragraph: Moves to U.S. and brings up main topic; summarizes and argues her position; adds quotation for support.
- Says, third paragraph: Some people think that children who don't speak Standard English will be helped by being made to use it in school, but that isn't the way to help them.
- Does, third paragraph: Gives an opposing argument and answers it.
- Says, fourth paragraph: Black children need to be taught Standard English too in order to be successful in society.
- Does, fourth paragraph: Emphasizes that the writer is not arguing an "either/or" position but a "both/and" position.
- Says, final paragraph: The strength and spirit of America have come from its acceptance of many cultures.
- Does, fifth paragraph: Summarizes and concludes by appealing to history and national pride.

Note: A descriptive outline isn't appropriate for a playful and indirect dialogue like "The Power of Sprinkles."

11. Criterion-Based Feedback

You may well have been getting a bit of this kind of feedback all along. No matter what kind of response you are asking for, it's hard not to ask your readers a few questions about aspects of your writing you feel uncertain about. "I've been trying to get this complicated piece clearly organized and easy to follow. Have I succeeded for you?" "I've done a lot of cutting. Does it feel too choppy?" "I want this to be fun to read, not a chore. Have I succeeded with you?"

The piece of writing itself will suggest certain of its own criteria, usually depending on function. For example, the main job might be to *convey information.* Or, as the writer, you can specify the criteria you consider most important, for example, tone or voice.

Criteria for Nonfiction Writing

The criteria traditionally applied to essays or nonfiction or expository writing are these:

- *Focus on task.* If the piece is written in response to an assignment, question, or task, does it squarely *address* it?
- *Content.* Are there good ideas, interesting or original insights? Are the ideas supported with reasons, evidence, examples?
- *Organization.* It's important to realize that even unconventional organization can be successful. The *real* questions about organization are always these: Does the *beginning* serve as a good way to bring readers in? Do the *middle parts* lead readers successfully where they need to go? Does the *ending* give a satisfying sense of completion or closure? Notice, for example, that many successful essays begin with an anecdote or example such that readers don't even know what the essay will be about, much less what it will be saying. The opening is successful because the anecdote works to get readers involved so that they don't mind not knowing where they are going.
- *Coherence among sentences.* Do sentences seem to follow satisfactorily from each other?
- *Clarity of language.*
- *Voice.* What is the voice or persona and the stance toward the reader, and do they work well?
- *Mechanics.* Spelling, grammar, punctuation; proofreading.

Criteria for Fiction Writing

The criteria that are traditionally applied to imaginative writing, such as fiction or narrative, are these:

- *Plot.* Is it a believable, interesting, or meaningful story?
- *Character.* Do we find characters real or interesting?
- *Description, vividness of details.* Do we *experience* what's there?
- *Language.* Not just "Is it clear?" but "Is it alive and resonant with meaning—perhaps through imagery and metaphor?"
- *Meaning; "So what?"* Is there a meaning or impact that makes the piece seem important or resonant?

Specifying Criteria Helps in Giving Feedback to Yourself

Criteria give you a kind of leverage or perspective, and help focus your attention on things you might otherwise miss when you read over what you've written. Before reading over a draft, you can pause and consciously ask yourself, "What criteria are the most important for this piece of writing?" or "What features of writing do I especially need to be careful about?" This will help you see more.

To Readers

You can make your criterion-based responses more valuable in two ways:

- Be specific: point to particular passages and words which lead you to the judgments you make.

- Be honest and try to give the writer the movies of your mind that lie behind these judgments. That is, what *reactions in you* led to these judgments? For example, if you felt the organization was poor, were you actually feeling lost as you read, or just somewhat distracted or merely disapproving?

SAMPLES OF FEEDBACK: CRITERION-BASED FEEDBACK

Criterion-Based Feedback for "What's Wrong with Black English?": One Reader:

- Clarity of sentences and ideas: I found it smooth to read, easy to follow. But I felt a bit confused in her use of the quotation at the end of the second paragraph.
- Voice: I found it ambitious, honest, quietly strong, confident.
- Ability to convince: For me, more explanations were needed and the original ideas need to be expanded.
- Techniques for arguing: a lot.
    - She used a novel approach by coming at a U.S. debate from a Japanese point of view.
    - She acknowledged an opposing argument, but only one.
    - She used quotations from published authors on both sides of the issue.
    - She appealed to history and national pride.
    - She tried to show how her position is not really one-sided.

Criterion-Based Feedback for "The Power of Sprinkles": One Reader:

- Style: Very creative.
- Clarity: The argument was easy to understand.
- Voice: Informal language used, but it is a personal conversation and would only be appropriate in such context.
- Tone: Sincere and yet also ironic and witty.
- Ability to convince: The voices gave good arguments and examples.
- Ability to throw light on the psychology of writing and dealing with assignment: Hearing two voices got at the complexity of inner struggle.

Final Word: Taking Charge of the Feedback Process by Choosing among These Techniques

We want to end by emphasizing the main point here: As writer, you need to take charge of the process of getting feedback on your work. We've created what could be called an artificial anatomy of *kinds* of feedback in order to help you take charge. For if you simply ask someone to give you feedback or response to what you've written and don't give any help or direction, they will probably just imitate the responses they remember getting from teachers. With the best will in the world, they will probably try to find things that are wrong or weak and then try to tell you how to fix them. Yet they are likely to do this badly: They may well call something wrong or weak in your writing that is in fact just fine. And even if they do it well, this may not be the kind of response that will help you most given your temperament and where you are with this piece.

Now that you've tried out these kinds of feedback—both getting them and giving them—you will be better at knowing what kind of feedback would help you most, and better at helping someone give it to you. And if you want feedback from someone outside your class who hasn't practiced these techniques, you can just show them samples in this book and they will get a pretty clear idea of what you are asking for.

Sometimes when you have a trusted reader or you feel pretty solid about the draft in hand, you might want to invite the reader to give whatever kind of feedback he or she most wants to give. And sometimes a writer will invite you to give whatever feedback you want. In such a situation it's helpful to realize that you can select among the kinds of feedback and give a kind of blend. We will end with an example of such a blending for each of the essays we've been dealing with.

We put this blend in the form of a letter since that's the form we use most often for giving feedback to our friends, colleagues, and students. And it's the form we usually ask our students to use with each other. The letter is a friendly and flexible form.

Dear Yoko,

I was impressed by your essay but it made me struggle too. I learned a lot from it and it made me think—think hard—but as I was reading I often wanted to argue against you. Now that I've read your essay a couple of times and thought about it, I don't resist you so much, but I still resist some. I don't feel as though I'm finished reacting and digesting your essay. Here are some responses at this point.

As I read your essay, I hear you arguing for the importance and value of Black English, arguing that it should be used and taught, and criticizing people who want to prevent that from happening.

Up till now, I've always considered Ebonics a type of slang; I've always been taught that it is simply "loose" or "bad" English—that the places where it differs from Standard English are "mistakes." But now you are making me think again. Is it a real language that follows a full set of rules? If so, I need to rethink my resistance, especially since my experience has come as a white person brought up in white neighborhoods and schools.

Despite any resistance, I had no trouble seeing lots of strong points in your essay. You'll see on your paper where I've put straight lines underneath words and phrases or alongside passages that I felt as especially strong or clear or striking. I used some wiggly lines at points where something didn't work so well for me.

Here are other strengths I felt:

It's clear, strong, sincere writing throughout. Impassioned but not shouting.

> You come at this issue from an outside angle. It's powerful to open with an image of kids in Japan and close by talking about the U.S. being valued by others for its diversity.
>
> I guess it's your outside point of view that helps you sidestep the either/or fight and stand up for both sides of the argument. That is, even though you are arguing for teaching Black English and inviting it to be used, still you are also saying that black children should be taught to be good at using Standard English. But maybe you could make this approach even clearer. For throughout my first reading, I thought you were only on the Black English side of the fight. I didn't quite figure out your middle position or double position till my second reading.

Here are some of the questions I had as I was reading:

> Can you say more about how society is hurting children's identity by not teaching Ebonics in schools? I agree with you that "children have the right to their own language," but can't they speak their language at home, with friends, and in the neighborhood? Will the language die if it isn't taught in class? Or do you think it will?
>
> Can you explain what you mean when you say, "When the bilingually educated blacks consist of the majority of the Black population of America, it will again change the white people's ways of thinking and the history of this country."
>
> Can you pay a bit more attention to arguments against bilingual education? This would have been helpful for me and might have helped other resistant readers.

Thanks for making me think so hard and making me open up an issue I thought was closed.

• • •

Dear Gabrielle,

It was a treat to read your essay. I never would have thought of fulfilling an essay assignment by writing something like this. I don't even know what to call it. My overall feeling is that *you* could get away with it, but *I* never could. But maybe your example will make me try to experiment. But I have a feeling I never could do it like you do.

I drew straight lines for words and passages that felt strong or hit home. Lots of them. Only one or two wiggly lines where I was confused.

When I started reading your piece, I said to myself, What is going on? But soon it all became very clear. You describe a struggle I often feel. I get sucked right in and it makes me want to read the rest. As I read on and the two voices continue to fight about writing the assignment, I begin to hear the words out loud in my head.

Actually everything about the essay seems strong to me. But I kept thinking about whether the teacher would accept this if the assignment was for an "essay." Really, my main question is, What happened when you turned this in?

I thought the voice that didn't want to write was the strongest, the loudest. It's so true about not being able to write what you want to write for teachers. And yet the other voice was more clever. In a way I was reluctant for that voice to trick the other one into writing. I wanted the other one to hold out and not give in.

As I tried to analyze your piece, my first thought was that it really does the job of an essay because it analyzes so well all the struggles and factors involved in writing for teachers. But then I thought that in a way it's really about something else: how the mind works—how we deal with difficulties. I wondered whether I actually talk to myself this way. I don't think I do. And yet your conversation somehow felt familiar to me.

What seemed particularly clever to me, after thinking about it for a while, was how this essay itself was a kind of example of what it's about. Just like the one part of you has to trick the other part into doing what she doesn't want to do, so this essay has to trick the teacher into accepting something that's different from a regular essay. You are trying to win the teacher over. I like how the essay is about trickery, creativity, and breaking the rules.

What's Wrong with Black English?

Yoko Koga

"Isn't America a diversified country?" When I learned that there were people who had to abandon their culture and language to be an American, I could not but ask this question. Then I asked, "What does it mean to be an American?" These questions had never come to a Japanese girl whose country consists of only one race and only one language.

Over the past five years or so, many fashionable streets in Tokyo have been flooded with young people wearing big sagging pants and knit caps. It was a fad for a while for girls to braid their hair with beads. They say that the fashion of blacks in the inner cities in America is cool. So they imitate them. Not only the fashion, they also love rap music, reggae, soul music, and Caribbean music. When a famous rap musician came to Budokan, the biggest concert hall in Tokyo, twenty thousand fans rushed to fill it. Every Sunday, Yoyogi Park, the central park of Tokyo, is filled with groups of young people dancing to rap music. They perform so wonderfully that many people stop and watch them. Huge crowds along the street enjoy these performances. Because of the revival of the 60s, films of Martin Luther King, Jr., and Malcolm X were big hits. Blacks of America and their culture have the power of attracting people, especially younger generations.

When I learned that there is a debate among educators whether they should educate black children in Black English or in Standard English, I was surprised. Why should they not educate their children in the children's own language? I thought it was everyone's basic right. Black children should be taught both in Black English (or Ebonics) and Standard English, the language of their own and the language of the country they live in. This bilingual approach helps build poor children's self-esteem immensely. Banning Black English and forcing them to learn Standard English only hurts the children's identity because it means to the children that their language and culture are rejected in the public place. Instead of banning the students' natural English, educators in the black population should teach how powerful Black English and culture are. They should encourage their students by teaching how black culture has influenced American history, has changed people's way of thinking, and attracts people like those in my country, Japan. The insight that originally inspired Lisa D. Delpit to write her seminal article, "Skills and Other Dilemmas" (1987) expresses the point of this issue very well. Although Delpit came to disagree with this formulation later, she stated it succinctly in her 1988 piece, "The Silenced Dialogue":

> Children have the right to their own language, their own culture. We must fight cultural hegemony and fight the system by insisting that children be allowed to express themselves in their own language style. It is not they, the children, who must change, but the schools. To push children to do anything else is repressive and reactionary. (280)

I think this statement represents the core idea of bilingual education and any argument should start from the belief that "children have the right to their own language."

There are some people who oppose the idea of bilingual education. They argue that the children whose native languages are not Standard English should be corrected at the beginning of their public education because those languages indicate that one is from the lower class of America, and that jeopardizes children's future success in this society. Richard Rodriguez opposes bilingual education in *Hunger of Memory:*

> I have heard "radical" linguists make the point that Black English is a complex and intricate version of English. And I do not doubt it. But neither do I think that Black English should be a language of public instruction. What makes Black English inappropriate in classrooms is not something in the language. It is rather what lower-class speakers make of it. Just as Spanish would have been a dangerous language to use in the schooling of teenagers for whom it reinforces feelings of public separateness. (101)

He claims that speaking the language of lower classes is the cause of public separation. I think, however, the feelings of public separateness do not come from the language only. The feeling arises in minority people, including African Americans, because they cannot be proud of themselves. It is because they know they are economically poor. If you could educate your next generation to be proud of their culture, they could get out of the vicious circle of "uneducated, poor, single mothers depending on welfare." You cannot abandon a language just because it is spoken by poor people. The language is used because there are people who need the language to express their feelings and to hand down their culture to the next generation. In a way, a language is a culture. Destroying a language is destroying people, because if you lose your language, you lose the way of expressing yourself. When the bilingually educated blacks consist of the majority of the black population of America, it will again change the white people's ways of thinking and the history of this country.

The argument that teaching Standard English to black children is important is understandable since Standard English and an understanding of white middle class rules and codes are necessary tools for social success. Children from the poor area should be taught these rules because, like it or not, they mark the place where "power" currently exists, and the children must get into there eventually. However, the children's own "English" should still be the public language in the classroom. Ideally the students should be taught by "bilingual" teachers who speak and understand the values and problems of both cultures, white middle class and black. As Delpit suggested in "The Silenced Dialogue":

> Appropriate education for poor children and children of color can only be devised in consultation with adults who share their culture. Black parents, teachers of

color, and members of poor communities must be allowed to participate fully in the discussion of what kind of instruction is in their children's best interest. Good liberal intentions are not enough. (282)

The advocates of nonbilingual education may believe that the only culture in this country should be the one of the dominant white middle class. Hence everybody should speak "their" English, the so-called Standard English. However, the cultures of America which people of other countries admire are not only the whites'. When many Japanese say they love America, they mention the "cultures" of America. The reason people love America is its diversity. And they are amazed at the generosity this country shows to its diverse population. America's capacity for holding so many different people and cultures has been one of the major attractions that draws so many people to this country. In the nineteenth century, many people came to the New World because they saw this country as a melting pot of many ethnic groups, and they thought there would be a room for them to live their lives. I think this is still the main reason for people coming to this country. If America starts denying its diversity by unifying its languages, it means it denies its history and the spirit of the country. To hold the richness of its culture, America should keep education its next generation in various languages. Coming from the racially homogeneous country like Japan, I see the standardization of America as a great loss to today's diversified world.

Works Cited

Delpit, Lisa D. "The Silenced Dialogue: Power and Pedagogy in Educating Other People's Children." *Harvard Educational Review* 58.3 (1988): 280–98.

Rodriguez, Richard. *Hunger of Memory: The Education of Richard Rodriguez.* Boston: D. R. Godine, 1982.

The Power of Sprinkles

Gabrielle Radik

"I don't want to do this! I'm bored, and I'm tired, and this thing doesn't make any sense, and everyone's watching the movie in the other room, and I want to watch too, and I don't want to do this I don't want to do this I don't want to do this!"

"We have to do this. It's important. If we don't turn in the essays then we don't do well in the class and we won't be able to participate in the discussion and our grade will go down and our GPA will suffer and we'll lose some of our scholarships."

"But you know I hate writing! Especially this kind, because we have to say things the way the teacher wants to hear them, and as often as not we have to do research and work it into the paper somewhere. Sometimes they make us argue a point, and I just don't like doing that."

"You're arguing a point right now. You argue all the time. And we've done writing before—we write to make lists, and give directions. Every now and again we take notes."

"When was the last time we took notes, I'd like to know? If we've taken notes recently, then I had nothing to do with it!"

"OK, never mind about the notes. Forget the notes. We write memos to the roommate, and we write stupid messages on the door."

"Yeah . . . but . . . but those don't take very long, and if we don't write the lists, then we forget things. And if we don't write directions, then no one can find us. And if we don't write the memos, then the roommate gets annoyed. And stupid messages aren't just stupid—they're fun!"

"We write e-mail. That takes a long time. We spend time every day writing e-mail."

"E-mail isn't the same! The messages are fun, like all those forwards we send. Besides, we're in a contest with the friend about how many e-mail forwards we can send each other! You know that! And when we write to the other friends it's because we can't talk to them because the phone is too expensive. You know I like people."

"Sometimes it isn't e-mail though. We've written letters to the friends. Those are always long. And what about the diary?"

"We only write to the friends when we can't talk to them or when there's a problem and we want them to listen to everything we have to say. And how often do we add to the diary? I'll tell you when. Only when we have stuff to argue about or when we've done something we don't want to forget. It only has five entries. It doesn't count."

"Well, if you can write for that, why can't you write for this?"

"Because this is assigned! It's something we were told we had to do; there's a certain way that we're supposed to do it. If we do it my way, it doesn't count. We have to finish it by a certain time, and anything I have to do by a certain time isn't fun. It's duty. And we have to make it a certain length; I can't just say what I want to say. We have to make sure we're saying enough or it'll look like we didn't put any work into it because it isn't long enough."

"Sometimes a minimum length is good. It tells us how much detail we're supposed to go into and how much we should say about something."

"Yeah, well, sort of. But then there's what happens when we've finished everything we want to say and we think it's good and it makes sense the way we have it and adding more would make it worse. But it isn't long enough! If we pass it in the way it is, we get marked down because we didn't do enough work. So we have to add stuff somewhere in the end, or somewhere in the thing, that really isn't important, just to make it longer. It's hard putting in bull_ _ _ _ without making it look like bull_ _ _ _. Or when we come to as long as it's supposed to be, and we still have more to say."

"All right, you have a point there. But the teacher-person has to penalize students for that sort of thing, or the stupid people would get away with too much."

"Yeah, I suppose."

"We've been writing them for years. Book reports, essays, research papers, thesis papers, lots of stuff."

"And I hated every minute of them. Remember, I put up a fight every time."

"You mean you whined every time."

"Hey! It's only because we never do things my way."

"We don't always have to do things the way we're supposed to. Sometimes it works much better if we do our own thing, and just make it look like what it's supposed to be. We've written those Green Eggs & Ham things. Those were sort of like essays. You enjoyed those."

"We didn't have to make those look like anything. They were just because we wanted to, and they were silly and random. I like random silly stuff. Like tapeworms and pickles and plungers and iguanas and anything beginning with J and . . ."

"OK, OK, I get the picture. How about we just do this assignment, and then we can go watch the movie. I want to see it, too, you know. We'll just make this one random somehow. Yeah, we'll put in something silly, just as long as the whole thing makes sense so that the teacher-person is happy. And as soon as it's over, we can get a Smurf sundae . . ."

"With sprinkles?"

"Of course."

"It's a deal. Let's get started . . ."

Works Cited

Anderson, Sherwood. "The Book of the Grotesque." *Winesburg Ohio,* New York: Viking-Penguin, 1919.

Austen, Jane. *Pride and Prejudice.* New York: Penguin, 1981.

Bacon, Francis. *Francis Bacon: A Selection of His Works.* Ed. Sidney Warhaft. Indianapolis: Odyssey, 1965.

Barnicle, Mike. "It Beats Going Home." *Boston Globe* 5 Jan. 1993: 21.

Bashō. *A Haiku Journey: Bashō's "The Narrow Road to the Far North" and Selected Haiku.* Trans. Dorothy Britton. New York: Harper and Row, 1974.

Belanoff, Pat, Betsy Rorschach, and Mia Oberlink. *The Right Handbook: Grammar and Usage in Context.* 2d ed. Portsmouth, NH: Boynton Cook, 1993.

Belenky, Mary, Nancy Goldberger, Blythe Clinchy, and Jill Tarule. *Women's Ways of Knowing.* New York: Basic Books, 1986. (We quote from pp. 17–18.)

Berthoff, Ann. "A Curious Triangle and the Double-Entry Notebook, or How Theory Can Help Us Teach Reading and Writing." *The Making of Meaning: Metaphors, Models, and Maxims for Writing Teachers.* Portsmouth, NH: Boynton Cook, 1981. 41–47.

Blau, Sheridan. "Invisible Writing: Investigating Cognitive Processes in Composition." *College Composition and Communication* 34 (1983): 297–312.

Boice, Robert, and Lyle R. Cramer. Appendix to Peter Elbow's "Making Better Use of Student Evaluations of Teachers." *Profession 92.* New York: Modern Language Association, 1992. 42–48.

Britton, James, et al. *The Development of Writing Abilities.* Urbana, IL: NCTE, 1975.

Burke, Kenneth. *Rhetoric of Motives.* Berkeley: U of California P, 1950. (We quote from p. 45.)

———. *Permanence and Change: An Anatomy of Purpose.* Berkeley: U of California P, 1984.

Cassidy, John. "Profile: Heights of Elegance." *The New Yorker* 30 Nov. 1998: 70–74.

Chi, Lu. "Rhymeprose on Literature: The *Wen Fu* of Lu Chi." Trans. Achilles Fang. *Harvard Journal of Asiatic Studies* 14 (1951): 527–566.

Clemens, Samuel L. *Selected Mark Twain-Howells Letters: 1872–1910.* Ed. Frederick Anderson et al. Cambridge, MA: Belknap Press, 1967. (In an Exploring the Writing Process box in Workshop 2, we quote from pp. 102–103; in an Exploring the Writing Process box in Workshop 5, we quote from pp. 370–371.)

———. *Adventures of Huckleberry Finn.* New York: Dodd, Mead, 1984.

Coleridge, Samuel Taylor. *Notebooks.* Ed. Kathleen Coburn. Bollingen series. New York: Pantheon, 1957.

Conrad, Joseph. Preface. *The Nigger of the Narcissus.* New York: Doubleday, 1954.

Coover, Robert. "An Interview with Robert Coover." *Anything Can Happen.* Eds. Tom LeClair and Larry McCaffery. Urbana: U of Illinois P, 1983. 63–78.

Crews, Frederick. *The Random House Handbook.* 6th ed. 1992. (We quote from p. 438.)

Darwin, Charles. *Autobiography of Charles Darwin.* Ed. Nora Barlow. New York: Norton, 1969.

Dillard, Annie. *The Writing Life.* New York: Harper and Row, 1989.

Doctorow, E. L. "An Interview with E. L. Doctorow." *Anything Can Happen.* Eds. Tom LeClair and Larry McCaffery. Urbana: U of Illinois P, 1983. 91–105.

Dunn, Stephen. "An Interview with Stephen Dunn" by Jonathan L. Thorndike. *AWP Chronicle* Oct./Nov. 1992: 14–16.

Elbow, Peter, ed. *Nothing Begins with an 'N': New Investigations of Freewriting.* Carbondale: Southern Illinois UP, 1991.

———. "Methodological Doubting and Believing: Contraries in Inquiry." *Embracing Contraries: Explorations in Learning and Teaching.* New York: Oxford UP, 1986. 254–300.

———. *Writing with Power.* New York: Oxford UP, 1973.

———. *Writing without Teachers.* New York: Oxford UP, 1981.

Federman, Raymond. "An Interview with Raymond Federman." *Anything Can Happen.* Eds. Tom LeClair and Larry McCaffery. Urbana: U of Illinois P, 1983. 126–151.

Fowler, H. W. *A Dictionary of Modern English Usage.* Oxford: Clarendon P, 1926.

Frost, Robert. "Introduction." *A Way Out.* New York: Seven Arts P, 1917.

Fulwiler, Toby. "Provocative Revision." *The Writing Center Journal* 12.2 (1992): 190–204.

Fulwiler, Toby, and Alan R. Hayakawa. *The Blair Handbook.* Englewood Cliffs, NJ: Blair Press/Prentice-Hall, 1998.

Gendlin, Eugene. "Experiential Phenomenology." *Phenomenology and the Social Sciences.* Ed. M. Natanson. Evanston, IL: Northwestern UP, 1973.

———. *Focusing.* 2d ed. New York: Bantam, 1981.

Gordimer, Nadine. *The Essential Gesture: Writing, Politics, Places.* Ed. Stephen Clingman. New York: Knopf, 1988.

Gray, Francine du Plessix. "I Write for Revenge against Reality." *New York Times Book Review* 12 Sept. 1982: 3.

Hailey, Arthur. *Airport.* New York: Doubleday, 1968.

Hardwick, Elizabeth. "Its Only Defense: Intelligence and Sparkle." *New York Times Book Review* 14 Sept. 1986: 1.

Hoffman, Eva. *Lost in Translation: A Life in a New Language.* New York: Penguin, 1989. (We quote from pp. 275–276.)

Hopkins, Gerard Manley. "Spring and Fall: To a Young Child." *Poems of Gerard Manley Hopkins.* London: Oxford UP, 1930.

Hull, John M. *Touching the Rock: An Experience of Blindness.* New York: Pantheon, 1990.

James, William. *The Variety of Religious Experience.* New York: Penguin, 1982.

Lucretius. "The Nature of Things." Trans. F. O. Copley. New York: Norton, 1977.

Maclean, Norman. *A River Runs Through It.* Chicago: U of Chicago P, 1976.

Macrorie, Ken. *Searching Writing.* Rochelle Park, NJ: Hayden, 1980.

———. *Writing to Be Read.* Rochelle Park, NJ: Hayden, 1968.

Michener, James A. *Hawaii.* New York: Random House, 1959.

Miller, Henry. Quoted in *The Paris Review* 107 (1998): 255.

Montaigne, Michel de. *Montaigne: Essays.* Trans. J. M. Cohen. New York: Penguin, 1959.

Moran, Charles. "Reading Like a Writer." *Vital Signs.* Ed. James. L. Collins. Portsmouth, NH: Boynton Cook, 1989. Earlier version: "Teaching Writing/Teaching Literature." *College Composition and Communication* 32 (1981): 21–30.

New York Daily News. Unsigned letter to the editor. 20 March 1986.

Noel, John V., and James Stavridis. *Division Officer's Guide.* Annapolis: Naval Institute P, 1989.

Pope, Alexander. "An Essay on Man." *Pope: Poems and Prose.* New York: Penguin, 1985.

Safire, William. "The Take on Voice." *New York Times Magazine* 28 June 1992: 14.

Schopenhauer, Arthur. *Parerga und Paralipomena.* Excerpted in *Best Advice on How to Write.* Ed. Gorham Munson. New York: Hermitage House, 1952: 61–77.

Schultz, John. *Writing from Start to Finish.* Portsmouth, NH: Boynton Cook, 1982.

———. *Writing from Start to Finish: The 'Story Workshop' Basic Forms Rhetoric-Reader.* Portsmouth, NH: Heinemann-Boynton Cook, 1990.

———. "Story from First Impulse to Final Draft." Videotape. Portsmouth, NH: Heinemann-Boynton Cook, 1992.

"Selling It: What's in a Name?" *Consumer Reports* Feb. 1999: 67.

Sheehy, Eugene P. *Guide to Reference Books.* Chicago: American Library Association, 1986.

Spender, Stephen. Quoted in *The Paris Review* 107 (1998): 259–260.

Stafford, William. "A Way Out." *Writing the Australian Crawl.* Ann Arbor: U of Michigan P, 1978. 17–20.

Stevens, Wallace. "Thirteen Ways of Looking at a Blackbird." *Harmonium.* New York: Knopf, 1950. 158.

Stowe, Harriet Beecher. *Uncle Tom's Cabin.* New York: Bantam, 1981.

Thomas, Dylan. "Poem in October." *Deaths and Entrances.* London: J. M. Dent & Sons, 1946.

Twain, Mark. *See* Clemens, Samuel L.

Warren, Robert Penn. Interview. *Paris Review Interviews.* 1st Series. Ed. Malcolm Cowley. New York: Viking, 1958. 183–208.

Welty, Eudora. *One Writer's Beginnings.* Cambridge, MA: Harvard, 1984. (We quote from p. 11.)

Williams, William Carlos. "How to Write." *New Directions Fiftieth Anniversary Issue.* Ed. J. Laughlin. New York: New Directions, 1986. 36–39.

Woolf, Virginia. "Sunday (Easter) 20 April." *The Diary of Virginia Woolf.* Vol. I: 1915–1919. Ed. Anne Olivier Bell. New York: Harcourt Brace, 1977.

Acknowledgments

W. H. Auden, "As I walked out one evening." From *W. H. Auden: Collected Poems* by W. H. Auden, edited by Edward Mendelson. Copyright © 1940 and renewed 1968 by W. H. Auden. Reprinted by permission of Random House, Inc.

Kate Barnes, "My Mother, That Feast of Light." Reprinted by permission of the author.

Elizabeth Bishop, "One Art." From the *Complete Poems 1927–1979* by Elizabeth Bishop. Copyright © 1979, 1983 by Alice Helen Methfessel. Reprinted by permission of Farrar, Straus & Giroux, LLC.

William F. Buckley, Jr., "With all Deliberate Speed: What's so Bad About Writing Fast?" Copyright © 1986 by William F. Buckley, Jr. First appeared in *The New York Times Book Review*. Used by permission of the Wallace Literary Agency, Inc.

Vern S. Bullough, "American Experience." Excerpt from *The Subordinate Sex* by Vern L. Bullough. Reprinted by permission of the author.

Mark Cassell, letter to the editor of *The New York Times* 16 Mar. 1999. Reprinted by permission of the author.

Mona Charen, "Aiming a Cannon at a Mosquito." By permission of Mona Charen and Creators Syndicate.

Bi Chen, "Wishing in the Dark." From *Shattered Reflections: An Anthology of Poetry from Independence High School, San Jose, California.* Ed. Ky Dang. San Jose: San Jose Center for Literary Arts, San Jose University, 1991.

Cindy Cheung, "I Am Sorrow." From *Shattered Reflections: An Anthology of Poetry from Independence High School, San Jose, California.* Ed. Ky Dang. San Jose: San Jose Center for Literary Arts, San Jose University, 1991.

Linda Miller Cleary, "The Social Consequences of Voicelessness." Reprinted by permission of Linda Miller Cleary. Excerpt from *The Other Side of the Writing Desk: Students Speak Out about Writing* (Boynton/Cook, a division of Reed Elsevier, Inc., Portsmouth, NH, 1991).

Cree Indians, "Quiet Until the Thaw" and "Rain Straight Down." From *The Wishing-Bone Cycle: Poems From The Swampy Cree Indians,* gathered and translated by Howard A. Norman.

Louise P. Dudley, letter to the editor of *The New York Times* 12 Oct. 1992. Reprinted by permission of the author.

Anne Fausto-Sterling, excerpt from *Myths Of Gender: Biological Theories about Women and Men.* Copyright © 1986 by Basic Books, Inc. Reprinted by permission of Basic Books, a member of Perseus Books, L.L.C.

Susan Faludi, "Speak for Yourself." From *The New York Times,* January 26, 1992. Reprinted by permission of the author.

"Gas Analgesia." Brochure from the offices of Jack H. Weinstein, D.D.S., and Ira H. Abel, D.D.S.

Sandra M. Gilbert and Susan Gubar, "A New World Beyond Snow White." Copyright © 1992 by The New York Times Company. Reprinted by permission.

Mark Goldblatt, letter to the editor of *The New York Times* 3 Feb. 1999. Reprinted by permission of the author.

Edmund Gosse, "The Essay." Reprinted with permission from *Encyclopaedia Britannica,* 11th edition (1910–11).

Michael Greenebaum, "Testing in Schools is Part of Problem, Not Solution." Reprinted by permission of *The Amherst Bulletin*.

Cathy Guisewite, "Cathy ("See what you can do with the Fallon project . . .")." CATHY © 1984 Cathy Guisewite. Reprinted with permission of UNIVERSAL PRESS SYNDICATE. All rights reserved.

John Hertzberg, "Composite Dream." © 1992 by John Hertzberg. Hertzberg, a collage artist, deals with metaphorical abstraction. More of his work can be viewed at www.JohnHertzberg.com.

Nazim Hikmet, "Autobiography." From *Poems of Nazim Hikmet,* translation copyright © 1986 by Randy Blasing and Mutlu Konuk. Reprinted by permission of Persea Books, Inc.

Edward Hoagland, "Essay: What I Think, What I Am." From *The Tugman's Passage* by Edward Hoagland. Published by Lyons and Burford. Copyright © 1976, 1995 by Edward Hoagland. This usage granted by permission.

David Ignatow, "Two Friends." From *Figures of the Human,* © 1964 by David Ignataw, Wesleyan University Press by permission of the University Press of New England.

Peter Jones, "DWIs and Lost Cars," letter to the editor of *Newsday* 1 Feb. 1999. Reprinted by permission of the author.

Lore Kramer, letter to the editor of *The New York Times* 3 Feb. 1999. Reprinted by permission of the author.

George Lakoff and Mark Johnson, excerpts from *Metaphors We Live By*. Reprinted by permission of the University of Chicago Press.

Mark Levensky, "A Letter." "Letter" by Mark Levensky from *Elementary English*.

Audre Lorde, "A Litany for Survival." From *The Black Unicorn* by Audre Lorde. Copyright © 1978 by Audre Lorde. Reprinted by permission of W. W. Norton & Company, Inc.

Laura Matthews, drafts and revisions of two short book reviews for *Glamour* magazine. Courtesy Glamour. Copyright © 1993 by Conde Nast Publications, Inc.

Sabra McKenzie-Hamilton, "got violence?" Op-ed, *The Catholic Worker* Aug.–Sept. 1998. Reprinted by permission of *The Catholic Worker.*

Marion Milner, "Loving and Destroying." Excerpt from *Eternity's Sunrise: A Way of Keeping a Diary* by Marion Milner. Used by permission of Virago Press.

James Moffet, "On Essaying." From Patricia L. Stock, editor: *Fforum: Essays on Theory and Practice in the Teaching of Writing,* 1983.

B. Mooney and K. Dimbleby, "Who Influences Children More: Their Parents or Their Peers?" Op-ed from *The Guardian* 22 Aug. 1998. Reprinted by permission of *The Guardian.*

Kay J. Moran, drafts and revisions of an editorial for *The Daily Hampshire Gazette*. Reprinted by permission of the author.

Donald Murray, "The Feel of Writing—and Teaching Writing." Excerpted from "The Feel of Writing—and Teaching Writing," in *Reinventing the Rhetorical Tradition* edited by Aviva Freedman and Ian Pringle (Conway, AR: L&S Books for the Canadian Council of Teachers of English, 1980), copyright © by the Canadian Council of Teachers of English and reprinted by permission.

Frank O'Hara, "Why I Am Not a Painter." From *Collected Poems* by Frank O'Hara. Copyright © 1958 by Maureen Granville-Smith, Administratrix of the Estate of Frank O'Hara. Reprinted by permission of Alfred A. Knopf, Inc.

Grace Paley, "A Conversation with My Father." From *Enormous Changes At The Last Minute* by Grace Paley. Copyright © 1974 by Grace Paley. Reprinted by permission of Farrar, Straus, Giroux, LLC.

Sondra Perl and Nancy Wilson, Composing Guidelines. From *Through Teachers' Eyes* by Sondra Perl and Nancy Wilson. Published by Heinemann Educational Books, Inc. Used by permission of Sondra Perl.

"Robert Bingham (1925–1982)." Reprinted by permission; copyright © 1982 by The New Yorker Magazine, Inc.

Robert Pool, excerpt from *Eve's Rib: The Biological Roles of Sex Differences*. Copyright © 1994 by Robert Pool. Reprinted by permission of Crown Publishers, Inc.

Adrienne Rich, "[Dear Adrienne]." Poem 6 of "Contradictions: Tracking Poems," reprinted from *Your Native Land, Your Life: Poems by Adrienne Rich.* Copyright © by Adrienne Rich. Reprinted by permission of W. W. Norton & Company, Inc.

Adrienne Rich, "[It's true, these last few years I've lived]." Poem 16 of "Contradictions: Tracking Poems," reprinted from *Your Native Land, Your Life, Poems by Adrienne Rich.* Copyright © by Adrienne Rich. Reprinted by permission of W. W. Norton & Company, Inc.

Richard Rodriguez, excerpt from *Hunger of Memory*. Copyright © 1981 by Richard Rodriguez. Reprinted by permission of David R. Godine, Publisher.

Gary Snyder, "Hay for Horses." From *Riprap and Cold Mountain Poems* by Gary Snyder. Copyright © 1990 by Gary Snyder. Reprinted by permission of North Point Press, a division of Farrar, Straus, and Giroux, LLC.

Gary Snyder, "How Poetry Comes to Me." From *No Nature* by Gary Snyder. Copyright 1992 by Gary Snyder. Reprinted by permission of Pantheon Books, division of Random House, Inc.

William Stafford, "A Way of Writing." First appeared in *Field.* Reprinted by permission of the estate of William Stafford.

Gary Stoner and Bill Matthews, "Measuring Students' Progress is not Antithetical to Learning." Reprinted by permission of *The Amherst Bulletin.*

Nate Stulman, "The Great Campus Goof-Off Machine." Op-ed, *The New York Times* 15 March 1999. Copyright © 1999 by The New York Times Co. Reprinted by permission of the author and The New York Times.

Jane Tompkins, "Reverie." From *A Life in School* by Jane Tompkins. Copyright © 1996 by Jane Tompkins. Reprinted by permission of Perseus Books Publishers, a member of Perseus Books, L.L.C.

Ludwig R. Vogel, letter to the editor of *The New York Times* 1 Nov. 1992. Reprinted by permission of the author.

Eudora Welty, "Is Phoenix Jackson's Grandson Really Dead?". From *The Eye Of The Story* by Eudora

Welty. Copyright © 1978 by Eudora Welty. Reprinted by permission of Random House, Inc.

Eudora Welty, "A Worn Path." From *A Curtain Of Green And Other Stories,* copyright 1941 and renewed 1969 by Eudora Welty, reprinted by permission of Harcourt, Inc.

Richard Wilbur, "The Writer." From *The Mind Reader,* copyright © 1971 by Richard Wilbur, reprinted by permission of Harcourt, Inc.

Simon Winchester, "Acknowledgments" from *The Professor and the Madman.* Copyright © 1998 by Simon Winchester. Reprinted by permission of HarperCollins Publishers, Inc.

William Zinsser, "Writing Mathematics and Chemistry." Excerpts from *Writing To Learn* by William Zinsser. Copyright © 1988 by William Zinsser. Reprinted by permission of the author.

Index